Introducing Transformational Grammar

Introducing Transformational Grammar

From Principles and Parameters to Minimalism

Second Edition

Jamal Ouhalla
**Reader in Linguistics,
Queen Mary and Westfield College,
University of London**

A member of the Hodder Headline Group
LONDON • SYDNEY • AUCKLAND
Co-published in the United States of America by
Oxford University Press Inc., New York

First published in Great Britain in 1994
Second edition published in Great Britain in 1999 by
Arnold, a member of the Hodder Headline Group,
338 Euston Road, London NW1 3BH

http://www.arnoldpublishers.com

Co-published in the United States of America by
Oxford University Press Inc.,
198 Madison Avenue, New York, NY 10016

British Library Cataloguing in Publication Data
A catalogue entry for this book is available from the British Library

Library of Congress Cataloging-in-Publication Data
A catalog record for this book is available from the Library of Congress

ISBN 0 340 74036 1

1 2 3 4 5 6 7 8 9 10

Production Editor: Rada Radojicic
Production Controller: Priya Gohil
Cover Design: Terry Griffiths

Typeset by J&L Composition Ltd, Filey, North Yorkshire
Printed and bound in Great Britain by
MPG Books Ltd, Bodmin, Cornwall

What do you think about this book? Or any other Arnold title?
Please send your comments to feedback.arnold@hodder.co.uk

Contents

For Sima

Acknowledgements

I owe a debt of gratitude to many individuals who have contributed directly or indirectly to this textbook. Most of these individuals are students who attended my classes at University College London, Queen Mary and Westfield College (QMW–London University), and, for one quarter, at the University of California at Los Angeles (UCLA). Unfortunately, the list is too long to reproduce here.

I am also indebted to Bettina Knipschild, Lluis Cabre and my daughter Sima for their help and patience.

1 Language and Linguistic Theory

Contents

1.1 *Language and mind*

1.1.1 Knowledge of language

Linguistics is usually defined as the discipline which concerns itself with the study of language, although what language is taken to be may differ from one school to another. In the Generative tradition, language is understood to refer to the knowledge that native speakers have which, together with other faculties of the mind, enables them to communicate, express their thoughts and perform various other functions. Accordingly, the task of the linguist is to characterise in one form or another the knowledge that native speakers have of their language.

Let us take Chris to be a native speaker of English and review certain 'things' that Chris knows by virtue of being a native speaker of English.

Obviously, Chris knows the words of the English language, the way they are pronounced, what they refer to, among other things. The word *pin*, for example, is pronounced in a particular way, and refers to a particular entity in the world. Words are basically sound symbols which bear an arbitrary relationship to whatever they refer to. As a matter of fact, Chris's knowledge of the words of the English language involves more subtle information. For example, the word *pin* is made up of discrete sound units, so that the initial sound /p/ can be replaced with the minimally different sound /b/ to obtain the different word *bin*.

Chris also knows that the word *unhappy*, for example, is made up of two smaller meaningful units, the negative **prefix** *un-* with the meaning 'not' and the adjective *happy*. Put together, they convey the meaning 'not happy'. The negative prefix can be attached to various other adjectives such as *kind* and *sympathetic* to derive the complex negative adjectives *unkind* with the meaning 'not kind', and *unsympathetic* with the meaning 'not sympathetic'. Interestingly, Chris knows that the negative prefix *un-* is different in meaning from the homophonous prefix found with complex verbs such as *unpack*, *unbutton* and *unzip*. The complex verb *unpack*, for example, does not mean 'not pack', but means roughly 'reverse the action of packing'. Somehow Chris knows that the negative prefix can only attach to adjectives. When Chris comes across a verb which includes the prefix *un-*, Chris interprets the prefix to mean 'reverse the action' and not to mean 'not'.

In addition to knowledge of words, Chris knows that words can be arranged together to form meaningful sentences, and that different arrangements (word orders) give rise to different meanings. Consider the examples in (1–5):

1. The the likes boy girl.
2. The boy likes the girl.
3. The girl likes the boy.
4. The girl is liked by the boy.
5. Boy girl likes the the.

If the words in these sentences are arranged as in (1) and (5) they do not make a meaningful sentence, but if arranged as in (2), (3) and (4) they make meaningful sentences. (2) means that *the boy* experiences a certain feeling towards *the girl*, and that this feeling is not necessarily shared by *the girl*. (3) has the (opposite) meaning that *the girl* experiences a certain feeling towards *the boy*, and that this feeling is not necessarily shared by *the boy*. Finally, (4) has a meaning which is similar to that of (2) rather than that of (3) even though it has a word order which is similar to that of (3) rather than that of (2).

As with knowledge of words, Chris's knowledge of sentences involves some quite subtle information. Consider now the pairs of sentences in (6a&b):

6a. The girl asked the boy to leave.
6b. The girl asked the boy to be allowed to leave.

(6a) can have the meaning whereby *the boy* is supposed to leave ('the girl ordered the boy to leave') or the (more subtle) meaning whereby *the girl* is supposed to leave ('the girl asked permission from the boy to leave'). However, if *to leave* is replaced with *to be allowed to leave*, as in (6b), only the meaning whereby *the girl* is supposed to leave is accessible.

Likewise, (7a) has the meaning whereby *the boy* is supposed to do the talking to somebody else. However, if *the girl* is dropped from the sentence, as in (7b), *the boy* changes from being the individual who is supposed to do the talking (to somebody else) to becoming the individual who is supposed to be talked to (by somebody else):

7a. The boy is too stubborn to talk to the girl.
7b. The boy is too stubborn to talk to.

In addition to what has been mentioned, Chris knows that sentences can convey different messages in different contexts. Consider the brief dialogue in (8a&b) from Sperber and Wilson (1986):

8a. The boy: Do you want some coffee?
8b. The girl: Coffee keeps me awake.

The girl's answer to *the boy*'s offer can mean 'yes, please' (acceptance) or 'no, thank you' (decline), depending on *the girl*'s intentions and plans, and the time in which the dialogue takes place. If *the girl* intends to stay up late in the night, (8b) is likely to convey an acceptance of the offer. However, if *the girl* intends to have a good night's sleep to be able to wake up early the next morning, (8b) is likely to convey a decline of the offer. Presumably, these two possibilities presuppose that the dialogue in (8a&b) takes place some time in the evening. If it is assumed to take place early in the morning a different message might be deduced from *the girl*'s answer.

The ability to infer the right message from the *the girl*'s answer depends on knowledge of contextual information relating to the time in which the dialogue takes place, the intentions and plans of *the girl*, as well as encyclopaedic knowledge relating to the fact that coffee contains a substance which can cause one to be awake. There is a sense in which this kind of knowledge is not of the same order as the formal knowledge of how to derive complex words from simpler units and how to arrange words together to form meaningful sentences. For example, it is possible that a native speaker of English will fail to infer the right message from *the girl*'s answer in (8b) (misunderstanding) for lack of the right background information. However, it is unlikely that the native speaker will fail to realise that *keeps* consists of the verb *keep* and the third person singular marker *-s*.

We can make a distinction between Chris's knowledge of the English language and Chris's ability to use this knowledge properly in different situations. The former includes knowledge of words and the rules which govern pronunciation, word formation, sentence formation, among other aspects of language. The latter, on the other hand, includes knowledge of language as defined, in addition to knowledge relating to people's beliefs, the rules that govern social behaviour, encyclopaedic knowledge, as well as rules of inference which enable people to interpret utterances in relation to a given context. We now have narrowed down the expression 'knowledge of language' to mean knowledge of the rules which govern pronunciation, word formation and sentence formation, in addition to knowledge of words. It is this specific definition of (knowledge of) language we are interested in here and which we will assume in the rest of this book.

1.1.2   Language and other faculties

The Chris we have been assuming so far could be a normal person with average intelligence. Now, Jane may be more skilful than Chris at knowing how to manipulate language to persuade, give good speeches, write detective stories, and so on. However, there is no sense at all in which Jane could be said to be more skilful than Chris at knowing, for example, that in (7a) above *the boy* is the individual who is supposed to do the talking to somebody else, whereas in (7b) *the boy* is the individual who is supposed to be talked to by somebody else. This kind of knowledge is common to all normal speakers of English irrespective of their other abilities and skills.

Now take Chris to be an adult with the mental age of a young child. Chris may have a few problems grasping the rules which govern social behaviour, and may also have difficulties with problem-solving tasks which are otherwise not supposed to be taxing for people at a similar biological age. However, it is quite possible that Chris knows, much as (skilful) Jane does, that sentence (4) above has a meaning which is similar to that of (2) rather than that of (3), even though (4) has a word order which is similar to that of (3) rather than that of (2). Smith and Tsimpli (1991) have reported the case of a '29-year-old man . . . whose non-verbal IQ averages between 60 and 70, who is institutionalised because he is unable to look after himself' (pp. 316–17). However, this man has a normal mastery of his native language English, and, more spectacularly, 'when given a passage written in any of some 15 or 16 languages simply translates it into English at about the speed one would normally read aloud a piece written in English' (p. 317). Other cases have been reported in the literature of people of varying ages who display a sharp discrepancy between their general cognitive abilities, including communicative skills, and their linguistic abilities or knowledge of their language (see e.g. Curtiss 1981, Yamada 1990).

Finally, take Chris to be somebody who, as a result of an accident or a stroke, has received physical damage to certain areas of the brain, and consequently is suffering from what is clinically known as Agrammatism in Broca's Aphasia. Chris may not have lost the ability to pick up hints from contexts to interpret sentences (in fact, this particular ability may become substantially enhanced), and may not have lost the ability to solve taxing problems, and so on. However, it is quite possible that Chris may have lost the basic ability to interpret sentence (4) as having a meaning similar to that of (2) rather than that of (3). Numerous studies have reported cases of aphasic patients who have difficulties interpreting sentences of the type in (4), though not necessarily sentences of the type in (2) and (3) (Caramazza and Zurif 1976, Grodzinsky 1990).

Interestingly, the difficulties mostly arise in relation to an identifiable sub-class of these sentences. Compare the sentences in (9a&b):

9a. The boy is kicked by the girl.
9b. The door is kicked by the girl.

(9a) is called a 'reversible passive', where either of the two individuals involved can in principle perform the action described by the verb (the kicking). The positions of *the boy* and *the girl* can be reversed to derive the equally plausible sentence *The girl is kicked by the boy.* (9b), however, is a 'non-reversible passive', where only *the girl* can perform the action described by the verb. Reversing the positions of *the door* and *the girl* results in the infelicitous sentences *The girl is kicked by the door.* The patients reported in the studies cited are likely to misinterpret (9a) as meaning 'the boy kicks the girl', but are not likely to misinterpret (9b) as meaning 'the door kicks the girl'. Presumably, this is because their knowledge of the world and their ability to reason (intact) enables them to exclude the infelicitous interpretation of (9b) whereby 'the door kicks the girl'.

The discussion so far should lead to the conclusion that knowledge of language is probably independent of the other faculties of the mind. It is independent of intelligence, can remain intact when other faculties are impaired, and can itself be impaired when other faculties are intact. The human mind is said to have a **modular** structure, where each faculty has an autonomous existence from the others, although the ability of humans to use their language normally involves an interaction between all of these autonomous modules. Because knowledge of language forms an autonomous module, it should be possible to study it separately from the other faculties of the mind. We will come back to this point later on in this chapter.

1.1.3 Grammar and Universal Grammar

We have defined knowledge of language as knowledge of words and knowledge of rules which govern pronunciation, word formation and sentence formation. Let us now try to classify this knowledge into identifiably distinct categories. Knowledge of words can be characterised in terms of an open-ended mental dictionary, technically called the **lexicon**. Like a commercial dictionary, the lexicon can be considered to consist of **lexical entries** for words, where each lexical entry specifies various types of information necessary for the proper use of the word. Knowledge of rules can be characterised in terms of the notion **'grammar'**. We can say that Chris knows the grammar of the English language to mean that Chris knows the rules of the English language.

The term 'grammar' is understood here to refer to the rules which govern pronunciation, word formation and sentence formation. The sub-component of grammar which includes the rules which govern pronunciation is called **phonology**. The sub-component which includes the rules which govern word formation is called **morphology**. Finally, the sub-component which includes the rules which govern sentence formation is called **syntax**. These terms are also used by linguists to refer to the sub-disciplines of linguistics which deal with each set of rules (more on this later on). Here, these terms are understood to refer to aspects of Chris's knowledge of English and therefore are components of Chris's mind. Accordingly, Chris's knowledge of English consists of an amalgam of more specialised types of knowledge together with the English lexicon.

Restricting our attention to grammar, let us now ask the following question: How did Chris come to have this intricate and highly specialised system of rules which we call 'the grammar of English'?

It is unlikely that Chris was taught this knowledge. Chris may have been instructed at an early age to say *brought* instead of *bringed* and *mice* instead of *mouses*, and at a later age to try to speak 'proper English' instead of 'teenage gibberish'. However, it is highly unlikely that Chris was taught that if one substitutes *to be allowed to leave* for *to leave* in (6), the meaning whereby *the boy* is supposed to leave disappears. This type of knowledge is subconscious, in the sense that although native speakers possess it and use it, they do not have direct access to it and therefore cannot teach it.

It is also highly unlikely, in fact practically impossible, that Chris came to know English by memorising all the sentences that exist in the English language. This is because the number of such sentences is infinite. An important property of human language is that a substantial number of sentences produced by speakers are **novel**, uttered for the first time. Human language is said to be **creative**, insofar as there is no limit to the number of novel sentences that can be produced by native speakers. The creative aspect of human language provides the strongest evidence that knowledge of language is essentially knowledge of rules, a computational system which makes it possible to **generate** an infinite number of sentences from a finite number of rules together with the lexicon.

A somewhat more plausible answer to the question raised above is that Chris came to know English by observing others speak it, deriving the rules from their speech, and then **internalising** those rules, all at a subconscious level. Granting this, one cannot help the feeling that there is something miraculous about this achievement. The examples discussed above give only a glimpse of the highly complex nature of human language, a fact which is all too clear to linguists, though not necessarily to people who do not undertake the task of analysing languages in search of rules and generalisations. Yet, Chris managed to master English at an age when certain much simpler tasks are beyond the reach of children. As a matter of fact, the complexity of human languages is such that learning them from scratch is beyond the reach of any living organism which does not have some kind of special predisposition, an **innate ability** of some sort.

Let us see what the nature of this predisposition or innate ability is likely to be. We have seen that knowledge of language is independent of the other faculties of the mind. Therefore, it is unlikely that this predisposition is common to all faculties of the human mind/brain. If it were, we would not expect the kind of selective impairment of faculties reported to exist. Rather, the predisposition in question must be a specialised one, specific to language. It is plausible to reason that to determine the nature of the predisposition in question we must look at the nature of language itself. The idea behind this reasoning is that the nature of the predisposition to develop language must somehow be reflected in the properties of language itself. We have seen that language basically consists of rules of various types which in combination with the lexicon make it possible for native speakers to produce an infinite number of sentences. On this basis, we can conclude, as a working hypothesis, that the innate predisposition to master language basically consists of a set of rules, i.e. a grammar.

Once we accept this conclusion, Chris's achievement in mastering the English language becomes amenable to a more rational explanation. Chris approached the task of mastering English already equipped with a rich system of rules. The learning process amounts to the comparatively more manageable task of learning certain aspects of the English lexicon and certain rules specific to the English language. Much of what remains of what we have been calling Chris's 'knowledge of English' was there right from the beginning, and could not possibly be said to have been learned in the way one learns how to drive or play chess, for example.

The grammar which characterises the innate predisposition to learn language is called **Universal Grammar (UG)**, where the term 'universal' is understood in terms of biological necessity. This is to say that UG is the set of rules that all humans possess by virtue of having certain common genetic features which distinguish them from other organisms. Consequently, UG rules are to be found in English, Berber, and indeed any human language, and form part of the knowledge that native speakers have of their own language. Thus, Chris's knowledge of English consists of the rules of UG, certain rules specific to the English language, in addition to the English lexicon. Likewise, Idir's knowledge of Berber consists of the rules of UG, certain rules specific to the Berber language, in addition to the Berber lexicon.

1.2 *Language and the linguist*

1.2.1 The task of the linguist

Assuming that there are good reasons to study human language, not least the prospect of learning something about the distinctive properties of the human mind, the task of the linguist can be described as an attempt to characterise in formal terms the knowledge that humans have of their language. The task is essentially one of reconstruction, in the sense that the linguist tries to reconstruct, via the process of analysing data, knowledge that exists in the mind of native speakers. In other words, the task of the linguist is to formulate a theory, sometimes called a model, of language, insofar as theories of natural phenomena in general are attempts at reconstructing the mechanisms underlying those phenomena. Needless to say, such theories and models are meant as approximations of reality supported by the evidence available, rather than exact replicas.

It is quite possible that the theories (approximations of knowledge of language) produced by the linguist may at some stage be wide of the mark. However, this is in the nature of scientific inquiry in general. The process of building a theory of language (or any other natural phenomenon, for that matter) consists of attempts to accommodate as many data as possible, including new data. In view of this, it is also possible that a revised version might reintroduce an idea that was previously rejected on the ground that there was not enough evidence to support it at the time. For example, new evidence might support an idea for which there was little evidence at an earlier stage in investigation, thereby justifying its resurrection.

We have characterised knowledge of language as involving, in addition to the lexicon, knowledge of universal and language-specific rules, i.e. knowledge of a grammar. It follows that a given theory of language is itself a grammar, insofar as it incorporates the rules which govern the various aspects of language. It is for this reason that the term 'grammar' is sometimes said to be used by (some) linguists with 'systematic ambiguity'. It is used to refer to the knowledge that native speakers have as a component of their mind/brain, as well as to the theory constructed by the linguist as an approximation of that knowledge.

The grammar constructed by the linguist should be able to distinguish the language-specific rules from the rules of UG, so that it is possible to have theories of particular languages and a theory of language or universal grammar. Obviously, sentences of particular languages do not come wearing on their sleeves the rules involved in generating them. These rules can only be arrived at via rigorous investigation. Moreover, once these rules have been identified they are not likely to be wearing labels which classify them as either universal or language-specific. The task of classifying a given rule as a rule of UG must take the form of a hypothesis to be tested against data from the same language, and ultimately against data from other languages.

A grammar which correctly describes a native speaker's knowledge of her/his language (i.e. a theory of a particular language) is said to meet the condition of **descriptive adequacy**. On the other hand, a grammar which correctly describes UG (i.e. a theory of UG), where UG is understood to be the set of rules which define human languages, is said to meet the condition of **explanatory adequacy**. The goal of achieving explanatory adequacy is very much tied to the question of how native speakers acquire their language. Recall that we came to the conclusion that Chris must have been born with a predisposition to learn language on the basis of the fact that the knowledge Chris has is highly complex. A theory which describes accurately the predisposition in question (i.e. UG), and explains how the knowledge that Chris currently has follows from this predisposition can be said to meet the condition of explanatory adequacy.

A distant goal is to construct a theory of language use, that is a theory which will characterise how knowledge of language interacts with other components of the human cognitive system in performing various functions. This theory entails individual theories which characterise the properties of the various interacting systems, including a theory of language. Because very little is known about the properties of some of these systems, the prospect of arriving at a theory of language use seems less realistic, for the time being.

1.2.2 Some necessary idealisations

We have seen that the ability to use language properly, for communication and other purposes, is the result of an interaction between different faculties of the mind, including the language faculty. Consequently, the speech produced by native speakers is likely to contain a jumble of information not all of which reflects their knowledge of language. Now, a linguist who is interested in studying native speakers' knowledge of their language obviously has a dilemma. The dilemma is basically to ensure that conclusions reached on the basis of an analysis of native speakers' speech reflects accurately and solely knowledge of their language.

In view of this, the linguist has to take certain steps to avoid drawing misguided conclusions on the basis of tainted speech. One such step, mentioned above, is to make a distinction between knowledge of language, that is knowledge of rules, and the use of language in particular situations which involves other faculties of the mind. This is the distinction between what Chomsky (*Aspects of the Theory of Syntax*, 1965) calls **competence** (knowledge of language) and **performance** (the actual use of language in concrete situations). Having made the distinction, the linguist can then be in a position to work out which properties of speech should be attributed to competence and which should be attributed to performance, by no means a straightforward task.

Chomsky explains that speech is usually affected by performance factors such as false starts, hesitation, memory lapses, and so on, all of which are extraneous to language itself, and therefore should be purged from the data to be analysed. In other words, the linguist should deal with an idealised form of speech hypothetically produced by an 'ideal speaker–listener', not affected by the performance factors mentioned. This is a necessary idealisation, designed to isolate for investigation only those aspects of speech which reflect the properties of language.

Another idealisation relates to the notion 'homogeneous speech community', that is a community where there are no individual or other types of variation. This idealisation is also a necessary procedural step designed to ensure isolation of properties which are common to all speakers of a given language. As a matter of fact, this abstraction away from individual or larger differences is routinely assumed in everyday life situations when people use the expression 'the English language', for example. There is no 'pure instantiation' of the English language in the outside world. Rather, English exists in the form of a collection of dialects (American English, Australian English, British English, Indian English, to mention just a few of the larger categories) which are collectively referred to as the English language.

Just as English, or any other language for that matter, has no 'pure instantiation', UG also has no 'pure instantiation'. UG is instantiated as a component of larger systems of rules which include language-specific rules. In other words, UG is instantiated as part of English, Berber, Japanese, etc. Thus, to be able to isolate the properties of UG when analysing data from individual languages (the only route), the linguist has to abstract away from the properties of those individual languages. Like the previous idealisations, this one is also a necessary procedural move, designed to isolate for investigation a specific component of language.

It is interesting to note that the data the linguist initially has to deal with, which as we have seen is generally 'degraded' in nature, is precisely the kind of data that the child is faced with when learning a language. Yet, on the basis of this 'poor evidence' the child succeeds in developing a rich and highly complex system of knowledge. This is one of the major arguments, usually known as the 'poverty of stimulus' argument, for the innateness hypothesis. Only if humans are assumed to be genetically predisposed in terms of a rich system of knowledge can this otherwise impossible achievement be rationally explained. Presumably, in learning a language the child undertakes a series of idealisations, abstractions away from the non-pertinent properties of speech similar in principle to the idealisations the linguist has to undertake. The difference, of course, is that in doing so the child is guided by UG (the innate predisposition), whereas for the linguist UG forms part of the object of investigation.

1.2.3   Speakers' judgements

Since the speech produced in normal conversations tends to be distorted by extraneous factors, it may include utterances which, under different circumstances, would be rejected by the same speaker. Data collected by observation or recording (sometimes called a corpus) will not be a reliable basis on which to draw conclusions about language, especially with respect to the subtle aspects of language. Thus, in addition to the necessary abstractions which need to be undertaken, the linguist has to resort to other means to ensure the database is reliable.

One such other means is called **native speakers' judgements**, that is the **intuitions** native speakers have about their language. Consider the sentences in (10a–c) and (11a–c):

10a. I think (that) John fixed the car with a crowbar.
10b. What do you think John fixed with a crowbar?
10c. How do you think John fixed the car?

11a. I wonder whether John fixed the car with a crowbar.
11b. ?What do you wonder whether John fixed with a crowbar?
11c. *How do you wonder whether John fixed the car?

Native speakers of English are likely to judge the questions in (10b) and (10c) as 'good' or acceptable. They are also likely to judge (11b) as being slightly deviant. The notion 'slightly deviant' is conventionally indicated by one or more question marks at the beginning of the sentence. (11b) is slightly deviant in that it is not as 'good' as (10b), but at the same time not as 'bad' as (11c), with *how* understood to modify the verb *fix*. (11c) is not acceptable, a property which is conventionally marked with an asterisk. These subtle judgements surely reveal crucial information about native speakers' knowledge of English, and therefore must be taken into consideration by the linguist.

Although these 'grammaticality judgements' may in certain cases be affected by certain irrelevant factors, there is a sense in which they are a reliable source of data. It is possible to think of 'grammaticality judgements' as the result of 'little experiments', whereby native speakers subject the sentences they are presented with to the test of whether they are generated by their mental grammar. A sentence that is judged as grammatical is a sentence that is generated by the native speaker's mental grammar, and a sentence that is judged as ungrammatical is a sentence that is not generated by the native speaker's mental grammar.

Now, since the grammar constructed by the linguist (the linguist's grammar) is intended to be a theory of the mental grammar, we should expect the linguist's grammar not to generate a sentence that is not generated by the mental grammar. The expression 'grammaticality judgement' is also systematically ambiguous, insofar as it relates to the linguist's grammar and to the mental grammar. If the expected parallelism between the linguist's grammar and the mental grammar does not hold with respect to a given sentence, the linguist will have to revise the model grammar to accommodate that particular sentence.

A linguist who is working on a language of which she/he is a native speaker can rely on her/his own judgements of sentences. In this case, the linguist is said to engage in the process of gathering data by 'introspection'. Although in principle introspection should be sufficient, it is sometimes useful and instructive to compare one's own judgements to those of other native speakers of the same language. However, by and large this would only be necessary in situations involving so-called borderline cases as opposed to clear-cut cases. For example, it is possible that some native speakers of English would find (11b) 'good' on a par with its counterpart in (10b). However, this is less likely to be the case with (11c). (11b) is a borderline case, but (11c) is a clear-cut case of an unacceptable sentence.

Borderline cases and clear-cut cases generally tend to elicit the same type of reaction across speakers: hesitation and certainty. To the extent that this is generally true for certain sentences, it implies a pattern, and therefore a piece of data which should be taken into consideration by the linguist. This is to say that we should expect an adequate theory of language (the linguist's grammar) to be able to distinguish between borderline cases and clear-cut cases. In view of this, what might otherwise look like 'conflicts of judgements' or 'disagreements on data' are in actual fact no more than a reflection of the borderline status of the sentences in question assigned to them by the (mental) grammar. Needless to say that clear-cut cases are not expected to, and usually do not, give rise to 'conflicts of judgements' or 'disagreements on data'.

1.3   *A brief historical overview*

Transformational Grammar is a version of a larger set of different versions of Generative Grammar. Generative Grammar developed in the 1950s in the context of what came to be known as 'the cognitive revolution', which marked a shift to focusing on the mental processes underlying human behaviour from a mere concern with human behaviour for its own sake. As far as language is concerned, it marked a shift from a concern with the mechanics of certain limited aspects of language (mostly, morphophonemics) to a concern with the mental processes underlying a broader range of the properties of language. This change led to the articulation of certain ideas about the mental processes underlying language, some of which have been mentioned in the previous sections. Here we will limit ourselves to a brief and broad description of the evolution of some of the major ideas which have influenced the development of Transformational Grammar. Inevitably, some of the specialised terminology will not be transparent to the uninitiated reader, but, hopefully, will become so in the course of reading this book.

Initially, grammar was considered to consist of a set of Phrase Structure (PS) rules which generate Phrase Markers called Deep Structures (DS), and a set of transformational rules which perform various types of operations on these Phrase

Markers to derive appropriately modified Phrase Markers called Surface Structures (SS). PS rules are 'rewrite' rules of basically two types. The 'context-free' type of the form X → Y, and the 'context-sensitive' type of the form X → WYZ, where W and Z represent the context. The former generate phrasal categories such NP, VP, S . . . etc. and the latter introduce lexical items into appropriate contexts in Phrase Markers. Transformations were largely construction-specific, so that there was a transformation for passives, a transformation for yes-no questions, and so on. UG was considered to contain a kind of blueprint which prescribes the types of possible rule systems, and an evaluation metric which restricts the range of possible grammars to the ones (ideally, one) compatible with the data available to the child.

At a later stage, it became clear that there was a conflict between the desire to provide a description of further phenomena, that is the desire to achieve descriptive adequacy, which resulted in the proliferation of rule systems, and the need to constrain this proliferation, that is the desire to achieve explanatory adequacy. The reaction to this conflict was basically to derive general principles with broad scope from existing ones and attribute them to UG. These principles would then serve as conditions on representations, the application of rules or their output, and perform a restricted range of operations. As components of UG, these principles also serve to define the notion 'possible human language'.

The developing theory went though successive stages with distinctive properties called the Standard Theory, the Extended Theory, Government and Binding Theory, the Principles and Parameters Theory and the Minimalist Program (or Minimalism). Each of these stages represented an improvement on the previous stage, where improvement is driven by the desire to achieve explanatory adequacy.

As the theory was developed, its empirical range was widened considerably to include a fairly broad range of diverse languages. This led to the sharpening of some of the existing ideas, but most prominently to the formulation of clearer ideas about the principles responsible for language variation. It turned out that some of the major aspects of language variation can be accounted for in terms of simple and well-defined sets of options, technically called **parameters**, which are largely determined by the lexical properties of a specific class of categories called functional or inflectional categories. The comparative work carried out within this framework has been largely successful in identifying common underlying properties of superficially different languages.

1.4   *About this book*

Although this book is intended as an introduction to Transformational Grammar, it also incorporates as a major objective an attempt to explain some of the fundamental shifts of perspective which have shaped its development up to Minimalism. These include the shift from a theory based on category-specific and construction-specific rules to one which is based on general rules with broader empirical range; the shift from a theory with a minimal (or no) internal structure to one which is highly structured; and the shift from a theory of grammar whose main focus was to provide an in-depth description of the grammars of a few individual languages to one which combines the task of describing the grammars of a broader range of individual languages with an attempt to account for language variation in terms of parameters which define and set the limits on linguistic variation.

Obviously, the task of presenting and illustrating these major shifts of perspective inevitably involves a process of selection of issues, data, hypotheses, opinions, bibliographical sources and so on. Combining this task with that of providing an introduction to the formal mechanisms of the theory sometimes inevitably involves a process of adapting ideas from previous frameworks in ways that affect mostly the format of their presentation, but sometimes also their content. For example, the task of justifying the eventual reduction of most transformations in earlier stages to a single operation has meant that the definitions of the relevant individual transformations in earlier chapters must emphasise their common aspects.

The book is divided into four parts. Part I includes a chapter on phrase structure (Chapter 2), a chapter on the lexicon (Chapter 3), a chapter on transformations which affect phrasal categories (Chapter 4) and a chapter on transformations which affect terminal categories (Chapter 5). Besides the task of introducing the nature of the rules involved in each of these components and their function, the presentation is also intended to give the reader an idea about how the theory looked in its earlier stages.

Part II outlines the stage of the theory known as the Principles and Parameters framework, with each chapter dealing with one of the modules of the framework. Chapter 6 deals with X-bar theory, Chapter 7 with θ-theory, Chapter 8 with Case theory, Chapter 9 with Binding theory and Control, and Chapter 10 with Movement theory. Here again, besides the task of explaining the major concepts of the Principles and Parameters framework, the presentation attempts to explain why these concepts came to be held and how they fit into the general aim of achieving descriptive and explanatory adequacy.

Up to this stage in the book all data discussed are from English. This is done to make the point that it is possible to construct a sufficiently abstract theory on the basis of an in-depth study of one language to be able to put forward hypotheses relating to the universal nature of some of its rules. Obviously, the hypotheses need eventually to be tested against data from other languages. This is done in Part III of the book, which deals exclusively with language variation across a fairly broad range of languages. It discusses some of the major parameters of variation discussed in the literature. Chapter 11 deals with variation relating to the order of heads in relation to their complement, variation relating to bounding nodes and Subjacency, and variation relating to whether the wh-phrase is moved or left in-situ in simple wh-questions. Chapter 12 deals with the phenomenon of null subjects and objects. Chapter 13 deals with the Verb Second phenomenon, VSO languages and NSO languages. Chapter 14 deals with Incorporation phenomena. Chapter 15 deals with clitics and cliticisation. Chapter 16 deals with variation relating to whether the verb is moved overtly or not.

Part IV outlines the broad aspects of the latest stage in the development of the theory called the Minimalist Program (or Minimalism). This new framework is still in its very early stages and therefore the presentation of it is generally sketchy, although there are attempts to explore some of its major implications. Chapter 17 presents the general organisation of grammar assumed by the Minimalist framework, as well as some of its technical concepts. Chapter 18 deals with the Copy theory of movement and its implications for Binding theory. Chapter 19 deals with Checking theory and how it accounts for certain aspects of language variation. Finally, Chapter 20 presents the theory of phrase structure known as Bare Phrase Structure and compares it with an alternative theory known as Antisymmetry.

The chapters in Parts I, II and III are each followed by a set of exercises. Some of the exercises are designed to test ideas discussed in the chapter. Other exercises invite the reader to think about possible problems and how they can be solved. Some of these exercises anticipate phenomena that are dealt with in subsequent chapters.

The chapters in Parts I and II each include a section at the end called 'Sources and further reading'. This section includes the bibliographical sources on which the discussion in the chapter is based, as well as related references. The reader is strongly urged to consult the original sources. The chapters in Parts III and IV adopt the style found in published material of including references in the text instead of in a separate section.

Sources and further reading

Discussions of the philosophical and methodological foundations of linguistic theory in general and Generative Grammar in particular can be found in Chomsky (1957, 1965, 1966, 1968, 1975b, 1980a, 1986a, 1987a, 1987b, 1988, 1991a, 1991b, 1995) and Chomsky *et al.* (1982). Smith and Wilson (1979) and Newmeyer (1983) include a summary of the core ideas, discussed and explained at a fairly accessible level. An equally accessible discussion of the underpinnings of linguistic theory and related issues can be found in Smith (1989).

Chomsky (1955/1975a), based on an unpublished text, includes an introduction which provides valuable information relating to the earlier stages of the development of (Transformational) Generative Grammar. A more up-to-date account of the development of the theory and reflections about its future shape can be found in Chomsky (1987a, 1987b, 1995). Newmeyer (1980) is an excellent historical account of the major debates which have shaped the evolution of Generative Grammar, and which have led to the development of other distinct, but equally important, versions.

A general discussion of the shift from a rule-based grammar to a principle-based grammar can be found in Chomsky (1986a). Chomsky (1981) is a detailed and highly technical account of the attempts to replace rules with general principles, and explain crosslinguistic variation in terms of parameters. An interesting and insightful evaluation of the principle-based model and its relationship to earlier models can be found in Newmeyer (1991).

Discussions of the issue of modularity can be found in most of Chomsky's references cited above, as well as in the references cited in the main text of this chapter, in particular Curtiss (1977, 1981, 1982, 1988), Yamada (1990) and Smith and Tsimpli (1991). A general discussion of the issue of modularity can also be found in Newmeyer (1983) and Smith (1989). For a philosophically oriented discussion, see Fodor (1983).

Part I
Phrase Structure, Lexicon and Transformations

2 Phrase Structure

Contents

2.1 *Preliminary remarks*

In Chapter 1, we characterised the native speaker's knowledge of English as consisting of rules in combination with the lexicon (a mental dictionary). The lexicon consists of lexical entries for words which specify various types of information necessary for the proper use of the word. A typical lexical entry will minimally include i) information relating to the pronunciation of the word (a phonetic representation); ii) information relating to the meaning of the word (a representation of meaning); and iii) information relating to whether the word is a verb, a noun . . . etc. (a categorial representation). As we proceed, information included in each of the representations mentioned will be made more precise and further information will be added.

So far, we have been using the term 'word' without defining it. As a matter of fact, it is hard, if not impossible, to find an accurate definition for this term. For example, *unhappy* and *unbutton* consist of two meaningful units each (Chapter 1), and yet they would normally be referred to as words. Likewise, *kicked* in (1) would normally be referred to as a word and yet it consists of the verb *kick* and the past tense marker *-ed*:

1. John kicked the white ball.

The category **Tense** specifies the time of the event described by the sentence (past, present or future) in relation to the time when the sentence itself is uttered. For example, the event of 'kicking' described in (1) takes place in the past in relation to the time when the sentence is uttered. It is not clear whether *-ed* is a word of the same order as *kick*, since, unlike *kick*, it cannot 'stand alone'. At the same time, the Tense marker *-ed*, like *kick*, is a meaningful unit in its own right, and contributes to the overall meaning of the sentence.

For the reasons explained, among many others, we will avoid the term 'word' here. Instead, we will use the less controversial term 'lexical item'. We will assume that *kick* and *-ed* each constitutes a lexical item with its own entry. As we proceed in this book, a distinction will emerge between lexical categories such as verbs and inflectional categories such as Tense.

Sentences are often said to have a structure. How do we know that this is the case? Our answer to this question will, for the moment, be that we simply do not know. We are using this claim as a hypothesis which we intend to verify against data. If it turns out that the data support the hypothesis, that is if we can show that the best way to explain certain properties of sentences is by assuming that they have a structure, our hypothesis will be valid. On the other hand, if it turns out that the data do not support the hypothesis, that is if we fail to show that properties of sentences can be explained in terms of a structure, we will either have to modify our hypothesis or give it up altogether. This is one of the main tasks of this chapter.

2.2 *Constituencies and hierarchies*

First, we need to clarify the expression 'sentences have a structure'. In the present context, we will understand this expression to mean that the lexical items which make up a given sentence are hierarchically ordered with respect to each other such that some are at a higher or lower level than other items, or at the same level of hierarchy. To illustrate with an abstract diagram, consider (2):

2.

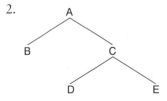

There is an obvious sense in which A is higher than B and C, and B and C are higher than D and E. There is an equally obvious sense in which B is at the same level of hierarchy as C, and D at the same level of hierarchy as E. Moreover, D and E are directly linked to C, while B and C are directly linked to A. Using more formal terminology, D and E are **constituents** (i.e. members) of C, and B and C are constituents of A. D and E, however, are not constituents of B for the simple reason they are not linked to B. It is these kinds of relations which we expect to find among lexical items which make up us sentences when we say that 'sentences have a structure'.

With this in mind, let us now try to work out the structure of the simple sentence (3):

3a. This boy can solve the problem.
3b.

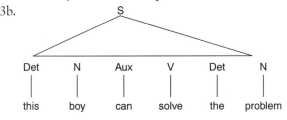

As a first step, we can assign each item in the sentence to its categorial class using the following abbreviations: **N** for nouns, **Aux** for modal auxiliaries, **V** for verbs, and **Det** for Determiners. These abbreviations are known as **categorial labels**. The categories in (3) together form the larger and more complex category **Sentence**, abbreviated as **S**. This preliminary information is represented in (3b).

The triangle in (3b) and other diagrams below is used to indicate that no specific claim is intended or made (yet) concerning the internal structure of the relevant category. On other occasions, the triangle will be used to include complex categories which are not directly relevant to the point being discussed.

A priori, there are a number of ways the categories in (3) can be hierarchically related to each other and, ultimately, to S. (4) and (5) represent two arbitrarily chosen possibilities, where the question mark stands for an unspecified categorial label:

4.

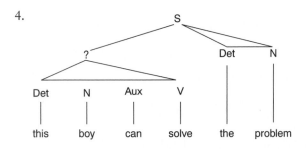

5.

(4) incorporates the claim that the determiner *this*, the noun *student*, the auxiliary modal *can* and the verb *solve* together form a constituent which excludes the determiner *the* and the noun *problem*. (5), on the other hand, incorporates the different claim that the verb *solve* and the determiner *the* together form a constituent which excludes the other categories in the sentence.

The correct structure of (3) is an empirical issue which can only be resolved on the basis of a proper investigation of relevant data. Our strategy will be to select strings of categories and see whether their members behave as a unit/block with respect to the phenomena listed in (6) known as **constituency tests/criteria**. If a string of categories can, in one block, move, delete, be co-ordinated with a similar string of categories, or be replaced with an appropriate pro-form, we will conclude that they form a single constituent:

6. i)   **displacement**
   ii) **deletion**
   iii) **co-ordination** and
   iv) **replacement with a pro-form.**

The string of categories we will select first is *solve the problem*, which we will examine in relation to the tests listed in (6). As shown in (7–10), the selected string of categories can be displaced in one block (7), deleted in one block (8), co-ordinated with a similar string of categories (9), and replaced with the pro-form *so* (10). The latter is a pro-form in the sense that it can stand for the string *solve the problem*. In (7) and (8), the symbol [—] marks the position where the displaced and deleted string is 'understood':

7. Displacement:
   This boy is determined to solve the problem and [solve the problem] he will [—].
8. Deletion:
   John cannot solve the problem, but this boy can [—].
9. Co-ordination:
   This boy will [solve the problem] and [win the prize].
10. Replacement with a pro-form:
    This boy can solve the problem and [so] can the others.

On the basis of the data in (7–10) we can conclude that the categories included in the string *solve the problem* together form a single constituent. In other words, we can think of the facts in (7–10) as empirical evidence in favour of postulating a structure for sentence (3) where the verb *solve*, the determiner *the* and the noun *problem* together form a single constituent which excludes the other categories in the sentence. This conclusion is represented in diagram (11), where the isolated constituent is labelled **Verb Phrase (VP)**. Pending the evidence, the remaining categories in the sentence, i.e. the determiner *this*, the noun *student* and the modal *will*, are linked to S by a triangle. Likewise, pending the discussion of the internal structure of VP, its constituents are linked to VP by a triangle:

11.

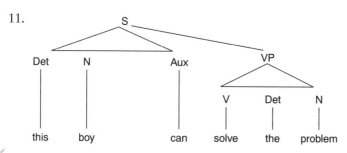

The conclusion we have reached on the basis of the data in (7–10) already excludes both (4) and (5) as possible structures for (3). This is because neither of these structures has the verb *solve*, the determiner *the* and the noun *problem* included under a single constituent. In other words, (4) and (5) make the wrong predictions with respect to the constituency tests discussed above. Because the categories in question are not included in a single constituent, they are not predicted to cluster together as a unit/block with respect to the phenomena of displacement, deletion, co-ordination, and replacement with a pro-form, contrary to what we saw above. Thus, structures (4) and (5) and the hypotheses they incorporate can be dismissed on the ground that they are empirically inadequate.

Following the same procedure, let us now select another string of categories to determine the structure of the rest of the sentence. This time we will select the string *this boy* which consists of the determiner *the* and the noun *boy*. The data in (12a&b) show that they form a constituent:

12a. [This boy] and [that girl] can solve the problem.
12b. [He] will solve the problem.

In (12a) the determiner and the noun are co-ordinated with a similar string of categories, and in (12b) they are together replaced with the pro-form (pronoun) *he*. Incorporating this conclusion into diagram (11), we obtain the more articulated structure shown in diagram (13). The larger category which includes the determiner and the noun is labelled **Noun Phrase (NP)**:

13.

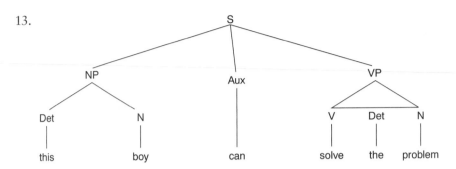

(13) also incorporates the implicit claim that Aux alone forms an autonomous constituent of S. Since Aux is the only category left, this claim seems to be warranted, if not inescapable. To make sure that there is an empirical basis for the claim, we can test it in terms of the constituency criteria. If the conclusion is correct, we expect Aux to be able, for example, to be displaced and to be co-ordinated with another Aux element independently of the categories which make up NP and indeed also VP. In (14a) *can* is displaced to the front of the sentence across the NP *this boy*. In (14b) the modal auxiliary is co-ordinated with another modal auxiliary, namely *will*:

14a. [Can] this boy [—] solve the problem?
14b. This boy [can] and [will] solve the problem.

Our remaining task with respect to (13) is to work out the internal structure of VP. That is, we need to determine whether each of the categories included under VP is an autonomous constituent of VP or whether some of them cluster together in the form of a constituent of VP. As a matter of fact, this task has already been carried out. Like their counterparts *this* and *boy*, the determiner *the* and the noun *problem* are likely to form an NP constituent too. Generalisations across categories of this type are expected on the grounds that categories of the same class tend to cluster together in the form of larger constituents. As it will transpire in this book, generalisations of this type form the backbone of linguistic research. On this basis alone, we can conclude that the determiner and the noun inside VP form an NP constituent of VP. The consequence of this conclusion is that V alone forms an autonomous constituent of VP. These conclusions are incorporated in diagram (15):

15.

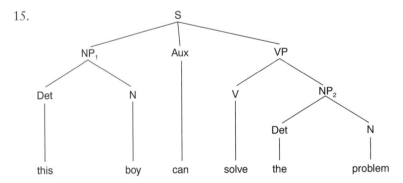

As in the previous situation, to make sure that there is an empirical basis for the conclusion that *the* and *problem* form a single constituent, we can test it in terms of the constituency criteria. (16a) shows that the determiner and the noun inside VP can be replaced with a pro-form. (16b) shows that the two categories can be co-ordinated with a similar string of categories. Finally, (16c) shows that they can be displaced together to the beginning of the sentence:

16a. This boy can solve [it].
16b. This boy can solve [this problem] and [that puzzle].
16c. [This problem], I believe the boy can solve [—].

(15) is a fully articulated structure of sentence (3). The numbers associated with NPs have no theoretical status. They are merely convenient devices to distinguish one NP from the other in the ensuing discussion. Diagram (15) is basically a graphic way of representing the conclusions we have reached concerning the con-stituent structure of sentence (3). The advantage of (15) is that it shows clearly (in visual terms) that categories are indeed hierarchically related to each other and, ultimately, to S. For example, V and NP_2 are not at the same level of hierarchy as NP_1, Aux and VP. This is because V and NP_2 are constituents of a constituent of S, whereas NP_1, Aux and VP are all constituents of S. V and NP_2 are said to be **immediate constituents** of VP. NP_1, Aux and VP are immediate constituents of S. Det and N are immediate constituents of NP.

The hierarchical relations between categories are expressed in terms of the relation of **dominance**. A category is said to **immediately dominate** its immediate constituents. Thus, S immediately dominates NP_1, Aux and VP. VP immediately dominates V and NP_2. NP (in both occurrences) immediately dominates Det and N. Note, however, that although S does not immediately dominate V and NP_2, because the latter are not its immediate constituents, it does dominate them. The distinc-tion here is between immediate dominance and (mere) dominance. A category is said to immediately dominate its immediate constituents, and to (merely) dominate the constituents of its constituents. The notion 'constituent of a constituent' is crucial in determining dominance relations. Because V and NP_2 are not constitu-ents of a constituent of NP_1, the latter does not dominate them.

(15) is called a **tree diagram,** as with family tree diagrams. As a matter of fact, terms used to refer to family relations, in particular **mother, daughter** and **sister,** are also used to refer to relations between categories in a tree diagram. Immediate constituents of a category are daughters of that category. For example, Det and N are daughters of NP. V and NP_2 are daughters of VP. Obviously, if Det and N are daughters of NP, then NP is their mother. If V and NP_2 are daughters of VP, then VP is their mother. Also, if Det and N are daughters of the same mother, then Det and N are sisters, and if V and NP_2 are daughters of the same mother, then V and NP_2 are sisters, and so on.

Tree diagrams such as (15) are not the only means to represent sentence struc-ture. Another equally frequently used means is known as **labelled brackets.** (17) represents exactly the same information as (15), using different notation:

17.   [$_S$ [$_{NP_1}$ [$_{Det}$ this] [$_N$ boy]] [$_{Aux}$ can] [$_{VP}$ [$_V$ solve] [$_{NP_2}$ [$_{Det}$ the]
      [$_N$ problem]]]]

In tree diagrams, categories are represented in terms of labelled **nodes**, and related to each other in terms of **branches**. In labelled brackets, categories are represented in terms of labelled brackets, and related to each other in terms of inclusion and exclusion relations. In (17), the bracket labelled VP, for example, includes the brackets labelled V and NP_2, meaning that V and NP_2 are constituents of VP. At the same time, the bracket labelled VP excludes the brackets labelled NP_1 and Aux, meaning that the latter are not constituents of VP. As expected, the bracket labelled S includes all the other brackets, reflecting the fact that all categories in the sentence are either constituents of S or constituents of constituents of S.

We will use both means of representing structure, with the choice being entirely a matter of convenience.

2.3   *Phrase Structure rules*

The claims about the structure of the sentence represented in diagrams (15) and (17) can be formulated in terms of 'rewrite rules' such as the ones in (18) (read '→' as 'rewrite as' or, less formally, 'goes to').

18a. S   → NP Aux VP
18b. NP → Det N
18c. VP → V NP

(18a–c) are **Phrase Structure (PS)** rules in the sense that they incorporate claims (specified to the right of the arrow) about the constituent structures of phrases (specified to the left of the arrow). PS rules are said to **generate** structures, where generate is understood to mean 'make explicit'. (18a), for example, generates the structure of S by making explicit the information that S consists of NP, Aux and VP. (18b), on the other hand, generates the structure of NP by making explicit the information that NP consists of Det and N. Finally, (18c) generates the structure of VP by making explicit the information that VP consists of V and NP. Tree diagrams and labelled brackets are (visual) devices of representing claims about constituent structures incorporated in PS rules.

The PS rules (18a–c) were based on sentence (3) in the previous section, reproduced in (19). However, their generative capacity goes well beyond (19), to include all possible sentences in the language with similar strings. (20a–d) are a few examples of such sentences. They all resemble (19) in that they include the same patterns of constituency for each category:

19a. This boy can solve the problem.
19b. [$_S$ [$_{NP}$ this boy] [$_{Aux}$ can] [$_{VP}$ [$_V$ solve] [$_{NP}$ the problem]]]

20a. The police will arrest the thief. [$_S$ [$_{NP}$ the police] [$_{AUX}$ will] [$_{VP}$ [$_V$ arrest]
20b. This man can drive that car.   [$_{NP}$ the thief]]

20c. The President will chair the meeting.
20d. The Parliament can impeach the President.

To generate a specific sentence of the set of sentences generated by rules (18a–c), another set of rules which generate specific lexical items can be added. (19), for example, is fully generated by the set of rules in (21):

21a. S   → NP Aux VP
21b. NP → Det NP
21c. VP → V NP
21d. Aux → can
21e. Det → the, this
21f. N   → student, problem
21g. V   → solve

Rules (21a–c) generate **phrasal categories** one constituent of which is a **terminal node**. Terminal nodes are nodes that do not branch and that immediately dominate the lexical item. For example, the phrasal category VP has the terminal node V as one of its constituents, and NP has the terminal node N as one of its constituents. S is called the **root node**. Rules (21d–g), on the other hand, generate terminal nodes by introducing corresponding lexical items in the sentence. The structures generated by both sets of rules are called **phrase markers**. (15) is the phrase marker of sentence (19), represented in the form of a tree diagram.

Obviously, there is also an equally large number of possible sentences which PS rules (21a–c) cannot generate, mainly because they have constituency patterns which differ from the ones in (19) and (20a–d). In the rest of this chapter, we will try to accommodate as many types of sentences as possible, essentially by enriching the system of PS rules developed so far. We will discuss each of the PS rules in (21a–c) separately and modify it in such a way that it can accommodate a broader range of constituency patterns for the category it generates, and therefore a broader range of sentences. Our first target will be the PS rule that generates Aux.

2.4 *Aux and Tense*

(22a&b) and many similar sentences differ from the ones discussed so far in that they apparently lack an Aux:

22a. The boy kicked the ball.
22b. The boy saw the girl.

(22a&b) are problematic for rule (21a) for the simple reason that the rule states that Aux is an obligatory constituent of S. To accommodate sentences such as (22a&b), as well as generate sentences with Aux, we need to modify rule (21a).

An obvious way of achieving the desired result is simply to make the occurrence of Aux optional. Notationally, this can be done by including Aux between parentheses roughly as follows: S → NP (Aux) VP. The latter states that S consists of NP, an optional Aux and VP. This version of the rule now generates sentences with an Aux as well as sentences without an Aux.

However, there is an alternative way of accommodating sentences such as (22a&b) which, when examined carefully, turns out to be more adequate than the solution which makes the occurrence of Aux optional. Examples (23a-d) show that Tense, the category which specifies the time of the event in relation to the time of the utterance, is a constituent of Aux rather than of V:

23a. The boy [will] kick the ball.
23b. The boy [doesn't/didn't] like the party.
23c. The girl [didn't] like the party, but the boy did.
23d. [Go to the party] I wonder whether the boy will [—].

In (23a), Tense shows up as the Modal *will*, while the main verb does not carry any Tense information. In (23b), Tense also shows up on the auxiliary *do*. In (23c), deletion of the verb and its complement (i.e. deletion of VP) does not affect Tense. Finally, in (23d), displacement of VP does not affect Tense.

Now, given that sentences invariably have a Tense category, and given that Tense is a constituent of Aux, it follows that all sentences have an Aux category. Sentences differ only in that some of them have a Modal auxiliary under the Aux node, in addition to Tense, as in (19), while others have only Tense under the Aux node, as in (22a&b). Thus, the optional occurrence of Aux implied by (22a&b) only reflects the optional occurrence of a Modal in addition to Tense. In view of this, our initial solution, which made the occurrence of Aux optional, is inadequate. This is because it was based on the assumption that Tense is not a constituent of Aux, contrary to what examples (23a–d) indicate. The solution which is consistent with the facts illustrated in (23a–d) is one which maintains Aux as an obligatory constituent of S on the grounds that it is the node under which Tense is located. The new version of the PS rule which generates Aux now looks as in (24b) where Tense is an obligatory constituent and the Modal an optional constituent. (24a) is the PS rule which generates S. This rule remains as we stated it originally, with Aux and obligatory constituent:

24a. S   → NP Aux VP
24b. Aux → Tense (Modal)

In view of (24b), in particular the idea that Tense is a constituent of Aux, we need to explain how it is that Tense shows up on the verb in sentences such as (22a&b). This task is carried out in Chapter 5. For the moment, note that Tense elements such as the past tense marker *-ed* are morphologically dependent morphemes or **bound morphemes**. They cannot stand alone, and need to attach to a verbal category such as a Modal or a verb. It is for this reason that Tense appears attached to the verb in sentences such as (22a&b). Obviously, Tense attaches to the verb only when Aux does not include a Modal category. In sentences where Aux includes a Modal category, e.g. *This boy will solve the problem*, Tense appears on the Modal category and the main verb appears unmarked for Tense.

The category **Neg(ation)** also belongs under Aux, irrespective of whether it has the full form *not* or the contracted form *n't*. This is shown in (25a), where the Modal and Neg are co-ordinated with a similar string of categories, and in (25b), where the Modal and Neg are displaced together to the beginning of the sentence:

25a. This politician [cannot] and [will not] solve the problem.
25b. [Can't] this politician [—] solve the problem?

The rule which generates Aux now looks as in (26a). Tense is an obligatory constituent present in all sentences, and Modal and Neg are optional. (26b) is the structure of Aux implied by rule (26a):

26a. Aux → Tense (Modal) (Neg)
26b.

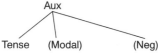

2.5   *Verb Phrase*

The PS rule which generates VP looks as in (28). The rule was established on the basis of the sentence reproduced in (27a), and states that VP consists of V and NP:

27a. This boy can solve the problem.
27b. this boy can [VP [V solve] [NP the problem]]

28.   VP → V NP

Sentences (29) and (30) appear to be inconsistent with (28). (29) and (30) seem to have a VP which consists of the verb only:

29a. The boy cried.
29b. the boy [VP [V cried]]

30a. The girl smiled.
30b. the girl [VP [V smiled]]

To accommodate sentences such as (29) and (30), the occurrence of NP in the rule which generates VP can be made optional by including it between parentheses. (31a) is the revised version of the VP rule. (31b&c) are the two VP structures generated by (31a). (31b) corresponds to sentences of the type illustrated in (27), and (31c) to sentences of the type illustrated in (29) and (30):

31a. VP → V (NP)
31b.   31c.

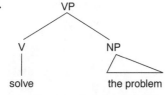

The form that VP takes is largely determined by the type of verb it includes. If the verb is of the type that takes an NP complement (or object), such as *solve* in (27), VP has the form seen in (31b). On the other hand, if the verb is of the type that does not take an NP complement, such as *cry* in (29) and *smile* in (30), VP has the form seen in (31c). Verbs which take an NP complement or object are called **transitive verbs** and the ones which do not take an NP complement are called **intransitive verbs**. Sometimes, the terms 'transitive' and 'intransitive' are also used to describe VPs. The VP in (31b) is transitive and the one in (31c) is intransitive.

Just as there are verbs which take NP as a complement, there are verbs which take other categories as a complement. For example, the verbs *hint* in (32) and *knock* in (33) take a complement which consists of a preposition and an NP. The preposition and its NP complement are said to form a Prepositional Phrase (PP), so that the verbs in (32) and (33) are said to take a PP as complement. PPs are generated by the PS rule seen in (34a), and have the structure shown in (34b):

32a. The teacher hinted at the solution.
32b. the teacher [$_{VP}$ [$_{V}$ hinted] [$_{PP}$ at the solution]]

33a. The girl knocked on the door.
33b. the girl [$_{VP}$ [$_{V}$ knocked] [$_{PP}$ on the door]]

34a. PP → P NP
34b.

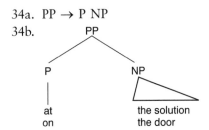

```
        PP
       /  \
      P     NP
      |    / \
     at   the solution
     on   the door
```

To generate sentences of the type illustrated in (32) and (33), the VP rule (28) needs to be revised to allow for the possibility that VP can consist of V and PP, in addition to the two other possibilities discussed. This can be done as in (35a). The PS rule in (35a) includes the information that VP can consist of V only, V and NP, or V and PP. The first two options are shown in (31b) and (31&c), and the third option required for sentences (32) and (33) is shown in (35b):

35a. VP → V ($\left\{ \begin{matrix} NP \\ PP \end{matrix} \right\}$)

35b.

```
          VP
         /  \
        V     PP
        |    / \
      hint  at the solution
      knock on the door
```

It is clear that the rule which generates VP becomes increasingly more complex as revisions are introduced to accommodate new types of VP. Although the complexity of a given rule only reflects the complexity of the various patterns of constituency it is intended to deal with, we will avoid formulating complex rules here. Instead, we will restrict ourselves to the version of the rule which is relevant to the example being discussed. Hopefully, the point that a given rule can be revised (made more complex) to accommodate a broader range of sentences is already clear.

Examples (36) and (37) imply the version of the VP rule in (38a) and the structure shown in (38b). The verb *send* in (36) and the verb *give* in (37) belong to a group of verbs which take two complements, an NP and a PP. Therefore, the VP which includes these verbs consists of V, NP and PP:

36a. The boy sent a letter to the girl.
36b. the boy [$_{VP}$ [$_V$ sent] [$_{NP}$ a letter] [$_{PP}$ to the girl]]

37a. The girl gave a present to the boy.
37b. the girl [$_{VP}$ [$_V$ gave] [$_{NP}$ a present] [$_{PP}$ to the boy]]

38a. VP → V NP PP
38b.

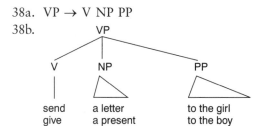

Examples (39) and (40) imply the rule in (41a) and the structure shown in (41b). The verbs *say* and *think* take S as a complement, implying that their VP has the form shown in (41b). That the complements in (39) and (40), included under S in (41b), are of the category S is shown by the fact that each one of them can stand alone as a complete sentence: *He would send a letter to the girl* and *She would give a present to the boy*:

39a. The boy said he would send a letter to the girl.
39b. the boy [$_{VP}$ said [$_S$ he would send a letter to the girl]]

40a. The girl thought she would give a present to the boy.
40b. the girl [$_{VP}$ thought [$_S$ she would give a present to the boy]]

41a. VP → V S
41b.

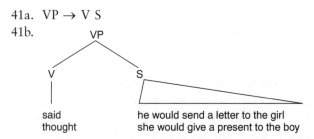

Now, compare (39) and (40) to their counterparts in (42) and (43), which differ only in that they include the extra item *that*, called **Complementiser** (**Comp**). Comp has the function of introducing the S-complement of the verb. For reasons which will become clear later on, Comp is not a constituent of S, but a constituent of another super category called **S'** (read S-bar). S' is generated by rule (44a) and has the structure shown in (44b):

42a. The boy said that he would send a letter to the girl.
42b. the boy said [that [he would send a letter to the girl]]

43a. The girl thought that she would give a present to the boy.
43b. the girl thought [that [she would give a present to the boy]]

44a. S' → Comp S
44b.

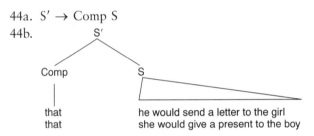

According to rule (44a), S is also a constituent of S' represented in (44b) as a sister to Comp. The VP in (42) and (43) therefore has the structure shown in (45b), generated by the rule in (45a):

45a. VP → V S'
45b.

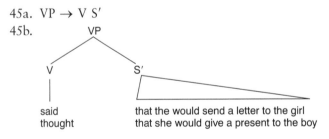

The (internal structure of the) S'-complement is generated by rule (44a), in combination with the rules which generate S and its major constituents. An S'-complement is sometimes called a **clausal complement**, or, alternatively, a **sentential complement**. The term 'clause' is sometimes used synonymously with 'sentence', so that (39), (40), (42) and (43) are said to be bi-clausal, meaning that they consist of two clauses. The larger clause (S) which includes the complement clause is called the **main** or **matrix** clause. It is also often referred to as the **root** clause. The complement clause is called the **subordinate** or **embedded** clause.

As things stand, it seems as though the complement of the verb in (39) and (40) is a different category from the complement of the same verbs in (42) and (43). In the former, the complement is S and in the latter it is S'. This would require a different version of the PS rule which generates VP for each set of examples. However, this may turn out to be an unnecessary complication. That is, it may turn out that the complement is the same category in both sets of examples, and that the presence and absence of *that* does not necessarily result in a different category. One could adopt the hypothesis that in both sets of examples the complement is S′ and that (42) and (43) differ only in that Comp is e(mpty), i.e. not filled with the complementiser *that*. This hypothesis is shown in (46):

46.

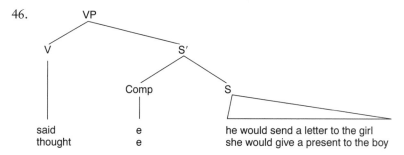

The advantage of the hypothesis represented in (46) is that only one version of the VP rule is needed for both types of example, namely (45a). Version (41a) can be dispensed with altogether, at least as far as the examples discussed are concerned. The hypothesis underlying (46) is desirable on grounds of economy, i.e. it allows us to dispense with one rule. However, like all hypotheses, it must be shown to be empirically correct, that is, we must be able to show that clauses have a Comp node even when they apparently do not include a complementiser. Unfortunately, we will not be able to discuss the relevant evidence till Chapter 5.

The PS rule which generates VP (45a) is a good example of a **recursive rule**. Recursive rules are thought to be responsible for the ability of native speakers to produce potentially indefinitely long sentences, e.g. *Mary thinks (that) Jane believes (that) John claims (that) Bill heard . . . (that) the witness will not testify*. The limits on such sentences are extraneous to language itself, such as memory, attention span and so on. This is another respect in which human languages are said to be 'creative'. By reintroducing S′ on the right of the arrow, rule (45a) makes it possible to reintroduce VP into the derivation which then makes it possible to reintroduce S′ into the derivation and so on.

2.6   *Noun Phrase*

The PS rule which generates NP established above on the basis of example (47) is reproduced in (48):

47a. This boy can solve the problem.

47b. [NP [Det this] [N boy]] can solve [NP [Det the] [N problem]]

48.   NP → Det N

Just as the constituent structure of VP depends on the type of verb it includes, the constituent structure of NP also depends on the type of noun it includes. (49) includes the noun *cancellation* which takes a PP complement as well as a Det. This means that the NP which includes this noun consists of Det, N and PP. (50)

includes the noun *claim* which takes an S'-complement as well as a Det, so that the NP which includes it consists of the categories Det, N and S':

49a. The cancellation of the party annoyed the boys.

49b. [NP the cancellation [PP of the party]] annoyed the boys

50a. The girl resents the claim that she likes the boy.

50b. the girl resents [NP the claim [S' that she likes the boy]]

The first NP has the constituent structure shown in (51b), generated by the version of the NP rule in (51a). The second NP has the constituent structure shown in (52b), generated by the version of the NP rule in (52a). The more general rule which generates both types of NP would therefore have to include the information that PP and S' are optional constituents of NP, although we will not try to spell it out here:

51a. NP → Det N PP

51b.

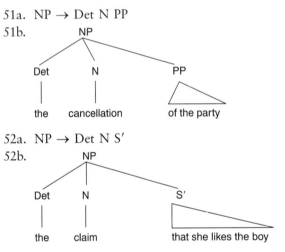

52a. NP → Det N S'

52b.

Examples (53) and (54) suggest that the occurrence of the category Det preceding the noun also needs to be made optional. (53) and (54) include NPs which consist of Det and NP, namely *the film* and *the boy*, and NPs which consist of the noun only, namely *Mary* and *bananas*. Both types of NP are generated by rule (55a). (55b) is the structure of NPs which consist of the noun only. Whether a determiner can occur in an NP depends on the noun, although determiners are not complements of the noun. In English, nouns such as *Mary*, i.e. names, do not tolerate a determiner, whereas nouns such as *boy* and *cancellation* require a determiner:

53a. Mary likes the film.

53b. [NP Mary] likes [NP the film]

54a. The boy likes bananas.

54b. [NP the boy] likes [NP bananas]

55a. NP → (Det) N
55b.
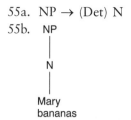

Not only determiners can precede N but full NPs as well. This is shown in (56) and (57). The relevant NPs in these examples have the structure shown in (58b) generated by rule (58a):

56a. John's cancellation of the party annoyed the boys.
56b. [NP [NP John's] cancellation of the party] annoyed the boys

57a. The girl resents the boy's behaviour.
57b. the girl resents [$_{NP}$ [$_{NP}$ the boy's] behaviour]

58a. NP → NP N . . .
58b.

```
                    NP
           _____/|_____
          /         |                 \
        NP          N                 (PP)
         |          |                 /\
       John's    cancellation      of the party
      the boy's  behaviour
```

The pre-nominal NPs in (56) and (57) are in complementary distribution (cannot co-occur) with determiners, as shown in (59) and (60). The rule which generates NP would therefore have to take this restriction into consideration. This can be done by including Det and NP in curly brackets as in (61), a notation which excludes co-occurrence. The formulation of the rule in (61) guarantees that NPs of the type illustrated in (59) and (60) are excluded:

59a. *John's the cancellation of the party annoyed the boys.
59b. [$_{NP}$ [$_{NP}$ John's] [$_{Det}$ the] cancellation of the party] . . .

60a. *The girl resents the boy's the behaviour
60b. . . . [$_{NP}$ [$_{NP}$ the boy's] [$_{Det}$ the] behaviour]

61. NP → $\left\{ \begin{array}{c} NP \\ Det \end{array} \right\}$ N . . .

2.7 *Adjectives and Adverbs*

Adjectives (A) and **adjectival phrases (AP)** typically occur in the positions indicated in (62) and (63):

62a. The boy is tall.

62b. the boy [$_{VP}$ is [$_{AP}$ tall]]

63a. The tall boy likes the girl.

63b. [$_{NP}$ the [$_{AP}$ tall] boy] likes the girl

In (62), AP is a constituent of VP together with the verb *is*. In this particular context, AP is said to have a **predicative function** for reasons that will be explained below in this chapter. In (63), AP is a constituent of NP together with the N it modifies and Det. In this context, AP is said to have an **attributive** function, in the sense that it specifies an attribute of the N it modifies.

As is the case with verbs and nouns, some adjectives take complements while others do not. The adjective *tall*, for example, does not take a complement. In contrast, the adjective *suspicious* takes a PP complement, as shown in (65). The appearance of the complement, however, is optional. This is shown in (64) which lacks a complement for the adjective:

64a. The suspicious girl is Mary.

64b. the [$_{AP}$ suspicious] girl is Mary

65a. The girl is suspicious of the tall boy.

65b. the girl is [$_{AP}$ suspicious [$_{pp}$ of the tall boy]]

The PS rule which generates AP must therefore be as in (66a), where PP is an optional constituent. (66b) and (66c) are the two structures of AP it implies:

66a. AP → A (PP)

66b.

66c.

Having established the rule which generates AP, we now turn to the rules which generate the phrasal categories which contain AP in (62–65). The rule which generates VP in (62) and (65) has the form shown in (67a), which implies the structure in (67b). On the other hand, the rule which generates the NP in (62) and (63) has the form shown in (68a), which implies the structure in (68b):

67a. VP → V AP

67b.

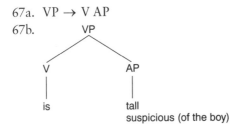

68a. NP → Det AP N
68b.

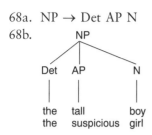

Det	AP	N
the	tall	boy
the	suspicious	girl

Turning now to **adverbs** (**ADV**), they typically occur in at least three major positions depending on the category they modify. In (69a), the adverb *quickly* appears between the subject and the main verb. In (69b), it appears in the sentence final position. The latter is also the position occupied by the adverb *evidently* in (70b). (70a) shows that an adverb can also appear in the sentence initial position:

69a. John quickly fixed the car.
69b. John fixed the car quickly.

70a. Evidently, John fixed the car.
70b. John fixed the car, evidently.

The adverb *quickly* in (69a&b) refers to the manner in which 'John fixed the car'. *Quickly* belongs to a group of adverbs which includes *cleverly, clumsily, deftly. . . etc.* called **manner adverbs**. Because manner adverbs modify the verb (and its complements), they are structurally represented as constituents of VP. For this reason, manner adverbs are sometimes also called **VP-adverbs**. The claim that manner adverbs are constituents of VP is confirmed by the fact that they can be displaced along with the constituents of VP as shown in (71):

71a. Fix the car quickly, I wonder whether John will.
71b. [VP Fix the car quickly] I wonder whether John will [—]

72a. VP → (ADV) V (NP) (ADV)
72b. 72c.

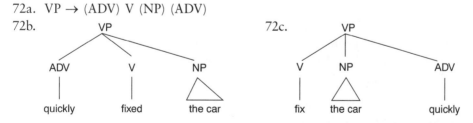

Manner adverbs are therefore generated by the VP rule (72a) which implies structures (72b) and (72c), depending on the linear position of the adverb in VP. (72b) is the structure of the VP in (69a), where ADV immediately precedes the verb. (72c) is the structure of the VP in (69b), where ADV is in the final position.

The adverb *evidently* in (70a&b) refers to a situation which suggests that 'John indeed fixed the car'. In this case, the adverb is said to modify the whole sentence rather than a specific constituent of the sentence. For this reason, *evidently* is classified as a S(**entence**)-**adverb**, together with other adverbs such as *presumably, ironically, probably* . . . etc. As constituents of S, S-adverbs are generated by the rule which expands S shown in (73a). (73b) and (73c) are the structures it generates. (73b) is the structure of (70a), where the S-adverb is in the initial position. (73c) is the structure of (70b), where the S-adverb is in the final position:

73a. S → (ADV) NP Aux VP (ADV)

73b.

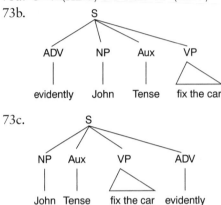

73c.

The adverbs discussed so far have in common the bound morpheme *-ly*, and hence the fact that they are sometimes called *ly*-adverbs. However, there are adverbs which do not have the suffix *-ly* such as *hard* and *fast* in (74) and (75). Like *quickly*, these adverbs are also manner adverbs in the sense that they describe the manner in which the event denoted by the verb is carried out. As such, they are constituents of VP generated by the PS rule (72a):

74a. John hit the nail hard.
74b. John [VP hit the nail hard]

75a. Mary ran fast.
75b. Mary [VP ran fast]

Note, finally, that in addition to the adverbs discussed, linguists sometimes talk about categories which have an 'adverbial function'. The most prominent examples of these adverbial functions relate to place and time. The bracketed constituents in (76) and (77) are said to have an 'adverbial function', although as categories they are PP (76a&b) and S′ (77a&b):

76a. John fixed the car [pp in the garage].
76b. John fixed the car [pp in the morning].

77a. John fixed the car [S′ where Bill had left it].
77b. John fixed the car [S′ when Bill was still sleeping].

Whether categories with the adverbial functions of place and time are constituents of S or VP is a difficult question which we are not going to address here. This does not prevent the reader from applying suitable constituency tests to find out for herself/himself.

2.8 *Co-ordinate structures*

Co-ordination is the device whereby two categories are joined together using *and* to form a complex category of the same type as the two co-ordinated categories. For example, the two NPs *the boy* and *the girl* in (78a) are co-ordinated to form a complex NP with the **co-ordinate structure** shown in (78c):

78a. The boy and the girl solved the problem.
78b. [NP [NP the boy] and [NP the girl]] solved the problem
78c.

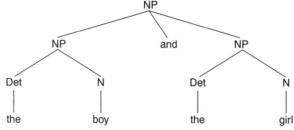

Any category can in principle be co-ordinated with another category of the same type to produce a co-ordinated category also of the same type. Numerous examples of co-ordination were cited in Section 2.2 above involving NP, VP and Aux. (79), for example, involves co-ordination of two PPs:

79a. Mary knocked on the door and on the window.
79b. Mary knocked [pp [pp on the door] and [pp on the window]]
79c.

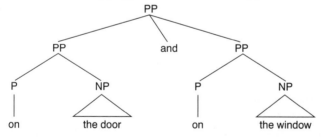

(80) involves co-ordination of two VPs:

80a. Mary opened the door and closed the window.
80b. John [VP [VP opened the door] and [VP closed the window]].

(81) involves co-ordination of two adverbial phrases:

81a. John resigned quickly and quitely.
81b. John resigned [ADV [ADV quickly] and [ADV quitely]].

Since all phrase structures are generated by PS rules, and since any category can be co-ordinated with another category of the same type, there must be a co-ordination rule for each category. However, instead of providing the relevant PS rule for each category, we can use the general and abstract rule in (82) where X stands for any category:

82 XP → XP and XP

Note that (82) must be interpreted in such a way that X is the same type of category on both sides of the arrow. This is because co-ordination can only involve categories of the same type. An NP can only be co-ordinated with another NP, a VP can only be co-ordinated with another VP, and so on. That two categories of different types cannot be co-ordinated is shown in (83) which involves co-ordination of an NP and a PP:

83a. *Mary plays the piano and at home.
83b. *Mary plays [[NP the piano] and [pp at home]]

2.9 *Grammatical functions and relations*

The terms '**subject**' and '**object**' are said to refer to the **grammatical functions** of categories. They are not categorial labels, and therefore should not be confused with categorial labels such as NP, VP, V . . . etc. In (84), *the boy* is an NP category which has the grammatical function 'subject', and *the ball* is another NP which has the grammatical function 'object':

84a. The boy will kick the ball.

84b.

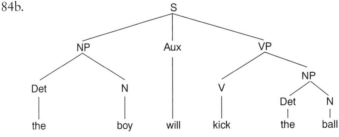

Moreover, the grammatical functions 'subject' and 'object' are structurally based. The subject is the 'NP-daughter-of-S', and the object the 'NP-daughter-of-VP'. In (84) *the boy* is the subject by virtue of the fact that it is the 'NP-daughter of S', and *the ball* the object by virtue of being 'the NP-daughter of VP'.

Grammatical functions such as 'subject' and 'object' are also said to be **relational**, and the expression **grammatical relations** is often used synonymously with grammatical functions. The NP *the boy* in (84) is the subject of the sentence in the sense that it is a subject in relation to the sentence S. On the other hand, the NP *the ball* is the object of the verb, that is, it is an object in relation to the verb or the VP that includes it. The relational nature of grammatical functions can be captured in terms of the formalism in (85):

85a. Subject-of-S: [NP, S]
85b. Object-of-V: [NP, VP]
85c. Predicate-of-S: [VP, S]

'**Predicate**' is another grammatical function which is also relational in nature. The predicate of a sentence is usually the string of categories which contains the verb and its complements, that is, the string of categories included under the VP node. For example, the predicate in (84) is *kick the ball*. It is for this reason that the AP in the sentence *The boy is tall* discussed earlier was said to be predicative.

Structural relations which determine grammatical functions are encoded in PS rules. For example, the structural relation 'NP-daughter-of-S' which underlies the grammatical function 'subject' is encoded in the PS rule which expands S (S → NP Aux VP). On the other hand, the structural relation 'NP-daughter-of-VP' which underlies the grammatical function 'object' is encoded in the PS rule which expands VP (VP → V NP). Thus, in addition to specifying the internal structures of phrasal categories, PS rules also specify the grammatical functions of categories.

Finally, it is important to bear in mind that linear-based notions such as 'precede' and 'follow' do not play a role in determining grammatical functions. Thus, 'subject' cannot be defined as the NP which precedes the verb, and 'object' cannot be defined as the NP which follows the verb. Although the two linear notions may apply to the sentences discussed so far, there are numerous other types of sentences to which they do not apply as will become clear in subsequent chapters. The fact that the subject precedes the verb and the object follows the verb in certain types of English sentences is a by-product of the geometrical aspects of the structures generated by PS rules. As we proceed, it will become clear that linear-based notions such as 'precede' and 'follow' do not play a role in grammar. Grammatical relations and rules are structurally based.

2.10 *Summary*

In this chapter we have postulated a set of rewrite rules called PS rules which generate (i.e. make explicit) the structure of the sentence. A subset of these rules generate phrasal categories such as S, VP, NP, and another subset generate specific lexical items. The latter rewrite a terminal node as a corresponding lexical item. Initially, the rules which generate phrasal categories were based on a single sentence. Then, it was shown that these rules could be revised in appropriate ways to generate phrasal categories with different constituency patterns, thereby accommodating a larger number of sentences. Each revision represents a small step towards the goal of developing a model of grammar which generates all and only grammatical sentences. We came across a situation where the rule which generates NP had to be revised in such a way as to exclude unwanted NPs where a prenominal NP co-occurs with a Det element. Thus, the revisions introduced are motivated not only by the need to accommodate new grammatical sentences, but also by the need to exclude ungrammatical sentences. We have also seen that grammatical functions such as 'subject' and 'object' are essentially structural rather than linear notions. Linear relations have no place in the grammar of human languages.

Exercises

Exercise 2.1

With reference to the diagram provided:

i)   Fill in all the missing nodes.
ii) List all phrasal nodes.
iii) List all terminal nodes.
iv) Identify the root node.
v)   List all constituents in the diagram.

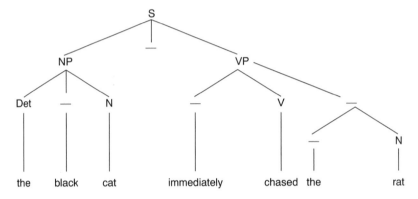

Exercise 2.2

Provide the information requested in (i–vii) in relation to the abstract tree diagram provided:

i)   List all the sisters of NP_2.
ii)   List all the daughters of S'.
iii) List all the categories of which S is the mother.
iv)   List all the categories that S dominates.
v)   List all the categories that S' immediately dominates.
vi)   List all the categories that are dominated by VP.
vii) List all the categories at are immediately dominated by NP_1.

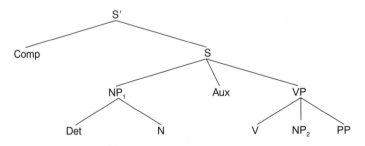

Exercise 2.3

Identify the categories described in (i–v) in the sentence provided:

i)   The subject of the sentence
ii) The object of the verb
iii) The predicate of the sentence
iv) The root clause
v)   The embedded clause

John believes sincerely that Bill knows the answer.

Exercise 2.4

Assign a structure to each of the sentences in (i–v) using both tree diagrams and labelled brackets:

i)   Bill thinks that John is clumsy.
ii) She cleverly avoided the question.
iii) Bill donated money to the charity.
iv) The tall building is new, obviously.
v)   The claim that John is incompetent is absurd.

Exercise 2.5

Sentences (i) and (ii) are said to be **structurally ambiguous**. Each sentence has two different meanings, each of which corresponds to a different structure. For each sentence, provide the two structures underlying its two different meanings:

i)   John saw a man with binoculars.
ii) The boy called the girl from London.

Exercise 2.6

Co-ordination is often said to involve only constituents, that is one or a string of categories exhaustively dominated by the same node. Explain if the sentences in (i) and (ii) are consistent with this idea about co-ordination:

i)   Mary sent a book to Bill and a postcard to Jane.
ii) John repaired and Bill washed the new car.

Exercise 2.7

The sentences in (i–iv) were used above as evidence in relation to constituency tests. Explain if these sentences can be generated by the PS rules discussed in this chapter or require a new type of rules. If they require a new type of rules, explain what form these rules would take:

i)   This problem, the boy can solve.
ii) Can the boy solve the problem?

iii) Solve the problem, I wonder whether the boy will.
iv) I wonder which problem the boy solved.

Sources and further reading

Chomsky (1957, 1965) include some of the early discussions of the general properties of phrase structure and the rules underlying it. The category AUX and its status in the phrase structure of the sentence has attracted a considerable amount of attention in the literature. For an overview of the major issues and views see Akmajian *et al.* (1979), Steele (1981) and Heny and Richards (1983). Jackendoff (1972) is the original source for most studies of the distribution of adverbs and their classification. Chomsky (1965) includes one of the earlier discussions of grammatical functions and relations in Transformational Grammar.

3 Lexicon

Contents

3.1 *Introduction*

Although the system of rules discussed in Chapter 2 generates a large number of grammatical sentences, it also generates a large number of ungrammatical sentences. In this section, we will discuss two major respects in which the system is said to **overgenerate**, and then seek possible ways of constraining it so that at least certain types of ungrammatical sentences are excluded.

One respect in which the system overgenerates concerns ungrammatical sentences such as (1) and (2), compared to (3):

1a. *The boy relied.
1b. the boy [VP relied]

2a. *The boy relied the girl.
2b. the boy [VP relied [NP the girl]]

3a. The boy relied on the girl.
3b. the boy [VP relied [pp on the girl]]

(1) is excluded because the complement required by the verb is missing. (2) is excluded because the complement of the verb, though present, is not of the type required by the verb *rely*. The latter requires a PP complement as shown in (3).

(1) and (2), though excluded, are both generated by the system of rules discussed in Chapter 2, as shown in (4) and (5):

4a. S   →   NP Aux VP
4b. VP   →   V (NP) (PP)

4c. NP → Det N
4d. V → rely
4e. Det → the
4f. N → boy, girl

5a. [$_S$ [$_{NP}$ [$_{Det}$ the] [$_N$ boy]] [$_{Aux}$ Tense] [$_{VP}$ [$_V$ relied]]]]
5b. [$_S$ [$_{NP}$ [$_{Det}$ the] [$_N$ boy]] [$_{Aux}$ Tense] [$_{VP}$ [$_V$ relied] [$_{NP}$ [$_D$ the] [$_N$ girl]]]]]

We continue to ignore the question of how Tense attaches to the verb until Chapter 5. (5a) is the structure of (1), generated by the set of rules in (4). (5b) is the structure of (2) generated by the same set of rules. Note that the options of having or not having a complement of the type NP are both allowed by rule (4b).

The other respect in which the system can be said to overgenerate concerns sentences such as (6), which are grammatically sound, but have an odd meaning. The notation ! is used here to indicate oddity of meaning, understood to be a different notion from 'ungrammaticality' (more on this point later):

6a. !The boy frightens sincerity.
6b. !Sincerity kicked the boy.

The oddity of (6a&b) arises from the fact that their meaning is inconsistent with our expectations in the real world. Given our knowledge of the world, we do not expect abstract concepts such as 'sincerity' to be frightened or to perform the act of 'kicking'. Obviously, (6a&b) would be interpretable in an imaginary world (of the type found in children's books, for example) but this does not alter the fact that they are odd in the context of the real world. (6a&b) are generated by the set of rules in (7a–f), and have the structures shown in (8) and (9):

7a. S → NP Aux VP
7b. VP → V (NP) (PP)
7c. NP → Det N
7d. V → frighten, kick
7e. Det → the
7f. N → boy, sincerity, girl

8a. !The boy frightens sincerity.
8b. [$_S$ [$_{NP}$ [$_{Det}$ the] [$_N$ boy]] [$_{Aux}$ Tense] [$_{VP}$ [$_V$ frightens] [$_{NP}$ sincerity]]]

9a. !Sincerity kicked the boy.
9b. [$_S$ [$_{NP}$ [$_N$ sincerity]] [$_{Aux}$ Tense] [$_{VP}$ [$_V$ kicked] [$_{NP}$ [$_{Det}$ the] [$_N$ boy]]]]

The reason (1) and (2) are excluded and (6a&b) are odd has to do with the properties of individual lexical items, in particular the verb. (1) and (2) are excluded because they are inconsistent with the fact that the verb *rely* requires a complement of the type PP. On the other hand, (6a&b) are odd because they are inconsistent with the fact that the verb *frighten* cannot be associated with an abstract object and *kick* cannot be associated with an abstract subject. This suggests that the revisions required to exclude the examples in question are not likely to affect the PS rules which generate phrasal categories. Recall that these rules were revised in the previous chapter with the purpose of enabling them to cater for different types of verbs. Rather, the revisions required are likely to affect the rules which generate individual lexical items, that is the rules which rewrite a terminal symbol as an appropriate lexical item.

3.2 *Subcategorisation restrictions*

Verbs are said to **subcategorise** into various sub-groups, depending on whether they require a complement, and if they do, what type of complement they require. The verb *kick*, for example, belongs to the sub-group of transitive verbs which require an NP complement. The verb *cry*, on the other hand, belongs to the sub-group of verbs which do not require an NP complement. Other sub-groups include verbs which require a PP complement, e.g. *rely* and *knock*, verbs which require both an NP and a PP complement, e.g. *put* and *give*, verbs which require an S'-complement, e.g. *think* and *believe* . . . etc.

The subcategorisation properties of verbs can be formally represented in terms of frames such as in (10), called **subcategorisation frames**:

10a. kick: [V;—NP]
10b. cry: [V;—]
10c. rely: [V;—PP]
10d. put: [V;—NP PP]
10e. think: [V;—S']

Subcategorisation frames specify the categorial class of the lexical item (the verb in (10)), and the environment in which it can occur. For example, (10a) specifies the information that *kick* is a verb, and that it requires a complement of the type NP. This information implies that *kick* can only be inserted under a V node in a VP structure where V has an NP sister. Given that subcategorisation frames specify (idiosyncratic) information relating to the properties of individual lexical items, they are associated with lexical items in their lexical entries. Thus, information concerning the subcategorisation properties of lexical items, which is necessary for their proper use, is an additional type of information to be added to the other types of information included in lexical entries and briefly discussed in the previous chapter. Obviously, similar subcategorisation frames exist for other categories: nouns, adjectives and prepositions. Verbs are used here merely for illustration.

Subcategorisation frames can form the basis on which a general **Subcategorisation rule** can be set up which would make rewriting a terminal symbol as a specific lexical item sensitive to the subcategorisation properties of the lexical item. More precisely, this rule would make it possible to rewrite a terminal symbol as a lexical item in association with its subcategorisation frame. The consequence of this rule is that a given lexical item can only be associated with a phrasal structure which is consistent with its Subcategorisation requirements. The rule in question can be formulated as in (11):

11. V → Y/ $\left\{\begin{array}{l} \text{—NP]} \\ \text{—]} \\ \text{— PP]} \\ \text{— NP PP]} \\ \text{— S']} \\ \ldots \end{array}\right\}$

(11) specifies the various environments in which a given verb, represented by the variable symbol Y, can be introduced. Which frame is chosen, obviously, depends on the subcategorisation properties of the verb which substitutes for the variable. If the verb is *rely* (i.e. if Y = *rely*), for example, the chosen subcategorisation frame would be —PP], and if the verb is *think* the chosen frame would be —S'], and so on.

With (11) incorporated into our system of rules, we guarantee that sentences such as (1) and (2), where the verb is associated with an inappropriate subcategorisation frame, are excluded. Because subcategorisation frames are chosen on the basis of the Subcategorisation properties of the verb, we ensure that verbs are paired with appropriate frames from the set specified in (11). To illustrate how the revised system works, example (12) is generated by the set of rules in (13a–g):

12.   The boy relied on the girl.

13a. S   →   NP Aux VP
13b. VP   →   V (NP) (PP) (S') . . .
13c. NP   →   Det N
13d. V   →   rely/—PP]
13e. P   →   on/—NP]
13f. Det   →   the
13g. N   →   boy, girl

Rule (13d) relating to the verb and rule (13e) relating to the preposition are instantiations of two of the options specified in the more general rule (11). Because (13d) specifies the frame of the verb it generates, we ensure that the verb is associated with this frame, thereby excluding sentences such as (1) and (2).

(11), of which (13d) and (13e) are instantiations, is a 'context-sensitive' rule in the sense that it specifies the context in which a given category can occur. In contrast, rules (13a-c) are 'context-free' since they do not specify contexts. They merely list the constituents that a given phrasal category can include.

3.3 *Selectional restrictions*

Let us now turn to (6a&b) and see how they too can be excluded. Since the problem they pose involves contextual information as well (i.e. which verbs can be paired with which nouns), the solution to the problem they present is likely to involve 'context-sensitive' rules as well.

As pointed out above, the odd nature of (6a&b), reproduced in (14a&b), seems to have to do with the fact that the verb *frighten* is inappropriately paired with an abstract or inanimate object and the verb *kick* is inappropriately paired with an abstract or inanimate subject. The solution to the problem posed by these examples will, therefore, consist of ensuring that the verbs *frighten* and *kick*, among others, are not associated with abstract nouns in certain positions. More generally, the system should include a mechanism which ensures that only nouns with appropriate properties are associated with given verbs in a given context:

14a. !The boy frightened sincerity.
14b. !Sincerity kicked the boy.

Features such as [+/−abstract], [+/−animate], among others, are inherent and idiosyncratic properties of nouns. Therefore, like subcategorisation properties, they are specified in the lexical entries of nouns. Thus, the lexical entry of *sincerity*, for example, includes the feature [+abstract], among other features, and the lexical entry of *boy* includes the feature [+animate], among others. Lexical information of this type can be used to set up a 'rewrite' rule of the type in (15), which specifies the contexts in which a given verb can occur. (15i) refers to the subject position and (15ii) to the object position:

15. $[V] \rightarrow Y /$
$$\begin{cases} \text{(i)} \quad [+/-\text{ abstract}] \text{ Aux} - \\ \text{(ii)} \quad - [+/-\text{ animate}] \end{cases}$$

(15) is called a **Selectional rule**, since it specifies certain selectional restrictions associated with verbs, and presumably other categories as well. Obviously, the version of the rule which would account for all possible combinations is much more complex than (15). The latter is simply an illustration of the form the rule can possibly take.

With respect to the verb *frighten*, the corresponding selectional rule would look, at least in part, roughly as in (16). The verb *frighten* can take either a non-abstract subject, as in *The girl frightened the boy*, or an abstract subject, as in *Sincerity frightens the boy*. However, it can only take an animate object, as in *The girl frightened the boy*. Consequently, (14a) is excluded, since it involves a non-animate object (i.e. *sincerity*), which is incompatible with the selectional restrictions of the verb *frighten*:

16. $V \rightarrow \text{frighten} /$
$$\begin{cases} [+/-\text{ abstract}] \text{ Aux} - \\ - [+\text{animate}] \end{cases}$$

The rule corresponding to the verb *kick* would look roughly as in (17). The verb *kick* can only take an animate subject as in *The girl kicked the boy*, and can only take a non-abstract object as in *The girl kicked the boy/chair*. (14b) is therefore excluded on the ground that it involves an abstract (or non-animate) subject (i.e. *sincerity*) which is incompatible with the selectional restrictions of the verb *kick*:

17. V → kick/ $\left\{\begin{array}{l} \text{[+animate] Aux —} \\ \text{— [− abstract]} \end{array}\right\}$

Like Subcategorisation rules, the Selectional rules (16) and (17) are 'context-sensitive'. They specify the environment in which a given verb can occur, where the environment is the subject and object positions.

One might wonder whether the problems posed by the odd examples (14a&b) are of the same order as the ones posed by ungrammatical examples such as (1) and (2). In other words, it is not clear whether selectional restrictions should be dealt with in terms of the same mechanisms (rules) which deal with subcategorisation requirements. Recall that while violations of subcategorisation requirements affect the grammatical status of the sentence, violations of selectional restrictions do not necessarily affect the grammatical status of the sentence. Rather, they affect the interpretation of the sentence in relation to a given world. In view of this, one could argue that selectional restrictions involve an aspect of language (meaning and interpretation) which is different from the one involved in subcategorisation. More precisely, selectional restrictions involve a different component of the grammar which exists over and above the component which deals with the grammatical properties of sentences.

It seems that we have to make a distinction between two different components of the grammar. One component comprises PS and subcategorisation rules and has the task of generating all and only grammatical sentences. We will call this component the **syntactic component**. The other component comprises a set of rules, whatever their nature, which assign an interpretation to sentences generated by the syntactic component in relation to a possible world. For the moment, we will call the component in question the **semantic component**, although the term 'semantic' may be misleading. The relationship between the two components is an input–output relationship, insofar as sentences generated by the syntactic component serve as input to the semantic component which then assigns them an interpretation. This relationship partly explains the remark made earlier that although sentences such as (14a&b) are semantically odd, they are syntactically sound. Such sentences are grammatically sound insofar as they are generated by the syntactic component.

In this chapter we will not have much to say about the rules of the semantic component. Our concern is with the syntactic properties of sentences, that is the properties which can be accounted for in terms of syntactic rules. In subsequent chapters we will learn more about the semantic component. One of the interesting conclusions which will emerge is that some of the mechanisms involved in assigning an interpretation to sentences are indeed syntactic in nature, and, therefore, should be dealt with in terms of the rules of syntax.

The broad picture of grammar we have so far is one where it consists of two components. One is the syntactic component which consists of PS rules and Subcategorisation rules and has the function of generating sentences (by making their structure explicit). The other is a semantic component which assigns an interpretation to sentences generated by the syntactic component. It is interesting to see where the lexicon fits in this broad picture. We turn to this question in the next section.

3.4 *Separating the lexicon from syntax*

Most of the revisions undertaken so far have been motivated by the twin need to accommodate further grammatical examples and exclude as many ungrammatical ones as possible. Each revision introduced results in strengthening the descriptive power of the grammar, and therefore represents a step towards the goal of achieving descriptive adequacy (Chapter 1). However, our success in accommodating certain types of new sentence required the introduction of new rule systems. For example, to exclude sentences where the subcategorisation properties of lexical items are not properly reflected, we had to introduce context-sensitive Subcategorisation rules to be added to the existing set of context-free PS rules. Given that the need to achieve explanatory adequacy depends on restricting the proliferation of rule systems (Chapter 1), it seems as though some of the steps we have taken towards the goal of achieving descriptive adequacy have resulted in corresponding steps away from the goal of achieving explanatory adequacy. We appear to have a dilemma.

One possible way out of this dilemma is to attribute some of the functions we have been attributing to the syntactic component to other components. For example, we have seen that the function of ensuring that the selectional restrictions of lexical items are properly reflected can be attributed to the semantic component which assigns an interpretation to sentences generated by the syntactic component. The consequence is that the context-sensitive rules required to accomplish this function can be eliminated from the syntactic component. Although this move has not resulted in the total elimination of context-sensitive rules from the syntactic component, it represents a step towards the goal of restricting the proliferation of the rule systems it includes. In view of this, it is desirable to eliminate the remaining set of context-sensitive rules, i.e. Subcategorisation rules, from the syntactic component. Let us see how this can be done.

Given their nature as rewrite rules, Subcategorisation rules have the curious effect of equating the rewriting of phrasal categories as individual constituents with the rewriting of terminal symbols as lexical items in association with their subcategorisation frames. In other words, Subcategorisation rules are syntactic in format, insofar as they are rewrite rules, but they differ from PS rules in that they make reference to lexical information. This implies a view whereby the syntactic component and the lexicon are somehow merged, which does not necessarily have to be the case. It is plausible to think of the lexicon as being independent of the syntactic component, insofar as it includes information which, though relevant to the syntactic representation of lexical items, is essentially lexical in nature. What is needed, then, is a general rule that will serve as a link between the lexicon and the syntactic component, that is a rule which will have the function of inserting lexical items under appropriate nodes in phrase markers generated by the PS rules of the syntactic component.

Let us call the rule in question the **Lexical Insertion Rule (LIR)**, and define it as in (18):

18. **Lexical Insertion Rule**

> Insert lexical item X under terminal node Y, where Y corresponds to the categorial properties of X, and YP corresponds to the subcategorisation properties of X.

LIR performs the operation of inserting lexical items under terminal nodes subject to two conditions. First, the terminal node must match the categorial class of the lexical item. This will ensure that verbs are inserted under V nodes, nouns under N nodes, and so on. The second condition is that the phrase containing the terminal node, i.e. the VP of V, the NP of N . . . etc., must match the subcategorisation properties of the lexical item. This means that if the lexical item is a verb which subcategorises for an NP, the VP containing V must include an NP, and if the lexical item is a verb which does not subcategorise for a NP complement, the VP containing V must not include an NP, and so on. Consequently, ungrammatical sentences where lexical items are associated with inappropriate subcategorisation frames are excluded.

It should be clear that LIR performs the functions that were previously performed by Subcategorisation rules, so that the latter can be dispensed with altogether. The syntactic component can now be thought of as consisting of one rule system, namely the context-free PS rules. It might be argued that in view of the fact that LIR is different in nature from PS rules, we have simply replaced one rule system with another. LIR differs from PS rules in that it performs an operation, as pointed above, unlike PS rules. We will see in Chapter 4 that such rules are needed in the grammar for quite independent reasons. Viewed in this wider context, the move to replace Subcategorisation rules with the single LIR does not, strictly speaking, amount to replacing one rule system with another, but to harnessing an independently needed rule system to perform additional tasks.

We now consider the lexicon as being separate from the syntactic component. The postulation of separate components should, in principle, be justifiable, preferably on the grounds that they have properties which distinguish them from other components. For example, the autonomy of the semantic component from the syntactic component is justifiable on the grounds that it includes rules of interpretation which are different in nature from the rules of syntax. Thus, we should expect the autonomy of the lexicon to be also justifiable on similar grounds. That is, we should expect the lexicon to include rules which are different in nature from the rules of syntax. We turn to this issue in the next section.

3.5 *Lexical derivation*

Our view of the lexicon so far is that it is an unordered list of lexical entries, with each entry specifying a range of information necessary for the proper use of the lexical item. Part of this information relates to the categorial property of the item, whether it is a verb, a noun . . . etc. Another part relates to its subcategorisation properties, whether it takes a complement or not and if it does what kind of complement it is. LIR makes crucial reference to both types of information in performing the operation of lexical insertion to ensure that lexical items are paired with appropriate contexts.

With this in mind, consider the derivation of complex categories roughly shown in (19a–c):

19a. translate +ion → translation (Verb-to-Noun)
19b. sheepish +ish → sheepish (Noun-to-Adjective)
19c. colony +-ise → colonise (Noun-to-Verb)

(19a–c) show that the process of forming complex categories from simpler lexical items can result in a change of the categorial class of the lexical item which serves as the **base** for the derivation. Thus, the **affixation** of the **suffix** -*ion* to a verb base results in the derivation of a noun (19a), the affixation of -*ish* to a noun base results in the derivation of an adjective (19b), and the affixation of -*ise* to a noun base results in the derivation of a verb (19c).

The derivation of complex categories not only affects categorial properties of lexical items, but also their subcategorisation properties. As shown in (20a&b), the presence of an NP complement is obligatory with the verb *translate* (20a), but apparently only optional with the noun *translation* derived from it (20b). The two categories, though derivationally related, have different subcategorisation properties which can be stated as in (21a&b):

20a. Mary translated *(the book).
20b. The translation (of the book) was awful.

21a. *translate*:   [V; — NP]
21b. *translation*:   [N; — (PP)]

Now, given that the rules of derivation affect the categorial class and the subcategorisation properties of lexical items, they must apply at a stage prior to their insertion into phrase markers. This is because, as pointed out above, LIR makes crucial reference to the categorial and subcategorisation properties of lexical items to ensure that they are inserted under appropriate nodes located in appropriate contexts. Presumably, the stage at which these rules apply is the lexicon, so that the lexicon is not merely a list of lexical entries. It also includes rules of derivation. Assuming that the syntactic component does not include rules of derivation which affect the categorial and the subcategorisation properties of lexical items, the autonomy of the lexicon is justifiable on the grounds that it includes rules which are distinct in nature from the rules of syntax. More on this point later on.

It is an interesting question whether derivationally related categories such as *translate* and *translation* have separate lexical entries which specify their categorial and subcategorisation properties, among other things. The alternative view would be that there is only one lexical entry for the base form, namely the verb *translate*, and that the complex noun *translation* is derived from it by a productive rule. The issue boils down to size, at least initially. The option of having lexical entries for derived forms as well as the base form implies an enormous lexicon. On the other hand, the option of having a lexical entry only for the base form and deriving the other forms from it by independently stated rules implies a comparatively smaller lexicon. However, there is more to this issue than just size. If it turns out that the process of deriving complex categories is governed by simple rules which apply across categories in a consistent manner, these rules must form an important component of human languages. Simply listing complex categories in the lexicon will amount to a failure to identify these rules. In view of this, the best course to follow is to try first to see whether the derivation of complex categories is subject to general rules.

It turns out that the derivation of complex categories is indeed subject to general rules. Judging from (19a–c) and (20a&b), the rules in question apparently have the effect of changing the categorial as well as subcategorisation properties of lexical items. For the moment, we will ignore the change in the subcategorisation properties and concentrate only on the change in the categorial properties. The change in subcategorisation properties is discussed in more detail in Chapter 6.

The suffixes listed in (19a–c) and others like them are consistent in more than one way. For example, when added to a base form they invariably result in the derivation of the same complex category irrespective of the base form. For example, when the suffix *-ion* is added to a verb, it invariably results in the derivation of a noun whatever the verb chosen. Likewise, when the suffix *-ise* is added to a noun, it invariably results in the derivation of a verb whatever the noun chosen. This consistent property of the suffixes can be explained by assuming that, like free morphemes such as *table* and *translate*, they too are specified for categorial information. Accordingly, *-ion* is specified as N; *-ish* is specified as A, and *-ise* as V. A more precise representation of the complex categories in (19a–c) would be as shown in (22a–c) and (23a–c). The representations in (22a–c) make use of labelled brackets and the ones in (23a–c) of tree diagrams:

22a. [N [V translate] [N -ion]]
22b. [A [N sheep] [A -ish]]
22c. [V [N colony] [V -ise]]

23a. 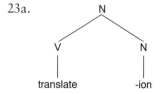   23b.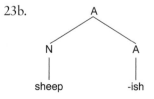

23c.

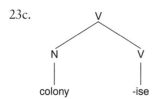

The next step is to explicate the process that we have been describing as change of category. Looking at the representations in (22) and (23), it is consistently the case that the category of the derived complex is the same as the category of the suffix. In other words, it is the category of the suffix that consistently predominates. For this reason, among others, the suffix is called the **head** of the complex category. The head of a complex category is basically the morpheme which imposes its own properties on the derived complex form. In English, the head of a complex category is the rightmost morpheme. This can be seen more clearly in complex categories with more than one suffix with different categorial properties, e.g. the adverb *sheepishly*. The latter has the structure shown in (24):

24a. [[[N sheep] [A -ish]] [ADV -ly]]

24b.

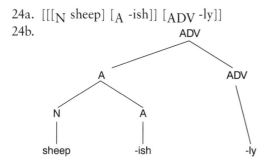

Sheepishly is a complex category of the type ADV by virtue of the fact that its rightmost morpheme is an ADV. *Sheepish* is a complex category of the type A by virtue of the fact that its rightmost morpheme is an A. This property of English complex categories can be stated in terms of the rule in (25) called the **Right Hand Head Rule** (**RHR**) (adapted from Williams 1981):

25. **Righthand Head Rule**

   The head of a complex word is its rightmost morpheme.

It turns out that, strictly speaking, there is no change in the category of the base form when a suffix is added to it. As shown in (22a–c) and (23a–c), the base form preserves its categorial identity. The (false) impression that it undergoes a change in category is due to the RHR (25) which results in the suffix imposing its categorial identity on the derived complex (by virtue of being the head of the derived complex).

The conclusion that affixes have a categorial property can be understood to imply that they have lexical entries on a par with free standing lexical items. This is already indicated by the fact that complex categories have a compositional meaning determined by both the base and the affix, suggesting that affixes have a sort of representation of meaning. In Chapter 1, it was pointed out that the complex adjective *unhappy* has the compositional meaning 'not happy' and the complex verb *unpack* has the compositional meaning 'reverse the action of packing'. There are reasons to believe that affixes have subcategorisation properties as well.

Affixes tend to be highly selective as to the categories they can attach to. The negative prefix *un-* attaches only to adjectives. Likewise, the suffix *-ion* usually attaches to verbs, whereas *-hood* can attach to nouns, as in *boyhood*, or to adjectives, as in *falsehood*. These idiosyncratic properties of affixes must be stated in their lexical entries, presumably in the form of subcategorisation frames. Using the suffixes *-ion* and *-hood* for illustration, their subcategorisation frames can be represented as in (26). The latter state the categorial identity of the suffix and the type of categories it can attach to:

26a. -ion: [N; [V] —]

26b. -hood: [N; $\left\{ \begin{matrix} [N] \\ [A] \end{matrix} \right\}$ —]

Subcategorisation by affixes targets lexical categories such as V, N . . . etc., rather than phrasal categories such as NP, PP . . . etc. Attaching an affix to a base results in the creation of a complex terminal category rather than a phrase. As such, it differs from subcategorisation by lexical categories of the type discussed earlier which targets phrasal categories and results in the creation of a phrasal category. To distinguish between the two types of subcategorisation we will refer to subcategorisation of lexical categories by affixes as **morphological subcategorisation**, and to the subcategorisation of phrasal (or syntactic) categories by lexical categories as **syntactic subcategorisation**. The former is relevant to the rules which form complex terminal categories applying in the lexicon, and the latter to rules of syntax.

Not all bound morphemes necessarily result in the derivation of a category different from that of the base. There are bound morphemes which consistently never have this effect. These include, among others, the plural marker *-s*, the past tense marker *-ed*, and the third person singular present tense marker *-s*. The plural marker attaches to nouns, e.g. *book*, to derive complex plural nouns, e.g. *books*. The past tense marker and the third person singular present tense marker attach to verbs, e.g. *kick*, to form complex verbs, e.g. *kicked*, *kicks*. These morphemes are called **inflectional morphemes**, to distinguish them from the **derivational morphemes** discussed above.

Although inflectional morphemes differ from derivational morphemes in the way indicated, they too are subject to the RHR. The plural character of the noun *books* is due to the fact that the number feature of the suffix is plural. Likewise, the past tense property of the verb *kicked* is due to the fact that the tense feature of the Tense suffix is past. This is shown more clearly in (27a&b):

27a. N[plural] — N book, -s[plural]   27b. V[past] — V kick, -ed[past]

The question of what exactly distinguishes inflectional morphemes from derivational morphemes has generated much discussion. The difference mentioned above, namely that derivational affixes result in the derivation of a category distinct from the base, is not absolute. For example, neither the negative prefix nor the reversative prefix results, in the derivation of a category distinct from the base. The former attaches to adjectives to derive adjectives, and the latter attaches to verbs to derive verbs. This follows from the RHR, since prefixes are not the rightmost morphemes in the complex categories which include them. However, one would be hard-pressed to call the prefixes in question 'inflectional morphemes'.

Another perhaps more useful way of distinguishing between the two types of morpheme is in terms of whether they are relevant to syntax or not. In Chapter 2 we discussed evidence that shows that Tense morphemes are generated under Aux separately from the verb. In Chapter 5 we will see that they are joined with the verb in terms of a rule of syntax. In subsequent chapters we will see that some rules of syntax make reference to whether a noun, and therefore the NP that includes it, is singular or plural, among other properties associated with inflectional morphemes. This picture is consistent with the view that inflectional morphemes are the morphemes that are relevant to syntax. There is no evidence that rules of syntax make reference to affixes of the type listed in (19a–c).

According to the scenario just outlined, it seems that the rules involved in the derivation of complex words are not restricted to the lexicon. They can also operate in syntax. This suggests that these rules may be part of a separate component, although one that is not in a strict feeding relationship with the other components. Its rules can apply either in the lexicon or in syntax. We will call the component in question the **morphological component**.

3.6   *Categories as feature complexes*

In the previous section, we classified the affix -*ion* as a noun and the affix -*ise* as a verb. This may appear strange, since it implies that we are putting these affixes on the same level as more familiar instances of nouns such as *table* and verbs such as *kick*. The use of categorial terms in relation to affixes reflects a crucial assumption underlying these terms, namely that they are understood merely as labels for **categorial features**. They have no implication whatsoever as to whether the labelled item refers to (or names) an entity or an individual or denotes an event or a state. Thus, *table*, for example, is a noun not because it refers to (or names) an entity, but because it is specified for the categorial feature [+N]. Likewise, *kick* is a verb not because it denotes an action (or event), but because it is specified for the categorial feature [+V]. In this context, it is not strange to classify affixes as nouns or verbs, meaning they are specified for the categorial features [+N] and [+V].

To be more precise, categorial labels are understood as 'bundles' of categorial features. The idea is borrowed from feature-based phonology where segments are understood as 'bundles' of distinctive features. For example, the vocalic sound /i/ is a 'bundle' of the features [+high, −low, −back, −round], and /u/ a 'bundle' of the features [+high, −low, +back, +round]. This decomposition of segments into features allows for the possibility of capturing certain common properties between segments which are otherwise different. For example, although /i/ differs from /u/ in terms of the values of the features [+/−back] and [+/−round], it is similar to /u/ in terms of the values of the features [+/−high] and [+/−low]. The sounds /i/ and /u/ are said to form a **natural class** with respect to their common features. One of the reasons underlying this view is that some rules of phonology make reference to specific features of segments, so that all segments which have a given feature referred to by a given rule will be subject to that rule, although the segments may differ with respect to other features.

The view that syntactic categories are also 'bundles of features' has been motivated on similar grounds. We cannot go into the details at this early stage, as we have not yet discussed the kind of rules that have been used to justify the assumption. Here, we will simply give the **feature matrix** of each categorial class, which we will assume in the rest of the book. Nouns have the categorial feature complex seen in (28a), verbs have the categorial feature complex seen in (28b), adjectives have the categorial feature complex seen in (28c) and prepositions have the categorial feature complex seen in (28d):

28a. N: [+N, −V]
28b. V: [−N, +V]
28c. A: [+N, +V]
28d. P: [−N, −V]

The classification in (28a–d) assumes that the nominal and verbal features are the only primitive categorial features, so that even categories such as A and P are 'bundles' of nominal and verbal features. Ns and As form a natural class in relation to the feature [+N], and Vs and Ps form a natural class in relation to the feature [−N]. Presumably, categories which form a natural class are expected to pattern together with respect to certain syntactic phenomena.

The idea that categories are essentially 'bundles of features' plays an important role in the theory outlined in this book. This will become clear in the subsequent chapters, where additional features are introduced that play a crucial role in the syntactic representation of categories. Thus, it is important to get used to thinking of categories as 'bundles' of features. For the moment, note that the idea applies not only to categorial features but other features as well. For example, we have been assuming that the Tense category is a bundle of the features [+/−Tense] with implied feature oppositions such as [+/−past]. Likewise, the plural inflectional morpheme is nothing more than the feature [+plural], and so on.

Categories as bundles of features are said to be spelled out by the rules of phonology. The latter is understood to be a separate component of grammar called the **phonological component**, with rules distinct in nature from the rules of syntax. Phrase markers derived by the syntactic component, where categories are represented in the form of feature complexes, are fed to the phonological component which spells out the feature complexes as morphemes, and assigns the phrase marker a phonological (or phonetic) interpretation.

3.7 *Summary*

We started this chapter by discussing two situations in which the system of rules developed in Chapter 2 is said to overgenerate. One situation concerns sentences where the subcategorisation properties of lexical items, in particular verbs, are not properly reflected. The other situation concerns sentences where the selectional properties of lexical items are not properly reflected.

The first situation was initially dealt with by adding to the existing set of context free PS rules, another set of context-sensitive rewrite rules called subcategorisation rules. The latter rewrite a terminal symbol as a given lexical category in association with its subcategorisation frame (the context). These rules ensure that verbs (and other categories) are paired with appropriate subcategorisation frames, thereby excluding sentences where verbs are associated with the wrong subcategorisation frames. Later on, we explored the possibility of eliminating these context-sensitive subcategorisation rules from the syntactic component. We have seen that they can be replaced with a single general rule called the Lexical Insertion Rule, which inserts lexical items under terminal nodes situated in contexts which are consistent with their categorial features and subcategorisation properties. The consequence of this move is that the syntactic component now consists of context-free PS rules only, and the lexicon exists separately from the syntactic component.

The situation which concerns sentences where the selectional properties of lexical items are not properly reflected was initially dealt with by including a set of selectional rules. The latter are context sensitive rules which operate in terms of binary semantic features such as [+/−abstract], [+/−human]. Their function is to ensure that lexical items such as verbs are paired with nouns with appropriate semantic features. Subsequently, it was decided that these rules do not belong to the domain of syntax, given that the problems they are supposed to deal with are not syntactic in nature. Instead, they belong to the semantic component which assigns interpretations to (grammatical) sentences generated by the (rules of) syntax.

Given that the LIR makes reference to the categorial and subcategorisation properties of categories, and given that both these properties may change as a result of the derivation of complex categories, the relevant rules of derivation must apply in the lexicon or at least prior to the insertion of complex categories into phrase markers. The rules in question could be regarded to belong to an autonomous morphological component. It was also pointed out that categories are essentially 'bundles of features', categorial or otherwise. The phrase markers derived in the syntax are fed to a phonological component, which spells out the feature bundles as morphemes. This is part of the general process of assigning the phrase marker a phonological or phonetic interpretation.

Exercises

Exercise 3.1

Work out the subcategorisation frame of each of the lexical items listed in (i–iv). Make sure you justify your proposals with relevant examples:

i)   fond
ii) declare
iii) transport
iv) within

Exercise 3.2

Using examples of your own, explain whether the derivationally related pairs of items in (i–v) have similar or different subcategorisation frames:

i)   derive/derivation
ii) believe/belief
iii) export/export
iv) fond/fondness
v)   eager/eagerness

Exercise 3.3

The verbs *believe* and *wonder* are similar in that they both subcategorise for a clausal complement (S'), as shown in (ia&b). However, each of the two verbs seems to be particular about the type of clause it takes as complement, as shown in (iia&b). Suggest a formal way of encoding this particular property in the subcategorisation frame of each verb such that the sentences in (iia&b) are excluded:

i)a. Bill believes that John left early.
i)b. Bill wonders if John left early.

ii)a. *Bill believes if John left early.
ii)b. *Bill wonders that John left early.

Exercise 3.4

Explain if examples (ia) and (iia), compared to (ib) and (iib), pose a problem for the claim that violation of the subcategorisation requirements of lexical items gives rise to ungrammaticality:

i)a. This problem, I can solve.
i)b. I can solve *(this problem).

ii)a. I wonder which city he comes from.
ii)b. He comes from *(London).

Exercise 3.5

Assign a tree structure to each of the complex categories listed in (i–v). Make sure you justify your proposals:

i) musical
ii) establishment
iii) modernisation
iv) interpretations
v) colonised (as a past tense verb)

Exercise 3.6

Think of possible arguments to decide between the two structures for the complex category *unhappiness* shown in (i) and (ii):

i)   ii)

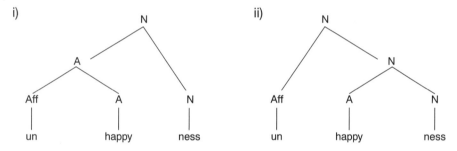

Exercise 3.7

The list in (i–v) includes **compounds**, which are complex categories formed with independent (i.e. non-affixal) lexical items. For example, the compound verb *dryclean* is made up of the adjective *dry* and the verb *clean* and has the structure [$_V$ [$_A$ *dry*] [$_V$ *clean*]]. Assign a tree structure to each of the compounds in (i–v). Try to justify your proposals with arguments:

i) crybaby
ii) bankroll
iii) overestimate
iv) steamboat
v) bluebottle

Sources and further reading

The discussion in this chapter of the problems posed by systems of rules that overgenerate is based on Chomsky (1965). The latter marks the first serious attempt to constrain the generative power of the theory, which led to the postulation of the semantic component and the separation of the lexicon from the syntax. The proposal to view categories as bundles of categorial features is outlined in Chomsky (1970, 1972). A recent evaluation of this proposal can be found in Muysken & van Riemsdijk (1985).

In addition to Chomsky (1965, 1970), a discussion of morphological derivation in relation to syntax can be found in Aronoff (1976), Selkirk (1982), Anderson (1982), Fabb (1984), Marantz (1984), Di Sciullo & Williams (1987), Zubizarreta (1987), and Baker (1988). For an overview of the major opinions relating to the nature of the rules of morphology see Bauer (1983), Scalise (1984), Jensen (1990), Spencer (1991) and Katamba (1993).

Kempson (1977) and Fodor (1982) include overviews of the issues considered to fall under the scope of Semantics. Larson & Segal (1995) and Heim & Kratzer (1998) are two of the most recent introductions to Semantic theory.

4 Transformations I: Phrasal Categories

Contents

4.1   *The nature of transformations*

4.1.1   Topicalisation

Compare the examples in (1) and (2):

1a. I can solve this problem.
1b. I can [$_{VP}$ solve [$_{NP}$ this problem]]

2a. This problem, I can solve.

2b. this problem, I can [$_{VP}$ solve]

The two sentences differ with respect to the position of the NP *this problem*. In (1) it is in the object position of the verb where it is expected to be given its function as the object of the verb *solve*. In (2), however, the NP *the problem* is in the initial position of the sentence, although it is understood as the direct object of the verb. As shown in (3a&b), the verb *solve* is transitive, and therefore associated with a transitive subcategorisation frame:

3a. I can solve *(this problem)

3b. solve: [— NP]

(1) is consistent with (3b), but (2) apparently is not. The absence of the object from the object position of the verb ([V —]) seems to imply an intransitive VP structure rather than the required transitive structure. Recall from Chapter 3 that situations where a given verb is associated with an inappropriate subcategorisation frame invariably give rise to unacceptable sentences, as shown in (3a). Recall also that sentences of this type are excluded by LIR reproduced in (4) for reference:

4.   Lexical Insertion Rule

Insert item X under terminal node Y, where Y corresponds to the categorial features of X, and YP corresponds to the subcategorisation properties of X.

It seems that the system of rules developed in the previous chapters cannot cope with (2) and similar sentences. (2) is expected to be ungrammatical on the grounds that the transitive verb *solve* is inappropriately associated with an intransitive frame, on a par with (3a). We therefore have to introduce a revision into the system such that sentences such as (2) are not excluded, without compromising its ability to exclude ungrammatical sentences such as (3a). Obviously, there is a clear difference between (2) and (3a), which suggests that the similarity is merely superficial, though not unproblematic. In (3a) the object of the verb is missing from the sentence altogether, whereas in (2) it is only missing from the (object) position of the verb. Moreover, although the NP *this problem* is not situated in the object position of the verb in (2), it is still interpreted as the object of the verb, i.e. 'the thing to be solved'.

A possible way of explaining this apparent inconsistency between the function of the NP and the position it occupies is to assume that the NP in question actually originates in the object position of the verb and is subsequently displaced to the sentence-initial position. In other words, we could postulate the derivation in (5a&b) for (2):

5a. I can solve [$_{NP}$ this problem]   →

5b. [$_{NP}$ this problem], I can solve [—]

(5a) is the underlying representation generated by PS rules in combination with LIR. In this representation the verb *solve* is correctly associated with a transitive frame. A rule of a different nature then applies to this underlying representation and displaces the NP *the problem* from the object position of the verb to the initial position of the sentence, deriving sentence (2a).

Before discussing the nature of the rule which displaces the object of the verb to the sentence initial position, it is important to see how the derivation outlined in (5a&b) solves the dilemma we faced above, i.e. the contrast between (2) and (3a). By assuming that the NP *this problem* originates in the object position of the verb in the representation generated by PS rules and LIR, the problem of the verb *solve* being associated with an inappropriate subcategorisation frame ceases to exist. As shown in (5a), the verb is correctly associated with a transitive VP. The rule which displaces the NP object to the initial position applies at a later stage. When compared to (2), the ungrammatical example (3a) involves a different situation. Because the NP object is missing altogether, the analysis outlined for (2) (in terms of 'displacement') does not extend to it. In other words, (3a) represents a situation where the (transitive) verb is indeed associated with an inappropriate (intransitive) subcategorisation frame in both the underlying representation and the derived representation.

The rule which displaces the NP *this problem* to the initial position shown in (5) is called a **transformation**. It transforms phrase marker (6a) generated by PS rules and LIR into the slightly different phrase marker (6b). The displaced NP is attached to the left side of S, a structural position which corresponds to its linear position in (2) as the leftmost constituent of the sentence. The symbol *t(race)* in the object position of the verb in (6b) marks the position from which the NP *this problem* has been displaced. The status and function of *trace* in the structural representation of sentences will be discussed in detail later on in this chapter:

6a.

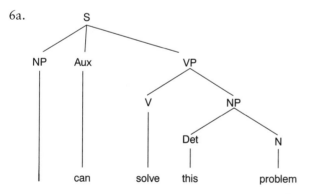

6b.

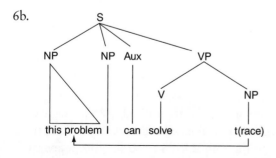

The transformational rule involved in the derivation of (2) is called **Topicalis-ation**. Its peculiar property is that it moves a category and attaches it to the left side of S. As we will see below, other transformational rules have different properties, having to do mainly with where they place the category they move. A possible way of formulating the transformational rule of Topicalisation is as in (7):

7.   X –   NP –   X   (Structural Description)
      1   2   3   →
      2   1 –   t –   3   (Structural Change)

Structural Description (SD) refers to the phrase marker generated by PS rules in combination with LIR and corresponds to the underlying representation (6a). NP is the category targeted by the transformation, and X is a variable which stands for the categories (including zero) to the left and to the right of NP. The numbers in (7) are simply devices which help us keep track of the changes which take place. **Structural Change (SC)** refers to the phrase marker derived by the application of Topicalisation, and therefore corresponds to the derived representation (6b). The targeted NP (designated by the number 2) has been displaced (topicalised) to the initial position of the sentence. The original position of the topicalised NP (i.e. the position it occupies in SD) is marked with the symbol *t(race)*.

The format used in (7) can be used to formulate all types of transformations. However, here we will define transformational rules using simple English prose. Topicalisation can be defined as in (8):

8.   Topicalisation

      Move XP and attach it as the leftmost constituent of S.

XP is a variable which stands for any phrasal category. This general definition of Topicalisation captures the fact that not only NPs but other phrasal categories can be topicalised. (9) involves Topicalisation of a PP and (10) Topicalisation of a VP. Other phrasal categories can also be subject to Topicalisation. However, the examples discussed so far are sufficient to justify the use of the variable XP in the definition of Topicalisation:

9a.   To John, Mary gave the book.
9b.   [pp to John], Mary gave the book [pp t]

10a. Fix the car, I wonder whether John will.
10b. [VP fix the car], I wonder [S' whether [S he will [VP t]]]

The S category to which the topicalised XP is attached can either be the first one which contains the XP in the underlying representation, or, in appropriate examples, a higher one. In (10), for example, the topicalised VP is attached to the root S, although it has been displaced from the embedded clause. The options of attaching the topicalised category to the embedded S or to the root S are more clearly illustrated in (11) and (12). The topicalised NP is attached to the root S in (11) and to the embedded S in (12):

11a. This problem, I believe that I can solve.
11b. [$_{NP}$ this problem], I believe [$_{S'}$ that [$_S$ I can solve [$_{NP}$ t]]]

12a. I believe that this problem, I can solve.
12b. I believe [$_{S'}$ that [$_S$ [$_{NP}$ this problem], I can solve [$_{NP}$ t]]]

4.1.2 Trace Convention

As pointed out above, *trace* designates the position from which the topicalised category is moved. Put differently, *trace* marks the position where the moved category is understood as far as its interpretation in the sentence is concerned. With respect to (2), reproduced in (13), the presence of *trace* in the object position of the verb helps explain the observation that the topicalised NP is interpreted as though it were in the object position of the verb:

13a. This problem, I can solve.
13b. [$_{NP}$ this problem]$_i$, I can [$_{VP}$ solve [$_{NP}$ t]$_i$]

The relation between a moved category and its *trace* is encoded in terms of **co-indexation**, as shown in (13b). Co-indexation of the topicalised NP and *trace* is intended to convey the information that the topicalised NP has the interpretation associated with the position occupied by *trace*. The moved category is said to be the **antecedent** of the *trace* it is related to (co-indexed with).

The category *trace* is said to have a full grammatical status. This means, first, that it has categorial features which are usually the features of the moved category it is related to. In (13), for example, *trace* is an NP, and in (9) and (10) it is a PP and a VP, respectively. Secondly, *trace* can enter into grammatical relations, and, as we will see below, also determine certain grammatical processes. In (13), for example, *trace* has the grammatical function 'object' by virtue of the fact that it occupies the object position of the verb. Since the antecedent of *trace* is co-indexed with it, the antecedent receives the status of object by inheritance from *trace*. These properties, among others which will transpire in the course of this book, all point to the conclusion that *trace* is a category in its own right. It differs from **lexical/overt** categories (i.e. categories which are spelled out) only in that it is **empty/null**, meaning it is phonetically unrealised.

Obviously, it is preferable, if not necessary, to have some clear evidence for the presence of *trace* in sentences which have undergone a movement transformation. A substantial amount of such evidence has been pointed out and evaluated in the literature, some of which is discussed in various places in this book. At this stage, we will discuss one such piece of evidence having to do with the phenomenon of *wanna*-contraction in Colloquial English, illustrated in (14a&b) and (15a&b):

14a. I want to read this novel.
14b. I wanna read this novel.

15a. I want this novel to be considered for a prize.
15b. *I wanna this novel be considered for a prize.

(14a&b) show that *want* and *to* can contract to *wanna* when they are adjacent. (15a&b) show that *want* and *to* cannot contract to *wanna* when they are not adjacent. In this example, the NP *this novel* intervenes between *want* and *to*, thereby preventing them from contracting to *wanna*. With this mind, consider now (16) and (17) which involve Topicalisation of the NP *this novel*:

16a. This novel, I want to read.
16b. This novel, I wanna read.
16c. [NP this novel]$_i$, I want to read [NP t]$_i$.

17a. This novel, I want to be considered for a prize.
17b. *This novel, I wanna be considered for a prize.
17c. [NP this novel]$_i$, I want [NP t]$_i$ to be considered for a prize.

In (16) *want* and *to* are adjacent and therefore can contract to *wanna,* as shown in (16b). The *trace* of the topicalised NP is in the object position following the verb, and therefore does not intervene between *want* and *to*. In (17), however, the *trace* of the topicalised NP intervenes between *want* and *to* as shown in (17c). For this reason, the two categories cannot contract to *wanna* as shown in (17b). What this fact shows is that *trace*, though a null category, is visible to the grammatical rule which contracts *want* and *to*.

The presence of categories in phrase markers have so far been motivated on the basis of PS rules in combination with LIR. However, the presence of *trace* cannot be motivated on similar grounds as it arises as a result of a movement transformation applying to the phrase marker generated by PS rules and LIR. It seems that we need a special mechanism to motivate the presence of *trace* in relevant sentences. For the moment, let us assume that the mechanism in question is simply the convention stated in (18):

18. **Trace Convention**

Movement transformations leave a trace behind.

Ideally, the presence of *trace* should follow from some general requirements of the grammar rather than be stipulated in terms of a convention such as (18). In the subsequent chapters, we will see that the presence of *trace* indeed follows from some general requirements of the grammar. Pending the discussion, we will continue to assume that moved categories leave a *trace* behind, by convention.

4.1.3 Levels of representation

The derivation of (2) outlined in (6a&b) assumes the existence of two phrase markers (or representations) for the sentence. One is an underlying representation where the NP *the problem* is in the object position of the verb. The other is a derived representation where the NP in question is attached to S and its position in the underlying representation is filled with a *trace*. (19a) corresponds to phrase marker (6a) and (19b) to phrase marker (6b). (19a) is the representation generated by PS rules and LIR. (19b) is the representation derived by applying the transformational rule Topicalisation to the underlying representation (19a):

19a. I can [VP solve [NP this problem]] $\qquad \rightarrow$
19b. [NP this problem]$_i$, I can [VP solve [NP t]$_i$]

The underlying representation (19a) is technically called the **Deep Structure (DS)**. The derived representation (19b) is called the **Surface Structure (SS)**. Extending the analysis to similar examples, their derivation involves two structures or levels of representation. One is DS where all categories are in the positions where they are expected to be by virtue of PS rules and the subcategorisation requirements. The other is SS where categories may appear in positions other than the ones where they are expected to be. In DS (19a), for example, the NP *this problem* is in the object position of the verb, as expected, whereas in SS (19b) it occupies the initial position of the sentence. Transformational rules such as Topicalisation represent the link between DS and SS representations. Transformational rules are said to **map** DS representations onto SS representations.

The idea that the derivation of sentences involves two levels of representation is a direct consequence of introducing transformational rules. The syntactic component of the grammar now comprises two sub-components. One sub-component, sometimes called the **Base**, includes context-free PS rules. The other sub-component includes transformational rules such as Topicalisation and others to be discussed below. The rules of the Base together with LIR are said to **base-generate** DS representations which serve as input to transformational rules. Transformational rules introduce modifications into DS representations, by, for example, moving a category from one position in the representation to another and derive SS representations. The organisation of the new-look system can be represented in roughly as in (20):

20.   Lexicon

DS   (PS rules and LIR)

         (Transformations)

SS

PF   LF

PF stands for **Phonetic Form**. This is the level where the sentence is assigned a phonetic representation in the sense explained in Chapter 3. It is important to make a distinction between SS and PF representations. SS is an abstract syntactic level of representation where categories have the form of feature bundles as explained in Chapter 3. These feature bundles are not assigned a phonetic representation till the level PF. The form of the sentence that is pronounced and heard is the output of PF, not SS. LF stands for **Logical Form**. This is the level where sentences are assigned a representation of meaning. Unlike the output of PF, the output of LF is not pronounced/heard. LF is often referred to as the **covert** level. The nature of this level of presentation and the reasons for assuming it will be discussed in detail in subsequent chapters. Note, finally, that the lexicon is not, strictly speaking, a level of representation. That is, there is no sense in which a phrase marker is mapped from the lexicon onto DS.

4.2   Wh-movement

4.2.1   Wh-questions

Compare the question–answer pair (21a&b) to the pair of statements in (22a&b):

21a. Question: Which problem did you solve?
21b. Answer: I solved the maths problem.

22a. Statement: I solved the maths problem.
22b. Statement: You solved which problem!

(21a) is a **wh-question**, used to ask for (new) information. The answer (21b) provides the information asked by the wh-question. (22b) is an **echo-question**, usually used to express surprise at information just made available to the speaker, such as the information in (22a). Although they are called questions, echo-questions do not seek (or ask for) new information. They are merely statements of surprise. However, they resemble questions in that they include **wh-phrases** such as *which problem* in (22b). For this reason, echo-questions are useful in shedding light on the derivation of wh-questions, which is our concern at the moment.

In the echo-question (22b), the wh-phrase appears in the object position of the verb, which is consistent with its interpretation as an object of the verb. In the wh-question (21a), however, the wh-phrase appears in the initial position of the sentence. Now, if the position occupied by the wh-phrase in the echo-question (22b) is assumed to be the DS position of the wh-phrase in the wh-question (21a), the latter can be said to be derived by a transformational rule which moves the wh-phrase from the object position of the verb to the initial position of the sentence.

Although echo-questions are useful in the way explained, we do not, as a matter of fact, need to appeal to them to reach the conclusion that the wh-phrase in the wh-question (21a) is moved from the object position of the verb. The reasoning adopted earlier with respect to topicalised objects also applies to the wh-phrase in (21a). The verb *solve* is transitive and therefore must be associated with a transitive frame in the lexicon and at DS. The verb *solve* has the (simplified) subcategorisation frame shown in (23a). (23b&c) show that *solve* takes an NP object obligatorily:

23a. solve: [V; — NP]
23b. I solved the problem.
23c. *I solved.

It follows from the information in (23a–c) that the verb *solve* must have an object in the wh-question (21a). Otherwise, the example should be excluded for the same reason as (23c). The object of the verb in (21a) is the wh-phrase base-generated in the object position of the verb and subsequently moved to the initial position of the sentence. The derivation of this example is as outlined in (24):

24a. Which problem did you solve?
24b. DS: $[_S$ you $[_{Aux}$ Tense$]$ $[_{VP}$ solve $[_{NP}$ which problem$]]]$
24c. SS: $[_{S'}[_{NP}$ which problem$]_i$ $[_S$ you $[_{Aux}$ Tense$]$ $[_{VP}$ solve $[_{NP}$ t$]_i]]]$

The transformation responsible for movement of the wh-phrase to the sentence-initial position is called **Wh-movement**.

The derivation in (24) ignores the Aux element *did*. Transformations which apply to Aux and other terminal categories are discussed in Chapter 5. There are contexts where Wh-movement does not affect the terminal category Aux. This is the case in sentences where it applies within the embedded clause called **indirect questions**. (25) is an example of an indirect question where the wh-phrase is Wh-moved from the direct object position of the verb to the initial position of the embedded clause:

25a. I wonder which problem Mary solved.
25b. I wonder $[_{S'}[_{NP}$ which problem$]_i$ $[_S$ Mary $[_{Aux}$ Tense$]$ $[_{VP}$ solved $[_{NP}$ t$]_i]]]$

Let us now try to define the transformational rule Wh-movement. To be able to do so we need first identify the position where the moved wh-phrase is placed. As far as Topicalisation is concerned, the conclusion that topicalised categories are attached to the left of S was somewhat dictated by the fact that the topicalised phrase occurs to the right of the complementiser *that* and to the left of the subject in embedded clauses. This is shown in example (12) above. Moved wh-phrases also occur to the left of the subject, but there is no point of reference to the left of the moved wh-phrase as there is with topicalised phrases. This is because interrogative clauses are incompatible with the complementiser *that*. For the moment, we will assume, as a working hypothesis, that moved wh-phrases are placed under Comp. The latter is the position that was said in Chapter 2 to be present in all clauses irrespective of whether they include a complementiser. Accordingly, the embedded wh-question in (25) has the more articulated representation shown in (26):

26.

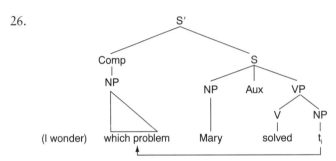

Having identified the landing site of the moved wh-phrase, we are now in a position to define Wh-movement. For the moment, Wh-movement can simply be defined as in (26):

26. **Wh-movement**

Move wh-XP to Comp.

The use of the variable XP in the definition is intended to capture the fact that wh-phrases other than NP can also undergo Wh-movement. (27) involves Wh-movement of an adjectival wh-phrase and (28) Wh-movement of an adverbial wh-phrase:

27a. I wonder how difficult the problem was.
27b. I wonder [$_{S'}$ [$_{AP}$ how difficult]$_i$ [$_S$ the problem was [$_{AP}$ t]$_i$]]

28a. I wonder when Mary solved the problem.
28b. I wonder [$_{S'}$ [$_{ADV}$ when]$_i$ [$_S$ Mary solved the problem [$_{ADV}$ t]$_i$]]

PPs can also undergo Wh-movement, as shown in (29). In English, the preposition has the option of staying behind, as in (30). The latter phenomenon is known as **preposition stranding**. Movement of the whole PP, seen in (29), is said to involve **pied piping** of the preposition along with the wh-phrase. The actual wh-phrase in this example is an NP object of the preposition:

29a. I wonder to whom Mary gave the book.
29b. I wonder [$_{S'}$ [$_{pp}$ to whom]$_i$ [$_S$ Mary gave the book [$_{pp}$ t]$_i$]]

30a. I wonder whom Mary gave the book to.

30b. I wonder [$_{S'}$ [$_{NP}$ whom]$_i$ [$_S$ Mary gave the book [$_{PP}$ to [$_{NP}$ t]$_i$]]]

Before we move on to discuss other issues relating to Wh-movement, a word about the internal structure of wh-phrases. For the moment, we will assume that wh-phrases which consist of both a wh-word and a noun, e.g. *which problem*, have the structure shown in (31a), where the wh-word occupies the Det position. On the other hand, wh-phrases which apparently consist of a wh-word only, e.g. *who, what*, have the structure shown in (31b) where the wh-word is under the N node:

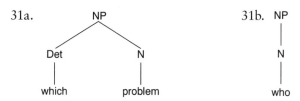

31a.

31b.

Note that in both (31a) and (31b) the wh-phrase is a phrasal category. Wh-movement, along with Topicalisation and other transformations discussed below, is an instance of the set of transformations which target phrasal categories.

4.2.2 Conditions on Wh-movement

4.2.2.1 *[+Q]-Comp Condition*   Compare (32) to (33):

32a. I wonder which problem Mary solved.

32b. I wonder [$_{S'}$ [$_{NP}$ which problem]$_i$ [$_S$ Mary Aux [$_{VP}$ solved [$_{NP}$ t]$_i$]]]

33a. *I believe which problem Mary solved.

33b. *I believe [$_{S'}$ [$_{NP}$ which problem]$_i$ [$_S$ Mary Aux [$_{VP}$ solved [$_{NP}$ t]$_i$]]]

Together, these examples show that Wh-movement cannot move a wh-phrase to any Comp position, contrary to what is implied by the preliminary definition of Wh-movement above. Wh-movement to the embedded Comp is allowed in (32) but not in (33). Our definition of Wh-movement therefore has to be revised to take into consideration the fact that not all Comps are legitimate targets for Wh-movement.

The difference between (32) and (33) lies in a difference in the subcategorisation properties of the verbs in the root clause. The verb *wonder* subcategorises for an interrogative clause. The verb *believe*, however, does not subcategorise for an interrogative clause. Instead, it subcategorises for a declarative clause, as in *I believe that Mary solved the problem*. The difference in the subcategorisation properties of the two types of verb can be encoded in terms of the feature [+/−Q(uestion)] associated with the Comp of the clause they subcategorise for. Interrogative clauses are marked with the feature specification [+Q] and declarative clauses with the negative feature specification [−Q]. Accordingly, the subcategorisation frames of the verbs in (32) and (33) are roughly as shown in (34):

34a. *wonder*: [— S′: [+Q]]
34b. *believe*: [— S′: [−Q]]

With this in mind, let us now go back to (32) and (33). In (32), the Comp of the embedded clause is marked with the feature [+Q] as required by the subcategorisation properties of the root verb *wonder*. In (33), however, the Comp of the embedded clause is marked with the feature [−Q] as required by the subcategorisation properties of the root verb *believe*. Now, if we assume that Wh-movement can move a wh-phrase only to a Comp which is [+Q], (33) will be excluded on the grounds that it involves Wh-movement to a [−Q]-Comp. We will call the condition in question the **[+Q]-Comp Condition**, and incorporate it into the definition of Wh-movement as shown in (35):

35. **Wh-movement**

Move wh-XP to Comp provided Comp is [+Q].

The idea that interrogative clauses are marked with the feature [+Q] plausibly extends to root interrogatives such as *Which problem did Mary solve?*. Like embedded clauses, root sentences can also be interrogative or declarative, among other possibilities. It is natural to assume that root sentences are distinguished in terms of the same mechanism as subcategorised clauses, so that root wh-interrogatives are marked with the feature [+Q] and root declaratives are marked with the feature [−Q]. Consequently, movement of the wh-phrase to Comp in root sentences is also consistent with (35). In (36), which is the direct question counterpart of (33), the root Comp is marked with the feature [+Q] and the embedded Comp with the feature [−Q]. This is the reason the wh-phrase moves to the root Comp instead of to the embedded Comp, although there are complications that will need to be sorted out later on:

36a. Which problem do you believe that Mary solved?
36b. [$_{S'}$ [$_{NP}$ which problem]$_i$ do [$_S$ you believe [$_{S'}$ that [$_S$ Mary solved [$_{NP}$ t]$_i$]]]]

Note, finally, that the feature [+/−Q] can also be used to distinguish between (genuine) wh-questions and echo-questions such as *John solved which problem!* discussed above. Echo-questions can be said to be [−Q], meaning they are not wh-questions even though they include a wh-phrase. Marking echo-questions with the feature [−Q] accounts for why the wh-phrase does not move to Comp in them. The wh-phrase remains in-situ in echo-questions. Thus, the fundamental difference between genuine wh-questions and echo-questions relates to the feature encoded in their Comp and not to whether the wh-phrase they include moves or does not move to Comp. Whether the wh-phrase moves to Comp is a consequential property which depends on the feature of Comp.

4.2.2.2 Wh-island Condition   Compare (37) and (38):

37a. How do you think (that) Mary solved the problem?
37b. [$_{S'}$ [how]$_i$ do [$_S$ you think [$_{S'}$ that [$_S$ Mary solved the problem [t]$_i$]]]]

38a. *How do you wonder whether Mary solved the problem?
38b. *[$_{S'}$ [[how]$_i$ do [$_S$ you wonder [$_{S'}$ whether [$_S$ Mary solved the problem [t]$_i$]]]]]

Both sentences involve movement of a wh-phrase out of the embedded clause to the root Comp. They differ in that the Comp of the embedded clause dominates the complementiser *that* in (37) and the wh-phrase *whether* in (38). This difference is the consequence of the difference in the type of the root verb discussed above.

The contrast between (37) and (38) illustrates the fact that it is generally more difficult to extract a wh-phrase out of a clause with a wh-phrase in its Comp position than it is from a clause without a wh-phrase in its Comp position. This fact is further illustrated by the contrast in (39) and (40). The Comp of the embedded clause dominates a wh-phrase in (39) but not in (40):

39a. Which way do you think (that) John went?
39b. [$_{S'}$ [[which way]$_i$ do [$_S$ you think [$_{S'}$ (that) [$_S$ John went [t]$_i$]]]]]

40a. *Which way do you wonder why John went?
40b. *[$_{S'}$ [[which way]$_i$ do [$_S$ you wonder [$_{S'}$ why [$_S$ John went [t]$_i$]]]]

Because it is difficult for a wh-phrase to escape out of a clause the Comp position of which dominates a wh-phrase, these clauses are called **wh-islands**. The condition on Wh-movement they illustrate is called the **Wh-Island Condition**. Continuing the strategy of incorporating conditions on transformations into their definitions, Wh-movement can now be defined as in (41):

41. **Wh-movement**

   Move wh-XP to Comp provided Comp is

   i)   [+Q]
   ii) not included in a wh-island that excludes the targeted Comp.

The revised version of Wh-movement in (41) now excludes (38) and (40) on the grounds that they involve wh-movement out of a wh-island, and therefore a violation of one of the conditions on wh-movement.

4.2.2.3 Complex Noun Phrase Condition   (42) illustrates another condition on Wh-movement called the **Complex Noun Phrase Condition (CNPC)**. (42) involves movement of a wh-phrase out of a complex noun phrase, where a complex noun phrase is a noun phrase which includes a clause (S') in addition to N and Det. The noun *claim* is of the type that subcategorises for a clausal complement (see Chapters 2 and 3):

42a. *Which way did you hear the claim that John went?
42b. *[$_{S'}$ [[which way]$_i$ did [$_S$ you hear [$_{NP}$ the claim [$_{S'}$ that [$_S$ John went [t]$_i$]]]]]]

The fact that it is difficult to extract a wh-phrase out of a complex noun phrase is further illustrated in (43). The noun *rumour* resembles *claim* in that it also subcategorises for a clausal complement:

43a. *Which way did Mary spread the rumour that John went?
43b. *[$_{S'}$ [[which way]$_i$ did [$_S$ Mary spread [$_{NP}$ the rumour [$_{S'}$ that [$_S$ John

went [t]$_i$]]]]]]

Incorporating CNPC into the definition of Wh-movement yields the more complex but more restrictive version in (44):

44.　**Wh-movement**

　　Move wh-XP to Comp provided Comp is

　　i)　[+Q]　　　　　　　　　　(the [+Q]-Comp Condition)
　　ii)　not included in a wh-island　　(the Wh-island Condition)
　　iii)　not included in a complex NP.　(the Complex NP Condition)

4.2.2.4　Cyclicity Condition and transformational cycle　One important characteristic of Wh-movement is that it seems to be **unbounded**, in the sense that it can operate across any number of clausal boundaries. This is partly illustrated in (45), where Wh-movement crosses at least three clausal boundaries:

45a. Which problem do you think (that) Jane believes (that) Bill claims (that) Mary solved?
45b. [$_{S'}$ [[$_{NP}$ which problem]$_i$ do [$_S$ you think [$_{S'}$ (that) [$_S$ Jane believes

[$_{S'}$ (that) [$_S$ Bill claims [$_{S'}$ (that) [$_S$ Mary solved [$_{NP}$ t]$_i$]]]]]]]]]]

There is a sense in which the impression that Wh-movement is completely free (unbounded) is false. We have already seen two contexts where it is restricted, namely the contexts where the wh-phrase is included inside a wh-clause or a complex NP. Wh-movement is not allowed to operate out of these two contexts. The Wh-island Condition and the CNPC are often called **locality conditions** on Wh-movement, insofar as they define certain local domains out of which Wh-movement cannot apply. In view of this, it may be that the seemingly unbounded Wh-movement in (45) applies in a series of local steps rather than in one step (or one swoop). Let us explore this possibility.

Compare (46) and (47). Both sentences include the verb *know* which sub-categorises for either a [+Q] or a [−Q] clause. The complement clause is interrogative in (46) and declarative in (47). In (47), it is the root sentence which is interrogative:

46a. John knows which problem Mary solved.
46b. John knows [$_{S'}$ [$_{NP}$ which problem]$_i$ [$_S$ Mary solved [$_{NP}$ t]$_i$]]

47a. Which problem does John know Mary solved?
47b. [$_{S'}$ [$_{NP}$ which problem]$_i$ does [$_S$ John know [$_{S'}$ [$_S$ Mary solved [$_{NP}$ t]$_i$]]]]

(46) is an indirect question and (47) is a direct question. However, let us assume for the sake of the argument that the derivation of (47) is partially similar to that of (46). The wh-phrase in (47) moves first to the position occupied by the wh-phrase in (46), i.e. the Comp of the embedded clause, then to the Comp of the root clause. This more detailed derivation is shown in (48):

48a. Which problem does John know Mary solved?
48b. [$_{S'}$ [$_{NP}$ which problem]$_i$ does [$_S$ John know [$_{S'}$ t$_i'$ [$_S$ Mary solved [$_{NP}$ t]$_i$]]]]

The *trace* in the embedded Comp position, marked with a prime, is called an **intermediate trace** to distinguish it from the **initial trace** in the original (object) position of the wh-phrase. Just as the initial trace marks the position from which the wh-phrase has been extracted, the intermediate trace marks the position through which the wh-phrase has passed on its way to the root clause. Traces are sometimes said to encode the 'history of movement'.

Nothing in the system developed so far forces the derivation in (48b). What we need to do is set up a condition on Wh-movement which will force it to move an embedded wh-phrase first to the Comp of the embedded clause before it moves it to the Comp of the root clause. The condition in question has to do with the notion **transformational cycle**. The latter is a domain within which a transformation can apply exhaustively. For example, S' is a transformational cycle because Wh-movement can apply within it (without leaving it). In (46), for example, Wh-movement applies exhaustively within the embedded clause. Let us now assume that Wh-movement is cyclical in nature, meaning it applies within the cycle that includes the wh-phrase before leaving it to the next cycle up, and so on. Let us then formulate this assumption into a condition on Wh-movement called the **Cyclicity Condition**. The consequence is that apparently unbounded instances of Wh-movement such as in (45) and (48) apply in successive cyclic steps, that is Wh-movement moves the phrase to the nearest Comp position and from there to the nearest Comp position up till it reaches the target Comp position marked with the feature [+Q]. The derivation outlined in (48b) now becomes the only legitimate derivation for (48a). The one swoop derivation in (47b) is illegitimate on the grounds that it violates the Cyclicity Condition on Wh-movement.

There are various ways the Cyclicity Condition can be incorporated into the definition of Wh-movement. A simple way of doing this which achieves the desired results is shown in (49 iv):

49. **Wh-movement**

Move wh-XP to Comp provided Comp is:

i)   [+Q]   ([+Q]-Comp Condition)
ii) not included in a wh-island   (Wh-island Condition)
iii) not included in a complex NP   (Complex NP Condition)
iv) the nearest to the wh-phrase.   (Cyclicity Condition)

We have not discussed ungrammatical sentences that would be excluded by the revised definition but not by the previous one. In other words, we have not discussed empirical evidence that Wh-movement indeed applies successive cyclically rather than in one step. We will postpone discussion of the relevant evidence to a later and more appropriate chapter. The point to keep in mind now is that the Cyclicity Condition imposes a relatively severe locality condition on Wh-movement, so that Wh-movement is not, strictly speaking, unbounded.

Finally, note that the newly introduced condition seems to clash with the condition that the Comp targeted by Wh-movement must be [+Q] ([+Q]-Comp Condition). To see why, consider the examples in (50) and (51). (50) illustrates the familiar fact that *believe* does not subcategorise for a [+Q]-clause. In view of this, the first step of Wh-movement involved in the derivation of (51) appears to target a Comp which is [−Q], apparently in violation of condition (49i):

50a. *I believe which problem Mary solved.
50b. *I believe [$_{S'}$ [$_{NP}$ which problem]$_i$ [$_S$ Mary solved [$_{NP}$ t]$_i$]]

51a. Which problem do you believe Mary solved?
51b. [$_{S'}$ [$_{NP}$ which problem]$_i$ do [$_S$ you believe [$_{S'}$ t$_i'$ [$_S$ Mary solved [$_{NP}$ t]$_i$]]]]

It is possible to solve the problem by rephrasing (49i) in such a way as to refer to the Comp position where the wh-phrase finally rests, with the intermediate Comp positions exempted. However, we shall not undertake this revision here.

4.2.3   Relatives

4.2.3.1   *Relatives with an overt wh-phrase*   Compare (52) and (53):

52a. John heard the claim that Bill made a cake.
52b. John heard [$_{NP}$ the claim [$_{S'}$ that [$_S$ Bill made a cake]]]

53a. John heard the claim which Bill made.

53b. John heard [$_{NP}$ the claim [$_{S'}$ which [$_S$ Bill made]]]

Both sentences include a (complex) NP with a clause (S′) inside it. In (52), S′ is the complement of the noun *claim* and therefore is a complement clause. In (53), however, S′ is not a complement of the noun *claim*. In this example, S′ has an adjective-like function whereby it modifies the noun *claim* by restricting its reference to a particular instance. Such a clause is called a **relative clause**, and the noun phrase which includes a relative clause is called a **relative noun phrase**.

The complement clause in (52) and the relative clause in (53) differ in one other important respect. In (52) the object of the verb *made* appears in its normal position immediately following the verb. However, in the relative clause (53) the object of the verb *made* is missing from its normal position. Instead, it appears in the form of the wh-phrase *which*, apparently situated under Comp. This property of the relative clause groups it together with wh-clauses even though, strictly speaking, the relative clause is not a wh-question. Let us take this similarity to mean that relative clauses of the type illustrated in (53) also involve Wh-movement in their derivation, as shown in (54):

54a. John heard the claim which Bill made.

54b. DS: John heard [$_{NP}$ the claim$_i$ [$_{S'}$ [$_S$ Bill made [$_{NP}$ which]$_i$]]]

54c. SS: John heard [$_{NP}$ the claim$_i$ [$_{S'}$ [$_{NP}$ which]$_i$ [$_S$ Bill made [$_{NP}$ t]$_i$]]]

Co-indexation between the moved wh-phrase and its *trace* is an automatic consequence of Wh-movement, as we have been assuming. Note, however, that (54) also shows co-indexation between the noun *claim*, called the head of the relative noun phrase, and the wh-phrase at both DS and SS. This particular co-indexation is intended to capture the fact that the wh-phrase has the same reference as the head N of the noun phrase. The head N is said to be the antecedent of the wh-phrase, although the two categories are not linked by a movement transformation. This is what is responsible for the impression that the head N is the direct object of the verb *made*. It is important to bear in mind that in relative noun phrases it is the wh-phrase co-indexed with the head N that undergoes movement not the head N itself. If it were the head N that undergoes movement, it would be hard to explain the presence of the wh-phrase, among other things.

The relative clause in (54) is called a **restrictive relative clause**. This is because, as pointed out above, it restricts the reference of the head N it modifies. There are other types of relative clause illustrated in (55) and (56):

55a. Mary, whom you will meet soon, is our president.

55b. Mary, [$_{S'}$ [$_{NP}$ whom]$_i$ [$_S$ you will meet [$_{NP}$ t]$_i$ soon]], is our president

56a. Whatever they say, we will press ahead with the project.

56b. [$_{S'}$ [$_{NP}$ whatever]$_i$ [$_S$ they say [$_{NP}$ t]$_i$]], we will press ahead with the project

The relative clause in (55) is called an **appositive relative clause**. Unlike restrictive relative clauses, appositive relative clauses do not necessarily restrict the reference of the head N they modify. They are essentially a kind of after-thought. The relative clause in (56), on the other hand, is called a **free relative clause**, mainly because it does not modify a N in the sentence in which it occurs (it does not have a head). Appositive and free relative clauses involve Wh-movement just as restrictive relative clauses do, although they have certain peculiar properties which need not concern us here. The rest of the discussion will be restricted to restrictive relative clauses.

4.2.3.2 *Relatives with a null wh-phrase* Compare now the relative noun discussed above, reproduced in (57a), to its synonymous counterparts in (57b) and (57c):

57a. John heard the claim which Bill made.

57b. John heard the claim that Bill made.

57c. John heard the claim Bill made.

(57b&c) apparently do not include a wh-phrase. (57b) includes the complementiser *that* instead of a wh-phrase, and (57c) appears to include neither a wh-phrase nor a complementiser.

In the discussion of (57a) above, it was pointed out that the wh-phrase functions as the object of the verb, meaning it is base-generated in the object position of the verb *made* and subsequently moved to Comp. The wh-phrase is co-indexed with the head N, and hence the interpretation whereby the object of the verb *made* has the same reference as the head N. The fact that the relatives in (57b&c) have exactly the same interpretation implies that they also include a wh-phrase with the same function. In other words, for the head N to be linked to the object position of the verb *made*, it needs to be co-indexed with an element which occupies the object position of the verb *made* at DS. Moreover, from a formal point of view, the system forces on us an analysis for (57b&c) which assumes the presence of an object for the verb *made*. The latter is a transitive verb, and therefore requires an object: *Bill made *(a claim)*. It follows that the verb *made* must have an object in (57b&c). Otherwise, (57b&c) should be excluded for the same reason that *Bill made* is excluded.

(57b&c) must therefore include a null object. Since the equivalent of this category in the synonymous relative clause (57a) is a wh-phrase, it is plausible to conclude that the null object in (57b&c) is a also wh-phrase. This null wh-phrase is base-generated in the object position of *made* and moved to Comp by Wh-movement. Accordingly, the derivation of (57b&c) is as shown in (58), where the null wh-phrase is represented with the symbol *Op(erator)*. An explanation of operators and their function is given in Chapter 7. When a null wh-phrase is moved to a Comp which already dominates the complementiser *that*, we will assume for the moment that Comp has the structure shown in (58c) where it dominates two categories:

58a. . . . the claim (that) Bill made
58b. . . . [$_{NP}$ the claim [$_{S'}$ [$_{NP}$ Op]$_i$ (that) [$_S$ Bill made [$_{NP}$ t]$_i$]]]
58c.

```
          Comp
         /    \
        /      \
      Op       that
```

According to the analysis outlined in (58), relatives with a null wh-phrase are identical to their counterparts with an overt wh-phrase. They differ only in that they include a null wh-phrase instead of an overt one. Although the similarity with relatives with an overt wh-phrase is sufficient to justify the analysis, it is desirable to seek further evidence. If relatives without an overt wh-phrase indeed include a null wh-phrase which undergoes Wh-movement, as claimed, we expect them to show the island effects. Recall that island effects are a reflection of some of the conditions on Wh-movement incorporated into its definition. To apply this test we need to embed a wh-island and/or a complex NP island inside the relative clause. (59) includes a wh-island inside a relative noun phrase. Its ungrammatical status is due to extraction of the null wh-phrase out of the wh-island:

59a. *I know the way (that) John wonders why Bill went.
59b. . . . [$_{NP}$ the way$_i$ [$_{S'}$ [Op]$_i$ [$_S$ John wonders [$_{S'}$ why [$_S$ Bill went [t]$_i$]]]]]]

Island conditions are essentially conditions on Wh-movement irrespective of whether the moved wh-phrase is overt or null. Island violations are good indicators for the presence of Wh-movement, and for this reason are often used as diagnostic criteria for the presence of Wh-movement in the derivation of sentences which do not include an overt wh-phrase.

4.2.3.3 Recoverability and the Doubly Filled Comp Filter

Two questions arise from our analysis of relatives without an overt wh-phrase. First, Why can't wh-questions have a null wh-phrase on a par with relatives? In other words, why is (60a) excluded with the analysis outlined in (60b&c) which assumes the presence of a null wh-phrase?

60a. *Did Mary solve? (with the meaning: What did Mary solve?)
60b. DS: [$_{S'}$ [+Q] [$_S$ Mary solved Op]
60b. SS: [$_{S'}$ [$_{NP}$ Op]$_i$ did [$_S$ Mary [Aux] [$_{VP}$ solve [$_{NP}$ t]$_i$]]]

Note that the reason (60a) is excluded cannot be attributed to a possible violation of the subcategorisation requirements of the verb *solve*. These are satisfied by the null wh-phrase *Op* in the same way they are in the relatives with a null wh-phrase discussed above.

The difference between the wh-question in (60) and the relatives with a null wh-phrase is that in the latter the null wh-phrase has an antecedent in the sentence, namely the head N it is co-indexed with. The head N is the antecedent of the null wh-phrase in the sense that it identifies the content of the null wh-phrase it is co-indexed with. In contrast, the null wh-phrase in the wh-question (60) does not have an antecedent in the sentence, with the consequence that its content remains unidentified or non-recoverable. (60) illustrates a general condition on the occurrence of null categories called the **Recoverability Condition**. The version of this condition we will assume here is stated in (61):

61.   **Recoverability Condition**

The content of a null category must be recoverable (from a co-indexed overt category in the sentence).

With (61) incorporated into the system, (60) is excluded on the grounds that it involves a violation of (61). Relatives with a null wh-phrase, however, do not violate (61), as the null wh-phrase is identified by the head N of the relative clause. (61) does not make reference to a specific class of null categories, and therefore is expected to hold of all types of null categories, including traces. Traces satisfy (61) in a trivial way because they are invariably identified by the moved category which functions as their antecedent. Traces of null wh-phrases in relatives are indirectly identified by the head N via the null wh-phrase.

The other question which arises from our analysis of relatives without an overt wh-phrase is the following: If a wh-phrase can co-occur with the complementiser *that* in Comp, as in (58) above, why is (62) excluded?

62a. *I know the problem which that Mary solved.
62b. *I know [$_{NP}$ the problem$_i$ [$_{S'}$ [$_{NP}$ which]$_i$ that [$_S$ Mary solved [$_{NP}$ t]$_i$]]]

(62) differs from (58) only in that the wh-phrase which co-occurs with the complementiser *that* under Comp is overt instead of null. For some reason, an overt wh-phrase cannot co-occur with the complementiser *that* under Comp, although a null one can. There are various ways to exclude examples such as (62). However, imposing a condition on Wh-movement preventing it from placing an overt wh-phrase under a Comp filled with *that* is not one of them. This is because this measure would render Wh-movement sensitive to whether the wh-phrase is null or overt, and therefore would undermine the idea that null and overt categories are treated equally by movement rules. In other words, transformational rules are not expected to discriminate between overt and null categories, on the grounds that they are not sensitive to whether a given category has or does not have a phonetic realisation.

A more plausible alternative is to formulate a condition on the co-occurrence possibilities in Comp, irrespective of whether the elements involved are base-generated there or moved to it. This condition will have the effect of excluding sentences where an overt wh-phrase co-occurs with *that* under Comp, that is sentences where Comp is 'doubly filled' in the intended sense. A possible way of defining the condition in question is as in (63).

63. **Doubly Filled Comp Filter**

   *[Comp wh-XP that], if wh-XP is overt (non-null).

(63) acts as a 'filter' on (SS) representations derived by Wh-movement, and has the effect of excluding phrase markers with a Comp filled by an overt wh-phrase and *that*.

Unlike the conditions which we have incorporated into the definitions of transformations, the Recoverability Condition and the Doubly Filled Comp Filter are not conditions on (the application of) transformations. Rather, they are conditions on representations (i.e. phrase markers) derived by transformations. The idea underlying conditions on representations such as these is that transformations can be allowed to overgenerate to a limited degree. The undesirable representations can then be excluded by conditions or filters which apply to the output of transformational rules. Thus, the Recoverability Condition and the Doubly Filled Comp Filter are new additions to our system, which previously consisted exclusively of rules.

4.3   *NP-movement*

4.3.1   Passives

Compare (64) and (65):

64a. Mary solved the problem.
64b. [$_S$ Mary [$_{Aux}$ Tense] [$_{VP}$ solved [$_{NP}$ the problem]]]

65a. The problem was solved (by Mary).
65b. [$_S$ [$_{NP}$ the problem] [$_{Aux}$ Tense] [$_{VP}$ was solved (by Mary)]]

(64) is an **active sentence**, where the subject and the object of the verb appear where they are expected to be. (65), on the other hand, is a **passive sentence**, where the object of the verb appears in the subject position and the subject appears, optionally, in the form of a **by-phrase** (*by Mary*) located at the end of the sentence.

The term 'subject' is used here in both its structural sense (i.e. 'NP-daughter-of-S') (see Chapter 2) and its semantic sense, referring to the individual who performs the act described by the verb. In the passive sentence (65) the NP *the problem* is a subject in the structural sense but not in the semantic sense. On the other hand, the NP *Mary* is the subject in the semantic sense but not in the structural sense. The same is true of the term 'object'. In (65) the NP *the problem* is the object of the verb in the semantic sense (i.e. it is the entity which undergoes the event described by the verb), but not in the structural sense since it is not in the object position of the verb, at least superficially. Semantic subjects and objects are sometimes called **logical subjects** and **logical objects**.

Putting aside the *by*-phrase for the moment, the analysis for (65), and passives in general, imposed on us by the system is one where the NP *the problem* is base-generated in the object position of the verb and subsequently moved to the subject position of the sentence. The reasoning behind this analysis is the same as for topicalised and wh-moved objects. The verb *solve* is transitive and there-fore expected to be associated with a transitive VP at DS. The object position in this representation is occupied by *the problem* which is the logical object of the verb. In the mapping from DS onto SS a transformational rule applies which moves the NP object to the subject position. The intended derivation is as shown in (66). (66d) is the SS representation in the form of a tree diagram where the auxiliary and the main verb are both included under V, pending the discussion of their properties in Chapter 5:

66a. The problem was solved (by Mary).

66b. DS: [$_S$ [$_{NP}$ e] [$_{Aux}$ Tense] [$_{VP}$ was solved [$_{NP}$ the problem]]]

66c. SS: [$_S$ [$_{NP}$ the problem]$_i$ [$_{Aux}$ Tense] [$_{VP}$ was solved [$_{NP}$ t]$_i$]]]

66d.

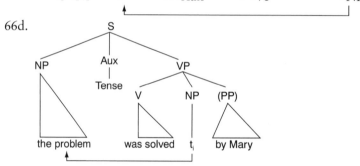

An important property of passives is that their subject position is empty (not filled) at DS, as shown in (66b). It gets filled as a result of movement of the object of the verb from the object position. The reason the subject position of passives is base-generated empty will be discussed in Chapter 7. Its relevance to the current discussion lies in that the definition of the rule which moves the object to the subject position makes reference to an empty subject position. The rule in question is called **NP-movement** and can be defined as in (67):

67.   **NP-movement**

Move NP to an empty subject position.

Unlike Topicalisation and Wh-movement, NP-movement, as its name suggests, applies only to NPs. A PP, for example, cannot be moved to the subject position in passives, as shown in (68):

68a. *To Mary was given the book (by John).

68b. [$_S$ [$_{PP}$ to Mary]$_i$ [$_{Aux}$ Tense] [$_{VP}$ was given the book [$_{PP}$ t]$_i$]]]

Although NP-movement applies only to NPs, the property which crucially distinguishes it from the other movement transformations, and the latter from each other, is the position in which the moved category is placed. The target of NP-movement is the (NP) subject position, whereas the target of Wh-movement, for example, is Comp.

Let us now turn to the *by*-phrase. Its occurrence is generally optional, and has the function of specifying the individual who performed the act undergone by the object-cum-subject. When the *by*-phrase is missing, as in *The problem was solved*, the 'implicit' logical subject is said to have an **arbitrary** interpretation roughly paraphrasable as 'someone or another'. As far as the structural status of the *by*-phrase is concerned, we will assume, for the moment, that it is base-generated as the rightmost constituent of VP, as shown in (66d). Passives which include a *by*-phrase are sometimes called **long passives** and the ones which do not include a *by*-phrase are called **short passives**.

4.3.2 Raising constructions

Compare (69) to (70):

69a. It seems (that) Mary has solved the problem.
69b. It seems [$_{S'}$ (that) [$_S$ [$_{NP}$ Mary] [$_{Aux}$ Tense] [$_{VP}$ has solved the problem]]]

70a. Mary seems to have solved the problem.
70b. [$_{NP}$ Mary] seems [$_S$ [$_{Aux}$ to] [$_{VP}$ have solved the problem]]

In (69), the NP *Mary* occupies the subject position of the embedded clause. The subject position of the root clause in this sentence is occupied by the 'semantically empty' NP *it*, called an **expletive** or **pleonastic** element. In (70), *Mary* occupies the subject position of the root clause even though it is related to the embedded clause by virtue of being the logical subject of the embedded verb. The two examples also differ in that the verb of the embedded clause is conjugated in (69) but not in (70). (70) is called a **raising construction** for reasons that will become clear shortly.

What we need to do with respect to (70) is reconcile the fact that *Mary* is the logical subject of the embedded verb with the fact that it is in the subject position of the root clause. This situation is not radically different from the situation encountered above with respect to passives, where an NP which is the logical object of the verb functions structurally as the subject of the sentence. This property of passives was accounted for by assuming that the NP in question is base-generated in the object position of the verb and subsequently moved to the subject position. This reasoning can be extended to (70). *Mary* can be assumed to be base-generated in the subject position of the embedded clause, and subsequently moved to the subject position of the root clause. The intended derivation is as shown in (71):

71a. Mary seems to have solved the problem.

71b. DS: [$_S$ [$_{NP}$ e] seems [$_S$ [$_{NP}$ Mary] to have solved the problem]]
71c. SS: [$_S$ [$_{NP}$ Mary]$_i$ seems [$_S$ [$_{NP}$ t]$_i$ to have solved the problem]]

The transformational rule shown in (71c) is an instance of NP-movement in that it targets an NP and raises it to an empty (NP) subject position. It differs from the instance of NP-movement involved in passives only in that the moved NP occupies the subject position of a different clause at DS. The instance of NP-movement involved in raising constructions such as (71) is called **subject-to-subject raising**, to distinguish it from the instance of NP-raising involved in passives which is called **object-to-subject raising**.

Just as object-to-subject raising in passives is associated with a particular type of verbs, i.e. passive verbs, subject-to-subject raising is also associated with a particular class of verbs called **raising verbs/predicates**. These include, in addition to *seem*, verbs such as *appear*, illustrated in (72), and complex predicates such as *be likely*, illustrated in (73):

72a. It appears (that) Mary has solved the problem.
72b. Mary appears to have solved the problem.

73a. It is likely (that) Mary will solve the problem.
73b. Mary is likely to solve the problem.

The main characteristic of raising predicates is that they can take the expletive element *it* as a subject. Thus, while *be certain*, for example, is a raising predicate, *be confident* is not. The predicate *be certain* can take an expletive subject, as shown in (74a), whereas the predicate *be confident* cannot, as shown in (75a):

74a. It is certain (that) Mary will win.
74b. Mary is certain to win.

75a. *It is confident (that) Mary will win.
75b. *Mary is confident to win.
75b. Mary is confident (that) she will win.

At the moment, the correlation between the ability to take an expletive subject and to host the subject of another embedded clause seems to be arbitrary. However, in Chapter 7 we will see that the two properties are intimately related in that one follows from the other.

Another property of raising predicates which will not be discussed in detail till Chapter 10 is that they can either subcategorise for S' or for just S. They subcategorise for an S' when no raising is involved, as in (69), and they subcategorise for an S when raising is involved, as in (70). It will transpire in Chapter 10 that whether the complement of raising predicates is S or S' is linked to whether NP-movement takes place.

4.3.3 Conditions on NP-movement

4.3.3.1 Tensed S Condition It was pointed out above that one of the differences between the raising sentence (70) and its non-raising counterpart (69) is that the verb of the embedded clause is not conjugated in the raising sentence. It turns out that this verb cannot be conjugated, as shown in (76):

76a. *Mary seems has solved the problem.
76b. [$_S$ [$_{NP}$ Mary]$_i$ seems [$_S$ [$_{NP}$ t]$_i$ [$_{Aux}$ Tense] [$_{VP}$ has solved the problem]]]

At the moment, we will understand by 'conjugated verb' a verb that bears Tense. A verb that bears Tense is a **tensed verb** and a verb that does not bear Tense is a **non-tensed verb**. Notice, however, that the term 'Tensed', strictly speaking, applies to S rather than to verbs. This is because Tense is a constituent of Aux, not V (see Chapter 2). Therefore, the more accurate terms are 'tensed clause' and 'non-tensed clause'. Tensed clauses have Tense under Aux, whereas non-Tensed clauses do not. Instead, they have the element *to* under Aux sometimes called the **infinitive marker**. We can think of the two types of Aux as being distinguished in terms of the feature complex [+/−Tense]. The value [+Tense] in turn implies the feature complex [+/−Past]. The value [+Past] is phonetically realised as *-ed* with the other tense morphemes realising the value [−Past]. The feature [−Tense] is realised as *to*. Accordingly, the raising sentence (70) has the representation shown in (77):

77.

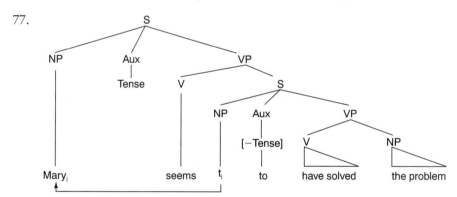

Going back to (76), this example illustrates a condition on the application of NP-movement known as the **Tensed S Condition** (TSC). The latter has the effect of preventing NP-movement from moving an NP out of a tensed clause. Pursuing the strategy of building conditions on transformations into their definition, the revised version of NP-movement can now be stated as in (78):

78. **NP-movement**

Move NP to an empty subject position, unless NP is contained in a Tensed S which excludes the targeted subject position.

4.3.3.2 *Specified Subject Condition*   (79) and (80) illustrate another condition on NP-movement:

79a. Mary appears to be likely to win.
79b. [$_S$ [$_{NP}$ Mary]$_i$ appears [$_S$ [$_{NP}$ t]$_i$ to be likely [$_S$ [$_{NP}$ t]$_i$ to win]]]

80a. *Mary appears it is likely to win.
80b. *[$_S$ [$_{NP}$ Mary]$_i$ appears [$_S$ [$_{NP}$ it] is likely [$_S$ [$_{NP}$ t]$_i$ to win]]]

In (79), the NP *Mary* moves from the subject position of the second embedded clause to the subject position of the first embedded clause up, and finally to the subject position of the root clause. In (80), *Mary* moves directly to the subject position of the root clause since the subject position of the intervening clause is filled with the expletive subject *it*. This type of movement is called **super-raising** and yields ungrammatical sentences.

(80) is excluded due the fact that the NP *Mary* has been moved across another subject, namely *it*. One might argue that (80) also involves a violation of TSC, given that the moved NP crosses the boundary of a tensed clause, namely the middle clause. There are other contexts which show that NP-movement cannot operate across an intervening subject. In (82), the direct object of the non-tensed embedded clause is moved to the subject position of the root passive clause across the intervening subject (of the embedded clause). In contrast, the NP-movement in (81) does not cross an intervening subject:

81a. John is believed to have seen Bill.
81b. [$_S$ [$_{NP}$ John]$_i$ is believed [$_S$ [$_{NP}$ t]$_i$ to have seen Bill]]

82a. *Bill is believed John to have beaten.
82b. *[$_S$ [$_{NP}$ Bill]$_i$ is believed [$_S$ John to have seen [$_{NP}$ t]$_i$]]

The condition on NP-movement illustrated in (80) and (82) is called the **Specified Subject Condition (SSC)**. A possible way of incorporating it into the definition of NP-movement is as in (83):

83.   **NP-movement**

Move NP to an empty subject position provided NP is

i)   not contained in a tensed S (TSC)
ii) not separated from the targeted position by a specified subject (SSC).

4.4 *Extraposition and Heavy NP Shift*

4.4.1 Extraposition

Compare the sentences in (84) and (85). The style in (85) is typical of news bulletins:

84a. Details of a secret plan to finance the rebels have emerged.
84b. details [pp of a secret plan to finance the rebels] have emerged

85a. Details have emerged of a secret plan to finance the rebels.
85b. details have emerged [pp of a secret plan to finance the rebels]

The PP included in brackets is the complement of the noun *details* in both (84) and (85). In (84) it appears where it is understood and expected to be, i.e. the complement position of the noun. However, in (85) it appears in the sentence-final position following the verb. Presumably, in (85) the PP complement of the noun has been moved from its DS position inside the NP containing *details* to the sentence-final position. The transformational rule responsible for this movement is called **Extraposition.**

   We will assume, for the moment, that extraposed phrases are attached as rightmost daughters of VP, so that (85) has the SS shown in (86):

86a. Details have emerged of a secret plan to finance the rebels.
86b. [s [NP details [pp t]i Aux [VP have emerged [pp of a secret plan . . .]i]]

Extraposition differs from the movement transformations discussed so far in that it operates rightward. It is an instance of rightward movement. Extraposition can be defined as in (87):

87. **Extraposition**

   Move XP and attach it as the rightmost constituent of VP.

As with the other transformations, the use of the variable XP is intended to capture the fact that categories other than PP can be extraposed. (88) involves extraposition of a relative clause (S'). Recall from above that the relative clause is a constituent of a complex NP and modifies the head N of the relative noun phrase:

88a. A man has come forward who claims to be the culprit.
88b. DS: [s [NP a man [s' who claims to be the culprit]] Aux [VP has come forward]]
88c. SS: [s [NP a man [s t]i Aux [VP has come forward [s' who claims to be the culprit]i]]

4.4.2   Heavy NP Shift

Compare (89) and (90):

89a. Mary returned all the books she had borrowed to the library.

89b. [$_S$ Mary Aux [$_{VP}$ returned [$_{NP}$ all the books she had borrowed] [$_{PP}$ to the library]]]

90a. Mary returned to the library all the books she had borrowed.

90b. [$_S$ Mary Aux [$_{VP}$ returned [$_{PP}$ to the library] [$_{NP}$ all the books she had borrowed]]]

The relative NP *all the books she had borrowed* is a complement of the verb *return*. The latter takes an NP and an (optional) PP complement, so that its subcategorisation frame is roughly of the form: [— NP (PP)]. In (89) the two complements of the verb appear in the order specified in the subcategorisation frame, with NP preceding PP. In (90), however, the order of the two complements is reversed, with NP following PP.

The order shown in (90) is the result of a transformational rule which moves the NP complement from its base-generated position immediately following the verb (and preceding the PP complement), and attaches it to the right side of VP. The transformational rule responsible for this operation is called **Heavy NP Shift**. The name of the transformation is intended to reflect the fact that the rule applies only to NPs which are 'heavy', where 'heavy' is vaguely understood to mean several constituents. The NP *the book*, for example, is not 'heavy' in the intended sense, and therefore cannot be subject to Heavy NP Shift, as shown in (91). When a direct object NP is not 'heavy' in the intended sense, only the order specified in the subcategorisation frame, seen in (92), is allowed:

91a. *Mary returned to the library the book.

91b. [$_S$ Mary Aux [$_{VP}$ returned [$_{NP}$ t]$_i$ [$_{PP}$ to the library] [$_{NP}$ the book]$_i$]]

92a. Mary returned the book to the library.

92b. [$_S$ Mary Aux [$_{VP}$ returned [$_{NP}$ the book] [$_{PP}$ to the library]]]

There are various ways of defining Heavy NP Shift, although the notion 'heavy' remains vague and difficult to define precisely. (93) is a possible version. The inclusion of the word 'heavy' in the definition ensures that sentences such as (91) are excluded:

93. **Heavy NP Shift**

Move a 'heavy' NP and attach it as the rightmost constituent of VP.

4.5 *Summary*

Sentences which involve a displaced category require a new set of rules called transformations. The latter apply to representations derived by PS rules and LIR, called Deep Structures (DS), and derive modified representations called Surface Structures (SS). To ensure that transformations do not overgenerate, conditions are built into their definitions. Basically, these inbuilt conditions help define the domains over which transformations (can) apply. On two occasions it was felt necessary to introduce conditions which differ from the previous ones in that they serve as 'filters' on representations derived by transformational rules rather than as conditions on the application of the transformations themselves. The underlying idea is that transformations can be allowed to overgenerate in a limited way, with the undesirable sentences excluded by conditions applying to representations derived by transformations.

Exercises

Exercise 4.1

Outline a derivation for each of the sentences in (i–v). Make sure you provide a separate representation for every step in the derivation, and explain whether and how each step satisfies the conditions on the application of the relevant transformational rule:

i) John wonders which match Bill saw.
ii) What did Mary buy?
iii) John knows the book which Bill bought.
iv) The play Bill wrote disappointed John.
v) Who did you think (that) Mary criticised?

Exercise 4.2

Explain how the sentences in (i–iv) are excluded in the system discussed in this chapter. Make sure you identify clearly the conditions violated with respect to the relevant transformation for each sentence:

i) *Mary thinks which English city Bill visited.
ii) *Why does Mary know John did it?
   (with *why* modifying the embedded verb)
iii) *How does Bill regret the claim that John treated him?
   (with *how* modifying the embedded verb)
iv) *In which direction does John know the people who went?
   (with *in which direction* modifying the verb *went*)

Exercise 4.3

Outline a derivation for each of the sentences in (i–iv). Make sure you identify the transformational rules involved in the derivation of each sentence and explain whether and how the conditions on each rule are or are not satisfied:

i)   Bill seems to have lost the match.
ii) Bill appears to have been excluded.
iii) The book was criticised strongly.
iv) Which author does Mary think has been praised?

Exercise 4.4

Explain why and how the sentences in (i–iv) are excluded in the system outlined in this chapter:

i)   *Bill is believed John to have criticised.
ii) *Mary seems (that) has left suddenly.
iii) *This is the book which that Mary wrote.
iv) *John appears it is likely to resign.

Exercise 4.5

Identify the transformational rules involved in the derivation of the sentences in (i–iv):

i)   I found a book in the library which I had not seen before.
ii) Mary donated to the library all the money she had inherited.
iii) These accusations, I resent very much.
iv) Who saw Bill?

Exercise 4.6

It has been claimed that the Wh-island Condition and the Complex NP Condition both reduce to the Cyclicity Condition and therefore may not be needed. Evaluate this claim in relation to the sentences in (i–iv):

i)   How do you know that John fixed the car?
ii) *How do you wonder whether John fixed the car?
iii) *How do you reject the rumour that John fixed the car?
iv) *How do you know the car that John fixed?

Exercise 4.7

Explain whether in your view the pairs of sentences in (ia&b) and (iia&b) should be related by a transformational rule, that is, whether they both derived from the same DS or from different DS representations. If you believe they should be, give an idea about what form the transformational rule should take. Make sure that your answer takes into consideration the pairs in (iiia&b) and (iva&b):

i)a. Bill sent a message to John.
i)b. Bill sent John a message.

ii)a. John gave money to the charity.
ii)b. John gave the charity money.

iii)a. Bill transmitted a message to John.
iii)b. *Bill transmitted John a message.

iv)a. John donated money to the charity.
iv)b. *Bill donated the charity money.

Sources and further reading

See 'Sources and further reading' at the end of Chapter 5.

5 Transformations II: Terminal Categories

Contents

5.1 *Preliminary remarks*

The previous chapter dealt with transformations that affect phrasal categories. This chapter deals with transformations that affect terminal categories such as Aux and V. Although it may not be clear by the end of this chapter, the two types of transformations have different properties. This will become clearer in Chapter 10 where we will discover that they are governed by different conditions.

Despite the differences, the theoretical machinery outlined in the previous chapter applies to both types of transformation. Transformations which apply to terminal categories apply to DS representations and may move one terminal catergory from one position to another. Movement of a terminal category also leaves a trace behind.

One of the new things we will learn in this chapter is that transformations can perform functions other than movement. We will discuss at least one transformation which inserts material into DS representations.

5.2 *Affix-hopping: main verbs*

In Chapter 2, it was concluded that Tense is an obligatory constituent of Aux, and that the PS rule which generates Aux is as in (1):

1. Aux → Tense (Modal) (Neg)

When Aux dominates a Modal in addition to Tense, Tense appears on the Modal and the main verb is unmarked for Tense. This is shown in (2). When Aux does not dominate a Modal, Tense appears on the main verb, as shown in (3):

2a. Mary will solve the problem.
2b. [S Mary [Aux [Tense] [Modal will]] [VP solve the problem]]

3a. Mary solved the problem.
3b. [S Mary [Aux] [VP solve+Tense the problem]]

The question how Tense, which is a constituent of Aux, ends up attached to the main verb in sentences such as (3) was left open. Now that we have introduced rules that can move a category from one position to another, we are in a position to address the outstanding question. Tense and the main verb could in principle be joined together in one of two possible ways. They could be joined either by movement of Tense (from Aux) to V or by movement of V to Tense (in Aux). The two options are outlined in (4) and (5):

4a. Mary solved the problem.
4b. DS: [S Mary [Aux -ed] [VP solve the problem]]
4c. SS: [S Mary [Aux tᵢ] [VP [V [V solve] [Tense]ᵢ] the problem]]]

4d.

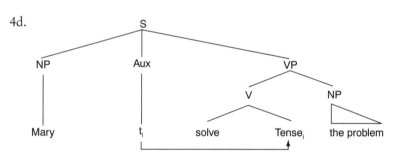

5a. Mary solved the problem.
5b. DS: [S Mary [Aux -ed] [VP solve the problem]]
5c. SS: [S Mary [Aux [V solve]ᵢ [Tense -ed]] [VP [V t]ᵢ [NP the problem]]]

5d.

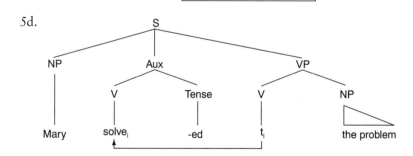

The two options have radically different consequences for the position of the complex [[V] [Tense]] at SS. According to option (4), the complex [[V] [Tense]] is located inside VP at SS. According to option (5), the complex [[V] [Tense]] is located outside VP and under Aux. Which of the two options is the correct one is an empirical question to be settled on the basis of evidence.

The evidence we will discuss here relates to the order of verbs in relation to VP-adverbs. Recall that VP-adverbs typically occur in the leftmost or rightmost positions of VP, as indicated by rule (6) from Chapter 2:

6. VP → (ADV) V . . . (ADV)

Concentrating on the leftmost (preverbal) position, we find the pattern shown in (7a&b) where the VP adverb precedes the complex [[V] [Tense]]:

7a. John cleverly avoided Bill.
7b. John rarely visited Bill.

The pattern in (7a&b) clearly favours the derivation outlined in (4) over the derivation outlined in (5). The former involves movement of Tense rightward across the adverb to the verb. This movement derives the order whereby the adverb is to the left of the complex [[V] [Tense]], as in (7a&b). The derivation in (5), however, involves movement of the verb leftward across the adverb to Aux. This particular movement derives the order whereby the adverb is to the right of the complex [[V] [Tense]]. This order is excluded in English as shown in (8) and (9):

8a. *John avoided cleverly Bill.
8b. *[S John [Aux [V avoid]ᵢ [Tense -ed]] [VP [ADV cleverly] [V t]ᵢ Bill]]

9a. *John visited rarely Bill.
9b. *[S John [Aux [V visit]ᵢ [Tense -ed]] [VP [ADV rarely] [V t]ᵢ Bill]]

(8) and (9) illustrate a general fact about English: VP-adverbs cannot intervene between a verb and its NP object. Here, we will take this fact to mean that V cannot raise to Aux in English. Instead, it is Aux that lowers to V.

Presumably, the rule which moves Tense and attaches it to V inside VP is a transformational one. To reach an adequate definition of this rule we need to take certain facts into consideration. One of these facts, mentioned above, is that when Aux dominates a Modal in addition to Tense, Tense appears on the Modal rather than on the verb. This is shown in (2) above which includes the Modal *will*. Thus, the rule which attaches Tense to V applies only when Aux does not dominate a Modal. Essentially, this observation amounts to a condition on the application of the rule in question. Continuing the strategy adopted in Chapter 4 of incorporating conditions on transformations into their definition, we can define the transformational rule that joins Tense with the verb in English, called **Affix-hopping**, as in (10):

10. **Affix-hopping**

    Move Tense (from Aux) to V provided Aux does not dominate a Modal.

The past Tense morpheme is an affix which morphologically subcategorises for a verbal category (see Chapter 3), hence the fact that it has to attach to a Modal or a verb. Affix-hopping is basically an inflectional rule which derives an inflected verb by attaching Tense to its base form. However, Affix-hopping is a (transformational) rule of syntax, not a lexical rule of derivation. This is because Affix-hopping, as defined in (10), is subject to a condition which is syntactically based, i.e. a condition which refers to a node in the phrase marker. This is consistent with the view discussed in Chapter 3 that inflectional morphemes are the morphemes which are relevant to syntax in the precise sense that rules of syntax make reference to them.

5.3   *V-raising: auxiliary verbs*

Consider now (12a&b) in comparison to (11a&b) from the previous section:

11a. *John avoided cleverly Bill.
11b. *John visited rarely Bill.

12a. Mary was often happy.
12b. John was rarely at home.

(12a&b) illustrates another general fact of English, namely that auxiliary verbs such as *be* can precede a VP adverb, unlike main verbs. According to our reasoning in the previous section, the order whereby an inflected verb precedes a VP-adverb, seen in (12a&b), must be derived by raising of the auxiliary verb to Aux across the VP-adverb. This is shown in (13):

13a. Mary was often happy.
13b DS: [$_S$ Mary [$_{Aux}$ [Tense]] [$_{VP}$ [$_{ADV}$ often] [$_V$ be] happy]]
13c. SS: [$_S$ Mary [$_{Aux}$ [$_V$ be]$_i$ [Tense]] [$_{VP}$ [$_{ADV}$ often] [$_V$ t]$_i$ happy]]

The observation that the auxiliary verb *be* can appear before a VP-adverb is also true of sentences where *be* is used together with a main verb in the participial form, such as (14a). It is also true of the other auxiliary verb *have*, as shown in (14b):

14a. Mary was often working at home.
14b. John has rarely visited Bill.

To be able to provide an adequate definition of the transformational rule that raises the auxiliary verb to Aux in appropriate contexts, we need first clarify the status of auxiliary verbs compared to main verbs. Contrary to what the expression 'auxiliary verb' might suggest, auxiliary verbs are not constituents of Aux at DS. Rather, they are verbs base-generated under a V node inside VP. This is the case not only in sentences such as (12a&b), which do not include a main verb in addition to an auxiliary verb, it is also true in sentences such as (14b). It would not make sense to treat *be*, for example, differently depending on whether the sentence includes a main verb or not. Sentences which include both an auxiliary verb and a main verb have the structure shown in (15). The latter includes two VPs, one for the auxiliary verb and the other for the main verb. Auxiliary verbs differ from main verbs in that they can subcategorise for a VP complement:

15.

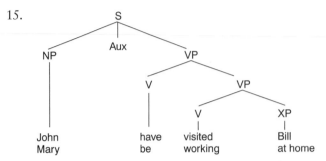

Assuming this to be the case, we need to make sure that the transformational rule which raises auxiliary verbs to Aux does not apply to main verbs as well. If it did, we would not be able to exclude sentences such as (11a&b) which are derived by raising of the main verb to Aux. This can be done by making a formal distinction between auxiliary verbs and main verbs that the transformational rule would make reference to. Here, we will make use of the feature complex [+/−AUX]. Auxiliary verbs have the value [+AUX] and main verbs the value [−AUX]. Now we can define the transformational rule which raises auxiliary verbs to Aux, called **V-raising**, as in (16):

16. **V-raising**

Raise V to Aux, provided V has the feature specification [+AUX].

As with other transformational rules we have discussed, further investigation reveals that other conditions on the application of V-raising must be incorporated into its definition. One has to do with the fact that V-raising does not apply when Aux dominates a Modal, i.e when Aux dominates a category capable of supporting Tense. This is shown in (17a–c) where the auxiliary verb is uninflected due to the presence of the Modal under Aux:

17a. John must be at home.
17b. Mary will be working.
17c. John should have visited Bill.

To account for the pattern in (17a–c) all we need to do is add the condition 'provided Aux does not dominate a Modal' to the definition of V-raising, as shown in (18):

18. **V-raising**

Raise V to Aux provided

i) V has the feature specification [+AUX]
ii) Aux does not dominate a Modal.

Going back to condition (18i), it was partly forced on us by the idea that auxiliary verbs originate inside VP under a V node. This idea equates auxiliary verbs with main verbs as far as their structural representation is concerned. In view of this, we had to ensure that V-raising does not apply to the wrong kind of V, that is, we had to ensure that it applies to auxiliary verbs but not to main verbs. Interestingly, the idea that auxiliary verbs originate inside VP under a V node also forces on us a revision of Affix-hopping discussed in the previous section. We now have to make sure that Affix-hopping does not apply to the wrong verbs, i.e. auxiliary verbs. This can be done by adding the condition 'provided that V has the feature specification $[-\text{AUX}]$' to the definition of V-raising, as in (19):

19. **Affix-hopping**

    Move Tense (from Aux) to V provided

    i)   Aux does not dominate a Modal
    ii) V has the feature specification $[-\text{AUX}]$.

Condition (19ii) ensures that sentences such as (13) which include only an auxiliary verb are not derived by Affix-hopping, but by V-raising. However, condition (19ii) is not sufficient to exclude other undesirable sentences such as (20) and (21), which include both an auxiliary verb and a main verb:

20a. *Mary be working at home.
20b. *[$_S$ Mary [$_{Aux}$ [Tense t]$_i$] [$_{VP}$ be [$_{VP}$ [$_V$ [$_V$ working] [Tense]$_i$] at home]]]

21a. *John have visited Bill.
21b. *[$_S$ John [$_{Aux}$ [Tense t]$_i$] [$_{VP}$ have [$_{VP}$ [$_V$ [$_V$ visited] [Tense]$_i$] Bill]]]

The application of Affix-hopping in (20) and (21) is consistent with both conditions in (19). Aux does not dominate a Modal and the targeted verb is not an auxiliary verb. (20) is assumed to have an abstract present tense marker which undergoes Affix-hopping onto the main verb.

To make sure (20) and (21) are properly excluded, we have to add yet another condition, which specifies that Affix-hopping does not apply when VP dominates a verb with the feature specification $[+\text{AUX}]$. A possible way of incorporating this condition into the definition of Affix-hopping is as in (22iii):

22. **Affix-hopping**

    Move Tense (from Aux) to V provided

    i)   Aux does not dominate a Modal
    ii)   V has the feature specification $[-\text{AUX}]$
    iii) VP does not dominate a V with the feature specification $[+\text{AUX}]$.

More conditions need to be built into the definition of Affix-hopping as we will see shortly.

5.4   Do-*support: negative sentences*

Consider now the negative sentences in (23a&b) in the light of the conclusion reached in the previous section relating to how Tense is merged with the verb:

23a. John did not avoid Bill.
23b. John does not like Bill.

In (23a&b) Tense appears on *do*, and the main verb is uninflected for Tense. Descriptively, the presence of Neg somehow results in Tense not being able to merge with the main verb. Formally, the presence of Neg under Aux appears to block Affix-hopping from applying. Application of Affix-hopping in this context yields undesirable sentences, as shown in (24) and (25):

24a. *John (do) not avoided Bill.
24b. *[$_S$ John [$_{Aux}$ ([do]) [$_{Neg}$ not] [$_{Tense}$ t]$_i$] [$_{VP}$ [$_V$ [$_V$ avoid] [Tense]$_i$] Bill]]

25a. *John (do) not likes Bill.
25b. *[$_S$ John [$_{Aux}$ ([do]) [$_{Neg}$ not] [$_{Tense}$ t]$_i$] [$_{VP}$ [$_V$ [$_V$ like] [Tense]$_i$] Bill]]

(24) and (25) can be excluded by adding the condition that Aux should not dominate Neg to the definition of Affix-hopping. A possible way of doing this is shown in (26):

26.   **Affix-hopping**

Move Tense (from Aux) to V, provided

i)   Aux does not dominate a Modal or Neg
ii)   V has the feature specification [−AUX]
iii) VP does not dominate a V with the feature specification [+AUX].

Having made sure that sentences such as (24) and (25) are excluded, we now have to explain how sentences such as (23a&b) are derived. They both include the item *do*, usually described as a 'dummy element' which is 'semantically vacuous'. In other words, *do* does not contribute anything to the meaning of the sentence. It is, in other words, a 'piece of semantic junk', but with a very useful and necessary mechanical role. Its role is to morphologically 'support' dependent Tense when the latter is 'stranded'. Tense is stranded in sentences with a main verb only as a result of Neg blocking the application of Affix-hopping. Note that when Aux dominates a verbal category capable of supporting Tense, *do* does not appear. This is shown in (27a&b):

27a. John should not avoid Bill.
27b. John cannot like Bill.

The element *do* does not appear either when the sentence includes an auxiliary verb, that is, a verb capable of raising to Aux to support Tense. This is shown in (28a&b):

28a. John has not avoided Bill.
28b. Bill is not working at home.

The semantically element *do* is said to be inserted into relevant phrase markers by a special transformational rule called **Do-support**. The latter can be defined as in (29). The word 'stranded' in the definition ensures that the rule applies only when Tense is left stranded, that is, only if Affix-hopping and V-raising fail to apply and Aux does not dominate a Modal:

29. **Do-support**

   Insert *do* to support stranded Tense.

Do-support is often described as a 'last resort', used only if derivational rules such as Affix-hopping and V-raising fail to apply. In the next section, we will discuss another context for *Do*-support which confirms its last resort character.

5.5 *Subject Aux Inversion: yes-no questions*

(30a&b) are examples of **yes-no questions**, i.e. questions which typically require 'yes' or 'no' for an answer:

30a. Can Bill solve the problem?
30b. Will John fix the car?

The main characteristic of yes-no questions is that Aux and the subject appear 'inverted' compared to their order in declarative sentences such as *Bill can solve the problem* and *John will fix the car*. Presumably, yes-no questions are derived from a DS representation where Aux is to the right of the subject seen in declarative sentences. Recall that the PS rule which generates S places Aux to the right of the subject. The PS rule is reproduced in (31):

31a. S → NP Aux VP
31b.
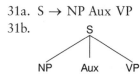

The inversion effect must therefore be the result of a transformational rule which applies in the mapping from DS onto SS in the derivation of yes-no questions. A priori, the transformational rule can either move the subject rightward to a position to the right of Aux, or move Aux leftward to a position to the left of the subject. We will choose the latter option. The reason is that there is no position to the right of Aux for the subject to move to, but there is a position to the left of the subject for Aux to move to. The position in question is Comp. As in wh-questions discussed in Chapter 4, the Comp of yes-no questions is marked with the feature

[+Q], and therefore requires movement to it. Accordingly, yes-no questions such as (30a&b) have the derivation shown in (32):

32a. Can Bill solve the problem?
32b. DS: [$_{S'}$ [+Q] [$_S$ Bill [$_{Aux}$ can] [$_{VP}$ solve the problem]]]
32c. SS: [$_{S'}$ [$_{Aux}$ can]$_i$ [$_S$ Bill [$_{Aux}$ t]$_i$ [$_{VP}$ solve the problem]]]

32d.

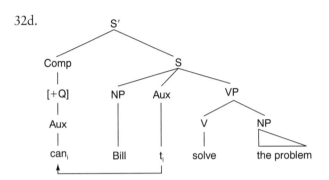

The transformational rule which raises Aux to Comp, shown in (32c&d), was originally called **Subject Aux Inversion (SAI)**. Here we will call it **Aux-raising**, a label which gives a clear indication as to which category moves and in which direction it moves. As with Wh-movement, Aux-raising only targets a Comp which has the feature [+Q], meaning it only applies in interrogative clauses. The requirement that Aux-raising only targets a Comp that has the feature [+Q] basically amounts to a condition on the application of Aux-raising, as with Wh-movement. Thus, our preliminary definition of Aux-raising can take the form shown in (33):

33. **Aux-raising**

Move Aux to Comp, provided Comp has the feature specification [+Q].

Since Aux-raising targets Comps with the feature specification [+Q], we expect it to apply in wh-questions as well. Recall from Chapter 4 that the Comp of wh-questions has the same feature specification. The prediction is borne out by wh-questions such as (34a), which has the derivation shown in (34b&c):

34a. Which problem can Bill solve?
34b. DS: [$_{S'}$ [+Q] [$_S$ Bill [$_{Aux}$ can] [$_{VP}$ solve which problem]]]
34c. SS: [$_{S'}$ [$_{NP}$ which problem]$_i$ [$_{Aux}$ can]$_i$ [$_S$ Bill [$_{Aux}$ t]$_i$ [$_{VP}$ solve [$_{NP}$ t]$_i$]]]

As with other transformations, further conditions need to be incorporated into the definition of Aux-raising. One such conditions relates to the fact that Aux-raising does not apply to embedded clauses. It is restricted to root clauses and for this reason it is said to be a 'root phenomenon'. Recall from Chapter 4 that the verb *wonder* subcategorises for a [+Q]-clause. The latter can either be a wh-question, as in (35), or a yes-no question, as in (36):

35a. I wonder which problem Bill can solve.
35b. DS: I wonder [$_{S'}$ [+Q] [$_S$ Bill [$_{Aux}$ can] [$_{VP}$ solve which problem]]]
35c. SS: I wonder [$_{S'}$ [[$_{NP}$ which problem]$_i$ [$_S$ Bill [$_{Aux}$ can] [VP solve [$_{NP}$ t]$_i$]]]

36a. I wonder if/whether Bill can solve the problem.
36b. DS: I wonder [$_{S'}$ [+Q] [$_S$ Bill [$_{Aux}$ can] [$_{VP}$ solve the problem]]]
36c. SS: I wonder [$_{S'}$ if [$_S$ Bill [$_{Aux}$ can] [$_{VP}$ solve the problem]]]

However, in neither situation can Aux-raising take place. This is shown in (37) and (38):

37a. *I wonder which problem can Bill solve.
37b. DS: I wonder [$_{S'}$ [+Q] [$_S$ Bill [$_{Aux}$ can] [$_{VP}$ solve which problem]]]
37c. SS: . . . [$_{S'}$ [[$_{NP}$ which problem]$_j$ [$_{Aux}$ can]$_i$ [$_S$ Bill [$_{Aux}$ t]$_i$ [$_{VP}$ solve [$_{NP}$ t]$_j$]]]

38a. *I wonder if/whether can Bill solve the problem.
38b. DS: I wonder [$_{S'}$ [+Q] [$_S$ Bill [$_{Aux}$ can] [$_{VP}$ solve the problem]]]
38c. DS: . . . [$_{S'}$ if [$_{Aux}$ can]$_i$ [$_S$ Bill [$_{Aux}$ t]$_i$ [$_{VP}$ solve the problem]]]

Embedded yes-no questions are introduced by the Comp elements *if* or *whether*. We will take these elements to correspond to [+Q]-Comp, in much the same way as *that* corresponds to [−Q]-Comp. Although the presence of *if/whether* may have something to do with the blocking of Aux-raising in (38), there does not seem to be any parallel reason in (37). Here we will take the root nature of Aux-raising to reflect a condition on its application which can be stated as in (39):

39. **Aux-raising**

   Move Aux to Comp, provided

   i) Comp has the feature specification [+Q]
   ii) Comp is situated in a root clause.

Aux-raising interacts with V-raising in a predictable way. We expect verbs which are able to raise to Aux to be affected by Aux-raising, and therefore end up in Comp. That is, if a verb moves to Aux by V-raising, it is expected to be able to end up in Comp by Aux-raising. Thus, we expect auxiliary verbs to be able to appear to the left of the subject in questions. This is shown in (40) and (41) which have the derivations indicated. VR in (40c) and (41c) stands for Verb-raising, and AR in (40d) and (41d) for Aux-raising:

40a. Was John at home?

40b. DS: [$_{S'}$ [+Q] [$_S$ John [$_{Aux}$ Tense] [$_{VP}$ be at home]]]

40c. VR: [$_{S'}$ [+Q] [$_S$ John [$_{Aux}$ [$_V$ be]$_i$ [Tense]] [$_{VP}$ [$_V$ t]$_i$ at home]]]

40d. AR: [$_{S'}$ [$_{Aux}$ [$_V$ be]$_i$ [Tense]]$_j$ [$_S$ John [$_{Aux}$ t]$_j$ [$_{VP}$ [$_V$ t]$_i$ at home]]]

40e. SS: [$_{S'}$ [$_{Aux}$ [$_V$ be]$_i$ [Tense]]$_j$ [$_S$ John [$_{Aux}$ t]$_j$ [$_{VP}$ [$_V$ t]$_i$ at home]]]

41a. Has John solved the problem?

41b. DS: [$_{S'}$ [+Q] [$_S$ John [$_{Aux}$ Tense] [$_{VP}$ has solve the problem]]]

41c. VR: [$_{S'}$ [+Q] [$_S$ John [$_{Aux}$ [V have]$_i$ [Tense]] [$_{VP}$ [$_V$ t]$_i$ solved NP]]]

41d. AR: [$_{S'}$ [$_{Aux}$ [V have]$_i$ [Tense]]$_j$ [$_S$ John [$_{Aux}$ t]$_j$ [$_{VP}$ [$_V$ t]$_i$ solved NP]]]

41e. SS: [$_{S'}$ [$_{Aux}$ [$_V$ have]$_i$ [Tense]]$_j$ [$_S$ John [$_{Aux}$ t]$_j$ [$_{VP}$ [$_V$ t]$_i$ solved NP]]]

However, we do not expect Aux-raising to interact with Affix-hopping, for obvious reasons. Affix-hopping destroys the context that Aux-raising applies to by lowering Tense onto V inside VP. Thus, we do not expect main verbs to be able to appear to the left of the subject in questions. This is shown in (42a). Assuming that (42a) has the derivation outlined in (42b–e), on a par with that of (40a) and (41a), the step shown in (42c) is illegitimate because it involves raising of a main verb to Aux:

42a. *Solved John the problem?

42b. DS: [$_{S'}$ [+Q] [$_S$ John [$_{Aux}$ Tense] [$_{VP}$ solve the problem]]]

42c. VR: [$_{S'}$ [+Q] [$_S$ John [$_{Aux}$ [$_V$ solve]$_i$ [Tense]] [$_{VP}$ [$_V$ t]$_i$ NP]]]

42d. AR: [$_{S'}$ [$_{Aux}$ [$_V$ solve]$_i$ [Tense]]$_j$ [$_S$ John [$_{Aux}$ t]$_j$ [$_{VP}$ [$_V$ t]$_i$ NP]]]

42e. SS: [$_{S'}$ [$_{Aux}$ [$_V$ solve]$_i$ [Tense]]$_j$ [$_S$ John [$_{Aux}$ t]$_j$ [$_{VP}$ [$_V$ t]$_i$ NP]]]

The acceptable version of (42) includes *do*, and therefore involves *Do*-support in its derivation. This is shown in (43), where DoS stands for *Do*-support:

43a. Did John solve the problem?

43b. DS: [$_{S'}$ [+Q] [$_S$ John [$_{Aux}$ Tense] [$_{VP}$ solve the problem]]]

43c. AR: [$_{S'}$ [$_{Aux}$ Tense]$_i$ [$_S$ John [$_{Aux}$ t]$_i$ [$_{VP}$ solve NP]]]

43d. DoS: [$_{S'}$ [$_{Aux}$ Tense]$_i$ [do] [$_S$ John [$_{Aux}$ t]$_i$ [$_{VP}$ solve NP]]]

43e. SS: [$_{S'}$ [$_{Aux}$ Tense]$_i$ [do] [$_S$ John [$_{Aux}$ t]$_i$ [$_{VP}$ solve NP]]]

Translating the derivation in (43) into English prose, we obtain the following scenario: Aux-raising moves Aux to Comp. This results in stranding Tense under Comp, thereby triggering *Do*-support which inserts *do* to support Tense under Comp.

In negative sentences with a main verb only discussed above, Tense gets stranded as a result of Neg blocking Affix-hopping. (43) does not include Neg, and yet Affix-hopping is blocked in this context as well. In (43), Tense is stranded as a result of being 'too far away' from the verb. Apparently, Affix-hopping can only apply when Aux is adjacent to VP. When Aux is moved away from VP, as in (43), Affix-hopping fails to apply. Thus, we need to incorporate a new condition into the definition of Affix-hopping. A possible way of formulating it is as in (44iv):

44. **Affix-hopping**

 Move Tense (from Aux) to V, provided

 i) Aux does not dominate a Modal or Neg
 ii) V has the feature specification [−AUX]
 iii) VP does not dominate a V with the feature specification [+AUX]
 iv) Aux is adjacent to VP which dominates the targeted V.

(43) confirms the last resort nature of *Do*-support. As in negative sentences, it only applies in (43) because Affix-hopping fails to apply.

5.6 *Summary*

Four different transformational rules have been identified and discussed in this chapter. All have in common the property of targeting a terminal category. Affix-hopping lowers Tense to the main verb in sentences which meet certain conditions. V-raising raises auxiliary verbs to Aux in sentences which meet certain conditions. Do-support applies to provide morphological support for stranded Tense by inserting the 'semantically vacuous' element *do*. Finally, Aux-raising (or Subject Aux Inversion) raises Aux to Comp in the derivation of interrogative clauses which meet certain conditions. The conditions that sentences have to meet for the relevant transformation to apply are incorporated into the definitions of the transformations themselves.

Exercises

Exercise 5.1

Outline a derivation for each of the sentences in (i–v). Make sure you provide a separate representation for every step in the derivation, and explain whether and how each step satisfies the conditions on the application of the relevant transformational rule:

i)   Bill went to the theatre.
ii) Mary did not see the play.
iii) Has John organised a party?
iv) Did Bill know about the party?
v)   Should Bill have told John?

Exercise 5.2

Explain how the sentences in (i–v) are excluded in the system discussed in this chapter. Make sure you identify clearly the conditions violated with respect to the relevant transformation for each sentence. Please note that the grammatical versions of the sentences are not necessarily relevant to the point of the exercise:

i)   *Bill plays frequently football.
ii) *John plays not football.
iii) *Did Bill be in the stadium?
iv) *Plays Bill football?
v)   *Does Bill will see the match?

Exercise 5.3

The issue of **rule ordering** generated a lot of discussion in the earlier stages of Transformational Grammar. The idea was that the transformational rules discussed in this chapter had to be ordered with respect to each other in the derivation of certain sentences. The transformational rules involved in the derivation of a given sentence may yield an acceptable or an unacceptable sentence, depending on the order in which they are applied. Using either the sentences discussed in this chapter or sentences of your own, try to figure out which rule must be ordered with respect to which other rule in the derivation of which sentence. Try also to reflect on the question whether rule ordering is really necessary.

Exercise 5.4

Explain whether in your view the negative questions in (i–iii) are problematic for the transformational rule Aux-raising as formulated in this chapter. Comparing the sentences in (i–iii) to their counterparts in (iv–vi), what conclusions can you draw about Neg?

i) Will John not go to the stadium?
ii) Was Mary not in the play?
iii) Did Bill not join the party?
iv) Won't John go to the stadium?
v) Wasn't Mary in the play?
vi) Didn't Bill join the party?

Exercise 5.5

Sentences (i) and (ii) are derived by long-distance Aux-raising from the embedded clause to the Comp of the root clause marked with the feature [+Q]. Explain whether this long-distance Aux-raising is consistent with the definition of Aux-raising provided in this chapter. One way of going about it is to check whether this instance of Aux-raising is consistent with each of the conditions on Aux-raising. If it is not consistent with one or more of them, that will explain why the sentences are excluded. If, on the other hand, it is consistent with all conditions, try to think of a way of preventing Aux-raising from applying long-distance. You may want to bring into the discussion the Cyclicity Condition and the notion 'transformational cycle' discussed in the previous chapter. It may or may not help, but try to check it out. The declarative counterparts of (i) and (ii) are *John wonders if Bill can fix the car* and *John thinks (that) Bill can fix the car*.

i) *Can John wonders if Bill fix the car?
ii) *Can John thinks (that) Bill fix the car?

Exercise 5.6

Examples (ia&b) illustrate another context for *Do*-support not discussed in this chapter. Sentences (ia&b) are said to have an **emphatic** or **focus** reading encoded in terms of heavier than normal stress on the complex *Do* + AUX. Explain how such sentences are derived by the system outlined in this chapter. You may want to take into consideration the fact that *Do*-support is excluded from emphatic sentences which include an auxiliary verb. In the latter, emphatic stress falls on the auxiliary verb. This is shown in examples (iia&b):

i)a. John DOES like football.
i)b. The children DO like ice-cream.

ii)a. *John DOES have seen Bill.
ii)b. John HAS seen Bill.

Exercise 5.7

Example (ia) illustrates yet another context for *Do*-support called **VP-deletion**. Sentences such as (ia) are said to derive from a richer DS representation by deletion of the VP-material of the second clause. This is roughly shown in (ib&c). Explain whether the appearance of *Do*-support in the second clause of sentences such as (ia) is consistent with the system outlined in this chapter. Here again, you may want to take into consideration the fact that *Do*-support is excluded when the sentence includes an auxiliary verb, as shown in (iia&b):

i)a.   John does not like football, but Bill does.
i)b.   DS: John does not like football, but [S Bill [Aux Tense] [VP like football]]
i)c.   SS: John does not like football, but Bill does.

ii)a. *John has not seen Mary, but Bill does (have).
ii)b. John has not seen Mary, but Bill has.

Sources and further reading

The role of transformations in the derivation of sentences is discussed in Chomsky (1957, 1965), Lees (1963), and Mathews (1964), although the idea had already been entertained in earlier work. At this stage, and in the subsequent years, transformations were said to have the format briefly discussed at the beginning of Chapter 4, which consists of a Structural Description (SD) and a Structural Change (SC). Moreover, different constructions were thought to involve different transformations, so that transformations were construction-specific. There was a transformation for passives, a transformation for raising constructions, a transformation for wh-questions, a transformation for yes-no questions, and so on. A good overview of these transformations can be found in Akmajian and Heny (1975) and Baker (1978).

Although the attempt to restrict the proliferation of transformations and to reduce some of them to fewer and more general transformations was already evident in Chomsky (1973), where the general rule NP-Movement is discussed, it did not materialise in a forceful way until Chomsky (1977b). The latter collapsed a number of individual transformations into the more general rule Wh-Movement which applies across a broad range of constructions as we saw in Chapter 4. That these constructions have similar underlying properties had already been clear from such major works as Ross (1967), Emonds (1970; 1976) and Chomsky (1973).

Most of the transformations discussed in Chapters 4 and 5 will be further discussed in the subsequent chapters. Topicalisation is discussed in Chomsky (1977b), and Extraposition in Baltin (1983, 1984), Guéron (1980), and Guéron and May (1984). The phenomenon of pied-piping and preposition-stranding and the structure of PPs in general are discussed in van Riemsdijk (1978) and references cited therein.

Early discussions of trace (or Trace Theory) can be found in Chomsky (1977a; 1977b), Fiengo (1977), Lightfoot (1977) and Wasow (1979). A survey of the literature which linked the phenomenon of *wanna*-contraction to Trace theory can be found in Postal and Pullum (1982).

The programme aimed at restricting the number of transformations, inevitably, was accompanied by a parallel attempt to collapse conditions on individual transformations into a fewer number of more general conditions applying to general transformations such as Wh-Movement and NP-Movement. The notion 'transformational cycle' as a condition on derivations is discussed in Chomsky (1965) and subsequent work. Other conditions not discussed in Chapters 4 and 5, such as the A-over-A condition, are discussed in Chomsky (1968, 1973). One of the most influential works as far as generalised conditions on Wh-Movement are concerned is Ross (1967). The latter identifies and discusses the island conditions, among many others.

Specified Subject Condition and the Tensed S Condition are introduced in Chomsky (1973). The conditions on the transformations which affect non-phrasal categories, e.g. SAI, are discussed in Emonds (1976), where the distinction between root and non-root transformations is introduced. The latter work was also influential in restricting movement of phrasal categories to specific positions already available in the structure. Emonds (1978) deals with the difference in behaviour between auxiliary verbs and main verbs.

Another landmark in the programme to restrict the power of transformations is Chomsky (1970), 'Remarks on Nominalisations'. Most of the arguments in this paper were directed towards a growing trend, known as Generative Semantics, which attributed what was seen by some linguists as 'excessive power' to transformations. The underlying idea was that meaning is exclusively determined at DS. Among other things, this idea led to the postulation of detailed DSs which included decomposed representations of complex predicates, with transformations having the role of assembling them into single syntactic units in the course of the derivation. The thrust of Chomsky's arguments is that (certain) morphological rules which derive complex categories must be confined to the lexicon, and that these categories are represented as single complex units in the syntax. This view came to be known as the Lexicalist Hypothesis, and has engendered an interesting debate about the scope of the rules of morphology and their place in the grammar (see references cited in the 'Sources and Further Reading section of Chapter 2).

The idea of surface filters as a means of restricting the power of transformations is discussed in Perlmutter (1971), and later (re)appeared in a more developed way in Chomsky and Lasnik (1977). The latter introduces the Doubly Filled Comp Filter together with a number of other filters. The filters-based model outlined in this paper was the precursor to the principle-based model (Principles and Parameters), discussed in Part II of this book.

Part II
Principles and Parameters

6 X-Bar Theory

Contents

6.1 *The redundant nature of PS rules*

We saw in Chapter 2 that the constituent structure of phrasal categories is largely determined by the subcategorisation properties of the terminal category. For example, the structure of VP including a transitive verb such as *hit* will consist of V and NP, and the structure of VP including an intransitive verb such as *smile* may consist of V only, and so on. There seems to be an implicational relationship between subcategorisation frames and PS rules, illustrated in (1) with respect to verbs:

1a. hit: [— NP]   →   1a.′ VP → V NP
1b. smile: [—]   →   1b.′ VP → V
1c. think: [— S′]   →   1c.′ VP → V S′
1d. give: [— NP PP] →   1d.′ VP → V NP PP
1e. rely: [— PP]   →   1e.′ VP → V PP

Each of the subcategorisation frames in the left column in (1) implies the PS rule in the right column. The subcategorisation frame of *think* in (1c), for example, implies the PS rule in (1c′); the subcategorisation frame of *give* in (1d) implies the PS rule in (1d′); and so on. The observed implicational relationship between subcategorisation frames and PS rules extends to other lexical categories: nouns, adjectives . . . etc.

In view of this, there is a sense in which PS rules simply duplicate information explicitly specified in subcategorisation frames. Most of the information about the constituent structures of phrasal categories can be derived from or 'read off' the subcategorisation frames of the corresponding lexical categories. Obviously, this duplication of information is undesirable, in that it makes the grammar unnecessarily complicated. We therefore should seek a way to eliminate it, presumably, by eliminating PS rules. If successful, this move will in actual fact result in the elimination of the whole component of the grammar called the Base in Part I of this book.

Obviously, the move to eliminate PS rules entails the availability of an alternative mechanism which would determine the structural representation of lexical categories on the basis of their lexical properties. Among other things, the mechanism will have to determine how complements are structurally represented in relation to the categories which subcategorise for them, as well as how non-complements such as adjectives and adverbs are structurally represented in relation to the categories they modify. The mechanism in question would also have to cater for the non-lexical categories S and S′, ideally on a par with lexical categories.

As a matter of fact, the implications of the move to eliminate the Base component go beyond PS rules to include LIR. Recall that the latter makes reference to terminal nodes in phrase markers generated by PS rules. The reference includes both the categorial features of the terminal node and the context in which it is situated in relation to the categorial features and the subcategorisation properties of lexical items. The function of matching lexical items with appropriate nodes situated in appropriate contexts is crucial. In view of this, any revision which will result in the elimination of LIR will have to a include a (substitute) mechanism which performs the functions previously performed by LIR.

The alternative mechanism which determines the structural representation of categories to be discussed in this chapter is called **X-bar theory**. The principle which ensures that the lexical properties of lexical items are accurately reflected in structural representations is called the **Projection Principle**. The revisions undertaken in this chapter will mark the beginning of a shift towards a system of grammar which operates in terms of general principles which function as conditions on representations rather than rules which perform operations.

6.2 *Projection Principle*

Part of the function of LIR was to ensure that sentences such as (2) are included and sentences such as (3) are excluded, given the subcategorisation frame of the verb *solve* shown in (4):

2a. Mary solved the problem.
2b. Mary Aux [$_{VP}$ solved [$_{NP}$ the problem]]

3a. *Mary solved.
3b. Mary Aux [$_{VP}$ solved]

4. *solve:* [+V; — NP]

Another part of the function of LIR is to introduce lexical items into phrase markers. In a sense, LIR has the nature of a transformational rule with conditions incorporated into it. It performs the operation of introducing lexical items into phrases markers subject to two conditions. One condition is that the terminal node must have the same categorial properties as the lexical items. The other is that the terminal node must be situated in a context which matches the subcategorisation properties of the lexical item. Note, however, that the desired result can be achieved simply by requiring that the lexical properties of lexical items be 'projected' onto structural representations, where 'projected' is understood to mean 'accurately reflected'. (4) includes information relating to the categorial features of the lexical item *solve* and its subcategorisation properties, both of which have to be accurately reflected in representations including the verb *solve*.

The requirement in question can take the form of a simple and general principle which will act as a condition on the structural representation of lexical categories. The principle in question is called the **Projection Principle** and can be defined as in (5) (adapted from Chomsky, 1981):

5. **Projection Principle**

   Representations at each syntactic level (i.e. LF, DS and SS) are projected from the lexicon, in that they observe the subcategorisation properties of lexical items.

The Projection Principle incorporates the condition that representations 'observe the subcategorisation properties of lexical items', where the term 'subcategorisation' is understood to include categorial features. Representations which do not observe this condition, such as (3), are therefore excluded. Another essential part of the condition is that the subcategorisation properties of lexical items be observed at 'each syntactic level (i.e. LF, DS and SS)'. DS and SS are syntactic levels in that they are characterised by syntactic rules (see Chapter 4). So far, we have not discussed evidence showing that LF is also syntactic in nature. Such evidence will be discussed in Chapter 7. For the moment, it is perhaps sufficient to remember that subcategorisation properties play a crucial role in determining meaning relations, particularly in sentences which involve a displaced complement. The fact that the topicalised object in *This problem, I can solve* is interpreted as the logical object of the verb is due to the transitive nature of the verb, among other things.

The property of the Projection Principle as a condition which holds of all syntactic levels of representation has an important consequence for the presence of traces in subcategorised positions. In Chapter 4 we discussed evidence showing that movement transformations leave a trace behind. The evidence consisted of examples where traces are visible to certain rules of the grammar, in particular the rule which contracts *want* and *to* to form *wanna* (wanna-contraction) in Colloquial English. Because traces arise at a post-DS level, we faced the problem of providing a formal motivation for their presence as legitimate categories in structural representations. At that stage, the formal motivation could only be provided in terms of a stipulation we called the Trace Convention reproduced in (6):

6. **Trace Convention**

    Movement transformations leave a trace.

We are now in a position to derive at least some of the effects of the Trace Convention from a general and independently needed principle of the grammar, namely the Projection Principle. Consider (7b&c) as candidates for the SS representation of (7a):

7a. This problem, I can solve.
7b. this problem, I can [$_{VP}$ [$_V$ solve]]
7c. this problem$_i$, I can [$_{VP}$ [$_V$ solve] [$_{NP}$ t]$_i$]

(7b) is excluded by the Projection Principle on the grounds that the subcategorisation properties of the transitive verb *solve* are not observed. (7c), however, is not excluded by the Projection Principle as the transitive verb *solve* has an NP object, namely the trace of the topicalised NP. Thus, the requirement that the topicalised NP leave a trace behind follows from the need that the subcategorisation properties of the verb be observed at SS as well as DS. The Trace Convention is not needed in this particular context to force the presence of a trace in the DS position of the topicalised noun phrase.

It seems, therefore, that, as far as subcategorised positions are concerned, the presence of traces follows from a general principle of the grammar. In other words, the effects of the Trace Convention with respect to subcategorised categories derive from an independent principle of the grammar. Obviously, the presence of the trace in non-subcategorised positions, e.g. the subject position of the sentence, cannot be motivated on the same grounds, as subjects do not figure in the subcategorisation frames of lexical items. However, although we cannot eliminate the Trace Convention completely yet, we have taken the first step towards achieving this goal. Further steps will follow later on in this chapter.

6.3   X-bar theory

While the Projection Principle ensures that the subcategorisation properties of lexical items are (accurately) reflected in all syntactic levels of representation, it does not specify how complements, for example, are structurally represented with respect to the lexical categories which subcategorise for them. This role is performed by different conditions, called the principles of X-bar theory or **X-bar schema**. In this section, we will discuss the nature and role of these schema. It will turn out that they are no more than formal statements of generalisations abstracted from PS rules.

6.3.1   Heads and maximal projections

PS rules generally recognise only one level of representation above the terminal node, namely the phrasal level VP, AP, PP. . . etc. (XP). This can be clearly seen in (8a–d) which are abstracted from the corresponding PS rules discussed in Chapter 2:

8a. VP → . . . V . . .
8b. NP → . . . N . . .
8c. AP → . . . A . . .
8d. PP → . . . P . . .

Read from right to left, rules (8a–d) encode the generalisation that the structural representation of every category includes a phrasal level, i.e. XP. For example, the structural representation of V includes VP, the structural representation of N includes NP, and so on. The phrasal level (XP) is called the **maximal projection** (of X) in X-bar terminology. Read from left to right, the rules in (8a–d) convey a different, but related, generalisation, namely that every XP has X as an obligatory constituent. For example, VP has V as an obligatory constituent, NP has N as an obligatory constituent, and so on. In X-bar terminology, the obligatory constituent of a maximal projection is called the **head** (of that maximal projection). This generalisation is related to the previous one in the sense that it actually follows from it. If the structural representation of every category includes a maximal projection, then every maximal projection will include the category (i.e. the head) of which it is the maximal projection.

This core property of PS rules can be captured in terms of the schema in (9), where X has the same categorial value on both sides of the arrow, e.g. if X = V, then XP = VP. (9) is a schema in the sense that it identifies a property which all members of the class of PS rules in question have in common. It is understood as a condition on the structural representation of categories insofar as it specifies the format that such representations must conform to:

9.   XP → . . . X . . .

Although (9) basically captures a common property of PS rules, there is a sense in which it is more restrictive than PS rules. Because the latter are rewrite rules, and because systems of rewrite rules generally make it possible in principle to rewrite a given symbol as one or a combination of any (number of) symbols, nothing seems to exclude unattested representations of the type illustrated by the rules in (10a&b). However, these rules are excluded by schema (9) on the grounds that they do not observe the condition that every maximal projection must have a head, and that a maximal projection exists insofar as it is a projection of a lexical head:

10a. *VP → N
10b. *NP → PP VP

6.3.2   Specifiers and complements

One of the serious shortcomings of PS rules is the fact that they do not reflect structurally the distinction between subcategorised and non-subcategorised categories in relation to the head. The PS rule which generates the NP in (11a), for example, has the form shown in (11b) and generates the structure shown in (11c):

11a. Mary's solution to the problem
11b. NP → NP N PP
11c.

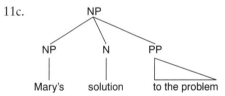

The PP *to the problem* is the complement of the noun *solution* and the NP *Mary* its (logical) subject. However, both the PP complement and the NP subject are sisters to the head N and therefore to each other. This is an undesirable situation, if only because it seems to undermine the claim that grammatical functions are structurally based. Under a structural definition of grammatical functions, subjects and complements are expected to have different structural or grammatical relations. In the structure of the sentence (S), the complement of the verb is a sister of the verb, but the subject of the sentence is not. The structure of NP needed is one where the subject and the complement have different structural relations with respect to the head N. Recall that the notions 'complement' (or object) and 'sister' are closely related. The complement of a head is structurally represented as its sister. In view of this, it seems that it is the structural relation that the subject has with the head N which needs to be modified in (11).

The required modification can be simply achieved by recognising an additional level of categorial representation intervening between the head and its maximal projection. This additional level is called X′ (read X-bar). The intervening level will include the head and its complement and exclude the subject. Incorporating this new level into (11c) yields the structure shown in (12) which makes a clear structural distinction between the subject of NP and the complement of N. The subject is the daughter of NP and sister of N′, and the complement is the daughter of N′ and sister of N:

12.

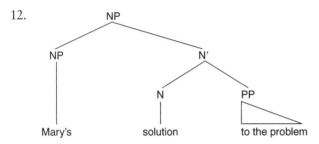

Pursuing our attempt to replace PS rules with general schema which act as conditions on the structural representation of categories, the schema underlying (12) can be stated as in (13a&b):

13a. XP → YP X′
13b. X′ → X ZP
13c.

(13c) is the abstract structure they generate. X, Y and Z are variables which stand for any category. In (12), for example, X = N (*solution*) with the inevitable consequence that X′ = N′ (*solution to the problem*) and XP = NP (*Mary's solution to the problem*).YP = NP (*Mary*) which is a subject by virtue of being daughter of NP and sister of N′. ZP = PP (*to the problem*) which is a complement of N by virtue of being a sister of N.

The intermediate level between the maximal projection XP and the head X is X′, called the **single bar projection**. The hierarchical relations between the three separate levels of categorial representation are sometimes represented in terms of the number of bars (or primes) associated with each level. This is shown in (14a&b), which are purely notational variants of (13a&b). The hierarchy is from 'double-bar' (X″ = XP) to 'single-bar' (X′ = X′) to 'zero-bar' (X⁰ = X) or vice versa. The double-bar projection is the maximal (or phrasal) projection and X⁰ the head. The asterisk associated with the complement category Z″ in (14b) means 'zero or more occurrences'. It is intended to reflect the (familiar) fact that the presence of complements, their number and their nature depends on the lexical item in the head position:

14a. $X'' \rightarrow \text{Spec*} X'$
14b. $X' \rightarrow X^0 Z''*$

Spec(ifier) is a functional term which refers to the category which is the daughter of XP and the sister of X'. Often the term 'Spec' is used interchangeably with the term 'subject' especially in relation to categories that are smaller than a clause/sentence. The Spec of an NP, for example, can be another NP as in (12), a determiner as in (15) or nothing as in (16):

15a. the solution to the problem
15b.

16a. Mary
16b.

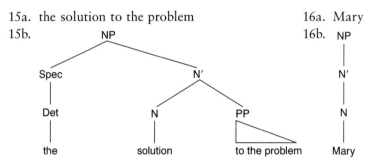

The option of not having a Spec at all is indicated by the asterisk in (14a), which has the same meaning as in (14b). Recall from Chapter 2 that determiners are determined by the type of N the NP includes. English names such as *Mary* do not take a determiner, unlike common nouns such as *solution* which can take either a determiner (15) or a whole NP Spec (12). Later on we will see that there is a limit on the number of Specifiers that a phrase could have such that a phrase cannot have more than one Specifier.

X-bar schema apply to all categories in the same way, as indicated by the use of variables in their formulation. Thus, V is expected to have the representation in (17a), A the representation in (17b), P the representation in (17c), and so on. Possible Specs for each one of these categories are discussed later on in this chapter:

17a.

17b.

17c.

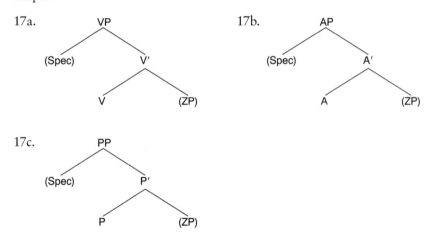

6.3.3   Adjuncts

6.3.3.1   Adjectives and adverbs   Adjectives and VP-adverbs are among the non-subcategorised categories. The PS rules which generate them are reproduced in (18) and (19):

18.   NP → $\left\{ \begin{array}{c} \text{NP} \\ \text{Det} \end{array} \right\}$ (A) N . . .

19.   VP → (ADV) V . . . (ADV)

   Because adjectives and VP-adverbs are not complements of the lexical categories they modify, they are excluded from the single-bar domain (N′ and V′) in the representation of NPs and VPs. Complements normally appear to the right of their head in English, which is not the case with adjectives and at least preverbal VP-adverbs. This property makes them possible candidates for specifiers of NP and VP, respectively, since specifiers usually appear to the left of the category they specify. Whether adjectives and adverbs are specifiers or not is an empirical question the answer to which requires consideration of some relevant data.
   Starting with adjectives, they differ from specifiers of NP in a number of respects, two of which will be discussed here. (20) illustrates the fact encoded in the PS rule (18) that Det and an NP subject cannot co-occur in the pre-N domain (see Chapter 2):

20a.   *Mary's the solution to the problem
20b.

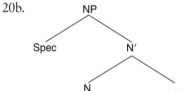

   Given structure (20b), the inability of Det and an NP subject to co-occur in the pre-N domain follows from the idea that they are both specifiers, i.e. categories which occupy the Spec position of NP. (20a) is excluded because there are two categories which compete for a single position. If adjectives were specifiers of NP, we would expect them to be unable to co-occur with either Det or an NP subject in the pre-N domain. However, we know (from Chapter 2) that this is not the case. As a matter of fact, it is quite usual for adjectives to co-occur with either of these categories, as shown in (21) and (22):

21a.   Mary's latest solution to the problem
21b.   [NP [NP Mary's] [AP latest] [N solution] [PP to the problem]]

22a.   The latest solution to the problem
22b.   [NP [Det the] [AP latest] [N solution] [PP to the problem]]

   Another respect in which adjectives differ from specifiers relates to the fact that specifiers tend to be unique. Each category can only have one specifier. (20a) is a good example of this restriction on the number of specifiers. In the X-bar system, this restriction on the number of specifiers follows from the existence of a single Spec position in every phrasal category. Adjectives differ in that they can be 'stacked', so that more than one adjective can be found in a single NP. (23a&b) are classic examples of 'adjective stacking':

23a. A tall dark handsome stranger
23b. The big red car

   The differences between adjectives and specifiers discussed are sufficiently compelling to warrant the conclusion that adjectives are not specifiers, and, therefore, do not occupy the Spec position of NP.
   The order of adjectives with respect to the specifier and the head N suggests that they occupy a position intervening between Spec and N. Looking at structure (20b), it is not clear what this position could be. The fact that adjectives can be 'stacked', as shown in (23a&b), indicates that we should not be looking for a unique position as such. Rather, adjectives should somehow be 'added' to the structure in (20b) with no limit on the number of additions that can be made. More formally, adjectives are said to be **adjoined** to a given category in terms of an **adjunction** structure. The term 'adjunction' can be loosely understood to mean 'extension' of a given category in the manner illustrated in (24), where N' is the extended category:

24.

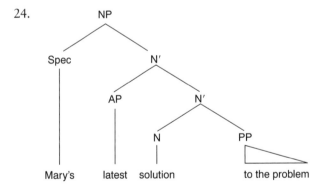

   'Extending' a category amounts to creating a copy of it, hence the fact that there are two occurrences of N' in (24). The newly created copy of N' serves as the mother node for the adjoined AP. Note, however, that because the newly created N' node is only an 'extension' of N', the adjunction structure in (24) means that AP has an ambiguous relationship with N'. AP is both the sister and the daughter of N'. Strange though this may sound from a real-life perspective, it is precisely this property of adjuncts which distinguishes them (in structural terms) from complements and specifiers. Complements and specifiers do not have ambiguous relationships. Complements are daughters of X' and sisters of X. Specifiers, on the other hand, are sisters of X' and daughters of XP. The important aspect of the adjunction structure illustrated in (24) is that it enables us to reflect in structural terms the fact that adjectives are neither complements nor specifiers of the noun they modify.

Turning now to VP-adverbs, we need to decide whether they are adjoined to a projection of V or occupy the Spec position of VP. Since we have not discussed specifiers of verbs yet, an examination of the data of the type carried out above with respect to adjectives and specifiers of nouns is not possible. Anticipating the discussion of specifiers of VP below and in Chapter 8, VP-adverbs do not occupy this position. They are more likely to be adjoined to a projection of the verb, on a par with adjectives in relation to nouns. There is a sense in which VP-adverbs parallel adjectives in function, as shown in (25) and (26):

25a. The army's total destruction of the city
25b. [NP [NP the army's] [N' [AP total] destruction of the city]]

26a. The army totally destroyed the city.
26b. [S [NP the army] Aux [VP [ADV totally] destroyed the city]]

The VP-adverb in (25) modifies the verb (or VP) in the same way its adjectival counterpart in (26) modifies the noun. If the modification relation in (25) is expressed in terms of an adjunction structure, as we have concluded, the parallel modification relation in (26) is likely to be expressed in terms of an adjunction structure too.

Another respect in which adverbs parallel adjectives relates to the fact that adverbs can also be 'stacked', although to a lesser degree than adjectives. (27) and (28) include (at least) two VP-adverbs each:

27a. John repeatedly viciously attacked Bill.
27b. John Aux [VP [ADV repeatedly] [ADV viciously] attacked Bill]

28a. Mary cleverly (only) partially solved the problem.
28b. Mary Aux [VP [ADV cleverly] [ADV partially] solved the problem]

It seems that, as with adjectives, adverbs do not occupy a unique (Spec) position, but are adjoined (added) to an existing projection of V.

The conclusion that adjectives are adjoined to N' was determined on the basis of the order of the adjective in relation to the specifier and the head noun. The order of VP-adverbs in relation to Aux elements and the verb suggests that it can be adjoined either to V' or to VP, as shown in (29):

29.

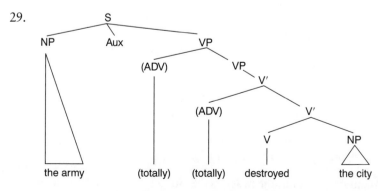

Both possibilities result in the VP-adverb following Aux elements and preceding the main verb. For reasons of uniformity and consistency, given the observed parallelism with adjectives, we will assume for the moment that VP-adverbs are adjoined to V′ rather than to VP.

Uniformity and consistency also dictate that the VP-adverb in (30) is adjoined to V′ even though it occupies a different linear position:

30a. John fixed the car quickly.

30b. John [vp fixed the car [ADV quickly]]

Recall (from Chapter 2) that some VP-adverbs can occur in the final position of VP, as shown in (30). This fact does not necessarily mean that VP-final adverbs have a different structural representation than VP-initial adverbs. The adjunction structures discussed so far are all instances of left-adjunction, in the sense that the 'extension' is located to the left of the extended category. There is no reason, though, why the 'extension' cannot be located to the right of the category adjoined to, as shown in (31):

31.

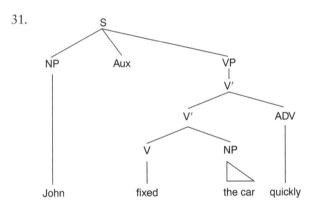

(31), the VP-adverb is **right-adjoined** to V′, whereas in (29) above the VP-adverb is **left-adjoined** to V′. The only difference between the two adjunction structures is in the directionality of adjunction. The VP-adverb has exactly the same structural status and the same ambiguous relationship with V′ in both structures.

6.3.3.2 *Relative clauses*

Recall from Chapter 4 that the bracketed clause has a different relation to the head N in (32) and (33). In (32), the clause is the complement of the noun *suggestion*, and in (33) it is a restrictive relative clause with an 'adjective-like' function:

32a. The suggestion that John should resign is absurd.

32b. [NP the suggestion [S′ that [S John should resign]]] . . .

33a. The suggestion that John made is absurd.

33b. [NP the suggestion$_i$ [S′ Op$_i$ that [S John made t$_i$]]] . . .

As the complement of the noun, the bracketed S′ in (32) is situated inside N′ as a sister of N. The structure of the NP in (32) is therefore as in (34):

34.

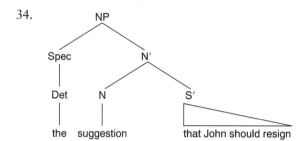

As an adjective-like modifier of the noun, the relative S′ in (33) is expected to have the same structural status as adjectives. The relative clause is neither the complement nor the specifier of the head N of NP. The relative clause is therefore an adjunct. Its linear order with respect to the head N, i.e. [N S′], suggests that the relative clause is right-adjoined to N′, unlike adjectives which are left-adjoined to N′. The relative NP in (33) therefore has the structure shown in (35):

35.

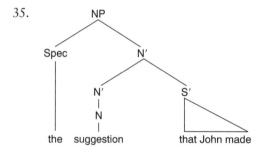

6.3.3.3 *Adjunction structures and X-bar theory*   The adjunction structures discussed so far can be captured in terms of the schema in (36a&b). (36a) underlies adjunction to the single-bar projection, and (36b) adjunction to the double-bar (phrasal) projection. The information included in brackets reflects the availability of right-adjunction in addition to left-adjunction.

36a. X′ → YP X′ (or X′ YP)
36b. XP → YP XP (or XP YP)

Strictly speaking, adjunction structures are inconsistent with the spirit of X-bar theory, namely the idea that each projection differs from the next projection in terms of the number of bars associated with it (X″ → X′ → X⁰). This is because adjunction does not result in the creation of a projection with one less (or more) bars, but in the creation of a projection with the same number of bars as the category adjoined to.

It could be argued on this basis that the adjunction schema in (36a&b) do not belong to the domain of X-bar theory. According to this view, adjunction structures, to the extent that they exist, will remain a mystery, insofar as they do not seem to form part of the set of permissible structures.

Another view would be to add the adjunction schema to the set of the X-bar schema discussed above, so that adjunction structures become part of the set of permissible structures. This will be the case despite the fact that the adjunction schema are somehow different in nature from the other X-bar schema.

A third view would be to argue that since adjunction structures are simply 'extensions' of the projections permitted by X-bar schema, there is a sense in which they are not necessarily inconsistent with the principles of X-bar theory. The logical outcome of this view is that the adjunction schema do not need to be added to the X-bar schema.

We are not going to resolve the issue here. We will continue to assume that adjunction structures exist and leave open the question of how they fit in with the principles of X-bar theory.

6.4   *X-bar theory and non-lexical categories*

The discussion so far has been restricted to lexical categories. It is important to see whether the non-lexical categories S and S' can be brought into line with the lexical ones. There are no a priori reasons to assume that non-lexical categories must have the same structural properties as the lexical categories. However, the principles of X-bar theory arguably will gain more credibility if it turns out that all categories, lexical and non-lexical, have fundamentally the same structural representation.

6.4.1   X-bar structure of S: IP

6.4.1.1   INFL as the head of S   To determine the X-bar structure of S, we need first decide which of its three major constituents is likely to be the head. Looking at (37a&b), the most likely candidate seems to be Aux:

37a. S → NP Aux VP
37b.

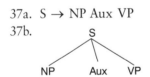

NP and VP are phrasal categories. Therefore, neither of them is likely to be the head of S. Given their status as phrasal categories (i.e. maximal projections) and their order in relation to Aux, NP and VP are more likely to be, respectively, the specifier and the complement of the head of S. On the other hand, the fact that Aux is not a phrasal category and that it occurs between the subject and the predicate VP suggests it is probably the head of S. Let us assume that Aux is indeed the head of S. The next step is to assign S a structure which is consistent with the principles of X-bar theory, i.e. a structure where Aux has a single-bar projection which dominates it and its complement (VP), and a maximal projection which dominates its single-bar projection and the specifier, i.e. the NP subject.

Before we take this step, let us first resolve a confusion surrounding the use of the term 'Aux'. The latter has been used so far to refer to a node in the structure of S and in its full form (auxiliary) to the verbs *be* and *have*. Recall from Chapter 5 that auxiliary verbs are not members of the Aux node at DS. Rather, they are base-generated inside VP and raised to Aux by V-raising. To avoid the confusion created by the term 'Aux' let us refer to the node which intervenes between NP and VP in (37a&b) with the term **INFLECTION**, usually shortened to **INFL** or just **I**. The term 'Inflection' can be justified on the grounds that the node in question hosts the inflectional category Tense (see Chapter 3).

As a matter of fact, Tense is not the only inflectional member of Aux. Another inflectional member of this node is the 'subject marker' -s, found with regular verbs in third person singular present tense conjugations. The distribution of this inflectional category is identical to that of Tense in most respects, as shown in (38):

38a. Mary does not like John, but Jane does.
38b. Does Mary like John?

In the two clauses of (38a) and in (38b) the inflectional category -s appears on *do*, presumably as a result of being left stranded (Chapter 5). In the first clause of (38a), -s is left stranded as a result of Neg blocking Affix-hopping. In the second clause of (38a), -s is left stranded as a result of the deletion of VP. Finally, in (38b) -s is left stranded as a result of Aux-raising (Subject Aux Inversion). All these facts show that the inflectional category -s is a member of Aux, on a par with Tense. This fact emphasises the inflectional character of Aux and arguably justifies renaming it **I(NFL(ECTION))**.

Although the inflectional morpheme -s is restricted to the present tense paradigm, there are reasons to believe that it is not a Tense morpheme. Consider the paradigm in (39):

39a. I smile	39c. You smile	39e. *She/he smile
39b. *I smiles	39d. *You smiles	39f. She/he smiles
39g. We smile	39i. You smile	39k. They smile
39h. *We smiles	39j. *You smiles	39l. *They smiles

The morpheme -s does not appear with any member of the present tense paradigm, but is restricted to the third person singular member. In other words, -s appears when the subject is third person singular. The subject and -s are said to agree in the features of person, gender and number, known as agreement or φ-features. The inflectional morpheme -s is said to belong to the inflectional category **Agr(eement)**, just as the past tense morpheme -ed is said to belong to the inflectional category Tense.

In languages which have richer inflectional paradigms, a different Agr morpheme appears with each member of the conjugation paradigm (see Chapter 13). Rather than assuming that English is different in that it includes the Agr category only in the third person singular conjugation, it is more plausible to assume that it includes the Agr category in every member of the conjugation paradigm. Unlike the third person singular morpheme, the others are simply abstract in nature. This view attributes the situation in English to the more general fact that its inflectional system is generally poorer compared to that of other languages, and not to some peculiar grammatical property. In subsequent chapters it will become clear that the Agr category plays an important role in the derivation and representation of sentences.

In Chapter 4 we used the expression 'tensed clause' to refer to clauses which include Tense under Aux, now I. A general property of English is that clauses which include Tense also invariably include Agr, and clauses which do not include Tense also invariably do not include Agr. Clauses which include Tense and Agr are called **finite clauses**, and clauses which do not include Tense and Agr are called **non-finite clauses**. Restricting our attention to finite clauses for the moment, they have the structure shown in (40), where I is the head and IP its maximal projection. VP is the complement of I. The NP subject is the Spec of IP:

40.

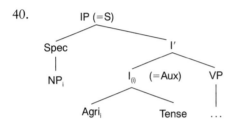

Co-indexation between the Agr category under I and the NP subject in Spec,IP encodes the agreement relation between them in φ-features. In this situation, the subject is said to be in a **Spec-head** agreement relation with (the Agr category of) I. The Spec-head agreement relation is mandatory, in the sense that the Agr category of I and the subject must bear the same or matching φ-features. Instances of non-agreement are excluded, as shown in (39). The notion that instances of non-agreement in features between the Agr category of I and the subject are excluded can be formalised in terms of a condition on representations along the lines of (41):

41. **Spec-Head Agreement**

   A head (X) and its specifier (Spec-XP) must agree in relevant features.

The relevant features for (the Agr category of) I and a subject in Spec, IP are the φ-features, among others to be discussed in the subsequent chapters. The relevant features for Determiners and N are number, e.g. *these/*this books* and *this/*these book*, possibly among others. Later on in this chapter, we will see that other types of features can enter Spec-head agreement relations.

6.4.1.2 Extended Projection Principle   It was pointed out earlier that specifiers are generally optional. However, IP seems to be an exception to this otherwise general property. Consider examples (42) and (43), discussed in Chapter 4 in the context of NP-movement:

42a. Mary seems to have solved the problem.
42b. [IP Mary_i seems [IP t_i [I' to [VP have solved the problem]]]]

43a. *(It) seems that Mary has solved the problem.

43b. [IP *(It) seems [S' that [IP Mary [I' I [VP has solved the problem]]]]]

Recall that the derivation of the raising sentence (42) involves movement of the subject NP *Mary* from the subject position of the non-finite embedded clause to the subject position of the root clause, as shown in (42b). This movement cannot apply in (43) because the embedded clause is tensed (or finite) (Tensed S Condition). In (43), *Mary* remains in the subject position of the embedded clause, and the subject position of the root clause is filled with the 'semantically empty' NP *it*.

The presence of a 'semantically empty' element in Spec,IP in the absence of a 'meaningful' subject can also be seen in sentences such as (44b). Like *it*, the NP *there* is also 'semantically empty'. This is partly shown by the fact that its absence in (44a) (or its presence in (44b)) does not have any effect on the meaning of the sentence. In (44a), the NP *a unicorn* occupies the subject position (i.e. Spec,IP). In (44b), however, the NP *a unicorn* occupies a lower position in the structure, the nature of which should not concern us at the moment:

44a. A unicorn is in the garden.

44b. *(There) is a unicorn in the garden.

One could ask with respect to (43) and (44b) why the presence of the expletive NP should be obligatory despite the fact that it is 'semantically empty'. A plausible answer to this question is that the presence of *it* is forced by some mechanical condition which requires Spec,IP (i.e. the subject position of the sentence) to be filled. The formal requirement in question is called the **Extended Projection Principle (EPP)**, and is sometimes defined as in (45):

45. **Extended Projection Principle**

Clauses must have a subject.

Recall from earlier that the Projection Principle requires subcategorised categories to be present in structural representations but says nothing about non-subcategorised categories such as subjects. (45) extends this requirement to subjects. However, we will assume here that the two principles are independent of each other, in the sense that EPP does not subsume the Projection Principle. Given its definition in (45), EPP is a condition on subjects, whereas the Projection Principle is a condition on the lexical properties of categories. Note that what is meant by 'subject' in (45) is a 'formal subject', that is a category which occupies the subject position of the clause, irrespective of whether the category is semantically empty or not.

One reason for keeping the two principles separate from each other relates to a difference in the level of representation at which they apply. We have seen that the Projection Principle applies at all levels of syntactic representation as specified in its definition. EPP, however, does not have the same scope. It does not hold of DS representations. The reason has to do with the derivation of raising sentences, outlined in (46b&c), and of passives outlined in (47b&c):

46a. Mary seems to have solved the problem.
46b. DS: [$_{IP}$ [$_{NP}$ e] seems [$_{IP}$ Mary [$_{I'}$ to [$_{VP}$ have solved the problem]]]]]
46c. SS: [$_{IP}$ Mary$_i$ seems [$_{IP}$ t$_i$ [$_{I'}$ to [$_{VP}$ have solved the problem]]]]]

47a. The problem was solved (by Mary).
47b. DS: [$_{IP}$ [$_{NP}$ e] I [$_{VP}$ was [$_{VP}$ solved [$_{NP}$ the problem]]]]]
47c. SS: [$_{IP}$ the problem$_i$ I [$_{VP}$ was [$_{VP}$ solved t$_i$]]]]

In the derivation of raising sentences and passives, the subject position which serves as a landing site for the moved NP is empty at DS, as shown in (46b) and (47b). In other words, the DS representation of raising constructions and passives lacks a subject. It follows that EPP does not hold of DS representations, unlike the Projection Principle, which holds of all syntactic levels of representation, including, crucially, DS. EPP holds of SS and LF representations only. The root clause in the SS representation (46c) satisfies EPP as a result of the movement of *Mary* to its subject position. The same is true for the SS representation of the passive (47c), where the sentence also acquires a subject via movement. The embedded clause in (46c) satisfies EPP via the trace in the subject position, left behind by movement of the NP subject to the root clause.

EPP has crucial implications for traces and the Trace Convention much like the Projection Principle. We concluded above that the presence of traces in sub-categorised positions follows from the Projection Principle, paving the way towards deriving the effects of the Trace Convention and consequently eliminating it. However, because the Projection Principle says nothing about non-subcategorised categories such as subjects, the presence of traces in subject positions of clauses does not follow from it. Now the presence of a trace in a subject position evacuated by movement follows from a general principle too, namely EPP. The presence of the trace in the subject position of the embedded clause in the SS representation (46c) is crucial for the clause to satisfy EPP. Thus, it seems that the effects of the Trace Convention are indeed derivable from general and independently needed principles.

Given the manner in which raising sentences and passives satisfy EPP, it is tempting to conclude at this stage that it is perhaps EPP which motivates (forces) NP-movement in raising sentences and passives. NP-movement enables the clauses with empty subject positions to acquire a subject, thereby avoiding a violation of EPP. When NP-movement cannot apply, as in (43a&b), a 'semantically empty' element is inserted in the subject position as a 'last resort' to save the derivation from being excluded by EPP. The question of what motivates movement transformations will be one of the most frequently recurring themes in the forthcoming chapters.

6.4.1.3   Non-finite clauses and PRO subjects   Consider the sentences in (48–50) in the light of the condition imposed by EPP. The embedded non-finite clause in (48–50) appears to lack a subject, apparently in violation of EPP:

48a. John tried to leave.
48b. John tried [$_{S'}$ [$_{IP}$ [e] to leave]]

49a. John persuaded Bill to leave.
49b. John persuaded Bill [$_{S'}$ [$_{IP}$ [e] to leave]]

50a. It is difficult to leave (in these circumstances).
50b. It is difficult [$_{S'}$ [$_{IP}$ [e] to leave . . .]]

EPP does not make a distinction between finite and non-finite clauses, and therefore is expected to hold of both types of clause. It follows that the embedded non-finite clauses in (48–50) must have a subject. Presumably, the subject is a null category. The null category in question is not a trace because none of the root verbs in (48–50) is a raising verb. The null category must therefore be base-generated, meaning it is present at DS much like the null wh-phrase found in relatives (Chapter 4). This null category is called *PRO*, a label which reflects the fact that it has certain properties in common with (overt) pronouns, shown in (51) and (52). (53a–c) are the structural representations of (48), (49) and (50), respectively, with *PRO* in the subject position of the embedded non-finite clause:

51a. John persuaded Bill that he should leave.
51b. John persuaded Bill$_i$ [$_{S'}$ that [$_{IP}$ he$_i$ should leave]]

52a. It is difficult for one/him to leave.
52b. It is difficult [$_{S'}$ for [$_{IP}$ one/him to leave]

53a. John$_i$ tried [$_{S'}$ [$_{IP}$ PRO$_i$ to leave]]
53b. John persuaded Bill$_i$ [$_{S'}$ [$_{IP}$ PRO$_i$ to leave]]
53c. It is difficult [$_{S'}$ [$_{IP}$ PRO to leave]]

Co-indexation between *PRO* and the root subject in (53a) and *PRO* and the root direct object in (53b) conveys the information that the two categories have the same reference. The NP in the root clause is said to be the antecedent of *PRO*. The antecedent is said to **control** *PRO*. (53a) is an instance of **subject control**, where the controller is the subject. (53b) is an instance of **object control**, where the controller is an object. (53c) is an instance of **arbitrary control**, where PRO does not have a controller and therefore receives an interpretation paraphrasable as 'one', as in (52). For reasons which will be discussed in detail in Chapter 9, *PRO* is restricted to the subject position of non-finite clauses.

Non-finite clauses differ from their finite counterparts in that they lack the Tense and Agr categories under I. Instead, they include the element *to* which is generally a marker of non-finiteness. Non-finite clauses have the representation shown in (54):

54.

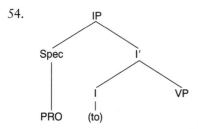

The reason *to* is included between parentheses has to do with the fact that there are other types of non-finite clauses which do not include this element. This is the case in **gerundive clauses**, for example. Gerunds bear the bound morpheme *-ing*, which differs from its counterpart in sentences such as *John is reading a book* in that it does not necessarily denote an ongoing event. The gerund in (55) and (56), for example, does not denote an event in the process of taking place when the sentence is uttered. As shown in (55b) and (56b), gerundive clauses have *PRO* as the subject. In (56) the gerundive clause is in the subject position of the sentence:

55a. John dislikes eating in public.
55b. John dislikes [$_{S'}$ [$_{IP}$ PRO eating in public]]

56a. Reading detective stories is fun.
56b. [$_{S'}$ [$_{IP}$ PRO reading detective stories]] is fun

One of the questions which arises with respect to gerundive clauses is what exactly occupies their head position I. Note that according to the principles of X-bar theory the head position has to be filled for X-bar structures to be licensed. In other words, the various levels of categorial representation, including the X^0 level, exist insofar as they are projections of a given head category (inflectional or otherwise). In finite clauses, I^0, I′ and IP are projections of the inflectional categories Agr and Tense. In non-finite clauses with *to* they are projections of *to*. It is conceivable that in gerundive clauses I^0, I′ and IP are the projections of the bound morpheme *-ing*. The latter could be assumed to be base-generated under I and subsequently Affix-hopped onto the verb inside VP. If this is the correct analysis for gerundive clauses, they do not give rise to a problem as far as the licensing of the X-bar projections of I is concerned.

The X-bar projections of I in gerundive clauses can be justified on independent grounds. Suppose that finiteness is encoded in the form of the feature [+/−FINITE], on a par with the feature [+/−Q] associated with the Comp of declarative and interrogative clauses (Chapters 4 and 5). The typology of I as determined by the feature complex [+/−FINITE] can be stated as in (57):

57a. I   → [+/−FINITE]
57b [+FINITE] → Agr, Tense
57c. [−FINITE] → to, ∅

(57a,b&c) can be understood to mean that the feature specification [+FINITE] is realised by Agr and Tense, and the feature specification [−FINITE] by either *to* (the marker of non-finiteness) or nothing. The idea is that the presence of a feature is sufficient to license X-bar projections, so that in gerundive clauses the X-bar projections of I are licensed by the feature [−FINITE]. Recall from Chapter 3 that even categories such as verbs and nouns are essentially bundles of features (with positive and negative values), so that their X-bar projections are in actual fact licensed by features. The same is true of Comp in relation to the features [−Q] (declarative clauses) and [+Q] (interrogative clauses).

6.4.2 Small clauses

Compare (58) and (59):

58a. John considers Bill to be incompetent.
58b. John considers [IP [NP Bill] [I′ to [VP be [AP incompetent]]]]

59a. John considers Bill incompetent.
59b. John considers [Bill incompetent]

The verb *consider* has a non-finite clause as complement in both (58) and (59). However, the two non-finite clauses differ in important respects. The finite clause in (58) includes *to* and the verb *be*, whereas the one in (59) apparently includes neither.

The embedded clause in (59) is called a **small clause**, partly because it lacks the I-element *to*. As a matter of fact, the small clause in (59) cannot include *to*, as shown in (60):

60. John considers Bill (*to) incompetent.

The small clause cannot include a complementiser either, as shown in (61), suggesting that it is perhaps smaller than an S′. However, this is also true of its non-small counterpart, as shown in (62):

61a. *John considers that/for Bill to be incompetent.
61b. *John considers [S′ for/that [IP Bill to be incompetent]]

62a. *John considers that/for Bill incompetent.
62b. *John considers [S′ that/for [IP Bill incompetent]]

The reason neither of the two clauses can take a complementiser is explained in Chapter 8. For the moment, it should be clear that the inability to take a complementiser is not what distinguishes the small clause in (59) from its non-small counterpart in (58).

The status of the constituent in brackets in (59b) as a clause has mainly been related to the fact that its NP constituent displays properties usually associated with subjects. We will not review the evidence here, although we will take this point into consideration in the analysis to be outlined. The question we will try to deal with first is whether the (obligatory) absence of *to* in small clauses affects the licensing of the X-bar projections of I. Given the discussion of gerundive clauses above, the absence of *to* does not necessarily imply the absence of I. However, the issue with respect to small clauses such as the one in (59) also involves the verb *be*. Like *to*, this verb is also excluded as shown in (63):

63. *John considers Bill be incompetent.

In the structure of IP outlined above, VP is the complement of I with the implication that I subcategorises for VP (like auxiliary verbs; Chapter 5). It follows that when I is present, VP is expected to be present too. Otherwise, the subcategorisation requirements of I would not be observed. In view of this, it remains mysterious why *be* cannot appear in small clauses. Reversing the argument, the fact that *be* cannot appear implies that VP is absent. If VP is absent then I is likely to be absent too, on the assumption that the absence of a complement implies the absence of the head which selects for it.

The plausible hypothesis seems to be that small clauses lack I and (therefore) its X-bar projections, as well as V and (therefore) its X-bar projections. Looking at the structure in (58b), the categories we are left with are the NP subject and the predicative AP. Bearing in mind that the NP subject must occupy a subject position, the small clause in (59) can be assigned the structure shown in (64). The status of the small clause as an AP is determined by the categorial property of the predicate, which is an adjective. The NP *Bill* has the status of a subject by virtue of occupying Spec,AP:

64.

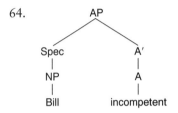

Categories other than AP can also function as a small clause complement. The small clause complement is a PP in (65) and a VP in (66):

65a. The captain expects the drunken sailor (*to) off the ship immediately.
65b.

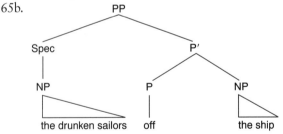

66a. John made Bill (*to) read the whole book.
66b.

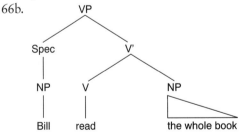

6.4.3   X-bar structure of S′: CP

6.4.3.1   Comp as the head of S′   As with S, we need to determine which category is the head of S′. The decision with respect to S′ is relatively straightforward. Looking at (67), the head is likely to be Comp, IP (alias S) being a maximal projection:

67a. S′ → Comp IP
67b.

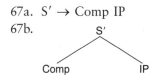

Assigning S′ a structure consistent with the principles of X-bar theory gives the result shown in (68). **C** is short for Comp(lementiser), and **CP** short for **Comp(lementiser) Phrase**:

68.

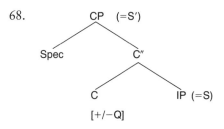

As explained in Chapters 4 and 5, declarative clauses are marked with the feature [−Q] and interrogative clauses with the feature [+Q]. Therefore, the X-bar projections of C actually are the projections of these features. As far as embedded clauses are concerned, the feature [−Q] is optionally realised as *that* when IP is finite, as shown in (69), and as *for* when IP is non-finite as shown in (70). The fact that the type of complementiser which appears under C depends on whether I is finite or non-finite implies a link between C and I, which we will not pursue here:

69a. I think (that) John should leave.
69b. I think [CP [C′ (that) [IP John should leave]]]
69c.

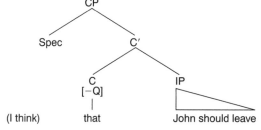

70a. I want (for) for John to leave.
70b.   want [CP for [IP John to leave]
70c.

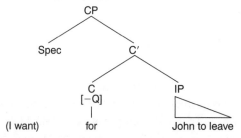

As for embedded yes-no clauses, the feature [+Q] can be realised as *if*, as shown in (71), or have its presence indicated by *whether*, as in (72). We will assume here that *whether* is a wh-phrase associated with yes-no questions and base-generated in Spec,CP. The important point to remember about (71) and (72) is that wh-phrases are located in Spec,CP, while complementisers, which are head categories, are located under C. This arrangement has important implications for the representation of moved wh-phrases and auxiliaries in wh-questions as we will see shortly:

71a. I wonder if John has left.
71b. I wonder [$_{CP}$ [$_{C'}$ [$_C$ if] [$_{IP}$ John has left]]]

72a. I wonder whether John has left.
72b. I wonder [$_{CP}$ whether [$_{C'}$ [$_C$ [+Q]] [$_{IP}$ John has left]]]

A major problem with the PS rules-based structure (67) is that it makes available only one position in the pre-S domain. The consequence is that in a wh-question such as (73) the moved wh-phrase and the auxiliary must share one position, namely Comp, an undesirable situation:

73a. Who did Mary see?
73b. [S' who$_i$ did$_j$ [$_{IP}$ Mary t$_j$ see t$_i$]]

Moreover, the two categories located under Comp belong to different levels of categorial representation. *Did* (i.e. Aux or I) is a head, while the wh-phrase is a phrasal category (maximal projection). Presumably, a given category cannot be both a head and a phrasal projection, as representation (73b) seems to imply with respect to Comp.

The structure of S'/CP based on the principles of X-bar theory shown in (74) does not have these problems. It makes available two positions in the pre-IP domain. Moreover, one of the two positions is a head (C) and the other a maximal projection (Spec,CP). The wh-phrase is located under Spec,CP and the head I (alias Aux) under C:

74.

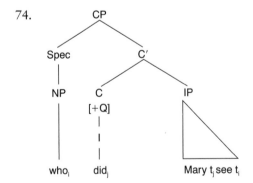

6.4.3.2   *Spec,CP in interrogative clauses*

We have seen that IP differs from other categories in that its Spec position is required (by EPP) to be filled at SS. Judging from some of the examples above, where Spec,CP is empty, it seems that CP is not subject to a similar requirement. However, this does not seem to be true for all types of CP. Apparently, CPs the head of which is marked with the feature [+Q], i.e. interrogative clauses, seem to be required to have their Spec position filled by a wh-phrase at SS. Consider the examples in (75) and (76):

75a. I wonder who Mary saw.
75b. DS: I wonder [CP e [C' [+Q] [IP Mary saw who]]]
75c. SS: I wonder [CP who$_i$ [C' [+Q] [IP Mary saw t$_i$]]]

76a. *I wonder Mary saw who.
76b. DS: I wonder [CP e [C' [+Q] [IP Mary saw who]]]
76c. SS: I wonder [CP e [C' [+Q] [IP Mary saw who]]]

The verb *wonder* subcategorises for a [+Q] clause. (76) shows that the Spec,CP of the complement [+Q]-clause cannot remain empty at SS. This is also true of root [+Q]-clauses, as shown in (78) compared to (77). The intended interpretation of (78) as a question is conveyed by the presence of the feature [+Q] in its representations. Obviously, (78) is possible with an echo-reading, but this is beside the point. Recall from Chapter 4 that echo-questions do not bear the feature [+Q]:

77a. Who did Mary see?
77b. DS: [CP e [C' [+Q] [IP Mary I [VP see who]]]]
77c. SS: [CP who$_i$ [C' did$_j$ [IP Mary [I' t$_j$ I [VP see t$_i$]]]]]
     SS: [CP who$_i$ [C' did$_j$ [IP Mary [I' t$_j$ [VP see t$_i$]]]]]

78a. *Mary saw who?
78b. DS: [CP e [C' [+Q] [IP Mary I [VP saw who]]]]
78c. SS: [CP e [C' [+Q] [IP Mary I [VP saw who]]]]

It seems that CPs the head of which is marked with the feature [+Q] are subject to the requirement that their Spec,CP be filled at SS. Here, we will call the requirement in question the [+Q]-CP Principle and define it as in (79):

79. **[+Q]-CP Principle**

     A [+Q]-CP must have a specifier.

Like EPP, (79) holds of SS and LF representations, but not of DS representations. Pursuing the parallelism with EPP, just as it is possible that NP-movement in raising constructions and passives is motivated by EPP, as pointed out above, it is equally possible that Wh-movement in wh-questions is motivated by (79). The wh-phrase has to move to Spec,CP to provide the [+Q]-CP with a specifier necessary for it to satisfy (79). Note that it is not necessary to specify that the specifier intended in (79) must be a wh-phrase. This will follow from the Spec-Head Agreement requirement discussed earlier. The relevant feature for C and a specifier occupying Spec,CP is [+/−Q]. Because C in questions bears the feature [+Q] only a phrase bearing the same feature, i.e. a wh-phrase, can occupy Spec,CP.

Finally, it is possible that (79) holds of yes-no questions as well. Recall from above that embedded yes-no questions can either include *if* under C or *whether* under Spec,CP. To the extent that *whether* is a wh-phrase, it seems that yes-no questions are possibly also specified for the feature [+Q]. Assuming this to be the case, it follows from (79) that all yes-no questions include a wh-phrase in Spec,CP. In embedded clauses, the wh-phrase can be realised either as *whether* or, presumably, as a null wh-phrase. In root sentences, it is invariably realised as a null wh-phrase. Evidence that embedded yes-no interrogatives probably include a null wh-phrase can be gleaned from sentences such as (80):

80a. *How do you wonder whether John fixed the car?
80b. *How do you wonder if John fixed the car?
80c. *how$_i$ do you wonder [$_{CP}$ wh-XP [$_{C'}$ if [$_{IP}$ John fixed the car t$_i$]]]?

(80a) involves a violation of the Wh-island Condition triggered by movement of the wh-phrase out of the embedded wh-island (Chapter 4). (80b) shows that the wh-island violation arises even when an overt wh-phrase is missing. Assuming that the defining characteristic of wh-islands is that they include a wh-phrase in Spec,CP, it follows that the embedded yes-no interrogative in (80b) includes a null wh-phrase in Spec,CP, as shown in (80c). The fact that an overt wh-phrase and *if* cannot co-occur, e.g. *I wonder whether if John fixed the car*, can be attributed to the Doubly Filled Comp Filter (Chapter 4). Questions such as *What if John fixes the car?* presumably have an (elliptical) structure where *what* and *if* do not necessarily share the same CP.

6.5   *Movement types*

6.5.1   Substitution movements

In this section, we address the important question whether the principles of X-bar theory hold of all levels of syntactic representation or just DS. If they hold of all levels of syntactic representation, the implication is that transformations do not have the power to modify DS representations in such a way as to derive SS and LF representations which are inconsistent with the principles of X-bar theory. If, on the other hand, the scope of the principles of X-bar theory is restricted to DS, the implication is that transformations can introduce modifications which result in violations of the principles of X-bar theory at the post-DS levels. The former scenario is arguably more desirable on the grounds that it places further constraints on the power of transformations and maintains a certain degree of uniformity of structure at all levels of representation. According to this view, the principles of X-bar theory turn out to have the additional function of restricting the permissible range of transformations such that only those which result in the derivation of structures consistent with them are allowed. The rest are excluded.

The idea that the principles of X-bar theory apply at all levels of syntactic representation implies that transformations 'preserve' DS representations. At this stage, this implication is basically a prediction. Its validity needs to be verified against the various types of transformations discussed in Chapters 4 and 5, among others. The hypothesis can be formulated as in (81) (adapted from Emonds 1976):

81. **Structure-Preserving Hypothesis**

Transformations are structure-preserving.

Here we will understand by a 'structure-preserving transformation' any transformation which leads to the derivation of a structure which is consistent with the principles of X-bar theory. Thus, all transformations which, for example, move a category to an empty position made available by the principles of X-bar theory are 'structure-preserving'. On the other hand, all transformations which require the creation of a new node which is not made available by X-bar theory are not 'structure-preserving'. The latter type of transformations are said to be 'structure-building'.

Transformations which move a category to an empty position are called **substitution transformations**. A prominent example of such transformations is NP-movement involved in the derivation of passives such as (82) and raising sentences such as (83). In both sentences, NP-movement moves an NP to a free (non-filled) Spec,IP position. Thus, NP-movement is trivially 'structure-preserving':

82a. The problem was solved (by Mary).
82b. DS: [$_{IP}$ e [$_{I'}$ I [$_{VP}$ was [$_{VP}$ solved the problem]]]]
82c. SS: [$_{IP}$ the problem$_i$ [$_{I'}$ I [$_{VP}$ was [$_{VP}$ solved t$_i$]]]]

83a. Mary seems to have solved the problem.
83b. DS: [$_{IP}$ e I [$_{VP}$ seems [$_{IP}$ Mary [$_{I'}$ to [$_{VP}$ have solved the problem]]]]]
83c. SS: [$_{IP}$ Mary$_i$ I [$_{VP}$ seems [$_{IP}$ t$_i$ [$_{I'}$ to [$_{VP}$ have solved the problem]]]]]

Another prominent example of a substitution movement is Wh-movement, illustrated in (84). Wh-movement moves the wh-phrase to a free Spec,CP position and therefore is trivially 'structure-preserving':

84a. Which problem did Mary solve?
84b. DS: [$_{CP}$ e [$_{C'}$ e [$_{IP}$ Mary [$_{I'}$ I [$_{VP}$ solve [NP which problem]]]]]]
84c. SS: [$_{CP}$ which problem$_i$ [$_{C'}$ did$_j$ [$_{IP}$ Mary [I' t$_j$ [VP solve t$_i$]]]]]

(84) also involves I-raising (alias Aux-raising) in its derivation, as shown in (84c). It is not entirely clear that I-raising is a substitution movement due to the fact that the position it targets includes the feature [+Q]. We will keep an open mind here on whether I-raising is a substitution movement or not. Both views have been advanced in the literature.

Thus, NP-movement and Wh-movement are 'structure-preserving', essentially because they are substitution movements. Let us now turn to the remaining transformations, i.e. Topicalisation, I-lowering (alias Affix-hopping), V-raising, Extraposition and Heavy NP Shift.

6.5.2   Adjunction movements

A typical example of a 'structure-building' transformation is Topicalisation, as formulated in Chapter 4. Recall that Topicalisation moves a category and attaches it to the (left side of) S (now IP), thereby creating a new node. (85a–c) are reproduced from Chapter 4:

85a. This problem, I can solve.
85b. I believe that this problem, I can solve.
85c.

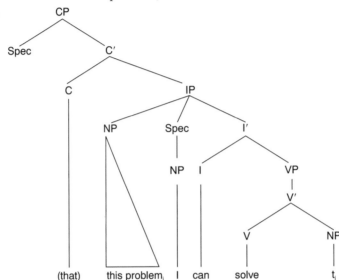

Structure (85c) is obviously inconsistent with the principles of X-bar theory, as the NP node created by Topicalisation is not licensed by any of the X-bar schema discussed above. The schema which deals with the branching of the XP node (XP → Spec X') specifies that XP can only have two daughter branches. In (85c), IP dominates three daughter branches. We therefore need to assign (85a&b) an alternative structure which is consistent with the principles of X-bar theory, if we are to maintain the position that all transformations are 'structure-preserving' in the sense explained above.

   To the extent that the schema which license adjunction structures can be considered to be among the principles of X-bar theory, (85a&b) can be assigned the structure shown in (86c), where the topicalised category is left-adjoined to IP:

86a. XP → YP XP (or XP YP)
86b. [$_{CP}$ (that) [$_{IP}$ this problem$_i$ [$_{IP}$ I [$_{I'}$ can [$_{VP}$ solve t$_i$]]]]]

86c.

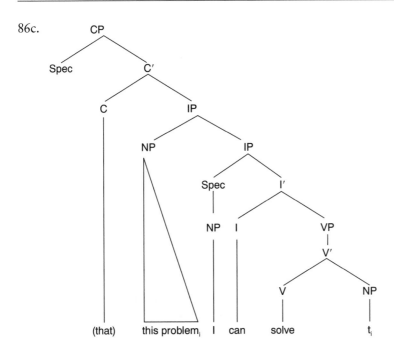

According to this analysis, Topicalisation can be said to be non-'structure-building', as, strictly speaking, it does not create a new node but simply 'extends' an existing node (IP). More generally, Topicalisation, as analysed in (86c), does not give rise to a structure which is inconsistent with the principles of X-bar theory, assuming that the latter include the adjunction schema in (86a), where XP = IP.

According to the analysis outlined in (86c), Topicalisation is an **adjunction** movement. Other 'structure-building' transformations can also be reanalysed as adjunction movements. These include Extraposition and Heavy NP Shift, which were said in Chapter 4 to attach the category they move as the rightmost constituent of VP. These transformations can now be said to right-adjoin the category they move to V' or VP, thereby deriving an adjunction structure. (87) and (88) are illustrative examples where the moved constituent is right-adjoined to VP:

87a. Details have emerged of a secret plan to finance the rebels.
87b. [IP [NP details ti] [I' I [VP [VP have emerged] [PP of a secret plan . . .]i]]]

87c.

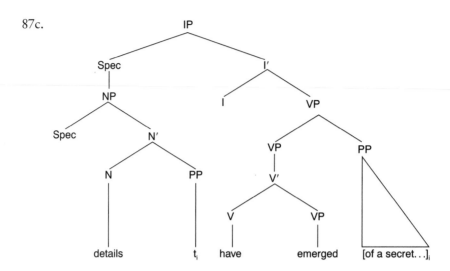

88a. Mary returned to the library all the books she had borrowed.
88b. [IP Mary I [VP [VP returned t_i [PP to the library]] [NP all the books . . .]_i]]
88c.

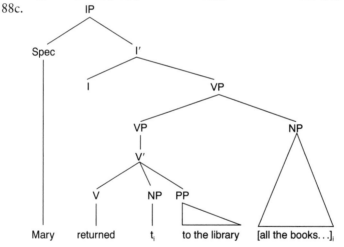

I-lowering and V-raising were said in Chapter 5 to attach the category they move to V and to I, respectively, as shown in (89) and (90):

89a. Mary solved the problem.
89b. [IP Mary [I' t_i [VP [V [V solve] [I]_i] the problem]]]

90a. Mary has solved the problem.
90b. [IP Mary [I' [V have]_i I [VP t_i [VP solved the problem]]]]

As a matter of fact, we have been vague about how exactly I and V are attached to each other in such examples. Now we are in a position to be more explicit about this process. The moved head can be said to adjoin to the host head category, deriving the complex head structures shown in (91a) and (91b). (91a) is the complex head structure derived by I-lowering, where V is the category adjoined to. (91b) is the complex head structure derived by V-raising, where I is the category adjoined to:

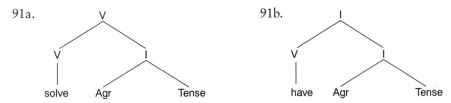

91a.   91b.

The adjunction schema discussed earlier in this chapter deal only with adjunction to single-bar projections and maximal projections. To accommodate the structures in (91a&b), we need to introduce a new adjunction schema for head-adjunction such as in (92):

92.   X → X Y (or Y X)

6.6   *Binary branching and VP-shells*

An interesting consequence of X-bar theory is that most nodes dominate no more than two branches, a phenomenon known as **binary branching**. To see this clearly, compare the structure of the sentence generated by the PS rule shown in (93) to the X-bar structure shown in (94):

93a. S → NP Aux VP
93b.

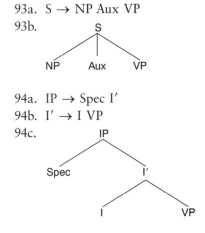

94a. IP → Spec I′
94b. I′ → I VP
94c.

In (93), S dominates three nodes, NP, Aux and VP. In (94b), however, IP (=S) dominates only two nodes, Spec (=NP) and I′. The head category I (=Aux) is included in a lower layer together with its complement VP, so that I too only dominates two nodes, I and VP.

The binary branching pattern is preserved even when a sentence-adverb is added. In the earlier system which included PS rules, sentence adverbs where simply added to the set of nodes dominated by S. The consequence is that in a sentence such as (95a), S dominates four nodes:

95a. Presumably, John fixed the car.
95b. S → (ADV) NP Aux VP
95c.

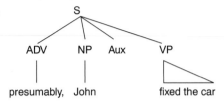

In the structure of the clause dictated by X-bar theory, sentence-adverbs can only have the status of adjuncts of IP, as shown in (96). The adjunction structure is binary in nature just like the structures discussed above. Each of the two segments of IP dominates no more than two branches:

96a. IP → ADV IP
96b.

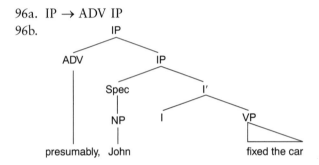

A theory of phrase structure which restricts branching to no more than two is to be favoured over a theory which does not include such a restriction. A theory with such a restriction puts a severe limit on possible structures compared to a theory without such a restriction. Although the binary branching pattern discussed is a consequence of assigning phrases structures consistent with X-bar theory, the latter actually does not include such a restriction. Recall that the asterisk associated with the complement YP in (97) was said earlier to mean 'zero or more occurrences'. In other words, this interpretation of the asterisk does not put a limit on the number of occurrences of the complement:

97a. XP → Spec X′
97b. X′ → X YP*

There are many ways of incorporating the intended restriction into the system. One obvious possibility is to reinterpret the asterisk to mean 'no more than one occurrence'. Another way is simply to state the intended restriction as a separate condition on structures along the lines of (98):

98.   **Binary Branching**

A node can dominate at most two branches.

The discussion of binary branching so far has carefully eschewed the most challenging cases which initially may give the impression of casting serious empirical doubt on the validity of (98). These are VPs headed by verbs which take two complements such as *give* and *put*, illustrated in (99) and (100).

99a. John put the book *(on the shelf).
99b. John put *(the book) on the shelf.

100a. Mary gave the book *(to John).

These verbs have the subcategorisation frame shown in (101a). The idea that complements of verbs are structurally represented as sisters to the verb (and to each other) implies that the VP which includes such verbs has the structure shown in (101b). The latter, however, is clearly inconsistent with (98) as V' dominates three nodes.

100b. Mary gave *(the book) to John.

101a. *put, give*: [— NP PP]
101b.

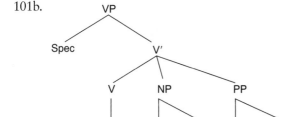

A possible (and by no means unreasonable) way of dealing with the challenge presented by (99) and (100) is to say that they constitute evidence against (98). Adopting this attitude would, however, amount to forsaking the significant economy gains that will follow from including (98) into the system. Another way of dealing with the challenge is to give prior importance to the economy gains which emanate from (98) and reanalyse (99) and (100) in such a way that they become consistent with (98). Adopting the latter attitude requires one to demonstrate that the new way of analysing (99) and (100) is consistent with the range of relevant facts, and preferably, makes it possible to account for additional facts which otherwise remain mysterious. In the next paragraphs we will discuss a new way of analysing (99) and (100) which is consistent with (98), although discussion of relevant facts will have to wait till later stages in this book.

The idea underlying the new analysis is that verbs such as *put* and *give* are more complex than they appear. More precisely, they are complexes which consist of two Vs. One is called a **light verb**, represented with the symbol *v*, and the other is an impoverished version of the verb itself, which we will represent here with an upper case version of the verb, e.g. PUT and GIVE. The consequence is that sentences which include these verbs, such as (99) and (100), actually include two VPs. This is shown in (102):

102.

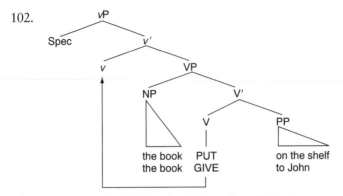

The upper VP is headed by the light verb and the lower one by PUT/GIVE. The NP complement is located in the Spec position of the lower VP (headed by PUT/GIVE) and the PP complement is a sister to PUT/GIVE. The order [V NP PP] is derived by movement of V to *v*. The VP structure in (102) is often called a **VP-shell**.

(102) is consistent with (98), since none of the nodes it includes dominates more than two branches. However, it raises some serious questions which must be addressed. For example, the NP *the book* is represented as the Spec of the lower VP. Consequently, it is a sister to neither *v* nor V. This representation amounts to the claim that NP is actually not a complement, but a kind of subject. For this claim to be valid it has to be shown that this NP shares some properties with subjects. It has also to be shown that NP is hierarchically higher than PP, contrary to what is implied by the earlier structure (101b) where they are at the same level of hierarchy. Another question relates to whether the occurrence of the light verb is restricted only to verbs with two complements or is also found with verbs with one complement and indeed also intransitive verbs. These questions and others will be addressed in relevant parts in subsequent chapters. One idea that will transpire clearly is that there are verbs which are morphologically or superficially simple (non-complex) but on closer inspection turn out to be semantically complex.

6.7   *Summary*

We started this chapter by considering the role of PS rules in the grammar. It transpired that their role was largely superfluous, as most of them simply duplicate information included in the lexical entries of lexical categories. This fact raised the possibility that PS rules could be eliminated completely, and with them the Categorial Component of the Base, leading to a major simplification of the grammar.

The role of ensuring that the subcategorisation properties of lexical items are properly reflected in structural representations has been attributed to a simple principle called the Projection Principle which applies at all levels of syntactic representation. The Projection Principle subsumes the role of LIR as well as derive the effects of the Trace Convention with respect to subcategorised positions.

The role of defining the major aspects of the structural representation of categories fell to a limited set of principles called the principles of X-bar theory. The latter mostly take the form of schema, in the sense that they capture certain common properties of phrase structures, and function as constraints on the structural representation of categories both lexical and non-lexical. The idea that these principles hold of all levels of syntactic representation leads to a situation where they also serve as conditions on the types of transformation allowed, such that only those which are 'structure-preserving' are possible.

In addition to these principles, there is the Extended Projection Principle (EPP) which requires (both finite and non-finite) clauses to have a subject. Non-finite clauses which do not have an overt subject have the null category *PRO* as the subject. Unlike the Projection Principle, EPP does not hold of DS representations. However, like the Projection Principle it derives some of the effects of the Trace Convention, this time with respect to the (non-subcategorised) subject position. Wh-questions (and possibly also yes-no questions) are subject to a condition called the [+Q]-CP Principle which requires them to have a (wh-)specifier at SS.

Exercises

Exercise 6.1

Assign an X-bar structure to the sentences in (i–v):

i) Bill remembers the unhappy experience.
ii) Incidentally, Bill left early.
iii) John genuinely believes that Bill should resign.
iv) Bill went to London to see his parents.
v) Bill arrived after John had left.

Exercise 6.2

Assign an X-bar structure to the sentences in (i–iv) and explain how the order inside VP is derived:

i) Bill sent a letter to John.
ii) Bill persuaded John to leave.
iii) Mary left the file on the desk.
iv) The player headed the ball into the net.

Exercise 6.3

Explain how the sentences in (i–v) are excluded. Bearing in mind that ungrammaticality results from the violation of a requirement of the grammar, make sure you identify the principle violated and explain how it is violated:

i) *The player headed.
ii) *Headed the ball.

iii) *Did in which match the player head the ball?
iv) *I wonder the player headed the ball in which match.
v) *Which way I wonder if the player headed the ball?

Exercise 6.4

Sentences (i–iv) have a clause for a subject, and (v) appears to have an adverb for a subject. Such sentences have been said to constitute empirical evidence in favour of the structure of the sentence determined by X-bar theory and against the structure determined by the relevant PS rule. Evaluate this claim:

i)   That John should leave suddenly is puzzling.
ii) To start with the simple exercises seems reasonable.
iii) Blaming others is not the solution.
iv) Bill believes that watching football is boring.
v)   Now is the time to do it.

Exercise 6.5

Example (i) shows that the predicate of a small clause can be an NP. Explain whether this example is consistent with the analysis of small clauses discussed in this chapter. Examples (ii) and (iii) include the modifiers *very* and *rather* which have been claimed to occupy the Spec position of the AP they are related to. Explain whether this claim is consistent with the analysis of small clauses outlined in this chapter:

i)   Bill considers John a genius.
ii) John considers Bill very intelligent.
iii) Bill finds John rather suspicious.

Exercise 6.6

Suggest a way of dealing with the sentences in (ia) and (iia) using the VP-shell structure discussed in this chapter. Explain whether these sentences can be derivationally related to their counterparts in (ib) and (iib), that is, whether both types of sentence can be derived from the same DS:

i)a. John sent Bill a message.
i)b. Bill sent a message to Bill.

ii)a. Mary gave John a book.
ii)b. Mary gave a book to John.

Exercise 6.7

Determine the structural status of the PP constituents *of Physics* and *with long hair* in the noun phrases (i-v). Make sure you explain why (ii) and (v) are excluded. You may want to consult the section on co-ordination in Chapter 2:

i)   The student of Physics with long hair

ii) *The student with long hair of Physics
iii) The student of Physics and Chemistry
iv) The student with long hair and (with) a big moustache
v) *The student of Physics and with long hair

Sources and further reading

The fundamentals of X-bar theory are outlined in Chomsky (1973) and later refined in Emonds (1976), Jackendoff (1977), Chomsky (1981) and Stowell (1981). Stowell (1981) and later Chomsky (1986b) were influential in extending the principles of X-bar theory to non-lexical categories, complementing earlier work by Bresnan (1970) and Fassi Fehri (1980) in relation to COMP and S'.

Discussions of the structure of small clauses can be found in Chomsky (1981), Stowell (1981) and Kayne (1984). A different view is expressed in Williams (1980, 1983). Chomsky (1986b) includes the analysis outlined in this chapter.

The Projection Principle and the Extended Projection Principle are discussed at length in Chomsky (1981). This is a highly technical piece of work which set research on the way to developing the Principles and Parameters framework. Most of the ideas discussed in Part II of this book can be traced to it.

The typology of movements discussed in this chapter is made more explicit in Chomsky (1986b). The latter also discusses the relevance of this typology to the Structure Preserving Hypothesis introduced in Emonds (1976).

Binary branching is introduced and applied to various contexts in Kayne (1984). The VP-shell structure for verbs with two complements is introduced in Larson (1988), although the discussion of it in this chapter took into consideration the version adopted in Chomsky (1995).

7 θ-Theory

Contents

7.1 *C-selection and s-selection*

In Chapter 4 we used the expressions 'logical subject' and 'logical object' to refer to the so-called semantic functions of categories. In active sentences such as (1), the semantic functions of the two NPs correspond to their grammatical functions. In passive sentences such as (2), however, the semantic and grammatical functions do not correspond:

1a. John hit Bill.
1b. [IP John I [VP hit Bill]]

2a. Bill was hit (by John).
2b. [IP Billi I [VP was hit ti (by John)]]

In the active sentence (1), *John* is both the logical subject and the grammatical subject of the sentence, and *Bill* both the logical and grammatical object of the verb. However, in the passive sentence (2) the semantic functions of the two NPs do not correspond to their grammatical functions. *Bill* is the logical object since it undergoes the act described by the verb. At the same time, it is the grammatical subject of the sentence by virtue of the fact that it occupies Spec,IP (the subject position) and is in a Spec-head agreement relations with (the Agr category of) I. The NP *John* inside the *by*-phrase appears to be the logical subject since it performs the act described by the verb. However, it is not the grammatical subject of the sentence for the simple reason that it is not located in the subject position and is not in a Spec-head agreement relation with (the Agr category of) I. This property of passives is reflected in the derivation outlined in (2b), whereby the NP *Bill* is base-generated in the object position of the verb and subsequently moved to the subject position of the sentence. The *by*-phrase is an optional adjunct.

There is a kind of implicational relation between selection in terms of semantic categories and subcategorisation in terms of syntactic categories. The transitive verb *hit* in (1) and (2) subcategorises for an NP because it selects a 'logical object' in the first place. An intransitive verb such as *smile* does not subcategorise for an NP because it does not select a logical object in the first place. Subcategorisation in terms of syntactic categories such as NP is called **categorial selection (c-selection)** and selection in terms of semantic categories is called **semantic selection (s-selection)**. S-selection is largely determined by the inherent meaning (sometimes called **conceptual structure**) of lexical items. The verb (or concept) *hit*, for example, entails two participants, a subject participant who performs the act of 'hitting' and an object participant who suffers the act of 'hitting'. On the other hand, the verb (or concept) *smile* entails only one subject participant, i.e. the individual who 'smiles'.

Just as c-selection operates in terms of syntactic categories, s-selection operates in terms of semantic categories called **thematic roles** or **θ-roles**. The verb *hit*, for example, is said to s-select two θ-roles, an **agent** (the subject participant) and a **patient** (the object participant). The verb *decide*, as in *Mary decided that John should leave*, also s-selects two participants, the second of which, i.e. the clause *(that) John should leave*, is called a **proposition**. Other verbs may select a different number of participants with different θ-roles, as we will see below.

The observation that c-selection seems to be based on s-selection is interesting insofar as it suggests that perhaps one is reducible to the other. The fact that the verb *hit* c-selects an NP arguably follows from the fact that it s-selects a participant with the θ-role patient in the first place. Similarly, the fact that the verb *smile* does not c-select an NP follows from the fact that it does not s-select an object participant in the first place. Suppose that a correspondence relation can be established between θ-roles and syntactic categories such that individual syntactic categories serve as the 'canonical structural realisation' (CSR) of specific θ-roles.

The CSR of agent, for example, will typically be NP, and the CSR of proposition will typically be a clause (CP). It follows from this situation that c-selection does not need to be stated in lexical entries. The c-selectional properties of lexical items are derivable from their s-selectional properties in terms of the relation CSR.

This conclusion, if correct, has important implications for the relevance of semantic categories to syntax. We have seen that subcategorisation properties play a crucial role in the syntactic representation of sentences. The relationship between the subcategorisation properties of lexical items and their syntactic representations is mediated by the Projection Principle. We will see below that the relationship between the thematic properties of lexical items and their syntactic representations is also mediated by a syntactic principle called the θ-**Criterion**. The latter interacts with the Projection Principle in a way that has implications for the level of representation at which it is supposed to apply.

The θ-Criterion belongs to a module of grammar called θ-**theory**, X-bar theory being the other module discussed so far. The Principles and Parameters framework outlined in this part of the book is said to have a **modular structure**. Each module is a self-contained autonomous component which consists of a set of principles which constrain relevant aspects of representations. The (principles of the) modules interact with each other to either include or exclude certain representations. Each chapter in this part of the book deals with one of the major modules of the Principles and Parameters framework.

7.2   *Arguments, quasi-arguments and operators*

7.2.1   Arguments and θ-roles

The semantic aspects of lexical items and their s-selectional properties are often described in terms of terminology borrowed from Logic. Verbs are called **predicates**. The participants involved in the event denoted by a predicate are called **arguments**. The verb *hit*, for example, is a predicate which takes two arguments, and the verb *smile* is a predicate which takes one argument. Verbs which take two arguments are called **two-place predicates,** and verbs which take one argument are called **one-place predicates**, where 'place' roughly corresponds to 'argument'. Information relating to arguments of predicates is called the **argument structure** (of predicates).

The number of arguments associated with a given lexical item determines the number of θ-roles the lexical item can assign, such that to every argument in the argument structure there corresponds a θ-role in the **thematic structure** of the lexical item. Lexical items are said to assign θ-roles to the arguments they select, subject to certain structurally based conditions to be discussed below. Here, we will adopt the notation in (3) to represent argument and thematic structures:

3a. hit: <1, 2>   (argument structure)
          <Agent, Patient>   (thematic structure)

3b. smile: <1>   (argument structure)
              <Agent>   (thematic structure)

Arguments are represented in terms of arabic numbers and θ-roles in terms of their individual names. The argument and thematic structures represent the selectional properties of lexical items included in their lexical entries along with other types of lexically determined information. Later on in this chapter, we will introduce a modification in representations (3a&b) which will distinguish between subject arguments and object arguments.

An argument is usually defined as a 'referring expression', i.e. an expression which corresponds to (or picks out) an individual or an entity in a given world (or discourse domain). In (4a) *the teacher*, *the book*, and *John* are all referring expressions in the sense defined, and therefore arguments. However, the expletive/ pleonastic (i.e. semantically empty) elements *it* in (4b) and *there* in (4c) and (4d) are not referring expressions in the intended sense, and therefore non-arguments:

4a. The teacher gave the book to John.
4b. It seems that Mary has solved the problem.
4c. There is a unicorn in the garden.
4d. There seems to be a unicorn in the garden.

Arguments can also be propositions, that is, clauses, both non-small, as in (5a) and (5c), and small, as in (5b). The verbs *consider* and *decide* each takes two arguments, one of which is a proposition. Propositions are arguments in the sense that they refer to a state of affairs in a given world:

5a. John considers Bill to be incompetent.
5b. John considers Bill incompetent.
5c. Bill decided that John should leave.

θ-roles can be collectively defined as the roles assigned to the arguments which participate in a given event. The definition of individual θ-roles, however, is much less clear in some cases. While some of the terms adopted are almost self-explanatory, e.g. agent/actor, others are much less so. Here we will content ourselves with illustrating the major θ-roles recognised in the literature. The illustrative examples are in (6–11):

6a. The boy likes the girl.
6b. The boy (**experiencer**), the girl (**theme**)

7a. Bill prepared the dinner for the guests.
7b. Bill (**agent**), the dinner (**patient**), the guests (**benefactive**)

8a. Mary put the book on the shelf.
8b. Mary (**agent**), the book (**theme**), the shelf (**location**)

9a. Bill gave the book to John.
9b. Bill (**agent**), the book (**theme**), John (**goal**)

10a. Mary stole the money from the thief.

10b. Mary (**agent**), the money (**theme**), the thief (**source**)

11a. John opened the door with a credit card.

11b. John (**agent**), the door (**patient/theme**), credit card (**instrumental**)

The patient role is generally understood to imply a change in state, and the theme role to imply a change in location or position. However, it is not clear sometimes whether the θ-role involved should be characterised as patient or theme. For example, it is not clear whether *the door* in (11) should be characterised as patient on the grounds that it has changed in state from being closed to being open, or as theme on the grounds that it has undergone a change in position, or both. Here, we will drop the term 'patient' and subsume the situation of change in state under the definition of 'theme'. The latter implies a change in position or state or both.

7.2.2   Quasi-arguments

Some expressions seem to share properties with both arguments and non-arguments. This is the case of the so-called 'weather-*it*', illustrated in (12a&b):

12a. It sometimes rains after snowing.

12b. It sometimes rains after [PRO snowing]

13a. It is difficult to predict their next move.

13b. It is difficult [PRO to predict their next move]

The weather-*it* in (12) is similar to the pure expletive *it* in (13) in that it is apparently a non-referring expression. However, the weather-*it* differs in that it can function as a controller of *PRO*, as shown in (12). The fact that the pure expletive *it* cannot function as a controller of *PRO* is shown in (13). In this sentence *PRO* has an arbitrary interpretation ('It is difficult for one to predict their next move') because it lacks a controller. The ability to function as a controller of *PRO* is a property of referring expressions (i.e. arguments), given that control is essentially a relation of reference assignment. The fact that weather-*it* can control *PRO* shows that it has argument properties even though it is apparently a non-referring expression.

Expressions with this type of ambivalent nature are sometimes called **quasi-arguments**. This term can be understood more generally to refer to expressions which function as arguments of a special class of verbs and have an interpretation peculiar to the situations described by those verbs. Like straightforward arguments, quasi-arguments are also assigned a θ-role, although the θ-role they are assigned is a special one in that it is peculiar to the situations they are associated with. Weather-*it*, for example, can be said to be assigned a 'weather' θ-role by the weather verb of which it is a special argument.

The term 'quasi-argument' is sometimes also used to refer to certain phrases in idiomatic expressions such as (14a&b):

14a. John took advantage of Bill.
14b. John kicked the bucket.

Idiomatic expressions are generally expressions the meaning of which does not derive (compositionally) from a combination of the literal meaning of its individual constituents. The idiomatic meaning 'exploit' cannot be derived compositionally from the meanings of the individual words in (14a). The same is true of the idiomatic meaning 'die' in relation to (14b). In the latter case, the expression *the bucket* does not refer to an entity in the real world (a 'vessel for holding or carrying water or milk'). The fact that the *bucket* is not a referring expression in the idiomatic meaning implies that it is not an argument. At the same time, the presence of *the bucket* is necessary for the idiomatic meaning to be conveyed. As shown in (15a&b), its absence or replacement with another expression results in ungrammaticality or the loss of the idiomatic meaning:

15a. *John kicked.
15b. John kicked the jug.

(15b) can only have the literal meaning, derived compositionally from the meanings of the individual words. This implies that although *the bucket* is a non-referring expression it functions as a special argument of the verb *kick* in its idiomatic use. The relationship between *the bucket* and the verb *kick* in the idiomatic meaning of (14b) is somewhat similar to the relationship between weather-verbs and weather-*it*, in that it is special and restricted to a peculiar interpretation. The verb *kick* can be said to assign a special θ-role to *the bucket* responsible for the idiomatic meaning.

Assuming this to be the case, the question arises as to whether the idiomatic *kick* is the same verb as the non-idiomatic *kick* which assigns a theme role to its object argument in non-idiomatic sentences such as (15b). To the extent that the two *kicks* differ in meaning, it could be argued that they have separate entries in the lexicon, just like homophonous words such as *bank* (of a river) and *bank* (of Scotland). On the other hand, given that the idiomatic meaning is the result of combining *kick* and the expression *the bucket* together, it could be argued further that the two items are entered together in the lexicon as a single complex item with the meaning 'die'. The status of *kick the bucket* as a lexical complex seems initially to be supported by the fact that unlike ordinary objects *the bucket* cannot undergo passivisation (NP-movement to the subject position). The passive sentence (16a) cannot have the idiomatic meaning that its active counterpart (14b) has. However, this is not true of all idioms. (16b) has the same idiomatic meaning as its active counterpart (14a):

16a. The bucket was kicked by John.
16b. Advantage was taken of John.

The properties of idioms, in particular variation in the properties of individual idioms, are still not well understood. We will have no more to say about them here (but see Part IV).

7.2.3   Operators and variables: Quantifier Raising

7.2.3.1   *Wh-phrases*   Wh-phrases are non-referring expressions. Unlike names
such as *Mary*, they do not pick out a specific individual or entity in a given world
(or domain of discourse). The wh-phrase *which problem* in (17a), for example,
does not refer to a specific problem. The speaker knows that *Mary* solved a
problem, but does not know which one. The same is true of simpler wh-phrases
such as *who, what . . .* etc.

17a. Which problem did Mary solve?
17b. DS: [$_{CP}$ e [$_{IP}$ Mary [$_{I'}$ did [$_{VP}$ solve which problem]]]]
17c. SS: [$_{CP}$ which problem$_i$ [$_{C'}$ did$_j$ [Mary [$_{I'}$ t$_j$ [$_{VP}$ solve t$_i$]]]]]

The nature of wh-phrases as non-referring expressions, and therefore non-
arguments, raises an interesting problem relating to the argument structure of
the verb *solve* in (17). The verb *solve* is a two-place predicate, and therefore
expected to have two arguments. Yet in (17) it apparently has only one argument,
namely *Mary*. The object *which problem* is a non-argument because it is a wh-
phrase. It appears that the argument structure of the verb is not properly reflected
in the syntactic representation. This state of affairs, if true, should result in
excluding the sentence. Notice, however, that in the SS representation (17c), the
wh-phrase does not occupy the object position of the verb. The latter is occupied
by the trace of the wh-phrase. Traces of wh-phrases (or **wh-traces**) are said to have
the status of **logical variables**. Logical variables can generally be assigned a value,
i.e. they can be translated as a referential expression in a given domain of
discourse. Using the terminology of Logic, the wh-question (17a) can be translated
as in (18), where the expression 'for which problem' corresponds to the wh-phrase
which problem and the variable x corresponds to the wh-trace. The expression 'for
which problem' is said to be the operator binding the variable:

18.   for which problem x [Mary solved x]

If the answer to the question is 'Mary solved the Maths problem', the variable in
the object position of the verb is assigned the value MATHS (PROBLEM). Wh-
traces are therefore (potential) arguments by virtue of being variables.

In view of this, the requirement that the argument structure of the verb be
accurately reflected holds of the SS representation (17c). To solve the problem
identified above, it appears that all we need to say is that the requirement in
question does not hold of DS representations such as (17b). However, there is
evidence that the requirement in question does not hold of SS representations
either. The evidence partly has to do with wh-questions which have more than
one wh-phrase called **multiple wh-questions**. (19a) is an (information-seeking)
multiple wh-question with one wh-phrase in Spec,CP and the other in situ at SS,
as shown in (19c):

19a. Who solved which problem?
19b. DS: [$_{CP}$ C [$_{IP}$ who I [$_{VP}$ solved which problem]]]

19c. SS: [CP who$_i$ [IP t$_i$ I [VP solved which problem]]]

In view of (19c), it appears that the requirement that a two-place predicate such as *solve* has two arguments does not hold of SS representations. The predicate *solve* has only one argument at SS, namely the wh-trace of *who* in the subject position. The requirement must therefore hold of a subsequent level of representation. Whatever the exact nature of this level of representation, something must happen that would result in removing the wh-phrase *which problem* from the object position and leaving a variable trace behind. In other words, the required representation must have the form shown in (20a), where the object wh-phrase is moved to Spec,CP leaving a variable trace behind:

20a. LF: [CP [who]$_i$ [which problem]$_j$ did [IP t$_i$ I [VP solve t$_j$]]]
20b. for which person x and which problem y [x solved y]

The need for the representation in (20a) is suggested by the logical translation in (20b), where the operator that corresponds to the wh-phrase *which problem* is placed at the beginning of the clause and the object position of the verb *solve* is occupied by a variable.

Movement of *which problem* in (20) does not have a 'visible' effect on word order, contrary to movement of *which problem* in the mapping from DS onto SS. Recall from Chapter 4 that the model of grammar branches off at the level of SS into the separate levels PF and LF. PF is the 'visible' level and LF the 'invisible' level. Any reordering (movement) process which takes place prior to or at the level of SS will be 'visibly' reflected (at PF). However, any reordering (movement) process which takes place in the mapping from SS onto LF will not be 'visibly' reflected. It follows that movement of the wh-phrase *which problem* which derives representation (20a) applies in the mapping from SS onto LF. The order in the PF representation of the multiple wh-question (19a) is as it is in the SS representation (19c), with *which problem* in the direct object position of the verb.

Movement processes which take place prior to or at the level of SS are called **overt** movements. Movement processes which apply in the mapping onto LF are called **covert** movements.

Given that the process which derives the LF representation (20a) involves movement of a wh-phrase to Spec,CP, it is tempting to call it Wh-movement. However, recall from Chapter 6 that Wh-movement is a substitution movement, which is not the case in (20a). The Spec,CP targeted by movement of *which problem* is already filled with the wh-phrase *who*, moved there overtly. The movement involved in (20a) must therefore be an adjunction movement, the only other type of movement allowed. Here, we will assume that this movement process adjoins the moved wh-phrase to the wh-phrase already in Spec,CP, deriving the adjunction structure shown in (21):

21.

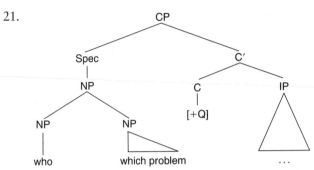

The process which moves categories in the mapping from SS onto LF is called **Quantifier Raising (QR)**. Wh-phrases are sometimes called **quasi-quantifiers**. True quantifiers are the subject of our next discussion.

7.2.3.2 Quantifiers (22) and (23) include the expressions *every(one)* and *some(one)*, called **quantifier phrases** or just **quantifiers:**

22a. John suspects everyone.
22b. SS: [$_{IP}$ John I [$_{VP}$ suspects everyone]]

23a. Mary likes someone.
23b. SS: [$_{IP}$ Mary I [$_{VP}$ likes someone]]

Quantifiers are non-referring expressions and therefore non-arguments. *Everyone* in (22) and *someone* in (23) do not pick out a specific individual but simply define the range of the object argument. (22) roughly means that if you find an individual (any individual), you can expect *John* to suspect him/her. (23) roughly means that of all the individuals in a given world there is/exists at least one whom *Mary* likes. *Every(one/thing/body/candidate)* is called a **universal** quantifier and *some(one/thing/body/book)* an **existential** quantifier.

As non-arguments, quantifiers present us with the same problem as wh-phrases in-situ in multiple wh-questions. If the LF representations of (22a) and (23a) remain as they are in (22b) and (23b), we will have a situation where the two-place predicates *suspect* and *like* have only one argument instead of the two arguments specified in their argument structure. The analysis outlined above for wh-phrases in situ carries over to quantifiers, so that quantifiers too undergo QR in the mapping from SS onto LF. QR leaves a variable trace behind which functions as the argument of the verb. The LF representations of (22) and (23), derived by QR, are as shown in (24) and (25), respectively. (24b) and (25b) are the interpretations of (22) and (23), where the operator expression 'for every person x/for some person x' corresponds to the moved quantifier, and the variable corresponds to its trace:

24a. [$_{IP}$ everyone$_i$ [$_{IP}$ John I [$_{VP}$ suspects t$_i$]]]
24b. for every person x, [John suspects x]

25a. [$_{IP}$ someone$_i$ [$_{IP}$ Mary I [$_{VP}$ likes t$_i$]]]
25b. for some person x [Mary likes x]

Unlike wh-phrases raised by QR, which are adjoined to Spec,CP, quantifiers raised by QR are adjoined to IP. A discussion of this discrepancy between wh-phrases and quantifiers raised by QR will take us too far afield. Here we will discuss one of the advantages of a QR-based analysis for quantifiers which has to do with sentences with more than one quantifier. This phenomenon is sometimes called **multiple quantification**. (26) is an example of a sentence with multiple quantification. It includes two quantifiers, one in the subject position and the other in the object position:

26a. Everyone suspects someone.

26b. SS: [$_{IP}$ [$_{NP}$ everyone] I [$_{VP}$ suspects [$_{NP}$ someone]]]

When pronounced with neutral intonation, (26) (and similar sentences) is ambiguous between at least two different meanings (or readings). It can have the so-called 'pair reading' whereby each individual suspects a different individual: *Mary* suspects *John*, *Bill* suspects *Donald*, *Jane* suspects *Fred*, and so on. It can also have the different reading whereby one and the same individual is suspected by everyone: *Mary, John, Bill, Donald, Jane, Mary* all suspect *Fred*. The first interpretation can be paraphrased as 'everyone has someone whom he/she suspects.' The second reading can be paraphrased as 'there is someone whom everyone suspects.'

More formally, in the first reading *everyone* is said to have **scope** over *someone*. In the second reading, the scope relation between the two quantifiers is the reverse, so that *someone* has scope over *everyone*. Using different terminology, in the first reading, *everyone* is said to have **wide/broad scope** and *someone* **narrow scope**. In the second reading, *someone* has wide/broad scope and *everyone* narrow scope. The notions 'wide/broad scope' and 'narrow scope' are in a sense visibly illustrated in the paraphrases given above. In the first paraphrase 'everyone has someone whom (s)he suspects', *everyone* is outside (wider than) *someone*, so that *someone* is within the scope of *everyone*. In the second paraphrase 'there is someone whom everyone suspects', *someone* is outside (wider than) *everyone*, so that *everyone* is within the scope of *someone*.

As with grammatical relations in general, we expect scope relations to have a structural basis. Scope can be defined as in (27):

27. **Scope**

   The scope of α is the set of nodes that α c-commands in the LF representation.

The notion 'c-command' used in (27) is defined as in (28):

28. **C-command**

   α c-commands β iff:

   i)   the first branching node dominating α also dominates β

   ii) α does not dominate β.

To illustrate the effects of these definitions, consider the abstract structures in (29a) and (29b):

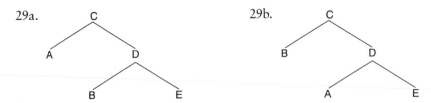

29a.   29b.

In (29a) A c-commands B because the first branching node which dominates A, namely C, also dominates B. Moreover, A does not dominate B. In (29b), however, A does not c-command B because the first branching node which dominates A, namely D, does not dominate B. Now, because A c-commands B in (29a), A has scope over B, and because A does not c-command B in (29b), A does not have scope over B.

Going back to (26), the different scope relations between the quantifiers which underlie the two different readings of the sentence can be represented in terms of the two different LF representations (30) and (31). (30) underlies the reading 'everyone has someone they suspect', and (31) the reading 'there exists someone such that everyone suspects him':

30a. [IP everyone$_i$ [IP someone$_j$ [IP t$_i$ I [VP suspects $_j$]]]]
30b.

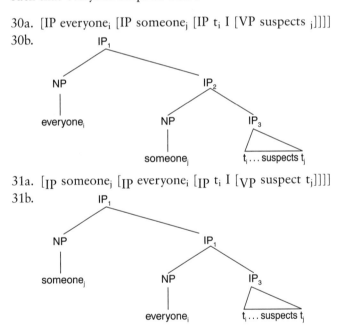

31a. [IP someone$_j$ [IP everyone$_i$ [IP t$_i$ I [VP suspect t$_j$]]]]
31b.

Both structures involve multiple adjunction to IP of the NP quantifier raised by QR. In (30), *everyone* has scope over *someone* since the first branching node which dominates *everyone*, namely IP$_1$, also dominates *someone*. Note that the reverse relation does not hold in this structure, that is, *someone* does not have scope over *everyone* as *someone* does not c-command *everyone*. In (31), *someone* c-commands *everyone*, and therefore has scope over it, but *everyone* does not c-command *someone*, and therefore does not have scope over it.

The conclusion which follows from this analysis is that the ambiguity of sentences with multiple quantifiers such as (26) is a function of their LF representations. In other words, the fact that such sentences have two possible interpretations follows from the fact that they can have two different LF representations which give rise to two different scope relations between the quantifiers. The possibility that ambiguous sentences such as (26) can have two LF representations is in turn made possible by the idea that quantifiers undergo a movement process (QR) in the mapping from SS onto LF. Note that in the SS representation (26b) of (26a), the quantifier in the subject position (Spec,IP) asymmetrically c-commands the quantifier in the object position. If the two quantifiers are not assumed to undergo movement in the mapping onto LF, the scope ambiguity of (26a) will be hard to explain in structural terms. The asymmetric c-command relation between the two quantifiers in the SS representation (26b) does not account for the reading whereby *someone* as scope over *everyone*.

7.3 *The structural representation of argument structures*

7.3.1 Internal and external arguments

In this section, we will discuss the question how the argument/thematic structures of lexical items are mapped onto structural representations such that an object argument/θ-role is assigned to an object position and a subject argument/θ-role to a subject position. In view of the fact that 'object' and 'subject' are structure-based (functional) terms, it is somewhat inaccurate to use them to refer to arguments/θ-roles in argument/thematic structures. The terms usually used in relation to argument/thematic structures are **internal argument/θ-role** and **external argument/θ-role**. In a simple sentence such as *The boy kicked the ball, the ball* is the internal argument of the verb *kick*, and *the boy* its external argument.

Structurally, the terms 'internal' and 'external' correspond to the complement position of the predicate and the subject position of the sentence, respectively, as shown in (32) and (33). The terms 'internal' and 'external' are defined relative to the maximal projection (or single-bar projection) of the verb. The internal argument position is located inside the maximal (or single-bar) projection of V and the external argument outside:

32a. The boy kicked the ball.
32b. [IP the boy I [VP kicked the ball]]
　　　　　Agent　　　　　　　　Theme

33.

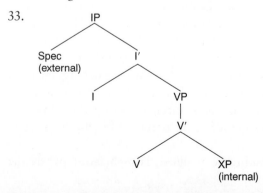

The next step is to set up a mechanism to ensure that arguments/θ-roles are assigned to appropriate positions. A general fact about certain arguments/θ-roles is that they have an invariable status with respect to the external/internal dichotomy. For example, an agent argument/θ-role is invariably assigned to an external position, and a theme argument/θ-role is invariably assigned to an internal position. One way of ensuring that arguments/θ-roles are assigned to appropriate positions is to assume that arguments/θ-roles are specified in lexical entries as to whether they are internal or external. Here, we will adopt the notation in (34) to distinguish between external and internal arguments/θ-roles:

34a. kick: agent <theme>
34b. smile: agent <∅>

The symbol ∅ indicates the absence of an argument/θ-role. The internal argument/θ-role is included inside (internal to) the brackets, and the external argument/θ-role outside (external to) the brackets. Given the argument/thematic structures in (34a&b), the external argument/θ-role will be mapped onto the subject position, and the internal argument/θ-role onto the complement position.

Lexical heads are said to **directly θ-mark** their internal arguments and **indirectly θ-mark** their external argument. As with certain other terms, there is both a structural basis and a semantic basis for this terminological distinction. Structurally, internal arguments are sisters to the lexical head which selects them, whereas external arguments are not. Recall from earlier that there is a close connection between the notion 'logical object' (internal argument) and the structural notion of sisterhood. The internal argument (object) has a closer structural relation to the lexical head than the external argument (subject). As far as meaning is concerned, there is evidence which suggests that the θ-role of the external argument is determined by a combination of the meanings of the lexical head and its internal argument. Consider the sentences in (35a&b) and (36a&b):

35a. John threw a ball.
35b. John threw a fit.

36a. John cut the bread.
36b. John cut his finger.

In (35a) *John* has an agent role in both the idiomatic and non-idiomatic meanings of the sentence. In (35b), however, *John* can hardly be said to have an agent role on the involuntary movement reading. Likewise, in (36a) *John* has the agent role, whereas in (36b), with the reading where it is John's finger which is cut, *John* does not necessarily have the agent role. Thus, the internal argument seems to play a role in determining the nature of the θ-role assigned to the external argument. In contrast, the external argument does not play a role in determining the nature of the θ-role assigned to the internal argument. Substituting the external argument in (35) and (36) with a different one does not affect the nature of the θ-role assigned to the internal argument.

The external θ-role is sometimes said to be assigned via **predication**, where the term 'predicate' refers to the verb and its internal arguments, i.e. VP. The θ-marking of the external argument is indirect in the sense that it is mediated by VP (or V'). In contrast, the theta-marking of the internal argument is not mediated by any (intermediate) category, as the internal argument is a sister to the lexical head.

7.3.2   Objects of prepositions

(37) and (38) include verbs such as *put* and *give* which take two internal arguments. These verbs were analysed in Chapter 6 as having a complex form which consists of a light verb and an impoverished version of the verb itself represented in uppercase letters. The predicate which includes such verbs has a VP-shell structure which consists of a higher *v*P headed by the light verb *v* and a lower VP headed by the upper-case verb. The direct object *the book* is located in the Spec position of the lower VP and the indirect object *on the shelf/to John* as a sister of the lower V:

37a. Mary put the book *(on the shelf).
37b. Mary I [*v*P [PUT]ᵢ [*v*] [VP [NP the book] [V' tᵢ [PP on [NP the shelf]]]]]
37c. put: agent <theme, location>

38a. Mary gave the book *(to John).
38b. Mary I [*v*P [GAVE]ᵢ [*v*] [VP [NP the book] [V' tᵢ [PP to [NP John]]]]]
38c. give: agent <theme, goal>

The status of the direct object as a specifier means that it is not an internal argument of either the light verb or the upper-case verb since it is a sister to neither of them. Rather, it is the external argument of the upper-case verb, indirectly θ-marked by the combination of the upper-case verb and its PP complement. We will ignore this issue here and concentrate instead on how the NP inside the PP complement receives its θ-role. For the purposes of the discussion we will assume that both the direct object and the indirect object are internal arguments of the (complex) verb.

In both (37) and (38), PP (the indirect object) is an obligatory complement of the verb. The θ-role assigned to the NP object of the preposition is part of the thematic structure of the verb, as shown in (37c) and (38c). This means that the object of the preposition is in actual fact an internal argument of the verb. However, the location argument in (37) and the goal argument in (38) are not structurally represented as sisters to the verb but as sisters to the preposition. In this situation, the verb is sometimes said to indirectly θ-mark the argument structurally represented as the object of the preposition. This relationship is indirect in the sense that it is mediated by the preposition in the way shown in (39):

39.   . . . [VP V NP [PP P NP]]
            └────→ └───→
              θ   θ

The verb θ-marks PP under sisterhood, and the head P of PP **transmits** this θ-role to its NP object also under sisterhood. The role of the preposition in this respect is restricted to transmitting to its object the θ-role originally assigned by the verb. The implication is that the preposition involved does not have an argument/ thematic structure of its own.

Now, compare (37) and (38) to (40) and (41):

40a. John baked fresh bread (for his guests).
40b. bake: agent <theme, (benefactive)>
40c. bake: agent <theme>

41a. John opened the door (with a credit card).
41b. open: agent <theme, (instrumental)>
41c. open: agent <theme>

The occurrence of PP is not obligatory in (40) and (41). In this situation, it is not clear whether the object of the preposition is an argument of the verb, so that the argument/thematic structure of the verb is as in (40b) and (41b), or it is not an argument of the verb, so that the argument/thematic structure of the verb is as in (40c) and (41c).

According to the scenario whereby the object of the preposition is an argument of the verb, the object will have a status similar to that of the object of the preposition in (37) and (38) above, except that its occurrence is optional. Its θ-marking by the verb will operate as shown in (39). However, on the scenario that the object of the preposition is not an argument of the verb, the object will not have a similar status. Its status will be similar to that of adjuncts, that is modifying constituents which are not part of the argument structure of the lexical head and which are generally optional. Its θ-marking will operate as shown in (42):

42. . . . [VP V [PP P NP]]

The implication of the scenario represented in (42) is that the benefactive and instrumental prepositions in (40) and (41) have an argument/thematic structure of their own, unlike the dative and locative prepositions in (37) and (38). While the dative and locative prepositions in (37) and (38) simply transmit to their object the θ-role originally assigned by the verb (to PP), the benefactive and instrumental prepositions in (40) and (41) assign a θ-role of their own to their object. We will not try to settle the issue here.

Remaining with the issue of prepositions, a distinction is sometimes drawn between prepositions which are semantically vacuous and prepositions which are not. For example, the dative preposition *to* in (38) is sometimes said to be semantically vacuous, partly on the grounds that the sentence has a close paraphrase which does not include the preposition: *Mary gave John the book* (more on these constructions later on). However, the same cannot be said about the locative preposition *on* in (37). Its occurrence is obligatory and, moreover, replacing it with a different preposition such as *under* leads to a change of meaning in location. This difference between the two prepositions shows that, to the extent that a genuine distinction can be made between prepositions which are semantically vacuous and prepositions which are not, it does not reflect the distinction between prepositions which do not have an argument/thematic structure and prepositions which do. According to the analysis outlined above, both the dative preposition and the locative preposition merely transmit to their object the θ-role originally assigned by the verb.

An often-cited instance of a (genuinely) semantically vacuous preposition is the preposition *of* found with complements of nouns such as *translation* in (43a), and with complements of adjectives such as *fond* in (43c):

43a. Mary's translation of the book
43b. Mary translated the book.
43c. Mary is fond of John.

The thematic relationship between the noun *translation* and *the book* in the NP (43a) is the same as the one between the verb *translated* and *the book* in the sentence (43b). The latter shows that this relationship does not need to be mediated by the preposition *of*, thereby suggesting that its presence in the NP (43a) is thematically superfluous. In Chapter 8, we will see that the presence of the preposition *of* in the NP (43a) and the AP (43c) is motivated by considerations which do not necessarily involve its thematic relation with the head N/A.

7.3.3 A-positions and θ-positions

The structural representation of argument/thematic structures gives rise to a typology of positions which turns out to play an important role in determining certain grammatical relations. Positions can now be classified as to whether they are **A-positions** (read argument positions) or **A'-positions** (read A-bar positions), and whether they are **θ-positions** (read theta positions) or **θ'-positions** (read theta-bar positions).

A-positions are usually defined as the positions where an argument can be base-generated, although perhaps it is more accurate to define them as the positions where an argument can be found in LF representations. Complement positions of lexical heads are A-positions occupied by the internal argument of the lexical head. The argument can either be a referential noun phrase such as *the problem* or a variable, that is the trace of a moved wh-phrase or a moved quantifier. The subject position of the clause (Spec,IP) is also an A-position. A'-positions are the positions where a non-argument can be found in LF representations. They include Spec,CP and adjoined positions. Spec,CP is usually filled with moved wh-phrases (non-arguments). Adjoined positions can either be filled by a moved category, as in the case of topicalised phrases and raised quantifiers (non-arguments), or base-generated modifiers (non-arguments), as in the case of adverbs and adjectives.

θ-positions are the positions which are assigned a θ-role. Thus, complement positions of lexical heads are θ-positions given that they are occupied by the internal arguments of the lexical head. However, not all subject positions are θ-positions. Whether the subject position is a θ-position in a given sentence depends on whether the lexical head assigns an external θ-role or not. In sentences which include a verb which assigns an external θ-role, the subject position is a θ-position. However, in sentences which include a verb which does not assign an external θ-role, the subject position is a θ'-position. Typical examples of verbs that do not assign an external θ-role are raising predicates. Recall that the subject position of clauses which include a raising predicate can be occupied either by a subject moved from the embedded clause, as in (44), or by the expletive *it*, as in (45):

44a. Mary seems to have solved the problem.
44b. Mary$_i$ seems [$_{IP}$ t$_i$ to have solved the problem]

45a. It seems that Mary has solved the problem.
45b. It seems [$_{CP}$ that [$_{IP}$ Mary has solve the problem]]

46.   seem: <∅> <proposition>

The subject *Mary* in (44) is the external argument of the embedded verb *solve*, which assigns it its external θ-role. The raising verb *seem* does not have an external θ-role of its own to assign, as shown in (46). This is why the subject position of the root clause that includes it can be occupied by an argument moved from another subject position, as in (44), or by non-argument, as in (45). Because raising predicates do not assign an external θ-role, the subject position of their clause is a θ'-position. We now have an explanation for the fact that raising verbs are characterised by their ability to take the expletive (non-argument) *it* as a subject.

The other θ'-positions are Spec,CP and adjoined positions which are usually occupied by non-arguments. Because these positions are occupied by non-arguments, they are not assigned a θ-role, and because they are not assigned a θ-role they are θ'-positions.

At this stage, it should be clear that while all A'-positions are also θ'-positions, not all A-positions are also θ-positions. While complement positions are invariably both A-positions and θ-positions, there is no similar complete overlap with respect to the subject position of the clause. We saw above that the subject position (Spec,IP) is an A-position. However, whether it is a θ-position or a θ'-position depends on whether the verb of the clause assigns an external θ-role or not. The subject position of a clause which includes a raising predicate is a θ'-position even though it is an A-position.

7.4   θ-Criterion

7.4.1   θ-Criterion and Projection Principle

Consider (47) which includes a raising verb and a base generated argument in the root clause:

47a. *John seems (that) Mary has solved the problem.
47b. *John seems [$_{CP}$ (that) [$_{IP}$ Mary has solved the problem]]

In (47) there is only one external θ-role available, assigned by the verb *solve* of the embedded clause to the argument *Mary*. Being a raising predicate, the verb *seem* of the root clause does not assign an external θ-role. However, the subject position of the root clause is occupied by an argument, namely, *John*. Recall that when this position is occupied by a non-argument the sentence is not excluded: *It seems that Mary has solved the problem*. Thus, (47) seems to be excluded due to the fact that it includes an argument which is not assigned a θ-role. This conclusion implies the condition that each argument must be assigned a θ-role.

Consider now (48) and (49):

48a. *There solved a problem.
48b. *[IP there I [VP solved a problem]

49a. *Mary solved there.
49b. *[IP Mary I [VP solved [there]]]

(48) and (49) represent the opposite situation, where the number of θ-roles available exceeds the number of arguments present. The verb *solve* has both an internal and an external θ-role to assign. However, (48) and (49) include only one argument each. The element *there* is a non-argument. (48) and (49) therefore seem to be excluded due to the fact that one of the θ-roles of the verb they include is not assigned to an argument. This conclusion implies the condition that each θ-role must be assigned to an argument.

The two conditions we have identified represent two clauses of a more general condition on the structural representation of thematic structures, called the θ-Criterion. The latter can be defined as in (50):

50. **θ-Criterion**

   i) Each argument must be assigned a θ-role.
   ii) Each θ-role must be assigned to an argument.

Like the other principles discussed so far, the θ-Criterion is a condition on representations. It has the function of ensuring that the thematic structures of lexical items are accurately reflected in structural representations such that each θ-role in the thematic structure is paired with an argument in the structural representation. As such, the θ-Criterion essentially holds of DS representations, i.e. the level where the argument structure of lexical items are first projected. The θ-Criterion also holds of SS and LF by virtue of the Projection Principle. Thematic structures are lexical properties of lexical items and like other lexical properties they fall under the scope of the Projection Principle.

However, the idea that the θ-Criterion holds of non-LF representations runs into the problem discussed above in relation to wh-in-situ and quantifiers. As shown in (51) and (52), reproduced from above, the noun phrases sitting in the subject and object position at DS are not arguments. Not until LF are the subject and object positions filled with arguments, namely the variable traces:

51a. Who solved which problem?
51b. DS: [CP e [IP who I [VP solved [which problem]]]]

51c. SS: [CP [who]i [IP ti I [VP solved [which problem]]]]
51d. LF: [CP [who]i [which problem]i [IP ti I [VP solved ti]]]

52a. John suspects everyone.
52b. DS: [CP e [IP John I [VP suspects [everyone]]]]
52c. SS: [CP e [IP John I [VP suspects [everyone]]]]
52d. LF: [CP e [IP everyonei [IP John I [VP suspects ti]]]]

It is perhaps possible to get around the problem by stipulating that the θ-Criterion requires that θ-roles be assigned to argument positions rather than to arguments. The job of ensuring that every argument position assigned a θ-role be filled with an argument is performed by some rules of interpretation applying at LF and which perhaps motivates movement of wh-in-situ and quantifiers. It remains to be seen whether this suggestion works. The point is that the idea that the θ-Criterion applies at DS creates a theory internal conflict which has been observed and discussed by some linguists (see Further Reading section).

7.4.2   θ-Criterion and chains

7.4.2.1   A-chains and A'-chains   Compare (53) and (54). (53) includes the raising verb *seem* in the root clause, and (54) includes the non-raising verb *believe* in the root clause:

53a. Mary seems to have solved the problem.
53b. [IP Maryi I [VP seems [IP ti to have solved the problem]]]

54a. *Mary believes to have solved the problem.
54b. [IP Maryi I [VP believes [IP ti to have solved the problem]]]

Recall that raising verbs such as *seem* do not assign an external θ-role, whereas non-raising verbs such as *believe* do. In view of this, the raised argument is assigned only one (external) θ-role (by the verb of the embedded clause) in (53). However, its counterpart in (54) is assigned two (external) θ-roles, one by the verb of the embedded clause and the other by the verb of the root clause. It seems, therefore, that (54) is excluded due to the fact that it includes an argument with two θ-roles, although there may be other considerations involved. This conclusion implies another condition on the assignment of θ-roles, namely that each argument be assigned one and only one θ-role. One way of incorporating this condition into the θ-Criterion is to include a **uniqueness condition** in its definition, as in (55):

55. **θ-Criterion**

   i)   Each argument must be assigned one and only one θ-role.
   ii) Each θ-role must be assigned to one and only one argument.

Note that (54) does not necessarily force a uniqueness condition on clause (ii), although it does force a uniqueness condition on clause (i). However, it is not difficult to see why a uniqueness condition should also be incorporated into clause (ii). The number of arguments associated with a given lexical head usually corresponds to the number of θ-roles the lexical head assigns. The possibility of allowing one θ-role to be assigned to more than one argument will mean that, in principle, a head can be associated with any number of arguments, an undesirable consequence. It will also lead to ambiguity of thematic functions in relation to individual arguments, such that an argument in a given sentence can have more than one role. This is also an undesirable consequence for obvious reasons.

Let us now go back to (53). The external θ-role of the verb of the embedded clause, strictly speaking, is assigned to the trace of the raised NP. Recall that the subject position of clauses containing a raising predicate is a θ'-position. The trace is said to **transmit** the θ-role it receives to its antecedent, located in a θ'-position. The trace and its antecedent are said to form a (movement) **chain**. The antecedent, i.e. the raised NP in (53), is the **head** (of the chain), and the trace is the **root/tail** (of the chain). The crucial implication of (53) is that the θ-Criterion should be viewed as a condition on the assignment of θ-roles to individual arguments as well as argument chains. As a matter of fact, the θ-Criterion can be exclusively viewed as a condition on chains if the notion 'chain' is extended to include non-moved categories such as {Mary} and {the problem} in Mary solved the problem. Chains will then differ as to whether they consist of one member or more. A chain which consists of one member, i.e. a chain not derived by movement, is called a **trivial chain**. A chain which consists of more than one member, e.g. {Mary, t} in (53), is called a **non-trivial chain**. Although this discussion requires that we substitute the expression 'argument chain' for the term 'chain' in the definition of the θ-Criterion, we will leave the definition of the θ-Criterion as it is in (55).

The idea that the θ-Criterion holds of chains implies a severe restriction on movement transformations such that only those which move an argument (from a θ-position) to a θ'-position are allowed. Movement of an argument (from a θ-position) to another θ-position will result in the derivation of a chain with two θ-roles in violation of the θ-Criterion. It is precisely for this reason that raising of the NP Mary to the subject position of the root clause is excluded in (54). The chain derived by this movement {Mary, t} has two θ-roles, the external θ-role of the embedded verb assigned to t, and the external θ-role of the root verb assigned to Mary. Our next step is to check whether the other movement processes we have identified so far are consistent with this requirement. The discussion of NP-movement in passives is postponed to a later section in this chapter. The movement processes which affect head categories such as I and V are ignored, as they are not directly relevant to the discussion.

Examples (56), (57) and (58) illustrate Topicalisation, Wh-movement and QR respectively. Although these movements do not affect arguments (topics have a non-argument status in LF) as such, they all have in common with NP-movement the fact that their target is a θ'-position. Recall that Spec,CP and adjoined positions are θ'-positions, so that the movement chains derived by Topicalisation, Wh-movement and QR all have a single θ-role each assigned to the trace:

56a. This problem, I can solve.

56b. [$_{CP}$ e [$_{IP}$ this problem$_i$ [$_{IP}$ I can [$_{VP}$ solve t$_i$]]]]

57a. Which problem did Mary solve?

57b. [$_{CP}$ which problem$_i$ did [$_{IP}$ Mary I [$_{VP}$ solve t$_i$]]]

58a. John suspects everyone.

58b. [$_{CP}$ e [$_{IP}$ everyone$_i$ [$_{IP}$ John I [$_{VP}$ suspects t$_i$]]]]

The chains derived by Topicalisation, Wh-movement and QR differ from the chains derived by NP-movement in one important respect. The target of NP-movement, i.e. Spec,IP, is an A-position. A chain derived by movement to an A-position is called an **A-chain**. Topicalisation, Wh-movement and QR differ in that their target is an A′-position. A chain derived by movement to an A′-position is called an **A′-chain**. As far as the θ-Criterion is concerned, the relevant member of A′-chains is the variable trace as the head is usually a non-argument.

7.4.2.2   *Raising to Object*   Consider (59a&b):

59a. John believes Bill to be a genius.
59b. John considers Bill to be a fool.

The NPs *Mary* and *Bill* are the external arguments of the embedded predicates *(be) a genius* and *(be) a fool*, respectively. Therefore, they are expected to occupy the external argument position (Spec,IP) of the embedded clause. However, these NPs exhibit certain properties which seem to suggest that they function grammatically as the direct object of the root verb even though they are thematically related to the predicate of the embedded clause. Some of the object-like properties of the NP in question are illustrated in (60a–c):

60a. John believes him/*he to be a genius.
60b. Bill is believed to be a genius.
60c. John (sincerely) believes (*sincerely) Bill to be a genius.

(60a) shows that when the NP in question is a pronoun, it is realised as the objective form of the pronoun *her/him/them*, instead of the subjective form *she/he/they*. This fact suggests that the NP is the direct object of the root verb. (60b) shows that the NP in question can move to the subject position of the root clause when the verb of this clause is in the passive form. This fact also suggests that the NP is the direct object of the root verb, as passivisation is exclusively a property of direct objects in (Standard) English. Finally, (60c) shows that a VP-adverb cannot intervene between the root verb and the NP in question, a property which characterises sequences involving a transitive verb and its direct object (see Chapter 5).

An obvious way of reconciling the fact that the NP in question is the external argument (subject) of the verb of the embedded clause with the fact that it has object-like properties is to assume that it is base-generated in the external argument position (subject position) of the embedded clause and subsequently moved to the object position of the root verb. This is shown in (61). This instance of NP-movement is called **Subject to Object raising** or **Raising to Object**:

61a. John believes Bill to be a genius.
61b. DS: [$_{IP}$ John I [$_{VP}$ believes [$_{NP}$ e] [$_{IP}$ Bill to be a genius]]]
61c. SS: [$_{IP}$ John I [$_{VP}$ believes Bill$_i$ [$_{IP}$ t$_i$ to be a genius]]]

62a. The problem was solved.
62b. DS: [$_{IP}$ [$_{NP}$ e] I [$_{VP}$ was [$_{VP}$ solved [$_{NP}$ the problem]]]]
62c. SS: [$_{IP}$ [the problem]$_i$ I [$_{VP}$ was [$_{VP}$ solved t$_i$]]]

The reasoning underlying the derivation in (61) is in essence similar to the reasoning underlying the derivation of passives in (62). Recall that the derivation of passives is intended to reconcile the status of the moved NP as the internal argument of the verb with the fact that it has subject-like properties, i.e. the fact that it is located in Spec,IP and that it is in a Spec-head agreement relation with (the Agr category of) I.

However, while the derivation of passives is consistent with the θ-Criterion, as we will see below, the derivation outlined in (61) is not. The analysis outlined in (61) assumes the presence of an empty object position in the root clause at DS, as shown in (61b), which is subsequently filled by the moved NP, as shown in (61c). In the current system, object positions exist insofar as they are the structural realisation (the projection) of the internal argument of the lexical head. It follows that every existing object (internal argument) position is by definition assigned a θ-role by the lexical head which selects it; otherwise it would simply not exist. In view of this, the movement process shown in (61), and in fact movement to a selected object position in general, inevitably leads to the derivation of a chain with two θ-roles. Such chains violate the θ-Criterion, and therefore are excluded.

The analysis of (59a&b) which is consistent with the θ-Criterion is the non-movement analysis shown in (63) and (64). The embedded subject remains in the embedded subject position at SS:

63a. John believes Bill to be a genius.
63b. DS: John believes [Bill to be a genius]
63c. SS: John believes [Bill to be a genius]

64a. John considers Bill to be a fool.
64b. DS: John considers [Bill to be a fool]
64c. SS: John considers [Bill to be a fool]

Although the analysis shown in (63) and (64) succeeds in avoiding a violation of the θ-Criterion, it still has the major task of explaining the object-like properties of the embedded subject noted above. In other words, the motivation for this analysis so far is purely theory-internal. It should be supported with empirical arguments (data). The arguments will have the task of explaining how come the subject of the embedded clause has object-like properties even though it occupies a subject position. Unfortunately, we will have to wait for the discussion of the arguments until the next chapter, where some notions crucially used by the analysis are introduced and explained. At the moment, note that the root verbs which occur in the constructions discussed belong to a limited class of verbs called **believe-type** verbs.

7.4.2.3 *Dative Shift*   Compare (65) and (66):

65a. Mary gave the book to John.
65b. Mary I [$_\nu$P [GAVE]$_i$ [ν] [VP [NP the book] [V' t$_i$ [pp to John]]]]

66a. Mary gave John the book.
66b. Mary I [$_\nu$P [GAVE]$_i$ [ν] [VP [NP John] [V' t$_i$ [NP the book]]]]

Both (65) and (66) have a VP-shell structure. The difference is in the placement of the two arguments in the two positions made available by the structure. In (65), the theme argument *the book* is the Spec of the lower VP. The goal argument *(to) John* is in the complement position of the lower V. In (65), however, the goal argument is in the Spec of the lower VP and the theme argument in the complement position of the lower V. Besides the difference in the position (order) of the two arguments, the two sentences also differ in that (65) includes the dative preposition *to* associated with the goal argument, whereas (66) does not. (66) is an instance of a phenomenon known as **Dative Shift** found with many verbs which take two internal arguments.

The apparent similarity in meaning between (65) and (66) suggests the possibility that the two constructions derive from one and the same underlying representation, namely (65b). Whether this is the case or not is an empirical question which we will not try to settle in this chapter. What should be clear is that the processes which derive (66) from (65) cannot take the form of switching the positions of the two arguments. This will lead to the derivation of ambiguous chains, i.e. chains with more than one θ-role, which are excluded. For the current purposes, we will assume that (65a) and (66a) derive from different DS representations shown in (65b) and (66b). In these DS representations, the two arguments have different positions, and therefore different grammatical functions.

There is evidence which suggests that the Dative Shift pattern [V NP$_{GOAL}$ NP$_{THEME}$] is unlikely to be derived from an underlying structure with the order [V NP$_{THEME}$ PP$_{GOAL}$] by a transformational rule. Although a substantial number of verbs which select two internal arguments allow the Dative Shift pattern, there are verbs which do not. For example, although the verb *donate* is close in meaning to *give*, it does not tolerate the Dative Shift pattern, as shown in (68b). Likewise, although the verb *transmit* is close in meaning to *send*, it does not tolerate the Dative Shift pattern, as shown in (69b):

67a. Mary sent the letter to John.
67b. Mary sent John the letter.

68a. Mary donated the money to the charity.
68b. *Mary donated the charity the money.

69a. Mary transmitted the message to John.
69b. *Mary transmitted John the message.

Transformations are usually not sensitive to individual lexical items, given that they operate on (classes of) categories. In view of this, it is unlikely that the Dative Shift pattern is derived by a transformation, as the transformation would have to be made sensitive to individual lexical items to exclude sentences such as (68b) and (69b). If the Dative Shift pattern is derived at all, it must be in terms of a rule which applies in the lexicon and affects the argument structure of certain verbs but not of others. Some of these rules are discussed in the next section.

7.5 *Argument structures and lexical rules of derivation*

7.5.1 Verbal passives

Compare the passive sentence in (70) to its active counterpart in (71):

70a. The problem was solved (by Mary).
70b. [IP the problemᵢ I [VP was [VP solved tᵢ (by Mary)]]]

71a. Mary solved the problem.
71b. [IP Mary I [VP solved the problem]]

The ability of the internal argument to move to the subject position in the passive sentence (70) implies, given the θ-Criterion, that the subject position of passives is a θ'-position, on a par with the subject position of raising predicates. However, looking at the active sentence (71), we see that the verb *solve* assigns an external θ-role to the subject position of its clause. Comparing the two sentences, it seems that the verb assigns its external θ-role to the subject position when it is in the active form, but not when it is the passive form. Why?

   Before we move on to a possible explanation for the observed difference between active and passive verbs, a word about the *by*-phrase. The optional presence of the *by*-phrase in passives, among other properties, suggests that it has the status of an adjunct. Its linear position suggests that it is right-adjoined to VP (or V'), as shown in (72):

72.

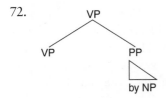

Although the *by*-phrase is somehow associated with the external argument of the passive verb, it is unlikely that it receives the external θ-role of the passive verb in the way external arguments receive theirs from active verbs. As a matter of fact, we are forced to assume, as pointed out above, that passive verbs do not assign an external θ-role. If they did, there would be no reason why it should not be assigned to the canonical external argument position (Spec,IP), instead of to an adjunct position.

Passive verbs are derived by attachment of the **passive morpheme** *-ed/-en* to the base (active) form of (regular) verbs. This process of affixation does not result in the derivation of a new category. Recall (from Chapter 3) that there are (derivational) affixes which do not change the categorial property of the base forms they attach to in the lexicon. In view of this, it is not implausible to conclude that the process which derives passive verbs from active verbs takes place in the lexicon. The lexical rule in question actually must do more than simply attach the passive morpheme to the base (active) form of the verb. More precisely, the rule in question affects the argument structure of the base verb in such a way as to eliminate its external argument. The complex rule involved in the derivation of passive verbs can be represented as in (73):

73a. solve: [+V; −N] (= V)
              agent <theme>   →

73b. solved: [+V; −N] (= V)
              ∅ <theme>

The derived passive form differs from the base active form in that its argument/ thematic structure lacks an external argument/θ-role. However, the two forms are identical categorially, even though the passive form has the additional passive morpheme. Now, since the argument/ thematic structure of the passive verb does not include an external argument/θ-role, the subject position of passive sentences is a θ′-position, and therefore a possible target for a moved argument. The chain derived by movement of the internal argument to the subject position in passives has only one θ-role, and therefore is consistent with the θ-Criterion.

7.5.2   Adjectival passives

Compare now the passive sentence above with (74a&b):

74a. The island was uninhabited.
74b. The performance was uninterrupted.

The complex forms *uninhabited* and *uninterrupted* in (74a&b) are said to be instances of **adjectival passives**. The latter are distinguished from the passive forms of verbs discussed above which are called **verbal passives**. The forms in (74a&b) are passive in the sense that their internal argument surfaces as the subject of the sentence, on a par with the verbal passive in (70). On the other hand, they are adjectival because they display properties usually associated with adjectives. We will discuss each of these properties separately.

One of the adjectival properties of the forms in (74a&b) relates to their ability to take the negative prefix *un-*. This prefix usually attaches to adjectives, as shown in (75a), but never to verbs, as shown in (75b) (Chapter 3). Recall from Chapter 3 that the negative prefix *un-* which appears with adjectival forms should be distinguished from the homophonous reversative prefix *un-* which appears with verbs such as *unzip*:

75a. unhappy, unkind, unsympathetic
75b. *to uninhabit (an island), *to uninterrupt (a performance)

The second adjectival property of the forms in (74a&b) relates to the fact that they can modify nouns, as shown in (76a&b). The ability to modify a noun is usually associated with adjectives (and relative clauses) and excludes verbs altogether:

76a. The uninhabited island
76b. The uninterrupted performance

The third property is that the forms in question can function as complement of verbs such as *remain* and *seem*, which select adjectives but not verbs. This is shown in (77a&b):

77a. The island seemed uninhabited.
77b. The performance remained uninterrupted.

The three properties discussed, among others, indicate that the forms in (74a&b) are adjectival in nature, and therefore categorially distinct from verbal passives. The relevant part of the rule involved in the derivation of adjectival passives from a base verb can be stated as in (78):

78a. inhabit: $[+V -N]$ (= V) →
78b. inhabited: $[+V +N]$ (= A)

Recall (from Chapter 3) that adjectives have the feature complex shown in (78b). Recall also that the categorial features of a derived complex are determined by the features of the affix which is the head of the derived complex. It follows that the adjectival features of the complex form in (78) are the features of the affix -*ed*, the base being a verb. Comparing the rule in (78) to the rule in (73) involved in the derivation of verbal passives, it seems that we are dealing with two different, though homophonous, affixes. The affix which appears on verbal passives has verbal features, so that when it is affixed to a verb, the derived complex is still a verbal category. On the other hand, the affix which appears on adjectival passives has adjectival features, so that when it is affixed to a verb the derived complex is an adjectival category.

Turning now to the argument structure of adjectival passives, we saw above that they resemble verbal passives in that their internal argument surfaces in the subject position of the sentence. Initially, this suggests that adjectival passives have a derivation similar to that of verbal passives. They undergo a lexical process which eliminates the external argument of the base verb, and a syntactic process (NP-movement) which moves their internal argument to the subject position of the sentence. However, for reasons which we will not get into here, adjectival passives are often assumed to have a different derivation, the main characteristic of which is that it is exclusively lexical. The steps of the derivation of adjectival passives relevant to our discussion so far are listed in (79):

79.   **Properties of Adjectival Passive Formation (APF)**

    i)   Affixation of the passive morpheme -*ed*/-*en*, e.g. interrupt → interrupted.

    ii)   Change of category, e.g. interrupt: [+V −N] → interrupted: [+V +N].

    iii) Suppression of the external argument of the base form,
          e.g. interrupt: agent <theme> → ∅ <theme>

    iv) Externalisation of the internal argument of the base verb,
          e.g. interrupted: ∅ <theme> → theme <∅>

Given the derivation in (79), sentences which include adjectival passives have the structural representation shown in (80):

80a. The performance was uninterrupted.

80b. DS: [$_{IP}$ the performance I [$_{VP}$ [$_V$ was] [$_{AP}$ uninterrupted]]]

80c. SS: [$_{IP}$ the performance I [$_{VP}$ [$_V$ was] [$_{AP}$ uninterrupted]]]

The derivation of adjectival passives does not involve movement of the internal argument to the subject position in syntax, contrary to the derivation of verbal passives. The externalisation of the internal argument of adjectival passives takes place in the lexicon. The internal argument is mapped directly onto the subject position of the sentence, as shown in (80b&c).

7.5.3   Implicit arguments

According to the analysis so far, the lexical derivation of both verbal passives and adjectival passives involves the elimination of the external argument of the base verb. However, there is evidence which suggests that while the derivation of adjectival passives indeed involves the elimination of the external argument, this is unlikely to be the case in the lexical derivation of verbal passives. Verbal passives appear to include an **implicit** external argument which does not have a counterpart in adjectival passives.

One piece of evidence relates to the *by*-phrase. Unlike verbal passives, adjectival passives do not seem to be compatible with the *by*-phrase, as shown in (81a&b):

81a. The ball was kicked (by Mary).

81b. The room was unoccupied (*by Mary).

The role of the *by*-phrase in verbal passives such as (81a) is to specify the identity of the individual who performs the act described by the verb, i.e. the external argument. When the *by*-phrase is missing, the external argument is said to have an arbitrary interpretation, roughly paraphrasable as '(some)one or other' (see Chapter 4).

The fact that the interpretation of verbal passives involves an external argument (even when the *by*-phrase is missing) implies that, contrary to what we assumed earlier, their external argument is not eliminated. In contrast, the interpretation of adjectival passives does not involve an external argument, hence the fact that they are incompatible with the *by*-phrase. Adjectival passives are sometimes said to have a **state** reading, as opposed to verbal passives, which tend to have an **event** reading. (81b), for example, describes the state of the room at a given point in time, rather than the event which led to the room being unoccupied. In contrast, (81a) describes an event, rather than a state.

Another piece of evidence relates to **subject-oriented** or **agent-oriented** adverbs such as *deliberately* and *intentionally*. These adverbs tend to modify the external argument, typically agent. They can occur freely with verbal passives, but not with adjectival passives, as shown in (82a&b):

82a. The ball was (intentionally) kicked (by Mary).
82b. The room was (*intentionally) unoccupied.

In the verbal passive (82a) the adverb modifies the external argument of the verb. Once again, this suggests that the external argument of verbal passives is somehow implicit. On the other hand, the fact that adjectival passives do not tolerate subject-oriented adverbs implies that they lack a corresponding implicit external argument.

The third piece of evidence relates to the phenomenon of Control, briefly discussed in Chapter 6 (and will be discussed in more detail in Chapter 9). Verbal passives allow control of the *PRO* subject of a non-finite purpose clause, as shown in (83). Adjectival passives do not, as shown in (84). The controller of *PRO* in the verbal passive (83) is the implicit external argument of the passive verb. (84) indicates that adjectival passives lack this argument:

83a. The ball was kicked (to make a point).
83b. the ball was kicked [PRO to make a point]

84a. The room was unoccupied (*to make a point).
84b. the room was unoccupied (*[PRO to make a point])

The evidence reviewed so far shows that it is inaccurate to assume, as we did above, that the external argument of the base verb is eliminated in the lexical derivation of verbal passives. The external argument of verbal passives is said to be merely 'suppressed' or 'suspended', meaning not mapped onto Spec,IP rather than completely eliminated. Recall that it is necessary to assume that the external θ-role is not assigned to Spec,IP in verbal passives as movement of the internal argument to this position would be incompatible with the requirement of the θ-Criterion. Obviously, it is desirable to clarify the status of the implicit argument in relation to the structural representation of passives. However, this task will not be carried out here. The reader is referred to the Further Reading section for some related references.

7.5.4 Unaccusatives and Middles

Compare the pair in (85a&b)

85a. John broke the vase.
85b. The vase broke.

English has a class of verbs which enter into a 'transitivity alternation' of the type illustrated in (85a&b). In (85a) the verb *break* has two arguments, an agent argument realised as the subject and a theme argument realised as the object. In (85b), however, the verb *break* has only the theme argument, this time realised as the subject. In (85b) the verb resembles verbal and adjectival passives, although, unlike verbal and adjectival passives, it does not seem to display a morpheme which could be related to this property. The verb is said to be **transitive** in (85a) and **unaccusative** in (85b) for reasons that will be clear in Chapter 8. Among the other verbs which enter into this particular alternation are *open, crack, bend, shorten, drop* and *spin*.

Two major questions arise in relation to transitive/unaccusative pairs. First, what is the status of the external argument in the unaccusative member of the pair (85b)? Is it eliminated as in adjectival passives or simply suspended as in verbal passives? Secondly, which of the two members of the pair is derived and which is basic? Is the unaccusative member derived from the transitive member or the other way round? Obviously, it is desirable not to have a separate entry for each member. Semantically related categories should be derivable one from the other, unless there are reasons to believe otherwise. Since the answer to the second question somewhat depends on the answer to the first, we will deal with the first question first.

An obvious way of checking whether the external argument in the unaccusative member of the pair is eliminated or simply suspended is to apply the tests discussed above in relation to verbal and adjectival passives. The relevant examples are in (86a–c):

86a. The vase broke (*by John).
86b. The vase broke (*intentionally).
86c. The vase broke (*to prove a point).

Unaccusative verbs are incompatible with a by-phrase (86a), with an agent-oriented adverb (86b) and with Control of the *PRO* subject of a purpose clause (86c). This means that unaccusative verbs pattern with adjectival passives rather than with verbal passives, leading to the conclusion that their external argument is eliminated rather than simply suspended.

There are in principle two possible ways of deriving (85b) where the internal argument occupies the (external) subject position. One is that the theme argument is externalised by a lexical rule of the type involved in the derivation of adjectival passives. According to this scenario, the theme argument is mapped directly onto the subject position at DS, as shown in (87):

87a. *break*: agent <theme> → theme <∅>
87b. DS: [$_{IP}$ [$_{NP}$ the vase] I [$_{VP}$ broke]]
87c. SS: [$_{IP}$ [$_{NP}$ the vase] I [$_{VP}$ broke]]

The other possibility is that while the external argument is eliminated, the theme argument remains unaffected, as in the derivation of verbal passives. According to this scenario, the theme argument is mapped onto an internal argument position at

DS and subsequently moved to the subject position by NP-movement. This scenario is shown in (88).

88a. *break*: agent <theme> → <∅> <theme>
88b. DS: [$_{IP}$ e [$_{VP}$ broke the vase]]
88c. SS: [$_{IP}$ [$_{NP}$ the vase]$_i$ I [$_{VP}$ broke [$_{NP}$ t$_i$]]]

(87) represents an exclusively lexical derivation, while (88) represents a partly lexical and partly syntactic derivation. The lexical part of the derivation eliminates the external argument of the transitive base, and the syntactic part moves the internal argument to the subject position. As far as English is concerned, it is not clear which of the two analyses is the more plausible. However, there is fairly strong evidence from other languages in favour of the mixed analysis outlined in (88). The reader is referred to the Further Reading section for references relating to this point.

Let us now turn to the second question: which of the two members of the pair is derived and which is basic? The idea that the external argument is eliminated, shared by the two analyses outlined in (87) and (88), presupposes that it is the unaccusative member which is derived from the transitive member. However, this is by no means the only possibility. It is conceivable that the transitive member is derived from the unaccusative member by a lexical operation which adds an external argument to the argument structure of the unaccusative member, as shown in (89):

89. *break*: ∅ <theme> →   agent <theme>

The analysis outlined in (89) implies that the semantic structure of the transitive *break* is more complex than it appears, so that example (85a) above means something like 'John caused the vase to be broken'. This reading is sometimes called the **causative** reading, and the lexical process shown in (89) is called **causativisation**. We will not try to decide between the two analyses here. A detailed discussion of causatives is included in Chapter 15.

Unaccusatives are traditionally distinguished from another class of verbs called **middles**. Middles resemble unaccusatives in that their internal argument appears in the subject position, and that, in English, they do not display a special morpheme which could be related to this property. The verbs *translate* and *bribe* in (90a&b) are said to have a middle use or middle reading:

90a. Greek translates easily.
90b. Bureaucrats bribe easily.

A distinctive property of middles is that they are usually 'adorned'. Most frequently, this is done with adverbs, as in (90a&b), but other elements can also serve this function. These include negation, as in (92a), a quantified subject, as in (92b), among others. (91a&b) show that adornment is obligatory with middles:

91a. *Greek translates.
91b. *Bureaucrats bribe.

92a. This bread doesn't/won't cut.
92b. Not many/few bureaucrats bribe.

Obviously, an adequate analysis of middles should be able to explain, among other things, why they have to be adorned. However, this task is beyond the limits of this book. Here, we will simply outline some basic properties of middles bearing on their argument structure.

Although middles resemble unaccusatives in that their subject is an internal argument, the interpretation of middles is said to differ fundamentally. The interpretation of middles involves an agent, on a par with that of verbal passives. The sentence in (90a), for example, means, roughly, 'It is easy for one to translate Greek'. No such reading is possible with unaccusatives, so that 'The vase broke' does not mean 'Someone broke the vase'. At the same time, the agent reading of middles is incompatible with the fact that they fail the usual tests for the presence of an implicit external argument, as shown in (93a–c):

93a. *The book sold (quickly) by Mary.
93b. *The book sold voluntarily.
93c. *The book sold (widely) [PRO to make money].

In this particular respect, middles pattern with unaccusatives and adjectival passives rather than with verbal passives. This is despite the fact that, as noted above, middles resemble verbal passives in that an agent argument seems to figure in their interpretation. A proper analysis of middles will, therefore, have to reconcile these apparently contradictory properties. As this task is beyond the limits of this book, we will leave the issue open and turn to a discussion of how middles can be derived.

As with unaccusatives, middles can, a priori, be derived in one of two possible ways. One possibility is that the internal argument of the base verb is externalised in the lexicon. According to this scenario, the theme role will be mapped directly onto the subject position at DS as shown in (94):

94a. *bribe*: agent <theme> → theme <∅>
94b. DS: [$_{IP}$ [$_{NP}$ bureaucrats] I [$_{VP}$ bribe easily]
94c. SS: [$_{IP}$ [$_{NP}$ bureaucrats] I [$_{VP}$ bribe easily]

The other possibility is that the internal argument of the base is not affected by the lexical rule. It is mapped onto the internal argument position at DS, and subsequently moved to the subject position by NP-movement, as shown in (95):

95a. *bribe*: agent <theme> → <∅> <theme>
95b. DS: [$_{IP}$ [$_{NP}$ e] I [$_{VP}$ bribe [$_{NP}$ bureaucrats] easily]]
95c. SS: [$_{IP}$ [$_{NP}$ bureaucrats]$_i$ I [$_{VP}$ bribe [$_{NP}$ t$_i$] easily]]

The analysis outlined in (94) represents an exclusively lexical derivation of middles, whereas the one in (95) represents a partly lexical and partly syntactic derivation of middles. Note with respect to the latter that, due to the θ-Criterion, the subject position has to be a θ'-position, even though the external argument figures in the interpretation of middles.

7.5.5   Derived nominals

Compare the sentences in (96a–c) to the noun phrases in (97a–c):

96a. The barbarians destroyed the city.
96b. *The barbarians destroyed.
96c. *There destroyed the city.

97a. The barbarians' destruction of the city
97b. The destruction of the city
97c. The destruction was awful.

(96a–c) illustrate the familiar fact that arguments of verbs must be syntactically realised, a consequence of the θ-Criterion and the Projection Principle. (97a–c), on the other hand, show that the corresponding arguments of derivationally related nouns do not have to be syntactically realised. This implies that the derivation of nouns from verbs affects the argument structure of the base verb such that the arguments somehow become optional.

As far as the external argument is concerned, it can be affected in one of the two possible ways discussed above. It can either be eliminated completely, as in the derivation of adjectival passives, or simply suspended, as in the derivation of verbal passives. The usual tests for detecting the presence of an implicit external argument give a positive result, as shown in (98a–c):

98a. The destruction of the city by the barbarians
98b. The deliberate destruction of the city
98c. The destruction of the city [PRO to prove a point]

It seems, therefore, that derived nominals resemble verbal passives in that their external argument is implicit. Presumably, whatever the nature of the analysis for verbal passives should extend to derived nominals.

Another respect in which derived nominals seem to resemble verbal passives, as well as other complex predicates, relates to the ability of the internal argument to appear in the subject position of NP. The NP in (99a) is sometimes referred to as a **nominal passive:**

99a. The city's destruction (by the barbarians)
99b. DS: [$_{NP}$ e [$_{N'}$ destruction [$_{NP}$ the city]]]
99c. SS: [$_{NP}$ the city$_i$'s [$_{N'}$ destruction t$_i$]]

If (99a) is an instance of passivisation in the sense associated with verbal passives, then it has the derivation outlined in (99b&c). The internal argument is base-generated in the complement position and subsequently moved to the subject position via NP-movement. However, there are reasons to doubt the apparent parallelism with verbal passives, chief among them the fact that complements of certain nouns cannot appear in the subject position of the NP (cannot be passivised). Compare the nominal passives in (100a&b) with their verbal counterparts in (101a&b):

100a. *The book's discussion (by Mary)
100b. *The issue's avoidance (by John)

101a. The book was discussed (by Mary).
101b. The issue was avoided (by John).

The contrast illustrated in (100) and (101) implies a restriction on the ability of internal arguments of nouns to appear in the subject position of the noun phrase known as the **Affectedness Constraint**. For an internal argument of a noun to be able to appear in the subject position of the NP, it has to be affected by the event denoted by the head noun, where an affected NP is, roughly, one which undergoes a change in state or location. The internal argument of *destruction*, for example, is affected in the intended sense, whereas the internal argument of *discussion* and *avoidance* arguably are not.

The Affectedness Constraint is not likely to be a condition on NP-movement since this would imply that NP-movement would have to be made sensitive to the categorial nature of the predicate (whether it is a verb or a noun). The Affectedness Constraint seems to suggest an exclusively lexical derivation for nominal passives such that the internal argument is directly mapped onto the subject position of NP. Notice that the definition of 'affected' is similar to the definition of 'theme', implying a lexical rule which makes specific reference to 'theme'. The status of the external argument in nominal passives remains somewhat obscure, as in verbal passives. A possible analysis for the status of implicit agentive arguments in NPs will be discussed in Chapter 9.

7.6   *Summary*

In this chapter we discussed the selectional properties of lexical items relating to their argument and thematic structures. Lexical categories are said to s-select a certain number of arguments to which they assign a corresponding number of θ-roles. To the extent that a correspondence relation can be established between semantic categories and syntactic categories, the selectional properties of lexical items can be reduced to their s-selectional properties.

Non-arguments such as wh-phrases and quantified phrases, called operators, undergo movement in the mapping from SS onto LF called QR. Movement of these categories leaves a trace behind which has the status of a variable, and therefore an argument. QR confirms the idea that LF is a syntactic level in much the same way as SS and DS.

The structural representation of thematic structures of lexical items is subject to a syntactic condition called the θ-Criterion. The latter establishes a one-to-one correspondence between θ-roles and arguments, such that every argument is assigned a single θ-role and every θ-role is assigned to a single argument. Essentially, the θ-Criterion is a well-formedness condition on argument chains, where the notion chain may include a moved argument and its trace (a non-trivial chain) or a non-moved argument alone (a trivial chain). The θ-Criterion essentially holds of DS, but it is also expected to hold of SS and DS by virtue of the Projection Principle.

A crucial consequence of the θ-Criterion is that movement of arguments is possible only to non-θ-marked positions, as movement to θ-marked positions would lead to the derivation of argument chains with more than one θ-role. All movements which affect arguments discussed so far appear to be consistent with this requirement. For example, the instance of NP-movement involved in the derivation of raising sentences is consistent with the θ-Criterion, as raising predicates do not assign an external θ-role as a lexical property.

Another consequence of the θ-Criterion, in combination with the Projection Principle, is that the processes which affect the argument/thematic structures of lexical items are confined to the lexicon. For example, the process which results in the inability of verbal passives to assign an external θ-role to the subject position of the sentence has to take place in the lexicon. This ensures that the subject position of verbal passives is a non-θ-marked position, and therefore a legitimate target for movement of the internal argument in syntax.

The θ-Criterion belongs to a module of the grammar called θ-theory. The latter has a status parallel to that of X-bar theory, another module. In the Principles and Parameters framework, grammar is said to have a modular structure, where each module deals with a different aspect of the representation and derivation of sentences. In the subsequent chapters we will discuss other modules which deal with different aspects of the representation and derivation of sentences, and see how the principles they incorporate interact with the principles of other modules.

Exercises

Exercise 7.1

First, identify the chains, both trivial and non-trivial, in each of the sentences in (i–v). Secondly, classify each chain as to whether it is an A-chain or an A'-chain. Thirdly, explain how each chain is consistent with the θ-Criterion:

i)   The match seems to have stopped.
ii) Who appears to be likely to win the match?
iii) Has Bill seen John?
iv) Who was arrested?
v)   Mary placed the file into the drawer.

Exercise 7.2

Explain how the sentences in (i–iii) are excluded in the context of the discussion in this chapter:

i) *John appears that Mary will see the play.
ii) *There thinks that the audience will like the play.
iii) *John believes [t to have seen the play].

Exercise 7.3

The θ-Criterion is said to exclude a raising analysis for the Control sentences in (i–iii). A raising analysis would involve movement of the root subject from the embedded subject position in (i) (Subject Control) and movement of the root direct object from the embedded subject position in (ii) (Object Control). Explain why the θ-Criterion rules out such an analysis, and explain how example (iii) fits into the picture:

i)   Bill tried to leave.
ii) John persuaded Bill to leave.
iii) It is difficult to leave (in these circumstances).

Exercise 7.4

Explain how the ambiguity of sentences with multiple quantification such as (i) is explained in the framework outlined in this chapter. Once you have done that, explain whether the analysis predicts the fact that sentence (ii) is not ambiguous. Sentence (ii) has only the reading whereby the wh-phrase has scope over *everyone*. Depending on the conclusion you reach with respect to (ii), explain whether the fact that sentence (iii) is ambiguous raises any problems. Sentence (iii) can either have the reading whereby the wh-phrase has scope over everyone or the reading whereby *everyone* has scope over the wh-phrase:

i)   Everyone bought some present.

ii) What did John buy everyone?
     Answer: John bought everyone a tie.

iii) What did everyone buy John?
     Answer: Everyone bought John a tie.
     Answer: Mary bought John a tie, Bill bought John a CD, Jane bought John a book . . . etc.

Exercise 7.5

Sentences such as (i–iv) include so-called secondary predicates, *angry* in (i), *exhausted* in (ii), *flat* in (iii) and *raw* in (iv). Like all predicates, secondary predicates have a θ-role to assign. Such sentences have been argued to require a relaxation of the uniqueness requirement incorporated into the θ-Criterion such that an argument can receive more than one θ-role. Explain why. If you have reasons to believe that the uniqueness requirement should not be relaxed, try to think of an analysis for (i–iv) which makes them consistent with the θ-Criterion:

i)   John left the room angry. (cf. John is angry.)
ii) Bill reached the finish line exhausted. (cf. Bill is exhausted.)

iii) Mary hammered the nail flat. (cf. The nail is flat.)
iv) John ate the fish raw. (cf. The fish is raw.)

Exercise 7.6

One of the consequences of the θ-Criterion is that expletives can only appear in non-θ-marked positions. The set of non-θ-marked positions excludes the complement positions. As pointed out in this chapter, complement positions are θ-marked by definition. Bearing this in mind, explain whether the sentences in (i–iv) are problematic:

i)   They mentioned it to him that he was not shortlisted for the job.
ii) John resents it very much that Bill is always late.
iii) John would hate it for Bill to resign.
iv) They require it of all students that they should attend regularly.

Exercise 7.7

Discuss the argument structure of the verbs in each of the pairs of sentences in (i–iii). Among other things, discuss whether the verbs in each pair should be derivationally related, and if so how:

i)a. The horse jumped (over the fence).
i)b. The rider jumped the horse (over the fence).

ii)a. The dog walked (to the park).
ii)b. Mary walked the dog (to the park).

iii)a. The horse raced across the barn.
iii)b. Mary raced the horse across the barn.

Sources and further reading

Allwood *et al.* (1977) discusses the relevance of logic to linguistics. See also Larson and Segal (1995) and Heim and Kratzer (1998). The terminology relating to θ-roles has been inherited from traditional grammar, and its relevance to linguistic theory within the generative tradition is established in Gruber (1965, 1976), Jackendoff (1972), and more formally in Freidin (1978) and Chomsky (1981). Higginbotham (1985) outlines a more comprehensive theory of θ-role assignment. Chomsky (1981) also includes an extended discussion of the typology of positions in relation to the dichotomies θ/θ'-positions and A/A'-positions.

   The properties of LF as presented in this chapter, in particular the idea that quantifiers undergo a movement (QR) in the mapping from SS onto LF, are discussed in Chomsky (1977a) and May (1977, 1985). The notion 'c-command' which plays a crucial role in the LF representation of sentences as well as in other aspects of the theory to be discussed in the next chapters appears in Reinhart (1976). The latter and also Reinhart (1983) represent a coherent alternative view of the interpretation of quantified expressions and the properties of logical representations in general. The issues relating to LF have given rise to a large body of literature, some of which will be mentioned in the relevant remaining chapters. Baker (1970), Bresnan (1970), Kuno and Robinson (1972) and Chomsky (1973) include some of the early discussions of the distribution of wh-phrases and the properties of multiple wh-questions. On the mechanisms underlying the movement of wh-phrases at LF, see Higginbotham and May (1981) and Aoun *et al.* (1981).

Raising to Object appeared in the typology of transformations outlined in Rosenbaum (1967) and has given rise to one of the most exciting controversies. Postal (1974) is a substantantial and formidable defence of Raising to Object. Evaluations of arguments for and against raising can be found in Bresnan (1976) and Lightfoot (1976). Some of the arguments against Raising to Object are outlined in Chomsky (1973, 1981). Dative Shift has also given rise to an exciting debate with arguments for and against. Among the early analyses are Chomsky (1965), Green (1974), Emonds (1976) and Oehrle (1976). Some of the more recent references on Dative Shift are Hornstein and Weinberg (1981), Stowell (1981), Chomsky (1981), Czepulch (1982), Kayne (1984), Larson (1988) and Baker (1988). For a recent debate see Jackendoff (1990) and Larson (1991).

The question relating to whether rules which affect the argument structure of lexical items should all be confined to the lexicon or distributed between the lexicon and syntax has given rise to a large body of data. Among the relevant references are Williams (1981, 1982), Chomsky (1981), Marantz (1984), Borer (1984), Keyser and Roeper (1984), Burzio (1986), Jaeggli (1986), Levin and Rappaport (1986), Roberts (1987), and Zubizarreta (1987). The view that all these rules, including the rule which results in the change of the grammatical function of the internal argument in passives, should be confined to the lexicon is one of the major tenets of Lexical Functional Grammar (LFG). Among the major references on this particular version of Generative Grammar are Bresnan (1982a and 1982b).

8 Case Theory

Contents

8.1 *Case Filter and Visibility Hypothesis*

8.1.1 Infinitives with an overt subject

Compare the examples in (1–3):

1a. *John to leave suddenly is foolish.
1b. *[CP [C′ e [IP John [I′ to [VP leave suddenly]]]]] is foolish

2a. For John to leave suddenly is foolish.

2b. [CP [C' for [IP John [I' to [VP leave suddenly]]]]] is foolish

3a. That John should leave suddenly is surprising.

3b. [CP [C' that [IP John [I' should [VP leave suddenly]]]]] is surprising

All three sentences have a clause (CP) for a subject. Each clausal subject has an overt NP subject of its own, *John*. In (1) and (2) the clausal subject is non-finite, whereas in (3) it is finite. Comparing the three examples, the following descriptive generalisation emerges: an overt NP cannot occur in the subject position of a non-finite (subject) clause, unless the overt NP is preceded by the prepositional complementiser *for*.

An early attempt to deal with (1) consisted of postulating the filter in (4) which has the effect of excluding representations with the sequence it specifies:

4. **NP-to-VP Filter**

   *NP-to-VP, except in the context [P (for) —]

Although (4) correctly rules out (1) and correctly rules in (2), it is somewhat ad hoc. It fails to explain, among other things, why and how the presence of the prepositional complementiser *for* in (2) succeeds in rescuing the sequence.

(4) also fails to explain why *PRO* can occur in the subject position of non-finite clauses, as shown in (5), contrary to overt NPs. Moreover, *PRO* is incompatible with the prepositional complementiser *for* in Standard English, as shown in (6):

5a. To leave suddenly is foolish.

5b. [CP e [IP PRO [I' to [VP leave suddenly]]]] is foolish

6a. *For to leave suddenly is foolish.

6b. *[CP [C' for [IP PRO [I' to [VP leave suddenly]]]]] is foolish

Presumably, a more desirable analysis would be one which explains why overt NPs cannot appear in the subject position of subject non-finite clauses unless they are preceded by a prepositional complementiser, and why *PRO* behaves differently, among other related issues.

8.1.2   Case Filter

As a first step towards developing such an analysis, consider (7), (8) and (9) along with the paradigm in (10):

7a. For him/*he/*his to leave suddenly is foolish.

7b. [CP for [IP him to [VP leave suddenly]]] . . .

8a. She/*her introduced him/*he/*his to them/*they/*their

8b. [CP [IP she I [VP introduced him [PP to them]]]]

9a. His/*he/*him attempt to leave suddenly surprised everybody.

9b. [IP [NP his [N' attempt [CP e [IP PRO to leave suddenly]]]]] . . .

10. *Subjective forms*	*Objective forms*	*Possessive forms*
a. I	a′. me	a″. my
b. you	b′. you	b″. your
c. he	c′. him	c″. his
d. she	d′. her	d″. her
e. we	e′. us	e″. our
f. you	f′. you	f″. your
g. they	g′. them	g″. their

Apart from certain exceptions (gaps in the paradigm), pronouns in Standard English generally have three different forms, a **subjective** form (10a–g), an **objective** form (10a′–g′), and a **possessive** form (10a″–g″). The subjective form occurs in the subject position of finite clauses, as shown in (8). The objective form occurs in the object position of verbs and prepositions, as shown in (8). Finally, the possessive form occurs in the subject position of NPs, as shown in (9). Thus, each form of the pronoun is associated with a specific syntactic environment.

The different forms of pronouns are said to reflect the **Case** properties of NPs. NPs are said to be **assigned** Case by a neighbouring head category which bears a specific structural relation of **locality** to the NP it **Case-marks**. Leaving aside possessive Case for the moment, an NP in the subject position (Spec,IP) of a finite clause is assigned subjective Case by finite I. However, an NP in the subject position of a non-finite clause is not assigned subjective Case. The reason is that non-finite I does not have the ability to assign (subjective) Case for reasons which will be discussed below. An NP in the object position of a transitive verb or a preposition is assigned objective Case by the transitive verb or the preposition. Unlike transitive verbs, intransitive verbs cannot assign objective Case. The relationship between transitivity and the ability to assign objective Case is discussed in detail later on in this chapter.

In a number of languages with rich inflectional morphology, e.g. Latin, (Modern) Greek, German, the Case properties of NPs are overtly reflected in terms of distinct morphological markers, called **Case-markers** or **Case-inflection**. In English, where inflectional morphology is comparatively poorer, the Case properties of NPs are overtly shown only in pronouns. On the understanding that Case is a property of NPs in general, it would be rather implausible to conclude that only pronominal NPs have Case in English. It is more plausible to take the view that all types of NP have Case, and that English differs in that Case is overtly reflected in pronominal NPs only. With non-pronominal NPs, the Case is encoded in terms of abstract Case-markers, much like the subject Agr marker discussed in Chapter 6.

Granting this, let us assume that all overt NPs have Case because they are required by a general principle of grammar to have Case. In other words, let us assume that the distribution of NPs is subject to a condition which requires them to have Case. The condition in question is called the **Case Filter** and can be formulated as in (11):

11. Case Filter

   *NP if NP has phonetic content and has no Case.

It is clear from its definition that the Case Filter is restricted to NPs which have phonetic content, i.e. overt NPs. Null NPs such as *PRO*, and possibly others, are not subject to the condition expressed by the Case Filter. Let us see how (11) helps explain the contrast between (1) and (3) above, and why the presence of the prepositional complementiser *for* in (2) makes it possible for an overt NP to occur in the subject position of the non-finite clause. The relevant parts of these examples are reproduced in (12–14):

12a. *John to leave suddenly . . .
12b. *[$_{CP}$ [$_{C'}$ e [$_{IP}$ John [$_{I'}$ to [$_{VP}$ leave suddenly]]]]]

13a. For John to leave suddenly . . .
13b. [$_{CP}$ [$_{C'}$ for [$_{IP}$ John [$_{I'}$ to [$_{VP}$ leave suddenly]]]]]

14a. That John should leave suddenly . . .
14b. [$_{CP}$ [$_{C'}$ that [$_{IP}$ John [$_{I'}$ should [$_{VP}$ leave suddenly]]]]]

   Recall that Case is assigned to an overt NP by a head category which bears a close structural relationship to it, to be defined below. Thus, an NP has Case if it is in the 'vicinity' of a Case-assigning category. Recall also that not all categories can assign Case. For example, non-finite I cannot assign (subjective) Case, and intransitive verbs cannot assign (objective) Case. In (14), the NP subject *John* is assigned subjective Case by finite I, and therefore satisfies the Case Filter. In (12), however, I is non-finite and therefore cannot assign subjective Case to the NP subject. Consequently, the NP subject *John* fails to be assigned Case in violation of the Case Filter. Finally, in (13), where I is also non-finite, the NP subject is assigned Case by the prepositional complementiser *for*, and therefore satisfies the Case Filter. This is precisely the sense in which the presence of the prepositional complementiser *for* helps rescue a representation with an overt NP in the subject position of a non-finite clause. In this particular context, the NP subject is assigned objective Case, indicated in example (8) above by the fact that only the objective form of the pronoun is allowed.

   The Case Filter does not apply to non-overt NPs such as *PRO* by definition (11). Consequently, *PRO* is expected to be able to occur in non-Case-marked environments. These include the subject position of a non-finite clause not preceded by the prepositional complementiser *for*, such as in (5). The reason *PRO*, unlike overt NPs, cannot be preceded by *for*, as shown in (6), will be discussed in Chapter 9 in the context of a broader account of the distribution of *PRO* and its referential properties.

   The idea that the Case Filter applies only to overt NPs can be understood to mean that it is a condition on the phonetic representation of (overt) NPs and therefore applies at the PF level. According to this view, the Case Filter is not relevant to LF representations. Initially, this view may look incompatible with the fact that Case encodes information relating to the grammatical functions of NPs. Recall that the terms 'subject(ive)' and 'object(ive)' refer to the grammatical functions of NPs. However, it is important to remember that the grammatical functions of NPs are determined by their structural positions (see Chapter 2), so that although Case encodes information about the grammatical functions of NPs it does not determine them. Moreover, there is no one-to-one correspondence between the various types of Case and grammatical functions. For example, objective Case does not necessarily invariably imply the grammatical function 'object'. In (7/13), for example, the NP *John/him* has the grammatical function 'subject' by virtue of the fact that it occupies Spec,IP (i.e. the subject position), but it bears objective Case rather than subjective Case.

According to the Case Filter and the theory underlying it, Case is a PF property of NPs. However, there have been attempts in the literature to make it relevant to LF and therefore to meaning relations. One such attempt is known as the **Visibility Hypothesis**.

8.1.3   Visibility Hypothesis

The Visibility Hypothesis incorporates the claim that the function of Case is to make NPs 'visible' for θ-marking at LF (see Chapter 7). The implication of this hypothesis is that Case is a property of arguments in general (i.e. expressions which receive a θ-role).

The Visibility Hypothesis has two major advantages. First, it makes it possible to dispense with the Case Filter altogether, since its effects, at least with respect to argument NPs, will derive from Visibility: an NP argument which does not have Case will not receive a θ-role and therefore is excluded by the θ-Criterion. The second major advantage of the Visibility Hypothesis is that it accounts for the fact that variables (traces of wh-phrases and quantified phrases) invariably occur in Case-marked positions even though they are null (or non-overt) categories. In (15) the subject position, occupied by the trace of *who*, and the object position of the verb, occupied by the trace of *what*, are Case-marked. The former by finite I and the latter by the verb. In (16) the trace of the raised quantifier *everybody* is located in a Case-marked position:

15a. Who bought what?
15b. LF: [$_{CP}$ [who]$_i$ [what]$_j$ [$_{IP}$ t$_i$ I [$_{VP}$ bought t$_j$]]]
15c. for which person x, for which thing y [x bought y]

16a. John suspects everybody.
16b. LF: [$_{CP}$ e [$_{IP}$ everybody$_i$ [$_{IP}$ John I [$_{VP}$ suspects t$_i$]]]]
16c. for every person x, [John suspects x]

Recall (from Chapter 7) that variables have the status of arguments, and therefore receive a θ-role at LF. In the context of the Visibility Hypothesis, the reason variables occur in Case-marked positions follows from the fact that they are arguments, and therefore need to be visible for θ-marking. The Case Filter fails to account for the fact that variable traces occur in Case-marked positions, because it is restricted to overt NPs by definition or by virtue of the fact that it applies at PF. Later on, we will discuss a definition of 'variable' which crucially relies on its Case property.

Although the Visibility Hypothesis has the two advantages mentioned, it leaves certain related facts unexplained. One such fact has to do with *PRO* and its distribution illustrated in (17) and (18):

17a. To leave suddenly is foolish.
17b. [CP e [IP PRO [I' to [VP leave suddenly]]]] . . .

18a. John planned to leave suddenly.
18b. John planned [CP e [IP PRO [I' to [VP leave suddenly]]]]

In both examples, *PRO* is an argument which receives a θ-role from the verb *leave*. Yet, *PRO* is in a non-Case-marked position, contrary to what is expected in the context of the Visibility Hypothesis. This problem is discussed in more detail in Chapter 9, where a possible solution to it is outlined and evaluated.

Another fact that the Visibility Hypothesis leaves unexplained relates to the expletive NPs *it* and *there*. The problem raised by these elements is the converse of the one raised by *PRO*. Expletive NPs usually occur in Case-marked positions, as shown in (19a&b), even though they are non-arguments, and therefore not assigned a θ-role:

19a. It seems that John is leaving soon.
19b. There is a unicorn in the garden.

It could be argued that the Case property of expletives is not necessarily incompatible with the Visibility Hypothesis. The latter implies the requirement that only NPs with Case can receive a θ-role. It does not necessarily follow from this requirement that all NPs which have Case will receive a θ-role. Recall that the θ-Criterion independently excludes assignment of θ-roles to non-arguments. Having said that, the fact that expletives invariably occur in Case-marked positions is significant and should be accounted for by an adequate theory of Case. A possible solution to the problem raised by expletive NPs will be discussed below. For the moment, note that a logical consequence of the Visibility Hypothesis is that propositional arguments, such as the embedded CP in (19a), are also expected to have Case.

We will not decide between the two approaches to Case here. We will use the expression **Case requirement** in a neutral way, leaving open the question whether it takes the form of a Case Filter or follows from the θ-Criterion by way of the Visibility Hypothesis.

8.2   *Government, Adjacency and Spec-head agreement*

We have been using the term 'objective' to refer to the Case assigned by transitive verbs and prepositions, and the term 'subjective' to the Case assigned by finite I. These are in fact cover terms for distinct individual Cases associated with each class of the categories mentioned. The (objective) Case assigned by transitive verbs is called **accusative** (Case). The (objective) Case assigned by prepositions is often called **oblique** (Case). Finally, the (subjective) Case assigned by finite I is called **nominative** (Case). In this section, we will discuss the structural conditions under which each of these Cases is assigned. The possessive Case assigned to subjects of NPs is discussed in a later section.

8.2.1   Government

Accusative Case and oblique Case are generally assigned by transitive verbs and prepositions, respectively, to their NP object. It could be concluded on this basis that, like internal θ-roles, these Cases are also assigned under the structural relationship of sisterhood. However, this conclusion would be inaccurate as far as (7) and (13) are concerned. In these examples, the NP subject is not a sister to the prepositional complementiser *for* which assigns it oblique Case. The relevant part of the structures is reproduced in (20):

20.

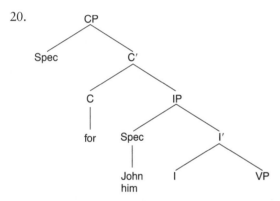

In view of this, what is needed is a structural relationship which includes sisterhood as well as the locality relationship of the type illustrated in (20). The structural relationship in question is called **government** and can, for the moment, be defined as in (21):

21. **Government**

α governs β iff:

i)   α is an X⁰ category
ii) α c-commands β.

The notion 'c-command', introduced in Chapter 7 for independent reasons, plays a crucial role in the definition of government. C-command defines the government domain of a head in much the same way that it defines the scope domain of quantifiers at LF. The definition of c-command is reproduced in (22):

22. **C-command**

α c-commands β iff:

i)   the first branching node dominating α also dominates β
ii) α does not dominate β.

Let us first see how government subsumes the relationship of sisterhood, using the diagrams in (23a) and (23b):

23a.   VP

23b.   PP

According to clause (i) of the definition of government (21), the class of **governors** is restricted to X^0 (i.e. head) categories. Thus, only V and P qualify as governors in (23a&b). In (23a), V governs NP because (i) V is a head category, and (ii) V c-commands NP. The same relationship exists between P and its NP complement in (23b). It should be clear that government indeed subsumes the relationship of sisterhood between heads and their complements. Heads assign Case to their NP complement under government.

Turning now to the configuration in (20), the prepositional complementiser *for* governs the NP in Spec,IP because (i) *for* is a head category, and (ii) *for* c-commands NP. The underlying generalisation here is that if a head governs a maximal projection, the head also governs the Spec position of that maximal projection. Because *for* governs IP in (20) it also governs the Spec position of IP. Thus, although *for* and the NP subject of the non-finite clause are not sisters, a government relationship exists between them which allows *for* to assign Case to the NP subject of the non-finite clause. Below, we will see other situations where a head category governs and assigns Case to an NP which is not its own object/sister. These considerations further highlight the need for the structural condition which subsumes sisterhood but extends beyond it to include other locality relationships. Government is precisely one such condition.

Although the definition of government in (21) accounts for the examples discussed so far, it is not sufficiently restrictive. For example, in a configuration such as (24), it allows the verb to govern and potentially assign Case to the NP complement of the preposition:

24.

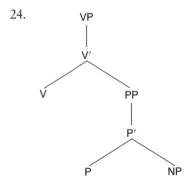

Since NP objects of prepositions receive their oblique Case from the preposition itself, the verb in (24) should be prevented from governing the NP complement of the preposition and potentially assigning it accusative Case. Thus, the definition of government should be made more restrictive, basically by incorporating into it a condition which would prevent a distant governor from governing a category which has a 'closer' governor. With respect to (24), V should be prevented from governing the NP complement of P on the grounds that NP has a closer governor, namely P.

The condition in question is known as **Minimality** and can be defined as in (25):

25. **Minimality (Condition)**

In the configuration [XP . . . X . . . [YP . . . Y . . . ZP] . . .] X does not govern ZP.

The configuration in (25) corresponds to the one in (24), where XP = VP, X = V, YP = PP, Y = P and ZP = NP. Minimality prevents the verb from governing the NP complement of the preposition in this configuration. Put more simply, Minimality prevents a head from governing into the (government) domain of another head category. There are various ways of incorporating the Minimality Condition into the definition of government, (26) being one of them:

26. **Government**

α governs β iff:

i)   α is an X^0 category
ii) α c-commands β
iii) Minimality is respected.

8.2.2 Adjacency

Government is the core condition which regulates Case assignment in general. It has been suggested that individual languages may choose to add another condition to the core condition of government on Case-assignment. For example, it has been suggested that English makes use of the condition of **adjacency**, in addition to government, in regulating Case-assignment. This means that a head category has to both govern and be adjacent to an NP to be able to assign it Case in English.

Consider sentences of the type illustrated in (27) and (28), discussed in Chapter 5 in relation to I-lowering (Affix-hopping). The sentences illustrate the general property of English that a VP adverb cannot intervene between the verb and its NP object:

27a. *John makes frequently mistakes.
27b. *[IP John [I′ [V make]i I [VP frequently [VP ti mistakes]]]]

28a. John frequently makes mistakes.
28b. [IP John [I′ ti [VP frequently [VP [V [V make][I]i] mistakes]]]]

Sentences such as (27) and (28) were cited in Chapter 5 as evidence that main verbs do not raise to I (leftward across the adverb) in English. Rather, I lowers to the main verb inside VP as in (28). (27) is derived by V-raising to I, which is illicit since the definition of the transformation which performs this operation includes the condition that it only applies to auxiliary verbs. Suppose now we ask why this transformation excludes main verbs in English. A plausible answer is that if a main verb is moved away from its NP object it will no longer be adjacent to the NP object and will therefore be unable to assign it Case.

This explanation gains credibility when (27) and (28) are compared to (29a&b):

29a. John knocked repeatedly on the door.
29b. John repeatedly knocked on the door.

In (29a&b), the complement of the verb is PP, i.e. a category that is not subject to the Case Requirement. In this context, a VP-adverb can appear intervening between the verb and its PP complement, as shown in (29a). The fact that a VP-adverb can intervene between the verb and a PP complement but not between a verb and an NP complement lends support to the Adjacency Condition on Case-assignment in English. The verb is required to be adjacent to its complement only in situations where the complement receives Case from the verb.

Note that (29a) seems to suggest that main verbs can move out of VP in English, after all. (29b) is consistent with the generalisation assumed up to this point that main verbs do not move out of VP in English. We will not pursue this issue here.

The Adjacency Condition on Case-assignment has also been credited with the advantage of determining the order of complements inside VP in situations where a verb selects more than one complement. Recall that the existence of apparent paraphrases such as (30a) and (30b) suggests that any of the two internal arguments of the verb can occupy any of the two positions made available by the VP-shell structure. However, when the goal argument is a PP, it is excluded from the position adjacent to the verb, as shown in (30c):

30a. Mary gave the book to John.
30b. Mary gave John the book.
30c. *Mary gave to John the book

(30a) has the representation shown in (31b):

31a. Mary gave the book to John.
31b. [$_{IP}$ Mary I [$_{vP}$ [$_{V}$ GAVE]$_i$ v [$_{VP}$ [$_{NP}$ the book] [$_{v'}$ t$_i$ [$_{PP}$ to John]]]]]

The NP object receives accusative Case from the complex verb [$_{v}$ [V] [v]] under government. The context involved is basically the same as the context which involves a prepositional complementiser and an NP subject, discussed earlier. Recall that if a head governs a maximal projection it also governs the Spec of that maximal projection. The PP complement is not subject to the Case Requirement, and hence the fact that the verb can move away from it.

(30c), on the other hand, has the structure shown in (32c). The NP object is not adjacent to the complex verb and therefore fails to be assigned Case. This leads to a violation of the Case Requirement, and hence the fact that (32a) is excluded:

32a. *Mary gave to John the book

32b. [IP Mary I [vP [V GAVE]i v [VP [PP to John] [v' ti [NP the book]]]]]

The Dative Shift pattern in (30b), which includes two NPs following the verb, appears to create a problem for the adjacency requirement on Case-assignment. However, this would be so only if the second NP is assumed to receive its Case from the verb. We will come back to this point in more detail later on this chapter.

8.2.3 Spec-head agreement

We have seen that nominative Case is assigned by finite I. A close look at the configuration involving an NP in Spec,IP and a finite I shown in (33) reveals that the definition of government needs to be revised to accommodate nominative Case-assignment:

33.

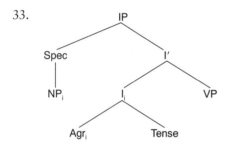

In (33), I does not c-command Spec,IP due to the intervening I' projection which is a branching node. Therefore, I does not govern the NP in Spec,IP and consequently should not be able to assign it (nominative) Case. If we maintain that all Cases are assigned under government, our task will be to revise the definition of government to accommodate the configuration in (33). If, on the other hand, we find reasons to believe that the assignment of nominative Case takes place under a different condition, we can maintain the definition of government as it is.

Let us start with the first view, that which maintains that all Cases are assigned under government. As pointed out above, this view requires a revision of the definition of government to accommodate configuration (33). A possible way of doing this is by revising the definition of c-command used in the definition of government. The definition of c-command adopted so far is one where a branching node such as I' in (33) can block c-command. According to this definition, I does not c-command NP in (33) because the first branching node which dominates I, namely I', does not dominate NP. Suppose now we assume that only a maximal projection can block c-command. Single-bar projections such as I' are invisible to this relation. Then I' will not count in calculating the c-command domain of I in (33). The first maximal projection which dominates I is IP which also dominates the NP subject. Therefore, I c-commands the NP subject. I therefore governs the NP subject and consequently assigns it nominative Case.

The definition of c-command which makes reference to maximal projection (instead of branching node) is sometimes called **m-command** and can be defined as in (34). (35) is the new definition of government which makes reference to m-command (instead of c-command):

34. **M-command**

   α m-commands β iff:

   i)   α does not dominate β and β does not dominate α
   ii) The first *maximal projection* dominating α also dominates β.

35. **Government**

   α governs β iff:

   i)   α is an X^0 category
   ii)   α m-commands β
   iii) Minimality is respected.

Recall that the original definition c-command was motivated by the need to account for the scope of raised quantifiers (Chapter 7). When the need arises to revise an existing definition which was originally motivated by a separate set of facts one has to make sure that the new version of the definition accounts for those facts as well as the new set of facts which have motivated its revision. You can check for yourself whether the new definition m-command compromises the account for quantifier scope in Chapter 7.

Let us now turn to the second view, that which maintains that nominative Case is assigned under a different condition, i.e. a condition other than government. What could this condition be? While the postulation of a new condition is inevitable sometimes, there are times when an existing condition would do. This is one of those situations. In Chapter 6 we concluded that the subject of a finite clause enters into a special relationship with (the Agr member of) I called Spec-head agreement. The principle which regulates this relationship is reproduced in (36). The facts of Standard English which necessitated it are summarised in (37a&b):

36. **Spec-Head Agreement**

   A head (X) and its specifier (Spec,XP) must agree in relevant features.

37a. I/you/we/they   like/*likes   them
37b. He/she   likes/*like   them.

(36) applies to all contexts involving a specifier, including wh-questions. The relevant features differ from one context to another and are largely determined by the features of the head. In finite clauses, the relevant features are the ones called φ-features in Chapter 6 (person, number and gender). We saw above that English pronouns also show an overt Case distinction which opposes the nominative forms, the objective forms and the possessive forms. In view of this, it is plausible to conclude that this distinction merely reflects a distinction in the Case feature of the pronoun in much the same way that the distinction between *I*, *you* and *he/she* reflects a distinction in the person feature, the distinction between *I* and *we* reflects

a distinction in the number feature and the distinction between *he* and *she* reflects a distinction in the gender feature. In other words, it is plausible to conclude that the set of φ-features includes a Case feature in addition to the person, number and gender features. The Case relationship between a finite I and an NP subject is therefore basically an agreement relationship. According to this scenario, nominative Case is assigned to the subject via Spec-head agreement, a structural relationship which is distinct from government.

The term 'assign' technically does not apply in situations of Spec-head agreement. The subject already has a Case feature of its own and the requirement is simply to make sure that the Case feature of the subject matches that of (the Agr member of) I. **Feature-matching** would be the more appropriate term to use in this situation. However, we will continue to use the term 'assign' for purely expository purposes.

In the rest of this book, we will assume the hypothesis that nominative Case is assigned via Spec-head agreement with finite I. This view makes is it unnecessary to replace the notion 'c-command' with the notion 'm-command' in the definition of government required for the purpose of Case-assignment.

8.3 *Objective Case*

8.3.1 Objective Case and transitivity

Traditionally, an intimate link is assumed to exist between the ability to assign objective Case and transitivity, such that transitive categories are the categories which assign objective Case. Prepositions usually take an NP object to which they assign oblique Case, so that prepositions are generally transitive in nature. As for verbs, there does not seem to be a strict correlation between the property of selecting an obligatory NP argument and the ability to assign accusative Case. A given verb may select an obligatory NP argument and not assign it Case. Examples of such verbs are *rely*, illustrated in (38), and *approve* in its use illustrated in (39):

38a. The boy relies on the girl.
38b. *The boy relies.

39a. Bill does not approve of John's behaviour.
39b. *Bill does not approve.

40a. John kicked the ball.
40b. *John kicked.

The function of the prepositions *on* and *of* in (38a) and (39a) is to assign Case to the NP argument selected by the verb. Unlike *rely* and *approve*, the verb *kick* in (40a) is transitive, and therefore does not need to rely on a preposition to assign Case to its internal NP argument. There is a parallelism between verbs such as *rely* and *approve*, on the one hand, and (derived) nouns and adjectives, on the other. Generally, nouns and adjectives cannot c-select an NP complement. Their internal argument cannot be realised as a bare NP. When the internal argument of a noun or an adjective is an NP, it is invariably preceded by a preposition, as shown in (41) and (42). To the extent that transitivity and the ability to assign objective Case are one and the same thing, it appears that nouns and adjectives are not transitive:

41a. The destruction *(of) the city
41b. The translation *(of) the book

42a. Mary is proud *(of) her achievements.
42b. Bill is keen *(on) soccer.

With respect to derived nouns such as *destruction* and *translation*, this is presumably the result of the lexical process which derives them from related transitive verbs. We saw in Chapter 7 that the lexical process which derives nouns from verbs affects the argument structure of the base verb. For example, the structural realisation of the otherwise obligatory (internal) argument of the base verb (e.g. *The army destroyed *(the city)* and *John translated *(the book))*) is optional with derived nouns. It seems that the lexical process which derives nouns from verbs also affects the Case properties of transitive base verbs such that an intransitive noun is derived from a transitive verb. It is possible that there is a link between the loss of the ability to assign objective Case and the optionality of internal arguments such that one follows from the other. However, we will not try to establish such a link here.

The correlation between transitivity and the ability to assign objective Case goes to some extent to solving certain problems raised by the attempt to reduce c-selection to s-selection discussed in Chapter 7. The idea underlying this attempt is that to each semantic category there corresponds a syntactic category which represents its Canonical Structural Realisation (CSR). A potential problem with this attempt is that two lexical items which s-select the same semantic category may c-select different syntactic categories. For example, the verbs *hear* and *listen* both s-select a theme argument. However, while *hear* can c-select an NP (*I heard him*), *listen* cannot (*I listened *(to) him*). Likewise, while the verbs *ask*, *wonder*, and *care* all s-select a proposition, only *ask* c-selects an NP, as shown in (43a&b), (44a&b) and (45a&b):

43a. Bill asked what time it was.
43b. Bill asked (about) the time.

44a. Bill wondered what time it was.
44b. Bill wondered *(about) the time.

45a. Bill didn't care what time it was.
45b. Bill didn't care *(about) the time.

Whether a given verb c-selects an NP or another category arguably follows from whether the verb is transitive, and therefore a Case-assigner, or intransitive, and therefore a non-Case assigner. The selectional properties of 'similar' verbs are basically the same, but differences in their Case properties may result in their internal argument being realised as an NP or an NP preceded by a preposition. Because *hear* and *ask* assign objective Case, their internal argument can be realised as a bare NP. On the other hand, because *listen, wonder* and *care* do not assign objective Case, their internal argument cannot be realised as a bare NP.

8.3.2   Exceptional Case Marking (ECM)

Two instances of objective Case-assignment have been discussed so far. One instance involves contexts where a transitive category assigns Case to an NP which is its (internal) argument. The other instance involves contexts where a transitive category assigns Case to an NP which is not its argument. The latter is found in examples where the subject of a non-finite clause is assigned objective Case by an external governor. In (46), reproduced from above, the subject of the non-finite clause is assigned objective Case by the prepositional complementiser *for*:

46a. For him to leave suddenly . . .
46b. [CP for [IP him [I' to [VP leave suddenly]]]]

The NP subject in (46) is thematically related to the predicate of the embedded clause, and does not bear any thematic relation to the category which assigns it Case. Case-assignment in contexts which do not involve a thematic relationship between the assigner and the assignee is known as **Exceptional Case Marking (ECM)**. The subject in (46) is called an ECM subject.

Although (46) is technically an instance of ECM, the term is more often associated with sentences such as (47) and (48):

47a. Bill believes John to be intelligent.
47b. Bill believes [John to be intelligent]

48a. Bill believes him/(*he) to be intelligent.
48b. Bill (sincerely) believes (*sincerely) him to be intelligent.
48c. He is believed to be intelligent.

We concluded in Chapter 7 that the analysis of (47a) consistent with the θ-Criterion is the one outlined in (47b), where the embedded subject remains in its DS position (i.e. does not move to a selected object position in the matrix clause). At the same time, it was pointed out that this analysis is apparently inconsistent with the fact that the embedded subject displays properties usually associated with direct objects rather than with subjects. (48a) shows that, when pronominal, the embedded subject appears in the objective Case form rather than the subjective Case form. (48b) shows that a VP-adverb cannot intervene between the root verb and the embedded subject, as is usually the case between verbs and their direct object in English. Finally, (48c) shows that the embedded subject can move to the subject position of the root clause when the verb of the root clause is in the passive form, a typical property of direct objects. All three properties indicate that the embedded subject is somehow also the object of the root verb.

The inconsistency disappears once we assume that the embedded subject, though thematically related to the predicate of the embedded clause, is assigned objective Case by the verb *believe* of the root clause, an instance of ECM. Because the ECM subject bears a Case relationship to the root verb which is identical to the Case relationship between verbs and their direct object, it is not surprising that the ECM subject behaves as if it were the direct object of the root verb. In other words, the ECM subject is a hybrid grammatical construct. It is a subject with respect to X-bar theory (it occupies Spec,IP) and θ-theory (it receives the external θ-role of the embedded verb), and an object with respect to Government theory (it is governed by the root verb) and Case theory (it is assigned Case by the root verb). In a modular system of the type discussed here, this situation is arguably expected.

The same situation is found in examples where the embedded clause is a small clause, such as (49) and (50):

49a. Bill considers John intelligent.
49b. Bill considers [$_{AP}$ John [$_{A'}$ intelligent]]

50a. Bill considers him/*he intelligent.
50b. Bill (sincerely) considers (*sincerely) him/John intelligent.

The relationship between the subject of the small clause and the root verb also exhibits the properties of verb–direct object relationships. As in the previous situation, this is due to the fact that the subject of the small clause is assigned objective Case by the root verb, even though it is thematically related to the predicate of the small clause and occupies the subject (Spec) position of the small clause.

Verbs that assign accusative Case to an NP that is not their internal argument are called **ECM verbs**. The transitive nature of these verbs is shown independently by the fact that they can take a bare NP object, as shown in (51), in addition to their ability to take a (small) clausal complement. The noun phrase (52a) shows that the (derived) nominal counterparts of ECM verbs cannot occur in an ECM context. This is to be expected in view of the conclusion that nouns do not assign (objective) Case:

51a. Bill believed it/him.
51b. Bill considered the offer seriously.
51c. Bill was expecting it/him.

52a. *Bill's belief John to be intelligent
52b. Bill's belief that John is intelligent

Recall from earlier that objective Case is assigned under the structural condition of government. Thus, in all ECM contexts discussed we expect the Case-assigner to govern the NP it Case-marks. With respect to (46), we have already seen that the prepositional complementiser governs the NP subject of the non-finite IP, part of a general pattern whereby if a head governs a maximal projection it also governs the Spec of that maximal projection. The context which involves a small clause is also part of this pattern, as shown in (53), where XP is the small clause:

53.   . . . [$_{VP}$ V [$_{XP}$ [NP] [$_{X'}$ X]]]

The context which involves a non-small clause complement needs clarification. Non-small clauses are canonically realised as CP. This fact implies the structure in (54b) where the ECM subject is separated from the ECM verb by both CP and IP:

54a. Bill believes John to be intelligent.
54b. Bill believes [$_{CP}$ [$_{C'}$ e [$_{IP}$ John to be intelligent]]]

The issue we need to address with respect to (54) is whether a head category should be allowed to govern across two maximal projections. Note that if C qualifies as a governor for the subject in (54), it will prevent the ECM verb from governing Spec,IP by Minimality: C is a closer governor of Spec,IP than the root verb. Consequently, the root verb would fail to assign Case to the ECM subject in Spec,IP. On a more general note, it is undesirable to allow a head category to govern across two maximal projections simply because this step would undermine the idea that government is essentially a locality relation. The root verb in (54) is simply 'too far away' from the ECM subject to govern it. Assuming this to be the case, (54b) is unlikely to be the structure underlying the ECM sentences (54a).

As a first step towards determining the structure of ECM sentences such as (54a), consider example (55):

55a. *Bill believes that John/him/he to be intelligent.
55b. *Bill believes [$_{CP}$ [$_{C'}$ that [$_{IP}$ John/him/he to be intelligent]]]

(55) illustrates the fact that the complementiser *that* is excluded from ECM contexts. Assuming that (55) is excluded on the ground that the NP subject of the embedded clause fails to be assigned Case, the following conclusion can be drawn: the presence of CP, implied by the complementiser *that* in (55), prevents the root verb from governing, and therefore assigning Case to, the subject of the embedded clause. It follows from this reasoning that the ECM sentence (54a), where the verb assigns accusative Case to the subject of the embedded clause, lacks CP. Accordingly, (54a) has the structure shown in (56b):

56a. Bill believes John to be intelligent.
56b. Bill believes [$_{IP}$ John to be intelligent].

In this configuration, the root verb governs the subject in the embedded Spec,IP for the same reason that the root verb governs the subject of the small clause in (49). As a matter of fact, the structure in (56b) is identical to the one in (53), where XP = IP.

ECM verbs such as *believe* are said to trigger **CP-deletion/reduction** as a lexical property. Alternatively, ECM verbs can be said to c-select either IP or CP (*I believe that John is intelligent*), depending on whether the selected clause includes a subject which is dependent on an external governor for Case. In a framework where c-selection reduces to s-selection, this will amount to saying that propositional arguments can be canonically realised as either as CP or IP, with the choice dependent on the context.

8.3.3 Dative Shift

It was pointed out earlier that Dative Shift constructions such as (57) present a problem for the adjacency requirement on Case-assignment in English on the assumption that the second (non-adjacent) NP receives its Case from the verb:

57a. Mary gave John a book.
57b. Mary I [$_{\nu}$P [$_V$ GAVE]$_i$ ν [VP [NP John] [$_{\nu'}$ t$_i$ [NP a book]]]]

The question we need to resolve is whether verbs which select two arguments assign two accusative Cases. If we maintain that the Case properties of lexical categories somehow reflect their argument structures, so that a given verb which selects two NP arguments can assign two Cases, it is possible that the two NPs in (57) are assigned one Case each by the verb. If, on the other hand, we maintain that lexical categories can only assign one Case, we need to work out the source of the Case assigned to the second NP in (57), its nature, and the condition under which it is assigned.

Starting with the first hypothesis, if the two NPs in (57) both receive their Case from the verb, we should expect both of them to behave like direct objects of the verb. For example, we should expect both NPs to be able to passivise, that is to move to the subject position of the sentence when the verb is in the passive form. It turns out, however, that only the first NP can passivise in Standard English, as shown in (58a&b):

58a. John was given a book.
58b. *A book was given John.

(58a&b) seems to suggest that the second non-adjacent NP does not have the property of a direct object, meaning it does not receive Case from the verb. However, there have been attempts in the literature to attribute verbs such as *give* in Standard English the ability to assign two Cases, although a distinction is drawn between the two Cases. For example, Chomsky (1981) suggests that these verbs have, as a lexical property, the ability to assign a 'secondary' Case to the second (non-adjacent) NP, in addition to the 'primary' Case assigned to the first (adjacent) NP. The difference in syntactic behaviour between the two NPs illustrated in (58a&b) follows from the distinction made between 'primary' and 'secondary' Case. Only object NPs with 'primary' Case qualify as true direct objects of the verb. According to this analysis, the ability to assign 'secondary' Case is lexically determined, so that verbs which select two internal arguments can be expected to differ as to whether they assign a 'secondary' Case. The advantage of this analysis is that it can account for the fact, pointed out in Chapter 7, that the verbs *donate* and *transmit* do not tolerate the Dative Shift pattern (*Mary donated the charity money* and *John transmitted Bill a message*) simply by assuming that these verbs lack the property of assigning a 'secondary' Case. On the other hand, to the extent that Case-assignment in English operates under adjacency, the analysis would either have to assume that the adjacency requirement holds only of 'primary' case or that it is somehow waved in Dative Shift constructions.

The second hypothesis, namely that the verb assigns only one Case, has also been suggested in the literature. Unfortunately, we cannot get into the details of the analyses based on this hypothesis here.

8.4   *Genitive Case and DP Hypothesis*

8.4.1   DP Hypothesis

The subject of NP's was said earlier to be assigned possessive Case. The technical term used to refer to this type of Case is **genitive**. (59–61) are examples of NPs with a subject in the genitive Case form:

59a. His/John's house
59b. [NP his/John's [N′ house]]

60a. Her/Mary's translation of the book
60b. [NP her/Mary's [N′ translation [of the book]]]

61a. Its/the city's destruction by the barbarians
61b. [NP its/the city's [N′ destruction [by the barbarians]]]

A genitive subject can have one of a number of possible θ-roles/readings. In (59), it is a possessor, in (60) an agent, and in (61) a theme. The genitive form of pronouns represents overt marking of the genitive Case assigned to the subject of NPs. Non-pronominal subjects are marked with 's, the nature of which has been subject to debate. It is possible to view 's as the overt realisation of the genitive Case assigned to the subject of NPs. If this idea is plausible, it turns out that Case is less abstract in English than we previously thought.

The questions we will concern ourselves with in this section are the following: First, What is the source of genitive Case in noun phrases? Secondly, Under which condition is genitive Case assigned? The NPs in (59a–61a) have the structures shown in (59b–61b). (62) is an abstract version of the structure of NP we have been assuming so far:

62.

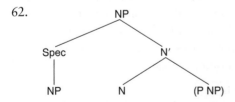

We concluded above that nouns do not assign Case on the grounds that their internal NP argument invariably appears preceded by a preposition. In view of this, the NP subject in (62) cannot be said to receive its genitive Case from N. Even if N did have the ability to assign Case, it would be rather bizarre that the Case of the head N is assigned to the subject rather than to the complement. Recall that it is generally the case that heads have a closer relationship with their complement than with the subject. This asymmetry between the complement and the subject is structurally reflected in (62) by the fact the complement is a sister to N whereas the subject is not.

It seems that there is no apparent source for the genitive Case assigned to the subject of noun phrases, and yet there must be one. As a first step towards resolving this paradox, we will discuss certain properties of noun phrases which indicate that they have a structure which is more complex than the one shown in (62). The revised structure suggested by these properties will reveal a clear source for the genitive Case assigned to the subject of noun phrases.

There are a number of respects in which noun phrases seem to resemble full clauses, suggesting that they have a structure which parallels that of a full clause. Initially, this can be seen simply by comparing the noun phrase in (63a) with its clausal counterpart in (63b):

63a. Mary's translation of the book
63b. Mary translated the book.

Like the clause (63b), the noun phrase (63a) has a propositional content. It includes a lexical category, a complement and a subject. It differs only in that its lexical category is a noun rather than a verb, and that the complement is preceded by a preposition. The second property follows from the first, on the assumption that nouns do not assign Case, unlike verbs. (63a) also differs from (63b), this time crucially, in that it lacks a Tense category. It is the ability of clauses to have Tense which enables them to function as complete sentences, assuming that a complete sentence is a proposition which is anchored in time in terms of Tense. The fact that noun phrases do not have Tense can be considered the reason they cannot function as complete sentences even though they may have a propositional content. Crucial though this difference is between noun phrases and clauses, it does not necessarily bear on the structural parallelism between them.

The similarities between noun phrases and clauses go much further than what has been mentioned. In Chapter 7 we discussed a construction called nominal passive where the internal argument of the noun appears in the subject position of the noun phrase and the external argument inside a *by*-phrase to the right of the noun. (61) is an example of such constructions, reproduced in (64) together with a corresponding verbal passive sentence. Although it was pointed out in Chapter 7 that nominal passives are arguably derived differently from verbal passives, the superficial similarities between the two constructions is suggestive of fundamental structural similarities between clauses and noun phrases:

64a. The city's destruction (by the barbarians)
64b. The city was destroyed (by the barbarians).

Yet another major similarity between clauses and noun phrases will emerge in Chapter 9 on Binding theory.

A plausible way of capturing the observed similarities between noun phrases and clauses is by assigning noun phrases a structure which parallels that of clauses. The intended structure is shown in (65a), where **D** is short for Det(erminer). (65b) is the structure of the clause (IP) provided for comparison:

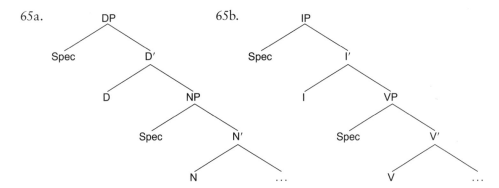

(65a) incorporates the claim that D is the head of the noun phrase rather than its specifier. D is the equivalent of I in IP. Like I, D is a non-lexical category which takes (the maximal projection of) a lexical category as its complement. The complement of D is NP. The subject position of the noun phrase is Spec,DP in much the same way that the subject position of IP is Spec,IP. The claim that noun phrases have the structure in (65a) is known as the **DP Hypothesis**. According to this hypothesis, noun phrases are actually DPs that include an NP in their structure. Although it is technically inaccurate to refer to (65a) as a 'noun phrase', the expression is still often used. We will continue to use the expression here as well, except that it will be written in lowercase letters: DP is a 'noun phrase', but NP is not a 'noun phrase'.

As pointed out, (65a) is basically a hypothesis. Whether it is correct or not depends on whether the structure it postulates solves the problems raised by the previous structure and accounts for the properties of noun phrases discussed so far, and possibly others. Our next task is therefore to check it out.

It was observed above that noun phrases differ from clauses in that they do not include the Tense category. However, there are reasons to believe that noun phrases include the category Agr under D which parallels the Agr category of I in IPs. There are languages where N carries overt agreement inflection which parallels the agreement inflection of V in sentences. In these languages, the Agr inflection of N is in agreement with the features of the subject, presumably an instance of Spec-head agreement. English, as we have seen, does not have rich agreement inflection. However, a residue of agreement in number between N and the subject arguably can still be seen in demonstrative noun phrases such as (66a&b). Presumably, Agr includes the other members of the set of ϕ-features, except that they do not have phonetic realisation in English:

66a. This/that book
66b. These/those books

According to this preliminary conclusion, (66a&b) have the structure shown in (67) where Dem(onstrative) is located in Spec,DP (the subject position) and is in Spec-head agreement with the Agr category of D. The internal structure of Dem is not crucially relevant to the point of the discussion. The question how Agr, realised as the plural number morpheme, ends up on N is discussed later on in this chapter:

67.

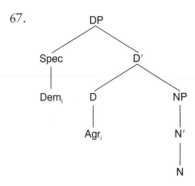

It is not difficult to see how (67) provides a solution to the problem identified above relating to the source of genitive Case and how it is assigned to the subject. Among the two theories entertained concerning subjective/nominative Case was one which claims that it is assigned via Spec-head agreement with the (Agr element of) I. The claim extends to the subjective/genitive Case of noun phrases. Genitive Case too is assigned via Spec-head agreement with the (Agr element of) D. The Agr of D and the Agr of I differ in that the Agr of D carries the genitive Case feature, while the Agr of I carries the nominative Case feature. Otherwise, they are similar in that they both carry a Case feature among other φ-features. Accordingly, a noun phrase such as (68a) has the structure shown in (68b) with the subject *Mary* in Spec,DP, and receives genitive Case via Spec-head Agreement with D. We will continue to assume that the morpheme *'s* is the spellout of the genitive Case:

68a. Mary's translation of the book
68b.

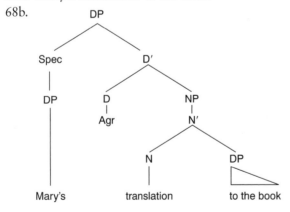

The similarities between the D of noun phrases and the I of IPs arguably run even deeper. In Chapter 6 we saw that I includes Agr (and Tense) in finite clauses but not in non-finite clauses. In the latter, I is spelled out as the infinitival marker *to*. The infinitival marker and Agr (and Tense) are therefore in complementary distribution. The subject of finite clauses is Case-marked internally (i.e. from inside the finite clause) via Spec-head agreement with I. This is not the case in non-finite clauses. When a non-finite clause has an overt subject, the subject can only be Case-marked by an external governor (ECM). Because non-finite clauses do not include Agr under I, they do not have an internal source of Case for the subject. This information is summarised and illustrated in (69a&b):

69a. Bill believes that John/he is incompetent.
69b. Bill believes John/him to be incompetent.

There is a fairly similar situation in noun phrases. Consider the familiar example in (70) which illustrates the familiar fact that an overt subject and a Det cannot co-occur in the pre-N domain:

70a. *Mary's the translation of the book
70b. *[$_{DP}$ Mary [$_{D'}$ the [$_{NP}$ translation of the book]]]

71. $DP \rightarrow \begin{Bmatrix} Det \\ DP \end{Bmatrix} D'$

Previously, this co-occurrence restriction was accounted for in terms of the (PS) rule shown in (71). Such rules are not available in the current system, and therefore an alternative account should be sought. Such an account is available on the assumption that Agr and Det, both members of D, are in complementary distribution. The presence of Det signals the absence of Agr. Accordingly, (70) lacks Agr under D, with the consequence that the subject does not have a source of Case, and hence the fact that (70) is excluded.

Thus, the idea that D includes Agr in some noun phrases but not in others not only enhances the parallelism with I, but also enables us to provide a natural explanation for why noun phrases such as (70) are excluded.

8.4.2 Gerundive noun phrases

(72–74) include the gerundive form briefly discussed in Chapter 6:

72a. John's keeping a rottweiler frightens his neighbours.
72b. [John's keeping a rottweiler] frightens his neighbours

73a. Bill resents John's keeping a rottweiler.
73b. Bill resents [John's keeping a rottweiler]

74a. Mary is against John's keeping a rottweiler.
74b. Mary is against [John's keeping a rottweiler]

Phrases which include a gerund fall into more than one type depending on a number of distinctive properties. The type of gerundive phrases we will concentrate on here have the following two crucial properties: their subject is in the genitive form, and the complement of the gerund is not preceded by a preposition. Both properties are illustrated in (72–74).

The gerundive phrases in (72–74) have certain properties usually associated with noun phrases. For example, they occur in positions typically reserved for noun phrases, such as the subject position of the sentence (72), the object position of transitive verbs (73), and the object position of prepositions (74). Moreover, the subject of these gerundive phrases bears genitive Case, which is a typical property of subjects of noun phrases, as should be clear by now. At the same time, these same phrases have other properties which are not typical of noun phrases. For example, the DP complement of the gerund in (72–74) is not preceded by a preposition, and therefore is different from complements of Ns which tend to be preceded by a preposition. This was attributed earlier to the fact that nouns do not assign Case. The form of the DP complement suggests that the gerund is a verb rather than a noun.

The gerundive phrases in question therefore have the properties of noun phrases, and at the same time appear to include a V(P) inside them. These mixed properties raise a serious problem relating to their structure. Prior to the DP analysis, they were assigned the structure shown in (75):

75.

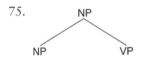

This structure accounts for the fact that they are basically noun phrases as well as for the fact that they include a V(P). The NP-daughter-of-NP is the position occupied by the genitive subject. However, (75) is clearly inconsistent with the principles of X-bar theory, and therefore excluded as a possible structure for gerundive noun phrases. The top node does not have a head. Moreover, (75) raises the same problem concerning the source of the genitive Case assigned to the subject. As a matter of fact, this problem arises in a more acute form in (75) since (75) does not include an N that could be claimed to be the source of the genitive Case of the subject.

In the context of the DP analysis the gerundive phrases in question can be assigned the structure shown in (76) which is consistent with both their apparently mixed properties as well as the principles of X-bar theory:

76.

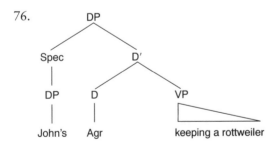

In (76) D takes VP as a complement which accounts for the internal verbal properties of the gerundive noun phrases in question. The subject is located in Spec,DP and is assigned genitive Case via Spec-head agreement with D. The complement of V is included inside VP and receives accusative Case under government by V.

It is an interesting question whether the *-ing* suffix of the gerundive form of the verb originates together with the verb or under D and subsequently attached to the verb. We will come back to this issue later on.

8.4.3 Pronouns as D elements

The term 'pronoun' suggests that pronouns are pro-forms for nouns. Strictly speaking, though, pronouns are pro-forms for noun phrases as they can stand for a whole noun phrase. The structural representation assigned to pronouns in the context of the NP-analysis is shown in (77). This representation is hopelessly confused, owing much to theoretical necessity and very little to empirical consider-ations. Because pronouns are noun phrases, their maximal projection must be NP. Since every maximal projection must have a head, there is no choice but to place the pronoun under N:

77.

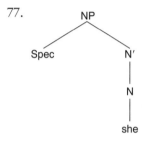

Our earlier discussion of pronouns suggests that they are best associated with the Agr category of D rather than with N, at least in English. Recall that pronouns show number, gender, person and Case distinctions. These are exactly the features associated with the Agr element of D. In other words, pronouns are no more than the spellout (i.e. phonetic realisation) of the bundle of features associated with (the Agr member of) D. Accordingly, a pronoun such as *she* has the representation shown in (78) which does not include a complement for D:

78.

There is some fairly robust evidence for the conclusion that pronouns are located under D. Some of the evidence has to do with noun phrases such as (79a&b). They consist of a pronoun and a noun with the pronoun having a Det-like function. These noun phrases have the structure shown in (79c), where the pronoun is located under D and is the spellout of Agr, and N is the head of the NP complement of D:

79a. we linguists
79b. you politicians
79c.

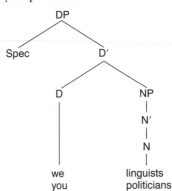

The claim that the pronoun is the head of the noun phrases in (79) is consistent with the fact that the pronoun displays the Case of the whole noun phrase. It is natural for the Case property of a noun phrase to be displayed by its head. When such noun phrases are in the subject position of a finite clause, as in (80), the pronoun has the nominative form. When they are in the object position, as in (81), the pronoun has the objective form. Finally, when they are in the subject position of an ECM clause, as in (82), the pronoun has the objective form:

80a. We politicians are disliked by most people.
80b. [IP [DP we politicians] I [VP are disliked by most people]]

81a. Most people dislike us politicians.
81b. [IP most people I [VP dislike [DP us politicians]]]

82a. Most people believe us politicians to be hypocritical.
82b. [IP most people I [VP believe [IP [DP us politicians] to be hypocritical]]]

The analysis outlined in (79c) makes the interesting prediction that the type of noun phrase in question is not expected to admit a Det in addition to the pronoun. Recall that Det is in complementary distribution with Agr. (83) and (84) show that the prediction is borne out. The examples are excluded with the intended reading, i.e. the reading where there is no intonational break between the pronoun and Det:

83a. we (*the) linguists
83b. [DP [D' we/*the [NP linguists]]]

84a. you (*the) politicians
84b. [DP [D' you/*the [NP politicians]]]

8.4.4 Head-movement in DPs

The parallelism we have drawn between noun phrases and clauses, in particular the idea that the D of noun phrases may include Agr, raises the interesting question of how Agr merges with N. It was suggested earlier that the plural number morpheme in noun phrases such as (85a) may originate under Agr/D and is subsequently merged with N. Singular nouns such as (85b) could be said to involve an abstract or a zero singular number morpheme with a bound property similar to that of the plural morpheme:

85a. the book
85b. the books

As with clauses, there are a priori two ways Agr could merge with N, either by Affix-hopping of Agr or N-movement to D. As with clauses too, the choice has to be determined on the basis of evidence. The evidence discussed in relation to clauses (Chapter 5) involved placement of VP-adverbs. The fact that VP-adverbs appear preceding main verbs in English was taken as evidence that I lowers to V inside VP. In Chapter 6 a parallelism was drawn between VP-adverbs in clauses, on the one hand, and adjectives in noun phrases, on the other. They both are modifiers adjoined to some projection of VP/NP. The parallelism is seen clearly in pairs such as (86) and (87). Just as VP-adverbs can appear before a main verb (86a), but not following it (86b), adjectives too can appear before the noun (87a), but not following it (87b):

86a. The army totally destroyed the city.
86b. *The army destroyed totally the city.

87a. The army's total destruction of the city
87b. *The army's destruction total of the city

(87a&b) do not include an overt number morpheme which would show overtly the nature of the movement involved. However, there are noun phrases with similar properties which include a plural number morpheme. (88a) is one example. (88b&c) also include a noun with plural morpheme following a modifying adjective:

88a. People's continuous donations to the fund
88b. Mary's fat/red books
88c. John's unfounded allegations

It seems that as in clauses, noun phrases involve a process of Affix-hopping (or D-lowering) in their derivation shown in (89):

89.

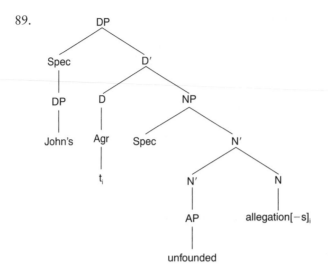

The fact that both clauses and noun phrases involve lowering of inflection to V/N instead of V/N-raising may be a pure accident, but it may also reflect some peculiar property of English such as the fact that it has poor inflection.

The analysis as presented so far, though attractive in many respects, is not without problems. We have been maintaining that Det and Agr are in complementary distribution. This idea proved useful in accounting for some significant properties of noun phrases. However, this idea appears to be inconsistent with the fact that Det can co-occur with a number morpheme on the noun, as shown in (90a–c):

90a. The continuous donations to the fund
90b. The fat/red books
90c. The unfounded allegations

It may be inaccurate to identify the number morpheme on nouns with Agr. If the number morpheme turns out to be independent of Agr, (90a–c) could be said not to involve Agr and therefore no D-lowering. On the other hand, it may be that Agr and D are not necessarily one and the same category, and that the impression that they are in complementary distribution reflects some selectional restrictions between two separate categories. We will leave these questions open here. An improved representation is discussed in Chapter 14 in the context of a comparison of English noun phrases with their counterparts in other languages.

8.5 *Case and Movement*

In this section we will discuss the ways in which Case theory interacts with movement transformations. We will start first with DP-movement (alias NP-movement), and then move on to Wh-movement and Quantifier Raising included under the general heading Op(erator)-movement.

8.5.1 DP-movement

8.5.1.1 Raising sentences Recall that raising sentences involve movement of a DP subject from an embedded non-finite clause to the subject position of the root (finite) clause. When the embedded clause is finite, DP-movement is prevented from taking place by TSC. Consequently, an expletive DP appears in the subject position of the root clause. This is shown in (91) and (92):

91a. John seems to be happy.
91b. $[_{IP} [_{DP} John_i]$ seems $[_{IP} t_i$ to be happy$]]$

92a. It seems (that) John is happy.
92b. $[_{IP} [_{DP} it]$ seems (that) $[_{IP} [_{DP} John]$ is happy$]]$

In Chapter 6 it was tentatively suggested that DP-movement in (91) is motivated by EPP, the principle which requires every clause to have a (formal) subject. Movement of the embedded subject to the subject position of the root clause enables the root clause to acquire a subject and thereby satisfy EPP. When DP-movement is prevented from taking place, as in (92), the expletive DP *it* is inserted in the subject position of the root clause for the purpose of ensuring that the root clause satisfies EPP. However, there are reasons which cast doubt on the possibility that DP-movement in (91) is motivated by EPP. Part of the reasoning underlying the EPP-based analysis is that EPP can be satisfied simply by inserting a formal, expletive DP in the subject position of the root clause, as in (92). It remains mysterious, though, why this process cannot apply to (91), thereby rendering movement of the embedded subject unnecessary. This alternative scenario is shown in (93):

93a. *It seems John to be happy.
93b. *$[_{IP} [_{DP} it]$ seems $[_{IP} [_{DP} John]$ to be happy$]]$

(93) is consistent with the EPP, and yet it is excluded. Somehow, it seems that DP-movement is obligatory in raising sentences whenever it is possible, that is whenever the embedded clause is non-tensed. A possible way of maintaining the EPP-based analysis is to argue that expletive-insertion is a last resort option, triggered only when a movement process is prevented from taking place by some principle of the grammar, much like *Do*-support (Chapter 5). When movement is possible, as is the case in (93), expletive-insertion is excluded, by last resort. In (92), expletive-insertion applies legitimately because DP-movement is prevented from taking place by TSC. Although this is not an implausible analysis, the standard view concerning the motivation behind DP-movement relies on Case rather than on EPP.

The reasoning underlying the Case-based scenario is as follows. When the embedded clause is non-finite, as in (91/93), its overt DP subject cannot receive Case (internally) via Spec-head agreement with (non-finite) I. To satisfy the Case Requirement, the DP subject moves to the subject position of the root finite clause where it receives nominative Case via Spec-head agreement with (finite) I.

(93) represents a situation where the embedded DP subject is located in a non-Case-marked position, and therefore excluded by the Case Requirement. In the context of this (Case-based) analysis, the fact that movement of the embedded DP subject results in the root clause acquiring a subject is simply a by-product of the need to circumvent the Case Requirement rather than the prime reason for the movement.

8.5.1.2 *Passives and unaccusatives*

Recall that passive sentences such as (94) involve movement of a DP object to the subject position. As in raising sentences, the DP in question cannot remain in its DS position even when the subject position is filled with a formal expletive subject. (95) is excluded in English:

94a. The ball was kicked.
94b. $[_{IP} [_{DP}$ the ball$_i]$ I $[_{VP}$ was $[_{VP}$ kicked $t_i]]]$

95a. *It was kicked the ball.
95b. *$[_{IP} [_{DP}$ it$]$ I $[_{VP}$ was $[_{VP}$ kicked $[_{DP}$ the ball$]]]]$

The parallelism with raising sentences suggests that DP-movement in passives is also motivated by Case considerations rather than by EPP. (95) appears to exclude the possibility that DP-movement in passives is motivated by EPP, unless, of course, one adopts the argument that expletive-insertion is a last resort strategy in the sense explained above. Evidence for the hypothesis that DP-movement in passives is motivated by Case can be gleaned from (extraposition?) examples such as (96a&b) where the complement of the passive verb is a clause rather than a DP:

96a. It was decided that John should resign.
96b. It was believed that John would resign.

Because the complement of the verb is not a DP, and therefore not subject to the Case Requirement, it does not move to Spec,IP. Consequently, the subject position is filled with an expletive DP for the purpose of satisfying EPP. (96a&b) suggest that movement of the complement of the passive verb to Spec,IP in passives is obligatory only when the complement is a DP. This observation confirms the Case-based analysis for DP-movement in passives: the DP object moves to Spec,IP to receive Case.

The idea that movement of the DP object in passives is motivated by Case implies inevitably that passive verbs cannot assign (accusative) Case. If the DP object could receive Case in its DS position, there would be no reason why it should move to the subject position. Later on we will discuss evidence that a DP cannot be assigned more than one Case, excluding the possibility that the DP in passives has two Cases. In view of the fact that the active counterpart of the verb *kick* in (94) assigns (accusative) Case, e.g. *John kicked the ball*, it appears that the inability of its passive counterpart to assign Case is due to the passive morpheme. In Chapter 7 we discussed evidence which showed that affixation of the passive morpheme to a an active base verb results in the derived (passive) verb being unable to assign its external θ-role to the subject position. Now we are led to conclude that affixation of the passive morpheme to a transitive base verb also results in the derived verbal passive being unable to assign accusative Case to its object. The passive morpheme is often said to 'absorb' the (accusative) Case of the passive verb, thereby forcing the DP object to move to the subject position in search for Case. The notion **Case-absorption** is a crucial element in the analysis of passives.

In addition to passives, Chapter 7 also discussed a class of verbs, called unaccusatives, which resemble passives in that their internal argument appears in the subject position. (97) includes one such verb. (97b) assumes the derivation of unaccusatives whereby the internal argument originates in the object position and is subsequently moved to the subject position by DP-movement. As with passives too, the internal argument of unaccusative verbs cannot surface in the object position as shown in (98):

97a. The vase broke.

97b. $[_{IP} [_{DP}$ the vase$_i] I [_{VP}$ broke $[_{DP} t_i]]]$

98a. *It broke the vase.

98b. *$[_{IP} [_{DP}$ it$] I [_{VP}$ broke $[_{DP}$ the vase$]]]$

If DP-movement is generally motivated by Case considerations, it follows that unaccusative verbs do not assign (accusative) Case to their object. As a matter of fact, this is the reason they are called 'unaccusative'. This is so despite the fact that, unlike passives, unaccusative verbs do not exhibit a morpheme which can be said to absorb the (accusative) Case. Besides their inability to assign (accusative) Case to their internal argument, passives and unaccusatives have in common the property that they do not assign an external θ-role either. This suggests the generalisation that verbs which do not assign an external θ-role to the subject position seem also to be unable to assign accusative Case to their internal argument (an vice versa). This generalisation was made in Burzio (1986) and came to be known as **Burzio's Generalisation**. (99) is a possible way of stating it:

99. **Burzio's Generalisation**

A verb (with an object) Case-marks its object iff it θ-marks its subject.

8.5.1.3 Subject-inside-VP Hypothesis So far, Spec,VP has not been attributed a role in the representation and derivation of sentences. This is a rather surprising gap which suggests that something has probably been overlooked. In this section, we will see that Spec,VP, far from remaining idle, plays a crucial role in the representation of subjects of sentences. The link between this issue and Case theory will become clear as we proceed.

Consider the pair in (100a&b) which include the **floating quantifier** *all* in different positions:

100a. All the travellers have drunk from the well.
100b. The travellers have all drunk from the well.

In both (100a) and (100b) the floating quantifier modifies (or quantifies over) the DP *the travellers*. However, only in (100a) is the quantifier adjacent to the DP it modifies. Assuming that modification relations are structurally based and imply adjacency (see Chapter 7), it follows that the quantifier in (100b) is somehow structurally related to the DP it modifies even though the two categories are separated by the auxiliary verb *have*. The situation we have here is no different from a number of other situations we have encountered so far where two related categories, e.g. a verb and its object in passives, appear separated from each other rather than adjacent. We have dealt with these situations by assuming that the two related categories are base-generated adjacent to each other, and that one of them is displaced by a movement process. The same reasoning can be applied to the quantifier in relation to the DP subject it modifies in (100b).

The question we need to answer is which of the two related categories is affected by movement, the quantifier or the DP it modifies. One possibility could be that the complex is base-generated in the position it occupies in (100a), namely Spec,IP. The derivation of (100b) will then involve lowering of the quantifier to a position intervening between the finite auxiliary, located under I (by V-raising), and the main verb. This process would be an instance of what is known as **Quantifier lowering**. Although this derivation both establishes a structural link between the quantifier and the DP it modifies and accounts for their order in (100a&b), there is an alternative analysis which implements one of the more familiar movement transformations, namely DP-movement. The alternative analysis is that the complex is base-generated in the position occupied by the quantifier in (100b) with the order in (100a) derived by DP-movement affecting *the travellers* and stranding the quantifier behind. According to this analysis, (100a) differs only in that the movement affects the whole of the complex instead of just *the travellers*. The derivations of (100a&b) implied by this analysis are roughly as outlined in (101) and (102), respectively. The complex which includes the quantifier and the DP subject is labelled Q(uantifier) P(hrase) purely for expository purposes. The movement process which affects the auxiliary is ignored:

101a. All the travellers have drunk from the well.
101b. [$_{IP}$ [$_{QP}$ all [$_{DP}$ the travellers]]$_i$ have [$_{VP}$ [$_{QP}$ t]$_i$ [$_{V'}$ drunk from the well]]]

102a. The travellers have all drunk from the well.
102b. [$_{IP}$ [$_{DP}$ the travellers]$_i$ have [$_{VP}$ [$_{QP}$ all t$_i$] [$_{V'}$ drunk from the well]]]

The position intervening between the auxiliary (under I) and the main verb (inside VP) where QP originates is likely to be Spec,VP. The latter is the only position in this environment made freely available by X-bar theory, short of adopting an adjunction structure. If the analyses outlined in (101b) and (102b) are the right analyses, (101a) and (102a) can be said to show that subjects are base-generated in Spec,VP and subsequently moved to Spec,IP. (102) is useful in that the position of the quantifier gives an indication as to the DS position of the subject in general. To the extent that this position is Spec,VP, it is the position occupied by subjects of sentences at DS in general. The reason DP subjects have to move to Spec,IP (from Spec,VP) can be related to Case theory if Spec,VP is assumed to be a non-Case-marked position. Spec,VP is outside the government domain of V if we adopt the definition whereby a branching node such as V' can block c-command. V therefore cannot assign Case to the subject in Spec,VP. Spe,VP is, however, within the government domain of I, but we have seen reasons to believe that I is only able to assign nominative Case via Spec-head agreement in English.

The idea that subjects of sentences originate in Spec,VP and move to Spec,IP is sometimes known as the **Subject-inside-VP Hypothesis**. According to this hypothesis, a simple sentence such as (103a) has the derivation shown in (103b). (104a&b) could be considered as evidence that movement of the subject to Spec,IP is motivated by Case rather than EPP-considerations:

103a. The boy kicked the ball.
103b. [$_{IP}$ [$_{DP}$ the boy]$_i$ I [$_{VP}$ t$_i$ [$_{V'}$ kicked the ball]]]

104a. *It/there have drunk all the travellers from the well.
104b. *It/there kicked the boy the ball.

The Subject-inside-VP Hypothesis arguably has other theoretical advantages. One could argue, for example, that the hypothesis makes possible a closer connection between the structural representation of lexical categories and their argument structure. By including all the arguments of lexical categories inside their X-bar projections (at DS), we are effectively implying that X-bar projections are basically the structural representations (domains) of lexical categories and their argument structure. Prior to the Subject-inside-VP Hypothesis, it was not possible to make this close connection between X-bar structures and argument structures as the subject was assumed to be base-generated outside VP. An interesting and perhaps advantageous implications of this idea is that expletive subjects do not originate in Spec,VP as they are not part of the argument structure of the verbs they occur with. Expletives are therefore inserted directly under Spec,IP for reasons having to do with the EPP applying at SS.

8.5.1.4 *Case and A-chains*

The idea that DP-movement is motivated by Case considerations implies that DP-movement takes place from a non-Case-marked position to a Case-marked position. Consequently, the A-chain derived by DP-movement has only one Case assigned to the head of the chain. This general property of A-chains suggests that there is probably a one-to-one correspondence between A-chains and Case which parallels the one-to-one correspondence between chains and θ-roles discussed in Chapter 7. Recall that the latter property of chains was encoded in (the definition of) the θ-Criterion in terms of a uniqueness condition such that a chain can have one and only one θ-role (or θ-position). To take a similar step with respect to the Case Requirement we need first check whether A-chains with two Case positions are indeed excluded.

Consider example (105), discussed in Chapter 4 in relation to the TSC on DP-movement:

105a. *John seems is happy.
105b. [IP [DP John]i seems [IP ti is happy]]

Up to this stage, we have been excluding this example in terms of TSC, that is the condition which prevents DP-movement from moving a DP out of a finite clause. Notice, however, that (105) also involves a situation where the DP *John* moves from one Case-marked position (the subject position of the embedded finite clause) to another Case-marked position (the subject position of the root finite clause). This movement results in the derivation of an A-chain with two Cases (or two Case positions). In view of this, (105) and similar examples actually show that A-chains are indeed subject to a uniqueness condition with respect to their Case properties. Once the Case Requirement is revised to this effect, TSC can then be dispensed with altogether. The condition it encodes is an epiphenomenon, insofar as it is part of a more fundamental restriction on the Case properties of A-chains.

There are various ways of incorporating the uniqueness condition in question into the definition of the Case Requirement. (106) is a possible version:

106. **Case Requirement**

A chain is Case-marked if it contains exactly one Case-marked position.

Recall that the notion 'chain' is understood in the broader sense which includes DPs not involved in movement. Such DPs form trivial one-member chains. (106), like the θ-Criterion, is best understood as a well-formedness condition on chains. For a chain to be well-formed with respect to its Case properties, it has to satisfy the requirement specified in (106). Note that (106) is not specific to A-chains, implying that it applies to A'-chains as well. We turn to A'-chains now.

8.5.2 Operator-movement

We have seen that DP-movement results in the derivation of A-chains where the head (i.e. the moved DP) is in a Case-marked position and the tail/root (i.e. the initial trace) is in a non-Case-marked position. This is to be expected on the assumption that DP-movement is motivated by Case considerations. A'-chains derived by Wh-movement and QR differ in that it is their root/tail position which is Case-marked. This property of A'-chains can be gleaned from (107) and (108):

107a. What did John kick?
107b. SS/LF: [CP whati [C' did [IP John I [VP kick ti]]]]
107c. for which thing x, John kicked x

108a. John suspects everyone.
108b. LF: [IP everyonei [IP John I [VP suspects ti]]]
108c. for every x, John suspects x

In (107) and (108) the trace of the A'-chain derived by Wh-movement in (107) and QR in (108) is situated in a Case-marked position. However, despite this fundamental difference between A-chains and A'-chains, the latter are also consistent with the Case Requirement in that they include a unique Case position, at least in examples of the type illustrated in (107) and (108). The reason A'-chains differ from A-chain with respect to their Case position is that movement of operators (wh-phrases and quantified phrases) is not motivated by Case considerations. Movement of wh-phrases in the syntax and at LF, and movement of quantifiers at LF are motivated by different considerations having to do with their scope.

There is perhaps a more fundamental reason why traces of operators are in Case-marked positions. Recall from Chapter 7 that traces of operators have the status of variables at LF, as shown in (107c) and (108c). Assuming an approach to Case in terms of the Visibility Hypothesis, variables have Case because as arguments they are required to be assigned a θ-role. Recall that in the context of the Visibility Hypothesis the assignment of θ-roles to arguments is dependent on arguments having Case which makes them visible to θ-marking. The fact that traces of operators have Case as a defining property then follows.

8.5.3 Expletive-argument chains

Consider the pairs in (109a&b) and (110a&b):

109a. Three girls arrived.
109b. There arrived three girls.

110a. A red car approached.
110b. There approached a red car.

The verbs *arrive* and *approach*, among others, belong to the class of verbs we referred to above as unaccusative. Their distinctive property is that their unique argument can either appear in the subject position (Spec,IP), as in (109a) and (110a), or in the postverbal position, as in (109b) and (110b). In the latter examples, the subject position is filled with the expletive element *there*. (109b) and (110b) raise the question how the DP in the postverbal position satisfies the Case Requirement given that the verb is unaccusative, i.e. does not assign accusative Case.

Various answers have been suggested, one of which relies on the notion of **Case-transfer**. The idea is that the expletive in the Case-marked subject position and the DP in the postverbal position are co-indexed and form an 'expletive-argument chain'. Within this chain, a process of Case transfer takes place whereby the expletive in the Case-marked subject position transfers the nominative Case it receives to the DP argument in the non-Case-marked postverbal position. This way, the postverbal DP, or rather the expletive-argument chain, can be said to satisfy the Case Requirement. An interesting consequence of the notion 'expletive-argument chain' is that it offers a possible solution to a problem that expletives raise for the Visibility Hypothesis pointed out earlier. The problem is that expletives invariably occur in Case-marked positions even though as non-arguments they are not assigned a θ-role, and therefore are not dependent on Case. If expletives can be shown to be invariably linked to an argument in a non-Case-marked position, as in (109b) and (110b), the fact that they occur in Case-marked positions can be said to follow from their role as the Case-marked member of the expletive-argument chain which makes the chain visible for θ-marking.

The analysis arguably extends to sentences such as (111) and (112):

111a. It is clear that John left suddenly.
111b. it_i is clear [_CP that John left suddenly]_i

112a. They consider it inappropriate that John left suddenly.
112b. they consider [_AP it_i [_A' inappropriate]] [_CP that John left suddenly]_i

(111) is said to involve extraposition of the clause from the subject position (cf. *That John left suddenly is clear*), understood as an argument of the predicate *be clear*. The clausal argument, though not a DP, is expected to have Case under the Visibility Hypothesis. The clausal argument can be said to satisfy the Case Requirement by being linked to the expletive element in the subject position in an expletive-argument chain. The expletive element is in a Case-marked position and transmits the nominative Case it receives to the extraposed clause. (112) involves a similar link. The expletive element in the subject position of the small clause complement receives accusative Case from the root ECM verb, and transmits it to the extraposed CP it is linked with in an expletive argument chain. The Case assigned to the expletive element in (111) and (112) makes the expletive-argument chain visible for θ-marking

Note that the position of the expletive in (112) is not only Case-marked, it is also θ-marked. It is unexpected for an expletive to appear in a θ-marked argument position. I leave you to think about the implications of this fact for θ-theory as presented here.

8.5.4 Structural versus inherent Case

Nominative and accusative Cases have two significant properties in common. One is that they do not necessarily involve a thematic relation between the assigner and the assignee. The other property is that they are both determined at SS.

Nominative Case is assigned to the subject via Spec-head agreement with finite I and does not involve a thematic relation between I and the DP subject. Nominative Case is determined at SS in the sense that it takes place subsequent to movement of the DP subject to Spec,IP. As for accusative Case, in most situations it involves DPs which are thematically related to the verb. However, it can also involve DPs which are not thematically related, as is the case in ECM contexts. The fact that accusative Case can be determined subsequent to movement, and therefore at SS, can be seen in examples such as (113) and (114):

113a. Bill believes John/him to have been sacked.
113b. Bill believes [_IP John/him_i [_I' to [_VP have [_VP been [_VP sacked t_i]]]]]

114a. Bill expected John/him to abandon the race.

114b. Bill expected [$_{IP}$ John/him$_i$ to [$_{VP}$ t$_i$ [$_{V'}$ abandon the race]]]

In (113) assignment of accusative Case to *John/him* by the ECM verb *believe* takes place subsequent to movement of *John/him* from the object position of the embedded passive verb to the subject position of the embedded clause. A similar situation exists in (114), except that movement takes place from Spec,VP to Spec,IP of the same (embedded) clause.

A Case that is determined at SS and does not necessarily involve a thematic relation between the assigner and the assignee is called **structural Case**. Nominative and accusative are therefore both structural Cases. A Case that is determined at DS and involves a thematic relation between the assigner and the assignee is called **inherent Case**. Of the Cases discussed so far, oblique Case assigned by prepositions to their object appears to be a candidate for inherent Case. However, the situation with prepositions is complicated by the fact discussed in Chapter 7 that some prepositions appear not to assign a θ-role to their object although they assign Case to it. This is the situation with the dative preposition *to* and the preposition *of* in noun phrases. Moreover, there are contexts where the Case assigned by a preposition to a DP appears to be determined at SS subsequent to movement. One such context is illustrated in (115):

115a. For John to be sacked is surprising.

115b. [$_{CP}$ for [$_{IP}$ John$_i$ [$_{I'}$ to [$_{VP}$ be sacked t$_i$]]]] is surprising

Despite the unclarity of the situation with prepositions, it is probably generally true that whenever the preposition assigns a θ-role to its object, the Case relationship between them is determined at DS.

There are other types of Case not discussed so far which have been suggested as possible candidates for inherent Case in the sense defined above. One such Case has been argued to be involved in sentences such as (116a&b) discussed above:

116a. There arrived three girls.

116b. There approached a red car.

An interesting property of such constructions not mentioned above is that the argument of the verb in the postverbal position must be indefinite. This is shown in (117a&b). This restriction does not hold of the argument when it is in the preverbal subject position as shown in (118a&b):

117a. *There arrived the girls.

117b. *There approached the red car.

118a. The girls/three girls arrived.

118b. The red car/a red car approached.

Belletti (1988) relates the indefiniteness requirement in (117a&b) to the fact that in Icelandic indefinite noun phrases generally have distinct Case properties from definite noun phrases. Indefinite noun phrases receive a special Case known as **partitive**, which Belletti argues is an inherent Case in the sense explained above.

Belletti generalises this property of indefinite noun phrases in Icelandic to all languages, arguing that in English it is simply masked by the fact that the language has poor Case morphology. Belletti argues further that all verbs have, as a lexical property, the ability to assign partitive Case to a noun phrase they θ-mark. However, only indefinite noun phrases are compatible with partitive Case. When the internal argument noun phrase of a given verb is not indefinite, assignment of partitive Case does not take place. According to this analysis, the postverbal noun phrase in (118a&b) receives partitive Case from the unaccusative verb by virtue of being θ-marked by the verb as well as by virtue of being indefinite. (117a&b) are excluded because the postverbal noun phrase does not receive partitive Case from the unaccusative verb on the grounds that partitive Case is incompatible with definite noun phrases.

8.6 *Summary*

This chapter discussed the Case properties of noun phrases and the mechanisms of the grammar which regulate them. Noun phrases are subject to a condition, called here the Case Requirement, which requires them to have Case. The Case Requirement can take the form of a Case Filter that applies at PF and excludes overt noun phrases which lack Case. Alternatively, it can be made to follow from the θ-Criterion in terms of the Visibility Hypothesis. Noun phrases, in particular arguments, need to have Case to be visible for θ-marking at LF.

The original empirical basis for the Case Requirement relates to the fact that when a noun phrase is in a non-Case-marked environment it gives rise to ungrammaticality. A noun phrase is in a Case-marked environment if it is in a specific structural relation of locality, called government, to a transitive category, or if it is in a Spec-head agreement relation with a non-lexical category which includes Agr. The Cases assigned under government alone are the accusative case assigned by transitive verbs, the oblique Case assigned by prepositions, and possibly also partitive Case assigned by unaccusative verbs to indefinite objects. The Cases assigned under Spec-head agreement are nominative and arguably also genitive.

The necessity to account for genitive Case-assignment, as well as certain significant structural similarities between noun phrases and clauses, led to the conclusion that noun phrases have a structure which parallels that of clauses. Noun phrases are DPs headed by the non-lexical category D which may have either NP or VP as its complement. D dominates Agr in some noun phrases but arguably not in others. Pronouns occupy the D position and are the spellout of Agr.

Cases fall under two major classes, structural and inherent. Structural Case is determined at SS and does not necessarily involve a thematic relation between the assigner and the assignee. Typical examples of structural Case are nominative and accusative. Inherent Case is determined at DS and involves a thematic relation between the assigner and the assignee. Examples of inherent Case are the oblique

Case assigned by prepositions which also assign a θ-role to their object, and arguably also partitive Case assigned by (un)accusative verbs to indefinite objects.

The Case Requirement is also responsible for DP-movement (alias NP-movement). DP-movement seems invariably to take place from a non-Case-marked position to a Case-marked position. This suggests that DPs move because they cannot receive Case in their DS position. The fact that DP-movement from a Case-marked position (to another Case-marked position) leads to ungrammaticality in turn suggests that there is a uniqueness condition on A-chains such that they can only have one Case-marked position. This requirement holds of A'-chains as well, although the latter differ in that their Case position is usually the root (i.e. the trace) rather than the head position.

The modular structure of the grammar assumed by the Principles and Parameters framework emerged more clearly in this chapter. For example, Case theory interacts with X-bar theory and Government theory insofar as the latter define the locality relations under which Case is assigned. The interaction between these theories is best illustrated in ECM contexts, where the ECM DP is a subject with respect to X-bar theory and θ-theory, but patterns with objects with respect to Government theory and Case theory. On the other hand, the Visibility Hypothesis establishes a clear dependency relation between Case theory and θ-theory such that assignment of a θ-role to a DP is made dependent on the DP having Case.

A third issue which illustrates clearly the interaction between separate modules of the grammar relates to DP-movement. The latter is motivated by Case considerations, in the sense that DPs move to a Case-marked position because they cannot receive Case in their DS position. The consequence is that the position to which DPs move need not be specified in the definition of DP-movement, thereby putting an end to the practice adopted in Part I of this book. Moreover, the fact that this position must be the subject position of a finite clause with a verb that does not assign an external θ-role follows from the principles of Case theory in combination with the principles of θ-theory. The condition that DP-movement cannot affect a DP included in a tensed clause (TSC) also does not need to be specified in the definition of DP-movement. This condition now follows from the principles of Case theory, in particular the requirement that chains have a unique Case position.

Exercises

Exercise 8.1

With reference to the abstract structure provided explain if:

i)   X c-commands YP
ii) X m-commands XP
iii) X m-commands YP
iv) Z c-commands WP

v) Z c-commands UP
vi) Z m-commands UP

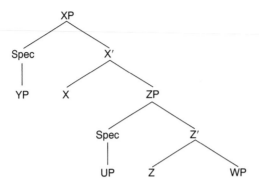

Exercise 8.2

Assuming a definition of government which incorporates the notion 'c-command', explain with reference to the abstract structure provided if:

i)   X governs ZP
ii) X governs YP
iii) X governs WP
iv) X governs UP
v)   YP governs X

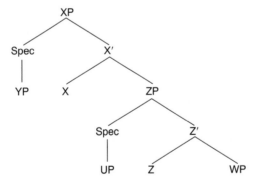

Exercise 8.3

With reference to examples (i–v) identify the Case of each DP, the source of each Case, the condition under which each Case is assigned, and explain whether each Case is structural or inherent:

i)   The wheel was spinning out of control.
ii) Bill wants for John to leave.
iii) There arose a problem during the discussion.
iv) Mary dislikes Bill's boss.
v)   Bill persuaded John to leave.

Exercise 8.4

Explain how the sentences in (i–v) are excluded in the context of the theory of Case outlined in this chapter:

i)   *Bill smiled John.
ii) *John to fail to attend is surprising.
iii) *Bill seems has lost his mind.
iv) *John is believed Bill has seen.
v)   *There arose the problem.

Exercise 8.5

Outline a derivation for each of the sentences in (i–iii) and explain how each movement step is motivated. Once you have done that, explain how example (iva) fits in with your analysis taking into consideration its close paraphrase in (ivb):

i)   The temperature appears to have dropped.
ii)   Bill is believed to have lost.
iii) Who seems to have arrived?

iv)a. John is easy to please.
iv)b. It is easy to please John.

Exercise 8.6

Sentences (i) and (ii) include a DP with an adverbial function called **Bare NP adverb**. Sentences (iii) and (iv) include a **cognate object** which is a DP with a noun that is etymologically related to the verb and serves to modify the verb. Explain whether the theory of Case outlined in this chapter accounts for the Case property of these DPs. If the theory accounts for them, explain how, and if not, try to think of a way of accommodating them. Make sure you consider both the Case Filter and the Visibility Hypothesis:

i)   Bill arrived this morning.
ii) John went that way.
iii) Mary smiled a strange smile.
iv) The athlete ran a good run.

Exercise 8.7

The verb *want* can take either of the complements shown in (i–iv). Discuss the Case properties of the verb *want* on the basis of the paradigm in (i–iv), together with some additional examples you may think of:

i)   John wants to see the match.
ii) Bill wants for John to see the match.
iii) Bill wants John to see the match
iv) John wants the present.

Sources and further reading

The theory of Case discussed in this chapter originated with Rouveret and Vergnaud (1980) and Vergnaud (1985) and was further refined in Chomsky (1981, 1986a). One of the original motivations for Case theory was the desire to handle the cases that Chomsky and Lasnik (1977) handled in terms of the NP-to-VP Filter. The Visibility Hypothesis appears in Chomsky (1981, 1986a) and is attributed to Joseph Aoun.

Government theory is developed in Chomsky (1981) and its precise definition has been the subject of debate. For a discussion of some definitions and their empirical implications see Aoun and Sportiche (1983). The issue of adjacency in relation to Case-assignment is discussed in Stowell (1981) and Chomsky (1981). The relevance of Spec-head agreement to Case is discussed in Chomsky (1986b), Koopman and Sportiche (1991) and Chomsky (1991c).

The idea that D is the head of the noun phrase (the DP Hypothesis), and the idea that pronouns are D elements were proposed in Postal (1966) and later in Brame (1981, 1982), Hudson (1987) and Abney (1987). The parallelism in structure between noun phrases and clauses, in particular the idea that noun phrases probably also include a COMP-like position, is discussed in Horrocks and Stavrou (1987) and Szabolcsi (1987). Abney (1987) includes an extended discussion of the structure of gerunds with external nominal properties.

The interaction between DP-movement and Case is discussed in Burzio (1986) and Chomsky (1981, 1986a). The idea that certain verbs which select an internal argument do not assign it Case (unaccusative verbs) appears in Perlmutter (1978). An alternative analysis for passives is presented in Baker *et al.* (1989). The Subject-inside-VP Hypothesis is discussed in Kitagawa (1986), Kuroda (1988), Mohammad (1989) and Koopman and Sportiche (1991).

The relevance of Case to variables is discussed in Chomsky (1981, 1982, 1986a). Chomsky (1986a) also includes a discussion of the distinction between structural and inherent Case.

9 Binding Theory and Control

Contents

9.1 *DP types*

Chapter 8 dealt with the distribution of DPs as determined by their Case properties in combination with the principles of Case theory. This chapter deals with the distribution of DPs as determined by their referential properties in combination with the principles of a module called **Binding theory.**

As far as their referential properties are concerned, overt DPs fall into three different classes: **anaphors, pronouns** and **r(eferential) expressions.** The group of anaphors includes **reflexives** such as *himself, themselves* and **reciprocals** such as *each other*. The group of pronouns includes the usual pronouns such as *she, him*. Finally, the group of r-expressions includes names such as *Mary* and *Bill*, and referring DPs such as *the coach* and *the players*.

Anaphors have the distinctive property that they are dependent on an antecedent included in the sentence for their reference. In other words, they must have an antecedent in the sentence in which they occur, as shown in (1) and (2):

1a. The players blamed themselves/each other.
1b. [IP the players; blamed themselves;/each other;]

2a. *The coach blamed themselves/each other.
2b. *[IP the coach; blamed themselves;/each other;]

In (1), the anaphor *themselves/each other* has an antecedent, namely *the players*. In (2), however, the anaphor does not have an antecedent, and hence the fact that the sentence is excluded. The subject *the coach* does not qualify as antecedent for the anaphor in (2) because the subject does not share the same number feature with the anaphor. Differences in the features of DPs imply differences in their referential values indicated in terms of indices. The subject and the anaphor have different features in (2), and therefore different indices.

Pronouns differ from anaphors in that they do not require an antecedent in the sentence, although they may have one. (3a), for example, can have the interpretation shown in (3b) where the pronoun refers back to the subject of the root clause. It can also have the interpretation shown in (3c) where the pronoun refers to an individual included in the discourse (i.e. an individual known to the participants in the discourse):

3a. The coach suspects that the players blame him.
3b. [IP the coach; suspects [CP that [IP the players blame him;]]]
3c. [IP the coach; suspects [CP that [IP the players blame him;]]]

Unlike anaphors and pronouns, r-expressions cannot have an antecedent in the sentence. (4a), for example, cannot have the interpretation shown in (4b) where the r-expression *the coach* is co-indexed with the pronoun in the subject position of the root clause. (4a) can only have the interpretation shown in (4c) where the pronoun *he* and *John* are not co-indexed:

4a. He suspects that the players blame John.
4b. *[IP he; suspects [CP that [IP the players blame John;]]]
4c. [IP he; suspects [CP that [IP the players blame John;]]]

The term 'antecedent' is understood for the moment to mean a DP which bears the same index as an anaphor, a pronoun or an r-expression. Later on, we will discuss a more precise definition of the term 'antecedent'.

The referential properties of DPs can be assumed to be encoded in them in terms of referential features. In Chapter 8, we saw that pronouns are basically the spellout of the features person, number, gender and Case. Since reflexives also include a pronominal element in English, e.g. *her-self*, they too include the same set of features as pronouns, and consequently perhaps also occupy the D position in DP. The difference between pronouns and reflexives lies with an additional feature complex relating to anaphoricity and pronominality formally represented as [+/−a(naphoric)] and [+/−p(ronominal)]. Anaphors have the feature specification [+a, −p]. Pronouns have the feature specification [−a, +p]. R-expressions differ from anaphors and pronouns in that they are neither anaphoric nor pronominal. They have the feature specification [−a, −p]. The fourth logical possibility, i.e. [+a, +p], does not seem to have a corresponding member among the set of overt DPs. It does, however, have one among the set of null DPs.

Assuming that the anaphoric and pronominal features are properties of all DPs, null DPs are expected to be specified for these features as well. So far, we have encountered three different types of null DPs: DP-traces, variables and *PRO*. DP-traces are found in raising sentences such as (5), and passive sentences such as (6), among others:

5a. The coach seems to have resigned.
5b. [IP the coach$_i$ seems [IP t$_i$ to have resigned]]

6a. The coach is believed to have resigned.
6b. [IP the coach$_i$ is believed [IP t$_i$ to have resigned]]

Because DP-traces arise as a result of DP-movement, they invariably have an antecedent in the sentence, namely the moved DP itself. Recall that movement involves automatic co-indexation between the moved category and the trace. Thus, DP-traces pattern with lexical anaphors in that they invariably have an antecedent in the sentence. We therefore conclude that DP-traces are anaphoric expressions with the feature specification [+a, −p].

Variables (i.e. traces of wh-phrases and quantified phrases) also arise as a result of movement applying either in the mapping onto SS (Wh-movement), as in (7), or in the mapping onto LF (QR), as in (8):

7a. Who does the coach blame?
7b. [CP who$_i$ does [IP the coach blame t$_i$]]

8a. The coach blames everyone.
8b. [IP everyone$_i$ [IP the coach blames t$_i$]]

Unlike DP-traces, variables cannot be said to depend on their antecedent for reference. This is because the antecedent of variables, in particular wh-phrases and quantified phrases, are not referential expressions. Recall (from Chapter 8) that in A′-bar chains involving an operator and a variable it is the variable which functions as the argument, occupying the Case-marked and θ-marked position of the chain. Variable traces are r-expressions, on a par with names and other referring expressions, and have the feature specification [−a, −p].

The third null DP is *PRO* found in the subject position of non-finite clauses situated in contexts such as the ones illustrated in (9) and (10):

9a. The coach tried to resign.
9b. [IP the coach$_i$ tried [CP C [IP PRO$_i$ to resign]]]
9c. *[IP the coach$_i$ tried [CP C [IP PRO$_j$ to resign]]]

10a. The coach doesn't know how to organise the team.
10b. [IP the coach$_i$ doesn't know [CP how [PRO$_i$ to organise the team]]]
10c. [IP the coach$_i$ doesn't know [CP how [PRO$_j$ to organise the team]]]

PRO seems to share properties with both anaphors and pronouns depending on the context in which it occurs. In (9), for example, *PRO* must have an antecedent in the sentence, as shown by the fact that the interpretation in (9c) is excluded. In this particular context, *PRO* seems to pattern with anaphors. In (10), however, *PRO* can either have an antecedent in the sentence or outside the sentence. (10b) represents the interpretation whereby *PRO* has an antecedent in the sentence, namely *the coach*: 'the coach doesn't know how he/the coach should organise the team.' (10c) represents the interpretation whereby *PRO* does not have an antecedent in the sentence. In this particular context, *PRO* has an arbitrary interpretation: 'the coach doesn't know how one should organise the team.' In context (10) *PRO* seems to pattern with pronouns. These conflicting properties of *PRO* suggest the conflicting feature specification [+a, +p]. This particular property of *PRO* is discussed in detail later on in this chapter.

The fourth logical combination [−a, +p] which underlies pure pronouns does not seem to have a corresponding member among the types of null DP discussed so far (but see Chapter 12). Nevertheless, the overt and null DPs discussed so far between them instantiate all the logical combinations of the anaphoric and pronominal features. The combination [+a, −p] is instantiated by reflexives, reciprocals and DP-traces. The combination [−a, +p] is instantiated by overt pronouns. The combination [−a, −p] is instantiated by r-expressions and variables. Finally, the combination [+a, +p] is instantiated by *PRO*.

As pointed out above, the distribution of anaphors, pronouns and r-expressions is regulated by the principles of Binding theory. The distribution of *PRO*, however, is thought to be regulated by a separate module sometimes called **PRO theory** for reasons that will become clear later on. We will discuss each of these modules separately, starting with Binding theory.

9.2   *Binding versus coreference*

The notion 'antecedent' was temporarily defined above as the category which bears the same index as an anaphor or a pronoun. This condition is met by *the coach* in relation to the anaphor *himself* in (11), and yet *the coach* cannot serve as a legitimate antecedent for the anaphor in (11):

11a. *The coach's assistants blame himself.
11b. *[$_{DP}$ the coach$_i$'s [$_{D'}$ D [$_{NP}$ assistants]]] blame himself$_i$

11c.

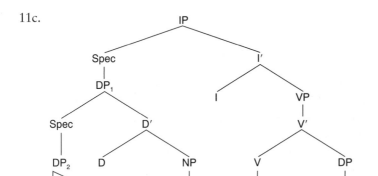

The reason *the coach* cannot serve as an antecedent for the anaphor in (11) is because *the coach* does not c-command the anaphor. As shown in (11c), the first branching node that dominates *the coach* is DP$_1$, and DP$_1$ does not dominate the anaphor. For a DP to serve as the antecedent of an anaphor, the DP has to c-command the anaphor. We now have a more precise definition of 'antecedent' which can be stated as in (12):

12. The antecedent of an anaphor or a pronoun must

    i) bear the same φ-features (or index) as the anaphor or pronoun
    ii) c-command the anaphor or pronoun.

Both conditions of (12) are met by the DP *the coach's assistants* in (13). The relevant node is DP$_1$ which bears the same index as the reflexive anaphor and c-commands the reflexive anaphor:

13a. The coach's assistants blame themselves.
13b.

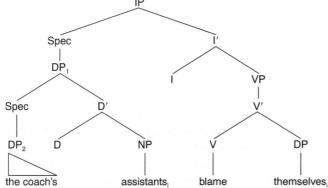

With this in mind, consider now (14). (14a) can either have the interpretation shown in (14b) or the one shown in (14c). The interpretation which concerns us here is the one in (14b), where the r-expression *John* has the same index as the pronoun *his*:

14a. His assistants blame John.
14b. [$_{DP}$ his$_i$ [$_{D'}$ D [$_{NP}$ assistants]]] blame John$_i$
14c. [$_{DP}$ his$_i$ [$_{D'}$ D [$_{NP}$ assistants]]] blame John$_j$

Initially, interpretation (14b) looks inconsistent with the conclusion reached earlier that r-expressions cannot have an antecedent in the sentence. However, a closer look at (14b) reveals that this is not the case. In (14b), the pronoun does not c-command the r-expression, and therefore does not qualify as an antecedent for the r-expression. In view of this, (14b) is quite consistent with the conclusion that r-expressions cannot have an antecedent in the sentence.

What needs to be explained with respect to (14b) is how come the pronoun can bear the same index as the r-expression. It seems that a pronoun can bear the same index as an r-expression as long as the pronoun does not c-command the r-expression. This fact seems to suggest that the combination of co-indexation and c-command results in a relationship which is distinct from the relationship which involves co-indexation only. The relationship which combines both co-indexation and c-command is called **binding**. The relationship which involves only co-indexation is called (mere) **coreference**. Binding is the relation which regulates the distribution of anaphors, pronouns and r-expressions. A formal way of defining it is as in (15):

15. **Binding**

α binds β iff:

i) α is co-indexed with β
ii) α c-commands β.

The relationship between the pronoun and the r-expression in (14b) is one of (mere) coreference not binding. This relationship falls outside the domain of Binding theory, and therefore outside the scope of this chapter.

Having defined the structural relation which regulates the distribution of anaphors, pronouns and r-expressions, we are now in a position to be more precise about the distribution of each of these DPs. Let us remind ourselves of the generalisations stated above. Anaphors must have an antecedent in the sentence. Pronouns do not have to have an antecedent in the sentence. R-expressions cannot have an antecedent in the sentence. These descriptive generalisations can now be formulated in the form of binding conditions on the distribution of anaphors, pronouns and r-expressions. The three binding conditions can be stated as in (15′), to be understood in association with the definition of binding in (15):

15′. BC A: An anaphor must have an antecedent in the sentence.
    BC B: A pronoun does not have to have an antecedent in the sentence.
    BC C: An r-expression cannot have an antecedent in the sentence.

The definitions in (15′) are preliminary. They need to be made more precise by making them consistent with all relevant contexts. This task is carried out for BC

A and BC B in the next section, and for BC C in the subsequent section. This division of the binding conditions is not arbitrary as will become clear.

9.3 *Anaphors and pronouns*

9.3.1 Binding Conditions A & B

Consider (16) and (17):

16a. The coach suspects (that) the players blame themselves.
16b. [$_{IP}$ the coach$_i$ suspects [$_{CP}$ that [$_{IP}$ the players$_i$ blame themselves$_i$]]]

17a. *The players suspect (that) the coach blames themselves.
17b. *[$_{IP}$ the players$_i$ suspect [$_{CP}$ that [$_{IP}$ the coach$_j$ blames themselves$_i$]]]

(16) shows that an anaphor can be bound in a domain which is smaller than a sentence, namely a clause. (17) shows that in this particular context the anaphor must be bound within the immediate clause that includes it. Although the DP *the players* c-commands and bears the same index as the anaphor in (17) it cannot bind the anaphor. BC A must therefore be revised to say that an anaphor must be bound within the clause that immediately includes it. The revision affects the part of the condition that states the domain in which the anaphor must be bound. It turns out that further revision is required.

(18) shows that an anaphor can be bound within a domain that is smaller than even a clause, namely a DP. (19) shows that the anaphor must be bound within DP in this particular context. Although the subject *the players* c-commands and is coindexed with the anaphor, it cannot bind the anaphor in (19):

18a. The coach heard the players' stories about each other.
18b. [$_{IP}$ the coach$_i$ heard [$_{DP}$ [the players']$_i$ stories about each other$_i$]]

19a. *The players heard the manager's stories about each other.
19b. *[$_{IP}$ the players$_i$ heard [$_{DP}$ [the coach's]$_j$ stories about each other$_i$]]

It should be clear that an adequate definition of BC A should provide a precise definition of the domain in which an anaphor must be bound. (16) and (17) suggest that the domain can be a clause, and (18) and (19) suggest that it can be a DP. (17) and (19) are excluded because although they include a potential antecedent for the anaphor, that is an expression which c-commands and is coindexed with the anaphor, the expression is not close enough to the anaphor. An anaphor must be bound within its 'local domain'. Pending a more precise definition of 'local domain', let us restate BC A as in (20) which is much more restrictive than the earlier definition:

20.   Binding Condition A

An anaphor must be bound within its 'local domain'.

Let us now turn to BC B. Recall that this condition states that a pronoun does not have to have an antecedent in the sentence. (21a) can either have the reading shown in (21b), where the pronoun is co-indexed with *the coach*, or the reading shown in (21c), where the pronoun is not co-indexed with any other DP in the sentence:

21a. The coach suspects (that) the players blame him.
21b. [$_{IP}$ the coach$_i$ suspects [$_{CP}$ (that) [$_{IP}$ the players blame him$_i$]]]
21c. [$_{IP}$ the coach$_i$ suspects [$_{CP}$ (that) [$_{IP}$ the players blame him$_j$]]]

Consider now (22) which involves the same context as (16). (22a) cannot have the reading shown in (22b) where the pronoun is bound by the subject of the embedded clause. (22b) suggests that a pronoun cannot be bound within the clause that includes it:

22a. The coach suspects (that) the players blame them.
22b. *[$_{IP}$ the coach suspects [$_{CP}$ (that) [IP the players$_i$ blame them$_i$]]]

Our earlier preliminary definition of BC B stated that a pronoun does not have to have an antecedent in the sentence. It turns out that this was the wrong way to approach the condition which regulates the distribution of pronouns. (22b) suggests that BC B should state that a pronoun cannot be bound within a certain domain. In other words, BC B should be defined in opposition to BC A which regulates anaphors. While an anaphor must be bound within the clause that immediately includes it, a pronoun must be free within the clause that immediately includes it. Anaphors are said to impose a locality condition on their antecedent, meaning they require their antecedent to be local. Pronouns are said to impose an anti-locality condition on their antecedent, meaning they require their antecedent to be non-local.

According to this reasoning, we should expect anaphors and pronouns to be in complementary distribution. We expect a pronoun to be excluded in exactly the same contexts where an anaphor is required. This is already shown in (22b) compared to (16), and is confirmed by (23b) compared to (17):

23a. The players suspect (that) the coach blames them.
23b. [$_{IP}$ the players$_i$ suspect [$_{CP}$ (that) [$_{IP}$ the coach$_j$ blames them$_i$]]]

(23) differs only in that includes a pronoun in the slot occupied by the anaphor in (17). Because *the players* is not included in the clause that immediately includes the pronoun, it can bear the same index as the pronoun. The pronoun is free in the (embedded) clause that immediately includes it.

The complementary distribution between anaphors and pronouns extends to the (other) domain, namely DP. Earlier we discussed contexts where an anaphor must be bound within the DP that includes it. The contexts are reproduced in (24) and (25) with a pronoun in the place of the anaphor. (24b) shows that a pronoun cannot be bound within the DP that includes it. (25b) is possible because the pronoun is free within the DP that includes it:

24a. The coach heard the players' stories about them.
24b. *[IP the coach heard [DP [the players']i stories about themi]]

25a. The players heard the coach's stories about them.
25b. [IP the playersi heard [DP [the coach's]j stories about themi]]

BC B can now be restated as in (26) which is both more restrictive and more accurate than our earlier definition:

26. **Binding Condition B**

A pronoun must be free in its 'local domain'.

Our next task is to try to find the appropriate definition of the notion 'local domain'. What we already know is that the 'local domain' can either be a clause or a DP. What we have yet to find out is what these two categories have in common that enables them to function as the 'local domain' for anaphors and pronouns.

9.3.2 NIC cases: the governor

Consider (27) and (28):

27a. The (two) coaches expected each other to resign.
27b. [IP the (two) coachesi expected [IP each otheri to resign]]

28a. The (two) coaches expected them to resign.
28b. *[IP the (two) coachesi expected [IP themi to resign]]

Both (27) and (28) include a non-finite clause embedded under an ECM verb. (27b) shows that an anaphor can occur in the ECM subject position and be bound by the subject of the root clause. Predictably, a pronoun is excluded from this context, as shown in (28b). (28a) has a possible reading whereby the pronoun in is not bound by the subject of the root clause. This reading has been ignored because it is irrelevant to the point of the discussion.

Now, compare (27) and (28) to (29) and (30) where the embedded clause is finite:

29a. *The (two) coaches expected (that) each other would resign.
29b. *[IP the (two) coachesi expected [CP (that) [IP each otheri would resign]]]

30a. The (two) coaches expected that they would have to resign.
30b. [IP the (two) coachesi expected [CP (that) [IP theyi would have to resign]]]

The striking fact about (29) and (30) is that they present a situation which is the reverse of the one in (27) and (28). An anaphor is excluded from the subject position of an embedded finite clause, whereas a pronoun is allowed. This contrast suggests that finiteness plays a role in determining 'local domain'.

An early attempt to deal with this contrast was based on a condition called the **Nominative Island Condition (NIC)**. The idea is that a subject position which is assigned nominative Case is an island with respect to binding, so that an anaphor cannot refer out of it. This is how (29) was excluded. In contrast, a subject position which is not assigned nominative Case is not an island, so that an anaphor can refer out of it. There is a clear sense in which NIC is to overt anaphors what TSC (the Tensed S Condition) is to DP-traces. Recall that TSC excludes DP-movement out of tensed (finite) clauses, as shown in (32) compared to (31). This parallelism was partly responsible for the idea that DP-traces are anaphors and that their distribution can be accounted for in terms of the same principle which accounts for the distribution of lexical anaphors:

31a. John seems to be happy.
31b. [$_{IP}$ John$_i$ seems [$_{IP}$ t$_i$ to be happy]]

32a. *John seems is happy.
32b. *[$_{IP}$ John$_i$ seems [$_{IP}$ t$_i$ is happy]]

Let us now tease out the content of NIC with the purpose of incorporating its effects in the definition of 'local domain'. Nominative Case is assigned to the subject position by finite I. The original analysis assumed that nominative Case-assignment takes place under government by finite I. In Chapter 8 we reached the conclusion that nominative Case assignment is best viewed as taking place under Spec-head agreement. However, this does not necessarily exclude the possibility that finite I governs the subject position. Let us assume that for the purpose of binding, finite I governs the subject position. We can then interpret NIC to mean simply that if the embedded clause includes a governor for the anaphor in the subject position, that is if the embedded clause is finite, an anaphor in the embedded subject position cannot be bound from outside the embedded clause. Because the embedded clause in (32) is finite, it includes a governor for the anaphoric DP-trace in the subject position. Consequently, the anaphor cannot be bound from outside the embedded clause. In (31), the embedded clause is non-finite, and therefore does not include a governor for the anaphor. Unlike finite I, non-finite I is not a governor. Consequently, the anaphor in the subject position can be bound from outside.

The important point to retain from this discussion is that the governor plays a role in defining the 'local domain' in which an anaphor must be bound. If a domain includes the governor of the anaphor, the anaphor must be bound within that domain; otherwise a violation of BC A arises. The embedded finite clause in (32) includes the governor of the anaphor, namely finite I. This means that the anaphor must be bound within the embedded clause. However, the anaphor is not bound within the embedded clause in (32), and hence the fact that the sentence is excluded. The embedded clause in (31) is non-finite. Non-finite I does not govern the subject. This means that the embedded clause does not include the governor of the anaphor in the subject position, and therefore does not qualify as the 'local domain' for the anaphor. The governor of the anaphor in (31) is the ECM verb which is included in the root clause. Therefore, the root clause is the 'local domain' of the anaphor in (31). The anaphor is bound within the root clause, and hence the fact that (31) is possible.

We have seen that the same notion 'local domain' is involved in the distribution of both anaphors and pronouns. Thus, although the discussion has been restricted to anaphors, it is likely that the governor plays the same rule in defining the 'local domain' of pronouns.

9.3.3   SSC cases: the subject

(33) and (34) were discussed in Chapter 4 in relation to SSC (the Specified Subject Condition) on DP-movement. In both examples, a DP is moved across a subject:

33a. *Mary appears it is likely to win.
33b. *[$_{IP}$ Mary$_i$ I appears [$_{CP}$ [$_{IP}$ it is likely [IP t$_i$ to win]]]]

34a. *Bill is believed John to have been beaten.
34b. *[$_{IP}$ Bill$_i$ is believed [$_{IP}$ John to have been beaten t$_i$]]

The SSC effect is derivable from Case theory in (34). However, the SSC effect is not derivable from Case theory in the super-raising example (33). The latter is arguably ruled out by TSC since DP-movement applies across the intermediate tensed clause. However, we have already come across more than one reason to eliminate TSC from the system.

The relevance of (33) and (34) to Binding theory is that SSC appears to play a role in regulating the distribution of anaphors and pronouns as well. This is to be expected at least as far as anaphors are concerned, on the assumption that DP-traces are anaphors. The SSC effect in the distribution of anaphors can be seen in (35):

35a. The (two) coaches expected the players to blame each other.
35b. [$_{IP}$ the (two) coaches$_i$ expected [$_{IP}$ the players$_j$ to blame each other$_j$]]
35c. *[$_{IP}$ the (two) coaches$_i$ expected [$_{IP}$ the players$_j$ to blame each other$_i$]]

(35a) can have the reading shown in (35b) where the anaphor is bound by the nearest subject to it, namely *the players*. However, (35a) cannot have the reading shown in (35c) where the anaphor is bound by the (more distant) subject of the root clause *the coaches*. In (35c), the subject of the embedded clause *the players* intervenes between the anaphor and the subject of the root clause.

Thus, just as a DP cannot be moved across an intervening subject, a lexical anaphor cannot be bound across an intervening subject either. Taking the relationship between a trace and its antecedent to be a relationship of binding, we can reinterpret SSC to mean that a trace cannot be bound across an intervening subject. We now have one general condition which applies to both lexical anaphors and DP-traces: an anaphor, be it lexical or a trace, cannot be bound across an intervening subject.

Recall that our aim is to identify the properties which determine the 'local domain' of anaphors and pronouns. We have already identified the governor as one such property. Now we are in a position to identify another property, namely the subject. If a domain includes a subject, the anaphor must be bound within that domain. Because the embedded clause in (35) has a subject, the anaphor must be bound within the embedded clause. The anaphor is bound within the embedded clause in (35b) but not in (35c). Notice that the embedded clause also includes the governor of the anaphor in (35), the embedded verb.

Let us test the hypothesis that the subject plays a role in defining 'local domain' by slotting a pronoun in the place of the anaphor in (35). If pronouns are truly in complementary distribution with anaphors, we expect the equivalent representation of (35b) to be excluded, and the equivalent representation of (35c) to be possible. This is shown in (36a-c):

36a. The (two) coaches expected the players to blame them.
36b. *[$_{IP}$ the (two) coaches$_i$ expected [$_{IP}$ the players$_j$ to blame them$_j$]]
36c. [$_{IP}$ the (two) coaches$_i$ expected [$_{IP}$ the players$_j$ to blame them$_i$]]

Because the embedded clause has a subject in (36), the pronoun must be free within the embedded clause. The pronoun is free in (36c) but not in (36b), and hence the fact that (36b) is excluded.

The idea that the subject plays a crucial role in defining 'local domain' is perhaps best seen in relation to DPs. Unlike clauses, DPs can have a subject optionally. We expect an anaphor included in a DP to be able to be bound from outside if the DP does not have a subject, but not if the DP has a subject. This is shown in (37) and (38). The DP which includes the anaphor does not have a subject in (37), but has one in (38):

37a. The players heard stories about each other.
37b. [$_{IP}$ the players$_i$ heard [$_{DP}$ [e] D [$_{NP}$ stories about each other$_i$]]]

38a. *The players heard the coach's stories about each other.
38b. *[$_{IP}$ the players$_i$ heard [$_{DP}$ [the coach's]$_j$ D [$_{NP}$ stories about each other$_i$]]]

Because DP does not have a subject in (37) it does not qualify as the 'local domain' for the anaphor. This is despite the fact that the DP includes the governor of the anaphor, the noun *stories*. The domain which includes the anaphor, its governor and a subject in (37) is IP. The anaphor is bound within IP. Turning now to (38), because DP includes a subject, in addition to the governor of the anaphor, it qualifies as the 'local domain' of the anaphor. The anaphor is not bound within DP in (38), and hence the fact that (38) is excluded.

9.3.4   Governing Category and Complete Functional Complex

The properties identified as playing a crucial role in defining 'local domain' of anaphors and pronouns are a governor and a subject. If a domain which includes the anaphor/pronoun also includes the governor of the anaphor/pronoun and a subject, it qualifies as the 'local domain' in which the anaphor must be bound and the pronoun must be free. Otherwise, it does not.

The technical term used to refer to such a domain is **Governing Category (GC)**. The latter can be defined as in (39a). (39b&c) are the definitions of Binding Conditions A and B which make reference to GC:

39a. **Governing Category**

The GC of α is the minimal domain which contains α, the governor of α, and a subject.

39b. **Binding Condition A**

An anaphor must be bound in its GC.

39c. **Binding Condition B**

A pronoun must be free in its GC.

Chomsky (1986a) uses the expression **Complete Functional Complex (CFC)** to refer to the domains in which an anaphor must be bound and a pronoun must be free. CFC is defined as in (40):

40. **Complete Functional Complex**

A CFC is a domain where 'all grammatical functions compatible with its head are realised in it–the complements necessarily, by the projection principle, and the subject, which is optional unless required . . .' (Chomsky, 1986a, p. 169).

The notion 'CFC' captures best, and perhaps in a simpler way, the property that clauses and DPs have in common which enables them to function as the 'local domain' of anaphors and pronouns. Recall that this was our chief concern. The key property seems to be the subject. All clauses have a subject by virtue of EPP. DPs may or may not have a subject, as there is no principle that requires them to have a subject. The point, though, is that only DPs with a subject, that is only DPs that are CFCs, function as 'local domain' for anaphors and pronouns.

9.4   *R-expressions*

9.4.1   A-binding versus A′-binding

We have seen that r-expressions cannot be bound in the sentence. This seems to be the case irrespective of the distance between the r-expression and a potential binder. In (41), the r-expression *the players* is separated from the pronoun *they* by three clausal boundaries, and yet the r-expression cannot be bound by the pronoun, as shown in (41b):

41a. They say (that) the journalists claim (that) the public thinks (that) the coach blames the players.

41b. *[IP they$_i$ say [CP (that) [IP the journalists claim [CP (that) [IP the public thinks [CP (that) [IP the coach blames the players$_i$]]]]]]]]

Recall that in (42) the pronoun does not bind the r-expression due to lack of c-command, even though the two categories are coreferential:

42a. His assistants blame John.

42b. [$_{DP}$ his$_i$ [$_{D'}$ D [$_{NP}$ assistants]]] blame John$_i$

(41) shows that GC/CFC, i.e. the notion 'local domain' discussed above in relation to anaphors and pronouns, does not play a role in the distribution of r-expressions. Therefore, BC C which regulates the distribution of r-expressions is not expected to make reference to GC/CFC. BC C is usually defined as in (43):

43. **Binding Condition C**

An r-expression must be free (everywhere).

Essentially, BC C amounts to the statement that r-expressions are incompatible with binding. This is not surprising on the understanding that binding is a relationship of reference-assignment and that r-expressions are inherently referential. Recall that reflexives and pronouns are no more than bundles of features which have the function of restricting the set of possible antecedents. For example, *herself* implies a feminine, singular antecedent, and *he* a masculine, singular antecedent. Anaphors and pronouns are dependent on an antecedent for reference, either directly as in *The coach blames himself* or indirectly as in *He blames himself*. In the latter example, the reflexive depends on the pronoun which in turn depends on a discourse antecedent for reference. In view of this, it is not surprising that r-expressions are incompatible with binding (cannot be bound). This conclusion can be understood to mean that, perhaps, BC C does not need to be stated as a binding condition. However, certain properties of r-expressions to be discussed below will show that BC C needs to be stated, albeit in a slightly different form than shown in (43).

The conclusion that r-expressions cannot be bound extends to variables as well, although initially this may not seem to be the case. (44) and (45) are reproduced from above:

44a. Who does the coach blame?

44b. [$_{CP}$ who$_i$ does [$_{IP}$ the coach blame t$_i$]]

44c. for which person x, the coach blames x

45a. The coach blames everyone.

45b. [$_{IP}$ everyone$_i$ [$_{IP}$ the coach blames t$_i$]]

45c. for every person x, the coach blames x

In each of these examples the variable is co-indexed with a c-commanding operator, the wh-phrase in (44), and the quantifier in (45). The relationship between an operator and a variable is traditionally called binding. In view of this, one might conclude that variables are inconsistent with BC C, with the implication that they are somehow different from overt r-expressions. However, there is a difference between the binding relation referred to by BC C and the binding relation in (44) and (45). The former, as pointed out above, is a relation of reference-assignment, whereby the antecedent assigns a reference to the bindee. The binding relation in (44) and (45), however, cannot be said to be one of reference-assignment for the simple reason that operators are not referential expressions, and therefore do not have a reference to assign.

We therefore need to make a formal distinction between two types of binding relations. The type of binding which involves reference-assignment is called **A-binding** (read A-binding). The type of binding which involves an operator and a variable is called **A'-binding** (read A-bar binding). In the former (A-binding), the binder is usually an argument located in an A-position. In the latter (A'-binding), the binder is usually an operator (a non-argument) located in an A'-position. Given this distinction, the binding conditions listed above are conditions on A-binding relations and do not hold of A'-binding relations. In other words, Binding theory which incorporates Binding Conditions A, B and C is a theory of A-binding. As such, it is irrelevant to A'-binding relations of the type in (44) and (45).

The conclusion that A'-binding relations are not relevant to Binding theory does not necessarily mean that BC C does not apply to variables at all. As r-expressions, variables are expected to be subject to BC C just like overt r-expressions. This is shown in (46):

46a. Who did John claim (that) the players blame?
46b. *[$_{CP}$ who$_i$ did [$_{IP}$ John$_i$ claim [$_{CP}$ t$_i$' (that) [$_{IP}$ the players blame t$_i$]]]]

(46a) cannot have the interpretation shown in (46b) where the individual wh-questioned (or enquired about) is the same as the individual who makes the claim. This particular interpretation involves the pattern of indexation shown in (46b) where the variable is co-indexed with the c-commanding subject of the sentence. This co-indexation results in the variable being A-bound by the subject in violation of BC C. Thus, like overt r-expressions, variables too cannot be bound (everywhere).

However, there are certain contexts where a variable is actually A-bound. One such context is illustrated in (47) which includes a relative noun phrase:

47a. The coach (whom/that) the players like most is Bill.
47b. [$_{DP}$ the coach$_i$ [$_{CP}$ Op$_i$ [$_{IP}$ the players like t$_i$ most]]] is Bill

As shown in (47b), the variable in the object position of the relative clause is A-bound (and assigned a referential value) by the head noun of the relative noun phrase. This relationship is clearly inconsistent with BC C as formulated above. (47) should be excluded for the same reason that (46) is excluded, among others. Thus, BC C should be revised so as to include (47) while still exclude (46) and similar examples.

There is a significant difference between (46) and (47) which gives an indication as to the nature of the revision required. In (46), the A-binder intervenes between the variable and its operator. In (47), the A-binder (*the coach*) does not intervene between the variable t$_i$ and its operator Op$_i$. This difference implies that a variable cannot be A-bound only if the A-binder intervenes between the variable and its operator. When the A-binder does not intervene in the intended sense, the variable can be A-bound by it. This amounts to saying that operators determine the 'local domain' in which variables must be free (cannot be bound). The definition of GC C must therefore make reference to this particular notion of 'local domain'. Chomsky (1986a) suggests the version shown in (48):

48. **Binding Condition C**

An r-expression must be A-free in the c-command domain of its operator.

The binding relation in (47) is consistent with (48) since the A-binder is not located in the (c-command) domain of the operator of the variable. However, the binding relation in (46) is inconsistent with (48) since the A-binder is located in the c-command domain of the operator of the variable. The c-command domain of the operator is the 'local domain' of r-expressions in which they cannot be bound.

Although the 'local domain' of r-expressions may initially appear to be different from that of anaphors and pronouns, a closer look reveals that this may not be the case. The 'local domain' of r-expressions is determined by an operator which is basically a subject/specifier of CP. The 'local domain' of anaphors and pronouns is also determined by a subject, either the subject of a sentence (IP) or the subject of a noun phrase (DP). This suggests that the same notion of 'local domain' applies to all DP-types. This possibility becomes more realistic if the notion 'governor' is eliminated from the definition of 'local domain'. The governor does not appear to play a role in the definition of the 'local domain' of r-expressions. We will come back to this issue in Chapter 10, where such a unified notion of 'local domain' is discussed.

9.4.2 Crossover and A′-bound pronouns

(49) and (50) illustrate a phenomenon known as **Crossover**:

49a. Who did he see?
49b. *$[_{CP}$ who$_i$ $[_{C'}$ did $[_{IP}$ he$_i$ see t$_i]]$
49c. for which person x, x saw x

50a. Who did his boss see?
50b. *$[_{CP}$ who$_i$ did $[_{IP}$ $[_{DP}$ his$_i$ $[_{D'}$ D $[_{NP}$ boss$]]]$ see t$_i]]$
50c. for which person x, x's boss saw x

(49a) cannot have the interpretation shown in (49b&c) where the pronoun in the subject position of the sentence is coindexed with the variable, and by transitivity, with the wh-phrase. (50a) cannot have the interpretation shown in (50b&c) with a similar pattern of indexation. In both examples, the wh-phrase has 'crossed over' a coindexed pronoun in the subject position. (49) is an instance of **Strong Crossover (SCO)** and (50) an instance of **Weak Crossover (WCO)**.

(49) is ruled out by BC C as it involves a situation where the variable is A-bound by the pronoun located in the subject position of the sentence. (50),

however, is not ruled out by BC C, nor by any other binding condition for that matter. The pronoun in the subject position of DP does not c-command the variable and therefore does not bind it in (50). The fact that the wh-phrase binds the pronoun should not be of significance as the binding relationship involved is an instance of A'-binding. Various analyses have been suggested in the literature to account for Crossover phenomena which we will not discuss here for lack of space. Descriptively, the condition involved in Crossover can be stated as in (51):

51. **Crossover**

A variable cannot be co-indexed with a pronoun to its left.

The Crossover effects also arise with quantifiers raised by QR in the mapping onto LF. (52a), for example, cannot have the interpretation shown in (52b&c), and (53a) cannot have the interpretation shown in (53b&c). (52) is an instance of SCO and (53) an instance of WCO:

52a. He saw everyone.
52b. *[$_{IP}$ everyone$_i$ [$_{IP}$ he$_i$ saw t$_i$]]
52c. for every x, x saw x

53a. His boss saw everyone.
53b. *[$_{IP}$ everyone$_i$ [$_{IP}$ [$_{DP}$ his$_i$ [$_{D'}$ D [$_{NP}$ boss]]] saw t$_i$]]
53c. for every x, x's boss saw x

The fact that variable traces of raised quantifiers pattern with the variable traces of wh-phrases should not come as a surprise at this stage. However, (52) and (53) represent evidence of a fairly strong nature for movement of quantifiers at LF, discussed in Chapter 7. Only if the quantifier is assumed to move and leave a variable trace behind can (52) and (53) be accommodated under the descriptive generalisation in (51). Moreover, although co-indexation with a quantifier is excluded in (53), co-indexation with an r-expression occupying the same position is not. Recall that the interpretation shown in (54b) of (54a) is possible as the subject pronoun does not bind the r-expression in the object position. Because r-expressions do not undergo QR at LF, the Crossover effect does not arise. Thus, the contrast between (53b) and (54b) strongly supports the hypothesis that quantified phrases undergo movement at LF:

54a. His boss saw John.
54b. [$_{DP}$ his$_i$ [$_{D'}$ D [$_{NP}$ boss]]] saw John$_i$

The expression 'to its left' in (51) is significant as a variable CAN be co-indexed with a pronoun to its right. (55a), for example, can have the interpretation shown in (55b&c), and (56a) can have the interpretation shown in (56b&c):

55a. Who claims (that) he is innocent?
55b. [$_{CP}$ who$_i$ [$_{IP}$ t$_i$ claims [$_{CP}$ (that) [$_{IP}$ he$_i$ is innocent]]]]
55c. for which person x, x claims x is innocent

56a. Everyone claims (that) he is innocent.
56b. [$_{IP}$ everyone$_i$ [$_{IP}$ t$_i$ claims [$_{CP}$ (that) [$_{IP}$ he$_i$ is innocent]]]]
56c. for every person x, x claims x is innocent

In (55) and (56), as in the Crossover examples above, the pronoun is A′-bound. A′-bound pronouns are sometimes said to have a **bound variable reading**, as shown in (55c) and (56c). Note, however, that if A′-bound pronouns are assumed to have the status of variables at LF, (55) and (56) will involve a violation of BC C. The pronoun-cum-variable will be A-bound by the variable trace of the operator in the domain of the operator. We will come back to this point later on.

9.4.3   Parasitic gaps and adjunct islands

(57) illustrates a phenomenon known as **parasitic gap**:

57a. Which article did John file without reading?
57b. [$_{CP}$ which article$_i$ did [$_{IP}$ John [$_{VP}$ file [e]$_i$] [without reading [e]$_i$]]]
57c. for which article x, John filed x without reading x

(57) includes two variables (or gaps) represented with the symbol [e]. One variable is in the object position of *file* and the other in the object position of *reading*. The presence of two variables in Case-marked argument positions should in principle imply two distinct operators. However, in (57) there apparently is only one operator, namely the wh-phrase *which article*.

An analysis of (57) along the lines outlined in (58) whereby the wh-phrase is base-generated in the position of the rightmost gap (the object position of *reading*), then moved to the position of the next gap (the object position of *file*), and finally to its surface position is excluded for a number of reasons some of which should be familiar:

58.   *[$_{CP}$ which article$_i$ did [$_{IP}$ John [$_{VP}$ file t$_i$] [without reading t$_i$]]]

First, movement into the second gap (the object position of *file*) is movement from a θ-marked position to another θ-marked position, and therefore is excluded by the θ-Criterion (see Chapter 7). Secondly, movement into the second gap is also movement from a Case-marked position to another Case-marked position which is excluded by the condition that chains have one Case position (see Chapter 8). Thirdly, this same movement would be movement out of an adjunct phrase which is generally excluded. Adjuncts are said to be islands, on a par with wh-clauses (the Wh-Island Condition) and complex noun phrases (the Complex Noun Phrase Condition), discussed in Chapter 4.

The fact that adjuncts are islands for movement is shown in (59):

59a. *How did John disappear after fixing the car?
59b. *[$_{CP}$ how$_i$ did [$_{IP}$ John [$_{VP}$ disappear] [after fixing the car t$_i$]]]

The phrase *after fixing the car t$_i$* is an adjunct, the verb *disappear* being intransitive. Because the phrase in question is an adjunct, it is an island for movement. (59) is excluded by a condition on movement which for the moment we will call the **Adjunct Island Condition (AIC)**. If the parasitic gap construction in (57) did involve wh-movement out of the (same) adjunct phrase as (59), (57) should be excluded for the same reason that (59) is excluded.

It must therefore be the case that Wh-movement of the wh-phrase *which article* in (57) takes place directly from the object position of the verb *file*, as shown in (60):

60. [CP which article$_i$ [C' did [IP John [VP file t$_i$] [without reading [e]]]]]

Given (60), the question we need to answer is how the gap inside the adjunct phrase arises. The answer outlined in (61) is suggested in (Chomsky 1986b):

61. . . . without [CP Op$_i$ [IP reading t$_i$]]

According to this analysis, the gap inside the adjunct phrase arises as a result of the movement of a null operator to the Spec,CP inside the adjunct phrase. Because this movement operates inside the adjunct phrase, it does not give rise to a violation of AIC.

An important aspect of the analysis outlined in (61) is that it assimilates (the adjunct phrase of) parasitic gap constructions to relative clauses with a null wh-phrase illustrated in (62). (63) is a parasitic gap construction which involves a relative clause with a null wh-phrase provided for comparison. The adjunct phrase of the parasitic gap construction is isolated in (63c):

62a. This is the article (that) John filed.
62b. this is [DP the article$_i$ [CP Op$_i$ [C' (that) [IP John filed t$_i$]]]]

63a. This is the kind of article you must read before you file.
63b. this is [DP the kind of article$_i$ [CP Op$_i$ [IP you must [VP read t$_i$]
       before [CP Op$_j$ [IP you file t$_j$]]] . . .

Recall that relatives such as the one in (62) involve movement of a null operator to the Spec,CP of the relative clause (see Chapter 4). The adjunct phrase in (61) and its counterpart in (63c) are claimed to involve a similar movement of a null wh-phrase.

In Chapter 4 we used island effects as diagnostic tests for the presence of Wh-movement in relatives without an overt wh-phrase. Now, if parasitic gap constructions do indeed involve movement of a null wh-phrase inside the adjunct phrase, we expect the island effects to show up if the gap is included in an island inside the adjunct phrase. What we need to do is make the adjunct phrase of the parasitic gap construction more complex by embedding a complex noun phrase or a wh-island inside it, as in (64) and (65):

64a. ??This is the report which John published before announcing the plan to discuss.
64b. ??. . . before [CP Op$_i$ [IP PRO announcing [DP the plan [CP t$_i$' [IP PRO to discuss t$_i$]]]]]

65a. ??This is the report which John filed before disclosing when to discuss.
65b. ??. . . before [CP Op$_i$ [IP PRO disclosing [CP when [IP PRO to discuss t$_i$]]]]

The adjunct phrase, which is the focus of our attention here, is represented separately in (64b) and (65b). (64b) includes a complex noun phrase out of which movement of the null wh-phrase has taken place. (65b) includes a wh-island out of which movement of the null wh-phrase has taken place. The fact that the adjunct phrase exhibits the island effects implies that it indeed involves movement of a null wh-phrase in its representation.

A salient property of parasitic gap constructions is that the two gaps (variables) have the same referential value (index). To account for this fact, Chomsky (1986b) suggests a mechanism of **chain composition** whereby the two independently derived A'-chains are merged together into a single complex chain. Technically, this merger results in a situation where the wh-phrase in (57), for example, is related to both gaps (via co-indexation), and therefore A'-binds both variables occupying them.

Parasitic gap constructions have a number of other properties which are by no means easy to account for. First, the gap (variable) inside the adjunct phrase is **parasitical** upon the presence of a variable inside the main clause. This is shown in (66) and (67), neither of which includes a variable inside the main clause. (66) has an overt DP in the object position of the main clause, and (67) has a DP-trace in this position. Because (66) and (67) do not include a variable in the main clause, the **parasitic gap** in the adjunct phrase is not licensed:

66a. *John filed the report without reading.
66b. *John filed the report [without reading [e]]

67a. *The report was filed without reading.
67b. *the report$_i$ was filed t$_i$ [without reading [e]]

Secondly, the licensing variable must not c-command the parasitic gap. In all examples of parasitic gap constructions discussed, the licensing variable is in the object position of the verb of the main clause. In this position, the variable does not c-command the adjunct phrase, assuming the latter is adjoined to VP/IP. In contrast, a variable in the subject position of the main clause would c-command the adjunct phrase, and, consequently, the parasitic gap. However, a variable in the subject position cannot license a parasitic gap as shown in (68). This condition on the licensing of parasitic gaps is sometimes called the **anti-c-command condition**: a parasitic gap is licensed by a variable which does not c-command it:

68a. *Who left before we could greet?
68b. *[CP who$_i$ [IP t$_i$ left [before we could greet [e]]]]

Thirdly, parasitic gaps are licensed by SS variables only. Variables which arise as a result of QR applying in the mapping onto LF seem to be unable to license a parasitic gap. The wh-phrase *which article* in (69b) and the quantifier phrase *every article* in (96c) raise at LF, leaving a variable behind which does not c-command the parasitic gap inside the adjunct phrase. However, this LF variable apparently is unable to license the parasitic gap. The fact that LF variables cannot license parasitic gaps whereas SS variables can suggests that parasitic gaps are licensed at SS:

69a. *John forgot who filed which/every article without reading.
69b. . . . [CP [which article]j [who]i [IP ti filed tj [without reading [e]]]] . . .
69c. . . . [CP whoi [IP every articlej [IP ti filed tj [without reading [e]]]] . . .

The conditions on the licensing of parasitic gaps discussed can be summarised in a single descriptive generalisation along the lines of (70):

70. **Parasitic Gaps**

A parasitic gap is licensed at SS by a variable which does not c-command it.

Obviously, (70) should be derivable from some general and independent principles, although it is not easy to see how. At any rate, to the extent that (70) is derivable from the principles of Binding theory, it shows that these principles arguably apply at SS. If this is the case, the possibility that A'-bound pronouns receive a bound variable interpretation at LF, pointed out above, would not necessarily give rise to a violation of BC C. This is because at the level where binding conditions apply (i.e. SS) the pronoun is still a pronoun and as such is subject to BC B rather than BC C.

9.5 PRO *and Control*

9.5.1 *PRO* Theorem

We have seen that *PRO* typically occurs in the subject position of non-finite clauses such as the ones in (71) and (72):

71a. The coach tried to blame the players.
71b. the coachi tried [CP C [IP PROi to blame the players]]

72a. Blaming the players won't help.
72b. [CP C [IP PROi blaming the players]] won't help

In (71) *PRO* has an antecedent in the sentence, namely the subject of the root clause *the coach*. In (72), *PRO* does not have an antecedent in the sentence. In a well-defined discourse context, *PRO* can have a specific antecedent in (72), e.g. 'the coach'. Otherwise, *PRO* is said to have an arbitrary reading. In view of the fact that *PRO* typically occurs in the subject position of non-finite clauses, it should be possible to determine the nature of the principle which governs the distribution of *PRO* by identifying the peculiar properties of the subject position of non-finite clauses.

The typical property of the subject position of non-finite clauses is that it is non-Case-marked. This is so, of course, unless the non-finite clause is introduced by a prepositional complementiser, as in (73), or embedded under an ECM verb, as in (74). In these examples, the subject position of the non-finite clause is assigned Case by an external governor:

73a. For the coach to blame the players is surprising.
73b. [CP for [IP the coach to blame the players]] is surprising

74a. The players believe the coach to be vindictive.
74b. the players believe [IP the coach to be vindictive]

PRO is excluded from these (ECM) positions, as shown in (75) and (76). The conclusion which emerges is that *PRO* occurs in non-Case-marked positions, and is excluded from Case-marked positions:

75a. *For to blame the players is surprising.
75b. *[CP for [IP PRO to blame the players]] is surprising

76a. *The players believe to be vindictive.
76b. *the players believe [IP PRO to be vindictive]]]

The conclusion that *PRO* is excluded from Case-marked positions is further supported by the fact that it cannot occur in the subject position of finite clauses, as shown in (77), together with the fact that it cannot occur in the object position of a transitive verb or a preposition either, as shown in (78) and (79):

77a. *Blamed the players.
77b. *[IP PRO I [VP blamed the players]]

78a. *The coach blamed.
78b. *the coach [VP blamed PRO]

79a. *The coach put the blame on.
79b. *the coach put the blame [pp on PRO]

The preliminary indications therefore seem to be that an account of the distribution of *PRO* lies with Case theory. However, there are reasons to believe that an account of the distribution of *PRO* lies with Government theory rather than Case theory. A fact about Case-marked positions is that they are also invariably governed given that Case is assigned under government. For the purposes of the current discussion we will adopt the view that finite I governs the subject position. The reverse is not true, that is, not all positions which are governed are also Case-marked. Case-marked positions form a subclass of the class of governed positions. Positions that are governed but non-Case-marked represent the real test for determining whether the distribution of *PRO* is regulated by Case theory or Government theory. If *PRO* cannot occur in a position that is governed but non-Case-marked, the conclusion will have to be that *PRO* is excluded from governed positions rather than Case-marked positions.

The object position of passive verbs is an instance of a position that is governed but not Case-marked (see Chapter 8). Consider (80) and (81):

80a. The player was sacked (by the coach).
80b. [IP the player$_i$ was sacked t$_i$]

81a. *It/there was sacked (by the coach).
81b. *[IP it/there was sacked PRO]

Recall that passive verbs do not assign Case to their object. The accusative Case of the base transitive verb is 'absorbed' by the passive morpheme. Recall also that it is for this reason that the object obligatorily moves to the subject position in passives giving rise to the derivation in (80b). Now, if *PRO* is excluded from Case-marked positions rather than governed positions there is no reason why it should not occur in the object position of passives. The absence of a possible controller for PRO in (81) is unlikely to be the reason it is excluded given the general availability of the arbitrary reading.

Further evidence for the hypothesis that *PRO* is excluded from governed positions rather than Case-marked positions can be gleaned from the noun phrases (82) and (83):

82a. *Their belief the coach to be vindictive
82b. *[DP their [D' D [NP belief [IP the coach to be vindictive]]]]

83a. *Their belief to be vindictive
83b. *[DP their [D' D [NP belief [IP PRO to be vindictive]]]]

(82) was cited in Chapter 8 as evidence that nouns lack the ability to assign Case, contrary to related transitive verbs. The fact that (82) is excluded is therefore attributed to the inability of the noun *belief* to exceptionally Case-mark the subject of the embedded non-finite clause. Note, however, that the noun governs the subject position of the embedded non-finite clause in (82). The reason N does not assign Case to the subject of the non-finite clause in (82) cannot therefore be attributed to a possible failure on the part of N to govern the subject position of the non-finite clause. (82) involves a genuine context where the subject position of the non-finite clause is governed but not assigned Case by N. The same context is involved in (83). There is no reason why (83) should be excluded on the view that *PRO* is excluded from Case-marked positions. The position occupied by *PRO* in (83) is non-Case-marked. It must therefore be the case that *PRO* is excluded in (83b) because the position it occupies is governed. It follows that *PRO* is excluded from governed positions rather Case-marked positions, and that an account of the distribution of *PRO* lies with Government theory rather than Case theory.

(84) is the condition on the distribution of *PRO* suggested in Chomsky (1981):

84. **PRO Theorem**

   PRO must be ungoverned.

As a theorem, (84) can presumably be shown to be true on independent grounds. That is, we should be able to show that (84) follows from some independent factors. We will come back to this issue later on. For the moment, the examples where *PRO* is situated in a governed position can be assumed to be excluded by (84).

9.5.2   *PRO in DP*

We saw above that DP can function as the 'local domain' (or GC) for an anaphor or a pronoun when it includes a subject, but apparently not when it does not include a subject. The relevant examples are reproduced in (85) and (86):

85a. The players heard stories about each other.
85b. the players$_i$ heard [$_{DP}$ [e] D [$_{NP}$ stories about each other$_i$]]

86a. *The players heard the coach's stories about each other.
86b. *the players$_i$ heard [$_{DP}$ [the coach]$_j$'s D [$_{NP}$ stories about each other$_i$]]

In (85) the DP containing the anaphor apparently does not have a subject, so that the anaphor can be bound by an antecedent located outside DP. In (86), however, the DP containing the anaphor includes a subject, and consequently the anaphor cannot be bound by an antecedent located outside DP.

However, there is a fact about the DP in (85) and (86), ignored above, which seems to cast doubt on this analysis. (87) and (88) show that a pronoun is also allowed in the position of the anaphor in both contexts:

87a. The players heard stories about them.
87b. the players$_i$ heard [$_{DP}$ [e] D [$_{NP}$ stories about them$_i$]]

88a. The players heard the coach's stories about them.
88b. the players$_i$ heard [$_{DP}$ [the coach]$_j$'s D [$_{NP}$ stories about them$_i$]]

The fact that a pronoun co-indexed with the subject of the sentence can occur in (88) is not surprising. The presence of the subject in the DP containing the pronoun means that the 'local domain' of the pronoun is DP. The pronoun *them* is free in DP, as expected. What is unexpected is the fact that a pronoun co-indexed with the subject of the sentence can occur in (87). In the latter, DP apparently lacks a subject, and therefore does not qualify as the 'local domain' for the pronoun. According to the analysis outlined earlier in this chapter, the 'local domain' of the pronoun in this example should be the whole IP. The pronoun appears to be bound inside this domain in violation of BC B.

Recall that BC A and BC B together predict that anaphors and pronouns should be in complementary distribution. However, this prediction appears to break down in (85) and (87) where the anaphor and the pronoun seem to be in free variation.

A possible solution to the problem lies with identifying a difference in interpretation between (85) and (87) which when taken into consideration reveals that these examples do not necessarily run counter to the otherwise general pattern of complementary distribution between anaphors and pronouns. In (85) the stories about the players are understood to be told by the players themselves, so that (85) can be paraphrased as meaning that 'the players heard their own stories about each other'. In (87), however, the stories are understood to be told by somebody else, so that the sentence can be paraphrased as meaning that 'the players heard somebody else's stories about them'. It is plausible to assume that this somebody else (i.e. the individual who tells stories about the players) is somehow structurally present in

DP in (87), presumably in the form of a null category. Taking on board Chomsky's (1986a) suggestion that the null category in question is *PRO*, (87) can be assigned the representation shown in (89). Now that DP has a subject, it qualifies as the 'local domain' for the pronoun. The pronoun is free in this domain, as required by BC B. The precise position of *PRO* inside DP is discussed below:

89a. The players heard stories about them.
89b. the players$_i$ heard [$_{DP}$ PRO$_j$ stories about them$_i$]

What about (85)? We could maintain the analysis outlined above for this example whereby the DP containing the anaphor does not have a subject, and therefore does not qualify as the 'local domain' of the anaphor. However, it is plausible to assume on grounds of consistency that the DP in this example also includes a null *PRO* subject on a par with its counterpart in (87)/(89). The fact that the story-telling is done by the players themselves in (85) will them mean that the *PRO* subject of DP is controlled by the subject of the sentence. The intended representation is as shown in (90):

90a. The players heard stories about each other.
90b. the players$_i$ heard [$_{DP}$ PRO$_i$ stories about each other$_i$]

According to the analysis in (90b), the 'local domain' of the anaphor is DP, not the whole sentence. The anaphor is bound in DP by the *PRO* subject of DP, as required by BC A. The fact that *PRO* is coindexed with (i.e. controlled by) the subject of the sentence means that the anaphor is also coindexed with the subject of the sentence. This is precisely the reason responsible for the initial impression that the anaphor is bound by the subject of the sentence.

Thus, what looked initially as a context where an anaphor and a pronoun are in free variation turns out to be a false impression caused by the Control properties of the lexical categories involved in the examples, in particular the verb. The fact that the choice of the verb determines the Control interpretations obtained and the representations underlying them is made more evident by (91) and (92), compared to (85) and (87):

91a. The players told stories about each other.
91b. the players$_i$ told [$_{DP}$ PRO$_i$ stories about each other$_i$]

92a. The players told stories about them.
92b. *the players$_i$ told [$_{DP}$ PRO$_i$ stories about them$_i$]

(92a) cannot have the interpretation shown in (92b) where the pronoun inside DP is coreferential with the subject of the sentence. This example contrasts sharply with the apparently similar example (87). The difference between the two is that (87) has the verb *hear*, while (92) has the verb *tell*; otherwise, the structures are virtually identical. In situations involving Control of a *PRO* subject of a DP, the verb *hear* seems to be a Free Control verb. The *PRO* subject of its DP object can either be controlled by the subject of *hear* or by a discourse controller. In the same context, however, *tell* seems to be a Subject Control verb. The *PRO* subject of its DP object is obligatorily interpreted as coreferential with the subject of *tell*. This means that *PRO* bears the same index as the subject of the sentence in both (91) and (92). This pattern of co-indexation gives rise to a situation where the pronoun is inappropriately bound inside its 'local domain' in (92). Thus, the contrast between (87) and (92) is a reflection of the contrast in the Control properties of the verbs they include.

The fact that verbs have different Control properties is true quite independently of the constructions discussed so far. For example, *persuade* is an Object Control verb, as shown in (93). In contrast, *ask* allows both Subject Control and Object Control, as shown in (94):

93a. The coach persuaded the players to leave.
93b. the coach$_i$ persuaded the players$_j$ [PRO$_j$ to leave]
93c. *the coach$_i$ persuaded the players$_j$ [PRO$_i$ to leave]

94a. The coach asked the players to leave.
94b. the coach$_i$ asked the players$_j$ [PRO$_i$ to leave]
94c. the coach$_i$ asked the players$_j$ [PRO$_j$ to leave]

(93a) cannot have the interpretation shown in (93c), where the Controller of *PRO* is the subject of the sentence. (94a), however, can have either of the two interpretations in (94b) and (94c).

This much is well known and relatively well understood. What is less understood is the range of factors which determine the choice of the Controller. For example, if the complement *to leave* is replaced with the passive version *to be allowed to leave* in (94), Subject Control becomes strongly favoured. Consequently, the interpretation shown in (95c) becomes harder to get (if not unavailable):

95a. The coach asked the players to be allowed to leave.
95b. the coach$_i$ asked the players$_j$ [PRO$_i$ to be allowed to leave]
95c. *the coach$_i$ asked the players$_j$ [PRO$_j$ to be allowed to leave]

The verb *tell* also seems to have different Control properties depending on the nature of the complement including *PRO*. We have seen that *tell* imposes Subject Control on the *PRO* subject of its DP object. However, when the complement including *PRO* is a non-finite clause as in (96), Object Control is strongly favoured. The interpretation shown in (96c) is harder to get (if not impossible):

96a. The coach told the players to leave.
96b. the coach$_i$ told the players$_j$ [PRO$_j$ to leave]
96c. *the coach$_i$ told the players$_j$ [PRO$_i$ to leave]

As a final point on the issue of *PRO-in-DP*, we need to determine the position of *PRO* in the structure of DP. Obviously, our decision on this matter is partly dictated by the PRO Theorem. *PRO* must be assigned to an ungoverned position. This has the immediate effect of ruling out Spec,DP as a possible position for *PRO* on the grounds that it is accessible to government from outside, at least in contexts where DP is in the object position. In view of this, the position we are left with is Spec,NP. Accordingly, a more detailed structure of (97a) is as shown in (97b):

97a. The players heard stories about each other.
97b. the players$_i$ heard [$_{DP}$ [e] [$_{D'}$ D [$_{NP}$ PRO$_i$ [$_{N'}$ stories about each other$_i$]]]]

Spec,NP could be thought of as the thematic subject position of DP where the subject is base-generated and may be raised to the grammatical subject position Spec,DP for Case reasons. Spec,NP would therefore be the equivalent of Spec,VP in clauses. Recall (from Chapter 8) that subjects of sentences are base-generated in Spec,VP (the thematic subject position) and move to Spec,IP (the grammatical subject position) for Case reasons. One could argue that since *PRO* is excluded from Case positions anyway, it does not raise to Spec,DP. However, the status of *PRO* with respect to Case theory is not as straightforward as it may seem, as we will see below.

9.5.3   Interpretation of *PRO*

We have seen that *PRO* shares properties with both anaphors and pronouns. In some contexts, *PRO* must have an antecedent in the sentence, whereas in other contexts it may not have an antecedent in the sentence. The Control properties of verbs, among other factors, play a crucial role in determining the interpretation of *PRO*. Here we will review other contexts which further illustrate the ambivalent nature of *PRO*, and then briefly discuss the issue of whether Control is reducible to Binding or should be kept separate as an independent module.

In addition to the fact that *PRO* has an obligatory antecedent in the sentence in some contexts, *PRO* also resembles anaphors in that it must be in the c-command domain of its antecedent. This is shown in (98) and (99):

98a.   *The coach's assistants tried to blame himself.
98b.   *[$_{DP}$ [the coach]$_i$'s D [$_{NP}$ assistants]] tried [PRO$_i$ to blame himself$_i$]

99a.   The coach's assistants tried to blame him.
99b.   [$_{DP}$ [the coach]$_i$'s D [$_{NP}$ assistants]]$_j$ tried [PRO$_j$ to blame him$_i$]

The subject of DP *the coach* does not c-command *PRO* in (98) and therefore does not Control it. Consequently, *PRO* cannot have the same index has *the coach*, and therefore cannot serve as a local antecedent for the anaphor. (99) shows that pronouns, contrary to anaphors, do not have to be in the c-command domain of their antecedent. In this respect, *PRO* patterns with anaphors rather than with pronouns. Anaphors require a c-commanding antecedent whereas pronouns do not.

However, in many other contexts *PRO* patterns with pronouns instead of with anaphors. In addition to the fact that *PRO* does not have to have an antecedent in the sentence in certain contexts, it can also have a 'remote' antecedent in some other contexts such as (100):

100a. The coach believes (that) it would be misleading to blame himself.

100b.   [IP the coach₁ believes [CP (that) [IP it would be misleading
        [PRO₁ to blame himself₁]]]]

PRO also resembles pronouns in that it can take a 'split antecedent', as shown in
(101). A 'split antecedent' is basically an antecedent which consists of two DPs. As
indicated by *together* in (101), PRO has a dual/plural interpretation, derived from
two separate singular antecedents *the coach* and *his assistant*. This is a property
which characterises pronouns, e.g. *John informed Bill that the coach disapproves
of them*, where *them* refers back to *John* and *Bill*:

101a.   The coach expected his assistant to accept the proposal to resign together.
101b.   the coach₁ expected his assistant₁ to accept the proposal
        [PRO₁ to resign together]

Recall that it was the fact that PRO seems to share properties with both
anaphors and pronouns which motivated the idea that it has the feature
specification [+a, +p]. Notice, however, that this feature specification gives
rise to a contradiction when considered in relation to BC A and BC B. The
feature [+a] implies that PRO is required (by BC A) to be bound in its GC. On
the other hand, the feature [+p] implies that it is required (by BC B) to be free
in its GC. Chomsky (1981) argues that the outcome of this contradiction is that
PRO never has a GC. In other words, the contradiction would not arise if PRO
did not have a GC, given that Binding Conditions A and B impose restrictions
on anaphors and pronouns in relation to GC. One way of guaranteeing that
PRO does not have a GC is if it does not have a governor. This is precisely the
way in which the content of the PRO Theorem (i.e. the requirement that PRO be
ungoverned) can be shown to be true. The reasoning is as follows: If PRO has a
governor it will have a GC, and if it has a GC a contradiction will arise in relation
to BC A and BC B. Therefore, PRO does not have a governor and therefore does not
have a GC.

This solution has been found unsatisfactory by a number of linguists. Some of
the alternative analyses offered have in common the attempt to treat PRO as a pure
anaphor with the feature specification [+a, −p]. The ultimate aim of this attempt
is to reduce Control (theory) to Binding (theory), a welcome simplification if
possible. The challenge for such attempts is to explain the pronoun-like properties
of PRO.

9.5.4   *PRO* and Case theory

One of the major issues still to be resolved is the status of PRO with respect to
the Case Requirement. If the Case Requirement is understood to take the form of a
Case Filter which applies to overt DPs only, the fact that PRO does not occur in
Case-marked positions does not raise a problem. If, on the other hand, the Case
Requirement is understood to hold of all argument DPs, null and overt, then PRO
raises an obvious problem.

Chomsky (1986a) suggests that PRO can be assumed to have 'inherent Case'.

The intended notion 'inherent Case' is understood differently from the one discussed in Chapter 8 in relation to oblique and partitive Case. The inherent Case associated with *PRO* is understood to take the form of a Case feature very much on the line of the discussion of the Case features in pronouns in Chapter 8. To the extent that this hypothesis is viable, it implies that *PRO* is not dependent for Case on a Case-assignor, and hence the fact that it occurs in non-Case-marked positions. However, as Chomsky points out, 'this decision conceals a problem rather than solving it.' In Chapter 8 we saw that overt DPs in general, including pronouns, also have a Case feature encoded in D, and that the assignment of nominative Case, for example, essentially amounts to a relationship of matching the Case feature of finite I with that of the subject. Yet, unlike *PRO*, overt DPs cannot occur in a non-Case-marked subject position of a non-finite clause (see Chapter 8).

The possibility that *PRO* is not dependent on a Case-assigner seems initially to be inconsistent with the fact that *PRO* would have to be assumed to move to Spec,IP in non-finite passives such as (102):

102a. The coach refused to be blamed.
102b. the coach$_i$ refused [$_{CP}$ C [$_{IP}$ PRO$_i$ to be blamed t$_i$]]

If it is generally the case that DP-movement to Spec,IP is motivated by Case, it is not clear why *PRO* should move in (102) on the assumption that it (already) has inherent Case. Note, however, that there are several possible arguments around this problem. First, it could be argued that movement of *PRO* in (102) is motivated by EPP rather than by the Case Requirement. Alternatively, the movement of *PRO* in (102) could be argued to be motivated by the *PRO* Theorem. *PRO* has to raise to Spec,IP because its DS position is governed. This argument entails that the *PRO* Theorem does not hold of DS representations.

A third argument could be constructed along the following lines. Although *PRO* bears a Case feature in the sense explained, it needs to have this feature matched with the Case feature of I under Spec-head agreement. This argument entails that non-finite I is marked for the Case feature, although not necessarily for the other agreement features. If we assume further that *PRO* differs from overt DPs in that it lacks the person, number and gender features, but is specified for the Case feature, we may well be in a position to account for the differences in the distribution of *PRO* and overt DPs, as well as for the status of *PRO* in relation to the Case Requirement.

9.6 Summary

In this chapter we discussed the distribution of DPs as determined by their referential properties in combination with the principles of Binding theory and Control theory. In addition to *PRO*, there are three classes of DPs: anaphors, pronouns and r-expressions. Anaphors have the feature-specification [+a, −p], meaning they are pure anaphors. Pronouns have the feature-specification

[−a, +p], meaning they are pure pronouns. R-expressions have the feature-specification [−a, −p], meaning they are neither anaphoric nor pronominal. Finally, *PRO* has the feature-specification [+a, +p], meaning it has properties in common with both anaphors and pronouns.

The class of anaphors includes reflexives, reciprocals and DP-traces. They have in common the fact that they require a c-commanding antecedent inside a well-defined 'local domain' called GC. This requirement takes the form of a binding condition, called Binding Condition A. The class of pronouns includes overt pronouns. Pronouns impose an anti-locality condition on their antecedent such that their antecedent, when present in the sentence, must be located outside their GC. The binding condition which encodes this requirement is called Binding Condition B.

The class of r-expressions includes names, referring expressions and variables. The binding condition which accounts for the properties of all these categories is called Binding Condition C. The latter stipulates that an r-expression cannot be bound in the domain of its operator. Variables, being traces of moved operators, are invariably bound by the operator. However, this particular relation of binding, called A′-binding, falls outside the scope of Binding theory. The latter concerns itself with A-binding relations, which are essentially relations of reference-assignment. Operators are not referential expressions and therefore cannot enter into relations of reference-assignment.

The feature-specification of *PRO* reflects the fact that it patterns with anaphors in certain contexts and with pronouns in others. The hybrid character of *PRO* gives rise to a contradiction in relation to BCs A & B. However, given that BCs A & B make reference to GC, the contradiction would not arise if *PRO* did not have a GC. *PRO* would not have a GC if did not have a governor. It is arguably for this reason that *PRO* is restricted to ungoverned positions (PRO Theorem). As for the interpretation of *PRO*, a number of factors seem to play a role which are still not well-understood. Moreover, the involvement of these factors seem to indicate that Control, that is the mechanism responsible for assigning an interpretation to *PRO*, is perhaps not reducible to Binding theory.

Exercises

Exercise 9.1

Show how the occurrence of the reflexive is consistent with the relevant binding condition in examples (i–iii), and explain why examples (iv–vi) are excluded:

i)   Bill believes himself to be a good soccer player.
ii) Bill resents John's criticism of himself.
iii) John admires himself.

iv) *Bill believes that himself is a good soccer player.
v)   *Bill resents Mary's criticism of himself.
vi) *Mary admires himself.

Exercise 9.2

Show how the occurrence of the pronoun is consistent with the relevant binding condition in examples (i–iii), and explain why examples (iv–v) are excluded. The intended interpretations are as indicated by the indices:

i)   Bill$_i$ appreciates his$_i$ supporters.
ii) Bill$_i$ believes that he$_i$ will be a good striker.
iii) John$_i$ does not admire him$_j$.

iv) *Bill$_i$ believes him$_i$ to be a good striker.
v)   *Bill$_i$ admires him$_i$.

Exercise 9.3

Explain how the examples in (i–v) are excluded by the theory outlined in this chapter. The intended interpretations are as indicated by the indices:

i)   *He$_i$ thinks that the fans admire Bill$_i$.
ii) *Which player$_i$ does he$_i$ admire most?
iii) *Which player$_i$ do his$_i$ fans admire?
iv) *His$_i$ fans admire everyone$_i$.
v)   *PRO left early.

Exercise 9.4

It was pointed out in this chapter that binding conditions probably apply at SS. Explain whether examples (i–iv) confirm this conclusion or suggest a different conclusion. Note that in (iv) the topicalised reflexive anaphor can have as antecedent either the subject of the root clause *John* or the subject of the embedded clause *Bill*. Both readings are possible. Make sure you take this fact into consideration:

i)   The players seemed to each other to be winning the match.
ii)   Which picture of himself does John like?
iii) Himself, John does not like.
iv)   John believes that himself, Bill doesn't like.

Exercise 9.5

Sentences (i) and (ii) are instances of what is sometimes called long-distance anaphor binding. Explain whether they are problematic for the theory of binding outlined in this chapter. If you reach the conclusion that they are problematic, try to think of a possible way of accounting for them:

i)   The players thought that pictures of themselves were on sale.
ii)   The players thought each other's pictures were on sale.

Exercise 9.6

Example (i) appears to include a reflexive anaphor without an antecedent. ((ii)b) appears to include a pronoun in an illicit domain. Explain whether in your view these examples are problematic for the theory of binding outlined in this chapter:

i)   Speaker: This paper is written by Mary and myself.

ii)a. Speaker A: I don't like you in this mood.
ii)b. Speaker B: I don't like me in this mood either.

Exercise 9.7

(i) is an example of parasitic gap constructions. Explain why (ii–v) are not possible parasitic gap constructions, and spell out what they reveal about the licensing of parasitic gaps:

i)   Which player did the coach sign without testing?
ii)   *Which player left before the coach could test?
iii) *Which coach signed which player without testing?
iv)   *The coach signed every player without testing.
v)   *The coach signed the player without testing.

Sources and further reading

The theory of Binding discussed in this chapter is the one outlined in Chomsky (1980b, 1981) and further refined in Chomsky (1982, 1986a). Prior to these works, there was a substantial amount of literature on anaphors and pronouns. Among the relevant works are Lakoff (1968), Dougherty (1969), Postal (1971), Jackendoff (1972), Chomsky (1973), Lasnik (1976) and Reinhart (1976).

The distinction between A-binding and A'-binding is discussed in Chomsky (1981, 1982, 1986a). The crossover phenomena were first identified in Postal (1971), and later discussed in more detail in Wasow (1972, 1979). A'-bound pronouns are discussed in Higginbotham (1980), Chomsky (1982) and Sells (1984). Parasitic gap constructions are discussed in Taraldsen (1981), Engdahl (1983, 1985), Chomsky (1982, 1986b), Kayne (1984), Bennis and Hoekstra (1984), Longobardi (1985), Browning (1987), Tellier (1988), Frampton (1989) and Postal (1993), among others.

The discussion of *PRO* and Control in this chapter is based on Chomsky (1980b, 1981, 1986a) and Manzini (1983). For more on the relationship between Binding and Control see Koster (1984) and Borer (1989). For a different view see Bresnan (1982a).

10 Movement Theory

Contents

10.1   *Move α*

In the course of this book we have identified a number of transformations responsible for the derivation of various kinds of construction. So far, the list includes Topicalisation, Wh-movement, DP-movement, Extraposition, Heavy NP-Shift, Quantifier Raising, I-lowering, V-raising, I-raising, *Do*-support, as well as the transformation which raises the uppercase verb to v in VP-shell structures. Apart from *Do*-support, all these transformations have in common the property of moving a category from one position to another in the phrase marker. This fact suggests the possibility of reducing all these transformations to a single, general process which performs all the operations previously performed by individual transformations. The general process is called **Move α**, where α is a variable which ranges over all categories. Move α can be simply defined as in (1):

1. Move α

Move any category anywhere.

To accommodate *Do*-support, as well as some deletion operations we will discuss in this chapter, Lasnik and Saito (1984) have suggested an even more general version of (1) called **Affect** α, where 'affect' ranges over the operations of movement, insertion and deletion. Since the discussion in this chapter is mainly concerned with movement processes, we will use the version Move α.

Contrary to individual transformations, as defined in Chapters 4 and 5 and others, Move α makes reference neither to the position targeted by the movement operation nor to the conditions on the movement operation. Recall from Chapter 4 that our definition of Wh-movement, for example, included a reference to the position it targets, as well as a reference to the Wh-island Condition, the Complex Noun Phrase Condition, and the Cyclicity Condition. On the other hand, our definition of DP-movement included a reference to the position it targets, i.e. an empty DP position, as well as to TSC and SSC. The definitions of other transformations also included reference to the same kind of information. The incorporation of this information into the definition of transformations was necessary to prevent them from overgenerating. In view of this, the fact that Move α does not incorporate any of the information mentioned means that it will inevitably overgenerate. Obviously, it is not the case that any category can move anywhere. An important fact we (are supposed to) have learned from our discussions in the previous chapters is that generally only certain categories move from certain positions to certain other positions over a certain distance.

Thus, we need to impose appropriate conditions on Move α to prevent it from overgenerating. The task involved here is similar in principle to the task carried out in Chapter 6 in relation to the replacement of PS rules with X-bar schema. The core properties of PS rules were factored out and stated as conditions on the structural representation of lexical items. The same thing can be done in relation to conditions on transformations. The core properties of these conditions can also be factored out and stated separately as conditions on the representations derived by Move α. This means, in essence, that we allow Move α to overgenerate in principle, but in practice we impose conditions on its output that will have the effect of excluding undesirable representations. This move is in keeping with the general attempt to replace construction-specific rules with general principles and conditions on representations.

As a matter of fact, a substantial part of this task has already been carried out with respect to the conditions on DP-movement and other processes now viewed as instances of Move α. In the previous two chapters we saw that the effects of TSC and SSC derive from BC A on the assumption that DP-traces are anaphors. The effects of TSC were also found in Chapter 8 to derive from the uniqueness requirement on the Case properties of chains. Movement of a DP from the Case-marked subject position of a tensed clause to the Case-marked subject position of a root clause leads to the derivation of a chain with two Case positions, an ill-formed chain. These independent conditions on representations have the effect of restricting DP-movement processes. Other conditions on representations also impose restrictions on DP-movement. For example, the uniqueness requirement on the thematic properties of chains restricts movement of DP-arguments to non-θ-marked positions. This has the effect of excluding (3) while allowing (2). (3) involves movement to a θ-marked position, leading to the derivation of a chain with two θ-positions, an ill-formed chain:

2a. John is certain to win.
2b. John$_i$ is certain [$_{IP}$ t$_i$ to win . . .

3a. *John is confident to win.
3b. *John$_i$ is confident [$_{IP}$ t$_i$ to win . . .

Not only DP-movement is constrained by independent conditions on representation but other movements as well. For example, in Chapter 6 we saw that the Structure Preserving Hypothesis (SPH) has the effect of forcing head categories to move to head positions and maximal projections to maximal (Spec) positions. The consequence is that (5) is excluded, while (4) is allowed:

4a. Which car will John fix?
4b. [$_{CP}$ [$_{DP}$ which car]$_i$ [$_{C'}$ [$_{I'}$ will]$_j$ [$_{IP}$ John [$_{I'}$ t$_j$ [$_{VP}$ fix t$_i$ . . .

5a. *Will which car John fix?
5b. *[$_{CP}$ [$_I$ will]$_j$ [$_{C'}$ [$_{DP}$ which car]$_i$ [$_{IP}$ John [$_{I'}$ t$_j$ [$_{VP}$ fix t$_i$ . . .

(5) is derived by I-raising to Spec,CP and movement of the wh-phrase to the head position C. These operations are excluded on the grounds that they give rise to representations which are inconsistent with the principles of X-bar theory. SPH restricts the set of positions which can be targeted by wh-movement and head-movement processes to the ones compatible with the category moved in X-bar terms.

Another consequence of the constraints on representations imposed by X-bar theory is the restriction of possible movements to substitution movements and adjunction movements. Recall from Chapter 6 that substitution and adjunction movements are structure-preserving and therefore compatible with SPH. Structure-building movements of the type discussed in Chapter 3, such as Topicalisation, are excluded.

The Spec-Head Agreement requirement (Chapter 6) also imposes stringent conditions on the positions which can be targeted by wh-movement. The latter can only target the Spec position of a CP marked with the feature [+Q]. This has the effect of excluding (7) while allowing (6):

6a. John wonders who Mary saw.
6b. John wonders [$_{CP}$ who$_i$ [$_{C'}$ [+Q] [$_{IP}$ Mary I [$_{VP}$ saw t$_i$ . . .

7a. *John believes who Mary saw.
7b. *John believes [$_{CP}$ who$_i$ [$_{C'}$ [−Q] [$_{IP}$ Mary saw t$_i$ . . .

In (6) the embedded C is [+Q], and therefore in Spec-head agreement with the wh-phrase in Spec,CP. In (7), however, the embedded C is [−Q], and therefore not in Spec-head agreement with the wh-phrase in Spec,CP.

Thus, the scope of Move α is already severely restricted by independent conditions on representations. As a matter of fact, the grammar in its current form goes beyond imposing conditions on Move α to arguably providing explanations for why its various instances take place. In Chapter 4 nothing was said in relation to why, for example, a DP object of a passive verb has to move to the subject position, and why the wh-phrase in a simple wh-question has to move to Comp (Spec,CP). In the subsequent chapters, it transpired that movement of these categories to the positions indicated was motivated by certain requirements of the grammar. DP objects of passives move to the subject position in order to satisfy the Case Requirement. Wh-phrases move to Spec,CP in simple wh-questions to satisfy the requirement we called the [+Q]-CP Principle. On the other hand, quantified phrases and wh-phrases in-situ move at LF for scope reasons. The end result is that most movement processes are motivated, in the sense that categories move because they have to.

Although some constraints on Move α are imposed by conditions belonging to various modules of the grammar, this does not necessarily have to be the case with all constraints on Move α. It is possible that some of these constraints belong to the **Movement theory** module itself, and function as conditions on the application of Move α or on the representations derived by Move α. In this chapter we will discuss one major principle called **Subjacency** which functions as a condition on Move α and another major condition called the **Empty Category Principle (ECP)** which serves as a constraint on representations derived by Move α. Subjacency is thought to belong to a module sometimes called **Bounding theory.**

The move to reduce all transformations to the single general principle Move α (or Affect α) is consistent with the general aim of the Principles & Parameters framework to eliminate construction-specific operations and replace them with general principles with broader scope. It is an interesting question, though, whether this move is consistent with the other aim of the framework to replace rules that perform operations with principles that serve as conditions on representations. Calling Move α a principle, obviously, does not alter the fact that it essentially performs an operation. A framework which incorporates Move α cannot be said to be purely representational. Rather, it is a mixed framework in that it incorporates representational elements (conditions on representations) and derivational elements (Move α). Transformational processes represent the real challenge for any theory which seeks to be purely representational. Removing the challenge they present will have to take the form of base-generating so-called moved categories in their SS positions and linking them to their trace with a mechanism of indexation of the type involved in Binding (Chapter 9). The relationship between the antecedent and the trace would then have to be regulated in terms of conditions on representations, possibly the same conditions involved in binding relations.

In the last section of this chapter we will discuss a theory called **Relativised Minimality** which comes very close to assimilating movement phenomena to binding phenomena, and another theory called **Generalised Binding** which does actually take this step.

10.2   *Bounding theory: Subjacency*

10.2.1   Island Conditions and Cyclicity

We saw in Chapter 4 that the Cyclicity Condition imposes the successive cyclic derivation outlined in (8b) on sentences such as (8a):

8a. Which car did you think (that) John would fix?
8b. [CP which car$_i$ [C′ did [IP you think [CP t$_i$′ (that) [IP John would fix t$_i$ . . .

The Cyclicity Condition imposes a successive cyclic derivation on (instances of long) wh-movement, with each step targeting the nearest Spec,CP position. (8b) includes two traces, the initial trace which marks the DS position of the moved wh-phrase, and the intermediate trace which marks the Spec,CP position of the embedded clause used by the wh-phrase on its journey up to the root Spec,CP position.

Now, compare (8) to (9):

9a. ?Which car do you wonder when John will fix?
9b. ?[CP which car$_i$ do [IP you wonder [CP when [IP John will fix t$_i$ . . .

(9) involves wh-movement out of a wh-island. The trace of *when* is ignored because it is irrelevant to the point of the discussion. The question mark associated with (9) encodes the information that the sentence is not as strongly deviant as sentences marked with two questions marks or an asterisk. Degrees of deviance is one of the major issues discussed in this chapter.

In Chapter 4, examples such as (9) were said to be excluded by the Wh-Island Condition on wh-movement. However, there is a sense in which the Wh-island Condition reduces to the Cyclicity Condition. The derivation outlined in (9b) involves a violation of the Cyclicity Condition as the wh-phrase moves directly to the root Spec,CP rather than in successive cyclic steps. The reason the wh-phrase is forced to move directly is that the embedded Spec,CP is filled with the wh-phrase *when*. Spec,CP is said to be an 'escape hatch' used by moved wh-phrases in order to get around the Cyclicity Condition. In (8) the embedded Spec,CP is empty, and therefore can be used as an escape hatch out of the embedded clause by the moved wh-phrase. In (9), however, the embedded Spec,CP is filled, and therefore cannot be used as an escape hatch by the moved wh-phrase to get around the Cyclicity Condition.

The Complex Noun Phrase Condition (CNPC) also appears to be reducible to the Cyclicity Condition, at least as far as complex noun phrases which include a relative clause are concerned. (10) includes a complex noun phrase with a relative clause:

10a. ??Which car have you met someone who can fix?
10b. ??[CP which car_i have [IP you met [DP someone [CP who_j [IP t_j can fix t_i . . .

Recall that relative clauses usually involve an internal process of wh-movement. The Spec,CP of the relative clause in (10) is filled with a wh-phrase, namely *who*. In view of this, the object wh-phrase *which car* cannot make use of the Spec,CP of the relative clause as an escape hatch out of the relative clause. Consequently, *which car* is forced to move directly to the root Spec,CP, thereby violating the Cyclicity Condition.

However, not all complex noun phrases include a relative clause. The complex noun phrase in (11) includes a CP-complement of a N and no wh-movement inside the complement clause:

11a. ?Which car did you hear the rumour that Bill fixed?
11b. ?[CP which car_i [C' did [IP you hear [DP the rumour [CP t_i' that [IP Bill fixed t_i . . .

In (11), the Spec,CP of the CP-complement of N is free and therefore can be used as an escape hatch by the object wh-phrase in moving to the root Spec,CP as shown in (11b). Unlike (10), (11) does not involve a violation of the Cyclicity Condition. It seems that the Complex Noun Phrase Condition is not fully reducible to the Cyclicity Condition, after all.

However, the similarities between the conditions on wh-movement discussed are sufficiently strong to motivate an attempt to reduce them all to a single underlying condition. Chomsky (1973) argues that they are indeed reducible to a single condition which he calls **Subjacency**. The definition of Subjacency we will adopt here is stated in (12):

12. **Subjacency**

    Movement cannot cross more than one bounding node in a single step, where bounding nodes are IP and DP

Let us see how Subjacency derives the effects of the three conditions discussed above. The derivations of the relevant examples are reproduced in (13) with bounding nodes included in a circle:

13a. [CP which car_i did [(IP) you think [CP t_i' (that) [(IP) John would fix t_i . . .
13b. ?[CP which car_i do [(IP) you wonder [CP when [(IP) John will fix t_i . . .
13c. ??[CP which car_i have [(IP) you met [(DP) someone [CP who [(IP) can fix t_i . . .
13d. ?[CP which car_i did [(IP) you hear [(DP) the rumour [CP t_i' that [(IP) Bill fixed t_i . . .

Starting with the Cyclicity Condition illustrated in (13a), Subjacency forces movement of the wh-phrase from the embedded clause to the higher clause to operate in two steps, i.e. successive cyclically. Each step crosses only one bounding node, namely IP. Movement of the wh-phrase to the root clause directly (in a single step) would result in crossing two IP nodes (the embedded IP and the root IP), and therefore is excluded. This is the sense in which Subjacency derives the cyclic effect of wh-movement.

Moving on to the Wh-island Condition illustrated in (13b), we have seen that this condition reduces to the Cyclicity Condition, and therefore is also derivable from Subjacency. Because Spec,CP of the embedded clause is filled in (13b), the wh-phrase is forced to move directly to the root clause in a single step, thereby crossing two IPs (bounding nodes).

Finally, the Complex Noun Phrase Condition illustrated in (13c) and (13d) also reduces to Subjacency. We have seen that the cases which include a relative clause such as (13c) reduce to the Cyclicity Condition, and therefore to Subjacency. In (13c), the wh-phrase is forced to move in a single step to the root clause, thereby crossing two IPs (bounding nodes) together. As a matter of fact, movement in this example crosses a third bounding node which is DP. This is precisely where Subjacency differs from the Cyclicity Condition, with the consequence that Subjacency accounts for cases of complex noun phrases with a CP-complement of N such as (13d). The first step of the movement crosses only one bounding node in (13d), i.e. the embedded IP, but the second step crosses two bounding nodes, i.e. the complex DP and the root IP.

Thus, the three major conditions on wh-movement are indeed reducible to a single condition. As defined in (12), Subjacency is basically a condition on movement (Move-α) rather than a condition on representations derived by movement. It is partly due to the fact that it is a condition on movement that Subjacency is sometimes thought to belong to a separate module of grammar called **Bounding theory.**

10.2.2 Subjacency and LF-movement

Compare (14) and (15) both of which involve a complex noun phrase with a relative clause. The declarative counterpart of the two sentences is *John wrote books that criticise Bill*:

14a. ??Who did John write books that criticise?

14b. SS: ??[$_{CP}$ who$_i$ did [$_{IP}$ John write [$_{DP}$ books [$_{CP}$ Op$_j$ that [$_{IP}$ t$_j$ criticise t$_i$ . . .

15a. Who wrote books that criticise who?

15b. LF: [$_{CP}$ [who]$_i$ [who]$_j$ [$_{IP}$ t$_j$ wrote [$_{DP}$ books [$_{CP}$ t$_k$ that [$_{IP}$ Op$_k$ criticise t$_i$ . . .

(14) is a simple wh-question where movement of the wh-object of the verb *hit* takes place in the syntax. The sentence exhibits a Subjacency violation since it involves extraction out of a complex noun phrase island. (15), on the other hand, is a multiple wh-question where the wh-object of *hit* remains in-situ at SS and does not move to the root Spec,CP till LF. The LF-movement of the object wh-phrase in (15), like that of its counterpart in (14), also crosses (the same) two bounding nodes. However, unlike (14), (15) does not exhibit an island effect, meaning it is not deviant. This difference between sentences such as (14) and (15) in English and

other languages led Huang (1982), among others, to conclude that Subjacency does not hold of LF-movement.

The lack of Subjacency effects with LF-movement apparently shows up in relation to other islands as well. (16) and (17) involve a wh-island. The declarative counterpart of both sentences is *I wonder where John met Bill*:

16a. ?Who do you wonder where John met?
16b. SS: ?[CP who_i do [IP you wonder [CP where [IP John met t_i . . .

17a. Who wonders where John met who?
17b. LF: [CP [who]_i [who]_j [IP t_j wonders [CP where [IP John met t_i . . .

Extraction of the wh-object of *meet* takes place in the syntax in (16) and at LF in (17). However, in both examples the movement crosses (the same) two bounding nodes. As with the complex noun phrase examples above, (16) and (17) exhibit a notable difference in status. This confirms the idea that Subjacency does not hold of LF-movement.

10.3   *Empty Category Principle (ECP)*

10.3.1 Subject–object asymmetries

Compare (18) and (19):

18a. ?Which car do you wonder how to fix?
18b. ?[CP which car_i do [IP you wonder [CP how [IP PRO to fix t_i . . .

19a. *Who do you wonder how will fix the car?
19b. *[CP who_i do [IP you wonder [CP how [IP t_i will fix the car . . .

(18) involves extraction of the wh-object of *fix* out of a wh-island. (19) involves extraction of the wh-subject of the embedded clause out of the same wh-island. The consequence of this difference in the grammatical function of the category extracted (the direct object in (18) and the subject in (19)) is that (18) exhibits a weaker degree of deviance compared to (19). (18) involves a violation of Subjacency which we will see later on typically gives rise to weaker degree of deviance. (19) also involves a Subjacency violation, but the stronger nature of its deviance implies the violation of some other principle which exists over and above Subjacency.

(18) and (19) illustrate the general fact that objects are much easier to extract than subjects, at least in languages such as English. This phenomenon is known as **subject–object asymmetry** with respect to extraction. One of the main aims of this chapter is to explicate the reasons behind it.

The observed asymmetry is not necessarily restricted to extraction out of islands. It also shows up in constructions which do not involve extraction out of an island such as (20) and (21). (21b) is the version of (21a) that does not include the complementiser *that* and (21c) the version that includes the complementiser:

20a. Which car did you say (that) John would fix?
20b. [CP which car_i did [IP you say [CP t'_i [C' (that) [IP John would fix t_i . . .

21a. Who did you say (*that) would fix the car?
21b. [CP who_i did [IP you say [CP t'_i [C' e [IP t_i would fix the car . . .
21c. *[CP who_i did [IP you say [CP t'_i [C' that [IP t_i would fix the car . . .

(20) shows that the object can be successfully extracted out of the embedded clause irrespective of whether the complementiser *that* is present or missing. (21), on the other hand, shows that a subject can only be successfully extracted out of the embedded clause if the complementiser *that* is missing. The phenomenon illustrated in (21c) is known as the **that-trace effect**, referring to the sequence *that-t* at the beginning of the embedded clause. In an earlier framework, that-trace effect cases were accounted for in terms of a special filter called the **That-trace Filter**. Later on, it turned that cases of the that-trace effect form part of a more general pattern revealing an asymmetry between subjects and objects with respect to extraction.

The fact that the deviance of (21c) is of the stronger type is significant. This example does not involve a Subjacency violation as the embedded clause is not an island. (21c) resembles (19) in that it also involves extraction of the subject, suggesting that they both involve a violation of the same principle. (21c) gives us an insight into the strong deviance of (19) in the sense that we now know that it is not due to the Subjacency violation it involves. Subjacency violations typically give rise to a weaker degree of deviance as pointed out above. The stronger deviance of (19) and (21c) is due to whatever principle makes it harder to extract subjects in general.

The explanation for the observed asymmetry between subjects and objects will presumably have to be based on differences in their respective structural properties. One such major difference relates to the fact that objects of verbs are usually governed by a lexical category, namely the verb, whereas subjects of finite clauses are governed by a non-lexical category, namely I. Let us assume that government by a lexical category is a 'stronger' form of government. Let us then call the 'stronger' form of government **proper government**, and define it as in (22):

22. **Proper Government**

    α properly governs β iff α governs β, and α is a lexical category.

Using the notion of proper government we can then set up a condition on traces which requires them to be properly governed. This condition is called the Empty Category Principle (ECP) and is defined as in (23):

23. **Empty Category Principle (ECP)**

    Non-pronominal empty categories must be properly governed.

ECP is usually conceived of as a condition on non-pronominal empty categories in general for reasons which we do not need to get into here. By 'non-pronominal empty categories' we will understand traces here. ECP differs from Subjacency in that it is a condition on the representation of traces derived by Move α rather than a condition on Move α itself.

Let us now see how ECP and Subjacency together account for the examples discussed above. On a general note, ECP discriminates between (traces in) the subject position and (traces in) the object position of the verb in terms of the notion 'proper government'. Traces in the object position are invariably lexically governed by the verb, and therefore will always satisfy ECP. In contrast, traces in the subject position are not lexically governed, their governor being a non-lexical category, and therefore will not satisfy ECP.

(18) and (19) are reproduced in (24) and (25) respectively:

24a. ??Which car do you wonder how to fix?
24b. ??[$_{CP}$ which car$_i$ do [$_{IP}$ you wonder [$_{CP}$ how [$_{C'}$ C [$_{IP}$ PRO to fix t$_i$ . . .

25a. *Who do you wonder how will fix the car?
25b. *[$_{CP}$ who$_i$ do [$_{IP}$ you wonder [$_{CP}$ how [$_{IP}$ t$_i$ will fix the car . . .

In (24) the trace satisfies ECP by virtue of being in the object position of the verb where it is lexically governed by the verb. The weaker deviance of this example is due to the Subjacency violation it involves, as explained above. In (25), however, the trace in the subject position does not satisfy ECP, as it is not lexically governed, and therefore not properly governed. Thus, (25) involves an ECP violation in addition to the Subjacency violation. The stronger degree of deviance it exhibits is due precisely to the fact that it involves an ECP violation and is not necessarily related to the fact it also involves a Subjacency violation.

Let us now move on to (20) and (21), reproduced in (26) and (27), respectively:

26a. Which car did you say (that) John would fix?
26b. [$_{CP}$ which car$_i$ did [$_{IP}$ you say [$_{CP}$ t$'_i$ [$_{C'}$ (that) [$_{IP}$ John would fix t$_i$ . . .

27a. Who did you say (*that) would fix the car?
27b. *[$_{CP}$ who$_i$ did [$_{IP}$ you say [$_{CP}$ t$'_i$ [$_{C'}$ that [$_{IP}$ t$_i$ would fix the car . . .
27c. [$_{CP}$ who$_i$ did [$_{IP}$ you say [$_{CP}$ t$'_i$ [$_{C'}$ e [$_{IP}$ t$_i$ would fix the car . . .

In (26), the trace is located in the object position of the verb *fix*, where it is lexically governed by the verb, and therefore properly governed. In (27b) the trace is located in the subject position, where it is not lexically governed, and therefore not properly governed. The sentence is therefore excluded as predicted with a stronger violation. (27c), however, is problematic. The trace in the subject position is apparently not properly governed and yet the sentence is perfect. Therefore something extra needs to be said about this example if the analysis in terms of ECP is to be maintained. Obviously, an explanation for the sharp contrast between (27b) and (27c) will have to rely on the fact that (27b) includes the complementiser *that* whereas (27c) does not.

The impeccable status of (27c) implies that an additional form of proper government needs to be recognised alongside lexical government. The additional form of proper government is called **antecedent-government** (i.e. government by an antecedent), and is defined as in (28). (29) is the revised definition of proper government:

28. **Antecedent-government**

    α antecedent-governs β iff:

    i)   α and β are co-indexed
    ii) α c-commands β
    iii) α is not separated from β by a barrier.

29. **Proper Government**
    α properly governs β iff:

    i)   α governs β and α is a lexical category   OR
    ii) α antecedent-governs β.

The definition of antecedent-government is said to be **conjunctive**, meaning that for a given category to satisfy antecedent-government all the conditions listed in (i), (ii) and (iii) have to be satisfied. The definition of proper government in (29) is said to be **disjunctive**, meaning that only one of the two conditions (i) and (ii) needs to be satisfied for proper government to hold.

Let us now see how our revised definition of proper government accounts for the data discussed so far. Clause (i) of the definition of proper government is our initial definition of proper government which accounts for all the cases above except (27c). The latter is the example which motivated the introduction of clause (ii) in the definition of proper government. The trace in the embedded subject position of this example now satisfies proper government via antecedent-government by the intermediate trace in the embedded Spec,CP. The intermediate trace satisfies all three conditions listed in (28), and therefore qualifies as an antecedent-governor for the initial trace. Condition (iii) referring to 'barrier' is the one responsible for the contrast between (27b) and (27c). The underlying idea is that the presence of the complementiser *that* renders C' a barrier to antecedent-government. This has the consequence that the intermediate trace does not antecedent-govern the initial trace in (27b). This is despite the fact that the intermediate trace is coindexed with and c-commands the initial trace. In other words, the intermediate trace in (27b) does not qualify as an antecedent-governor for the initial trace because the intermediate trace does not satisfy condition (iii) of the definition of antecedent-government. In (27c), C' is not a barrier to antecedent-government by the intermediate trace because C is not filled with the complementiser *that*.

10.3.2 Adjunct-traces: *that*-deletion and γ-marking

We have seen that there is an asymmetry between subjects and objects with respect to extraction. Subjects are less easily extractable than objects. It is not surprising to learn that adjuncts pattern with subjects in this respect rather than with objects. This is because adjuncts are not governed by a lexical head. Traces in adjunct positions therefore can only satisfy ECP via antecedent-government, like traces in the subject position.

With this in mind, consider (30) and (31). (30a) cannot have the interpretation shown in (30b), and (31a) cannot have the interpretation shown in (31b). The possible interpretation whereby the adjunct wh-phrase is understood to modify the root clause is ignored because it is irrelevant to the point of the discussion:

30a. *How do you wonder whether John fixed the car?
30b. *[CP how$_i$ do [IP you wonder [CP whether [IP John fixed the car t$_i$ . . .

31a. *How have you met someone who could fix the car?
31b. *[CP how$_i$ have [IP you met [DP someone [CP who$_j$ [IP t$_j$ could fix the car t$_i$ . . .

(30) includes a wh-island and (31) a complex noun phrase island. The stronger nature of the violation shown by these examples means that the initial trace is not antecedent-governed. For the moment, we will assume that this is because the antecedent of the trace is 'too far away'. To be a bit more precise, an antecedent is 'too far away' if it is not included in the same clause (CP) as the trace. Another way of putting it is to say that CP is a barrier to antecedent-government. According to this particular explanation, condition (iii) in the definition of proper government above is not satisfied by the antecedent in (30b) and (31b).

With this in mind, consider now (32) in comparison to (33):

32a. How did you think (that) John fixed the car?
32b. [CP how$_i$ did [IP you think [CP t$'_i$ that [IP John fixed the car t$_i$ . . .
32c. [CP how$_i$ did [IP you think [CP t$'_i$ e [IP John fixed the car t$_i$ . . .

33a. Who did you think (*that) would fix the car?
33b. *[CP who$_i$ did [IP you think [CP t$'_i$ [C$'$ that [IP t$_i$ [I$'$ would fix the car . . .
33c. [CP who$_i$ did [IP you think [CP t$'_i$ [C$'$ e [IP t$_i$ would fix the car . . .

(32a) can have the interpretation shown in (32b&c), where the adjunct wh-phrase *how* modifies the embedded verb. This shows that the adjunct wh-phrase can be extracted out of the embedded clause irrespective of whether the complementiser *that* is present, as in (32b), or absent, as in (32c). In this respect, adjunct-extraction differs from subject-extraction as the latter is sensitive to the presence/absence of the complementiser, as shown in (33b&c). Recall that (33b) is excluded on the grounds that the presence of the complementiser *that* renders C$'$ a barrier to antecedent-government of the initial trace by the intermediate trace. Notice, however, that this explanation predicts (32b) to be on a par with (33b), that is, the presence of the complementiser in (32b) should block antecedent-government of the initial adjunct-trace by the intermediate trace just as it does in (33b). Thus, more needs to be said to account for the contrast between (32b) and (33b). This contrast is sometimes said to show that adjunct-extraction does not give rise to the that-trace effect.

To account for this contrast, Lasnik and Saito (1984) suggest an analysis which makes a crucial distinction between the levels at which argument traces and adjunct traces are licensed with respect to ECP. The licensing mechanism takes the form of assigning the feature $[+/-\gamma]$ to the trace. A trace is licensed with respect to ECP if it bears the (positive) feature specification $[+\gamma]$, and not to satisfy ECP if it bears the (negative) feature specification $[-\gamma]$. Argument traces such as subject and object traces must be licensed (i.e. must satisfy ECP) at SS. However, adjunct traces need not be licensed (i.e. need not satisfy ECP) until LF. Put differently, argument traces must be properly governed at SS whereas adjunct traces do not have to be properly governed at SS although they must be properly governed at LF. The underlying idea is that all traces must satisfy ECP at LF by virtue of bearing the feature specification $[+\gamma]$.

Let us now see how this analysis accounts for the contrast between (32b) and (33b). (33b) is reproduced in (34):

34a. *Who did you think that would fix the car?
34b. SS: γ-marking applies $\rightarrow [-\gamma]$
 *[$_{CP}$ who$_i$ did [$_{IP}$ you think [$_{CP}$ t$'_i$ [$_{C'}$ that [$_{IP}$ t$_i$ would fix the car . . .
   $[-\gamma]$

The trace is an argument trace, and therefore must satisfy proper government at SS. However, in SS (34b) the subject trace is not antecedent-governed by the intermediate trace due to the presence of the complementiser *that*. The latter turns C' into a barrier to antecedent-government. Consequently, the trace is assigned the feature $[-\gamma]$ which seals its fate with respect to ECP in the negative sense. Thus, the explanation for (34) remains much as it was earlier.

(32b) is reproduced in (35):

35a. How did you think (that) John would fix the car?
35b. SS: γ-marking does not apply as trace is an adjunct
 [$_{CP}$ how$_i$ did [$_{IP}$ you think [$_{CP}$ t$'_i$ [$_{C'}$ that [$_{IP}$ John would fix the car t$_i$ . . .
35c. LF: *that*-deletion applies followed by γ-marking $\rightarrow [+\gamma]$
 [$_{CP}$ how did [$_{IP}$ you think [$_{CP}$ t$'_i$ [$_{C'}$ e [$_{IP}$ John would fix the car t$_i$ . . .
   $[+\gamma]$

The trace involved is an adjunct-trace and therefore does not have to satisfy ECP until LF. Consequently, although the adjunct-trace is not properly governed at SS (35b), the mechanism of γ-marking does not apply to it at SS. Lasnik and Saito suggest that at the LF level the complementiser *that* deletes (Affect α) on the grounds that it is semantically empty and does not play a role in interpretation. Once the complementiser is deleted, C' ceases to be a barrier to antecedent-government of the initial trace by the intermediate trace. Consequently, the initial trace is assigned the feature $[+\gamma]$, thereby satisfying ECP.

Obviously, the mechanism of *that*-deletion at LF is available to (34) as well. However, because (34) involves an argument trace, and because the fate of argument traces is sealed at SS with respect to ECP, *that*-deletion does not result in rescuing (35) at LF. The argument trace is already assigned the negative feature specification $[-\gamma]$

10.3.3   Intermediate traces: trace-deletion and θ-government

So far, the discussion has been restricted to initial traces. However, as formulated above, ECP applies to all traces, including intermediate traces. In this section, we will discuss the status of intermediate traces with respect to ECP.

Consider the contrast between (36) and (37) noted by Lasnik and Saito (1984):

36a. *How do you wonder whether John said Bill solved the problem?
36b. [CP how$_i$ do [IP you wonder [CP whether [IP John said
      [CP t$_i$′ [IP Bill solved the problem t$_i$ . . .

37a. ??Who do you wonder whether John said solved the problem?
37b. ??[CP who$_i$ do [IP you wonder [CP whether [IP John said
      [CP t$_i$′ [IP t$_i$ solved the problem . . .

The extracted wh-phrase is an adjunct in (36) and an argument (subject) in (37). In both examples, the initial trace is antecedent-governed by the intermediate trace, and yet (36) is notably worse than (37). Presumably, (36) involves an ECP violation, in addition to the Subjacency violation. On the other hand, (37) involves only a Subjacency violation, induced by the presence of *whether*. Lasnik and Saito argue that in view of the fact that the initial trace is properly governed in the two situations, the 'offending trace' must be the intermediate trace.

The solution Lasnik and Saito offer is as follows. Starting with (37), because the initial trace is an argument it receives the feature specification $[+\gamma]$ at SS by virtue of being antecedent-governed by the intermediate trace. Having already done its job, the intermediate trace can then delete at LF. Note that intermediate traces do not have the status of variables at LF, and therefore do not contribute to the interpretation of sentences, unlike initial traces. Since the intermediate trace is the 'offending trace', i.e. the trace that does not satisfy proper government, its deletion at LF eliminates the problem. In (36) the initial trace is an adjunct and therefore does not have to satisfy proper government until LF. The initial trace is crucially dependent on the intermediate trace to be able to satisfy ECP at LF, given that adjunct-traces can only satisfy proper government via antecedent-government. The consequence of this situation is that the intermediate trace in (36) cannot delete at LF, unlike its counterpart in (37). Since the intermediate trace is the 'offending trace', it is the one responsible for the ungrammaticality of (36).

Presumably, the 'offence' of the intermediate trace is that it is not properly governed. The antecedent of this trace (i.e. the wh-phrase itself) is 'too far away' on the assumption that antecedent-government is a local relation confined to a clause. How about lexical government? According to the definition of proper government adopted so far, the intermediate trace in (36) and (37) should be able to satisfy proper government via lexical government by the verb *say*. The configuration involved is shown in (38):

38.   . . . said $[_{CP}$ t_i' $[_{C'}$ e $[_{IP}$ . . .

We have been assuming all along that specifiers are usually accessible to government from outside, so that in (38) the verb lexically governs the intermediate trace in Spec,CP. This implies that the intermediate trace is properly governed, contrary to what was concluded on the basis of the contrast between (36) and (37). It seems that the definition of proper government needs to be revised once more to ensure that the verb does not properly govern the intermediate trace in configuration (38). The revision needs to be undertaken to maintain the analysis outlined for (36) and (37) which is predicated on the idea that the intermediate trace is the 'offending trace' by virtue of being not properly governed.

The required relation is one which does not result in the proper government of the trace in (38) while still guaranteeing that verbs generally properly govern their object. Recall that objects of verbs usually satisfy proper government and are generally easier to extract. The difference between the trace in (38) and a trace in the object position of a verb is that the latter is assigned a θ-role by the verb. In (38), however, the trace is not assigned a θ-role by the verb. Let us then substitute the notion 'θ-**government**' for the notion 'lexical government' in the definition of proper government. The definition of θ-government we will adopt is as stated in (39). (40) is the revised definition of proper government forced by the conclusion to substitute θ-government for lexical government:

39. θ-**Government**

   α θ-governs β iff α is an X^0 category that θ-marks β.

40.   **Proper Government**

   α properly governs β iff:

   i) α θ-governs β OR
   ii) α antecedent-governs β.

The previous definition of proper government allowed a lexical category, such as the verb in (38), to properly govern the specifier of an XP simply by virtue of (lexically) governing it. The new definition incorporating the requirement of θ-government does not have this specific consequence. For a lexical category to properly govern another category it has to both govern it and θ-mark it. Thus, a verb will always properly govern its object by virtue of governing it and θ-marking it. The verb in configuration (38), however, does not properly govern the trace in Spec,CP, although it (merely) governs it. This is because the verb does not θ-mark Spec,CP.

We therefore obtain the desired result which is to prevent the 'offending' intermediate trace in (36) and (37) from being properly governed.

Before we move on to discuss DP-traces, a word about a problem which arises from the assumption that antecedent-government is confined to the clause/CP. Consider example (41a) with the interpretation shown in (41b):

41a. How did you think John would fix the car?
41b. [CP how$_i$ did [IP you think [CP t$_i'$ [IP John would fix the car t$_i$ ...

The initial adjunct-trace satisfies the ECP at LF by virtue of being antecedent-governed by the intermediate trace. The problem raised by (41b) relates to the status of the intermediate trace with respect to ECP. Note, first of all, that this trace cannot delete at LF as the initial trace is dependent on it for antecedent-government. On the other hand, the verb does not properly govern the intermediate trace simply because the verb does not θ-govern the intermediate trace. Finally, the wh-phrase does not antecedent-govern the intermediate trace either, on the grounds that the wh-phrase is 'too far away'. The consequence is that the intermediate trace is not properly governed in (41), and yet the sentence does not exhibit any violation.

The issue concerning this example boils down to finding an appropriate definition for the expression 'too far away'. Let us assume as a working hypothesis that an antecedent is 'too far away' if it is separated from its trace by another wh-phrase. This definition would work for wh-islands which invariably involve a situation where the moved wh-phrase (the antecedent) is separated from its trace by an intervening wh-phrase. In (36) and (37), the intervening wh-phrases separates the moved wh-phrase from the intermediate trace, resulting in a failure of antecedent-government and therefore proper government. In (41), however, the wh-phrase is not 'too far away' from the intermediate trace as no wh-phrase intervenes between the moved wh-phrase and the intermediate trace. The role of intervening wh-phrases in breaking chain-links (i.e. antecedent-government) will be discussed in more detail later on in this chapter.

10.3.4   DP-traces: CP-reduction and improper movement

The fact that ECP does not discriminate between types of traces means that it also applies to DP-traces in a similar way. In this section, we shall discuss the status of DP-traces with respect to ECP.

DP-movement is generally a local operation. In view of this, DP-traces are expected to satisfy ECP via antecedent-government in a trivial way. Where DP-movement takes place from the object position of a verb, the DP-trace is also θ-governed. This is the case in (42) and (43):

42a. The vase was broken (by John).
42b. the vase$_i$ I was broken t$_i$ (by John) ...

43a. The vase broke.
43b. the vase$_i$ broke t$_i$ ...

44a. John is believed to have resigned.
44b. John$_i$ is believed [$_{IP}$ t$_i$ to have resigned . . .

In (44), the DP-trace is not θ-governed even though it is governed by the ECM verb. Recall that the typical property of ECM contexts is that the verb governs and assigns Case to a DP it does not θ-mark. In all three examples, the DP-trace is antecedent-governed by the moved DP, as the two categories are both included in the same clause/CP. Recall from Chapter 8 that the complement is IP (not CP) in ECM contexts.

The situation with respect to DP-traces in raising constructions needs clarification. Consider (45b,c&d) as alternative derivations for (45a):

45a. Mary seems to be happy.
45b. Mary$_i$ seems [$_{CP}$ [$_{C'}$ e [$_{IP}$ t$_i$ [$_{I'}$ to [$_{VP}$ be happy. . .
45c. Mary$_i$ seems [$_{CP}$ t$'_i$ [$_{C'}$ e [$_{IP}$ t$_i$ to be happy. . .
45d. Mary$_i$ seems [$_{IP}$ t$_i$ to be happy. . .

(45b) does not include an intermediate trace in the embedded Spec,CP, implying that DP-movement operates directly out of the embedded clause. The trace in the subject position is not θ-governed, and therefore can only satisfy ECP via antecedent-government. If CP is a barrier to antecedent-government, then, obviously, the trace is not antecedent-governed by the moved DP. If, on the other hand, CP is not a barrier to antecedent-government, as concluded above, then antecedent-government holds in (45b). Note, however, that derivation (45b) is independently excluded by BC A in combination with the assumption that DP-traces are anaphors. The GC of the DP-trace in (45b) is the embedded clause in which the DP-trace is not bound. The root clause would qualify as the GC of the DP-trace if the root verb could govern the DP-trace. However, the root verb does not govern the DP-trace in (45b) due to the presence of CP.

As for (45c), this derivation includes a trace in the embedded Spec,CP, implying that DP-movement operates via this position. This kind of movement, i.e. movement from an A-position to an A'-position and then to an A-position again (A → A' → A) is called **improper movement**. The impropriety relates to the fact that this kind of movement gives rise to an unusual chain, as well as a situation where the initial anaphoric trace is A'-bound by the intermediate trace. Although this relationship helps the initial trace satisfy ECP (via antecedent-government), it does not help it satisfy BC A. Recall that A'-binding is irrelevant to Binding theory which is essentially a theory of A-binding. Thus, derivation (45c) is excluded for the same reason as (45b), among other reasons we have not discussed. The DP-trace is not bound within its GC, namely the embedded clause, in violation of BC A.

We are then left with derivation (45d). The latter involves a representation which differs from the others in that it lacks CP in the embedded clause. The consequence is that the trace in the embedded subject position is governed by the root verb. Government of the DP-trace by the root verb in turn results in the root clause being the GC of the DP-trace by virtue of being the domain which includes the governor of the DP-trace. The DP-trace is bound in the root clause by the moved DP, thereby satisfying BC A. As for its status with respect to ECP, although the DP-trace is not θ-governed by the root verb, it is antecedent-governed by the moved DP. Thus, raising constructions also involve a process of **CP-reduction** affecting the embedded non-finite clause, as with ECM constructions (Chapter 8).

10.3.5   ECP and LF-movement: superiority effects

Compare (46) and (47). Both sentences are instances of multiple wh-questions:

46a. Who saw what?
46b. SS: $[_{CP}$ who$_i$ $[_{IP}$ t$_i$ saw what . . .
46c. LF: $[_{CP}$ [what]$_j$ [who]$_i$ $[_{IP}$ t$_i$ saw t$_j$ . . .

47a. *What did who see?
47b. SS: *$[_{CP}$ what$_j$ did $[_{IP}$ who see t$_j$ . . .
47c. LF: *$[_{CP}$ [who]$_i$ [what]$_j$ did $[_{IP}$ t$_i$ see t$_j$ . . .

In (46) the subject wh-phrase moves to Spec,CP and the object wh-phrase remains in-situ at SS, as shown in (46b). Movement of the object wh-phrase to Spec,CP does not take place until LF, as shown in (46c). In (47) the two wh-phrases move in the reverse order. The object wh-phrase moves to Spec,CP at SS, as shown in (47b), and the subject wh-phrase does not make this movement until LF, as shown in (47c). The contrast between the two examples is a further illustration of the subject–object asymmetry with respect to extraction, this time holding at the LF level. An object wh-phrase can move to a Spec,CP already filled with another wh-phrase (46), whereas a subject wh-phrase cannot (47). This phenomenon is called **superiority** (**effects**).

As expected, adjunct wh-phrases pattern with subject wh-phrases with respect to (covert) extraction at LF, as shown in (48) and (49):

48a. Why did you say what?
48b. SS: $[_{CP}$ why$_i$ did $[_{IP}$ you I say what . . . t$_i$ . . .
48c. LF: $[_{CP}$ [what]$_j$ [why]$_i$ did $[_{IP}$ you say t$_j$ . . . t$_i$ . . .

49a. *What did you say why?
49b. SS: *$[_{CP}$ what$_j$ did $[_{IP}$ you say t$_j$ . . . why . . .
49c. LF: *$[_{CP}$ [why]$_i$ [what]$_j$ did $[_{IP}$ you say t$_j$ . . . t$_i$ . . .

(48) shows that an object wh-phrase can move to a Spec,CP position already filled with another wh-phrase. (49) shows that an adjunct wh-phrase cannot move to a Spec,CP position already filled with another wh-phrase. Thus, adjunct wh-phrases pattern with subject wh-phrases with respect to (covert) LF-movement, just as they do with respect to (overt) SS-movement. Presumably, an account of this asymmetry with respect to LF-movement is expected to operate on the same lines as the parallel asymmetry with respect to SS-movement. Recall that the difference between the two types of wh-phrase is that object wh-phrases can satisfy proper government via antecedent-government or θ-government or both, whereas subject and adjunct wh-phrases can only satisfy proper government via antecedent-government.

One of the accounts of the observed asymmetry relies partly on the **COMP-indexing** rule suggested in Aoun *et al.* (1981) and adapted in (50):

50. **COMP-indexing**

    [COMP... XP_i ...] → [COMP ... XP_i ...]$_i$
    iff COMP dominates only i-indexed elements.

For the moment we will ignore the condition relating to indexing. We will understand (50) to mean, simply, that COMP acquires the index of the first category that moves to it. Obviously, (50) was based on the earlier structure of the clause where COMP was the only node in the pre-IP domain (see Chapters 2–5). In the current structure of the clause, COMP can be understood to refer to Spec,CP, the position occupied by moved wh-phrases.

Given (50), the LF representations of (46) and (47) have the patterns of indexation shown in (51) and (52), respectively:

51a. Who saw what?
51b. SS: [$_{CP}$ [$_{Spec}$ who$_i$]$_i$ [$_{IP}$ t$_i$ see what$_j$ ...
51c. LF: [$_{CP}$ [$_{Spec}$ [what]$_j$ [who]$_i$]$_i$ [$_{IP}$ t$_i$ see t$_j$ ...

52a. *What did who see?
52b. SS: *[$_{CP}$ [$_{Spec}$ what$_i$]$_i$ [$_{C'}$ did [$_{IP}$ who see t$_i$ ...
52c. LF: *[$_{CP}$ [$_{Spec}$ [who]$_j$ [what]$_i$]$_i$ did [$_{IP}$ t$_j$ see t$_i$ ...

Because it is the subject wh-phrase which moves first (overtly) to Spec,CP in (51), Spec,CP acquires the index of the subject wh-phrase. This is shown in (51b&c). Assuming that the antecedent-government relation holds between Spec,CP and a trace, the subject wh-trace in (51c) is antecedent-governed by Spec,CP, thereby satisfying ECP. The object wh-trace, however, is not antecedent-governed by Spec,CP simply because Spec,CP does not bear the index of the object wh-phrase. However, being in the object position of the verb *see*, the object wh-trace satisfies ECP via θ-government.

Turning now to (52), Spec,CP acquires the index of the object wh-phrase since it is the object wh-phrase which moves to it first, as shown in (52b&c). Consequently, the subject wh-trace in (52c) is not antecedent-governed by Spec,CP, and therefore excluded by ECP. In other words, because Spec,CP acquires the index of the object wh-phrase, rather than that of the subject wh-phrase, the trace of the subject wh-phrase is deprived of the only mechanism whereby it can satisfy ECP, namely antecedent-government by Spec,CP.

On a general note, the ability of an object wh-phrase to move to a Spec,CP position already filled with another wh-phrase is due to the fact that its trace is not crucially dependent on antecedent-government to satisfy ECP. It can always satisfy ECP via θ-government. On the other hand, the inability of a subject wh-phrase to move to a Spec,CP position already filled with another wh-phrase, and therefore bearing a different index, is due to the fact that its trace is crucially dependent on antecedent-government to satisfy ECP. The same account extends to (48) and (49), where the contrast is between the trace of an adjunct wh-phrase which is crucially dependent on antecedent-government and the trace of an object wh-phrase which is not. Thus, the comparatively privileged status of the trace of object wh-phrases with respect to ECP is responsible for the observed asymmetry with respect to LF-movement.

The analysis outlined makes an interesting prediction. Multiple wh-questions which involve a subject wh-phrase and an adjunct wh-phrase are expected to be impossible, irrespective of which of the two categories moves to Spec,CP first. This is because in this situation the traces of both wh-phrases are dependent on antecedent-government to satisfy ECP. Since Spec,CP can bear the index of only one of them, the trace of the other wh-phrase will always fail to satisfy ECP. (53) and (54) show that the prediction is borne out:

53a. *Who disappeared why?
53b. SS: *[$_{CP}$ [$_{Spec}$ who$_i$]$_i$ [$_{IP}$ t$_i$ I disappeared . . . why$_j$ . . .
53c. LF: *[$_{CP}$ [$_{Spec}$ [why]$_j$ [who]$_i$]$_i$ [$_{IP}$ t$_i$ disappear . . . t$_j$ . . .

54a. *Why did who disappear?
54b. SS: *[$_{CP}$ [$_{Spec}$ why$_j$]$_j$ did [$_{IP}$ who$_i$ disappeared . . . t$_i$ . . .
54c. LF: *[$_{CP}$ [$_{Spec}$ [who]$_i$ [why]$_j$]$_j$ did [$_{IP}$ t$_i$ disappear . . . t$_j$ . . .

In (53) the trace of the subject is antecedent-governed by the co-indexed Spec,CP and therefore satisfies ECP. However, the trace of the adjunct wh-phrase is not antecedent-governed and therefore does not satisfy ECP. In (54) it is the trace of the adjunct wh-phrase which satisfies ECP via antecedent-government by Spec,CP. The trace of the subject wh-phrase is not antecedent-governed and therefore does not satisfy ECP.

10.4   *Unifying Subjacency and government: Barriers framework*

Subjacency and ECP were said above to be two separate conditions. The former is a condition on movement, and the latter a condition on the representation of traces. The difference between them is reflected in their respective definitions. The definition of Subjacency does not make reference to government, whereas the definition of ECP relies crucially on the notion of government: proper government is a 'stronger' form of government. It is perhaps desirable to have a unified approach to government (ECP) and movement (Subjacency), such that Subjacency would make reference to the same structural relations as government. One such approach is outlined in Chomsky (1986b) and is often called the **Barriers** framework. In this section, we will discuss the general characteristics of this framework, simplifying to a considerable degree a fairly complex system of ideas and relations. A useful guiding principle to keep in mind is that the term 'government' is understood to include both head-government and antecedent-government, and can mean either depending on the issue being discussed.

Note that from now on the index of traces will be represented in a subscript form of the antecedent itself, e.g. the trace of a moved wh-phrase such as *who* will have the form t_{who} and the trace of a moved DP such as *Mary* will have the form t_{Mary} and so on. This change is purely notational and has no theoretical implications in the discussion in the rest of this chapter.

10.4.1 Defining barriers

Central to the Barriers framework, as its name suggests, is the notion 'barrier'. The intuitive idea underlying it is that a given maximal projection may not be a barrier to government inherently, but may become a barrier as a result of being in the proximity of another maximal projection which is a barrier. Consider the familiar examples in (55a–e):

55a. Mary believes [$_{IP}$ them [$_{I'}$ to [$_{VP}$ be clever . . .
55b. I consider [$_{DP}$ them [$_{NP}$ great athletes . . .
55c. I find [$_{AP}$ them [$_{A'}$ crazy . . .
55d. I want [$_{PP}$ them [$_{P'}$ out of my room now . . .
55e. They made [$_{VP}$ us [$_{V'}$ leave immediately . . .

(55a–e) illustrate the fact pointed out in various parts of this book that specifiers of XPs are generally accessible to government from outside. In all five examples, the subject of the embedded XP is governed (and assigned Case) by the root verb. This means that maximal projections are usually not barriers to government from outside, so that IP, DP, AP, PP and VP are not barriers to government in (55a–e). It is plausible to assume that this is true of CP as well by virtue of being true of all maximal projections in general.

With this in mind, consider now the equally familiar example (56):

56a. John decided to leave.
56b. [$_{IP}$ John decided [$_{CP}$ e [$_{IP}$ PRO to leave . . .

The root verb *decide* does not govern *PRO* in the subject position of the embedded clause in (56) (recall that *PRO* can only occur in non-governed positions). In view of this, the question which arises is the following: Why is *PRO* not governed in (56) despite the fact that, as we saw above, neither CP nor IP is a barrier to government from outside? The difference between (55a) and (56) lies in the fact that the subject is separated from the root verb by both IP and CP in (56), but only by IP in (55a).

Capitalising on this difference, let us try to work out why government of the subject is blocked in (56) but not in (55a), and by extension other examples in (55). In (55a) the embedded IP is governed by the root verb, which is a lexical category. In (56) the embedded IP is governed by C, which is a non-lexical category. Using the terminology discussed in the previous section, IP is θ-governed by the verb in (55a) but not in (56). In the latter example, IP is governed, if at all, by a functional category, namely C. Let us call the relation of θ-government **L-marking**, and define it as in (57). (58) is the definition of θ-government, reproduced here for reference:

57.   **L-marking**

α L-marks β if α θ-governs β.

58.   **θ-government**

α θ-governs β iff α is an X^0 category that θ-marks β.

In (55a) IP is L-marked because it is θ-governed by the root verb. In (56) IP is not L-marked because it is not θ-governed. The governor of IP is C in (56) which is a non-lexical category and therefore does not θ-mark IP.

Let us now assume further that maximal projections which are L-marked are never barriers. Accordingly, IP is not a barrier in (55a), given that it is L-marked (by the root verb). This is the reason the root verb can govern across IP in (55a). It is tempting to assume the reverse, that is maximal projections which are not L-marked are invariably barriers. This would mean with respect to (56) that IP is a barrier, and hence the fact that the root verb does not govern Spec,IP. In configuration (56b) CP is not a barrier as it is L-marked by the root verb. However, there are familiar reasons to believe that IP alone is never a barrier to government even when it is non-L-marked. Consider (59) bearing in mind that antecedent-government is a form of government. The moved adjunct-phrase *how* antecedent-governs its trace across IP. This implies that IP is not a barrier to government. This appears to be the case even though IP is not L-marked in (59):

59a.   How did John fix the car?
59b.   [CP how did [IP John fix the car t_{how} . . .

Rather than concluding from (59) that maximal projections which are not L-marked are not barriers, let us assume instead that IP is an exception. Chomsky calls IP a 'defective' category. Let us assume further that IP is an exception only in a partial way. More precisely, although IP is never a barrier when it is not L-marked, it can cause a maximal projection which immediately dominates it to be a barrier. To put it in more mundane terms, although IP has the capacity to be a barrier, it never takes the responsibility to block government. At the same time, it is always happy to pass the responsibility onto the maximal projection immediately dominating it. We now have two distinct notions of 'barrier'. One is the notion 'inherent barrier' which is a maximal projection that is a barrier by virtue of being non-L-marked. The other is the notion 'barrier by inheritance' which is a maximal projection that is a barrier by virtue of immediately dominating IP or a maximal projection which is a barrier. Accordingly, 'barrier' can be defined as in (60):

60.   **Barrier**

α is a barrier (for β) iff:

i)   α is not L-marked   OR
ii) α immediately dominates IP   OR
iii) α immediately dominates a non-L-marked category.

Were it not for the 'defective' nature of IP, we would not need clause (ii) in (60). IP differs from the other categories in that it never is a barrier inherently even when it is non-L-marked.

Let us now see how (60) accounts for the examples above. (55a) and (56) are reproduced in (61) and (62), respectively:

61a. Mary believes them to be clever.
61b. Mary believes [$_{IP}$ them [$_{I'}$ to [$_{VP}$ be clever . . .

62a. John tried to leave.
62b. John tried [$_{CP}$ e [$_{IP}$ PRO [$_{I'}$ to [$_{VP}$ leave . . .

In (61) IP is not a barrier both because it never is inherently anyway, and, redundantly, because it is L-marked by the root verb. Thus, the verb governs and assigns Case to the subject of the embedded clause. In (62) IP is not a barrier either and neither is CP since CP is L-marked by the root verb. However, because CP immediately dominates IP, and because IP usually transmits barrierhood to the maximal projection immediately dominating it, CP inherits barrierhood from IP and becomes a barrier itself (by inheritance). In other words, CP is barrier by virtue of clause (ii) in the definition of 'barrier' (60). This is an example of situations where a given category which is not a barrier inherently may become one by virtue of being in the vicinity of a certain category, in this case IP. Thus, the root verb does not govern *PRO* in the subject position of the embedded clause in (62).

The relation of inheritance between CP and IP is basically intended to capture the generalisation that the relation of government (both head-government and antecedent-government) can hold across each of these categories individually but not across both of them together. The fact that (antecedent-) government can hold across IP and CP individually but not across both of them together is further illustrated in (63):

63a. How did you say (that) she solved the problem?
63b. [$_{CP}$ how did [$_{IP}$ you say [$_{CP}$ t$_{how}$' [$_{IP}$ she solved the problem . . . t$_{how}$ . . .
63c. *[$_{CP}$ how did [$_{IP}$ you say [$_{CP}$ [$_{IP}$ she solved the problem . . . t$_{how}$ . . .

(63b) and (63c) represent different derivations only one of which is legitimate. (63b) inlcudes an intermediate trace in the embedded Spec,CP, whereas (63c) does not. In (63b) the intermediate trace antecedent-governs the initial trace across the embedded IP and the moved wh-phrase antecedent-governs the intermediate trace across the embedded CP. In (63c), where movement of the wh-phrase applies directly, the antecedent in the root Spec,CP does not govern its initial trace inside the embedded IP. This is because the embedded CP and IP both intervene between them, resulting in a situation where CP inherits barrierhood from IP. Thus, the Barriers system derives the cyclicity effects of Subjacency with respect to movement. In (63c) CP is a barrier both to antecedent-government (ECP) and to movement (Subjacency). This is precisely the sense in which a given maximal projection can be a barrier to both government and movement in the Barriers framework.

10.4.2 Barriers and adjunction

Consider the simple example (64):

64a. Who did John meet?
64b. [$_{CP}$ who did [$_{IP}$ John [$_{VP}$ meet t$_{who}$ . . .

IP is not a barrier in (64) for the reasons mentioned above. VP, on the other hand, is the archetypal example of an inherent barrier. Its governor, namely I, is a functional category which does not L-mark it. Now, since IP immediately dominates VP, IP inherits barrierhood from VP. Consequently, (64) includes two barriers between the antecedent and the trace, namely VP (inherently) and IP (by inheritance from VP). It does not necessarily follow from this that (64) involves an ECP violation. As a matter of fact, (64) does not involve an ECP violation. The trace is in the object position of the verb and therefore θ-governed by the verb. However, (64) does indeed involve a Subjacency violation by virtue of the fact that the movement it involves crosses two barriers, VP and IP. (64) is therefore expected to exhibit at least a slight degree of deviance. However, (64) is perfectly grammatical. The Barriers system as conceived so far predicts (64) to exhibit a Subjacency type violation which it does not. It needs to be fixed.

Compare (64) to (65). (65) involves an adjunct wh-phrase instead of an object wh-phrase:

65a. How did John fix the car?
65b. [$_{CP}$ how did [$_{IP}$ John [$_{VP}$ fix the car . . . t$_{how}$ . . .
65c.

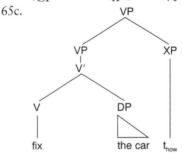

The trace of the adjunct wh-phrase is right-adjoined to VP, as shown in (65c). Recall (from Chapter 6) that adjuncts have a special status with respect to the categories they adjoin to. An adjunct is both a sister to and a daughter of the category it is adjoined to. Using different terminology, although adjuncts are constituent members of the categories they are adjoined to, they are not full members. V and DP are full members of VP in (65), but the adjoined category is not. We will call the adjoined category in (65) an 'associate member' of VP, just for clarification.

Let us now assume that maximal projections are barriers only for their full members. Associate members are governed by different regulations. It follows that VP is not a barrier for the adjoined trace in (65) simply because the adjoined trace is not a full member of VP. This accounts for the fact that this trace is antecedent-governed by the moved adjunct wh-phrase. With this in mind, let us go back to (64), where the wh-phrase is a full member of VP. Suppose now that the object wh-phrase in this example exploits the associate-membership status temporarily, as an escape hatch out of VP. In other words, suppose that in moving out of VP, the object wh-phrase adjoins to VP first, so that a more detailed derivation of (64a) is as in (66b):

66a. Who did John meet?
66b. [$_{CP}$ who did [$_{IP}$ John [$_{VP}$ t$_{who}$' [$_{VP}$ meet t$_{who}$ . . .

Because the intermediate trace is not a full member of VP in (66b), VP is not a barrier for it. The consequence is that no barrier intervenes between the intermediate trace and the initial trace and between the antecedent and the intermediate trace. Consequently, (66b) satisfies both ECP and Subjacency.

The essence of the analysis outlined in (66b) is that it is always possible to circumvent the barrierhood of a maximal projection simply by adjoining to it. Adjunction creates a structure where an intermediate trace is neither in nor out.

In situations of long extraction, adjunction to VP takes place in both the embedded clause and the root clause. Thus, (67a), for example, has the derivation shown in (67b). The intermediate traces are distinguished from each other in terms of increasing numbers of primes:

67a. Who did you say (that) John met?
67b. [$_{CP}$ who did [$_{IP}$ you [$_{VP}$ t$_{who}$''' [$_{VP}$ say [$_{CP}$ t$_{who}$'' [$_{IP}$ John [$_{VP}$ t$_{who}$' [$_{VP}$ met t$_{who}$ . . .

Just as the moved object wh-phrase has to adjoin to the embedded VP containing it to circumvent its barrierhood, it also has to adjoin to the root VP to circumvent its barrierhood. In the meantime, the wh-phrase moves to the embedded Spec,CP to avoid crossing IP and CP together for reasons that should be familiar by now.

Note, however, that for the analysis outlined in (67b) to go through, adjunction to both IP and CP has to be banned. This is because if adjunction to these categories were possible, their barrierhood could be circumvented simply by adjoining to them, and movement through Spec,CP would become unnecessary.

The need to ban adjunction to IP and CP is more evident with examples involving extraction out of a wh-island such as (68):

68a. *How do you wonder whether John fixed the car?
68b. *[$_{CP}$ how do [$_{IP}$ you [$_{VP}$ t$_{how}$' [$_{VP}$ wonder [$_{CP}$ whether
     [$_{IP}$ John [$_{VP}$ fixed the car . . . t$_{how}$ . . .

Recall from earlier that extraction of an adjunct out of an island invariably gives rise to a strong ECP-type violation. Recall also that examples such as (68) also involve a Subjacency violation, although this is masked by the strong nature of their deviation. The strong nature of (68) means that its derivation involves an 'offending trace', that is a trace which fails to be (antecedent-) governed due to some intervening barrier. The 'offending trace' is the initial trace which is separated from the intermediate trace by IP and CP together. Recall that this situation always results in CP becoming a barrier by inheritance from IP. Recall also that it is possible to circumvent this situation by moving through Spec,CP. However, this option is not available to the moved adjunct wh-phrase in (68) because the most embedded Spec,CP is already filled with another wh-phrase (*whether*). This is how the Barriers system derives the strong island effects with respect to adjuncts.

We are now in a position to demonstrate why adjunction to IP and CP should be banned. If the moved wh-phrase in (68) is allowed to adjoin to IP and to CP, the barrierhood which otherwise results from crossing them together would be circumvented. Consequently, we would not have an explanation for the deviant nature of (68). In other words, an explanation of (68) in the Barriers system is crucially dependent on disallowing adjunction to IP and CP by moved categories.

As a matter of fact, not only adjunction to IP and CP has to be banned, but also adjunction to DP. The ban on adjunction to DP is needed to account for complex noun phrase island violations of the type illustrated in (69) (The declarative counterpart is: *I have seen the car which John was driving.*)

69a. *Who have you seen the car which was driving?
69b. *[$_{CP}$ who have [$_{IP}$ you [$_{VP}$ t$_{who}$' [$_{VP}$ seen [$_{DP}$ the car
       [$_{CP}$ which [$_{IP}$ t$_{who}$ [$_{VP}$ was driving t$_{which}$ · · ·

(69) involves two barriers between the intermediate trace adjoined to the root VP and the initial trace in the subject position of the relative clause. CP is a barrier both by inheritance from IP and by being non-L-marked. Recall (from Chapter 6) that relative CPs are adjuncts and therefore not θ-marked by the noun they modify. DP is also a barrier by inheritance from the relative CP it immediately dominates. Now, for this explanation to go through, not only adjunction to IP and CP should be banned, but also to DP. If wh-movement were allowed to adjoin to these three maximal projections in (69), no barrier would be involved. Consequently, we would not have an explanation for its deviance.

10.4.3   Subjacency violations: degrees of deviance

In addition to an attempt to unify government and Subjacency, the Barriers system incorporates an attempt to relate the degree of deviance in cases of Subjacency violations to the number of barriers crossed in a movement derivation. The expectation is that movement which crosses only one barrier should give rise to a less severe degree of deviance than movement which crosses two barriers, and so on. In other words, the more barriers are crossed the more degraded the status of the sentence becomes. The issue is mainly restricted to examples which involve Subjacency violations.

We have seen that Subjacency violations typically give rise to weaker effects. What we have not seen yet is that among the class of Subjacency violations itself, there appear to be varying degrees of deviance. Subjacency violations involving wh-islands are felt to be weaker than Subjacency violations involving complex noun phrase islands with relative clauses. Thus, (70), for example, is felt to be less bad (one question mark) than (71) (two questions marks):

70a. ?Which car don't you know how to fix?
70b. ?$[_{CP}$ which car don't $[_{IP}$ you $[_{VP}$ t$_{which\ car}$"$[_{VP}$ know
   $[_{CP}$ how $[_{IP}$ PRO to $[_{VP}$ t$_{which\ car}$' $[_{VP}$ fix t$_{which\ car}$ · · ·

71a. ??Which car have you met someone who can fix?
71b. ??$[_{CP}$ which car have $[_{IP}$ you $[_{VP}$ t$_{which\ car}$"$[_{VP}$ met $[_{DP}$ someone
   $[_{CP}$ who $[_{IP}$ t$_{who}$ can $[_{VP}$ t$_{which\ car}$' $[_{VP}$ fix t$_{which\ car}$ · · ·

Recall from above that examples of wh-island violations such as (70) involve a single barrier. On the other hand, examples of CNPC island violations such as (71) involve two barriers. The single barrier in (70) is CP, which inherits barrierhood from IP. The two barriers in (71) are the (adjunct) relative CP and DP, the former by being non-L-marked and the latter by inheritance from CP. Thus, the varying degree of deviance exhibited by (70) and (71) reflects the varying number of barriers each one of them involves.

In Chapter 9 we briefly discussed another island for extraction called the adjunct-island, illustrated in (72). (73) illustrates a fourth island for extraction known as the **subject-island**. These two islands are sometimes referred to as cases of **Conditions on Extraction Domains (CED)**, after Huang (1982) (The declarative counterparts are: *They disappeared without greeting John* and *Reading this book would be fun*):

72a. ??Who did they disappear without greeting?
72b. ??$[_{CP}$ who did $[_{IP}$ they $[_{VP}$ disappear $[_{PP}$ without
   $[_{CP}$ t$_{who}$"$[_{IP}$ PRO I $[_{VP}$ t$_{who}$' $[_{VP}$ greeting t$_{who}$ · · ·

73a. ??This is the book which reading would be fun.
73b. ?? · · · $[_{CP}$ which $[_{IP}$ $[_{CP}$ t$_{which}$" $[_{IP}$ PRO $[_{VP}$ t$_{which}$' $[_{VP}$ reading t$_{which}$ · · ·

In (72) the wh-phrase is extracted out of the PP adjunct. We will assume here that the PP in question is adjoined to VP, although this many not be entirely clear. (73) involves extraction out of a clausal (CP) subject to the Spec,CP of the relative clause modifying the noun *book*. Since the movement takes place inside the relative CP in (73), only the relative CP is represented in (73b). The two examples appear to involve the same degree of deviance as the complex noun phrase case discussed above. Therefore, they are both expected to involve two barriers each. The two barriers in (72) are the PP adjunct and the IP immediately dominating it. The PP adjunct is a barrier by virtue of being non-L-marked (adjuncts are non-L-marked). IP is a barrier by inheritance from the adjunct PP. The two barriers in (73) are the CP of the clausal subject and the IP of the relative clause immediately dominating it. The CP of the clausal subject is a barrier inherently as it is not L-marked. The IP of the relative clause is a barrier by inheritance from the relative CP.

10.4.4 Head movement: Head Movement Constraint (HMC)

So far the discussion of movement in the Barriers system has been restricted to movement of maximal projections, in particular wh-movement. Our next task is to work out how the Barriers system deals with instances of movement that involve heads or X^0 categories.

Compare (74), (75) and (76):

74a. How tall will John be?
74b. [$_{CP}$ how tall [$_{C'}$ will [$_{IP}$ John [$_{I'}$ t$_{will}$ [$_{VP}$ be . . . t$_{how\ tall}$ . . .

75a. How tall is John?
75b. [$_{CP}$ how tall [$_{C'}$ is [$_{IP}$ John [$_{I'}$ t$_{is}$ [$_{VP}$ t$_{be}$ . . . t$_{how\ tall}$ . . .

76a. *How tall be John will?
76b. *[$_{CP}$ how tall [$_{C'}$ be [$_{IP}$ John [$_{I'}$ will [$_{VP}$ t$_{be}$ . . . .t$_{how\ tall}$ . . .

(74) involves I-raising and (75) involves V-raising followed by I-raising. (76) shows that the verb cannot raise directly from inside VP to C. As shown in (75), raising of the verb to C has to go through I. In Chapters 5 and 6 raising of the verb to I on its way to C was said to be motivated by the need to 'support' the inflectional elements of I. Note, however, that this argument does not extend to (76) where I includes a Modal and the inflectional elements of I do not need 'support' by the verb. There seems to be no reason why the verb should not move directly to C, and yet this movement is not allowed. What (76) demonstrates is that raising of the verb to I on its way to C is forced by some consideration, a constraint, which exists over and above the need for I elements to be supported.

The constraint in question is known as the Head Movement Constraint (HMC). There are many ways it can be formulated (see Travis 1984 and Baker 1988). The version in (77) is adapted from Chomsky (1986b):

77. **Head Movement Constraint (HMC)**

Movement of an X^0 category α is restricted to the position of a head β that governs the maximal projection of α.

The head category which governs the maximal projection of the verb (VP) is I, and the head category which governs the maximal projection of I (IP) is C. According to HMC, movement of the verb is restricted to I. If the verb moves directly to C without going through I, a violation of HMC arises. Thus, movement of the Modal (I) to C in (74), and movement of the verb first to I and then to C in (75) are all consistent with HMC. However, movement of the verb directly to C in (76) is not consistent with HMC. In more general terms, movement of a head is restricted to the nearest head above it. Skipping an intervening head category results in the violation of HMC. Let us now see how the constraint encoded in HMC follows from the Barriers system.

Starting with (76), recall that VP is usually a barrier unless it is adjoined to. Recall also (from Chapter 6) that SPH (Structure Preserving Hypothesis) requires that maximal projections can only adjoin to maximal projections and heads can only adjoin to head categories. It follows that the verb in (76), being a head category, cannot adjoin to VP to circumvent its barrierhood. Therefore, the verb has to move across VP on its way to C. Consequently, VP is a barrier for movement of the verb to C. Note that in moving to C, the verb also crosses IP. The latter is also a barrier by inheritance from VP. Thus, (76) actually involves two barriers, and hence the fact that it is excluded.

Note, however, that the barrierhood of VP should also block movement of the verb to I in (75). However, it apparently does not. It seems that when the verb moves only as far as I, the barrierhood of VP gets nullified somehow.

To account for the contrast between (75) and (76), the Barriers system introduces the idea that I θ-marks and therefore θ-governs its complement VP. The consequence of this idea is that VP is now L-marked and therefore ceases to be a barrier. Movement of the verb to I becomes legitimate under this view. However, there is an obvious sense in which this cannot be the whole story. Notice that movement of the verb directly to C, seen in (76), also becomes legitimate, with the consequence that the explanation for the ungrammatical status of (76) is lost. Something extra needs to be said to achieve the desired result, which is that the barrierhood of VP is nullified when the verb moves only as far as I, and preserved when the verb moves directly to C skipping over I. The desired result can be achieved by maintaining the idea that I θ-governs VP and introducing a slight revision in the definition of L-marking such that the class of L-marking categories is restricted to lexical categories which θ-govern their complement. The required definition is as stated in (78):

78. **L-marking**

α L-marks β iff α is a lexical category that θ-governs β.

In principle, I is a non-L-marking category by virtue of being a non-lexical category. Thus, even though I θ-governs its complement VP, it does not L-mark it. However, when the verb moves to I, the latter becomes 'lexicalised', meaning it acquires the status of a lexical category. This means that in situations where the verb moves to I such as (75), VP ceases to be a barrier because it is now L-marked by ('lexicalised') [$_I$ [V] I]. This is not the case in situations where the verb moves directly to C, as in (76). In (76) I is filled with a modal which is not a lexical category. In view of this, I is not 'lexicalised' in (76), with the consequence that VP remains a barrier and moreover transmits its barrierhood to IP. (76) therefore involves two barriers, as concluded earlier. This is the sense in which the revised definition of L-marking in (78) together with the idea that I θ-governs VP ensure that VP ceases to be a barrier when the verb moves to I but remains a barrier when the verb does not move to I. This is also the sense in which the Barriers system derives the effects of HMC.

10.5 *Unifying antecedent-government and binding*

In this section we will discuss the possibility of unifying (antecedent-) government and Binding. First, we will discuss an approach outlined in Rizzi (1990) and known as **Relativised Minimality.** This approach reveals a significant parallelism between (antecedent-) government and binding which represents a tempting invitation to reduce one to the other. Although Rizzi does not actually undertake the task of unifying the two, he clearly points out the parallelism between them: 'The analogies with the theory of binding look more than superficial, and suggest the possibility of a partial unification of government and binding . . .' (p.8). In the second part of this section we will discuss another approach outlined in Aoun (1985, 1986) known as **Generalised Binding.** This approach actually takes the step of unifying (antecedent-) government and binding.

10.5.1   Relativised Minimality: Rizzi (1990)

Rizzi starts by making the important observation that the phenomena of adjunct-extraction out of wh-islands, super-raising, and violations of HMC, illustrated in (79–81), have an underlying common denominator:

79a. *How do you wonder why John fixed the car?
79b. [$_{CP}$ how [$_{C'}$ do [$_{IP}$ you wonder [$_{CP}$ why [$_{IP}$ John fixed the car t_{how} . . .

80a. *John seems it is likely to solve the problem.
80b. [$_{IP}$ John seems [$_{IP}$ it is likely [$_{IP}$ t_{John} to solve the problem . . .

81a. *How tall be John will?
81b. [$_{CP}$ how tall [$_{C'}$ be [$_{IP}$ John [$_{I'}$ will [$_{VP}$ t_{be} . . . $t_{how\ tall}$ . . .

In each of these cases a category of the same type as the antecedent intervenes between the antecedent and its trace. In (79) the wh-phrase *why* intervenes between the moved adjunct wh-phrase *how* and its trace in the embedded clause. In (80) the DP *it* in Spec,IP of the middle clause intervenes between the moved DP *John* in the root clause and its trace in the most embedded clause. Finally, in (81) the X^0 category *will* (I) intervenes between the moved X^0 category *be* and its trace inside VP.

   The fact that an intervening category seems to interfere with the relation between an antecedent and its trace suggests the involvement of a Minimality effect. The antecedent fails to antecedent-govern its trace because a category of the same type as the antecedent (a potential antecedent) intervenes between the two of them. The notion 'same type' is crucial. Consider (82) and (83):

82a. How did you think (that) John fixed the car?
82b. [$_{CP}$ how did [$_{IP}$ you think [$_{CP}$ (that) [$_{IP}$ John fixed the car . . . t_{how} . . .

83a. Will John fix the car?
83b. [$_{CP}$ [$_{C'}$ will [$_{IP}$ John [$_{I'}$ t_{will} [$_{VP}$ fix the car . . .

In (82) two subjects intervene between the wh-phrase and its trace. Yet, they do not block the antecedent-government relation between the wh-phrase and its trace. This is because the two subjects are not of the same type as the antecedent. While the subjects are A-specifiers, meaning they occupy a Spec position which is an A-position (Spec,IP), the wh-phrase is an A'-specifier, meaning it occupies a Spec position which is an A'-position (Spec,CP). (83) shows that a subject does not block antecedent-government of an X^0 trace by its antecedent either, because the subject is not of the same type as the moved X^0 category. The moved category (antecedent) is a head while the subject of the sentence is an XP-specifier.

Since antecedent-trace relations seem to be sensitive to the peculiar properties of antecedents and intervening categories, Rizzi has argued that the version of the Minimality Condition required must be a **relativised** one instead of the **rigid** version provided in Chapter 8 and reproduced in (84):

84. **Minimality Condition**

> In the configuration [XP . . . X . . . [YP . . . Y . . . ZP] . . .] X does not govern ZP.

Definition (84) is rigid in the sense that it does not distinguish between the types of categories which can function as minimal intervening governors. The required definition of Minimality must be relativised in the precise sense that only a category of the same type as the antecedent can serve as a minimal governor for the trace of the antecedent. Rizzi then formulates a relativised version of Minimality which includes both head-government and antecedent-government. The adapted version given in (85), however, is restricted to antecedent-government, as head-government is not crucially relevant to the ensuing discussion. (86) is the definition of antecedent-government incorporating Relativised Minimality:

85. **Relativised Minimality (RM)**

> α antecedent-governs β only if there is no γ such that

> i)   γ is a typical potential antecedent-governor for β
> ii) γ c-commands β and does not c-command α.

86. **Antecedent-government**

> α antecedent-governs β iff:

> i)   α and β are co-indexed
> ii)   α c-commands β
> iii) No barrier intervenes
> iv)   Relativized Minimality is respected.

Clause (ii) of the definition of Relativised Minimality in (85) defines the notion 'intervene'. An intervening element is one which c-commands the trace and is c-commanded by the antecedent. Clause (i), on the other hand, defines the relativised aspect of Minimality. A typical potential governor for the trace of an A'-specifier is another A'-specifier, and a typical potential governor for the trace of an A-specifier is another A-specifier.

With this in mind, let us now go back to (79), (80) and (81). In (79) antecedent-government of the wh-trace by the antecedent *how* is blocked by the wh-phrase *why*. The latter intervenes between the antecedent and the trace in the sense defined above. Moreover, *why* is of the same type as the antecedent, i.e. an A'-specifier. In (80) antecedent-government of the DP-trace by its antecedent *John* is blocked by the intervening A-specifier *it*. Thus, both examples are excluded on the grounds that the antecedent-trace relation they involve does not respect the Relativised Minimality Condition on antecedent-government. In the grammatical example (82), no A'-specifier intervenes between the wh-trace and its antecedent *how*, and therefore no Relativised Minimality effect is involved.

It is interesting to recall that the super-raising example reproduced in (87) is a typical example of the SSC on binding relations discussed in Chapter 9:

87a. *John seems it is likely to solve the problem.
87b. *[$_{IP}$ John seems [$_{IP}$ it is likely [$_{IP}$ t$_{John}$ to solve the problem . . .

The DP-trace, being an anaphor, is not bound in the (c-command) domain of the nearest subject *it*. This means that (87) is excluded by BC A, although it may also involve a violation of a condition on movement. Recall that the SSC pattern is part of a more general pattern which also involves lexical anaphors as shown in (88):

88a. *The players expected the coach to blame each other.
88b. *[the players$_i$ expected [$_{IP}$ the coach$_j$ to blame each other$_i$ . . .

This is the sense in which Relativised Minimality patterns, except for the one involving heads, are basically the same patterns found in binding relations involving lexical anaphors and accounted for in terms of the principles of Binding theory. The Relativised Minimality patterns can quite easily be reduced to binding patterns and accounted for in terms of the principles of Binding theory, although, as explained above, Rizzi does not take this step. Note, however, that the theory of binding required is one which incorporates both A-binding relations as well as A'-binding relations. Recall that the theory of binding outlined in Chapter 9 is a theory of A-binding and does not include A'-binding relations. In the next section, we will discuss a theory of binding which incorporates both relations and which reduces cases of antecedent-government to a generalised version of Binding Condition A.

10.5.2 Generalised Binding: Aoun (1985; 1986)

Recall from Chapter 9 that the origins of the theory of Binding outlined there were rooted in earlier accounts which made use of SSC on DP-movement (or DP-traces) and NIC on lexical anaphors. Variable traces (or wh-movement) are not subject to SSC and NIC as shown in (89) and (90), with SSC understood at that time to refer only to A-specifiers. It was for this reason that the theory of binding that developed from these earlier accounts was essentially a theory of A-binding:

89a. Who did you say (that) Mary saw?
89b. [$_{CP}$ who did [$_{IP}$ you say [$_{CP}$ (that) [$_{IP}$ Mary saw t$_{who}$ . . .

90a. Who did you say solved the problem?
90b. [$_{CP}$ who did [$_{IP}$ you say [$_{CP}$ [$_{IP}$ t$_{who}$ solved the problem . . .

Aoun (1986) argues that a closer look at other examples reveals that variables are indeed subject to SSC and NIC. The examples he discusses with respect to SSC relate to extraction out of noun phrases in French and Italian which we are not going to discuss here. On the other hand, the examples he discusses with respect to NIC are the familiar ones in (91), (92) and (93):

91a. *Who do you wonder how solved the problem?
91b. *[$_{CP}$ who [$_{C'}$ do [$_{IP}$ you wonder [$_{CP}$ how [$_{IP}$ t$_{who}$ solved the problem . . .

92a. *Who do you think that saw Bill?
92b. *[$_{CP}$ who do [$_{IP}$ you think [$_{CP}$ that [$_{IP}$ t$_{who}$ saw Bill . . .

93a. *It is unclear what who saw.
93b. SS: *it is unclear [$_{CP}$ what [$_{IP}$ who saw t$_{what}$ . . .
93c. LF: *it is unclear [$_{CP}$ [who] [what] [$_{IP}$ t$_{who}$ saw t$_{what}$ . . .

All three examples involve a variable in a nominative island. Ignoring the fact that all three examples also involve material in the pre-IP domain of the embedded clause, they at least superficially show that variables are subject to some form of NIC. As a matter of fact, the *that*-trace effect case (92) was previously treated, e.g. in Chomsky (1981), as a residual case of NIC.

To the extent that this conclusion is warranted, it indicates that the distribution of variables with respect to their A'-antecedent is regulated by the same conditions of Binding theory which regulate the distribution of lexical anaphors. This in turn indicates that the theory of A-binding should be generalised to include A'-binding relations, with the rather attractive consequence that the effects of antecedent-government (more generally, ECP) are derivable from a generalised binding theory. Aoun suggests to replace the conditions of A-binding, discussed in Chapter 9, with the generalised conditions of X-binding in (94):

94. **Generalised Binding Conditions**

    A. An anaphor must be X-bound in its GC
    B. A pronoun must be X-free in its GC
    C. A name (r-expression) must be A-free.
       (where X = A or A')

95. **Governing Category**

    β is the GC for α iff β is the minimal maximal projection containing α, a governor for α, and a SUBJECT accessible to α.

96. Accessibility

> α is accessible to β iff β is in the c-command domain of α, and co-indexing of (α,β) would not violate any grammatical principle (e.g. BC C).

A SUBJECT (read big subject) can be either a normal subject (a specifier of IP) or the Agr element of I. (94), (95) and (96) are intended to account for all the elements which enter into binding relations, but the discussion here will be restricted to variables.

Two important assumptions play a crucial role in the theory of Generalised Binding. First, variables are subject to both BC A and BC C. They are subject to BC A because they are anaphoric in nature and resemble anaphors in that they require an antecedent in the sentence, albeit an A′-antecedent. On the other hand, they are subject to BC C because they are variables, and they are variables by virtue of being A′-bound. The second assumption is that it is CP (S′ in the structure used by Aoun) rather than IP (S) which counts as the GC for variables. This is clearly shown in (97). If variables must have an antecedent inside their GC, then the GC of the variable in (97) must be CP rather than IP:

97a. Who left?
97b. $[_{CP}$ who $[_{IP}$ t_{who} $[_{I'}$ Agr $[_{VP}$ left . . .

A consequence of the assumption that variables are subject to both conditions A and C is that variables in non-subject positions in embedded domains have the whole sentence as the GC. (98) is reproduced from above:

98a. Who did you say (that) Mary saw?
98b. $[_{CP}$ who did $[_{IP}$ you say $[_{CP}$ (that) $[_{IP}$ Mary AGR saw t_{who} . . .

The definition of GC above specifies that GC must include an accessible SUBJECT. The definition of accessibility, on the other hand, specifies that co-indexation between SUBJECT and the variable must not violate any condition. Now, if the variable in (98) were to be coindexed with Agr, the variable would also be co-indexed with the subject *Mary*. This is because the subject and Agr are co-indexed for independent reasons having to do with the mandatory relationship of Spec-head agreement between a head and its specifier (see Chapter 6). Consequently, the variable in (98) would be A-bound by *Mary* in violation of BC C. The variable in (98) does not have an accessible subject in the embedded clause resulting in a situation where the embedded clause cannot be its GC. Its GC is the whole sentence, where it is A′-bound by the antecedent wh-phrase.

In contrast to variables in non-subject positions, variables in the subject position of an embedded clause can have an accessible SUBJECT in the embedded clause, and consequently be A′-bound in it. In (99) co-indexation between the variable and Agr would not give rise to a violation of BC C. This is because Agr cannot be an A-binder as it does not occupy an A-position. Therefore, Agr qualifies as an accessible SUBJECT for the variable trace, and the embedded clause as its GC. The variable is A′-bound in the embedded clause by the intermediate trace:

99a. Who did you think solved the problem?

99b. [CP who did [IP you think [CP t~who~' [IP t~who~ AGR solved the problem . . .

Let us now see how the theory accounts for the NIC-cases above. The account relies on a mechanism which is best illustrated in relation to examples of superiority effects such as (100). Recall from earlier that superiority cases are accounted for in terms of the COMP Indexing mechanism, reproduced in (101). By virtue of (101), Spec,CP in (100) acquires the index of the object wh-phrase *what*, moved to it first in the syntax. Consequently, movement of the subject wh-phrase *who* to Spec,CP at LF results in a situation where its trace is not A'-bound by Spec,CP:

100a. *It is unclear what who saw.

100b. SS: *it is unclear [CP [Spec [what]]~what~ [IP who saw t~what~ . . .

100c. LF: *it is unclear [CP [Spec [who] [what]]~what~ [IP t~who~ saw t~what~ . . .

101. **COMP-indexing**
[COMP. . . XP~i~ . . .] → [COMP. . . XP~i~ . . .]~i~
iff COMP dominates only i-indexed elements.

With this mind, consider now the NIC cases reproduced in (102) and (103):

102a. *Who do you wonder how solved the problem?

102b. SS: *[CP who do [IP you wonder [CP [Spec how]~how~ [IP t~who~ solved the problem . . .

102c. LF: *[CP who do [IP you wonder [CP [Spec how]~how~ [IP t~who~ solved the problem . . .

103a. *Who do you think that saw Bill?

103b. SS: *[CP who do [IP you think [CP that [IP t~who~ saw Bill . . .

103c. LF: *[CP who do [IP you think [CP that [IP t~who~ saw Bill . . .

The situation in (102a) is identical to the one in (100). Spec,CP bears the index of the adjunct wh-phrase *how* moved to it first in the syntax, resulting in a situation where the variable trace in the subject position is not A'-bound in the embedded CP (its GC). To account for (103), Generalised Binding relies on the idea that the complementiser *that* is a non-index-bearing element. Its presence in CP therefore prevents the COMP-indexing mechanism from applying. COMP-indexing does not apply if COMP (CP) dominates a non-i-indexed element such as *that*. This leads to a situation where the variable in the subject position of the embedded clause is left without an A'-antecedent in the embedded clause.

It should be clear that Generalised Binding can successfully handle various cases that have otherwise been analysed in terms of special government-based requirements. The theory extends to other cases not discussed here with minimal additional assumptions. The element that seems to be missing from it in the form presented is the Minimality effect on A'-binding relations discussed above in relation to Relativised Minimality. This is the effect whereby a closer A'-specifier disrupts the A'-binding relation between an antecedent and a variable. The Minimality effect on A'-binding relations in the context of Generalised Binding has been extensively investigated by Aoun and Li in various papers over the recent years (see Sources and further reading). It turns out that not only wh-phrases but various other types of intervening A'-specifiers give rise to a Minimality effect on A'-binding relations.

As a final remark, note that when taken to its logical limit, Generalised Binding does away completely with at least movement processes affecting XPs. The antecedent of a trace is base-generated in its SS position and linked to its trace in terms of the mechanism of indexation involved between lexical anaphors and their antecedent. Terms such as 'movement' and 'trace' become metaphors with a historical value but no theoretical significance.

10.6   *Summary*

We started this chapter by observing that most of the transformational rules discussed in the previous chapters had in common the property of moving a given category from one position to another. This fact raised the possibility of reducing all these transformational rules to a single general principle called Move α. The transformational rules which insert or delete material in representations could be accommodated by adopting an even more general version of Move α called Affect α. The move to replace the transformational rules with a general principle was part of the broader attempt to replace construction-specific rules with general principles.

Since the definitions of transformations in Chapters 4 and 5 included references to landing sites and conditions on the application of the transformations, there was the prospect that Move α would overgenerate. However, it turned out that the scope of Move α was already severely restricted by various conditions on representations belonging to different modules of the grammar. Some other conditions could simply be factored out of the definitions of transformations themselves and stated either as conditions on the application of Move α or as conditions on representations derived by Move α.

Two major conditions have been identified and discussed, Subjacency and ECP. Subjacency is a condition on (the application of) Move α, and is itself a general version of a number of individual conditions previously thought to be unrelated. ECP, on the other hand, is a condition on the representation of traces. These two conditions were initially thought to be independent of each other, and to belong to separate modules. However, we have seen that it is perhaps possible to design a system (e.g. the Barriers system) where the two conditions could be merged, in the sense that they would make reference to the same notions and structural relations.

In the last section of the chapter we discussed two approaches to antecedent-trace relations. One approach reveals a significant and inviting parallelism between (antecedent-) government and binding (Relativised Minimality). The other approach literally reduces the conditions of government on antecedent-trace relations to binding conditions (Generalised Binding). To the extent that the latter approach is viable, it shows that phenomena which superficially and initially may look different are related at a deep and abstract level, and that the common patterns underlying them can be captured in terms of simple and general principles with broader scope.

Exercises

Exercise 10.1

Identify the island involved in each of the examples in (i–iv) and explain which islands can be collapsed together under one condition and which cannot. Make sure you justify your answer:

i)   ?What does John wonder whether Bill likes?
ii)   ??What does Bill know someone who likes?
iii) ??What does Bill think that seeing is fun?
iv)   ??What did Bill disappear before seeing?

Exercise 10.2

Explain the contrast between the pairs of examples in (i) and (ii), and show how this contrast is accounted for by the analysis outlined in this chapter:

i)a. Which film does John think Bill likes?
i)b. Which film does John think that Bill likes?

ii)a. Who does Bill think likes the film?
ii)b. *Who does Bill think that likes the film?

Exercise 10.3

Identify the phenomenon illustrated in examples (i–iv) and explain how it is accounted for by the analysis outlined in this chapter:

i)   Who saw which film?
ii)   *Which film did who saw?
iii) When did Bill see which film?
iv)   *When did who see the film?

Exercise 10.4

Identify the type of movement illustrated in examples (i–iii) and discuss the condition on it cited in this chapter:

i)   Bill is in the cinema.
ii)   Could Bill be in the cinema?
iii) *Be Bill could in the cinema?

Exercise 10.5

Examples (i) and (ii) show that subject relatives do not exhibit the *that*-trace effect. As a matter of fact, the presence of the complementiser is even obligatory. Discuss the problems that such examples raise for the analysis of the that-trace effect outlined in this chapter. You may want to consider the possibility that it is the analysis of relatives that needs to be modified rather than the analysis of the *that*-trace effect:

i)   the car *(that) chased Bill.
ii)   the problem *(that) bothered Mary.

Exercise 10.6

The discussion of the complex noun phrase island cases in the context of the Barriers framework in this chapter did not include noun phrases involving a CP-complement of a noun such as (i)a and (i)b. The latter exhibit a milder violation of the type found with wh-islands indicated by the single question mark. Examples (iia) and (iib) differ in that they involve extraction of an adjunct out of the complex noun phrase island, and as expected they exhibit a stronger type of violation. This suggests that complex noun phrase islands involve at least one barrier. In view of this, explain whether the Barriers framework does indeed account for the presence of a barrier in complex noun phrase contexts involving a CP-complement of a noun:

i)a. ?Which car did you hear the rumour that John fixed?
i)b. ?Which problem do you resent the claim that Bill solved?

ii)a. *How did you hear the rumour that John fixed the car?
      (Answer: with a crowbar)
ii)b. *How do you resent the claim that Bill solved the maths problem?
      (Answer: with a pen and paper)

Exercise 10.7

The paradigm in (i–iv) involves Topicalisation, an instance of Move α not discussed in this chapter. Explain whether the paradigm is consistent with the analysis outlined in this chapter on the basis of other instances of Move α:

i)   This problem, Bill can solve.
ii)   ?This problem, John wonders whether Bill can solve.
iii) ??This problem, John knows someone who can solve.
iv)   *This problem, John thinks that bothers Bill a lot.

Sources and further reading

The attempt to unify some of the earlier constraints on movement, including some of Ross's island constraints, appeared in Chomsky (1973). Subjacency, and more generally the issue of bounded versus unbounded movement, has generated a large amount of literature which is hard to represent in terms of a few selected references. The claim that Subjacency does not hold of LF-movement is made in Huang (1982) and Lasnik and Saito (1984).

Although subject–object asymmetries with respect to movement had been noted in earlier work, their formal treatment in terms of the ECP appears in Chomsky (1981) and Belletti and Rizzi (1981). The mechanisms of γ-marking and trace-deletion are discussed in Lasnik and Saito (1984), as noted in the main text, as well as in Chomsky (1986b). An attempt to extend the ECP to LF-movement is made in Kayne (1984). An early discussion of superiority effects in English multiple wh-questions appears in Chomsky (1973). Later discussions of this phenomenon include Jaeggli (1980), Aoun *et al.* (1981) and Pesetsky (1987).

The original sources relating to the Barriers system, Relativised Minimality and Generalised Binding are as mentioned in the main text. The Head Movement Constraint is discussed in Travis (1984), Koopman (1984), Chomsky (1986b) and Baker (1988).

Part III
Language Variation

11 Head-Complement Order, Bounding Nodes, and Wh-in-situ

Contents

11.1 *The nature and function of parameters*

An adequate theory of language has to address two major issues. The first issue relates to the fact that languages, despite their superficial differences, are identical at a deep and abstract level. In the Principles and Parameters theory outlined in Part II of this book, this property of human languages is accounted for by postulating the existence of a set of abstract principles common to all languages called Universal Grammar (UG). In the various chapters of Part II, we identified a number of such principles on the basis of an in-depth analysis of a broad range of facts in English. Although the investigation has been restricted to one language, some of the principles isolated and tested for validity are deep and general enough to warrant the hypothesis that they are principles of UG. Obviously, these hypothetical principles of UG are open to further testing against data from other languages which may either confirm their universal character, possibly in a modified form, or reveal their language-specific character. They may also force their rejection altogether. In this part of the book, we will test the validity of some of these principles of UG against data from a relatively broad range of related and unrelated languages.

The second issue that an adequate theory of language has to address is the converse of the first one. Despite the fact that languages are identical at a deep and abstract level, they exhibit significant differences at the surface level. A close examination of some of these differences across languages reveals that they are not arbitrary, and in most parts not isolated either. The patterns revealed by crosslinguistic differences seem to suggest that variation is restricted, presumably by a predetermined set of constraints. The task of a theory of language is then to find out the nature of these constraints and explain how they relate to the system of principles we call UG. This is one of the major issues we will be concerned with in this part of the book.

In the Principles and Parameters framework, language variation is accounted for in terms of **parameters**. A parameter is understood to be a restricted set of options/values associated with a given principle or category. Choice of one option/value yields a given pattern, and choice of a different option/value yields a different pattern. The metaphor sometimes used to explain parameters is an (old-fashioned) light switch with two options – on and off, each of which yields a different state of affairs. Whether the values of parameters are binary or have more than two options/values is an interesting question which has received attention in the literature, although a clear answer to it remains elusive. We will discuss parameters which lend themselves to a binary division of options/values and others which do not.

Parameters are said to be set (or fixed) on the basis of the properties of surface PF-strings. The latter are the only representations directly available (visible) to the language learner. Languages are not expected to differ with respect to the properties of the (invisible) LF level. It is unlikely that two languages would differ with respect to the representation of certain types of sentences at the LF level. At this level, sentences with similar scope properties from different languages are expected to have identical LF-representations in the relevant respects. We will discuss constructions where a certain key constituent with semantic scope occupies different positions in two different languages at SS (and PF) but occupies the same position in both languages at LF.

One of the questions discussed in the literature in relation to parameters is whether they are associated with the principles of UG (Chomsky 1986a), or with individual categories in their lexical entries (Borer 1984). In order to be able to empirically evaluate these two views, and in order to have a perspective over the types of parameters suggested in the literature, we will start this part of the book by briefly discussing three different parameters as representative examples. The first parameter is called the **Head (or Directionality) parameter** and is intended to account for differences among languages relating to the order of complements with respect to their heads. The second parameter is sometimes called the **Subjacency parameter** and is intended to account for differences among languages relating to bounding nodes. The third parameter, which we will call here the **Wh-movement parameter**, is intended to account for differences among languages relating to whether a wh-phrase is left in-situ at SS or fronted to Spec,CP in simple wh-questions.

11.2 *Head-Complement order*

Languages differ as to whether they have the order [Verb Object] (VO), as in English, or the order [Object Verb] (OV), as in German. The OV character of German can be seen in embedded clauses such as in (1). The order in German root clauses is discussed in Chapter 13:

1a. Mary sagt, dass Hans den Ball   kaufte.
    Mary said that Hans the ball   bought
    'Mary said that Hans bought the ball.'

1b. . . . dass Hans [$_{VP}$ [$_{DP}$ den Ball] [$_V$ kaufte]]

Chomsky (1986a) suggests that the difference between English-type languages and German-type languages, illustrated in (1), can be accounted for in terms of the parameter shown in (2), understood to be associated with X-bar theory:

2. **Head parameter**

   i) Head-first
   ii) Head-last

The Head parameter has two values: Head-first (or Head-initial) and Head-last (or Head-final). The first value yields the structure and order shown in (3a) found in English-type languages. The second value yields the structure and order shown in (3b) found in German-type languages. Accordingly, the difference between English and German responsible for the observed difference in order reduces to the idea that English selects value (i) of the Head parameter, whereas German selects value (ii) of the Head parameter.

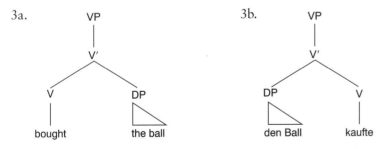

It is plausible to argue that if a language is claimed to select a given value of the Head parameter, all head categories in the language are expected to select their complement in the same direction. This expectation seems to be fulfilled by the functional category I in both languages. In English, where heads select their complement to the right, VP is located to the right of I. In German, where heads select their complement to the left, VP is located to the left of I. The idea that I is located to the right of VP in German is based on the fact that finite auxiliary verbs appear to the right of the non-finite main verb in German, as shown in (4). It is plausible to assume that German finite auxiliaries are located under I at SS, on par with their English counterparts:

4a. . . . dass Hans   den Ball   gekauft hat
    . . . that Hans   the ball   bought has
    '. . . that Hans has bought the ball'

4b.

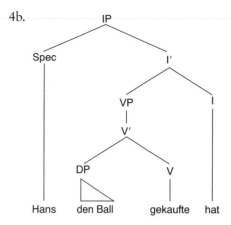

However, not all head categories select their complement in the same direction as V and I in German. The order of the complementiser *dass* 'that' in relation to IP in (4a) is the same as in English: *[CP dass [IP]]*. This suggests that C selects IP to the right in German, as shown in (5):

5a. . . . [$_{CP}$ dass [$_{IP}$ Hans den Ball kaufte]]
5b.

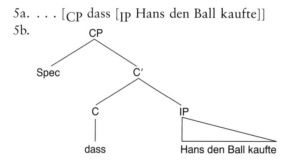

Other categories select their complement to the right as well. This is the case with nouns, adjectives and prepositions, as shown in (6), (7) and (8), respectively, from Webelhuth (1989). Note that example (6) also shows that D selects its NP complement to the right in German (Gloss: GEN stands for genitive Case):

6a. die Zerstörung der Stadt
    the destruction the city (GEN)
    'the destruction of the city'

6b.

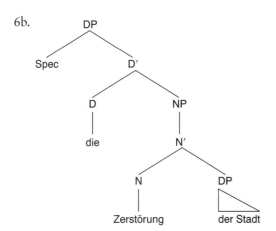

7a. stolz auf Maria
    proud of Mary

7b.

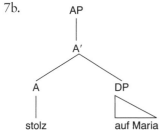

8a. mit einem Hammer
    with a hammer

8b.

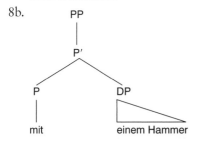

German appears to be a mixed order language, unlike English which is consistently head-initial. The facts of German suggest that categories in the same language may select different values of the Head parameter. This seems to support the view that parameters are associated with individual categories as part of the set of idiosyncratic properties specified in their lexical entries. Just as individual categories differ with respect to whether they select a complement and whether they assign Case to the complement they select, they also differ with respect to the direction in which they select their complement.

There have been attempts in the literature to derive the effects of the Head parameter from parametrised restrictions on the directionality of the assignment of θ-roles and/or Case (see Koopman 1984 and Travis 1984, among others). The idea is that if a given category selects to assign its internal θ-role and/or Case to the right, its complement will appear to its right (Head-initial), and if a given category selects to assign its internal θ-role and/or Case to the left, its complement will appear to its left. We have already seen that I assigns Case to the subject (Chapter 8) and possibly also a θ-role to VP (Chapter 10). In later chapters in this part of the book, we will discuss situations where C and D have been claimed to assign Case. In view of this, it seems that the functional categories I, C and D can also be accommodated under a parametrised restriction on the directionality of at least Case-assignment which determines order at SS and therefore PF.

An interesting fact about human languages is that although they differ with respect to the order of heads in relation to their complement, they do not appear to differ with respect to the order of specifiers in relation to the X′ projection. For example, despite the noted order differences between English and German, Spec,IP appears to the left of I′ in both languages. There is in principle no reason why Spec,IP should not appear to the right of I′ yielding the order [X′ Spec], but it apparently does not. If true, this is a remarkable fact of human languages which must conceal some significant property yet to be unravelled.

11.3   *Bounding nodes*

The Italian example (9), discussed in Rizzi (1982), involves extraction out of a wh-island but does not exhibit a Subjacency violation. (9) is in marked contrast with its English counterpart, shown in the gloss (see Chapter 10 for discussion of Subjacency violations in English):

9a.   tuo fratello,   a cui   mi domando   che storie   abbiano raccontato
      your brother   to whom   myself I-ask   which stories   they-have told
      ?'your brother, to whom I wonder which stories they told'

9b.   . . . [CP a cui [IP mi domando [CP che storie [IP abbiano raccontato t$_{che\ storie}$
      . . . t$_{a\ cui}$ . . .

Initially, this difference between English and Italian may seem to suggest that Subjacency is a language-specific principle after all. However, Rizzi argues that such a conclusion would be inaccurate, as extraction out of other islands indeed gives rise to a Subjacency violation in Italian. (10) involves extraction out of a complex noun phrase island and exhibits the same type of violation found in similar English examples:

10a. ??Tuo fratello a cui   temo la possibilità   che   abbiano raccontato tutto
      your brother   to whom I-fear the possibility that they-have told everything
      ??'your brother, to whom I fear the possibility that they have told everything'

10b. . . . [CP a cui [IP temo [DP la possibilità [CP t$_{a\ cui}$ che [IP abbiano racontato
      t$_{a\ cui}$ tutto . . .

The fact that extraction out of a complex noun phrase island gives rise to a Subjacency violation in Italian, as it does in English, shows that Subjacency is not likely to be a language-specific condition on movement. An adequate account of the difference between Italian and English would have to be based on the assumption that Subjacency constrains movement in both English and Italian. On this basis, Rizzi (1982) suggests that Italian differs from English with respect to which categories count as bounding nodes. In English the bounding nodes are IP and DP, as concluded in Chapter 10. In Italian, however, the bounding nodes are CP and DP. The underlying idea is that while Subjacency specifies that movement cannot cross two bounding nodes together, it does not specify which categories count as bounding nodes. Languages can differ as to which categories they choose as bounding nodes. English chooses IP and DP, whereas Italian chooses CP and DP.

Let us now see how this suggestion accounts for the data above. In (9) wh-movement crosses two IPs but only one CP. Because IP does not count as a bounding node in Italian, no Subjacency violation arises. On the other hand, because IP counts as a bounding node in English, a Subjacency violation arises in the English equivalent example shown in the gloss. In (10), wh-movement crosses one CP, one DP and one IP together. Such a movement is bound to give rise to a Subjacency violation in both Italian and English, and hence the fact that Italian and English are similar with respect to extraction out of complex noun phrase islands.

It is not clear whether the Subjacency parameter is associated with a principle of UG (Subjacency) or with relevant individual categories. To the extent that the formulation of Subjacency does not offer a choice between potential bounding nodes, the Subjacency parameter can be said to be associated with the relevant individual categories. However, the categories which function as bounding nodes are not lexical categories (heads), but phrasal categories: DP, CP and IP. We leave the issue open.

11.4 *Wh-in-situ*

Languages differ as to where they place the wh-phrase in simple wh-questions. We already know that English obligatorily moves the wh-phrase to Spec,CP in overt syntax (see Chapters 5 and 6). Japanese differs radically in that it apparently never moves the wh-phrase to Spec,CP in overt syntax. Colloquial French, on the other hand, can either move the wh-phrase or leave it in-situ in overt syntax. In this section we will compare these three languages with the aim of identifying the parameter responsible for variation between them. The discussion is based on the seminal work of Huang (1982) which compared Chinese to English, as well as the work of Lasnik and Saito (1992) on Japanese. The latter is the source of the Japanese examples in this section.

Compare the Japanese example (11) to the English examples in (12) and (13). In considering the Japanese example (11), it is important to bear in mind that

Japanese is a (consistently) head-final language. The wh-phrase *nani-o* 'what-ACC' occupies the object position situated to the left of the verb: $[_{VP} [DP] V]$. On the other hand, the question marker *ka* occupies the C position situated to the right of IP: $[_{CP} [IP] C]$ (GLOSS: *-TOP* stands for 'topic marker', *-ACC* for 'accusative Case marker', and *Q* for 'question marker').

11a. John-wa   nani-o   kaimasita ka?
      John-TOP   what-ACC   bought Q
      'What did John buy?'

11b. SS: $[_{CP} [_{IP}$ John-wa $[_{VP} [_{DP}$ nani-o] $[_V$ kaimasita]]] ka/[+Q]]

12a. What did John buy?
12b. SS: $[_{CP}$ what $[_{C'}$ did/[+Q] $[_{IP}$ John I $[_{VP}$ buy t_{what} . . .

13a. *John bought what?
13b. SS: $[_{CP}$ [+Q] $[_{IP}$ John I $[_{VP}$ bought what . . .

(11) shows that the wh-phrase remains in situ in overt syntax in Japanese simple wh-questions. Lasnik and Saito (1992) argue that Japanese lacks overt wh-movement altogether. This situation is the opposite of the one found in English, where the wh-phrase has to undergo overt wh-movement in simple wh-questions. While (12) is a genuine (information-seeking) wh-question in English, (13b) is not (see Chapter 6).

Besides English and Japanese, which represent the opposite ends of a continuum, there exist languages where overt movement of the wh-phrase is possible but not obligatory. Colloquial French is an often cited example of this type of languages. (14) and (15) are both possible wh-questions in Colloquial French:

14a. Qui   as -tu   vu?
      who   have-you   seen
      'Who have you seen?'

14b. SS: $[_{CP}$ qui $[_{C'}$ as $[_{IP}$ tu $[_{I'}$ t_{as} $[_{VP}$ vu t_{qui} . . .

15a. Tu   as   vu   qui?
      you   have   seen   who
      'Who have you seen?'

15b. SS: $[_{CP} [_{C'}$ [+Q] $[_{IP}$ tu $[_{I'}$ as $[_{VP}$ vu qui . . .

In (14) the wh-phrase is fronted to Spec,CP in overt syntax. As in English, overt movement of a non-root subject wh-phrase triggers SAI in Colloquial French. (14) is identical in order to the English example (12). In (15), however, the wh-phrase remains in situ in overt syntax as in the Japanese example (11). (Colloquial) French is a VO language, like English. (15) has the (declarative-like) order of the English example (13). Yet, while (15) is a possible wh-question in French, (13) is not a possible wh-question in English.

The contrast between the English root sentences (12) and (13), as well as the embedded clauses in (16) and (17) below, was accounted for in Chapter 6 in terms of the principle reproduced in (18):

16a. I wonder who Mary saw.
16b. SS: I wonder [$_{CP}$ who [$_{C'}$ [+Q] [$_{IP}$ Mary saw t$_{who}$ . . .

17a. * I wonder Mary saw who.
17b. *I wonder [$_{CP}$ e [$_{C'}$ [+Q] [$_{IP}$ Mary saw who . . .

18.   A [+Q]-CP must have a [+Q]-specifier.

(12), (13) and the embedded clause in (16) and (17) all include the feature [+Q] in their C. (12) and (16) are consistent with (18) whereas (13) and (17) are not, and hence the fact they are excluded. Recall that we are assuming that wh-phrases include the feature [+Q], possibly spelled out as the wh-morpheme in English and its equivalent in other languages.

The Japanese example (11) and the Colloquial French example (15) are also inconsistent with (18) and yet they are both possible. It appears that (18) does not hold of Japanese and Colloquial French. As far as Japanese is concerned, (18) apparently does not hold of selected/embedded [+Q]-clauses either, as shown in (19) and (20). Lasnik and Saito (1992) explain that the verb *kiite iru* 'heard' in (19) allows for a [+Q]-CP complement, while the verb *siritagatte iru* 'want-to-know' in (20) requires a [+Q]-CP complement. (20a) is excluded because the complement clause is not [+Q]. However, in neither (19b) nor (20b) does the wh-phrase occupy the Spec position of the selected [+Q]-CP at SS. Instead, the wh-phrase remains in-situ (-*NOM* stands for 'nominative Case marker'):

19a. Mary-ga   John-ga   hon-o   katta   to   kiite iru   koto
     Mary-NOM   John-NOM   book-ACC   bought   Comp   heard   fact
     'the fact that Mary heard that John bought a book'

19b. Mary-ga   John-ga   nani-o   katta   ka   kiite iru koto
     Mary-NOM   John-NOM   what-ACC   bought   Q   heard fact
     'the fact that Mary heard what John bought'

20a. *Mary-ga   John-ga   hon-o   katta   to   siritagatte iru koto
     Mary-NOM   John-NOm   book-ACC   bought   Comp   want-to-know fact
     Lit. 'the fact that Mary wants to know that John bought a book'

20b. Mary-ga   John-ga   nani-o   katta   ka   siritagatte iru koto
     Mary-NOM   John-NOM   what-ACC   bought   Q   want-to-know fact
     'the fact that Mary wants to know what John bought'

Although the wh-phrase is in-situ at SS in Japanese and Colloquial French simple wh-questions, it must move to the relevant Spec,CP at LF for reasons having to do with the interpretation of wh-questions. The latter, in particular the requirement that the wh-operator be a situated in a position where it has scope over the whole sentence, are the same in all languages (see Chapter 7). At LF, Japanese and Colloquial French simple wh-questions have a representation which is identical to that of their English counterparts with the wh-phrase located in the relevant Spec,CP. This is shown in (21), (22) and (23). In all representations, the wh-phrase occupies the scope-taking position that corresponds to the position of the logical operator in the logical representation:

21a. John-wa　　nani-o　　　kaimasita ka?
　　 John-TOP　what-ACC　bought　　Q
　　 'What did John buy?'

21b. SS: [$_{CP}$ [$_{IP}$ John-wa [$_{VP}$ [$_{DP}$ nani-o] [$_V$ kaimasita]]]] ka/[+Q]]
21c. LF: [$_{CP}$ nani-o [$_{IP}$ John-wa [$_{VP}$ t$_{nani-o}$ kaimasita]] ka/[+Q]]
21d. for which thing x, John bought x.

22a. Tu　　as　　vu　　qui?
　　 you　have　seen　who
　　 'Who have you seen?'

22b. SS: [$_{CP}$ [+Q] [$_{IP}$ tu as vu qui . . .
22c. LF: [$_{CP}$ qui [$_{C'}$ [+Q] [$_{IP}$ tu as vu t$_{qui}$ . . .
22d. for which person x, you saw x.

23a. What did John buy?
23b. SS: [$_{CP}$ what [$_{C'}$ did/[+Q] [$_{IP}$ John buy t$_{what}$ . . .
23c. LF: [$_{CP}$ what [$_{C'}$ did/[+Q] [$_{IP}$ John buy t$_{what}$ . . .
23d. for which thing x, John bought x.

　　In view of this, it could be concluded, along with Lasnik and Saito (1992), that languages differ as to the level at which (18) must be satisfied. In English and similar languages with obligatory overt wh-movement, (18) must be satisfied at SS (overt syntax). In Japanese and similar languages which lack overt wh-movement, (18) is satisfied at LF (covert syntax). Finally, in Colloquial French and similar languages with optional overt wh-movement, (18) can either be satisfied at SS or at LF.

　　The Wh-movement parameter cannot be said to be associated with a given category, in this case C. It is unlikely that Japanese wh-interrogative clauses, for example, differ from English wh-interrogative clauses in that they lack the feature [+Q] under C. This is because the presence of this feature is necessary to characterise the clauses in question as wh-interrogative, and therefore to be distinguished from declarative clauses and others. Moreover, the presence of the feature [+/−Q] in selected clauses is necessary to account for the difference in the selectional properties of verbs in Japanese shown (19) and (20). We will come back to this parameter in Chapter 19.

　　The Japanese examples above have the **Q(uestion) morpheme** *ka* situated under C to the right of IP in a head-final structure of CP: [$_{CP}$ [$_{IP}$] C]. This property of Japanese questions illustrates what seems to be a general correlation between wh-in-situ and the Q-morpheme. Languages that have wh-in-situ in simple wh-questions tend also to have the Q-morpheme (Cheng 1991). The Q-morpheme is sometimes said to license the wh-phrase in situ in the sense that the Q-morpheme somehow makes wh-movement of the wh-phrase unnecessary. However, there are exceptions, as is often the case with typological generalisations, which is why they are usually described as 'tendencies'. The dialect of French illustrated above is one such language. The examples provided do not include an equivalent of the Japanese Q-morpheme.

In addition to languages which have a Q-morpheme and the ones which do not, there is a third group of languages which make use of a (dummy) wh-phrase in Spec,CP, often 'what', instead of a Q-morpheme in C. This is the case in Hungarian, for example, illustrated with the example in (24) from Horvath (1996). The root Spec,CP is filled with the inanimate wh-phrase *mit* 'what' bearing accusative Case. The real wh-phrase in (24) is the animate *kit* 'who', situated inside the embedded clause. The (dummy) wh-phrase which licenses the real wh-phrase lower in the sentence is sometimes called a **wh-expletive**:

24a. Mit   gondolsz, hogy kit   látott   János?
     what-ACC   think-2S   that   who-ACC   saw-3S   John-NOM
     'Who do you think that John saw?'

24b. [CP mit gondolsz [CP hogy kit latott Janos . . .
24c. for which person x, you think that John saw x

There is a kind of parallelism between Hungarian questions such as (24) and English multiple wh-questions such as *Who bought which book?* The latter are often described as involving a situation where the object wh-phrase is licensed in situ by the subject wh-phrase in Spec,CP. In other words, a wh-phrase can remain in situ in contexts where Spec,CP is filled with another wh-phrase. This description applies to the Hungarian example (24) as well. The difference is that Hungarian makes use of the wh-expletive to create this pattern even in non-multiple wh-questions such as (24). The reason English lacks the pattern in (24) is possibly due to the fact that English lacks a corresponding wh-expletive element.

Recall from Chapter 7 that English multiple wh-questions such as *Who bought which book?* undergo covert movement of wh-in-situ. The latter adjoins to the subject wh-phrase in Spec,CP, thereby deriving a representation which is consistent with the logical interpretation: *for which person x, for which book y [x bought y]*. Note that a similar process has to apply in the derivation of the Hungarian wh-question (24), as indicated by its logical interpretation roughly shown in (24c). The real wh-phrase *kit* 'who' moves at LF and adjoins to the wh-expletive in Spec,CP. The wh-expletive actually does not play a role in the interpretation of the wh-question, and therefore can be assumed to delete. A similar process has been argued by Chomsky (1986a) to be involved in the derivation of English sentences with an expletive subject such as *There is a unicorn in the garden.* The postverbal subject *a unicorn* moves and adjoins to (or replaces) the expletive subject *there* at LF, deriving a representation which is similar to its superficially synonymous counterpart *A unicorn is in the garden.* This process is discussed in more detail in Part IV of this book.

11.5   *Summary*

In the Principles and Parameters framework, differences among languages are accounted for in terms of parameters. A parameter is a well-defined set of options each of which gives rise to a specific pattern. Three different parameters have been discussed in this chapter.

The first parameter, called the Head/Directionality parameter, is intended to account for differences among languages relating to the order of the head in relation to its complement. VO languages such as English select the Head-first option of the parameter, and OV languages such as German select the head-last value of the parameter. However, we have seen that while all heads select their complement in the same direction in English, this is not the case in German. Some heads select their complement to the right in German, as in English. This fact was tentatively said to suggest that parameters are perhaps associated with individual categories rather than with principles of UG.

The second parameter, which we called the Subjacency parameter, is intended to account for differences among languages relating to which categories they choose as bounding nodes. English selects IP and DP as bounding nodes, whereas Italian selects CP and DP as bounding nodes. This explains the fact that English exhibits a Subjacency effect with wh-islands whereas Italian does not.

The third parameter, which we called here the Wh-movement parameter, is intended to account for differences between languages relating to whether they move or do not move the wh-phrase in simple wh-questions. It turned out that there is a three-way variation in this respect found in English, Japanese and Colloquial French. English moves the wh-phrase obligatorily, Japanese leaves it in situ obligatorily and Colloquial French can either move the wh-phrase or leave it in situ. This variation was attributed to variation relating to the level at which the principle which requires a [+Q]-CP to have a wh-specifier is satisfied. In English, the principle is satisfied at SS. In Japanese it is satisfied at LF. Finally, in Colloquial French it can be satisfied either at SS or at LF.

Exercises

Exercise 11.1

The examples in (i–iv) are from Dutch (Webelhuth 1989). Assign a structure to each example, and compare the order in each phrase to the order found in its counterpart in the closely related language German discussed in this chapter:

i) . . . dat Jan een boek lezen kan
    . . . that Jan a book read can

ii) het huis
    the house

iii) tevreden met hem
     satisfied with him

iv) de verovering van de stad
    the conquest of the city

Exercise 11.2

German verbs were said in this chapter to select their complement to the left. This conclusion was based on the fact that a verb and its direct object appear in the order OV in embedded clauses. However, when the complement of a verb is a finite clause, it appears following the verb (as in English) rather than preceding it. This is shown in (i) and (ii). It seems that there is order variation in German depending on the nature of the complement of the verb. Try to think of a way of bringing some order to German order by, for example, making the facts in (i) and (ii) consistent with the idea that German verbs invariably select their complement to the left:

i) Mary glaubt, dass John gesagt hat, dass   Bill früh geht.
    Mary believes that John   said   has, that   Bill early leaves
    'Mary believes that John said that Bill leaves early.'

ii) Mary sagte, dass John gehen will.
     Mary said   that John to-go   wants
     'Mary said that John wants to go.'

Exercise 11.3

Examples (ia&b) and (iia&b) are from French. (ia&b) show that a non-pronominal complement appears following the verb and cannot appear preceding the verb. (iia&b) show that a pronominal complement cannot appear following the verb and must appear preceding the verb. Do French verbs select a different value of the Head parameter depending on the nature of their complement? Is there a way of accounting for the facts in (ia&b) and (iia&b) while maintaining the view that French verbs consistently select their complement in one direction?

i)a. Jean a vu les enfants
      Jean has seen the children

i)b. *Jean les enfants a vu.
      Jean the children has seen.

ii)a. *Jean a vu les.
       Jean has seen them

ii)b. Jean les a vus.
       Jean them has seen

Exercise 11.4

Examples (i) and (ii) are from Iraqi Arabic (Wahba 1991). Outline a derivation for each question and discuss the status of Iraqi Arabic in the typology of languages relating to wh-questions:

i) meno Mona shaafat?
    who Mona saw
    'Who did Mona see?'

ii)   Mona shaafat meno?
      Mona saw who
      'Who did Mona see?'

Exercise 11.5

Examples (i–iii) are from Chinese (Huang 1982). (ii) and (iii) are the type of examples that led Huang to conclude that Subjacency does not hold of LF movement (Chapter 10). Outline an analysis for each example, and explain why Huang reached the conclusion that Subjacency does not hold of LF movement:

i) ni   kanjian-le shei?
    you   see-ASP   who
    'Who did you see?'

ii) ni   xiang-zhidao shei   mai-le   sheme?
    you   wonder   who   buy-ASP   what
    'What is the thing x such that you wonder who bought x'

iii) shei xie   de   shu zui youqu?
     who   write DE   book most interesting
     'Books that who wrote are interesting'

12 Null Subjects and Objects

Contents

12.1 *Null subjects*

12.1.1 *Pro*

Compare the Italian examples in (1) and (2):

1a. Lui   ha   telefonato.
    he   has   phoned

1b. [$_{IP}$ lui I [$_{VP}$ ha telefonato . . .

2a. Ha   telefonato.
    has   phoned

2b. [$_{IP}$ e I [$_{VP}$ ha telefonato . . .

Pronominal subjects are optional in Italian finite clauses. They can either be present, as in (1), or absent, as in (2). Italian is said to allow subject pronouns to 'drop' and therefore is a **pro-drop** language. The phenomenon is the same in embedded clauses, as shown in (3) and (4):

3a. Gianni ha   detto che   lui   ha   telefonato.
    Gianni has   said   that   he   has   phoned

3b. [$_{IP}$ Gianni I [$_{VP}$ ha detto [$_{CP}$ che [$_{IP}$ lui I [$_{VP}$ ha telefonato . . .

4a. Gianni ha   detto che   ha   telefonato.
    Gianni has   said that   has phoned

4b. [$_{IP}$ Gianni I [$_{VP}$ ha detto [$_{CP}$ che [$_{IP}$ e I [$_{VP}$ ha telefonato . . .

This property of Italian is not found in English, so that English is not a pro-drop language. As we saw in Chapter 6 and others, English finite clauses must have an overt subject. Sentences such as (5a&b) were said to be excluded by EPP:

5a. *(He) has phoned.
5b. John said that *(he) has phoned.

This contrast between Italian and English again raises the possibility that a principle which was thought to be a component of UG and therefore holds of all languages may turn out to be specific to English. As with other situations discussed in the previous chapter, a closer look reveals that this is not necessarily the case.

Let us first address the question why Italian allows subject pronouns to 'drop' in finite clauses and English does not. Initially, the answer to this question seems to be straightforward. Italian allows subject pronouns to 'drop' because their content can be recovered from the subject Agr morpheme on the verb. As shown in (6), Italian has rich Agr inflection where each member of the paradigm is clearly distinguishable from the others in terms of at least person and number features:

	Singular			*Plural*	
6a.	(Io) mangio	'I eat'	6d.	(Noi) mangiamo	'we eat'
6b.	(Tu) mangi	'you eat'	6e.	(Voi) mangiate	'you eat'
6c.	(Lui/lei) mangia	'he/she eats'	6f.	(Essi) mangiano	'they eat'

The agreement features overtly encoded in the Italian Agr category make the presence of subject pronouns with identical agreement features redundant. In comparison, the English Agr paradigm is largely poor (or abstract), so that the feature-content of a dropped subject pronoun cannot be recovered from it. This appears to be the reason Italian is a pro-drop language whereas English is not. The phenomenon of pro-drop is allowed only in languages where the feature-content of the dropped pronoun can be recovered from Agr.

With this in mind, let us now go back to the issue relating to EPP. Rizzi (1982) suggests that, contrary to appearances, examples with a dropped subject pronoun indeed have a subject realised as a null category. Some of the evidence for this claim is discussed later on in this chapter. Pending the discussion, the questions we need to sort out now is what is the nature of this null category. Let us start by examining each of the null categories identified in Part II. The list includes DP-trace which has the feature specification [+a, −pro], variable trace which as the feature specification [−a, −pro] and *PRO* which has the feature specification [+a, +pro]. The first two are excluded on the grounds that the pro-drop examples cited above do not show any sign of movement. This is not to say that null arguments never imply movement. We will see later on in this chapter that this is not the case. The null category *PRO* is also excluded, this time on the grounds that the subject position of finite clauses is governed (the *PRO* Theorem, see Chapter 9). The null category which occurs in the subject position of finite clauses must therefore be a new one.

In Chapter 9 it was pointed out that the repertoire of null categories identified up to that stage lacked a member corresponding to the fourth logical combination [−a, +p], i.e. a pure pronominal category which would correspond to overt pronouns. The 'missing' subject in the pro-drop examples above clearly has the interpretation of a pure pronominal, on a par with its overt counterpart in the examples with an overt pronominal subject. Rizzi suggests that a pure pronominal null category is precisely the one that functions as the subject in pro-drop sentences. The pure pronominal null category is represented as *pro* (read small/ little *pro*). Accordingly, (2) and (4) above have the more accurate representations shown in (7) and (8), where the subject is a null category. In (7) the null subject *pro* has an antecedent in the discourse much like overt pronouns in the same context. In (8), *pro* can be coreferential with the subject of the root clause, again much like an overt pronoun in the same context:

7a. Ha   telefonato.
     has phoned

7b. [$_{IP}$ pro I [$_{VP}$ ha telefonato . . .

8a. Gianni ha   detto che   ha   telefonato.
     Gianni has said   that has   phoned

8b. [$_{IP}$ Gianni ha detto [$_{CP}$ che [$_{IP}$ pro ha telefonato . . .

Having identified the nature of the null category in null subject sentences, we now need determine the conditions under which it appears. This is necessary to account for the difference between Italian and English, that is to explain why *pro* cannot occur in the subject position of English finite clauses, as shown in (9) and (10):

9a. *Has phoned.
9b. *[$_{IP}$ pro I [$_{VP}$ has phoned . . .

10a. *John said that has phoned.
10b. *[$_{IP}$ John said [$_{CP}$ that [$_{IP}$ pro I [$_{VP}$ has phoned . . .

Presumably, the explanation would have to depend on the conclusion reached above that the option of allowing a null subject in finite clauses is crucially dependent on the presence of an overt (rich) Agr category capable of identifying the feature content of the null subject. This conclusion can be stated in the form of a licensing condition on the appearance of *pro* along the lines of (11). Co-indexation between Agr under I and *pro* in Spec,IP is part of the mandatory Spec-head agreement relation characteristic of finite clauses (see Chapter 6):

11. **Condition on the licensing of *pro***

     pro is licensed by an overt (rich) Agr category co-indexed with it.

Because the English Agr category is largely abstract (poor) it cannot license *pro*. This is the reason English does not allow null subjects in finite clauses.

12.1.2   Free Inversion

It has been observed that the phenomenon of null subjects does not occur in isolation, but as part of a cluster of properties (e.g. Taraldsen 1981, Rizzi 1982). One such property is called **Free Inversion**. The latter is the process whereby an overt subject of a finite clause can appear freely in the clause final position following the verb and other VP-material. This is shown in the Italian example (12). The process of inversion is free in the sense that it can occur with all types of verbs:

12a. Ha   telefonato   Gianni.
     has telephoned   Gianni'
     'Gianni has phoned.'

12b. Hai   detto che ha   telefonato   Gianni.
     have-2S said   that has telephoned   Gianni
     'You said that Gianni has phoned.'

The phenomenon of Free Inversion is not found in English. The equivalents of (12a&b) are both excluded in English, as shown in (13a&b):

13a. *Has phoned John.
13b. *You said that has phoned John.

It seems that the phenomena of null subjects in finite clauses and Free Inversion indeed cluster together such that one implies the other. If a language allows null subjects in finite clauses, e.g. Italian, it also allows Free Inversion. On the other hand, if a language does not allow null subjects in finite clauses, e.g. English, it does not allow Free Inversion either. A proper analysis for Free Inversion would therefore have to link it the null subject phenomenon.

Rizzi (1982) suggests the analysis outlined in (14) for Italian sentences with an inverted subject. The derivation in (14) is for both root and embedded clauses with an inverted subject:

14a. Ha   telefonato   Gianni.
     has phoned   Gianni

14b. DS: [$_{IP}$ Gianni I [$_{VP}$ ha telefonato . . .
14c. FI: [$_{IP}$ pro$_i$ I [$_{VP}$ [$_{VP}$ ha telefonato] Gianni$_i$ . . .
14d. SS: [$_{IP}$ pro$_i$ I [$_{VP}$ [$_{VP}$ ha telefonato] Gianni$_i$ . . .

At DS the subject is situated in Spec,IP, the canonical subject position, as shown in (14c). Move α then applies to the subject and right-adjoins to VP (the postverbal subject position), as shown in (14c). The movement involved is a lowering one. The landing site of the moved subject (the VP-adjoined position) does not c-command the initial (DS) position of the subject. In view of this, the null category left behind in the subject position cannot be a trace. A trace in the subject position would need to be antecedent governed to satisfy ECP. Recall from Chapter 10 that subject-traces can only satisfy the ECP via antecedent government and that antecedent government requires c-command. The null category left behind by subject inversion is *pro*, as shown in (14c&d). The category *pro* is pronominal and therefore not subject to ECP. Recall that the definition of ECP given in Chapter 10 refers to non-pronominal empty categories. As in null subject sentences, *pro* in (14) is licensed by the overt/rich Agr category.

It is not difficult to see how the analysis outlined in (14) makes the phenomenon of Free Inversion crucially dependent on the phenomenon of null subjects in finite clauses. The subject position vacated by the inverted subject can only be filled with *pro*. On the other hand, *pro* is subject to licensing by overt/rich Agr. It follows that only languages which allow null subjects, that is languages which license *pro* in the subject position of a finite clause, are expected to have Free Inversion. Italian is one such language. English is not.

12.1.3   THAT-trace effect

Another property which clusters together with the null subject property and Free Inversion is sometimes called 'the apparent lack of the THAT-trace effect', where THAT is mnemonic for the English *that* and its equivalent in other languages. As shown in (15), it is possible to extract the subject of a clause introduced by the complementiser THAT in Italian. This property is missing in English as we saw in Chapter 10. Extraction out of this context gives rise to the THAT-trace effect and ultimately to an ECP violation in English:

15a. Chi   hai   detto che   ha   telefonato?
    who   have-2S said that has phoned

15b. [$_{CP}$ chi hai detto [$_{CP}$ t$_{chi}$' [$_{C'}$ che [$_{IP}$ t$_{chi}$ ha telefonato . . . .

Rizzi (1982) argues that the ECP violation seen in the Italian example (15) is only apparent. Such sentences have a (roundabout) derivation that yields an LF-representation consistent with the ECP. The derivation in question is outlined in (16). It consists of two steps. The first step, shown in (16c), involves inversion of the subject to the VP-adjoined position following the verb. The second step, shown in (16d), involves wh-movement of the inverted subject from the postverbal VP-adjoined position:

16a. Chi   hai   detto che   ha   telefonato?
    who   have-2S said that has phoned

16b. DS: [$_{IP}$ pro hai detto [$_{CP}$ che [$_{IP}$ chi I [$_{VP}$ ha telefonato . . .

16c. FI: [$_{IP}$ pro hai detto [$_{CP}$ che [$_{IP}$ pro$_i$ I [$_{VP}$ [$_{VP}$ ha telefonato] chi$_i$ . . .

16d. Wh-mov.: [$_{CP}$ chi$_i$ ha detto [$_{CP}$ t$_{chi}$' che [$_{IP}$ pro$_i$ I [$_{VP}$ [$_{VP}$ ha telefonato] t$_{chi}$ . . .

16e. SS: [$_{CP}$ chi$_i$ ha detto [$_{CP}$ t$_{chi}$' che [$_{IP}$ pro$_i$ I [$_{VP}$ [$_{VP}$ ha telefonato] t$_{chi}$ . . .

Rizzi's analysis is couched in a theoretical framework which assumes, first, that traces can satisfy the ECP via lexical government and not necessarily θ-government, and secondly, that the VP-adjoined position is lexically governed by the verb. The consequence is that the trace in the VP-adjoined position shown in (16d) satisfies the ECP. In contrast, a trace in the subject position gives rise to the THAT-trace effect and does not satisfy the ECP for the same reason as in English. The presence of the complementiser *che* 'that' blocks antecedent-government of the trace in Spec,IP by the intermediate trace in Spec,CP. This is the reason wh-movement cannot proceed directly from the subject position Spec,IP in Italian (as in English). This is also the sense in which that the absence of the THAT-trace effect in (16) is said to be only apparent.

It should be clear how the analysis outlined in (16) relates the phenomenon of the (apparent) lack of the THAT-trace effect to the null subject property and Free Inversion. The lack of the THAT-trace effect is dependent on the ability of the subject to undergo Free Inversion. The ability of the subject to undergo Free Inversion is in turn dependent on the ability of Agr in the language to license *pro* in the subject position of a finite clause. Because English lacks the phenomenon of null subjects it also lacks the phenomenon of Free Inversion, and because it lacks the phenomenon of Free Inversion, it also lacks the phenomenon of the apparent absence of the THAT-trace effect.

12.1.4 Null expletives

Languages which allow null subjects in finite clauses have also been claimed to allow null expletive subjects in finite clauses (Safir 1985, Travis 1984). This phenomenon is illustrated with the Spanish example in (17) from Jaeggli and Safir (1989). The root clause shows that Spanish allows null thematic subjects, and the embedded clause shows that it also allows null expletive subjects:

17a. (El) dijo que le   parece que Juan mató al perro.
     he said that to-him seems that Juan killed the dog
     'He said that it seems to him that Juan killed the dog.'

17b. [IP pro dijo [CP que [IP pro le parace [CP que [IP Juan mató al perro . . .

The fact that null subject languages allow null expletive subjects is not surprising. Just as Agr can identify the features of a thematic *pro* it can also identify the features of an expletive *pro*. The issue of null expletives becomes more interesting when one learns that some non-null subject languages also allow it. For example, German is not a null subject language, but it allows a null expletive subject in finite clauses, as shown in example (18) from Jaeggli and Safir (1989). The root clause shows that German does not allow a null thematic subject in finite clauses, and the embedded clause shows that it allows a null expletive subject in finite clauses:

18a. *(Er) sagt, dass ihm   scheint, dass Hans den Hund getötet hat.
     he said   that him-DAT seemed that Hans the dog   killed has
     'He said it seemed to him that Hans killed the dog.'

18b. [IP Er sagt [CP dass [IP pro ihm scheint [CP dass . . .

The generalisation seems to be that languages which allow null thematic subjects in finite clauses, e.g. Italian and Spanish, also allow null expletive subjects in finite clauses. However, languages which allow null expletive subjects in finite clauses, e.g. German, do not necessarily allow null thematic subjects in finite clauses. The first part of the generalisation follows from the parameter that underlies the null subject phenomenon and related phenomena, but the second one does not. One could perhaps surmise that null expletive subjects are allowed in languages which are not null subject languages because the features of null expletive elements are predictable and therefore do not require rich Agr to be identified. Expletive elements, whether null or overt, tend to have the same features across languages, usually third person singular.

12.2   *Null objects*

12.2.1   Identified null objects

Italian is one of the languages which have overt agreement between the subject of a finite clause and the Agr category on the verb. This is called (overt) subject agreement. There are languages which, in addition to overt subject agreement, also have what is often called overt **object agreement**. The latter refers to the agreement relationship between the direct object of a transitive verb and an Agr morpheme usually attached to the verb. Chichewa (Bantu) is one such language, as shown in examples (19a&b) from Baker (1988) (SP stands for 'subject agreement prefix', OP for 'object agreement prefix', and ASP for aspect):

19a. Mikango   yanu   i- na- thamangits-a   mbuzi   zathu.
     lions   your   SP-PAST-chase-ASP   goats   our
     'Your lions chased our goats.'
19b. Mikango   yanu   i- na- zi- thamangits-a   mbuzi   zathu.
     lions   your   SP-PAST-OP-chase-ASP   goats   our
     'Your lions chased our goats.'

Object agreement, that is the presence of an object agreement morpheme which agrees with the direct object of the verb, is actually optional in Chichewa. (19a) includes only one Agr morpheme, namely the subject agreement morpheme glossed as SP. (19b), however, includes two distinct Agr morphemes, one agrees with the subject of the sentence (SP) and the other with the direct object of the verb (OP). To distinguish between the two types of agreement morpheme, we will refer to the subject Agr morpheme as **Agr$_S$** and to the object agreement morpheme as **Agr$_O$**. Pending a detailed discussion of the theoretical status of Agr$_O$ in Chapter 16, we will assume for the moment that Agr$_O$ is base-generated attached to the verb. Agr$_S$ is base-generated under I, as we have been assuming.

The relevance of object agreement to the issue of null arguments lies in the fact that languages which have overt/rich object agreement inflection allow null objects with a pronominal interpretation. For example, the DP object in the Chichewa example (19b) can be 'dropped', as shown in (20a). The fact that the 'missing' object has a pronominal interpretation implies that it is structurally present in the form of *pro*, as shown in (20b):

20a. Mikango   yanu   i- na- zi- thamangits-a.
     lions   your   SP-PAST-OP-chase-ASP
     'Your lions chased them (the goats).'
20b. [IP mikango yanu [VP [V i-na-zi$_i$ – thamangits-a] pro$_i$]

Besides considerations having to do the pronominal interpretation of the missing direct object, there are other reasons for including *pro* in the direct object position in (20b). The verb 'chase' is transitive and therefore must have a structurally represented internal argument required by the Projection Principle and the θ-Criterion. The mechanism which licenses *pro* in the subject position of Italian finite clauses also licenses *pro* in the direct object position of the Chichewa null object sentence (20). The Agr$_O$ element on the verb is sufficiently rich to make the features of the direct object *pro* recoverable.

Thus, there seems to be a complete parallelism between Italian null subjects and Chichewa null objects. They are both made possible by the presence of a co-indexed overt/rich Agr morpheme. As a matter of fact, the parallelism goes further than this. Bresnan and Mchombo (1987) show that when the Agr$_O$ morpheme is present in Chichewa sentences, an overt object is free to appear in positions other than the canonical direct object position immediately following the verb. This property of objects in Chichewa is arguably the equivalent of the Free Inversion property of overt subjects in Italian. It is plausible to attribute the freedom of ordering objects in Chichewa examples with overt object agreement to the same reason responsible for the freedom of ordering subjects in Italian. However, we will not attempt to explicate the link here.

12.2.2   Arbitrary null objects

Unlike Chichewa, Italian and English do not have overt object agreement inflection. Consequently, they are not expected to allow null objects, just as languages which do not have overt/rich subject agreement inflection, e.g. English, were shown above not to allow null subjects. On the assumption that the null object would be *pro*, as in Chichewa null object sentences, its occurrence would not be licensed in the absence of overt Agr$_O$ morpheme. However, it turns out that while the prediction is borne out in essence, there are certain complications that need to be ironed out.

Consider the Italian examples in (21) and (22), discussed in Rizzi (1986a):

21a. Questo   conduce   la gente   a concludere   quanto segue.
      this   leads   the people   to conclude   what follows

21b. Questo   conduce   la gente a [PRO concludere quanto segue]

22a. Questo   conduce   a concludere   quanto   segue.
  this   leads   to conclude   what   follows

22b. Questo conduce [e]$_i$ a [PRO$_i$ concludere quanto segue]

The transitive verb *conduce* 'leads' has an overt object in (21), namely *la gente* 'the people'. However, it apparently does not have an object in (22). Rizzi (1986a) argues that (22) must be assumed to include a null object necessary to explain the fact that the PRO subject of the embedded clause is understood to have the implicit object of the root verb as an antecedent (a controller). Given that Control is essentially a relation between two A-positions (see Chapter 9), the Italian example in (22) must have a structurally represented object.

 Further evidence for the presence of a null object in sentences of the type illustrated in (22) can be gleaned from examples such as (23):

23a. La buona musica   reconcilia   con   se stessi.
  the good music   reconciles   with   themselves

23b. La buona musica reconcilia [e]$_i$ con se stessi$_i$

For the reflexive anaphor *se stessi* 'themselves' in (23) to satisfy BC A, it has to have a binder in the sentence. The binder of the reflexive anaphor is understood to be the object of the verb *reconcilia* 'reconcile'. The subject *la buona musica* '(the) good music' cannot be the antecedent for a number of reasons among them the fact that it is singular while the reflexive anaphor is plural. Together, these facts show that (22) and (23) must include a null object.

 Assuming that the null category in question is *pro* (PRO is excluded because the position is governed), it seems that the prediction spelled out above is only partially fulfilled. The prediction is fulfilled in English, where the lack of overt object agreement seems to result in the lack of null objects. The English equivalents of the Italian null object examples shown in (24) are excluded:

24a. *This leads to conclude what follows.
24b. *Good music reconciles with oneself.

 However, the prediction is not fulfilled in Italian, which seems to allow null objects even though it resembles English in that it lacks overt object agreement. Technically, the problem is that *pro* seems to occur in an environment where it is not licensed, given the condition on the licensing of *pro* above. The licensing condition on *pro* must therefore be revised. An indication as to the nature of the revision required comes from the fact that null objects in Italian have an arbitrary interpretation, contrary to their counterparts in Chichewa which have a specific interpretation. The null object in the Italian examples above is understood to mean 'people in general' or 'one'. It seems that whether the null object has a specific interpretation, as in the Chichewa example, or an arbitrary one, as in the Italian examples, depends on the presence or absence of overt object agreement. The specific interpretation associated with null objects in the Chichewa example is the consequence of the restrictions on the reference of *pro* imposed by the Agr$_O$

morpheme. On the other hand, the arbitrary interpretation associated with null objects in Italian is the consequence of the absence of restrictions on the reference of *pro* due to the absence of an overt Agr$_O$ morpheme in the language.

To a large extent, the mechanism responsible for the assignment of an interpretation to *pro* is parallel to (or the same as) the mechanism responsible for the assignment of an interpretation to *PRO*, discussed in Chapter 9 (Huang 1984). *PRO* has a specific interpretation when it has an antecedent in the sentence, as in (25), and an arbitrary interpretation when it does not have an antecedent in the sentence, as in (26):

25a. John tried to leave.
25b. [$_{IP}$ John$_i$ I tried [$_{CP}$ C [$_{IP}$ PRO$_i$ to leave . . .

26a. It is difficult to predict their next move.
26b. [$_{IP}$ it is difficult [$_{CP}$ C [$_{IP}$ PRO to predict their next move . . .

Two conclusions can be drawn from the comparison made between null objects in Chichewa and Italian. First, it seems that a distinction needs to be made between the mechanism responsible for the formal licensing of *pro* and the mechanism responsible for the assignment of an interpretation (reference) to *pro*. The latter is arguably the mechanism responsible for the assignment of an interpretation to all (base-generated) null categories. Secondly, overt object agreement inflection seems to relate to the interpretation of *pro* rather than to its formal licensing. This is shown by the fact that *pro* can be licensed even in the absence of overt object agreement inflection, as in Italian null object sentences. The effect that overt object agreement inflection has on *pro* is simply to restrict its interpretation to a specific reference. Rizzi (1986a) suggests a theory of *pro* which makes a clear distinction between its formal licensing and its interpretation. (27a) and (27b) are adapted from this theory:

27a. **Pro-drop parameter**

   pro is governed by a designated X^0 (formal licensing).

27b. **Identification Convention**

   pro has the feature complex specified on X^0; otherwise, it has arbitrary features.

(27a) is a licensing schema, where 'designated head' is a head which, as a lexical property, can license *pro* under government. The consequence of associating the licensing of *pro* with specific categories is that the class of designated heads may vary from one language to another. In Italian, for example, it includes finite I and V, given that *pro* is allowed in both the subject position of finite clauses and the object position of a class of transitive verbs. In English, however, the class of designated heads has zero-members, given that *pro* is allowed neither in the subject position of finite clauses nor in the object position of any verb. (27b) is the convention which specifies the conditions under which *pro* has a given interpretation, which is presumably part of a more general convention on the identification of null categories. The null category *pro* has a specific interpretation in situations where its licensing head incorporates an overt Agr morpheme, and an arbitrary interpretation when its licensing head does not incorporate such an element.

According to the theory outlined in (27a&b), the fact that English does not allow null arguments is not so much due to the absence of overt (subject and object) agreement inflection. Recall that Italian allows null objects even though it lacks overt object agreement inflection. Rather, it is due to the idea that English lacks categories which can license *pro* as a lexical property. It is this lexical property which accounts for the parametric distinction between English, on the one hand, and Italian and Chichewa, on the other.

12.2.3 Null operator objects

Italian is not unique among members of the Romance family in allowing null objects. European Portuguese has also been reported to allow null objects (Huang 1984, Raposo 1986). This is shown in (28) and (29). The object in (28) belongs to a group of pronouns called clitic pronouns discussed in Chapter 15:

28a. A Joana   viu-o   na televisao   ontem e noite.
     the Joana   saw-him   on television   last the night

28b. [$_{IP}$ A Joana I [$_{VP}$ [$_V$ viu] [$_{DP}$ o] [$_{PP}$ na televisao] [ontem e noite] . . . .

29a. A Joana   viu   na televisao   ontem e noite.
     the Joana   saw   on television   last the night

29b. [$_{IP}$ A Joana I [$_{VP}$ [$_V$ viu] [e] [$_{PP}$ na televisao] [ontem e noite] . . . .

Unlike (28), (29) lacks an overt object for the verb *viu* 'saw'. Superficially, it looks as though European Portuguese resembles Italian in this respect, with the possibility that the analysis outlined above for Italian null objects can perhaps be extended to European Portuguese examples such as (29). However, there are reasons to believe that European Portuguese null objects are different in nature from the Italian null objects discussed above.

First of all, European Portuguese null objects tend not to have an arbitrary interpretation, contrary to their Italian counterparts. European Portuguese null objects tend to be understood to refer to an individual (or entity) understood in the discourse context sometimes called a **zero-topic**. Secondly, European Portuguese null objects cannot co-occur with a (fronted) wh-phrase in the same sentence, again contrary to their counterparts in Italian. This is shown in (30), compared to the Italian example in (31) from Rizzi (1986a):

30. *Para   qual   d-os filhos   é   que a Maria comprou?
     for   which   of-her children   is that   Maria bought

31. Quale musica   riconcilia   con se stessi?
    which music   reconciles   with themselves

The fact that European Portuguese null objects cannot co-occur with a wh-phrase is interesting insofar as it gives us an indication as to the nature of the null category. Suppose the null category is assumed to be a null operator of the type found in English relatives such as *the book [CP Op$_i$ [IP Mary bought t$_i$]]*. The fact that it cannot co-occur with a wh-phrase in European Portuguese would then follow from the general constraint that only one operator category can be in Spec,CP at SS. On the other hand, the fact that Italian null objects can co-occur with a wh-phrase, shown in (31), confirms that null objects in this language are not null operators.

The conclusion that European Portuguese null objects are null operators which move to the relevant Spec,CP is supported by a number of other facts discussed in Huang (1984) and Raposo (1986). Here we will mention only two of them. First, when the null object is situated inside an island, a Subjacency effect arises. Recall that this test was used in Chapter 4 to detect the presence of a null operator in relatives without an overt wh-phrase. The context for the European Portuguese example (32) is a 'conversation . . . about some important documents'. The null object in this example, represented as *e* in the object position of the verb *guardado* 'kept', is included inside a complex noun phrase island. The fact that the sentence exhibits a Subjacency violation shows that the null object moves out of the island, and therefore is a null operator:

32a. ??Eu informei   a policía   da possibilidade   de o Manel
    I informed   to the police   of the possibility   that the Manel

    ter guardado   no cofre da sala de jantar
    had kept   in safe of room of dining

32b. ??Eu informei a policia da [DP possibilidade de
    [CP C [IP o Manel ter guardado [e] no cofre da sala de jantar . . .

Secondly, when null objects are co-indexed with a c-commanding subject, a Strong Crossover effect arises (see Chapter 9 for discussion of Crossover). Thus, (33a) cannot have the interpretation shown in (33b):

33a. Joao   disse   que   Pedro viu.
    Joao   said   that   Pedro saw

33b. *[IP Joao$_i$ I [VP disse [CP que [IP Pedro viu e$_i$ . . .

The situation in (33) is identical to the situation found in English Strong Crossover cases such as *Who$_i$ does he$_i$/John$_i$ like t$_i$*. This indicates that the null object is a null operator which moves to Spec,CP, crossing over the subject and leaving behind a variable trace situated to the right of a co-indexed A-specifier.

Thus, there are good reasons to conclude that European Portuguese null objects are different in nature from their Italian counterparts. In European Portuguese, they are null operators which move to an appropriate Spec,CP in the syntax. In Italian, they are realised as *pro* which receives an arbitrary interpretation for lack of identification. European Portuguese null objects do not fall under the scope of the pro-drop parameter. Recall that null operators are also allowed in English, although their occurrence is much more restricted. In English, their occurrence is restricted to contexts where the null operator has an antecedent (an identifier) in the sentence. In relatives, for example, the null operator is co-indexed with the head N of the relative noun phrase which identifies it (see discussion in Chapter 4).

European Portuguese belongs to a group of languages which have been described as 'context-oriented'. In these languages, null categories can rely on antecedents understood in the context and not necessarily present in the sentence. There may be a parametric distinction between such languages and languages where null categories must be identified in the sentence such as English, although it is not easy to see what form the parameter will take.

12.3 *Summary*

It seems that there is not necessarily a link between overt (rich) Agr inflection and null arguments. Null arguments can be found in contexts which are not related to overt agreement inflection. The role of overt agreement inflection is to restrict the reference of a given null argument rather than to license it in formal terms. The licensing of null arguments seems to depend on the properties of individual categories related to the argument. Two types of null arguments have been identified. One type is realised as a pronominal null category and the other as a null operator. The former falls under the scope of the *pro*-drop parameter, whereas the latter falls under the scope of a more general parameter which distinguishes between 'context-oriented' languages and 'non-context-oriented' languages.

Exercises

Exercise 12.1

Explain on the basis of examples (i), (ii) and (iii) whether French patterns with Italian or English with respect to null subjects. When thinking about example (iii) bear in mind that the French complementiser THAT has the form *que* which is not the form that appears in (iii):

i) *(Il) a appelé.
    he has called

ii) *A appelé Jean.
     has called Jean

iii) Qui as-tu   dit   qui a appelé?
     who have-you   said that has called
     'Who have you said (*that) has called?'

Exercise 12.2

Examples (i) and (ii) are from French (Authier 1989). Outline an analysis for each example, and explain whether French patterns with Italian or English with respect to null objects:

i) L'ambition   amène (les gens)   à commetre des erreurs.
   the ambition   leads (the people)   to commit errors
   'Ambitions leads people to commit errors.'

ii) Une bonne thérapeutique   réconcilie   avec soi-même.
    a good therapy   reconciles   with oneself
    'Good therapy reconciles one with oneself.'

Exercise 12.3

Explain what examples (ii) and (iii) reveal about the status of the implicit object in example (i), and suggest an analysis for example (i):

i)   This fact leads (one/people) to the following conclusion.
ii) *This fact leads to conclude what follows.
iii) *This realisation leads to appreciate oneself.

Exercise 12.4

Examples (i–iv) are from Chinese (Huang 1989). Chinese is a language which allows both null subjects and null objects. Huang explains that the null category [e] in the subject position of the embedded clause in (iii) can have the root subject *Zhangsan* as an antecedent. However, the null category in the object position of the embedded verb in (iv) cannot have the root subject *Zhangsan* as an antecedent. Explain what this fact reveals about the nature of the null categories in the subject and object position in Chinese (PERF stands for 'perfective aspect'):

i) (ta)   kanjian (ta)   le.
    he   see   he   PERF
    'He saw him.'

ii) wo   xiang (ta)   kanjian (tat)   le.
     I   think he   see   he   PERF
     'I think he saw him.'

iii) Zhangsan   shuo   [[e]   hen   xihuan Lisi].
     Zhangsan   say   very like   Lisi
     'Zhangsan said that he liked Lisi.'

iv) Zhangsan   shuo   [Lisi   hen   xihuan [e]].
    Zhangsan   say   Lisi   very like
    'Zhangsan said that Lisi liked him.'

Exercise 12.5

Examples (i–iii) are from a dialect of Arabic called Levantine Arabic, and examples (iv–vi) are from another dialect of Arabic called Bani-Hassan Arabic (Kenstowicz 1989). The examples show that the two dialects behave differently with respect to the null subject parameter in embedded clauses. Explain how:

Levantine Arabic

i) Fariid kaal inn *(ha) ishtarat l-fustaan.
   Farrid said that (she) bought the-dress
   'Fariid said that she bought the dress.'

ii) Fariid kaal innu (l-bnt) ishtarat l-fustaan (*l-bnt).
    Fariid said that (the-girl) bought the-dress (the girl)
    'Fariid said that the girl bought the dress.'

iii) ?ayy bint Fariid kaal inn *(ha) ishtarat l-fustaan?
     which girl Fariid said that (she) bought the-dress
     Which girl did Fariid say bought the dress?'

Bani Hassan Arabic

iv) al-binit gaalat innu ishtarat al-libaas.
    the-girl said that bought the-dress
    'The girl said that she bought the dress.'

v) Fariid gaal innu ishtarat al-binit al-libaas.
   Farrid said that bought the-girl the-dress
   'Fariid said that the girl bought the dress.'

vi) wayy binit Fariid gaal innu ishtarat al-libaas?
    which girl Fariid said that bought the-dress
    'Which girl did Fariid say bought the dress?'

13 Verb Second, VSO and NSO

Contents

13.1   *Verb Second*

The Verb Second phenomenon is often associated with Continental Germanic languages. In these languages the finite verb is required to be in the 'second position', roughly immediately following the first constituent. In some languages, e.g. German, this phenomenon is restricted to root clauses. In others, e.g. Yiddish and Icelandic, it is found in both root and embedded clauses. English is not a Verb Second language, but it is sometimes said to be a 'residual Verb Second language' on the grounds that the Verb Second constraint can still be seen in some restricted contexts.

13.1.1   Verb Second in root clauses

We saw in Chapter 11 that the unmarked order in German embedded clauses is for the verb to follow its complement and for the finite auxiliary to follow the main non-finite verb. This is shown in (1) and (2):

1a. . . . dass   Hans   den Ball   kaufte.
    . . . that   Hans   the ball   bought

1b. [$_{CP}$ dass [$_{IP}$ Hans [$_{VP}$ [$_{DP}$ den Ball] [$_V$ kaufte]]]].

2a. . . . dass   Hans   den Ball   gekauft   hat.
    . . . that   Hans   the ball   bought   has

2b. [$_{CP}$ dass [$_{IP}$ Hans [$_{VP}$ [$_{DP}$ den Ball] [$_V$ gekauft]] [$_I$ hat]]]

The order patterns in (1) and (2) were accounted for by assuming that V and I select their complement to the left in German. In contrast, C selects its complement IP to the right, as indicated by the fact that the complementiser *dass* 'that' appears clause-initially. With this in mind, consider now examples (3a&b) and (4a&b), all of which are root sentences:

3a. Hans   kaufte   den Ball.
    Hans   bought   the ball

3b. *Hans   den Ball   kaufte.
    Hans   the ball   bought

4a. Hans   hat   den Ball   gekauft.
    Hans   has   the ball   bought

4b. *Hans   den Ball   gekauft   hat.
    Hans   the ball   bought   has

In (3a) the verb precedes its direct object instead of following it. (3b) shows that the OV order characteristic of embedded clauses is in fact excluded in this particular example. In (4a) the order of the verb and its object is consistent with the order found in embedded clauses. In this example, it is the order of the finite auxiliary with respect to the main verb which is inconsistent with the [[VP] Aux] order characteristic of embedded clauses. (4b) shows that the [[VP] Aux] order typical of embedded clauses is excluded in this particular example.

The observed order differences between embedded and root clauses present an obvious dilemma. We either abandon the conclusion that the underlying order in German is [OV] and [VP I] or maintain this conclusion and explain the order differences between root and embedded clauses in terms of some peculiar property of root clauses. It is important to realise that the possibility that V and I select their complement in different directions depending on whether they are located in the embedded clause or the root clause is a non-starter. In addition to the fact that it is extremely add-hoc (non-explanatory), it is empirically inaccurate. (4a), for example, shows that the OV order typical of embedded clauses is also found in root clauses.

A closer look at (3a&b) and (4a&b) leads to the observation that the finite verb is required to immediately follow the first constituent of the sentence. (3a) and (4a) have in common the fact that the finite verb immediately follows the first constituent of the clause. On the other hand, (3b) and (4b) have in common the fact that the finite verb does not immediately follow the first constituent of the clause. This observation is confirmed by the examples in (5a&b) and (6a–c):

5a. Gestern   kaufte   Hans   den Ball.
    Yesterday   bought   Hans   the ball

5b. *Gestern   Hans   den Ball   kaufte.
    Yesterday   Hans   the ball   bought

6a. Im Park   hat   Hans   den Ball   gekauft.
    In the park has   Hans   the ball   bought

6b. *Im Park   Hans   den Ball   gekauft   hat.
    In the park Hans   the ball   bought   has

6c. *Im Park   Hans   hat   den Ball   gekauft.
    In the park Hans   has   the ball   bought

German seems to have an order constraint which requires the finite verb to be in the 'second position' in root clauses. This constraint is known as the **Verb Second (V2) Constraint**. An essential part of the attempt to explicate the nature of this constraint and explain why it is restricted to root clauses is to identify the nature of the so-called 'second position'. This is our next step.

(5a) and (6a) indicate that the 'second position' must be in the pre-IP domain. In all these examples the finite verb precedes the subject located in its canonical position Spec,IP. The fact that the finite verb is a (complex) head category implies, by virtue of SPH (Chapter 6), that the 'second position' is unlikely to be any category other than C, the only head position in the pre-IP domain. On the other hand, the fact that the category in the 'first position' is a maximal projection implies that the 'first position' is Spec,CP, the only phrasal position in the pre-C domain. Presumably, the finite verb reaches C via movement from its canonical position inside VP through I.

In view of this, the order properties of root clauses cannot be said to reflect the underlying order of V in relation to its complement, and I in relation to its complement. Both V and I are displaced by the V-raising and I-raising processes involved in the derivation of root clauses. Thus, the fact that the verb does not follow its direct object in (3a) cannot be said to argue against the conclusion reached in Chapter 11 on the basis of embedded clauses that the verb follows its direct object in the structure of German. Likewise, the fact that the finite auxiliary does not follow the main verb in (4a) cannot be said to argue against the conclusion reached in Chapter 11 on the basis of the word order in embedded clauses that I follows its VP-complement in the structure of German. The more optimal view to pursue is that the underlying order of V in relation to its direct object, and I in relation to its VP-complement is the same in both embedded and root clauses. Moreover, the exact nature of this order is reflected more directly in embedded clauses than in root clauses. The canonical order of German is distorted in root clauses by the requirement that the finite verb must move from its canonical position inside IP to C.

According to the reasoning outlined in the previous two paragraphs, (7a) has the structure and derivation roughly shown in (7b):

7a. Den Ball   hat   Hans   gekauft.
    the ball   has   Hans   bought

7b. [$_{CP}$ den Ball [$_{C'}$ hat [$_{IP}$ Hans [$_{VP}$ [$_{DP}$ t$_{den Ball}$] [$_V$ gekauft]] t$_{hat}$]]]

The structure shown in (7b) is the same structure reached in Chapter 11 for embedded clauses, where V is to the right of its direct object, I is to the right of its VP-complement and C to the left of its IP-complement. The XP in Spec,CP (the 'first position') is the direct object of the verb moved from its canonical position inside IP in terms of a process known, somewhat misleadingly, as topicalisation. German topicalisation is a substitution movement, contrary to English topicalisation which is an adjunction movement (Chapter 6). Raising of the finite auxiliary verb from inside VP to I is ignored in (7b) as it is not directly relevant to the point of the discussion.

Assuming that the V2 Constraint applies to all root clauses, sentences with the deceptive English-like surface order SVO such as (8a) also undergo movement of the finite verb to C and topicalisation of the subject to Spec,CP. (8a) has the structure and derivation shown in (8b):

8a. Hans kaufte den Ball.

8b. [$_{CP}$ Hans [$_{C'}$ kaufte [$_{IP}$ t$_{Hans}$ [$_{VP}$ [$_{DP}$ den Ball] [$_{V}$ t$_{kaufen}$]] t$_{kaufte}$]]]

The essentials of the analysis of German order outlined here are based on work as early as Bierwisch (1963) through Koster (1975), Thiersch (1978), den Besten (1983), among others. One of its major advantages is that it maintains a uniform view with respect to the underlying order of constituents in both root and embedded clauses. The order differences between root and embedded clauses are the consequence of V-raising to C and topicalisation of an XP-constituent to Spec,CP in root clauses. V-raising to C in root clauses is motivated by the V2 Constraint which holds of root clauses but not embedded clauses. In German C is located to the left of IP, and hence the linear notion 'verb second'.

The reason the V2 Constraint does not hold of embedded clauses receives a plausible explanation on the basis of the hypothesis that the 'second position' is C. Because embedded clauses tend to have their C position filled with a complementiser, the verb cannot move to it (den Besten, 1983). Interestingly, when the complementiser is missing from the complement clause of a restricted class of verbs called 'bridge verbs' (Grewendorf 1988), the V2 effect can be observed in embedded clauses as well. This is shown in (9) and (10) (Vikner 1990):

9a. Er   sagt, dass die Kinder   diesen Film   gesehen   haben.
     he   says   that the children this film   seen   have

9b. . . . [$_{CP}$ dass [$_{IP}$ die Kinder [$_{VP}$ [$_{DP}$ diesen Film] [$_{V}$ gesehen]] [$_{I}$ haben]]]

10a. Er   sagt   diesen Film   haben   die Kinder   gesehen.
     he   says   this film   have   the children seen

10b. . . . [$_{CP}$ diesen Film [$_{C'}$ haben [$_{IP}$ die Kinder [$_{VP}$ [$_{DP}$ t$_{diesen Film}$]
     [$_{V}$ gesehen]] [$_{I}$ t$_{haben}$]]]

(9) includes the complementiser *dass* 'that' in the embedded clause and consequently the embedded clause does not exhibit the V2 effect. (10), however, does not include the complementiser *dass* 'that', and consequently the embedded

clause exhibits the V2 effect. This confirms the view that the so-called 'second position' is indeed C.

The question we still need to address with respect to V2 languages of the German type is the following: Why does the finite verb have to move to C in root clauses? The answer to this question will effectively amount to an explanation of the parametric difference between V2 languages such as German and non-V2 languages such as English. Various hypotheses have been suggested in the literature which have in common the idea that C in V2 languages, when not filled with a complementiser, has a special property which forces the finite verb to move to it (e.g. Koopman 1984, Travis, 1984, Holmberg 1986, Platzack 1986a, 1986b, Grewendorf 1988, Rizzi 1990). Some of these hypotheses relate the parametric distinction in question to a restriction in the directionality of Case-assignment by finite I. In V2 languages, finite I assigns Case strictly leftward under government instead of via Spec-head agreement. Consequently, finite I must be located to left of the subject by SS. This hypothesis motivates raising of finite I to C, though not necessarily raising of the verb to I. To tie them together, it has been suggested that finite I alone cannot assign nominative Case. It must be 'supported' by the verb to be able to do so, and hence the fact that the verb ends up in C along with finite I.

Recall from Chapter 11 that restrictions on directionality of Case-assignment were also invoked to explain directionality of complementation. German verbs select their DP object to the left because they assign Case strictly to the left. This argument has also been invoked to account for the order of C in relation to its IP complement, although the account requires the auxiliary assumption that finite I supported by the verb assigns Case under the condition of adjacency. The combination of these ideas forces C to be to the left of IP instead of to the right. If C were located to the right of IP, the finite I which moves to it would not be adjacent to the subject. Check for yourself!

13.1.2 Verb Second in embedded clauses

We have seen that V2 is allowed in the complement clause of a restricted class of verbs in German, provided C is not filled with a complementiser. However, there are V2 languages in the Germanic family which allow, indeed require, V2 in embedded clauses in the presence of the complementiser 'that'. Yiddish and Icelandic are two such languages as shown in (11) and (12), respectively (Vikner 1990):

11a. *... az   dos yingl   oyfn veg   vet   zen   a kats.
    ... that   the boy   on-the way   will   see   a cat

11b. ... az   dos yingl   vet   oyfn veg   zen   a kats.
    ... that   the boy   will   on-the way   see   a cat

12a. *... ad   Helgi aldrei   hevur   hitt   Mariu.
    ... that   Helga never   has   met   Maria

12b. ... ad   Helgi hevur   aldrei   hitt   Mariu.
    ... that   Helga has   never   met   Maria

Unlike German, Yiddish and Icelandic have the (English-like) underlying orders [VO] and [I VP]. The order of adverbial expressions such as 'on the way' in (11) and 'often' in (12) is used as a diagnostic for the V2 effect. Clauses are concluded to exhibit the V2 effect when the finite verb precedes the adverbial expression, and not to exhibit the V2 effect when the finite verb follows the adverbial expression. Accordingly, (11b) and (12b) exhibit the V2 effect, whereas (11a) and (12a) do not. The latter are excluded because they are in violation of the V2 Constraint which in Yiddish and Icelandic holds of embedded clauses as well. The fact that the V2 effect holds even in the presence of the complementiser 'that' poses a serious problem for the analysis outlined above on the basis of German where the 'second position' is assumed to be a C not filled with the complementiser 'that'. At least two alternative analyses have be suggested in the literature which we will discuss here briefly.

The first hypothesis, advocated in Diesing 1990, Santorini 1990, Rognvaldsson and Thrainsson 1990, among others, rests on two assumptions. First, the 'second position' is finite I rather than C in both root and embedded clauses. Secondly, Spec,IP is or can be an A′-position occupied by topicalised categories. According to this hypothesis, (11b) and (12b) have the representations shown in (13b) and (14b). The adverbial expressions are assumed to be left-adjoined to VP. The representations are basically identical to the representations of the equivalent English sentences:

13a. . . . az   dos yingl   vet   oyfn veg   zen   a kats.
     . . . that the boy   will   on-the way see   a cat

13b. . . . [$_{CP}$ az [$_{IP}$ dos yingl [$_{I'}$ vet [$_{ADV}$ oyfn veg] [$_{VP}$ t$_{vet}$ [$_{VP}$ zen a kats . . .

14a. . . . ad   Helgi   hevur   aldrei   hitt   Mariu.
     . . . that Helga   has   never   met   Maria

14b. . . . [$_{CP}$ ad [$_{IP}$ Helgi [$_{I'}$ hevur [$_{ADV}$ aldrei] [$_{VP}$ t$_{hevur}$ [$_{VP}$ hitt Mariu . . .

Examples (15a) and (16a), where the category in the 'first position' is not the subject of the sentence, have the representations shown in (15b) and (16b):

15a. . . . az   morgn   vet   dos yingl   oyfn veg   zen   a kats.
     . . . that tomorrow will   the boy   on-the way see   a cat

15b. . . . [$_{CP}$ az [$_{IP}$ morgn [$_{I'}$ vet [$_{VP}$ dos yingl [$_{ADV}$ oyfn veg] [$_{V'}$ t$_{vet}$ zen
     a kats . . .

16a. . . . ad   Mariu   hevur   Helgi   aldrei   hitt.
     . . . that Mariu   has   Helga   never   met

16b. . . . [$_{CP}$ ad [$_{IP}$ Mariu [$_{I'}$ hevur [$_{VP}$ Helgi [$_{ADV}$ aldrei] [$_{V'}$ t$_{hevur}$
     hitt t$_{Mariu}$]]]]]

In the Yiddish example (15), Spec,IP (the 'first position') is occupied by the adverb 'tomorrow'. The adverb is possibly topicalised from an IP internal position, although this is not shown in (15b) as it is not crucially relevant. In the Icelandic example (16), Spec,IP is occupied by the object of the verb topicalised from the direct object position. The subject is located in Spec,VP, the DS position of subjects (see Chapter 8). The adverbial expression is assumed to be left-adjoined to V', one of the options entertained in Chapter 6 for so-called VP-adverbs.

It should be clear how the hypothesis that the 'second position' is finite I rather than C manages to solve the problem raised by languages such as Yiddish and Icelandic, which have V2 in embedded clauses introduced by a complementiser. In the context of this hypothesis, the co-occurrence of V2 with a complementiser not only ceases to be a problem, it even becomes expected. It remains to be explained, though, why V2 is incompatible with clauses introduced by a complementiser in German and other Continental Germanic languages. We will not pursue this question here.

The second hypothesis rests on the assumption that the 'second position' in embedded V2 clauses is the head of an additional category intervening between CP and IP with properties similar to those of CP (Holmberg, 1986). The category in question is sometimes thought to be no more than a second occurrence of CP itself, which is why this hypothesis is called **CP-recursion**. Here, we will call the category in question XP, leaving open the question whether it is a second occurrence of CP or an entirely different category with properties (partly) similar to those of CP. In the context of this hypothesis, the Yiddish and Icelandic examples discussed above have the representations shown in (17b) and (18b). The adverbial expression is assumed to be left-adjoined to I':

17a. . . . az   dos yingl   vet   oyfn veg   zen   a kats.
     . . . that   the boy   will   on-the way   see   a cat

17b. . . . [$_{CP}$ az [$_{XP}$ dos yingl [$_{X'}$ vet [$_{IP}$ t$_{dos\ yingl}$ [$_{I'}$ [oyfn veg] [$_{I'}$ t$_{vet}$ [$_{VP}$ t$_{vet}$ zen a kats . . .

18a. . . . ad   Helgi   hevur   aldrei   hitt   Mariu.
     . . . that   Helga   has   never   met   Maria

18b. . . . [$_{CP}$ ad [$_{XP}$ Helgi [$_{X'}$ hevur [$_{IP}$ t$_{Helgi}$ [$_{I'}$ [aldrei] [$_{I'}$ t$_{hevur}$ [$_{VP}$ t$_{hevur}$ hitt Mariu . . .

13.1.3   Residual Verb Second

Studies on the V2 phenomenon have mostly concentrated on providing an answer to the question: Why does the finite verb have to move to the 'second position' in V2 clauses? Note, however, that this question represents only part of the picture. The other part relates to the following question: Why does the 'first position' invariably have to be filled with a topicalised category in declarative V2 clauses? The German examples (19) and (20) lack a topicalised constituent in the 'first position', and consequently are excluded as declarative sentences. (19) and (20) cannot be said to involve a violation of the V2 Constraint, if the latter is understood as the requirement that the finite verb be in C:

19a. *Kaufte   Hans   den Ball.
     bought   Hans   the ball

19b. *[CP e [C' kaufte [IP Hans [VP [DP den Ball] [V tkaufen]] tkaufte]]]

20a. *Hat   Hans   den Ball   gekauft.
     has   Hans   the ball   bought

20b. *[CP e [C' hat [IP Hans [VP [DP den Ball] [V gekauft]] that]]]

Once the second question just raised is taken into consideration, a third question becomes obvious, namely: Which of the two categories involved in V2 pulls the other to the pre-IP domain? Is it topicalisation of the 'first constituent' which triggers raising of the finite verb to C or the other round? A possible answer to this question can be gleaned from the facts of English. For reasons which will become clear shortly, English is said to be a 'residual V2 language' (Rizzi 1991).

English is obviously not a V2 language in the sense that German and other Continental Germanic languages are. This is trivially shown by the order of constituents in (21a&b):

21a. Mary often reads the *Socialist Worker*.
21b. To John, Mary gave a book.

The counterparts of (21a&b) with similar orders are excluded in V2 languages for the simple reason that the finite verb is not in the 'second position'. However, English exhibits what looks like the V2 effect in root wh-questions. Movement of a wh-phrase to the root Spec,CP (root wh-subjects excepted, see Chapter 4) generally triggers movement of the finite auxiliary to C (SAI) in English. This is shown in (22) and (23):

22a. Why has John left early?
22b. [CP why [C' has [IP John [I' thas [VP thave [VP left early. . . twhy. . .

23a. *Why John has left early?
23b. *[CP why [C' e [IP John [I' has [VP left early. . . twhy. . .

Recall (from Chapter 4) that SAI (or I-raising) is a root phenomenon (Emonds 1980), as shown in (24) and (25):

24a. *I wonder why has John left early.
24b. *[IP I wonder [CP why [C' has [IP John [I' thas [VP thave [VP left early. . .
     twhy . . .

25a. I wonder why John has left early.
25b. [IP I wonder [CP why [C' e [IP John [I' has [VP thave [VP left early. . . twhy. . .

If V2 is understood to mean the obligatory presence of the finite verb in root C, there is a sense in which English can be said to exhibit the V2 phenomenon at least in wh-questions. As a matter of fact, the V2 effect is not necessarily restricted to wh-questions in English. It also arises in sentences involving topicalisation of a constituent with negative content, as shown in (26) and (27):

26a. Never have I seen anything like that.
26b. [CP never [C′ have [IP I [I′ thave [VP thave [VP seen anything like that . . .

27a. *Never I have seen anything like that.
27b. *[CP never [C′ e [IP I [I′ have [VP thave [VP seen anything like that . . .

(26) and (27) show that topicalised negative phrases also trigger SAI in English. This gives rise to an effect which to all intent and purposes is similar to the V2 effect. Interestingly, this effect can also be seen in embedded clauses introduced by the complementiser *that*, as shown in (28) and (29) (Culicover 1992):

28a. The committee resolved that under no circumstances would John be allowed to continue in his work

28b. . . . [CP under no circumstances [C′ would [IP John [I′ twould [VP be allowed. . . .

29a. ??The committee resolved that under no circumstances John would be allowed to continue in his work.

29b. ?? . . . [CP [under no circumstances] [C′ e [IP John [I′ would [VP be allowed. . . .

Assuming that the subject of the embedded clause occupies its canonical position Spec,IP, the inversion effect in (28) and (29) appears to give credence to the hypothesis that the 'second position' is the head position of a category which exists over and above the CP selected by the root verb.

To the extent that SAI can be considered a manifestation of the V2 effect, it is clear, as far as English is concerned, that the V2 effect is triggered by the presence of an operator in Spec,CP. The operator can be either a wh-phrase or a negative phrase, but apparently not a category of the type illustrated in (21b). It would be interesting to know why topicalised non-negative phrases do not have the same effect in English. In Chapter 6 topicalised non-negative phrases were said to left-adjoin to IP instead of substitute into Spec,CP. In view of this, one could put forward the hypothesis that topicalised non-negative phrases do not trigger SAI because they do not occupy Spec,CP. Only categories that are moved to Spec,CP trigger SAI such as wh-phrases and negative topics. However, this only begs the question why topicalised non-negative phrases do not occupy Spec,CP. The contrast between topicalised phrases which are located in Spec,CP and the ones which are left-adjoined to IP and their effect on interpretation can be seen in the pair (30) and (31). (30) has the meaning 'there is no score that would make the coach feel satisfied' whereas (31) has the meaning 'the coach would feel satisfied if there was no score':

30a. With no score would the coach be satisfied.
30b. [CP with no score [C′ would [IP the coach [I′ twould [VP be satisfied . . .

31a. With no score, the coach would be satisfied.
31b. [IP with no score [IP the coach [I′ would [VP be satisfied . . .

If the conclusion that the V2 effect arises only when Spec,CP is filled were to extend to languages with a generalised V2 effect (i.e. so-called V2 languages), the parametric distinction between these languages and languages with limited V2 would hinge on an answer to the second question raised above: Why does the 'first position' have to be filled with an operator in declarative sentences? Raising of the finite verb to the C when Spec,CP is filled with an operator is not an exclusive property of V2 languages. In other words, the V2 effect, understood as the obligatory raising of the finite verb to C, seems to be a by-product of the parameter underlying the V2 phenomenon rather than its core property. The core parameter would have to distinguish between languages such as German where Spec,CP has to be filled with an operator in declarative clauses and languages such as English where it does not have to be filled with an operator in declarative clauses.

13.2   *VSO*

VSO languages can be loosely characterised as the languages where the most natural (or unmarked) position for the subject is to immediately follow the finite verb. However, there are significant differences between VSO languages regarding the order of the subject. Some VSO languages, e.g. Welsh (Celtic), do not allow SVO as an alternative order in neutral finite sentences at all. Other VSO languages, e.g. Standard Arabic (Semitic), allow SVO as an alternative order in neutral finite sentences. We will discuss two major hypotheses concerning the parametric distinction between VSO languages and SVO languages such as English. The first hypothesis, which we will call here **V-raising to C,** will be discussed in relation to Welsh. The second hypothesis, which we will call here **Subject in VP,** will be discussed in relation to Standard Arabic.

13.2.1   Verb-raising to C

(32a&b) are representative examples of two types of VSO sentence in Welsh (Sproat 1985):

32a. Gwelodd Siôn ddraig.
　　 saw　　　 Siôn dragon
　　 'Siôn saw a dragon.'

32b. Gwnaeth Siôn weld draig.
　　 did　　　 Siôn see　 dragon
　　 'Siôn saw a dragon.'

(32a&b) appear to be synonymous, although they differ slightly in their constituent structures. (32a) has a simple structure where the inflectional elements of I appear on the main verb. (32b) has what is called a **periphrastic structure,** where the main verb is uninflected and the inflectional elements of I appear on an auxiliary verb with properties arguably similar to those of English *do*-support. The two sentences display the VSO order in the sense that the subject immediately follows the finite verb, although in (32b) the subject precedes the non-finite main verb.

Some of the early work on VSO languages concentrated on the question whether they have a hierarchical structure with a VP which excludes the subject, or have what is sometimes called a 'flat structure' which does not include a VP and where all major constituents of the sentence are sisters (McCloskey 1983). This question was obviously motivated by the fact that VP constituents, in particular the verb and its complements, are discontinuous in VSO languages with the subject intervening between them. Starting with Emonds (1980), the focus of attention shifted to trying to work out how the VSO order is derived from a structure where the verb and its complements form a VP and are adjacent at DS. Underlying this attempt is the idea that all languages have a unique underlying sentence structure and that order differences involving specifiers are merely surface phenomena which result from the application of certain movement processes in some languages but not in others.

The essence of Emonds' proposal is that the VS(XP) order in VSO languages such as Welsh is derived by raising of the verb to C (via I) from an underlying structure which is identical to that of English in relevant respects. Accordingly, (32a) has the derivation shown in (33b), and (32b) the derivation shown in (34b). It is not clear whether the auxiliary in (34) originates inside VP and moves to C via I or is directly inserted under I or under C (as with English *do*-support). Whatever the right analysis, it is not crucial to the discussion here:

33a. Gwelodd Siôn ddraig.
    saw   Siôn dragon
    'Siôn saw a dragon.'

33b. [$_{CP}$ e [$_{C'}$ gwelodd [$_{IP}$ Siôn [$_{I'}$ t$_{gwelodd}$ [$_{VP}$ t$_{gwelodd}$ ddraig . . . .

34a. Gwnaeth Siôn weld draig.
    did   Siôn see   dragon
    'Siôn saw a dragon.'

34b. [$_{CP}$ e [$_{C'}$ gwnaeth [$_{IP}$ Siôn [$_{I'}$ t$_{gwnaeth}$ [$_{VP}$ weld draig . . .

According to the analysis outlined in (33b) and (34b), the order [V S (XP)] in VSO languages such as Welsh is derived by the same process responsible for the derivation of the order [Wh-XP V S (XP)] in English wh-questions and the order [XP V S (YP)] in V2 languages. The difference is that while raising of the finite verb to C in English, and arguably also V2 languages, is triggered by the presence of an operator in Spec,CP, in VSO languages such as Welsh it applies irrespective. According to this analysis, VSO languages are basically V2 languages, in the sense that their finite verb invariably moves to C.

Sproat (1985) attributes this property of VSO languages to a parametrised restriction on the directionality of nominative Case-assignment to the subject by finite I. In Welsh, finite I can only assign nominative Case rightward under government. For I to be able to do so, it has to raise to C located to the left of the subject. Raising of the verb to C along with finite I is needed to 'lexically support' I, either for purely morphological reasons or in order to enable finite I to assign Case. When 'support' for I is provided by an auxiliary, as in (34), raising of the main verb becomes unnecessary. The parameteric difference between VSO and SVO languages, therefore, reduces to a parametrised restriction on the directionality of Case-assignment by I. Recall from above that a similar parameter has been invoked to account for the difference between V2 languages and non-V2 languages, emphasising the parallelism between the V2 phenomenon and the VSO phenomenon.

The analysis outlined and the parallelism it (implicitly) draws with V2 languages is supported by two important properties of Welsh. First, finite clauses do not allow SVO as an alternative order. In sentences such as (35), where the subject precedes the finite verb, the subject is topicalised/focused and has an operator reading rather than a neutral reading (Jones and Thomas 1977). The status of the preverbal subject as a topic/focus category arguably located in Spec,CP is also indicated by the presence of the particle *a*. The latter is found in contexts which clearly involve an operator in Spec,CP such as relatives (Jones and Thomas 1977):

35a. Mair a   fydd   yn aros   am John.
     Mair PRT   will-be   in wait   for John
    'It is Mair who will be waiting for John.'

The other property of Welsh which supports the analysis outlined in (33b) and (34b) relates to a sharp contrast between finite and non-finite clauses in order. We have seen that finite clauses have the VSO order and exclude the SVO order. In contrast, embedded non-finite clauses have the SVO order as shown in (36):

36a. Dymunai Wyn i   Ifor   ddarllen y llyfr.
     wanted   Wyn for   Ifor   read   the book
    'Wyn wanted for Ifor to read the book.'

36b. $[_{IP}$ dymunai Wyn $[_{CP}$ e $[_{C'}$ i $[_{IP}$ Ifor I $[_{VP}$ ddarllen y llyfr . . . .

According to Sproat's (1985) analysis, the complex [[V] I] raises to C in finite clauses in order to enable I to assign nominative Case to the subject rightward under government. Non-finite I lacks the ability to assign Case, as in English and other languages. Therefore, there is no reason for non-finite I to raise to C in the embedded non-finite clause in (36). The subject is assigned Case by the prepositional complementiser *i* 'for' very much as in the equivalent English example in the gloss.

The SVO order of non-finite clauses confirms the analysis whereby the VSO order of finite clauses is derived by raising of [[V] I] to C to enable I to assign nominative Case to the subject in Welsh.

13.2.2 Subject in VP

As pointed out above, Standard Arabic belongs to the group of VSO languages which allow SVO as an alternative order in finite clauses. (37a) and (37b) are basically synonymous in Standard Arabic, and there seems to be no reason to suspect that (37b) with the SVO order has a non-neutral reading:

37a. raʔa-a   l-ʔawlaad-u   Zayd-an.
    saw-3S   the-boys-NOM   Zayd-ACC
    'The boys saw Zayd.'

37b. l-ʔawlaad-u   raʔa-w   Zayd-an.
    the-boys-NOM   saw -3PL   Zayd-ACC
    'The boys saw Zayd.'

Although (37a) and (37b) appear to be synonymous, they differ in one important respect. In the VSO example (37a) the subject does not agree in number with the Agr$_S$ category on the verb. The subject is (masculine) plural while Agr$_S$ is (masculine) singular. In the SVO example (37b), however, the subject agrees with the Agr$_S$ category on the verb. Both the subject and Agr$_S$ are (masculine) plural. Capitalising on this difference in number agreement between postverbal and preverbal subjects, Mohammad (1989) argues that agreement between the subject and Agr$_S$ in SVO sentences implies that the subject is in a Spec-head relation with I and therefore located in Spec,IP. On the other hand, the lack of number agreement between the subject and Agr$_S$ in VSO sentences implies that the subject is not in a Spec-head relation with I and therefore not located in Spec,IP. In VSO sentences the subject remains inside VP, where it is base-generated according to the Subject-inside-VP Hypothesis (Chapter 8). According to this analysis, (37a) has the derivation shown in (38b), and (37b) the derivation shown in (39b):

38a. raʔa-a   l-ʔawlaad-u   Zayd-an.
    saw-3S   the-boys-NOM   Zayd-ACC
    'The boys saw Zayd.'

38b. [$_{IP}$ e [$_{I'}$ raʔaa [$_{VP}$ l-ʔawlaadu [$_{V'}$ t$_{raʔaa}$ Zaydan . . .

39a. l-ʔawlaad-u   raʔa-w   Zayd-an.
    the-boys-NOM   saw -3PL   Zayd-ACC
    'The boys saw Zayd.'

39b. [$_{IP}$ l-ʔawlaadu [$_{I'}$ raʔaw [$_{VP}$ t$_{l-ʔawlaadu}$ [$_{V'}$ t$_{raʔaw}$ Zaydan . . .

(38) and (39) share the property that the verb moves to I, thereby acquiring its finite character. They differ in whether the subject remains in its DS position Spec,VP or moves to Spec,IP. In (38), the subject remains in its DS position, with the consequence that the order derived at SS is VSO. In (39), the subject moves to Spec,IP resulting in the derivation of the SVO order at SS. Because the subject is not in a Spec-head relation with I in (38), number agreement between the subject and Agr$_S$ is not expected in VSO sentences. On the other hand, because the subject is in a Spec-head relation with I in (39), number agreement between the subject and Agr$_S$ is expected in SVO sentences.

A crucial idea of the analysis outlined in (38) and (39) is that Standard Arabic I can assign Case either rightward (under government), as in (38), or leftward (under Spec-head agreement), as in (39). This is the basic parametric difference which distinguishes Standard Arabic from other VSO languages such as Welsh, as well as from strictly SVO languages such as English.

The analysis outlined in (38b) and (39b), besides accounting for the two basic orders of Standard Arabic and the agreement patterns they are associated with, makes two important predictions discussed in Mohammad (1989). First, if the VSO order is derived due to failure of the subject to move to Spec,IP instead of by verb-raising to C, we expect VSO clauses to be able to appear embedded under the complementiser 'that'. We also expect SVO clauses to be able to occur in the same context. This is shown in (40) and (41):

40a. za'amu-u   ?anna-u   ra?a-a   l-?awlaad-u   Zayd-an.
     claimed-3PL   that-it   saw-3S   the-boys-NOM   Zayd-ACC
     'They claimed that the boys saw Zayd.'

40b. [IP za'amuu [CP ?anna-hu [IP thu [I′ ra?aa [VP l-?awlaadu [V′ tra?aa Zaydan . . .

41a. za'amu-u   ?anna   l-?awlaad-a   ra?a-w   Zayd-an.
     claimed-3PL   that   the-boys-ACC   saw-3PL   Zayd-ACC
     'They claimed that the boys saw Zayd.'

41b. [IP za'amuu [CP ?anna [IP l-?awlaada [I′ ra?a-w [VP tl-?awlaad [V′ tra?aw Zaydan . . .

The second prediction is that VSO sentences must have an expletive subject in Spec,IP required by EPP (Chapter 6). SVO sentences, on the other hand, are not expected to have an expletive subject. This prediction arises from the idea that the thematic subject does not move to Spec,IP in overt syntax in VSO sentences but it does in SVO sentences. The relevant contexts are illustrated in (40) and (41). In (40) the embedded VSO clause includes the expletive element *-hu* 'it' which appears attached to the complementiser *?anna* 'that'. The expletive element cliticises onto the complementiser from Spec,IP (see Chapter 15 on cliticisation). In contrast, the embedded SVO clause in (41) does not include the expletive element.

In root VSO sentences such as (38) the expletive subject is realised as a null category, more precisely *pro*. Recall from Chapter 12 that null subject languages usually have null expletive subjects. Standard Arabic is a null subject language, as shown in the root clause of examples (40) and (41). For different views on the derivation of VSO and SVO clauses in Arabic see Benmamoun (1992), and Shlonsky (1997), among others.

13.3   *NSO*

NSO languages can be loosely characterised as the languages where the subject of a DP appears following the head N rather than preceding it. The difference in the order of the subject in relation to N can be seen in simple possessive DPs such as (42a) from Hebrew compared to its English counterpart in (42b):

42a. mixtav ha-mora
     letter   the-teacher

42b. the teacher's letter

The NSO order is found in a number of languages. The discussion in this section will be based on data from Hebrew and ideas suggested in Ritter (1991) to account for them. The parallelism with the VSO order in clauses discussed in the previous section will become clear as we proceed, although there are differences as well.

Let us start by recalling the major ideas of the analysis of English DPs outlined in Chapter 8. The subject is located in Spec,DP where it is assigned genitive Case via Spec-head agreement with D. Let us assume that the subject of DP, like the subject of the clause, starts in a thematic position lower in the structure and moves to Spec,DP for Case reasons. The lower thematic subject position is Spec,NP. The head N was concluded in Chapter 8 not to raise to D on the grounds that adjectives precede the head N in English, as shown in (43a). Adjectives are left-adjoined to NP, on a par with VP-adverbs in relation to VP in clauses. (43a) therefore has the derivation shown in (43b):

43a. the army's brutal destruction of the city
43b. [$_{DP}$ [the army's] D [$_{NP}$ [$_{AP}$ brutal] [$_{NP}$ t$_{the\ army}$ [$_{N'}$ destruction of the city . . .

In view of the analysis outlined in (43b), it is possible to conceive of a derivation for NSO DPs of the type found in Hebrew which parallels the derivation of VSO clauses in Standard Arabic discussed in the previous section. As in Standard Arabic VSO clauses, the subject of DP remains in situ (Spec,NP). As in Standard Arabic VSO clauses, too, the head of the 'predicate' raises to the head position above its maximal projection. In DPs this means that the head N raises to D. Thus, a Hebrew DP such as (44a) has the derivation shown in (44b):

44a. axilat   Dan   et ha-tapuax
     eating   Dan   ACC the apple
     'Dan's eating of the apple'

44b. [$_{DP}$ [$_{D'}$ [$_N$ axilat] [$_{NP}$ Dan [$_{N'}$ t$_{axilat}$ et ha-tapuax . . .

Note that the object inside the DP in (44) bears accusative Case, suggesting (44) has an internal structure similar to that of English gerunds (Chapter 6) (see Hazout 1990 and Siloni 1994 on this type of DP in Hebrew).

One could then go on to conclude that NSO DPs differ in that D assigns genitive Case strictly rightward under government. This would force the subject to remain in Spec,NP and arguably also motivate N-raising to D to 'support' D.

Ritter (1991) points out that deriving the NSO by N-raising to D accounts for an important property of Hebrew DPs such as (44a) called **Construct State** DPs (Borer 1984, 1996). The head N in (44a) does not bear the definite article, and as shown in (45a&b), cannot bear the definite article when the DP is definite. This would follow from the idea entertained in Chapter 8 that the (in)definite article is in complementary distribution with Agr under D:

45a. *ha-axilat   Dan   et ha-tapuax
      the-eating   Dan   ACC the apple
      'Dan's eating of the apple'

45b. *ha-mixtav ha-mora
    the-letter the-teacher

However, this cannot be the whole story. The analysis outlined in (44b) predicts that it is possible for an adjective left-adjoined to NP to intervene between the head N under D and the subject in Spec,NP. (46a) shows that this order is excluded:

46a. *axilat hamenumeset Dan et ha-tapuax
    eating polite   Dan ACC the apple
    'Dan's polite eating of the apple'

46b. axilat   Dan hamenumeset et ha-tapuax
    eating Dan polite   ACC the apple

In Hebrew Construct State DPs, an adjective cannot intervene between the head N and the genitive subject, as shown in (46a). The adjective must follow the subject, as shown in (46b). The fact that the adjective follows the head N confirms the idea that the head N moves out of NP to a higher position, contrary to the situation found in English DPs. To explain the facts in (46a&b), Ritter suggests that DP includes an additional functional category called **Num(ber)** situated between D and NP, as in (47b):

47a. axilat   Dan hamenumeset et ha-tapuax
    eating Dan polite   ACC the apple

47b.

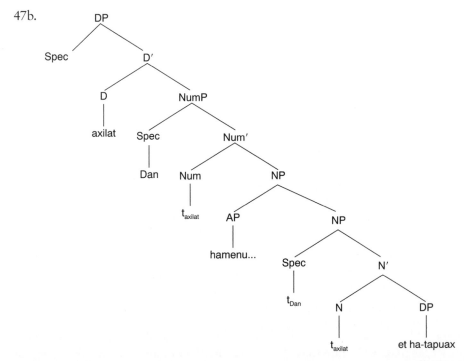

N raises to D as in the analysis above. The new element in the analysis is that the subject does not remain in Spec,NP but moves to Spec,NumP leaving the adjective behind. The subject in Spec,NumP receives genitive Case under the same condition as in the analysis above. The derivation of (47a) is as outlined in (47b) which is consistent with the order shown in (46b).

Hebrew has another type of DP called **Free State**. Free State DPs resemble Construct State DPs in that the subject also appears following the head N. However, they differ in that the subject is preceded with the preposition *shel* 'of' and the head N carries the definite article when DP is definite. Free State DPs also differ with respect to the order of the adjective in relation to the subject. As shown in (48a), the adjective can precede the subject, contrary to the situation found in Construct State DPs. Free State DPs such as (48a) have the derivation and representation shown in (48b):

48a. ha-axila   hamenumeset shel   Dan   et ha-tapuax
     the-eating   polite   of   Dan   ACC the-apple
     'Dan's polite eating of the apple'

48b. [$_{DP}$ Det [$_N$ axilat] [$_{NumP}$ t$_{axilat}$ [$_{NP}$ [AP] [$_{NP}$ shel Dan [$_{N'}$ t$_{axilat}$ et ha-tapuax . . .

Assuming that *shel* 'of' is a 'semantically vacuous' preposition which has the function of assigning Case to the subject, its appearance in Free State DPs can plausibly be taken as an indication that the subject does not occupy a Case-marked position. In other words, the subject remains in its thematic (DS) position Spec,NP, as shown in (48b). This accounts for the fact that the adjective left-adjoined to NP precedes it. The reason the subject does not move to the structurally Case-marked position Spec,NumP can be linked to the appearance of the definite article. On the view that the definite article is in complementary distribution with Agr, Spec,NumP is not a Case-marked position in Free State DPs.

13.4   *Summary*

Verb Second languages fall into two major groups. In one group, the V2 Constraint holds mainly of root clauses. In the other group, the V2 Constraint holds of both root and embedded clauses in a parallel way. The first group suggests that the 'second position' is C occupied by the complementiser in embedded clauses. The finite verb and the complementiser are in complementary distribution in relation to the 'second position'. The second group, however, where V2 clauses co-occur freely with the complementiser, suggests that the 'second position' is a position which exists over and above the C position of the complementiser. English is a 'residual V2 language' in the sense that the finite verb is required to be in the 'second position' in certain restricted contexts.

Some VSO languages seem to lend themselves to an analysis which groups them with V2 languages. The analysis claims that the VSO order is derived by raising of the finite verb to C. Other VSO languages seem to be consistent with the view that the VSO order results from failure of the subject to move from Spec,VP to Spec,IP.

The latter scenario is also consistent with the NSO order found in Hebrew Construct State DPs, although the order of the adjective in relation to the head N suggests the presence of an addition functional head intervening between D and NP.

Most of the parameters suggested in the literature to account for V2, VSO and NSO seem to rely on the notion 'directionality of Case-assignment'. In V2, VSO and NSO languages, assignment of subjective Case operates strictly rightward under government, and hence the need for the lexical category which bears the Case assigning head to move to a position to the left of the subject.

Exercises

Exercise 13.1

Examples (i–iv) are from Dutch (adapted from Koopman 1984). (i) is an embedded clause and (ii–iv) are root sentences. Compare the order in Dutch root sentences to the order in German root sentences discussed in this chapter and outline an analysis for the Dutch examples (i) and (ii) on the basis of this comparison:

i) . . . dat Marie   gisteren   een boek   aan Jan   gegeven   heeft.
    . . . that Marie   yesterday   a book   to Jan   given   has

ii) Marie heeft   gisteren   een boek   aan Jan   gegeven.
    Marie has   yesterday   a book   to John   given

iii) *Marie gisteren   een boek   aan Jan   gegeven   heeft.
     Marie yesterday   a book   to Jan   given   has

iv) *Gisteren   Marie   heeft   een boek   aan Jan   gegeven.
    yesterday   Marie   has   a book   to Jan   given

Exercise 13.2

Examples (ia&b) and (iia&b) are from Tarifit Berber, a strictly VSO language. (ia) and (iia) show that the VSO order is found in root sentences as well as embedded clauses introduced with the complementiser *qa* 'that'. (ib) and (iib) show that the postverbal subject must agree with the Agr$_S$ category on the verb in number (and other φ-features), contrary to the situation found in Standard Arabic and discussed in this chapter. Try to think of an analysis for VSO in Tarifit Berber which is consistent with the fact that the postverbal subject must agree with the Agr$_S$ category on the verb:

i)a. zra-n   ifruxn   argaz.
     saw-PL   children   man
     'The children saw the man.'

i)b. *y-zra   ifruxn   argaz.
      S-saw   children   man

ii)a. y-nna   Idir   qa   zra-n   ifruxn   argaz.
     S-said   Idir   that   saw-PL   children   man
     'Idir said that the children saw the man.'

ii)b. *y-nna   Idir   qa   y-zra   ifruxn   argaz.
     S-said   Idir   that   S-saw   children   man

Exercise 13.3

Examples (ia&b) and (iia&b) are from Italian (Cinque 1995a). (ia&b) include thematic APs and (iia&b) include attributive APs. Cinque explains that the attributive AP in (iia&b) has a different interpretation according to whether it precedes or follows the head N. When it precedes the head N it has a 'subject-oriented' interpretation and when it follows the head N it has an attributive interpretation. Outline an analysis for Italian DPs on the basis of examples (ia&b) and explain how they differ from their English counterparts. Once you have done that, explain whether the apparent fact that AP can either precede or follow N in (iia&b) presents a problem for the analysis:

i)a. L'invasione   italiana   dell'Albania
     the invasion   Italian   of Albania

i)b. *L'italiana   invasione   dell'Albania
     the Italian   invasion   of Albania

ii)a. La   loro   brutale   aggressione   all'Albania
      the their brutal   aggression   against Albania

ii)b. La   loro   aggressione   brutale   all'Albania
      the their aggression   brutal   against Albania

Exercise 13.4

Examples (ia–d) and (iia&b) are from Moroccan Arabic. (ia-d) are instances of Construct State DPs, and (ii)a&b instances of Free State DPs. Compare these DPs to their Hebrew counterparts discussed in this chapter, and outline an analysis for Moroccan Arabic DPs on the basis of your comparison. The fact that the noun *risala(t)* 'letter' includes a *t* in (ia–d) but not in (iia&b) is not necessarily relevant to the point of the exercise:

i)a. risalat   l-mudrris
     letter   the-teacher
     'the teacher's letter'

i)b. *l-risalat   l-mudrris
     the-letter   the-teacher

i)c. risalat   l-mudrris   ttwila
     letter   the-teacher   long
     'the teacher's long letter'

i)d. *risalat ttwila l-mudrris
    letter   long   the-teacher

ii)a. l-risala   dyal l-mudrris
    the-letter of   the-teacher

ii)b. l-risala   ttwila dyal l-mudrris
    the-letter long   of   the-teacher
    'the teacher's long letter'

Exercise 13.5

Examples (i–iii) are from Irish (Bobaljik and Carnie 1996). Bobaljik and Carnie argue that example (iii), with an embedded VSO clause, shows that the VSO order is not derived by verb-raising to C in Irish. Explain why, and suggest an alternative analysis on the basis of the examples provided:

i) Chonaic   Seán an madra
    see(PAST) John the dog
    'John saw the dog.'

ii) *Seán chonaic   an madra
    John   see(PAST) the dog
    'John saw the dog.'

iii) Ceapaim   go bhfaca   sé an madra
    think(PRES.1S) that see(PAST) he the dog
    'I think he saw the dog.'

14 Incorporation Phenomena

Contents

14.1 *Incorporation theory: Baker (1988)*

In this chapter, we will outline the broad lines of a syntactic approach to the derivation of complex predicates called **Incorporation theory**. The latter is developed in Baker (1988), a substantial and impressive piece of work not easy to summarise and present in a textbook. Baker's work should be considered in relation to a previous tradition which claimed that complex predicates are derived in the lexicon and base-generated as such. Baker argues that the derivation of complex predicates takes place in syntax in terms of the general syntactic process Move α. The latter moves a category and incorporates it into a predicate category deriving a complex predicate. Some of the arguments previously used as evidence for a lexical analysis are shown by Baker to be consistent with a syntactic analysis of predicates. In this chapter we will discuss some instances of Noun Incorporation, Verb Incorporation and Preposition Incorporation.

Compare the examples in (1a&b) from Mohawk (Iroquoian) (N: 'neuter agreement', SUF: 'nominal inflection suffix'):

1a. Ka-rakv ne   sawatis   hrao-**nuhs** -a?
    3N-be-white   John   3M- house-SUF
    'John's house is white.'

1b. Hrao-**nuhs** -rakv ne   sawatis
    3M- house-be-white   John
    'John's house is white.'

(1a) and (1b) appear to be thematically synonymous, but differ with respect to the position of the noun *nuhs* 'house'. In (1a) the noun is situated inside the noun phrase complement of the stative verb *-rakv* 'be white'. In (1b), however, the noun *nuhs* 'house' appears incorporated into the verbal complex and is situated between the verb and the Agr$_O$ morpheme.

A major consequence of the incorporation of the noun into the verb in (1b) is a change in object agreement. In the non-incorporation example (1a), the verb carries the neuter Agr_O morpheme and agrees with the noun phrase 'John's house' headed by the neuter noun 'house'. In the incorporation example (1b), however, the verb carries the masculine Agr_O morpheme and agrees with 'John'. Assuming, as is standardly the case, that object agreement is a manifestation of direct-objecthood (object agreement is usually restricted to the direct object), it seems that the possessor in (1b) acquires the status of a direct object as a result of the incorporation of the noun into the verb. In other words, incorporation of the noun into the verb apparently results in a change of the grammatical function of the possessor from being the subject of the noun phrase to becoming the direct object of the verb.

The change in the grammatical function of the possessor which accompanies incorporation of the noun into the verb has been used as a major argument for an exclusively lexical derivation of complex predicates with an incorporated noun. An exclusively lexical derivation of such predicates would involve deriving the complex predicate in terms of morphological rules of derivation applying in the lexicon. According to this analysis, sentences such as (1b) are base-generated as they are with the 'possessor' in the direct object position of the complex predicate.

In the Principles and Parameters framework, it is possible for a change in the grammatical function of a noun phrase to take place as a result of syntactic movement. In the derivation of passives and unaccusatives, for example, the internal argument changes from being the direct object of the verb to becoming the subject of the sentence as a result of syntactic movement to the subject position (Chapter 8). However, the situation with respect to the possessor in N-incorporation constructions such as (1b) is different. The possessor cannot be said to acquire the status of the direct object of the verb as a result of moving from the subject position of the noun phrase to a base-generated empty direct object position. Such a movement is excluded by the θ-Criterion (Chapter 7). Baker argues that the apparent change in the grammatical function of the possessor is not necessarily a problem for a syntactic derivation of complex predicates with an incorporated noun. Baker argues further that there is evidence which indicates that N-incorporation must be syntactic rather than lexical. Before we discuss the evidence, let us first outline Baker's syntactic analysis for N-incorporation and the effect it has on the possessor.

At the heart of Baker's Incorporation Theory is the hypothesis stated in (2):

2. **Uniformity of Theta Assignment Hypothesis (UTAH)**

    Identical thematic relationships between items are represented by identical structural relationships between those items at the level of D-structure.

The effects of UTAH can be simply illustrated in terms of a passive sentence such as (3) compared to an active sentence such as (4):

3a. The ball was kicked (by John).
3b. [IP the ball was kicked $t_{the\ ball}$ (by John) . . .

4a. John kicked the ball.

4b. [IP John kicked the ball . . .

By virtue of UTAH, *the ball* must bear the same structural relationship to the verb at DS in both (3) and (4). The consequence is that *the ball* should be in the direct object position of the verb in the DS representation of the passive example (3), just as it is in the active example (4). This is basically the reasoning behind the standard analysis of passives (Chapter 7).

With respect to N-incorporation examples such as (1b), UTAH implies that the noun 'house' occupies the same position as its non-incorporated counterpart in (1a) at DS. Incorporation of N into the verb therefore must take place at the post-DS level, presumably in the mapping from DS onto SS. Accordingly, (1b) has a derivation roughly along the lines shown in (5b), where the noun phrase in question is considered to be the internal argument of the stative verb 'be-white'. Note that Baker uses an NP structure of the noun phrase. It is an interesting question whether the analysis carries over using a DP structure instead. We will not pursue this issue here:

5a. Hrao-**nuhs** -rakv ne   sawatis
    3M- house-be-white   John
    'John's house is white.'

5b.

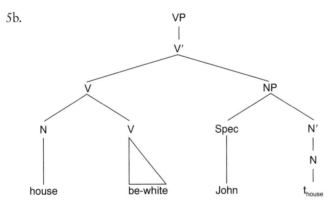

N-incorporation into V is an instance of head-to-head movement, whereby the head N moves out of NP and head-adjoins to V. The moved N antecedent-governs its trace inside NP, presumably for the same reason that the verb antecedent governs its trace in instances of V-raising to I, and instances of I-raising to C (Chapter 10).

To account for the effect of N-incorporation on the possessor, Baker suggests the statement in (6):

6. **Government Transparency Corollary (GTC)**

    A lexical category which has an item incorporated into it governs everything which the incorporated item governed in its original structural position.

Assuming that N governs Spec,NP, the verb in (5) governs the possessor in Spec,NP by virtue of the fact that it has N incorporated into it. The government relation between the derived complex predicate and the possessor is reflected by object agreement, a standard assumption. This is how the possessor, which is structurally the specifier of NP, acquires the status of the direct object of the derived complex predicate.

An apparently robust generalisation about N-incorporation is that only internal arguments, most typically patients of transitive verbs, can incorporate. External arguments cannot incorporate (Mithun 1984). This contrast is illustrated with the Mohawk examples in (7a–c). (7b) involves N-incorporation out of the direct object position, and (7c) incorporation out of the subject position (ASP: 'aspect', PRE: 'nominal inflection prefix'):

7a. Yao-wir-aʔa   ye-nuhweʔ-s   ne ka-**nuhs**-aʔ.
     PRE-baby-SUF   3FS/3N-like-ASP   the PRE-house-SUF
     'The baby likes the house.'

7b. Yao-wir-aʔa   ye- **nuhs**-nuhweʔ-s.
     PRE-baby-SUF   3FS/3N-house-like-ASP
     Lit. 'The baby house-likes.'

7c. *Ye-**wir**-nuhweʔ-s   ne ka-nuhs-aʔ.
     3FS/3N-baby-like   PRE-house-SUF
     Lit. 'Baby-likes the house.'

Baker argues that the restriction on N-incorporation illustrated in (7b) and (7c) is syntactic in essence. It reflects the restriction on head-movement imposed by the HMC/ECP. Incorporation of a noun from the subject position (Spec, IP) into the verb, outlined in (8b), is a lowering movement which results in a situation where the incorporated N does not antecedent-govern its trace for lack of c-command:

8a. *Ye-**wir**-nuhweʔ-s   ne ka-nuhs-aʔ.
     3FS/3N-baby-like   PRE-house-SUF
     Lit. 'Baby-likes the house.'

8b. $[_{IP} [_{NP} t_N] \text{ I } [_{VP} [_V [\text{ V}] [N]] \ldots$

The generalisation that external arguments do not incorporate turns out, according to Baker, to be a strong argument in favour of a syntactic derivation of N-incorporation in terms of Move-α.

Another major argument for a syntactic analysis of N-incorporation relates to another generalisation, namely that objects of prepositions do not incorporate into V, unlike direct objects of verbs. This is shown in examples (9a&b) from Niuean (Austronesian) (ABS: 'absolute Case marker'):

9a. Ne tutala a au ke he tau **tagata**.
     PAST-talk ABS-I to PL-person
     'I was talking to (the) people.'

9b. *Ne tutala **tagata** a au (ke he).
PAST-talk-person ABS-I (to)
Lit. 'I was people-talking (to).'

9c. [IP I [VP [V [V] [N]] [PP P [NP [N tN . . .

On the assumption that N-incorporation is a head-to-head movement process, (9b) falls under the scope of the HMC. As shown in (9c), movement of N to V across P gives rise to a violation of the HMC. The incorporated N does not antecedent-govern its trace inside PP due to the intervening P. The latter creates a (Relativised) Minimality effect in the sense explained in Chapters 6 and 10.

Before we move on to discuss other instances of incorporation, a word about N-incorporation and Case theory. In the Mohawk example (1b) with the structure shown in (5b), the verb is unaccusative and therefore does not assign Case to the noun phrase in the object position (Chapter 8). In view of this, the question arises as to how the noun phrase satisfies the Case Requirement. Baker argues that the noun phrase satisfies the Case Requirement via incorporation of its head N into the verb. The idea is that there are various ways in which a noun phrases can satisfy the Case Requirement which relate to the various types of existing Cases, e.g. inherent Case, structural Case . . . etc. Incorporation of the head N of the noun phrase into the verb is one of the permissible ways in which a given noun phrase can satisfy the Case Requirement. Thus, although the verb in (1b) does not assign Case, its noun phrase complement satisfies the Case Requirement by virtue of the incorporation of its head N into the verb. Baker outlines a well developed, and in many respects novel, approach to Case spelling out its relevance to PF and LF. Unfortunately, we cannot go into the details of this approach here for lack of space.

14.2 *Verb Incorporation*

Compare the examples in (10a) and (10b) from Chichewa (Bantu):

10a. Mtsikana   ana-chit-its-a   kuti mtsuku   u-**gw**-e.
      girl   AGR-do-make-ASP   that waterpot   AGR-fall-ASP
      'The girl made the waterpot fall.'

10b. Mtsikana   anau-**gw**-ets-a   mtsuko.
      girl   AGR-fall-make-ASP   waterpot
      'The girl made the waterpot fall.'

(10a) and (10b) are different instances of the **causative construction**. In (10a) the **causativised** verb *gw* 'fall' appears in the embedded clause and is inflected separately from **the causative** verb *its* 'make' of the root clause. (10a) appears to be similar to the type of causative construction found in English with a bi-clausal structure. In (10b), however, the causativised verb appears incorporated into the causative verb and is inflected together with it. (10b) is an instance of so-called **morphological causatives**. The latter appear superficially to have a mono-clausal structure.

As with N-incorporation, V-incorporation in (10b) results in an apparent change in the grammatical function of the subject of the incorporated verb. The noun phrase 'the waterpot', situated in the subject position of the embedded clause in (10a), exhibits the properties of a direct object in the incorporation example (10b). This is shown by the fact that it can trigger object agreement with the verb (OP) and can become the subject of the sentence when the verb is in the passive form. These two properties are illustrated in (11a&b):

11a. Mphunzitsi   a-na-wa-**lemb**-ets-a   ana.
      teacher   SP-PAST-OP-write-CAUS-ASP   children
      'The teacher made the children write.'

11b. Ana   a-na-**lemb**-ets-edw-a   ndi mphunzitsi
      children   SP-PAST-write-CAUS-PASS-ASP   by teacher
      'The children were made to write by the teacher.'

Note that in Chichewa, as in many other languages, the passive is not peri-phrastic, meaning it does not consist of an auxiliary and a main verb in the participial form as it does in English. The Chichewa passive is an instance of what are called **morphological passives** which consist only of a main verb with a passive morpheme (see Exercises).

Baker argues that morphological causatives such as (10b), though superficially mono-clausal, have a bi-clausal structure identical to the one of the periphrastic causative construction in (10a). This analysis is forced by UTAH, given that the two constructions in (10a) and (10b) are thematic paraphrases of each other. The fact that the embedded causativised verb appears incorporated into the root causative verb in (10b) is the result of a syntactic head-to-head movement process affecting the causativised verb. Morpholgical causatives such as (10b) have the derivation outlined in (12b):

12a. Mtsikana   anau-**gw**-ets-a   mtsuko.
      girl   AGR-fall-make-ASP   waterpot
      'The girl made the waterpot fall.'

12b.

The causativised verb moves in a successive cyclic fashion consistent with the requirements of HMC (Chapter 10). Baker argues that this V-movement process creates, by virtue of GTC, an ECM-like structure, where the root verb governs and assigns Case to the subject of the embedded clause. This accounts for the direct object-like properties of the thematic subject of the causativised verb, illustrated in (11a&b). In other words, the thematic subject of the causativised verb has direct object-like properties for the same reason that English ECM subjects do (Chapter 8).

In the causative example (10b) the causativised verb is intransitive. Languages which have morphological causatives display a striking degree of similarity with respect to causativisation of intransitive verbs. The thematic subject of the causativised verb invariably has direct object-like properties in causative constructions. However, when the causativised verb is transitive, languages tend to differ as to whether the thematic subject or the thematic object of the causativised verb has direct object-like properties in causative constructions. Baker illustrates this difference with two different dialects of Chichewa which he refers to simply as Chichewa-A and Chichewa-B.

In Chichewa-B it is the thematic subject of the causativised verb which has direct object-like properties in causative constructions. This is shown by the fact that it can trigger object agreement (OP) with the complex verb, and can move to the subject position when the complex verb is in the passive form. These two properties are illustrated in (13b) and (13c), respectively:

13a. Catherine a-na-mu-**kolol**-ets-a   mwana   wake   chimanga.
     Catherine SP-PAST-OP-harvest-CAUS-ASP   child   her   corn
     'Catherine made her child harvest the corn.'

13b. Mnyamata   a-na-**kolol**-ets-edw-a   chimanga ndi Catherine.
     boy   SP-PAST-harvest-CAUS-PASS-ASP   corn   by   Catherine
     'The boy was made to harvest the corn by Catherine.'

The thematic object of the causativised verb has none of the direct object-like properties illustrated in (13a&b). It cannot trigger object agreement (OP) with the complex verb, as shown in (14a), nor can it move to the subject position when the complex verb is in the passive form, as shown in (14b):

14a. *Catherine   a-na-chi-**kolol**-ets-a   mwana   wake   chimanga.
     Catherine   SP-PAST-OP-harvest-CAUS-ASP   child   her   corn
     'Catherine made her child harvest the corn.'

14b. *Chimanga chi-na-**kolol**-ets-edw-a   mwana wake ndi Catherine.
     corn   SP-PAST-harvest-CAUS-PASS-ASP child   jer   by   Catherine
     'The corn was made to be harvested by her child by Catherine.'

Since causatives of transitive verbs of the type found in Chichewa-B resemble causatives of intransitive verbs in that it is the subject of the causativised verb that has direct object-like properties, they have the derivation outlined in (12b) for causatives of intransitive verbs. The thematic object of the causativised verb, located inside the embedded VP, is not accessible to exceptional Case-marking by the derived verb, and hence the fact that it does not have direct object-like properties. In contrast, the subject of the causativised verb is accessible to exceptional Case-marking from the root verb, and hence the fact that it has direct object-like properties.

In Chichewa-A and other languages (see Gibson 1980), it is the thematic object of the causativised verb (rather than the thematic subject) which has direct object-like properties in causative constructions. This is shown in examples (15a&b) by the fact that the thematic object of the causativised can trigger object agreement (OP) with the complex verb (15a) and the fact that it can move to the subject position when the complex verb is in the passive form (15b):

15a. Anyani   a-na-wa-**meny**-ets-a   ana   kwa   buluzi.
     baboons   SP-PAST-OP-hit-CAUS-ASP   children   to   lizard
     'The baboons made the lizard hit the children.'

15b. Ana   a-na-**meny**-ets-edw-a   kwa   buluzi (ndi anyani).
     children   SP-PAST-hit-CAUS-PASS-ASP   to   lizard (by baboons)
     'The children were made to be hit by the lizard (by the baboons).'

The thematic subject of the causativised verb has none of the direct object-like properties illustrated in (15a&b). It cannot trigger object agreement (OP) with the complex verb, as shown in (16a), and neither can it move to the subject position when the complex verb is in the passive form, as shown in (16b):

16a. *Anyani   a-na-zi-**meny**-ets-a   ana   kwa   mbuzi.
     baboons   SP-PAST-OP-hit-CAUS-ASP   children   to   goats
     'The baboons made the goats hit the children.'

16b. *Buluzi   a-na-**meny**-ets-edw-a   ana   ndi   anyani.
     lizard   SP-PAST-hit-CAUS-PASS-ASP   children   by   baboons
     'The lizard was made to hit the boys by the baboons.'

Besides the differences discussed between causatives of transitive verbs in the two
dialects of Chichewa, there are other related differences. In the Chichewa-A
example (15a) the thematic object precedes the thematic subject of the causativised
verb in linear order. Moreover, the thematic subject is preceded by the preposition
'to'. The Chichewa-B example (13a) differs in both respects. The thematic subject
precedes the thematic object of the causativised verb (reverse) and neither the
thematic subject nor the thematic object is preceded by a preposition.

Baker argues that the noted differences between the two types of causative of
transitive verbs suggest that they have different derivations. We concluded above
that Chichewa-B causatives of transitive verbs are similar to causatives of intransitive verbs in that it is the thematic subject of the causativised verb which has
direct object-like properties. They therefore have the same derivation as causatives
of intransitive verbs, namely the one outlined in (12b). Chichewa-A causatives of
transitive verbs have a different derivation shown in (17b):

17a. Anyani   a-na-wa-**meny**-ets-a   ana   kwa   buluzi.
     baboons   SP-PAST-OP-hit-CAUS-ASP   children   to   lizard
     'The baboons made the lizard hit the children.'

17b.

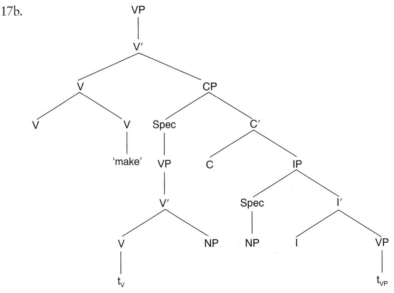

Prior to incorporation of the causativised verb into the root causative verb, the
VP containing the causativised verb and its thematic object moves to the embedded
Spec,CP. The consequence of VP-movement to embedded Spec,CP is that the

thematic object of the causativised verb, located inside the moved VP, becomes accessible to exceptional Case-marking from the complex verb in the root clause. This is the reason the object of the causativised verb shows direct object-like properties of the complex verb. The other consequence of VP-movement to embedded Spec,CP is that the thematic subject of the causativised verb, located in the embedded Spec, IP, is not accessible to exceptional Case-marking from the derived root verb. This is the reason it does not have direct object-like properties in relation to the complex verb. The preposition 'to', seen (17a), is inserted by a special mechanism for the purpose of assigning Case to the thematic subject of the causativised verb. The derivation shown in (17b) also derives the order whereby the thematic object precedes the thematic subject of the causativised verb.

Thus, the difference between the two types of causative of transitive verbs relates to whether the VP containing the causativised verb moves to the embedded Spec,CP prior to incorporation of the causativised verb or it does not. In Chichewa-B transitive causatives, only the verb moves successive cyclically to the root V. In Chichewa-A transitive causatives, however, the whole VP moves to the embedded Spec,CP followed by incorporation of the causativised verb into the causative verb in the root clause. The ability of the derived complex verb to govern the thematic object NP inside VP in Spec,CP and assign it Case is the result of V-incorporation in combination with GTC. Recall that the latter makes it possible for a complex predicate derived by incorporation to govern into the domain of the head category incorporated into it.

14.3 *Preposition Incorporation*

Compare the examples in (18a&b) from Chichewa:

18a. Mbidzi zi-na-perek-a   msampha **kwa**   nkhandwe.
     zebras SP-PAST-hand-ASP   trap   to   fox
     'The zebras handed the trap to the fox.'

18b. Mbidzi zi-na-perek-**er**-a   nkhandwe   msampha.
     zebras SP-PAST-hand-to-ASP   fox   trap
     'The zebras handed the fox the trap.'

In (18a) the goal argument (indirect object) appears inside a PP headed by the preposition 'to' and following the direct object (theme). In (18b), however, the goal argument appears adjacent to the verb and preceding the theme argument. Moreover, the preposition 'to' is absent and the verb shows an extra morpheme called the **applied morpheme**. The goal argument in (18b) is called the **applied object**. (18b) is called an **applicative construction.**

(18a&b) are thematic paraphrases of each other, where the arguments bear the same thematic relationship to the verb. In view of this, UTAH requires that they have identical DS representations with the consequence that differences between them must be the result of syntactic processes applying in the mapping onto SS.

Baker argues that the applicative construction (18b) is derived by a process of P-incorporation into the verb, roughly along the lines shown in (19b). Note that the framework adopted by Baker (1988) does not include a binary branching restriction, and hence the structure of VP in (19b):

19a. Mbidzi zi-na-perek-er-a　　　　　　nkhandwe　msampha.
　　　zebras SP-PAST-hand-to-ASP　　fox　　　　trap
　　　'The zebras handed the fox the trap.

19b.

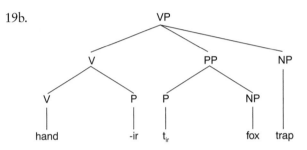

The fact that PP is ordered before the theme argument in (19a), contrary to what is found in the non-applicative counterpart (18a), does not necessarily follow from UTAH, nor for that matter from HMC. The order in (19b) could be forced in terms of the assumption that Case-assignment by the complex verb to the complement of P is subject to adjacency. A crucial assumption in Baker's system, not mentioned so far, is that traces of incorporated categories cannot act on behalf of their antecedents as far as Case-assignment is concerned. Thus, the trace of the incorporated preposition in (19b) does not assign Case to the applied object. Rather, it is the derived complex verb [$_V$ [P] V] which assigns Case to the applied object. Baker argues that it is this property of applicatives which accounts for the general fact that applied objects invariably display direct object-like properties (Marantz 1984). In Chichewa, this is shown by the fact that the applied object can trigger object agreement with the verb, shown in (20a), and the fact that it can move to the subject position when the verb is in the passive form, shown in (20b):

20a. Amayi a-ku-mu-umb-ir-a　　　　　　　mtsuko　　mwana.
　　　woman SP-PRES-OP-mold-for-ASP　waterpot　child
　　　'The woman is moulding the waterpot for the child.'

20b. Mbidzi　zi-na-gul-ir-idw-a　　　　　　　　nsapato　(ndi kalulu).
　　　zebras　SP-PAST-buy-for-PASS-ASP　shoes　　by hare
　　　'The zebras were bought shoes by the hare.'

The theme argument shows none of the direct-object like properties illustrated in (20a&b). It cannot trigger object agreement on the verb, as shown in (21a), nor can it move to the subject position when the verb is in the passive form, as shown in (21b):

21a. *Amayi　a-na-u-umb-ir-a　　　　　　　　mwana mtsuko.
　　　woman　SP-PAST-OP-mould-for-ASP　child　waterpot
　　　'The woman is moulding the waterpot for the child.'

21b. *Nsapato   zi-na-gul-**ir**-idw-a   mbidzi   (ndi kalulu).
     shoes   SP-PAST-buy-for-PASS-ASP   zebras   (by hare)
     'Shoes were bought for the zebras by the hare.'

Note, finally, that, contrary to the cases of N and V incorporation discussed above, there is no obvious morphological relationship between the preposition in (18a) and the applied morpheme in (18b). In cases of N-incorporation and V-incorporation, the same recognisable root appears in both the incorporation examples and their non-incorporation paraphrases. This is not the case in applicatives. The preposition in (18a) does not seem to be morphologically related to the applied morpheme in (18b). Baker argues that this difference simply reflects the fact that the preposition in (18b) is an affix, whereas the one in (18a) is not. Because the preposition in (18b) is an affix it is forced to attach to the verb by virtue of an interaction between its morphological selectional properties and the general condition on the representation of affixes stated in (22):

22. **Stray Affix Filter**

     *X if X is a lexical item whose morphological subcategorisation frame is not satisfied at S-structure.

V-incorporation in morphological causatives could also be justified along similar lines. In morphological causatives, the causative verb tends to be an affix with morphological selectional properties which require it to attach to a verb root. Because lowering processes are generally excluded in Baker's system, it is the causativised verb which moves up to the causative verb in the root clause rather than the other way round. It is not clear, though, that N-incorporation could be justified along similar lines. The complex derived by N-incorporation is similar to compounds formed out of two categories none of which is an affix.

14.4 *Summary*

N-incorporation constructions, morphological causatives and applicatives, among other phenomena not discussed here, seem to be amenable to a syntactic analysis in terms of head-to-head movement processes (Incorporation) in so far as the domains of incorporation parallel those of Move α. The apparent changes in the grammatical functions of certain noun phrases triggered by incorporation processes can be attributed to a rearrangement in government relations which follows from the process of incorporation rather than from a change in the position of those noun phrases.

N-incorporation involves movement of the head N of a noun phrase object and its incorporation into the verb. If the incorporated N has a subject, the subject acquires direct object-like properties in relation to the derived complex verb. This apparent change in the grammatical function of the subject is the consequence of a principle called GTC which makes it possible for the derived complex verb to govern into the domain of the incorporated head.

V-incorporation is involved in the derivation of morphological causatives. Causatives of intransitive verbs across languages have in common the property that the thematic subject of the causativised verb acquires direct object-like properties in relation to the derived verb. This is due to the fact that the subject is situated in a context which is identical to that of ECM subjects. In contrast, causatives of transitive verbs differ across languages as to whether it is the subject or the object of the causativised verb that acquires direct object-like properties in relation to the derived complex verb. Baker (1988) reduces this difference to a difference in whether only the verb or the whole VP of the embedded clause moves prior to incorporation of the verb into the root causative verb.

P-incorporation is involved in the derivation of applicative constructions. Incorporation of the preposition into the verb creates a configuration whereby its object acquires the status of direct object of the derived verb.

Exercises

Exercise 14.1

Baker (1988) extends his analysis of applicative constructions to English Dative Shift constructions such as (i) even though they do not exhibit an applicative morpheme. Baker argues that the analysis accounts for the fact that the goal argument appears adjacent to the verb and the fact that it exhibits direct object-like properties such as the ability to passivise. Try to reconstruct the analysis for the English Dative Shift Construction on the basis of the discussion of applicative constructions in this chapter. As pointed out in this chapter, Baker does not assume a binary branching restriction in his analysis of sentences with a ditransitive verb. You may want to try recasting Baker's analysis in terms of a VP-shell structure:

i)   John gave Bill the book.
ii)   *John gave the book Bill.
iii)   Bill was given the book.
iv)   *The book was given Bill.

Exercise 14.2

Examples (ia&b), (iia&b) and (iiia&b) are from Italian (Baker 1988). Baker argues that Italian causatives have the same syntax as Chichewa causatives and therefore the same derivation. They only differ in that the Italian causative verb is not an affix. Explain on the basis of the examples provided in what sense Italian causatives have the same syntax as Chichewa causatives discussed in this chapter, and outlined a derivation for examples (ia&b):

i)a. Maria   fa   lavorare   Giovanni.
     Maria   makes   work   Giovanni
    'Maria makes Giovanni work.'

i) b. Maria   a   fatto riparare   la macchina   a Giovanni.
       Maria   has   made fix   the car   to Giovanni
       'Maria made Giovanni fix the car.'

ii) a. Maria   lo   fa lavorare.
        Maria   him   makes work
        'Maria makes him work.'

ii) b. Maria   la fa   riparare   a Giovanni.
        Maria   it makes   fix   to Giovanni
        'Maria makes Giovanni fix it.'

iii) a. Giovanni   è stato fatto   lavorare   (molto).
         Giovanni   was made   to work   (a lot)
         'Giovanni was made to work (a lot).'

iii) b. La macchina   fu fatta   riparare   a Giovanni.
         the car   was made   fix   to Giovanni
         'The car was made to be fixed by Giovanni.'

Exercise 14.3

Example (i) is from Southern Tiwa (Kiowa-Tanoan), and shows that noun incorporation can feed verb incorporation. Example (ii) is from Tuscarora (Iroquian), and shows that noun incorporation can also feed preposition incorporation. Outline a derivation for each example showing clearly the two incorporation processes involved in each example, and explain how exactly noun incorporation feeds the other incorporation process:

i)   I-**'u'u**-kur-**'am**-ban.
      1sS: 2sO-**baby**-hold-**CAUS**-PAST
      'I made you hold the baby.'

ii)   Wa?-khe-**ta?nar**-atya?t-**hahθ**.
      PAST-1sS/3fO-**bread**-buy-**APPL/PUNC**
      'I bought her some bread.'

Exercise 14.4

Examples (i) and (ii) are from Greenlandic Eskimo. (ii) is an example of a construction known as the **antipassive**. Antipassives are derived by adding an affix to a transitive verb and (consequently) relegating the direct object to an oblique phrase. The oblique status of the direct object in (ii) is marked with the morpheme glossed as INSTR. Baker argues that the antipassive is derived by noun incorporation. Try to reconstruct the analysis on the basis of the discussion of noun incorporation in this chapter. You may want to consider assigning the oblique phrase a status similar to that of the *by*-phrase in passives. Note that Greenlandic Eskimo is an OV language. It is also an ergative language, but this should not matter to the purpose of the exercise (ERG stands for ergative Case, ABS for absolutive Case, APASS for antipassive morpheme):

i)   Angut-ip   arnaq   unatar-paa.
     man-ERG   woman(ABS)   beat-INDIC: 3sS/3sO
     'The man beat the woman.'

ii) Angut   **arna-mik**   unata-**a**-voq.
     man (ABS)   **woman-INSTR**   beat-**APASS**-INDIC: 3sS
     'The man beat a woman.'

Exercise 14.5

Examples (ia&b) and (iia&b) are from Tarifit Berber. (ib) and (iib) illustrate two different types of causatives of transitive verbs. Berber allows causativisation of only a restricted class of transitive verbs with the pattern determined by the type of transitive verb (Guerssel 1986). In (ib) the subject of the causativised verb shows up as the direct object of the complex verb, and the direct object of the causativised verb shows up as an oblique phrase with the dative preposition i 'to'. In (iib), the direct object of the causativised verb shows up as the direct object of the complex verb, and the subject of the causativised verb as an oblique phrase. Compare the two types of causative of transitive verbs in Tarifit Berber to the ones from Chichewa discussed in this chapter and outline a derivation for each of them. Berber is a VSO language, but this property of the language does not necessarily impinge on the point of the exercise:

i)a   y-awd   ufrux   taddart.
      3S-reach   boy   house
      'The boy reached the house.'

i)b. y-**ss**-awd   wargaz afrux   i taddart.
      3S-CAUS-reach   man   boy   to house
      'The man caused/helped the boy (to) reach the house.'

ii)a. y-sha   ufrux   tafirast.
      3S-ate   boy   pear
      'The boy ate the pear.'

ii)b. t-**ss**-sha   tmghart   tafirast i ufrux.
      3S-CAUS-eat   woman   pear   to boy
      'The woman made the boy eat the pear.'

15 Clitics and Cliticisation

15.1   *Clitics and syntax*

English has pronouns which differ along the dimensions of number, gender, person and Case (see Chapter 8), although the paradigms are not as transparent as in other languages. Some languages have an additional series of pronouns which differ along the dimension of phonological strength. These languages are said to have a series of **strong pronouns** and another series of **weak pronouns** or **clitics**. In French, this distinction opposes *moi* 'I/me' to *me* 'me' and *toi* 'you' to *te* 'you', for example:

1a. À toi   de   décider.
     to you   Comp   to-decide
     'The decision is yours.'

1b. Jean **te** connaît.
     Jean you knows

Note that *moi/me* and *toi/te* are morphologically related. The second member of each pair appears to be a reduced form of the first member, although the relationship between other pairs is not as transparent, e.g. *eux* 'they' as opposed to *les* 'them'.

     As shown in (1a&b) and (2a&b), direct object clitic pronouns appear before the finite verb and cannot appear following the verb in French:

2a. Jean **te** connaît.
    Jean you knows

2b. *Jean connaît **te**.
    Jean knows you

There is a marked order contrast between clitic and non-clitic direct objects. The latter appear following the verb and cannot appear preceding the verb, as shown in (3a&b):

3a. *Jean Marie connaît.
    Jean Marie knows

3b. Jean connaît Marie.
    Jean knows Marie

It is unlikely that French verbs select both values of the Head parameter, [OV] and [VO], depending on whether the direct object is a clitic or a non-clitic pronoun. It is more likely that French verbs select the Head-first [VO] value of the Head parameter, and that the [OV] order is derived by movement of the clitic pronoun to a position preceding the finite verb. Since the [OV] order is only found in contexts where the direct object is a clitic pronoun, the implication is that clitic pronouns have a peculiar property which forces them to move to the preverbal position.

It is very important not to confuse clitics with affixes. Although the two resemble each other in that they are both dependent elements, they are different in many respects. For example, affixes are usually very particular about the type of lexical categories they can attach to (see Chapter 3). However, clitics are comparatively more promiscuous as will transpire later on. Their placement is largely determined by syntactic considerations, although it involves some prosodic considerations as well. More on this later on.

Clitics have many properties which show that they are dependent on the verb and cannot stand alone as well-formed units. For example, when the verb is moved to C (SAI) in (literary style) questions such as (4a), the clitic must raise along with the verb. It cannot be stranded behind, as shown in (4b). (5a&b) show that a clitic pronoun cannot be used alone as an answer to a question, in contrast to strong pronouns:

4a. **Les** a-t-elle vus?
    them has-she seen

4b. *A-t-elle **les** vus?
    has-she them seen

5a. Qui a-t-elle vu?
    who has-she seen

5b. ***Les**/eux.
    them/them.

At this stage one could ask why French clitics lean on the verb from the front/left instead from the back/right which would be a shorter route. Put differently, one could ask why cliticisation of the pronoun in French results in the order [CL V] instead of the order [V CL]. There is variation among Romance languages in this respect. Apart from non-negative imperatives (see Exercises), French clitics appear before the verb in both finite clauses, as shown in the examples above, and non-finite clauses as shown in (6):

6a. Marie veut **les** voir.
    Marie wants them to-see

6b. *Marie veut voir **les**.
    Marie wants to-see them

However, Spanish (and Italian, among others) clitics appear before the verb only in finite clauses. In non-finite clauses, they appear following the verb. This is shown in the Spanish examples (7) and (8):

7a. Maria **los** ha visto.
    Maria them has seen

7b. *Maria ha visto **los**.
    Maria has seen them

8a. Maria quiere ver**los**.
    Maria wants to-see-them

8b. *Maria quiere **los** ver.
    Maria wants them to-see

It is unlikely that the difference between French and Spanish in clitic-placement in non-finite clauses is due to some purely phonological considerations. It is more likely to be due to some syntactic difference between the two languages affecting non-finite clauses. That clitic-placement is determined at least in part by syntactic considerations will become clearer as we proceed in this chapter. To anticipate, it will turn out that clitic-placement involves two major steps. One step involves movement of the clitic to a designated position in the structure. This step will be called **syntactic cliticisation** and is arguably largely uniform across contexts and across languages. The second part involves prosodic association of the clitic with a neighbouring category. This step will be called **phonological cliticisation** and it may vary from one context to another and one language to another.

15.2   *Types of clitics*

The clitics discussed in the previous section correspond to the direct object of the verb. For this reason they are called **accusative clitics**. There are clitics which correspond to the indirect object of the verb called **dative clitics**. The latter are illustrated with the French examples in (9a&b):

9a   Marie **lui** a donné un livre.
    Marie him$_{DAT}$ has given a book

9b.   Marie **le lui** a donné.
    Marie it him$_{DAT}$ has given

10.   Marie a donné le livre a Jean.
    Marie has given the book to Jean

It is not clear whether dative clitics correspond to DP or PP. Non-clitic indirect objects are realised as PPs in French, as shown in (10). French and Romance languages in general lack the Dative Shift pattern. This seems to suggest that the dative clitic possibly corresponds to a PP. However, there is evidence that the French dative preposition *a* does not project a PP structure and is probably only a surface marker of Case (Vergnaud 1985). According to this view of the dative preposition, dative clitics could correspond to a DP instead of a PP.

There are clitics which are arguably clearer candidates for PP-clitics. In French, these include the partitive clitic *en* 'of them', seen in (11a), and the locative clitic *y* 'in it', seen in (12a):

11a.   Marie **en** a vu trois.
    Marie of-them has seen three

11b.   Marie a vu trois de ces livres.
    Marie has seen three of these books

12a.   Marie **y** a vécu.
    Marie in-it has lived

12b.   Marie a vécu a Londres.
    Marie has lived in London

The PP nature of the French *en* and *y* cannot be directly gleaned from their morphological shape. They do not compositionally consist of a preposition and a pronominal object. Their status as PP clitics is deduced from the fact that they correspond to PP in non-clitic contexts, shown in (11b) and (12b).

PP clitics with a transparent morphological shape are found in the VSO language Berber (Afroasiatic) (Ouhalla 1989). The locative clitic *x-s* in (13a) is made up of the preposition *x(f)* 'on', seen in (13b), and the dative clitic *s* 'to-it/him/her', seen in (13c). (13a–c) are from the dialect called Tarifit Berber:

13a. ur   **x-s**   yqqim   wargaz.
     Neg   on-it$_{DAT}$ sat   man
     'The man did not sit on it.'

13b. yqqim   wargaz   **x** ughyur
     sat   man   on donkey
     'The man sat on the donkey.'

13c. ysqad   (a)**s**   wargaz   tabrat.
     sent   her$_{DAT}$ man   letter
     'The man sent a letter to her.'

The clitics discussed so far correspond to VP-related constituents. There are clitics which correspond to the subject of the sentence called **subject clitics**. For some reason, subject clitics tend to be rare compared to VP-related clitics. For example, Spanish and Italian (and Berber) have VP-related clitics but do not have (a full paradigm of) subject clitics. French, however, has (a full paradigm of) subject clitics, two of which are illustrated in (14):

14a. **Elle/il**   a   acheté   le livre.
     she/he   has   bought   the book

14b. A-t-**elle/il** acheté le livre?
     has-she/he bought the book

French subject clitics appear before the verb in declarative clauses, such as (14a), but after the verb in interrogative clauses involving SAI, such as (14b). This property sets subject clitics apart from VP-related clitics which appear before the verb in both declarative and interrogative clauses. More on this distinction later on.

Besides clitics which clearly correspond to VP-related positions and clitics which clearly correspond to the subject, there are clitics the status of which appears to vary or is at least unclear. An example of such clitics is the Italian *si* illustrated in examples (15a–c) from Cinque (1995b):

15a. Loro **si** sono feriti.
     they CL be wounded
     'They wounded themselves.'

15b. **Si** lavora sempre troppo.
     CL work always too much
     'One always works too much.'

15c. Non **si** è mai contento.
     not CL is never satisfied
     'One is never satisfied.'

In (15a) the clitic *si* is said to have a reflexive reading (a reflexive clitic), and in (15b&c) it is said to have an arbitrary reading. The French equivalent of (15a) has a similar reflexive clitic *se*, e.g. *Ils **se** sont blessés*, 'They CL were wounded', whereas the equivalents of (15b) and (15c) include the subject clitic *on*, e.g. **On** *travaille trop [ici]* 'One works too-much [here]'.

The clitics discussed so far all have in common the property of being related to the verb or the verbal complex. There are clitics which are both syntactically and phonologically related to other lexical categories such as the noun and the preposition. Clitics related to a noun usually correspond to the possessor and are often called **possessive or genitive clitics**. These are illustrated with the French example in (16a):

16a. **son** estomac
    his stomach

16b. Le docteur **lui** a examiné l'estomac.
    the doctor him$_{DAT}$ examined the stomach
    'The doctor examined his stomach.'

It is an interesting question why possessive clitics remain inside the noun phrase and do not cliticise (out of the noun phrase) onto the verb. This question is sometimes discussed in relation to examples such as (16b), where the dative clitic appears on the verb but has a possessive reading related to the direct object. This raises the possibility that the dative clitic originates inside the direct object noun phrase as a possessor and cliticises onto the verb. However, the issue is very complicated and we will have nothing to say about it here (see Vergnaud and Zubizarreta 1992).

French and other Romance languages appear not to have clitics corresponding to the object of a preposition. A language which has such clitics is Tarifit Berber, illustrated in (17). These contexts also raise the question why the clitic remains inside PP and does not cliticise (out of PP) to higher positions:

17. tjja   tmghart   arfruz zdath **s.**
    kept   woman   child   next   her$_{DAT}$
    'The woman kept the child next to her.'

The clitics discussed so far either correspond to a pronoun (pronominal clitics) or in the case of PP-clitics to a category which includes a pronominal object. There are clitics which do not correspond to a pronoun, i.e. **non-pronominal clitics**. For example, some Slavic languages have clitics that correspond to a finite auxiliary verb (see Halpern 1995). As far as the Romance languages are concerned, non-pronominal clitics would arguably include the preverbal negation element *ne* in French (and its counterparts in other Romance languages). We will not have much to say about non-pronominal clitics here.

15.3 *Types of clitic languages*

Languages with clitics (clitic languages) are sometimes classified on the basis of the distribution of their clitics. Unfortunately, apart from one group which is reasonably well-defined, the others are not so easy to classify. The group that appears to be well-defined consists of languages often called **Clitic Second (CL2) languages.** Here we will identify two other groups of clitic-languages which, for lack of standard terminology, will be called Non-CL2 languages and Fixed Position clitic languages.

We have seen that clitics appear before the verb in both finite and non-finite clauses in French. In Spanish and Italian, they appear before the verb in finite clauses and following the verb in non-finite clauses. Despite this diversity, all these languages have in common the property that a clitic can be the first (overt) category in the sentence/clause. This is trivially shown in the Spanish example (18a) and the Italian example (18b). Because French is not a pro-drop language, unlike Spanish and Italian, it is not possible to have a declarative clause starting with an object clitic. However, the property in question can be seen in interrogative clauses such as (19a). French subject clitics, though different from VP-related clitics, can also be said to illustrate this property, as shown in (19b):

18a. **Los** ha visto Maria.
   them has seen Maria

18b. **Li** ha visti Maria.
   them has seen Maria

19a. **Les** a-t-elle vus?
   them has-she seen

19b. Elle **les** a vus.
   she them has seen

The property of Spanish, Italian and French illustrated in (18) and (19) is put into sharp focus when the distribution of clitics in European Portuguese is brought into the picture. In European Portuguese, a clitic cannot be the first category in a sentence/clause. The [CL V] pattern with a finite verb found in French, Spanish and Italian is excluded in European Portuguese contexts of the type illustrated in (20). In this particular context, the clitic must follow the finite verb, as shown in (20a). The European Portuguese examples (20a&b) and others below are adapted from Madeira (1993):

20a. Deu   **lhe**   uma prenda.
   gave-3S   him$_{DAT}$ one present
   'He gave him a present.'

20b. *****Lhe**   deu   uma prenda.
   him$_{DAT}$ gave-3S   one present

European Portuguese belongs to the group of clitic languages called CL2 languages. Various interpretations have been suggested in the literature for the expression 'CL2' (see Halpern 1995). The interpretation given to it here is that CL2 languages are the languages where a clitic cannot occur as the first constituent in a sentence/clause. This is what distinguishes European Portuguese from French,

Spanish, Italian and others. However, this is not the whole picture. The whole picture must also include the contexts illustrated in (21a–c):

21a. Não **lhe**   deu   uma prenda.
    not   him$_{DAT}$ gave-3S   one present
    'She did not give him a present.'

21b. Onde a   encontrou O João?
    where her   met-3S   the John
    'Where did John meet her?'

21c. A alguém   **as**   ofreceram.
    to someone   them$_{DAT}$ offered3PL
    'They offered them to someone.'

When the verb is preceded by the sentence negation element, as in (21a), a wh-phrase, as in (21b), or a topicalised/focused category, as in (21c), the clitic is forced into the preverbal position. However, the distribution of the clitic in (20a) as well as (21a-c) is consistent with the CL2 restriction understood in the linear sense, namely that the clitic is not the first constituent in the clause/sentence.

It is an interesting question whether the categories in (21a–c) which force the clitic into the preverbal position form a natural class and if so what kind of natural class it is. Madeira (1993) reaches the conclusion that the categories in question are all operators, located in Spec,CP or thereabouts. This conclusion is consistent with the fact that preverbal subjects do not force the clitic into the preverbal position as shown in (22), unless they are topicalised/focused, in which case they are operators located in presumably the same operator position as the categories in (21a-c):

22. O Pedro   deu   **lhe**   uma prenda.
    the Pedro   gave   him$_{DAT}$ one present
    'Pedro gave him a present.'

There is at least one context which appears, at least superficially, to be in-consistent with Madeira's generalisation. Embedded clauses introduced by the complementiser 'that' exhibit the order [CL V] even though they apparently do not include an operator. This is shown in (23):

23. O Jorge   disse   que   O Pedro   **lhe**   deu   uma prenda.
    the Jorge   said   that   the Pedro   him$_{DAT}$ gave   one present
    'Jorge said that Pedro gave him a present.'

Contexts such as (23) would presumably have to be assumed to include a null operator to make them consistent with the generalisation that it is operators which force the clitic into the preverbal position in European Portuguese.

The third group of languages, which we have called (somewhat awkwardly) Fixed Position Clitic languages, involves a pattern whereby the clitic invariably appears following a verb, a noun or a preposition. This pattern is usually associated with the Semitic languages Arabic and Hebrew, although it is arguably also found in other languages (see Roberts and Shlonsky 1995). Hebrew does not tolerate clitics on the verb, and for this reason we will use data from Standard Arabic to illustrate this particular pattern. (24a) involves a direct object clitic, (24b) a possessive clitic, and (24c) an object of preposition clitic:

24a. raʔa-w-**hu.**
   aw-3PL him
   They saw him.'

24b. kitaabu-**hu**
   book his

24c. sallamuu ʿalay-**hi.**
   greeted-3PL on him
   'They greeted him.'

The pattern of clitic placement found in Arabic and Hebrew is fundamentally different from the other two patterns discussed above. This difference perhaps calls for an analysis which makes a fundamental distinction in nature between the clitics found in Arabic and Hebrew, and the ones found in the other languages cited above. More on this later on.

15.4   *Cliticisation*

15.4.1   Local cliticisation

The contexts of cliticisation discussed above are all local. They involve displacement of the clitic inside the same clause. To give a formal explanation to the process of cliticisation we need to provide answers to a number of questions. We need to know, among other things, whether pronominal clitics are maximal projections or heads, whether they move as maximal projections or as heads, and whether the category they move to is a maximal projection or a head. The discussion of cliticisation in the Romance languages will draw heavily on work by Kayne (1975, 1989). In contexts where Kayne's analyses assume ideas we have not discussed yet at this stage of the book, the analyses are simplified and slightly modified, hopefully without compromising the main ideas. Once again the reader is strongly advised to consult the original sources cited.

In Chapter 8, it was concluded that pronouns are of the category D, that is they occupy the D position of a DP. Presumably, this conclusion extends to pronominal clitics, their dependent nature being no bar to their status as D. As a matter of fact, there is a more transparent morphological link between object clitic pronouns and determiners in French than there is in English. The French third person masculine and feminine accusative clitics *le* 'him' and *la* 'her' are identical to the masculine and feminine definite articles *le* 'the(masc)' as in *le livre* 'the book', and *la* 'the(fem)', as in *la table* 'the table'.

Assuming that clitic pronouns are of the category D, it does not necessarily follow that clitics move as heads (head-movement) instead of as maximal projections (XP-movement). Other considerations have to be brought into the picture. Kayne (1989) argues that one such consideration is the fact that clitics appear associated with head categories such as the verb or, in the case of other languages, nouns and prepositions. Assuming that what underlies the notion 'association with a head' is head-adjunction, it follows that clitics move as heads and that cliticisation is an instance of head-movement.

This conclusion may initially appear not to extend to cases of PP-clitics. However, it is argued in Ouhalla (1988) that they too involve head-movement, along the lines outlined in (25). The pronominal clitic moves from D to P forming with it a complex head [p [P] [D]] which subsequently head-moves to a higher position in the structure of the clause. Note that the transparent composition of Berber PP clitics is consistent with this analysis, in fact requires it:

25. ... [p^0 [P] [CL]]. ... [$_{VP}$ ... [$_{PP}$ t$_{[P [P] [CL]]}$ [$_{DP}$ [D' t$_{CL}$]] ...

Kayne goes on to argue that once cliticisation is taken to be an instance of head-movement, the facts of French illustrated in (26a&b) follow without the need for a special statement about ordering of clitics:

26a. Jean ne **les** voit pas.
　　 Jean not them sees not

26b. *Jean **les** ne voit pas.
　　 Jean them not sees not

(26b) shows that a VP-related clitic cannot precede the preverbal negation element *ne* in French. It must follow the preverbal negation element, as shown in (26a). (26b) is excluded due to the fact that the clitic head-moves across the sentence negation element. As in English negative sentences (Chapter 5), sentence negation in general blocks head-movement across it. This property of sentence negation is discussed in more detail in Chapter (16) in relation to negative sentences in both English and French.

Having established the categorial identity of pronominal clitics, and the type of movement they undergo, we now need to identify the category they move to (the host). Kayne (1989) suggests that clitics left-adjoin to I, possibly subsequent to verb-raising to I, as shown in (27):

27. [$_{IP}$ SUBJ [$_{I'}$ [CL] [$_{VP}$ V [$_{DP}$ [D' t$_{CL}$]] ...

This derivation is consistent with the pattern [CL V] typical of finite clauses in French, Spanish and Italian, among others.

The idea that clitics left-adjoin to I carries straightforwardly to French non-finite clauses since they too exhibit the pattern [CL V]. They differ only in that the non-finite verb does not raise to I, as shown in (28b):

28a. **Lui**　　 parler　　 serait　　 une erreur.
　　 him$_{DAT}$　 to-speak　 would-be　 a mistake

28b. [$_{IP}$ SUBJ [$_{I'}$ [CL] [$_{VP}$ V [$_{DP}$ [$_{D'}$ t$_{CL}$]] . . .

Kayne points out that the analysis outlined in (28b) is consistent with the pattern shown in the Literary French example (29), where an (VP-adjoined) adverb intervenes between the clitic and the non-finite verb:

29. . . . en   bien   parler . . .
     . . . of-it   well   to-speak

The analysis appears not to carry over to non-finite clauses in Spanish and Italian since they exhibit the pattern [V CL], shown in the Italian example (30a):

30a. Parlargli   sarebbe   un errore.
      to-speak-him$_{DAT}$ would-be   an error

30b. [$_{IP}$ SUBJ [$_{I'}$ [V] [$_{I'}$ [CL] [$_{VP}$ t$_V$ [$_{DP}$ t$_{CL}$] . . .

Assuming right-adjunction of the clitic to the verb in (30a) would be ad hoc for many reasons, among them the fact that it would remain mysterious why this process should be restricted to non-finite clauses. Instead, Kayne suggests that the clitic left-adjoins to I in Italian and Spanish non-finite clauses, as it does in French non-finite clauses. Italian and Spanish non-finite clauses differ in that they undergo verb-raising and left-adjunction to I', shown in (30b). This additional process is responsible for placing the non-finite verb to the left of the clitic in Italian and Spanish non-finite clauses. Thus, the relevant difference between French non-finite clauses, on the one hand, and their Italian and Spanish counterparts, on the other, is due to a difference in the scope of verb-raising rather than to a difference in the scope and/or directionality of syntactic cliticisation.

Kayne does not include European Portuguese in his analysis. The CL2 nature of European Portuguese complicates the situation considerably, and it is not clear whether one could maintain the view that the clitic consistently left-adjoins to I with the pattern [V CL] derived by verb-raising to a position higher than I (see Madeira 1993 for discussion). On a more general note, the CL2 phenomenon remains largely a mystery, perhaps due to the fact that it involves prosodic considerations which are still less well understood. The restriction that the clitic, a prosodically non-prominent element, cannot be the first constituent in the sentence/clause appears to be phonological rather than syntactic. We will have no more to say about CL2 here (see Halpern 1995 and Klavans 1980, 1985 for discussion).

15.4.2   Clitic climbing

Italian, among other Romance languages, has constructions where a clitic which is thematically related to an embedded non-finite clause appears associated with the root finite verb. This phenomenon is known as **clitic climbing** and is illustrated with the Italian example in (31a). (31b) shows that the clitic also has the option of staying within the embedded clause in this particular context:

31a. Gianni **li** vuole vedere.
       Gianni them wants to-see

31b. Gianni vuole veder**li**.
       Gianni wants to-see-them

Interestingly, French lacks the phenomenon of clitic climbing, at least in the context illustrated in (31a&b). The French counterpart of (31a) is excluded, as shown in (32a). Only the option whereby the clitic remains in the embedded clause, shown in (32b), is allowed:

32a. *Jean **les** veut voir.
       Jean them wants to-see

32b. Jean veut **les** voir.
       Jean wants them to-see

Clitic climbing appears to be an instance of long distance movement. As such, it is apparently inconsistent with the view that cliticisation is an instance of head movement. Head movement processes are usually local, due to the restriction imposed on them by HMC (see Chapter 10). While it looks plausible to view local cliticisation as an instance of head movement, it is arguably less plausible to view clitic climbing as an instance of head-movement as well. At the same time, conceding that clitic climbing is an instance of XP-movement while local cliticisation is an instance of head movement does not seem to be a coherent view to take. Kayne (1989) argues that clitic climbing too is an instance of head movement which applies in short successive cyclic steps. Before we trace the steps of clitic movement in clitic climbing constructions, let us first discuss the evidence that Kayne cites for the claim that clitic climbing is also an instance of head movement.

Kayne cites at least two major pieces of evidence. The first piece of evidence relates to the interaction between clitic climbing and sentence negation. Just as local cliticisation is blocked by negation, as we saw above, clitic climbing is also blocked by negation. When the embedded non-finite clause is negative, the clitic cannot climb across it, as shown in (33b). In this context, only the non-climbing option, shown in (33a), is allowed:

33a. Gianni vuole non veder**li**.
       Gianni wants not to-see-them

33b. *Gianni **li** vuole non vedere.
       Gianni them wants not to-see

The second piece of evidence relates to the fact that a wh-phrase such as 'what' does not block clitic climbing, whereas a Comp element such as 'if' does. This is shown in (34a–c). In other words, clitic climbing is blocked by a head category but not by a non-head category. It follows that clitic climbing is an instance of head-movement:

34a. Non **ti** saprei che dire.
    not to-you would-know what to-say
    'I would not know what to say to you.'

34b. Non so se far**li**.
    not know-1S if to-do-them
    'I don't know whether to do them.'

34c. *Non **li** so se fare.
    not them know-1S if to-do

According to Kayne (1989) clitic climbing proceeds as in (35). The clitic moves through each intervening head, including C, and ultimately left-adjoins to the I of the root finite clause. Each step is arguably consistent with HMC:

35a. Gianni **li** vuole vedere.
    Gianni them wants to-see

35b. [$_{IP}$ SUBJ [$_{I'}$ [CL] [$_{VP}$ V [$_{CP}$ [$_{C'}$ t$_{CL}$ [$_{IP}$ SUBJ [$_{I'}$ t$_{CL}$ [$_{VP}$ V [DP t$_{CL}$] . . .

Besides attempting to make explicit the process of clitic climbing in Italian (and similar languages), Kayne also attempts to explain why French lacks clitic climbing. This difference between Italian and French is linked to another difference between them, namely the fact that Italian is a null subject language whereas French is not. Kayne takes the null subject nature of Italian to mean that non-finite I is 'strong' and therefore L-marks VP (see Chapter 10 on L-marking). This enables the clitic to escape out of the infinitival VP in Italian clitic climbing contexts and subsequently move to the root clause. Because French is not a null subject language, its non-finite I is not 'strong' and therefore does not L-mark VP. Consequently, a clitic cannot escape out of the infinitival VP in French. For a clitic to be able to climb to a root clause, it has to be able to escape out of the infinitival VP that includes it in the first place.

15.4.3 Clitics as Agr elements

Let us now see whether the analysis suggested by Kayne for Romance clitics in terms of head-movement extends to the type of clitics found in the Semitic languages Arabic and Hebrew, briefly discussed above. It turns out that Arabic and Hebrew so-called clitics may not be clitics in the same sense as the Romance ones. Roberts and Shlonsky (1995) have carried out a detailed comparative study of clitics in Arabic and Hebrew, on the one hand, and Romance on the other which leads to the conclusion that Arabic and Hebrew so-called clitics are best analysed as base-generated object agreement markers rather than as D categories which undergo head-movement. We will go through their arguments here, once again using data from Arabic. Recall the observation that Hebrew does not tolerate clitics on the verb.

The list of properties of Arabic and Hebrew clitics compiled by Roberts and Shlonsky (1995) is reproduced in (36):

36. a. They occur on the right of their host, never on the left.
    b. They are always attached to the closest c-commanding head.
    c. They appear on all lexical categories and on certain functional ones.
    d. They do not manifest Case distinctions.
    e. They never cluster, i.e. a single clitic per host.
    f. They bear no morphological resemblance to nominal determiners.

Property (36a) was illustrated above with data from Standard Arabic. The relevant examples are reproduced in (37) together with the additional example (37d), where the clitic is hosted by the complementiser:

37a. raʔa-w-**hu**.
     saw-3PL him
     'They saw him.'

37b. kitaabu-**hu**
     book his

37c. sallamuu ʿalay-**hi**.
     greeted-3PL on him
     'They greeted him.'

37d. zuʾima ʔanna-**hum** wasal-uu
     claimed that-them arrived
     'It is claimed that they have arrived.'

In all contexts illustrated in (37a–d), the clitic consistently appears to the right of the head category it is related to. This is not the case at least in Italian and Spanish, where the clitic appears to the left of the verb in finite clauses and to the right of the verb in non-finite clauses.

Property (36b) is illustrated with the Palestinian Arabic example (38) cited in Roberts and Shlonsky (1995). Recall that in Romance finite clauses which include both an auxiliary and a main verb, the clitic is associated with the finite auxiliary rather than with the main verb:

38. kaan bixayyt **ha**.
    was sewing it
    'He was sewing it.'

Property (36c) is illustrated in the Standard Arabic examples (37a–d). The clitic appears on the verb in (37a), the noun in (37b), the preposition in (37c) and the functional category C in (37d).

Property (36d) is illustrated in example (39) from Cairene Arabic cited in Roberts and Shlonsky (1995):

39. fahhim-**u**   la-**ha**.
    make-understand3MS-it   to-her
    'He made her understand it.'

Arabic clitics all have the same Case form irrespective of context. Arabic does not have a distinct clitic corresponding to dative arguments. In sentences which include a verb with two arguments such as the causative verb *fahhim* 'cause to understand' in (39), the indirect object pronoun appears as a clitic on the preposition 'to'. Romance languages have a morphologically distinct form for dative clitics as we saw above.

Property (36e) is also illustrated in the Cairene example (39). The presence of the dative preposition 'to' is obligatory in (39) and other relevant contexts in Arabic. The relevant French sentences above, e.g. (9b), do not include a preposition. Rather they involve a situation where the dative clitic and accusative clitic cluster together in the preverbal position.

As for property (36f), the definite article has an invariable form in Arabic, e.g. *l-mudarris/a/iin* 'the-teacher(MS)/MF/PL' which does not appear to be morphologically related to clitics. This is contrary to the situation found in French and pointed out above, where at least some clitics are transparently related to the definite article.

Roberts and Shlonsky (1995) go on to conclude that Arabic and Hebrew so-called clitic pronouns are actually object Agr elements, base-generated on the head they are associated with, rather than pronouns base-generated under the D of a DP and moved to their host. In Roberts and Shlonsky's analysis, the argument position is occupied by a null pronominal element *pro* identified by the Agr element. The basic configuration is as outlined in (40), where X stands for any lexical category and at least some functional categories. The CL/Agr$_O$ element agrees in relevant features with *pro* in the argument position indicated with co-indexation:

40. ... X+CL$_i$/Agr$_{Oi}$ ... pro$_i$

(40) recalls an earlier analysis suggested in Aoun (1982) for Arabic clitics and in Borer (1984) for Hebrew clitics. More on this analysis later on in the section dealing with clitic doubling.

15.4.4 Subject clitics

As an introduction to the discussion of subject clitics, let us briefly go back to clitics in Arabic and Hebrew. In these languages, clitics are prosodically related to the category to their left rather than to the category to their right. This fact is reflected in transcription conventions where the clitic is linked to the category to its left with a dash. This pattern of association is arguably expected in Arabic and Hebrew under the analysis that clitics are actually agreement markers. However, it may not be so for Italian and Spanish non-finite clauses in view of Kayne's argument that clitics invariably left-adjoin to their host. In Italian and Spanish non-finite clauses, the clitic is prosodically related to the verb situated to its left. This is reflected in writing conventions whereby the verb and the clitic are written together as one word, as shown in (8a) and (30a). In finite clauses, the clitic is prosodically related to the verb situated to its right, which is apparently consistent with the argument that clitics left-adjoin to the their host.

However, prosodic association with a category situated to the left of the clitic is not necessarily inconsistent with left-adjunction, especially if one keeps in mind the distinction made earlier between clitics and affixes, and by implication cliticisation and affixation. Although both processes involve head-adjunction, clitics do not determine the properties of the derived complex head in the way affixes do (Chapter 3). The complex [V CL] has none of the nominal properties of CL. In thinking of clitics one needs to make a clear distinction between cliticisation at the syntactic level (syntactic cliticisation) and cliticisation at the PF level (phonological cliticisation). The former is an instance of head-movement determined by syntactic considerations in the sense discussed above. The latter, however, is determined by prosodic considerations which take context into consideration and may vary from one language to another. A clitic may be placed in the same position by syntactic cliticisation, but may end up associated with different categories in different contexts by phonological cliticisation.

There is evidence to suggest that subject clitics do not undergo syntactic cliticisation, unlike VP-related clitics. Their association with their host is due solely to phonological cliticisation. This is basically the claim made by Kayne (1975) for subject clitics in French.

In French, subject clitics appear to the left of the verb, VP-related clitics, and the preverbal negation element. This is shown in (41a), (41b) and (41c), respectively:

41a. **Il** a vu Jean.
    he has seen Jean

41b. **Il** l'a vu.
    he her has seen

41c. **Il** ne l'a pas vu.
    he not her has not seen.

The negative context (41c) illustrates a clear distinction between subject clitics and VP-related clitics. Recall that VP-related clitics cannot appear to the left of the preverbal negation element in French, as shown in (26b).

Another context which illustrates an equally clear distribution distinction between subject clitics and VP-related clitics is the SAI context, illustrated in (42):

42a. L'a-t-**il** vu?
    her has he seen

42b. Ne l'a-t-**il** pas vu?
    not her has he not seen

VP-related clitics, as well as the preverbal negation element, appear to the left of the inverted verb. Presumably, this shows that VP-related clitics and the negation element raise along with the verb to C. The subject clitic, however, appears to the right of the verb in SAI contexts. This suggests that the subject clitic does not adjoin to the verbal complex prior to the latter's raising to C. Rather, the subject clitic is prosodically associated with the verbal complex to its left subsequent to the latter's raising to C.

There are other reasons why subject clitics are not likely to be derived by head-raising. In Chapter 14, we saw that incorporation of true subjects is not attested because it would involve a lowering head-movement process which is excluded by the ECP. A syntactic derivation for subject clitics along the lines suggested by Kayne for VP-related clitics would also involve lowering, and therefore is excluded.

As with object clitics, it seems that there are languages where so-called subject clitics are best treated as Agr$_S$ elements rather than as clitics in the French sense. This is the conclusion that Rizzi (1986b) reaches in relation to some Northern Italian dialects compared to French. Rizzi outlines numerous arguments for his conclusion, only three of which will be reproduced here (for lack of space).

The basic pattern in the Northern Italian dialects said to have subject clitics is illustrated in example (43) from Trentino. First, the subject clitic co-occurs with a DP subject, and secondly, the subject clitic appears to be obligatory:

43a. El Gianni **el** magna.
   the Gianni CL eats

43b. **El** magna.
   CL eats

43c. *Magna.
   eats.

44a. *Jean **il** mange.
   Jean he eats

44b. Jean, **il** mange.
   Jean, he eats

The pattern seen in (43a) is possible in French only if the DP subject is followed by a prosodic break, as shown in (44a&b). The prosodic break signals that the subject in (44b) has the status of a left-dislocated DP rather than a subject. If the DP subject in the Trentino example (43a) can be shown not to be a dislocated DP, we will have a clear difference between French subject clitics and their Trentino counterparts.

Rizzi argues that there is good evidence that the DP subject in (43a) and similar examples from other Northern Italian dialects is not a dislocated DP. Quantifier DPs such as 'nobody' and 'everything' cannot be left-dislocated in French, as shown in (45a). However, they can appear in the preverbal position in Fiorentino, as shown in (46a), and in Trentino, as shown in (46b):

45. *Personne (,) **il** n'a rien dit.
   nobody he not has anything said

46a. Nessuno **l'**ha detto nulla.
   nobody CL said anything
   'Nobody said anything.'

46b. Tut l'e capita' de not.
  everything it happened in the night
  'Everything happened in the night.'

Simplifying to some extent, another argument presented by Rizzi consists of showing that the subject clitic can appear inside the preverbal negation element in some Northern Italian dialects. This is illustrated with the Trentino example in (47). Recall that French subject clitics appear outside or to the left of the preverbal negation element, and cannot appear inside the negation element:

47. (La Maria) no **la** parla.
  the Maria not CL speaks

A third argument consists of showing that a conjunction of VPs cannot be predicated of a subject clitic in Trentino, for example, as shown in (48a). However, a conjunction of VPs can be predicated of a subject clitic in French, as shown in (48b):

48a. *__La__ canta e balla.
  CL sing and dance

48b. **Elle** chante et danse.
  She sings and dances

The three major differences discussed clearly point to the conclusion that so-called subject clitics in the Northern Italian dialects cited have the status of Agr_S elements generated under I and joined with the verb via verb-raising. True subject clitics of the French type are base-generated in the subject position and only join the verbal complex via phonological association at PF. This difference is represented in structures (49a) and (49b):

49a. $[_{IP} [_{DP} CL] [_{I'} [Agr] [_{VP} V \ldots$
49b. $[_{IP} [_{DP} pro] [_{I'} [Agr} CL] [_{VP} V \ldots$

(49a) is the configuration that underlies French subject clitics. The subject clitic is located in the subject position and only cliticises onto the verbal complex till PF. (49b) is the configuration underlying so-called subject clitics in the Italian dialects discussed by Rizzi. CL is located under Agr and is essentially an Agr_S element which merges with the verb via verb-raising to I.

15.5   *Clitic doubling*

Clitic doubling refers to the phenomenon whereby a pronominal clitic co-occurs with a thematically related DP. Most clitic languages allow doubling involving a dative clitic and an indirect object. However, not many clitic languages allow doubling involving an accusative clitic and a direct object. Other languages allow clitic doubling involving a possessive clitic and a possessor. Here, we will concentrate our attention on doubling involving an accusative clitic and a direct object.

The earliest languages cited in the relevant literature include River Plate Spanish (Rivas 1977, Jaeggli 1980), Romanian (Steriade 1980) and Lebanese Arabic (Aoun 1982). Example (50a) is from River Plate Spanish and (50b) from Lebanese Arabic. (50c) is from Modern Hebrew (Borer 1984) and illustrates doubling of the possessor:

50a. **Lo** vimos   a Juan.
     him saw-1PL   to Juan
     'We saw Juan.'

50b. shuft **o**   la Kariim.
     saw-1S him   to Kariim
     'I saw Kariim.'

50c. beit-**o**   shel ha-more
     house-his   of the-teacher
     'The teacher's house'

The phenomenon of clitic doubling raises a number of issues. One issue relates to the question how to deal with a situation where two nominal categories appear to compete for one and the same argument position, and one and the same θ-role. This situation potentially gives rise to a θ-Criterion violation. The references cited above resolved this problem by assuming that the clitic is base-generated together with its host. The argument/θ-position is filled with the related DP, with the two categories linked by co-indexation. In view of subsequent and more recent work reported in this chapter, this analysis is consistent with the properties of clitics in Arabic and Hebrew, where there is evidence that they are probably Agr$_O$ elements. It remains to be seen, however, whether it works as well for the Romance languages River Plate Spanish and Romanian. There is the possibility that these languages may simply have reanalysed clitics as Agr$_O$ elements, but this conjecture needs to be supported with independent evidence of the type that Roberts and Shlonsky (1995) have adduced in relation to Arabic and Hebrew.

Another issue raised by clitic doubling relates to the question why the DP is obligatorily preceded by a preposition, as shown in (50a-c). This property of clitic doubling came to be known as Kayne's Generalisation. It is less transparent in the Spanish example because Spanish requires the dative preposition with animate direct objects anyway, independently of doubling. The obligatory presence of the preposition in clitic doubling configurations was accounted for in Aoun (1982) and Borer (1984) in terms of the notion 'Case absorption.' The idea is that the clitic absorbs the Case of the host normally assigned to the DP in the argument position in much the same way that the passive affix is said to absorb the Case of transitive verbs (Chapter 8). Case absorption by the clitic results in a situation where the DP in the argument position must have an independent Case-assigner. This is the role of the preposition construed as a semantically vacuous Case-assigner.

A substantial amount of the discussion relating to clitic doubling concentrates on extraction. Jaeggli (1982) observes that extraction of the DP direct object, allowed in non-doubling contexts, is excluded in clitic doubling contexts in River

Plate Spanish. This is shown in (51a&b). In contrast, extraction of the indirect object is allowed in clitic doubling contexts, as shown in (51c):

51a. A quien vimos?
     to who saw-1PL
     'Who did we see?'

51b. *A quien **lo** vimos?
     to who him saw-1PL
     'Who did we see?'

51c. A quien **le** han regalado ese libro?
     to whom to-him have send this book
     'To whom did they send this book?'

Jaeggli outlines an ECP-based analysis for the data in (51a–c). According to this analysis, extraction out of clitic doubling configurations involves a situation where the argument position occupied by the trace is never governed for reasons we cannot get into here. Thus, (51b) is ruled out on the grounds that it involves an ECP violation. The reason (51c) is not ruled out along with (51b) is due to the fact that the trace it involves is of the category PP and therefore is not subject to the ECP. The latter is restricted to NPs/DPs, as clearly shown in some of its earliest definitions.

Various other analyses have been suggested in the literature for why extraction is not possible out of clitic doubling contexts. Dobrovie-Sorin (1990) reviews some of these analyses and outlines an alternative analysis based on Romanian.

15.6 *Summary*

The distribution of VP-related clitics is largely determined by syntactic considerations, although it also involves prosodic considerations applying that the PF level. At the syntactic level, cliticisation takes the form of a syntactic movement to a functional category higher up in the structure. At the PF level, cliticisation takes the form of prosodic association with a category which can be located either to the left or to the right of the clitic, depending on prosodic considerations which may vary from one context to another and one language to another.

There is evidence that cliticisation at the syntactic level takes the form of head-movement and left-adjunction to I. This is the case not only in contexts of local cliticisation within the same clause, but also contexts of long distance cliticisation (or clitic climbing) from an embedded non-finite clause to the root clause.

Clitic languages can be classified on the basis of the distribution of their clitics. In some languages, clitics can appear either before or after the verb, depending on the syntactic context. In a second group of languages, clitics invariably appear in what is called 'the second position' which may either precede or follow the verb depending on the context. In a third group of languages, clitics invariably appear following the category they are associated with. There is evidence that the clitics in the latter group are best analysed as Agr$_O$ elements rather than as clitics.

Unlike VP-related clitics, subject clitics appear not to undergo cliticisation at the syntactic level. They display properties which suggest that they are simply prosodically associated with their host at the PF level.

Exercises

Exercise 15.1

VP-related clitics have a variable distribution in French imperatives depending on whether the imperative is negative or non-negative. In non-negative imperatives the clitic appears following the verb, as shown in (i). In negative imperatives, however, it appears preceding the verb, as shown in (ii). Explain whether this distribution is consistent with Kayne's analysis of cliticisation outlined in this chapter:

i) Arrêtez **le**!
   stop him

ii) Ne **l'**arrêtez pas!
    not him stop not
    'Don't stop him!'

Exercise 15.2

It was pointed out in this chapter that French lacks clitic climbing of the type found in Italian. However, it has been claimed that French allows clitic climbing in causative sentences of the type illustrated in (i–iv). Assuming that (ii–iv) are genuine cases of clitic-climbing, explain whether they present a problem to Kayne's account of why French lacks clitic-climbing in the contexts discussed in this chapter. You may want to refer to the discussion of causative constructions in Chapter 14:

i)   Jean a fait   écrire   la lettre   a Pierre.
     Jean has made   write   the letter   to Pierre
     'Jean made Pierre write the letter.'

ii) Jean **lui**   a fait   écrire la lettre.
     Jean him$_{DAT}$ has made   write the letter
     'Jean made him write the letter.'

iii) Jean **l'**a fait   écrire a Pierre.
     Jean it$_{ACC}$ has made   write to Pierre
     'Jean made Pierre write it.'

iv) Jean   **la lui**   a fait   écrire.
     Jean   it$_{ACC}$ him$_{DAT}$ has made   write
     'Jean made him write it.'

Exercise 15.3

Examples (i–iv) are from Tarifit Berber. Examine the properties of Tarifit Berber clitics in the light of the criteria suggested by Roberts and Shlonsky (1995) and discussed in this chapter. Note that the clitics are linked with a dash to the category to their left. This encodes the fact that clitics are prosodically associated with the category to their left in Tarifit Berber. Discuss this property of Berber clitics in the light of Kayne's claim that clitics left-adjoin to their host:

i) ushan-**as-t**.
   gave3PL-him$_{DAT}$-it$_{ACC}$
   'They gave it to him.'

ii) ur-**as-t** ushan.
   not-him$_{DAT}$-it$_{ACC}$ gave3PL
   'They did not give it to him.'

iii) mlmi ay-**as-t** ushan?
   when Comp-him$_{DAT}$-it$_{ACC}$ gave3PL
   'When did they give it to him?

iv) t-nna qa ushan-**as-t**.
   3FS-said that gave3PL-him$_{DAT}$-it$_{ACC}$
   'She said that they gave it to him.'

Exercise 15.4

Examples (i–iii) are from Serbo-Croatian (Halpern 1995). The clitic in these examples is a verbal clitic corresponding to the finite auxiliary (AUX). Discuss the implications of such clitics for the question whether clitics are heads which undergo head-movement or XPs which undergo XP-movement:

i) Čovek **-je** voleo   Mariju.
   man   -AUX loved   Mary
   'The man loved Mary.'

ii) Voleo **-je**   čovek Mariju.
   loved -AUX   Man   Mariju
   'The man loved Mary.'

iii) Mariju -je   voleo   čovek.
   Mary -AUX   loved   man
   'The man loved Mary.'

Exercise 15.5

CL2 languages seem to differ as to whether they require the clitic to follow the first constituent in the sentence/clause or the first phonological word in the sentence/clause. In Serbo-Croatian, for example, the clitic can either follow the first phonological word or the first constituent as shown in (ia&b). In Czech, however, the clitic must follow the first constituent as shown in (iia&b) (Halpern 1995). Explore the implications of these two patterns for the claim discussed in this chapter that clitics undergo prosodic association subsequent to their syntactic movement:

i)a. Taj **-je**   čovek voleo Mariu.
    that   -AUX man   loved Mary
    'That man loved Mary.'

i)b. Taj čovek **-je**   voleo   Mariu.
    that man   -AUX   loved   Mary
    'That man loved Mary.'

ii)a. Ten básník **-mi**   čte   ze   své knihy.
    that poet   to-me   reads   from   his book
    'That poet reads to me from his book.'

ii)b. *Ten **-mi**   básník čte   ze   své knihy.
    that   -to-me   poet   reads   from   his book

16 I-lowering versus V-raising

Contents

16.1 *Weak versus strong Agr$_S$*

16.1.1 Main verbs

In Chapter 5 we saw that English applies I-lowering (or Affix-hopping), and disallows V-raising with main verbs, as shown in (1) and (2):

1a. John often kisses Mary.
1b. [$_{IP}$ John [$_{I'}$ t$_I$ [$_{VP}$ often [$_{VP}$ [$_V$ kiss [I]] Mary . . .

2a. *John kisses often Mary
2b. [$_{IP}$ John [$_{I'}$ [$_V$ kiss] I [$_{VP}$ often [$_{VP}$ t$_{kiss}$ Mary . . .

In Chapter 8 it was pointed out that the reason English disallows V-raising with main verbs may have to do with the adjacency requirement on Case-assignment it incorporates. V-raising would result in a VP-adverb intervening between the verb and its direct object. However, this is unlikely to be the right explanation for a number of reasons. The adjacency requirement is a linear notion, and therefore is likely to be only a reflection of a more fundamental structural reason. Moreover, main verbs appear unable to raise to I even in the absence of a VP-adverb, that is even in the absence of a category that would break adjacency between the verb and its direct object. In this section, we will outline an alternative account for this property of English which relies on non-linear notions. The account is based on a comparison between English and French which was first undertaken in Emonds (1978).

The situation in French is the reverse of the one found in English. The equivalent of (1) is disallowed, while the equivalent of (2) is allowed. This is shown in (3) and (4):

3a. *Jean souvent embrasse Marie.
    Jean often kisses Marie

3b. *[IP Jean [I' tI [VP souvent [VP [V embrasser [I]] Marie . . .

4a. Jean embrasse souvent Marie.
    Jean kisses often Marie

4b. [IP Jean [I' [V embrasser] I [VP souvent [VP tembrasser Marie . . .

The properties of French illustrated in (3) and (4) translate formally into the scenario that French disallows I-lowering and requires V-raising with main verbs in finite clauses. To account for the contrast between main verbs in English and French, Pollock (1989) capitalises on the difference in the categorial property of the complex head derived by I-lowering to V and the complex head derived by V-raising to I, together with an assumption bearing on the nature of Agrs in the two languages. I-lowering and adjunction to V results in the derivation of a complex V shown in (5). In contrast, V-raising and adjunction to I results in the derivation of a complex I shown in (6):

5a. [V [V] [I]]   : I-lowering
5b.

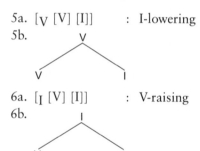

6a. [I [V] [I]]   : V-raising
6b.

The assumption bearing on the nature of Agrs in the two languages is as follows. In English, Agrs is 'opaque' arguably due to its largely abstract nature. The opaque nature of English Agrs has the effect of 'confining' categories adjoined to it in such a way that they cannot transmit their lexical properties, in particular their θ-roles, to their arguments. In contrast, French Agrs is 'transparent' arguably due to its comparatively less abstract nature especially with respect to the plural members of the paradigm. The transparent nature of French Agrs means that it does not confine lexical categories adjoined to it, contrary to its English counterpart. A verb adjoined to French transparent Agrs will therefore be able to transmit its θ-roles to its arguments.

Let us now see how the two assumptions account for the data above. Starting with English, (2) involves V-raising of the main verb and its adjunction to I/Agrs. Because English Agrs is opaque, the main verb is confined and consequently cannot transmit its θ-roles to its arguments. Thus, this example is excluded on the grounds that the arguments of the verb fail to be assigned their respective θ-roles, and therefore fail to satisfy the θ-Criterion. On a more general level, main verbs cannot raise to I in English because if they do so they will be confined inside an opaque Agr$_S$ which will prevent them from transmitting θ-roles to their arguments. In contrast, the process of I-lowering involved in the derivation of (1) does not result in the confinement of V. In this situation, V itself is the host and the complex head has the structure shown in (5). Consequently, V can transmit its θ-roles to its arguments. Turning now to French, recall that French Agr$_S$ is transparent, unlike English Agr$_S$. Consequently, although the head complex derived by V-movement to I is the one shown in (6), Agr$_S$ does not prevent the verb from transmitting its θ-roles to its arguments. It is for this reason that movement of main verbs to I is possible in French, as shown in (4).

The next step is to explain why I-lowering is excluded in French. The generalisation underlying the French facts that needs to be captured is that V-raising is obligatory whenever it is possible. Because V-raising is possible with main verbs in French, it is obligatory. V-raising is not possible in English anyway for the reasons mentioned above.

To explain the generalisation underlying the French facts, let us have a closer look at the SS representation of the English example (1), reproduced in (7):

7a. John often kisses Mary.
7b. SS: [$_{IP}$ John [$_{I'}$ t$_{[I]}$ [$_{VP}$ often [$_{VP}$ [$_V$ [$_V$ kiss] [I]] Mary . . .

Chomsky (1991c) remarks that this representation involves an ill-formed chain where the trace of the lowered I is not c-commanded and therefore not antecedent-governed by I. Since head-traces can only satisfy the ECP via antecedent-government (Chapter 10), (7b) involves an ECP violation. Assuming that the ECP holds at LF (Chapter 10), Chomsky suggests that the derivation of (7) involves an additional head-movement step at LF, whereby the complex [V+I] raises (back) to I and eliminates the offending trace in I. The derived LF-representation is roughly as shown in (8c):

8a. John often kisses Mary.
8b. SS: *[$_{IP}$ John [$_{I'}$ t$_I$ [$_{VP}$ often [$_{VP}$ [$_V$ [$_V$ kiss] [I]] Mary . . .
8c. LF: [$_{IP}$ John [$_{I'}$ [$_V$ [$_V$ kiss] [I]] [$_{VP}$ often [$_{VP}$ t$_{[V [kiss] [I]]}$ Mary . . .

The head-movement process which applies at LF in the derivation of (8) is basically 'corrective' in nature. It is intended to correct chains that would otherwise not satisfy the conditions on chain formation (ECP) applying at LF.

The derivation of the English example (8a) outlined in (8b&c) initially seems to complicate significantly the prospect of explaining why I-lowering is not possible in French. The French example (9a) could be assigned a legitimate derivation along the lines of (8b&c) with the consequence that it remains mysterious why it is excluded. The derivation is shown in (9b&c):

9a. *Jean   souvent   embrasse   Marie.
    Jean   often   kisses   Marie
9b. SS: *[$_{IP}$ Jean [$_{I'}$ t$_{[I]}$ [$_{VP}$ souvent [$_{VP}$ [$_V$ [$_V$ embrasser] [I]] Marie . . .
9c. LF: [$_{IP}$ Jean [I' [$_V$ [$_V$ embrasser] [I]] [$_{VP}$ souvent [$_{VP}$ t$_{[V [embrasser] [I]]}$ Marie . . .

If the corrective measure of LF-raising is available in French, there appears to be no reason why (9a) should not be assigned the legitimate derivation in (9b&c). An account of why lowering is excluded in French must therefore ensure that the derivation outlined in (9) is not possible.

To exclude the derivation in (9), Chomsky (1991c) suggests a condition on derivations called the **Least Effort Condition**, understood as part of an overarching principle of **economy of derivation**. The interpretation of this condition relevant to the present discussion is that 'shorter derivations are always chosen over longer ones.' In a situation where more than one derivation are possible for a given sentence, the one which involves less movement steps is chosen over the others. Recall that the acceptable version of (9a), reproduced in (10), is derived by overt V-raising, French Agr$_S$ being transparent:

10a. Jean   embrasse   souvent   Marie.
    Jean   kisses   often   Marie

10b. SS: [$_{IP}$ Jean [$_{I'}$ [$_V$ embrasser] I [$_{VP}$ souvent [$_{VP}$ t$_{embrasser}$ Marie . . .

The chain derived by overt V-raising is well-formed, and therefore no corrective covert V-raising is required in the derivation of (10). In contrast, the derivation of (9) with a well-formed chain requires a corrective V-raising process, shown in (9c), and therefore involves one extra movement step. For this reason, the derivation in (9) is excluded by the Least Effort Condition in favour of the derivation for the same example, shown in (10), which involves overt V-raising and no subsequent corrective covert raising.

On a more general level, a derivation which involves overt lowering inevitably involves subsequent covert raising, whereas a derivation which involves overt raising does not. Thus, if overt V-raising is possible, as is generally the case in French, any alternative derivation which involves overt I-lowering, and therefore subsequent covert raising, will be excluded in favour of one which involves legitimate overt raising.

According to the analysis outlined, the parametric difference between English-type languages, sometimes called 'lowering languages', and French-type languages, sometimes called 'raising languages', reduces to a difference in the properties of Agr$_S$. Because English Agr$_S$ is opaque, main verbs cannot move to it, and because French Agr$_S$ is transparent main verbs can move to it. On the other hand, because main verbs in French can move to I overtly, they have to do so by the Least Effort Condition. The alternative derivation which makes use of overt lowering would involve more steps.

Following Belletti (1990), Chomsky (1991c) uses the terms 'weak' (instead of 'opaque') for the English Agr$_S$, and the term 'strong' (instead of 'transparent') for the French Agr$_S$. The reason these terms are applied to Agr$_S$ rather than I will become clear later on. The terms 'strong' and 'weak' will figure prominently in this chapter as well as in Part IV of this book. Arguments based on economy of derivation will also figure prominently in the remainder of this book.

16.1.2 Auxiliary verbs

Although English and French differ with respect to main verbs, they are similar as far as auxiliary verbs are concerned. Both languages allow overt V-raising with auxiliary verbs in finite clauses, as shown in (11) and (12):

11a. John has completely lost his mind.
11b. [$_{IP}$ John [$_{I'}$ [$_V$ have] I [$_{VP}$ completely [$_{VP}$ t$_{[have]}$ lost his mind . . .

12a. Jean a   complètement perdu la tête.
     Jean has   completely   lost   the head

12b. [$_{IP}$ Jean [$_{I'}$ [$_V$ avoir] I [$_{VP}$ complètement [$_{VP}$ t$_{[avoir]}$ perdu la tête . . .

English and French also resemble each other in that they both exclude overt I-lowering with auxiliary verbs in finite clauses, as shown in (13) and (14):

13a. *John completely has lost his mind.
13b. *[$_{IP}$ John [$_{I'}$ t$_{[I]}$ [$_{VP}$ completely [$_{VP}$ [$_V$ [have] [I]] lost his mind . . .

14a. *Jean complètement a   perdu la tête.
     Jean completely   has lost   the head

14b. *[$_{IP}$ Jean [$_{I'}$ t$_{[I]}$ [$_{VP}$ complètement [$_{VP}$ [$_V$ [$_V$ avoir] [I]] perdu la tête . . .

The similarity in behaviour between English and French auxiliary verbs illustrated in (11&12) and (13&14) follows from the analysis developed on the basis of main verbs. In (11), overt raising of the auxiliary verb to I results in the derivation of a complex I where the auxiliary verb is confined. Recall that English Agr$_S$ is opaque, arguably by virtue of being weak. However, because auxiliary verbs do not assign θ-roles (they do not take arguments), their confinement inside the English opaque Agr$_S$ does not give rise to a violation of the θ-Criterion. This is precisely the reason auxiliary verbs can move to I in English, contrary to main verbs. What remains to be explained is why example (13) is excluded, that is why overt I-lowering is not possible with auxiliary verbs in English. We will come back to this point below. Let us now discuss parallel examples in French.

Not much needs to be said about the derivation of the French example (12). Recall that French Agr$_S$ is transparent anyway. Given that even a main verb can overtly raise to it, it is not surprising that auxiliary verbs can too. The explanation for why overt I-lowering is excluded with auxiliary verbs in French, as shown in (14), must be the same as the explanation for why the same process is excluded in English.

As a matter of fact, the explanation for why overt I-lowering is excluded with auxiliary verbs in English and French must be the same as the explanation for why overt I-lowering is excluded with main verbs in French outlined above. All three contexts involve a situation where overt V-raising is obligatory by virtue of being possible. Thus, (13) and (14) are excluded by the Least Effort Condition. Their derivation involves an unnecessary extra step. Recall that overt I-lowering leads to a situation where covert V-raising becomes necessary as a corrective measure to ensure that the representation satisfies ECP at LF.

16.2 *Neg Phrase*

16.2.1 Negation in English

Consider (15), (16) and (17):

15a John does not like his teacher.
15b. [IP John [I′ [do] I [NEG not] [VP like his teacher . . .

16a. *John not likes his teacher.
16b. *[IP John [I tI [NEG not] [VP [V [like] [I]] his teacher . . .

17a. *John likes not his teacher.
17b. *[IP John [I′ [V like] [NEG not] [VP [V tlike] his teacher . . .

These examples illustrate the fact that Neg forces *do*-support with main verbs (Chapter 5). Somehow, Neg prevents I from merging with the verb, a fact we have yet to explain. Neg appears to prevent I from merging with the verb irrespective of whether I is assumed to lower to V, as in (16), or V is assumed to raise to I, as in (17). Both processes appear to be excluded in negative sentences. Only the application of *do*-support appears to derive an acceptable sentence, as shown in (15).

Note that while (17) can be said to be independently excluded by the fact that main verbs cannot raise overtly to I anyway it is not clear why (16), where I lowers to V, should be excluded. The ill-formed chain that results from overt I-lowering could in principle be corrected by subsequent covert raising of [V [V] [I]] to I at LF, as in the derivation of affirmative sentences with a main verb discussed in the previous section. It seems as though the covert raising of [V [V] [I]] to I is blocked in negative sentences for some reason.

So far, we have been assuming that Neg is base-generated under I, along with Agr₅ and Tense. However, it is not clear whether *not* is an inflectional category of the same order as Agr₅ and Tense. From a morphophonological point of view, *not* (at least in its non-contracted form) is an autonomous category, not dependent on a verb in the manner Agr₅ and Tense are. The strongest evidence for the independence of Neg, however, relates to its syntactic behaviour. Pollock (1989) argues that the blocking effect that Neg has on the process which merges I with the main verb is best explained by assuming that Neg is an independent category which projects its own X-bar structure NegP, separate from that of I. Given that Neg superficially appears intervening between the I elements (Agr₅ and Tense) supported by *do*-support and the main verb, NegP is located between I and VP in the sentence structure. This is shown in (18):

18.

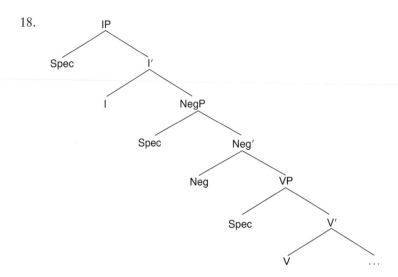

How does the revised structure of negative sentences in (18) explain the fact that Neg blocks merger between I and the main verb in English? Recall that in affirmative sentences, I merges with the main verb via overt I-lowering to V. Recall also that this lowering movement creates an ill-formed chain which is subsequently corrected by raising the complex [$_V$ [V] [I]] to I at LF. Applying this derivation to the DS representation of a negative sentence yields the unacceptable sentence shown in (19d):

19a. DS: [$_{IP}$ John [$_{I'}$ I [$_{NegP}$ [$_{Neg'}$ not [$_{VP}$ like his teacher . . .

19b. SS: *[$_{IP}$ John [$_{I'}$ t$_I$ [$_{NegP}$ [$_{Neg'}$ not [$_{VP}$ [$_V$ [$_V$ like] [I]] his teacher . . .

19c. LF: *[$_{IP}$ John [$_{I'}$ [$_V$ [$_V$ like] [I]] [$_{NegP}$ [$_{Neg'}$ not [$_{VP}$ t$_{[V\ [V\ like]\ [I]]}$ his teacher. . .

19d. *John not likes his teachers.

Recall that (19d) is the sentence that raises a problem for the analysis outlined in the previous section for sentences with a main verb. If covert raising of [$_V$ [V] [I]] is available in principle, as it is in affirmative sentences with a main verb, there is no reason why (19d) should be excluded. The conclusion reached above is that for some reason the corrective covert raising of [$_V$ [V] [I]] (back) to I appears to be blocked in negative sentences though not in affirmative sentences. The reason it is blocked in negative sentences is now made explicit in the LF representation (19c). Raising of [$_V$ [V] [I]] to I skips over the intervening head category Neg, a violation of the HMC. Neg creates a Minimality effect that prevents the raised [$_V$ [V] [I]] from antecedent governing its trace inside VP (Chapter 10). Because affirmative sentences do not include Neg or any other intervening head between V and I, covert raising of [$_V$ [V] [I]] is not blocked and therefore possible.

The reasons which exclude covert raising of [$_V$ [V] [I]] involved in the derivation of (16/19d) also exclude overt V-raising across Neg involved in the derivation of (17). The latter is reproduced in (20) with a structure that includes Neg as a separate category. V-raising across Neg gives rise to an HMC/ECP violation and therefore is excluded, although (20) is also independently excluded by whatever excludes overt V-raising to I in English in general:

20a. *John likes not his teacher.
20b. *[IP John [I' [V like] I [NegP [Neg' not [VP [V t_like] his teacher . . .

In view of the fact that neither overt I-lowering followed by covert raising nor overt V-raising to I are possible in negative sentences with a main verb, English makes use of *do*-support to salvage negative sentences with a main verb. *Do*-support is a language-specific rule used as a last resort strategy to save negative sentences which cannot otherwise be derived by UG-determined processes such as head-movement. According to Chomsky (1991c), the use of language-specific rules such as *do*-support is subject to economy conditions such that they apply only if UG-determined processes such as head-movement are blocked. This particular view of language-specific rules makes it possible to rule out sentences such as (20) with a non-emphatic reading. Because non-emphatic affirmative sentences such as *John likes his teacher* can be derived in terms of head-movement processes, as we have seen, the application of *do*-support in the derivation of (21) is excluded by economy considerations:

21a. *John does like his teacher.
21b. *[IP John [I' [do] I [VP like his teacher . . . .

16.2.2 Negation in French

In Standard French finite clauses, sentence negation is marked with two element *ne* and *pas*. The former appears preceding the finite verb and the latter following the finite verb. In Colloquial French, the preverbal negation element *ne* tends to be dropped in finite clauses, leaving the postverbal negation element *pas* as the only marker of sentence negation. This is shown in (22a):

22a. Les enfants   (n')aiment   pas   Jean.
      the children   like   not   Jean

22b. *Les enfants   pas   aiment   Jean.
      the children   not   like   Jean

Presumably, French negative sentences involve overt V-raising in their derivation just like affirmative sentences. V-raising to I is the process responsible for placing the finite verb before *pas* in (22a). This is confirmed by the fact shown in (22b) that negative sentences which involve overt I-lowering are excluded, on a par with affirmative sentences.

(22a) appears to raise a problem for the analysis of English negative sentences outlined in the previous section. If Neg projects its own X-bar structure in French as it does in English, V-raising across *pas* is expected to give rise to an HMC/ECP violation. Recall that a similar derivation for English negative sentences was excluded above on the basis of HMC/ECP. (22a) appears to give the impression that for some reason French Neg does not block V-raising across it, unlike English

Neg. To explain why, we need first examine the order of the verb with respect to Neg and VP-adverbs in French non-finite clauses.

In French non-finite negative clauses both Neg elements appear preceding the verb as shown in (23a). The pattern whereby the verb precedes *pas* typical of finite clauses is actually excluded in non-finite clauses, as shown in (23b). Non-finite clauses also differ in that they allow the dropping of *ne* with more difficulty than finite clauses in Colloquial French, although we will have nothing to say about this property here:

23a. Ne pas paraître   triste . . .
     not   to-appear   sad

23b. *Ne paraître   pas   triste . . .
     not to-appear   not   sad

(23a&b) appear to suggest that the verb does not raise overtly in French non-finite clauses, contrary to the situation found in finite clauses. However, the order of the non-finite verb in relation to the VP-adverb in (24) seems to suggest otherwise. Recall that the order [V ADV] usually implies that the verb has raised out of of VP across the VP-adjoined adverb, as shown in (24b). The landing site of the raised verb is represented as X in (24b), pending identification of its exact nature:

24a. Paraître   souvent   triste . . .
     to-appear   often   sad

24b. $[_{IP}$ e $[_{I'}$ I $[_{XP}$ $[_V$ paraître] X $[_{VP}$ $[_{ADV}$ souvent] $[_{VP}$ t$_{paraître}$ triste . . .

Pollock (1989) argues that the paradox raised by (23) and (24) together is only apparent. The apparent paradox reveals the existence in the structure of the sentence of an additional position which is lower than Neg, as suggested by the order [Neg V] in (23a), and higher than VP, as suggested by the order [V ADV] in (24). Pollock identifies the position in question as Agr which Chomsky (1991c) suggests is Agr$_O$ rather than Agr$_S$. Accordingly, French non-finite negative clauses have the representation shown in (25b). The order of constituents in this representation is confirmed by examples such as (25a). V-raising to Agr$_O$ is sometimes called 'short verb movement':

25a. Ne pas paraître   souvent   triste . . .
     not   appear   often   sad

25b. $[_{IP}$ PRO I $[_{NegP}$ ne pas $[_{Agr_OP}$ $[_V$ paraître] Agr$_O$ $[_{VP}$ souvent $[_{VP}$ t$_{[V\ paraître]}$ triste . . .

Before we move on to explain how the conclusion about the structure of the clause outlined in (25) makes it possible to explain why the verb is able to raise across *pas* in French finite clauses, a word about the idea that the structure of the clause includes Agr$_O$. We saw in Chapter 11 that there are languages, e.g. Chichewa, which have overt Agr$_O$, just as there are languages, e.g. Italian, which have overt Agr$_S$. The existence of overt subject agreement in some languages is often used to justify the idea that languages with poor or no subject agreement inflection such as English have an abstract version of Agr_S. The argument extends to Agr_O in a natural way. The existence of overt Agr_O in some languages can be used to justify the existence of an abstract version of it in languages that lack overt object agreement inflection.

Chomsky (1991c) argues that as far as French is concerned, there is independent evidence for an Agr_O. The evidence is based on data having to do with participle agreement in French discussed in Kayne (1987) and illustrated in (26a&b):

26a. Paul les   a repeintes.
      Paul them(f.pl) has repainted(f.pl)

26b. **Combien de tables**   Paul a repeintes?
      how-many of tables(f.pl) Paul has repainted(f.pl)

In (26a) the participle agrees with the preposed direct object clitic pronoun in number and gender. In (26b) the participle agrees with the moved direct object wh-phrase also in number and gender. If this type of agreement is the same type of agreement between Agr_O and the direct object in languages such as Chichewa, then it represents overt evidence for the existence of Agr_O in the structure of French sentences.

Let us now go back to the question why the verb appears to be able to move across Neg to I without giving rise to an HMC/ECP violation in French finite clauses. The relevant example is reproduced in (27a) together with a representation which includes NegP and Agr_OP:

27a. Marie aime pas Jean.
      Marie likes not Jean

27b. SS: *$[_{IP}$ Marie $[_{I'}$ $[_{Agr_O}$ $[_V$ aimer] $Agr_O]$ I $[_{NegP}$ pas $[_{Agr_OP}$ $t_{[AgrO\ [V]\ AgrO]}$ $[_{VP}$ $t_{[V]}$ Jean . . .

27c LF: $[_{IP}$ Marie $[_{I'}$ $[_{Agr_O}$ $[_V$ aimer] $Agr_O]$ I $[_{NegP}$ pas $[_{Agr_OP}$ $[_{VP}$ $t_{[V]}$ Jean . . .

Chomsky's (1991c) explanation of (27a) rests on two crucial assumptions concerning the nature of traces and their relevance at LF. First, traces have the categorial identity of their antecedent. The trace of V is V represented as $t_{[V]}$, the trace of Agr_O is Agr_O represented as $t_{[AgrO]}$, and so on. In situations where the moved category is a complex head such as $[_{Agr_O}$ $[V]$ $Agr_O]$ in (27b), its trace has the categorial identity Agr_O as shown in (27b). Recall that the category of a complex head derived by head-adjunction is determined by the host category. This means that verb-movement to Agr_O in (27b) results in the derivation of a complex Agr_O category. The second assumption is that traces of categories that do not play a role in the interpretation of the sentence at LF are deletable while traces of categories that play a role in the interpretation of the sentence are not. The trace of a verb is not deletable at LF because obviously the verb plays a role in interpretation. In contrast, the trace of Agr_O is deletable at LF on the grounds that Agr_O does not play a role in interpretation. This is the reason the trace $t_{[AgrO\ [V]+AgrO]}$ is missing in the LF representation (27c).

The SS representation (27b) involves an offending trace, namely $t_{[AgrO\ [V]+AgrO]}$. The latter arises as a result of raising of the complex head $[_{Agr_O}$ [V] $Agr_O]$ to I across the intervening head Neg. Neg creates a Minimality effect which prevents the complex head $[_{Agr_O}$ [V] $Agr_O]$ situated under I from antecedent-governing its trace under Agr_O. Chomsky (1991c) suggests that this representation can be corrected by deletion of the offending trace $t_{[AgrO\ [V]+AgrO]}$ on the grounds that it does not play a role in interpretation. This deletion results in the derivation of the LF representation (27c) consistent with the ECP. The verb trace $t_{[V]}$ inside VP in (27c) satisfies the ECP in terms of the mechanism of γ-marking (Chapter 10), whereby it is assigned the feature $[+\gamma]$ under antecedent-government by $t_{[AgrO\ [V]+AgrO]}$. Presumably, γ-marking applies prior to deletion of $t_{[AgrO\ [V]+AgrO]}$ at LF.

As is often the case in comparative work, resolving a problem in one language raises a question with respect to the other language. The question that has to be answered now is: Why can't the same mechanism of trace-deletion be applied to salvage the derivation of English negative sentences such as (28a)?

28a. *Mary not likes John.
28b. SS: *$[_{IP}$ Mary $[_{I'}$ $t_{[I]}$ $[_{NegP}$ not $[_{Agr_OP}$ Agr_O $[_{VP}$ $[_V$ $[_V$ like] [I]] John . . .
28c. LF: $[_{IP}$ Mary $[_{I'}$ $[_{Agr_O}$ $[_V$ like] $Agr_O]$ I $[_{NegP}$ not $[_{Agr_OP}$ $t_{[AgrO]}$ $[_{VP}$ t_v John . . .

(28a) has the SS and LF representations shown in (28b) and (28c) which include Agr_OP. (28c) includes an offending trace in exactly the same position as the LF representation of the French example (27), namely $t_{[AgrO\ [V]\ AgrO]}$ under Agr_O. If this offending trace is deletable at the LF representation of the English example (28), as it is in the LF representation of the French example (27), there is no reason why (28a) should be excluded.

The answer to the question raised relies on yet another stipulation relating to a difference between overt V-raising and covert V-raising to Agr_O. The idea is that while overt V-raising to Agr_O is an adjunction movement, covert V-raising to Agr_O is a substitution movement. This means that covert V-raising to Agr_O and subsequently to I in (28) leaves a trace under Agr_O which is of type $t_{[V]}$ rather than type $t_{[AgrO]}$. Accordingly, (28a) has the LF-representation shown in (29c), where the trace under Agr_O is of type $t_{[V]}$:

29a. *Mary not likes John.
29b. SS: *$[_{IP}$ Mary $[_{I'}$ $t_{[I]}$ $[_{NegP}$ not $[_{Agr_OP}$ Agr_O $[_{VP}$ $[_V$ $[_V$ like] [I]] John . . .
29c. LF: *$[_{IP}$ Mary $[_{I'}$ $[_{Agr_O}$ $[_V$ like] $Agr_O]$ $[_{NegP}$ not $[_{Agr_OP}$ $t_{[V]}$ $[_{VP}$ t_v John . . .

Now, traces of the type $t_{[V]}$ are not deletable at LF as claimed above. This is the reason (29a) with the LF representation in (29c) is not rescuable by the mechanism of trace-deletion. The offending trace under Agr_O is not deletable and therefore remains in violation of the ECP.

16.3 *Agr$_S$, Agr$_O$ and structural Case*

16.3.1 Agr$_S$, Tense and nominative Case

The move to dissociate Neg from I and assign it the status of a head category in its own right removes one of the major anomalies of the I category with respect to the principles of X-bar theory. In the previous structure of the sentence, the 'dual headedness' of I, as dominating inflectional categories as well as non-inflectional ones, was inconsistent with the one-to-one relation between categories and projections implicit in X-bar theory. However, it is important to bear in mind that the main reasons for dissociating Neg from I were empirical in nature in the form of evidence which shows that Neg behaves syntactically like an independent head category rather than as a member of the category I. Similarly, the postulation of an Agr$_O$ category which projects its own X-bar structure was motivated on empirical grounds having to do with 'short movement' in French non-finite clauses supported with evidence from participle agreement.

The structure of the sentence that has emerged from these major revisions is one where I dominates Agr$_S$ and Tense only. However, it could be argued that the 'dual headedness' problem is not entirely eliminated as I still dominates two arguably distinct categories, Agr$_S$ and Tense. The logic of the argument of dismantling I, sometimes referred to as the **Split Infl Hypothesis**, seems to lead to the conclusion that Agr$_S$ and Tense are probably also independent categories each of which projects its own X-bar structure. Agr$_S$ heads a maximal projection of its own (Agr$_S$P) and Tense heads a maximal projection of its own (T(ense)P). Accepting the logic of the argument, the question arises as to how these two categories are ordered with respect to each other: Is Agr$_S$ higher than T or vice versa?

Belletti (1990) argues that the order of the inflectional elements corresponding to Agr$_S$ and T in Italian finite clauses such as (30a&b), where Agr$_S$ is outside T, suggests that Agr$_S$ is higher than T:

30a. Legg-eva-no.
    read-T(imperfect)-Agr$_S$(1PL)
    'They read.'

30b. Parl-er-o.
    speak-T(future)-Agr$_S$(1S)
    'I will speak.'

In (30a&b), the inflectional morpheme corresponding to T is closer to the verb root than the inflectional morpheme corresponding to Agr$_S$. This suggests that the verb first adjoins to T forming with it the complex [[V] T] which then adjoins to Agr$_S$ to derive the surface complex [[[V] T] Agr$_S$]. By virtue of HMC, which prevents a head from moving across another head, the fact that V adjoins to T first implies that T is lower than Agr$_S$. According to this evidence, the structure of the sentence looks as in (31) with Agr$_S$ higher than T:

31.

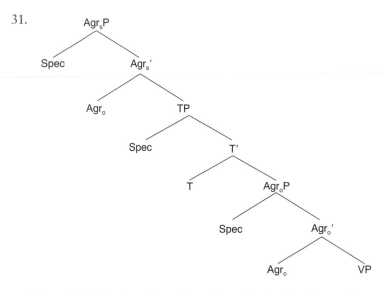

Although (31) is based on the order of inflectional morphemes in Italian, it is plausible to assume that it generalises to other languages, at least those of the same typological group as Italian. Spec,AgrsP is the canonical subject position where the subject is in a Spec-head agreement relation with Agrs. A running theme in the linguistics tradition associated with languages such as English is that nominative Case is dependent not just on Agrs (subject agreement) but also on T (tense). Nominative subjects are only found in finite clauses which include both Agrs and T. Subjects of non-finite clauses usually do not bear nominative Case. They can bear accusative Case assigned by an ECM verb or oblique Case assigned by a preposi-tional complementiser (Chapter 8). To capture this fact, Chomsky (1991c) suggests that nominative Case is assigned to the subject vial Spec-head agreement with the complex $[_{Agr_S} [T] Agr_S]$, that is a complex which includes T as well as Agrs. Agrs encodes the ϕ-features and T the nominative Case feature. The complex $[_{Agr_S} [T]$ Agrs] is derived by head-raising of T to Agrs in English.

16.3.2   Agr$_O$, V and accusative Case

In Chapter 8, a distinction was made between two types of Case, inherent and structural. Inherent Case is determined at DS and involves a thematic relationship between the assigner and the assignee. Structural Case, on the other hand, is determined at SS or LF and does not necessarily involve a thematic relationship between the assigner and the assignee. The typical examples of structural Case are nominative and accusative. Restricting ourselves to these Cases, nominative was said to be assigned under Spec-head agreement with I and accusative under government by a transitive verb. It is desirable to have a unified approach to structural Case such that all structural Cases are assigned under the same condi-tion. This unified approach was not possible in the context of the previous structure of the sentence as it did not include an Agr$_O$ category parallel to the Agr$_S$ category. However, now that the structure of the sentence has been revised to include an Agr_O category, accusative Case can be said to be assigned under Spec-head agreement with Agr_O. The consequence is that structural Case basically reflects a Spec-head agreement relation between the categories involved.

As with nominative Case, accusative Case can also be said to be assigned under Spec-head agreement with a complex Agr_O category which includes the verb, that is, a complex of the form $[_{Agr_O} [V] Agr_O]$. Accusative marked DPs agree with Agr_O in ϕ-features and with V in accusative Case feature. This scenario preserves the traditional idea that transitive verbs play a role in accusative Case-assignment. The complex $[_{Agr_O} [V] Agr_O]$ is presumably derived by V-raising to Agr_O, which in English does not apply till LF. Movement of the direct object DP to Spec,Agr_OP also does not apply till LF in English. If the direct object moved overtly to Spec,Agr_OP, English sentences would be expected to exhibit the OV order rather than the VO order. The implication is that Case relations are determined at LF rather than at SS.

One other important implication of the idea that accusative Case is determined at Spec,Agr_OP via Spec-head agreement with $[_{Agr_O} [V] Agr_O]$ is that a Raising to Object analysis for ECM constructions such as (32) becomes possible:

32a. John believes Bill to be intelligent.

32b. John believes [$_{IP}$ Bill to be intelligent]

32c. LF: [$_{IP}$ John [$_{I'}$ [$_V$ believes] [$_{Agr_O P}$ Bill [$_{Agr_O'}$ $t_{believes}$ [$_{VP}$ $t_{believes}$ [$_{IP}$ t_{Bill} . . .

In Chapters 7 and 8 ECM sentences such as (32a) were said to have the representation shown in (32b). The direct object-like properties of the ECM subject are due to the fact that it is governed and assigned Case by the root verb. A Raising to Object analysis was excluded on the grounds that it would require a base-generated direct object position in the root clause for the ECM DP to move to. Since a base-generated direct object position is θ-marked by definition, Raising to Object is inconsistent with the θ-Criterion. However, this argument no longer holds in a structure where the target of Raising to Object is Spec,Agr_OP, a non-θ-marked position. In the context of the theory of structural Case outlined here, the ECM DP actually has to raise to Spec,Agr_OP in the root clause for its Case properties to be determined. Raising to Object becomes necessary.

Presumably, Raising to Object (where Object is Spec,Agr_OP) applies covertly at LF for the same reason that movement of direct objects in general was said above to apply at LF. If the ECM DP raises overtly with the verb remaining inside VP, the wrong order will be derived. There seems to be a correlation between movement of objects to Spec,Agr_OP and V-raising such as that they either apply together or do not apply together. We turn to this correlation in the next section.

16.4 *Object Shift in Continental Germanic*

Consider example (33) from Danish (Vikner 1991). Bear in mind that Danish is a Verb Second VO language:

33a. Peter købte **den** ikke.
     Peter bought it not
     'Peter did not buy it.'

33b. Peter købte **den** [VP ikke [VP t$_{købte}$ · · · t$_{den}$ · · ·

The finite verb moves out of VP to C. As a result of this movement, the pronominal direct object also moves out of VP to a position just above VP which we will assume here to be Spec,Agr$_O$P. This particular movement is known as **Object Shift**. The analysis of (33) and other examples below on which this presentation is based assumes Neg to be an adverbial element left-adjoined to VP, and is used as a diagnostic for Object Shift. An object that appears to the left of the negation element is assumed to have undergone Object Shift.

With this in mind, compare now (33) to (34) and (35). (34) is a root sentence which includes an auxiliary verb. In this type of sentence, the finite auxiliary raises to C and the main verb remains inside VP, as in German (Chapter 13). (35) includes an embedded clause which lacks the V2 effect, as in German:

34a. Hvorfor har Peter ikke købe **den**?
     why   has Peter not   bought it
     'Why hasn't Peter bought it?

34b. Hvorfor har Peter [VP ikke [VP købe **den** . . .

35a. Det var godt at   Peter ikke købte **den**.
     it   was good that Peter not   bought it
     'It was good that Peter did not buy it.'

35b. Det var godt [CP at [IP Peter [VP ikke [VP købte **den** . . .

(34) and (35) show that when the main verb does not move out of VP, the direct object does not undergo Object Shift either.

The facts of Danish just reviewed confirm that there is a correlation between V-raising and Object Shift. Object Shift applies only when the verb raises out of VP. This generalisation came to be known as **Holmberg's Generalisation** (Holmberg 1986). (36) is the version of it provided in Bobaljik (1995):

36. **Holmberg's Generalisation**

   Object Shift is possible only if the main verb raises out of VP.

The situation in English described in the previous section is consistent with (36). The main verb does not move overtly in English and neither does the direct object. The situation in French, however, is not so clear-cut. We have discussed evidence that the verb moves out of VP in finite clauses and indeed also non-finite clauses. However, the order [SUBJ V ADV OBJ] typical of French finite clauses suggests that the direct object does not move out of VP. However, this situation is not necessarily inconsistent with (36). It does not necessarily follow from (36) that if the verb moves out of VP, the direct object must follow.

16.5   *Summary*

Differences between languages in the order of the verb in relation to VP-adverbs and Neg elements can be accounted for in terms of a parameter relating to the 'strength' and 'weakness' of Agr$_S$. In English-type languages Agr$_S$ is weak and therefore does not attract the verb to it. In French-type languages, Agr$_S$ is strong and consequently attracts the verb to it. Derivations are guided by an overarching principle of economy which has the effect of forcing the choice of economical derivations over less economical ones, where economy is defined in terms of the number of steps involved in the derivation. A closer investigation of the way V-raising interacts with I-elements such as Neg, together with certain theoretical considerations, has led to a major revision of the structure of the sentence. In the revised structure, each of the elements previously thought to belong under I projects its own separate X-bar structure. This view of the clause structure came to be known as the Split Infl Hypothesis.

Exercises

Exercise 16.1

The Pollock–Chomsky analysis outlined in this chapter derives the adjacency requirement on accusative Case-assignment in English discussed in Chapter 8. Part of the evidence for the adjacency requirement on accusative Case assignment in English consisted of examples such as (i–iv), where the complement of the verb is a PP. In such contexts, a VP-adverb can intervene between the verb and its PP complement. Explain whether these examples are problematic for the Pollock–Chomsky analysis outlined in this chapter:

i)   John knocked repeatedly on the door.
ii) Mary waved frantically at Jane.
iii) Bill looked suspiciously at John.
iv) Jane leaned carefully on the wall.

Exercise 16.2

The discussion of negative sentences in this chapter did not include examples with an auxiliary verb. Explain whether the Pollock–Chomsky analysis which assumes NegP extends to the English and French examples in (i–iv):

i)   John has not lost his mind.
ii) John is not at home.
iii) John n'a pas perdu la tête.
     John Neg has not lost the head
iv) Jean n'est pas chez lui.
     Jean Neg is not at home

Exercise 16.3

Examples (i–iv) are from Standard Arabic. The negative sentences (ii–iv) have the peculiar property that T(ense) appears on Neg rather than on the verb, contrary to the situation in non-negative sentences such as (i) where T(ense) appears on the verb. In (ii–iv) the verb is uninflected for T(ense), although it is inflected for Agr$_S$. Benmamoun (1992) explains that this apparently peculiar pattern actually masks a familiar phenomenon, namely the fact that Neg blocks V-raising across it. The reason T(ense) does not appear on the verb is because this would require V-raising to T across Neg, a HMC violation. Benmamoun goes on to explain that an analysis along these lines requires a structure of the sentence where Agr$_S$ is lower than T and Neg. Try to reconstruct the analysis on the basis of the examples and information provided:

i) qara?a   l-tullaab-u   l-kitaab-a.
    read-3S   the-students-NOM   the-book-ACC
    'The students read the book.'

ii) lam   y-aqra?   l-tullaab-u   l-kitaab-a.
    not+PAST   3S-read   the-students-NOM   the-book-ACC
    'The students did not read the book.'

iii) lan   y-aqra?a   l-tullaab-u   l-kitaab-a.
    not+FUT   3S-read   the-students-NOM   the-book-ACC
    'The students will not read the books.'

iv) laa   y-aqra?u   l-tullaab-u   l-kutub-a.
    not+PRES   3S-read   the-students-NOM   the-books-ACC
    'Students don't read books.'

Exercise 16.4

Bobaljik (1995) argues that Holmberg's Generalisation discussed in this chapter fails systematically to hold in OV languages. This is shown in example (i) from Afrikaans, (ii) from Dutch, and (iii) from German. Explain how these examples show that Holmberg's Generalisation does not hold of OV languages. Bear in mind that all three languages are Verb Second languages:

i) Ons   het   al die bier   gister   gedrink.
    we   have   all the beer   yesterday   drunk
    'We drank all the beer yesterday.'

ii) . . . dat   veel mensen   dat boek   gistern   gekocht hebben.
    . . . that   many people   that book   yesterday   bought have
    . . . 'that many people bought the book yesterday'

iii) . . . dass   viele Leute   die Zeitung   ganz   gelesen   haben.
    . . . that   many people   the article   completely   read   have
    . . . 'that many people have completely read the article'

Exercise 16.5

The French examples in (ia&b) and Italian examples in (iia&b) were cited in Chapter 15 as evidence for Kayne's (1989) argument that syntactic cliticisation is an instance of head-movement. Explain whether the conclusion reached in this chapter that Neg projects its own X-bar structure enhances this argument or weakens it:

i) a. Jean   ne   **les**   voit   pas.
    Jean   not   them   sees   not

i) b. *Jean   **les**   ne   voit   pas.
     Jean   them   not   sees   not

ii) a. Gianni vuole   non   veder**li**.
     Gianni wants   not   to-see-them

ii) b. *Gianni   **li**   vuole   non vedere.
      Gianni   them   wants   not to-see

Part IV
Minimalism

17 Minimalist Program

Contents

17.1 *Levels of representation*

The Principles and Parameters framework outlined in Parts II and III of this book postulated three levels of syntactic representation, DS, SS and LF, in addition to PF. LF and PF are external interface levels, the former relates to the conceptual-intentional system and the latter to the articulatory-perceptual system. DS is a kind of internal interface level which links syntax to the lexicon. There is a sense in which the interface levels LF and PF are independently needed and therefore should be assumed by any theory of language. This is not so for DS and SS which are arguably theoretical artefacts set up on the basis of theory internal evidence. DS is the level where the Projection Principle and the θ-Criterion apply, and SS is the level where various modules are said to apply such as Binding theory, Case theory, the *pro* module. A minimalist theory of language, that is a theory which tries to minimise the theoretical machinery needed as much as possible, should therefore seek to eliminate DS and SS. The challenge then is to develop an alternative system which relies solely on the necessary interface levels LF and PF and at the same time accounts in a non-costly way for the phenomena that were thought previously to apply at DS and SS.

In addition to the fact that the evidence for DS and SS is largely theory internal, the postulation of at least DS raises some serious internal problems. One such problem was identified in Chapter 7 having to do with the tension created by the requirements of the Projection Principle and the θ-Criterion in relation to operators. Among other things, the θ-Criterion regulates the representation of the thematic structure of lexical items. The thematic structure of lexical items is a lexical property which therefore falls under the scope of the Projection Principle. The latter requires that lexical properties of lexical items must be reflected at all levels of syntactic representation, including DS (Chapter 6). The consequence is that the DS representation of examples such as (1) and (2) includes an operator (a non-argument) in a θ-marked position (Brody 1993):

1a. Who did Mary see?
1b. DS: [Q [Mary saw who . . .

2a. Mary suspects everyone.
2b. DS: [Mary suspects everyone . . .

Another problem is identified and discussed originally in Chomsky (1981) and later in Chomsky (1993). It has to do with **complex adjectival constructions** such as (3):

3a. John is easy to please.
3b. SS: [John$_i$ is easy [Op$_i$ [PRO to please t$_{Op}$ . . .

4a. It is easy to please John.
4b. SS: [It is easy [PRO to please John . . .

(3a) has the SS representation shown in (3b) which includes a null operator coindexed with the subject of the root clause. The subject position of the complex adjectival predicate occupied by *John* at SS is a non-θ-marked position. This is shown in (4) by the fact that it can host an expletive subject. The property of the root subject position as a non-θ-marked position means that *John* cannot appear in it at DS. Non-θ-marked positions (such as the subject position of passives and raising predicates) are empty at DS by definition. DS is said to be a pure representation of thematic structures.

To solve the problem raised by (easy-to-please) constructions such as (3), Chomsky (1981) suggests that the argument *John* is inserted in the course of the derivation (at SS) and assigned a θ-role at LF. However, this account requires the weakening of the notion that DS is a pure representation of thematic structures and moreover leads to the kind of tension described above in relation to examples (1) and (2).

Thus, besides the fact that DS and SS are theory-internal, the postulation of at least DS seems to give rise to empirical problems.

Chomsky (1993) sketches the broad lines of a minimalist system which came to be known as the **Minimalist Program (MP)** (or just **Minimalism**). Its title is an indication of the fact that it is an embryonic system, a programme, rather than a well articulated theory. MP does away with DS and SS and relies solely on the interface levels LF and PF which are necessary by what Chomsky calls 'virtual conceptual necessity.' MP takes language to consist of the lexicon and a **computa-**

tional system (CS). CS selects items from the lexicon and constructs derivations. Each derivation determines a **structural description (SD)**. SD includes a pair of representations, LF and PF, which must satisfy the interface conditions which apply to each one of them. Some of the interface conditions applying at LF are discussed later on in this chapter and in subsequent chapters.

The computation of a derivation proceeds in a deterministic way selecting freely from the lexicon at any stage. At any point in the derivation, an operation called **Spell-Out** may be applied which has the consequence of creating a new dimension for the derivation which leads to the interface level PF. If the ultimate representation reached at PF satisfies the interface conditions of PF, the derivation is said to **converge** at PF. If, on the other hand, it does not meet the interface conditions of PF, the derivation is said to **crash** at PF. At the point of Spell-Out, the computation continues towards LF with the condition that it no longer has access to the lexicon. New lexical items cannot be inserted after Spell-Out, for obvious reasons. If the ultimate representation reached at LF satisfies the interface conditions of LF, the derivation is said to converge at LF, and if it does not satisfy the interface conditions of LF, the derivation is said to crash at LF.

Although most of the major aspects of MP are yet to be presented, it should be clear from this brief presentation that the system does not assume any levels of presentation over and above the interface levels PF and LF. DS and SS disappear. Our next step is to make explicit how the computation constructs derivations, and later on identify some of the major interface conditions that have to be met by derivations at LF.

17.2 *Generalised Transformation and Move α*

It was said above that the derivation selects items from the lexicon up to Spell-Out. Each item is assigned a representation consistent with X-bar theory. The core structures of X-bar theory are the maximal projection, the single bar projection and the head. A selected lexical item assigned an X-bar structure is a kind of small phrase marker. The small phrase markers of selected lexical items are assembled together in the form of a (larger) phrase marker by an operation called **Generalised Transformation (GT)**. The latter has been revived from an earlier stage in the development of Transformational Grammar. In its original form, GT performs a fairly complex operation which consists of more than one step. Here we will adopt a simpler and modified version of it, whereby it has the function of selecting items from the lexicon, assigning them X-bar structures and then merging them together into larger phrase markers. In Chapter 20, this complex operation will be divided into separate simpler operations which are independent of each other. For the moment, note that merger applies from bottom to top for reasons that will become clear later on. GT is said to **extend** SDs.

To illustrate with a concrete example, let us try to trace the derivation of (5a). Recall we are assuming here that X-bar structures assigned to lexical items include all the usual projections. Recall also that derivations apply bottom up:

5a. The boy likes the girl.
5b. [NP [N' girl]]
5c. [DP the [NP girl]]
5d. [VP like [DP the girl]]
5e. [VP [DP the boy] [V' likes [DP the girl]]]
5f. [IP e [I' I [VP [DP the boy] [V' likes [DP the girl]]]]]

GT selects *girl* with the structure *[NP [N' girl]]*, then merges it with the determiner *the* to form the DP *[DP the [NP girl]]*. The latter is then merged with the verb *likes* to form the VP *[VP [V' likes [DP the girl]]]*. The phrase marker of the DP *the boy* is formed as for the DP *the girl* and then merged into Spec,VP. VP is merged with I (understood as a collective term for inflectional categories) to form IP. This leads to the intermediary SD shown in (5f).

Besides GT, computation also makes use of the more familiar operation Move α. While GT deals with the introduction of newly selected items into the derivation, Move α deals with items already in the phrase marker and moves them to another position in the phrase marker. In most of its applications, Move α is essentially a substitution operation. It selects an item, targets a category in the phrase marker and substitutes the selected item into the Spec position of the targeted category leaving a trace behind. Like GT, Move α is also said to extend its target, basically by adding a specifier to it. In derivation (6), Move α selects the [DP *the boy*] in (5f), targets IP and substitutes the selected DP into Spec,IP, deriving the modified SD shown in (6c):

6a. The boy likes the girl.
6b. [IP e [I' I [VP [DP the boy] [V' likes [DP the girl . . .   (GT)
6c. [IP [DP the boy] [I' I [VP t_the boy [V' likes [DP the girl . . . (Move α)

The requirement that both GT and Move α extend their target has two crucial consequences. One consequence has to do with the notion '**strict cycle**' discussed in Chapter 4. This notion subsumes cases which were said to fall under the Cyclicity Condition, but extends to other cases. Let us first start with the more familiar case of adjunct-extraction out of a wh-island illustrated in (7a):

7a. *How does John wonder what Mary fixed?
7b. [CP C [IP John wonder [CP C [IP Mary fixed what . . . how . . .
7c. [CP how C [IP John wonder [CP C [IP Mary fixed what . . . t_how . . . .
7d. [CP how C [IP John wonder [CP what C [IP Mary fixed t_what . . . t_how . . . .

Suppose that in the derivation of (7a) we reach the stage in (7b). We then apply Move α to substitute the adjunct wh-phrase *how* into the root Spec,CP, as in (7c). Later on, we apply Move α again to substitute the wh-phrase *what* into the embedded Spec,CP, as shown in (7d). None of these two movements crosses over an intervening c-commanding wh-phrase, strictly. The first application of Move α affecting the adjunct wh-phrase is legitimate because it extends its target (it applies at the top of the SD). The second application of Move α, however, is not legitimate as it applies to a cycle that has already been completed.

There is an alternative derivation for (7a) which is consistent with the requirement that GT and Move α extend their target. Before merging the embedded CP with the root verb *wonder*, we could apply Move α and substitute *what* into the embedded Spec,CP. Once the root CP is formed, we could apply Move α again and substitute *how* into the root Spec,CP. Both applications of Move α are consistent with the extension requirement. This particular derivation must be excluded by some other condition which mimics the effects of Relativised Minimality in a derivational way. Note that the second application of Move α which substitutes *how* into the root Spec,CP operates across a c-commanding wh-phrase, namely *what* in the embedded Spec,CP. The condition which excludes this particular step is introduced and discussed later on in this chapter. The same reasoning extends to the derivation of examples (8a) and (9a) below.

The extension requirement on GT and Move α also excludes the derivation outlined in (8b-d) for the super-raising example (8a):

8a. *John seems it is certain to be here.
8b. [$_{IP}$ I [$_{VP}$ seems [$_{IP}$ is certain [$_{IP}$ John to be here . . .
8c. [$_{IP}$ John I seems [$_{IP}$ is certain [$_{IP}$ t$_{John}$ to be here . . .   (Move α)
8d. [$_{IP}$ John I seems [$_{IP}$ it is certain [$_{IP}$ t$_{John}$ to be here . . . (GT)

Suppose that in the derivation of (8a) we reach the stage shown in (8b). We could apply Move α to substitute *John* into the subject position of the root clause, as shown in (8c). Later on, we apply GT to introduce the expletive *it* into the subject position of the middle clause, as shown in (8d). The application of Move α is legitimate because it extends the target in the intended sense. The application of GT, however, is not legitimate in the sense explained above in relation to (7). This yields the Relativised Minimality effect in super-raising instances such as (8a), with the proviso that (8a) has a derivation which is consistent with the extension requirement and which must be excluded by some other condition.

Finally, the extension requirement on GT and Move α exclude the derivation outlined in (9b–d) for the HMC example (9a):

9a. *Be John will in his office?
9b. [$_{CP}$ C [$_{IP}$ John I [$_{VP}$ be in his office . . .
9c. [$_{CP}$ be [$_{IP}$ John I [$_{VP}$ t$_{be}$ in his office . . .   (Move α)
9d. [$_{CP}$ be [$_{IP}$ John [$_{I'}$ will [$_{VP}$ t$_{be}$ in his office . . . (GT)

Suppose that in the derivation of (9a) we reach the stage shown in (9b). We apply Move α to raise *be* to C, as shown in (9c). Later on, we apply GT to insert *will*, as shown in (9d). Once again, the application of Move α is legitimate whereas the application of GT is not, yielding the HMC violation.

The second crucial consequence of the requirement that GT and Move α extend their target is that introduction of an item into the complement position of a category is excluded. That is, given a structure such as [X′ X YP] we cannot introduce a new item ZP to form [X′ X YP ZP], irrespective of whether the new item is introduced directly from the lexicon (GT) or via movement (Move α). Such an operation does not meet the requirement of extension. The aspect of this restriction relating to Move α amounts to the exclusion of raising to the complement position of a head. In the Principles and Parameters framework (P&P), this particular process was excluded in terms of a conspiracy between the Projection Principle and the θ-Criterion applying at DS (Chapter 7). Deriving this particular effect of these two principles must therefore be a welcome consequence in a system that does away with DS.

The discussion so far has excluded adjunction structures of the type shown in (10a) (adjunction to a head) and (10b) (adjunction to a maximal projection). It is not clear that adjunction to the single bar projection is needed or even allowed at all:

10a. $[_X$ [Y] X]
10b. $[_{XP}$ [YP] XP]

To the extent that the adjunction structures (10a&b) are licensed by X-bar theory, it should be possible to derive them in terms of both GT and Move α. Adjunction structures derived by GT (i.e. base-generated adjunction structures) are needed for adverbs, adjectives, among other modifying categories (Chapter 6). Adjunction structures derived by Move α are needed for adjunction movements, including head movement (Chapter 6).

Chomsky (1993) points out that adjunction structures do not extend their target in the intended sense. Consequently, they are not subject to the extension requirement. The latter is very much tied to the notion of 'strict cycle' and therefore not relevant to contexts involving adjunction. The implication is that an adjunct can be inserted in a non-cyclical way, that is, it can be merged into a cycle that has already been completed. In Chapter 18, we will discuss a specific situation where this idea seems to give the right result.

17.3   *LF interface conditions*

17.3.1   X-bar theoretic relations

(11) is the core structure defined by X-bar theory:

11. $[_{XP}$ YP $[_{X'}$ X ZP]]

(11) defines two crucial relations of locality. One is the spec-head relation holding between YP and X. The other is the head-complement relation holding between X and ZP. Chomsky (1993) argues that the head-complement relation is 'more fundamental', and that the spec-head relation is a kind of 'elsewhere' relation.

The spec-head relation underlies agreement in φ-features and Case. In Chapter 16 it was concluded that this involves subject agreement as well as object agreement, assuming a (Split Infl) structure of the type illustrated in (12):

12. $[_{CP}$ C $[_{Agr_sP}$ Spec $[_{Agr_s'}$ Agr_s $[_{TP}$ T $[_{Agr_oP}$ Spec $[_{Agr_o'}$ Agr_o $[_{VP}$ . . .

13a. $[_{Agr_S} [T] Agr_S]$
13b. $[_{Agr_O} [V] Agr_O]$

Recall that T plays a role in determining the nominative Case assigned to the subject of finite clauses. T enters into a spec-head relation with the subject as a result of head-movement and adjunction to Agr_S. This process results in the derivation of the complex head (13a) with Agr_S determining agreement in ϕ-features and T agreement in nominative Case. A similar scenario and pattern is involved with respect to (structural) accusative Case. Movement of the verb and its adjunction to Agr_O creates the complex head structure shown in (13b) where Agr_O determines agreement in ϕ-features and V determines accusative Case.

The Spec-head relation between the subject and the complex $[_{Agr_S} [T] Agr_S]$ obtains subsequent to movement of the subject to Spec,Agr_SP, and raising of T to Agr_S. The two processes derive the configuration $[_{Agr_S P} DP_{NOM} [_{Agr_S'} [Agr_S T Agr_S]]]$. On the other hand, the Spec-head relation between the direct object and $[_{Agr_O} [V] Agr_O]$ obtains subsequent to movement of the direct object to Spec,Agr_OP and raising of V to Agr_O. The derived configuration has the form $[_{Agr_O P} DP_{ACC} [_{Agr_O'} [_{Agr_O} V Agr_O]]]$.

(13a&b) are head-adjunction structures which have to be assumed to belong to the core relations allowed by X-bar theory. Head-adjunction defines the relationship head-head. The head-head relation and the spec-head relation define the domains for inflectional morphology. The latter deals with the relationship between an inflectional category and a verb within the head-head adjunction structures derived by raising, as well as with the relationship between an inflected verb and an agreeing subject or object within the spec-head relation.

Chomsky (1993) suggests that the spec-head relation also underlies the agreement relation between a predicate adjective and a noun phrase subject. Although this relationship is abstract in English, it is overt in languages such as French, as shown in (14):

14a. Jean est intelligent.
     Jean is intelligent(M)

14b. Marie est intelligente.
     Marie is intelligent(F)

The relevant part of the structure underlying (14a&b) is as shown in (15):

15. . . . $[_{Agr_A P}$ Spec $[_{Agr_A'}$ Agr$_A$ $[_{AP} [_{DP}$ Jean] $[_{A'} [_A$ intelligent] . . .

A is mnemonic for the set of ϕ-features associated with adjectives. A moves and head-adjoins to Agr_A to derive the complex head structure $[_{Agr_A} [A] Agr_A]$. The DP subject moves to Spec,AP where it enters into a Spec-head relation with the complex head $[_{Agr_A} [A] Agr_A]$. In the complete derivation of (14a&b), the subject moves further up to Spec,Agr_SP.

The licensing of *pro* (see Chapter 12) can also be subsumed under the spec-head relation. In the subject position of finite clauses, *pro* is licensed and identified via a spec-head relation with 'strong' Agr_S incorporating finite T: $[_{Agr_S} [T] Agr_S]$. In the direct object position, *pro* is licensed and identified via a spec-head relation with Agr$_O$ incorporating a designated V*: [$_{Agr_O}$ [V*] Agr$_O$].

Note that some relations which were accounted for in terms of the notion 'head government' in the P&P framework are now subsumed under the spec-head relation. These include the Case relation between a verb and an accusative object, including the relation between a verb and an ECM subject (Chapter 16). They also include the relation between a designated V* and a *pro* object, among others. This fact raises the prospect of eliminating the notion 'head-government' completely. The broader notion of 'government', however, is much more pervasive, playing a role in the relationship between an antecedent and its trace (antecedent government), among others. Antecedent-trace relations are discussed later on in this chapter. Our next step is to discuss X-bar theoretic relations which define domains of heads and head-chains.

17.3.2   Domains

Consider the abstract structure in (16) which involves adjunction to XP, adjunction to the Spec of XP, and adjunction to the head X:

16.

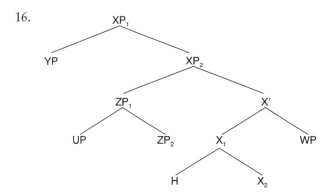

Adjunction to a category is said to lead to the derivation of a category with two **segments**. In (16) XP has two segments, XP$_1$ and XP$_2$. ZP has two segments, ZP$_1$ and ZP$_2$. Finally, X has two segments, X$_1$ and X$_2$.

A category α is said to dominate another category β if every segment of α dominates β. Thus, XP$_2$ dominates all categories in (16) except YP. This is because YP is adjoined to XP$_2$, and therefore is only dominated by one segment of XP. Also, X does not dominate H because one segment of X, namely X$_2$, does not dominate H. A category α is said to **contain** another category β if a segment of α dominates β. Thus, although XP does not dominate YP, XP contains YP, and although X does not dominate H, X contains H.

The **domain** of a head category α is said to include all the categories contained by all segments of all projections of α. The domain of X in (16) therefore includes YP, ZP, UP, WP and H. WP is the **complement domain** or **internal domain** of X which defines the head-complement relation. ZP, UP and YP represent the **checking domain** of X which defines the spec-head relation. It is important to keep in mind that not only the specifier ZP of X can enter into a spec-head relation with X in (16), but also UP (the category adjoined to the specifier of XP) and YP (the category adjoined to the maximal projection of X).

The need for the adjoined category UP in (16) to enter into a spec-head relation with the head X can be seen in the LF representation of English multiple wh-questions such as (17a):

17a. Who bought what?
17b. [$_{CP}$ who [$_{C'}$ [+Q] [$_{IP}$ t$_{who}$ bought what . . .
17c. LF: [$_{CP}$ [$_{Spec}$ what [who]] [$_{C'}$ [+Q] [$_{IP}$ t$_{who}$ bought t$_{what}$ . . .

English multiple questions undergo covert raising of wh-in-situ and adjunction to the wh-phrase already in Spec,CP (Chapters 6 and 10). This is shown in (17c). The covertly moved (second) wh-phrase should be able to check its [+Q] feature against C under the Spec-head relation.

The need for YP adjoined to XP in (16) to enter into a spec-head relation with X would arise from situations where a category adjoined to the XP of X shows an agreement relation with X together with the specifier ZP. These are situations which are sometimes said to involve multiple specifiers claimed to exist in head-final languages such as Japanese (Fukui 1992, 1993).

The domains of X identified above are uniquely defined for X. Even though X contains H in (16), the internal and checking domains of X are not shared by H. H has no internal or checking domain in (16). This is irrespective of whether H is newly introduced from the lexicon (by GT) or moved by Move α. In situations where H is moved by Move α, H can have a domain only by virtue of being a member of the chain which includes it and its trace. In other words, a moved head does not have a domain in its landing site. Only the chain that includes the raised head has domains. Take X in (16) to be Agr$_O$, H the verb raised and adjoined to Agr$_O$, and ZP a non-complex DP direct object as in (18):

18a. . . . [$_{Agr_OP}$ [DP] [$_{Agr_O'}$ [$_{Agr_O}$ [V] Agr$_O$] [$_{VP}$ . . . t$_V$ . . . t$_{DP}$ . . .
18b.

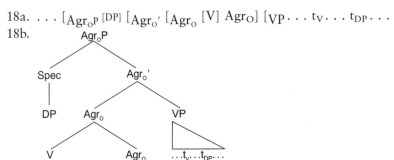

DP will have agreement features by virtue of its checking relation with Agr$_O$, and the Case feature by virtue of its checking relation with the head chain that includes V. DP is within the checking domain of the chain which includes the raised V. Let us now define domains of head-chains.

To define domains of head-chains, Chomsky (1993) uses example (19a) with the partial VP-shell structure shown in (19b) (Chapter 6). V$_2$ moves out of VP$_2$ and adjoins to v_1 in vP$_1$ leaving a trace behind, as shown in (19c):

19a. John put the book on the shelf.
19b. $[_{vP_1} [_{DP_1} \text{John}] [_{v'} v_1 [_{VP_2} [_{DP_2} \text{the book}] [_{v'} [_{v_2} \text{put}] [PP] \dots$
19c.

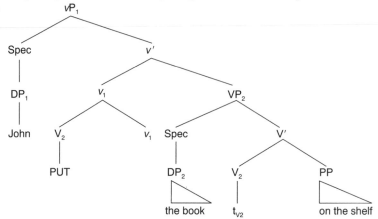

The domain of the chain $\{V_2, t_{V2}\}$ in (19c) is the set of nodes that are contained in vP_1 and which do not contain either V_2 itself or its trace. The set includes DP_1, DP_2 and PP. vP_1 is not in the domain of the chain because it includes V_2 (and its trace), and VP_2 is not in the domain of the chain because it includes the trace of V_2. The internal domain of the chain $\{V_2, t_{V2}\}$ is the set of nodes contained in the complement domain of its host which do not dominate its trace. The complement domain of the host of V_2 is VP_2 which includes DP_2 and PP. VP_2 itself is not in the internal domain of the head chain because VP_2 dominates the trace of V_2. This leaves us with DP_2 and PP as the members of the internal domain of the chain. The checking domain of the head chain $\{V_2, t_{V2}\}$ includes the set of nodes which are external to the host of V_2, namely DP_1 in (19c).

A useful way to think about the basic idea behind domain of a chain is to take V_2 inside VP_2 in (19b) to be a trivial (one member) chain $\{V_2\}$. In (19c) V_2 is a member of a non-trivial chain $\{V_2, t_{V2}\}$. The trivial chain $\{V_2\}$ in (19b) does not include DP_1 in its domain. However, the non-trivial chain $\{V_2, t_2\}$ in (19c), derived by raising of V_2 to V_1, has access to DP_1 in Spec,VP_1.

The definition of domain discussed attempts to achieve two main aims. One is to incorporate the spirit of Baker's (1988) GTC (Chapter 14). The other aim is to explain Holmberg's Generalisation (Chapter 16). Recall that according to this generalisation, a direct object can only move out of VP to Spec,AgroP if the verb also moves out of VP. We turn to this issue in the next section.

17.3.3 Shortest move

(20) and (21) are instances of superiority (Chapter 10):

20a. Whom did John persuade to visit whom?
20b. whom$_1$ did John persuade t_{whom1} [to visit whom$_2$]

21a. *Whom did John persuade whom to visit?
21b. *whom$_2$ did John persuade whom$_1$ [to visit t$_{whom2}$]

(20) involves overt movement of *whom$_1$* from the direct object position of the root verb. (21) involves movement of *whom$_2$* from the direct object position of the embedded verb across *whom$_1$* to the root Spec,CP. Movement of *whom$_1$* in (20) is 'shorter' than movement of *whom$_2$* in (21). Movement of *whom$_1$* in (20) is 'shorter' in the precise technical sense that it does not cross over a c-commanding wh-phrase. In contrast, movement of *whom$_2$* in (21) crosses over a c-commanding wh-phrase, namely *whom$_1$*.

Chomsky (1993) suggests that the movement in (21) can be excluded in terms of a simple condition which he calls the **Shortest Move Condition (SMC)**. Later on we will discuss a more precise version of this condition. For the moment, we will understand SMC to require that a moved category cannot cross over another c-commanding category of the same type. The link between SMC and Relativised Minimality should be obvious. Indeed, Chomsky points that the Relativised Minimality cases discussed above all involve a violation of SMC. The relevant examples are reproduced in (22–24):

22a. *How does John wonder what Mary fixed?
22b. *how$_1$ does John wonder [$_{CP}$ what$_2$ [$_{IP}$ Mary fixed . . . t$_{how1}$ . . .

23a. *John$_1$ seems it$_2$ is certain to be here.
23b. *John$_1$ seems [it$_2$ is certain [t$_{John1}$ to be here . . .

24a. *Be John will in his office?
24b. *[$_{CP}$ [$_{C'}$ Be$_1$ [$_{IP}$ John [$_{I'}$ will$_2$ [$_{VP}$ t$_{be1}$ in his office . . .

In (22), the wh-phrase *how$_1$* has moved across the c-commanding wh-phrase *what$_2$*. In (23), the DP *John$_1$* has moved across the c-commanding DP *it$_2$*. Finally, in (24) the head category *be$_1$* has moved across the c-commanding head category *will$_2$*.

However, there are legitimate derivations which appear to violate SMC, including the derivation of simple sentences such as (25a):

25a. John kicked the ball.
25b. [$_{IP}$ [John] I [$_{AgroP}$ the ball [$_{Agro'}$ kicked [$_{VP}$ t$_{John}$ [$_{V'}$ t$_{kicked}$ t$_{the ball}$ . . .

The subject *John* raises overtly to Spec,IP. The verb raises covertly to Agr$_O$, and ultimately to I. The direct object *the ball* raises covertly to Spec,Agr$_O$P. Movement of the direct object to Spec,Agr$_O$P operates across the Spec,VP position occupied by t$_{John}$. This movement is apparently in violation of SMC. The DP direct object moves across a c-commanding DP specifier.

To explain why the crossing pattern in (25) is possible, Chomsky suggests a precise definition of the notion 'shortest movement' reproduced in (26):

26. If α, β are in the same minimal domain, they are equidistant from γ.

The basic idea is that two positions are equidistant if they are both included in the same minimal domain of a head-chain. Recall from above that raising of the verb to

Agr$_O$ extends the minimal domain of the verbal chain to include Spec,Agr$_O$P. As far as (25b) is concerned, the minimal domain of the chain {kicked, t$_{kicked}$} includes both Spec,VP and Spec,Agr$_O$P. Thus, these two positions are equidistant by virtue of being both included in the minimal domain of the verbal chain. Now, because Spec,Agr$_O$P and Spec,VP are equidistant, Spec,VP is technically not closer to the DP direct object than Spec,Agr$_O$P. Consequently, movement of the DP direct object to Spec,Agr$_O$P in (25b) does not constitute a violation of SMC.

Besides making movement of the direct object to Spec,Agr$_O$P in (25) legitimate as far as SMC is concerned, (26) also derives the effect of Holmberg's Generalisation. The latter and the Danish examples which illustrate it are reproduced here from Chapter 16:

27.   **Holmberg's Generalisation**

Object Shift is possible only if the main verb raises out of VP.

28a.   Peter   købte   **den**   ikke.
       Peter   bought   it   not
       'Peter did not buy it.'

28b.   Hvorfor   har   Peter   ikke   købe   **den?**
       why   has   Peter   not   bought   it
       'Why hasn't Peter bought it?

28c.   *Hvorfor   har   Peter   **den**   ikke   købe.
       why   has   Peter   it   not   bought

Assuming that Object Shift is movement to Spec,Agr$_O$P, (28c) is excluded because movement of the direct object is not accompanied by movement of the main verb out of VP. According to (26), Spec,Agr$_O$P becomes equidistant in relation to the direct object only if the verb moves to Agr$_O$. In (28a), the verb moves out of VP, and consequently the direct object can move to Spec,Agr$_O$P without violating SMC. In (28b&c), however, the main verb does not move out of VP. Consequently, movement of the direct object to Spec,Agr$_O$P will give rise to a violation of SMC, and hence the fact that (28c) is excluded.

17.3.4   Form Chain and Minimal Link Condition

SMC is basically an economy measure. As such it appears to be in conflict with the economy idea discussed in Chapter 16 which favours derivations with fewer steps. SMC gives rise to derivations with many steps in situations of long distance movement. Direct movement in these cases would give rise to fewer steps (one), but it will be inconsistent with SMC. Chomsky argues that this paradox is resolved if Move α is construed as an operation which forms chains called **Form Chain**, instead of as an operation which moves a category in single successive steps. Form Chain applies to a representation such as (29b) in one step and yields the representation shown in (29c) with the chain {John, t', t}:

29a. John seems to be likely to win.

29b. [seems [to be likely [John to win . . .

29c. [John seems [t′$_{John}$ to be likely [t$_{John}$ to win . . .

Since Form Chain does not involve movement steps, the notion 'shortest move' and the SMC it incorporates are restated as 'minimal link' and **Minimal Link Condition (MLC)**. MLC can be understood to mean that given two convergent derivations with the same number of steps, the one that involves shorter links is favoured over the one that involves longer links.

17.4 *Summary*

MP assumes only two levels of representation, the necessary interface levels LF and PF. As such it represents a radical departure from the P&P framework. MP takes language to consist of the lexicon and a computational system. The computational system selects items from the lexicon and constructs derivations that have to meet the interface conditions at LF and PF. Derivations are built in terms of the operation GT which selects items from the lexicon and merges them to form phrase markers, and in terms of Move α which moves a category and merges it with a targeted category in a strictly cyclical way. Among the interface conditions applying at LF are X-bar theoretic relations which define spec-head, head-complement and head-head relations, among others, as well as domains of chains. Move α is understood as an operation which creates a chain subject to MLC. The latter is an economy condition which favours derivations with shorter links.

18 Copy Theory of Movement, and Binding

Contents

18.1 *Copy theory of movement*

In the Principles and Parameters framework outlined in Parts II and III of this book movement was said to leave a trace behind, where trace is construed as an independent category with its own properties. Traces have different properties depending on the nature of their antecedent, that is whether the antecedent is an A-antecedent or an A′-antecedent, among other considerations (Chapters 9 and 10). According to this framework, (1a) has the LF representation shown in (1b), and (2a) the LF representation shown in (2b):

1a. What did John buy?
1b. [what] did John buy [t]

2a. Which book did Mary read?
2b. [which book] did Mary read [t]

Chomsky (1993) suggests replacing the notion 'trace' by the notion 'copy'. Movement of a category leaves a copy of the moved category behind with properties identical to the antecedent. This is known as the 'copy theory of movement', another idea resurrected from an earlier stage of Transformational Grammar. One of the two copies is deleted at PF in terms of some special deletion rules applying to chains at that level. The deleted copy, at least in English, is the (lower) copy in the original position. However, at LF both copies remain on the grounds that they both play a crucial role in interpretation, as we shall see below. According to the copy theory of movement, (1a) will have the LF representation shown in (3b) and the PF representation shown in (3c). (2a), on the other hand, will have the LF representation shown in (4b) and the PF representation shown in (4c):

3a. What did John see?
3b. LF: [what] did John see [what]
3c. PF: [what] did John see

4a. Which book did Mary read?
4b. LF: [which book] did Mary read [which book]
4c. PF: [which book] did Mary read

The copy theory of movement has many advantages some of which are discussed in the sections below. For the moment, note that the LF derivations of (3a) and (4a) shown in (3b) and (4b) are still incomplete. The target is an LF representation which includes an operator–variable link with the operator in the initial scope position and the variable in the argument position. Some rules of interpretation need to apply to the representation to derive the operator–variable link. Concentrating on (4a), the next step towards the derivation of the target representation could be said to involve local movement of the wh-operator to a higher position inside the wh-phrase. This movement leaves a category behind which is interpreted as x, and yields the representation shown in (5a&b). The second step involves deletion of the wh-operator [*which x*] and the restriction *book* from the copy in the argument position, yielding the representation shown in (5c):

5a. [[which x] [x book]]
5b. [[which x] [x book]] Mary read [[which x] [x book]]
5c. [[which x] [x book]] Mary read [x]

The same processes could be applied to (3a). One could assume that *what* has a complex form *wh-at*. The wh-morpheme *wh-* corresponds to the operator, and the morpheme *-at* to the restriction 'thing'. (3a) could then be said to have the derivation shown in (6a&b). The wh-morpheme is moved to a higher position inside the wh-phrase, leaving a variable behind. Later on in this chapter, we will discuss other contexts where the wh-morpheme is assumed to undergo movement alone:

6a. [[wh x] [x thing]]
6b. [[wh x] [x thing]] John bought [[wh x] [x thing]]
6c. [[wh x] [x thing]] John bought [x]

There is another possible derivation for (3a) and (4a) which shares the step shown in (5a) and (6a) and (the inevitable) deletion of the wh-operator from the copy in the argument position, but differs with respect to the instance of the wh-phrase that undergoes deletion of the restriction [*x book*] and [*x thing*]. Suppose that it is the higher instance of the wh-phrase in the operator position which undergoes deletion of the restriction, yielding the representations shown in (7a&b). (7a&b) differ in that the restriction is expressed in-situ rather than in the operator position:

7a. [which x] Mary read [x book]
7a. [wh x] John bought [x thing]

It is an interesting question whether the representations in (5c) and (6c), on the one hand, and the representations in (7a) and (7b), on the other, have two different meanings or are simply notational variants. One could perhaps argue that (5b) is compatible with the answer 'War and Peace', where the variable ranges over the whole phrase. (7a), on the other hand, is compatible with the answer 'THAT book', where the variable ranges over the determiner only. What will become clear later on in this chapter, is that the derivation of the target LF representation sometimes requires deletion of the restriction in the instance of the wh-phrase in the operator position and on other times deletion of the restriction in the copy in the argument position.

18.2   *Reconstruction*

Reconstruction refers to the process whereby an overtly moved wh-phrase is returned to its original position at LF for reasons having to do with interpretation. The archetypal examples of reconstruction usually involve anaphors (BC A) and r-expressions (BC C). However, we will first discuss reconstruction in relation to pied piping of the type illustrated in (8):

8a. (guess) in which house John lived(?)
8b. (guess) [in which house] John lived [t]

Chomsky (1993) observes that the chain which involves the moved PP and its trace in (8) is not an operator–variable construction. The target representation necessary for convergence at LF should have the form shown in (9a) or the form shown in (9b), both of which involve reconstruction of PP:

9a. [[which x] [x house]] John lived [in [x]]
9b. [which x] John lived [in [x house]]

In (9a), the variable x could be said to range over 'houses' and to correspond to a DP. This is suggested by the fact that 'the old one' is a felicitous answer to the question. In (9b), the variable x could be said to range over entities and to correspond to the determiner D. This particular interpretation is as suggested by fact that 'that (house)' is also a felicitous answer to the question.

Reconstruction is a strange process for reasons over and above the fact that it is a lowering process. It is not clear how it leads to the required operator–variable link with the operator in its scope position and the variable in the argument position. Chomsky (1993) argues that reconstruction can be eliminated altogether under the copy theory of movement enriched with the rules of interpretation discussed above. Under the copy theory of movement, (8a) could have either the derivation shown in (10) or the derivation shown in (11). In (10) the restriction is deleted from the copy in the argument position, whereas in (11) the restriction is deleted from the operator position:

10a. [[which x] [x house]] [in [x]]
10b. [[which x] [x house]] John lived [in x]

11a. [[which x] [in [x house]]]
11b. [which x] John lived [in [x house]]

As pointed out above, reconstruction is often associated with examples involving anaphors, pronouns and r-expression, i.e. binding phenomena. (12a) is one such example involving an anaphor:

12a. Which picture of himself did John buy?
12b. SS: [which picture of himself] did John buy [t]
12c. LF: [Q [John bought [which picture of himself]]]

The reflexive anaphor inside the overtly moved wh-phrase has *John* as its antecedent. However, *John* does not c-command the anaphor in (12b). To obtain the right representation at LF, where the anaphor is c-commanded by *John*, the whole wh-phrase is lowered back to the argument position, as shown in (12c). This scenario fits in with the Principles and Parameters framework which assumed SS and LF as separate levels of representation.

Under the copy theory of movement, (12a) will have the LF representation shown in (13d):

13a. Which picture of himself did John buy?
13b. [which picture of himself] did John buy [which picture of himself]
13c. [[which x] [x picture of himself]] did John buy [[which x] [x picture of himself]]
13d. [which x] did John buy [x picture of himself]

Copying of the wh-phrase into the Spec,CP yields the representation shown in (13b). The LF rules of interpretation then apply to assign both copies of the wh-phrase the representation shown in (13c). This is followed by deletion of the restriction from the operator position yielding the targeted representation shown in (13d). In the latter, the reflexive is c-commanded and bound by *John*.

The copy theory of movement has other advantages discussed by Chomsky (1993). One of them relates to the pair (14) and (15), originally discussed in Freidin (1986) and Lebeaux (1988):

14a. Which claim that John was asleep was he willing to discuss?
14b. [which claim [that John was asleep]] was he willing to discuss

15a. Which claim that John made was he willing to discuss?
15b. [which claim [that John made]] was he willing to discuss

(14) and (15) have different interpretations even though they superficially appear to be identical. In (14), the pronoun does not take *John* as its antecedent suggesting that reconstruction is obligatory with this example. Reconstruction will derive an LF representation where the pronoun c-commands *John*, with the consequence that co-indexation between them will give rise to a BC C violation. In (15),

however, the pronoun can take *John* as its antecedent, at least on one reading, suggesting that reconstruction does not take place under the intended reading. If reconstruction did take place under the intended reading, we would have a BC C violation, and consequently fail to explain the fact that the pronoun can take *John* as its antecedent.

The explanation that Chomsky suggests for (14) and (15) is essentially the one outlined in Lebeaux (1988) which relies on the operation GT. The clause inside the wh-phrase is a complement of the noun *claim* in (14), but an adjunct relative clause in (15). The extension condition on GT discussed in Chapter 17 excludes the possibility of introducing the complement clause after wh-movement has applied in (14). The complement clause must be introduced cyclically, i.e. before wh-movement applies. (14a) has the representation shown in (16b) under the copy theory of movement. Both instances of the wh-phrase include the complement clause subsequent to copying of the wh-phrase. This accounts for the observation that (14a) involves obligatory reconstruction, meaning it has an LF representation where the pronoun c-commands *John*:

16a. Which claim that John was asleep was he willing to discuss?
16b. [which claim [that John was asleep]] was he willing
        to discuss [which claim [that John was asleep]]

As for (15a), recall from Chapter 17 that adjunction is not subject to the extension requirement. Adjuncts do not have to be introduced cyclically. They can be introduced non-cyclically, in this case after wh-movement. Consequently, the instance of the wh-phrase in the argument position does not include the relative clause. (15a) has the derivation outlined in (17b&c). (17b) represents the stage before the adjunct relative clause is introduced into the wh-phrase in the operator position. At no stage in the derivation does the pronoun c-command *John*, accounting for the possible coreference relation between them (i.e. lack of reconstruction):

17a. Which claim that John made was he willing to discuss?
17b. [which claim] was he willing to discuss [which claim]
17c. [which claim [that John made]] was he willing to discuss [which claim]

Let us explore this account further. Presumably, (16b) is not the target representation for (16a). The LF rules of interpretation apply to (16b) to derive the intermediate representation shown in (18c):

18a. Which claim that John was asleep was he willing to discuss?
18b. [which claim [that John was asleep]] was he willing
        to discuss [which claim [that John was asleep]]
18c. [[which x] [x claim [that John was asleep]]] was he willing
        to discuss [[which x] [x claim [that John was asleep]]]
18d. [which x] was he willing to discuss [x claim [that John as asleep]]
18e. [[which x] [x claim [that John was asleep]] was he willing to discuss [x]]

Recall that it is possible in principle to delete the restriction from either instance of the wh-phrase. Deleting the restriction from the operator position yields the representation shown in (18d). This representation is consistent with the fact that the pronoun cannot be co-indexed with *John*. The pronoun c-commands *John*. Suppose now we apply the option of deleting the restriction in the argument position, deriving the representation shown in (18e). This particular representation is not consistent with the fact that the pronoun cannot be co-indexed with *John*. The pronoun does not c-command *John*. Thus, it seems that the option of deleting the restriction in the argument position must be excluded for the correct target representation to be uniquely derived. It is not clear what would exclude this option in this particular case. However, later on we will discuss examples where the required option is dictated by independent considerations.

18.3 *Idioms*

Idioms were said in Chapter 7 to be inserted as a single lexical unit at DS. This is the most commonly held view in the P&P framework. Chomsky (1993) suggests that the idiomatic interpretation is actually determined at LF, and moreover requires that the elements which determine the idiomatic interpretation be adjacent at LF. This suggestion potentially faces a problem with situations where a member of the idiomatic expression is overtly displaced by movement. This problem does not arise under the copy theory of movement.

Among the examples that Chomsky discusses in relation to this issue is the one reproduced in (19):

19a. John wondered which picture of himself Bill took.
19b. John wondered [which picture of himself] Bill took [t]

(19) is ambiguous in at least two ways. One involves the antecedent of the reflexive pronoun, and the other idiomatic versus literal meaning of 'take picture'. The reflexive pronoun can have as its antecedent either *John* (the subject of the root clause) or *Bill* (the subject of the embedded clause). On the other hand 'take picture' can either have the idiomatic meaning 'photograph' or the literal meaning 'pick up and walk away with'.

Chomsky observes that there is an interesting correlation between the choice of the antecedent for the reflexive anaphor and the idiomatic versus literal interpretation in (19). In the version where *John* is the antecedent of the reflexive anaphor, the idiomatic interpretation is excluded. In the version where *Bill* is the antecedent of the reflexive anaphor, the idiomatic meaning is possible. Under the copy theory of movement, (19) can either have the representation shown in (20), where the restriction is deleted from the argument position, or (21), where the restriction is deleted from the operator position:

20a. John wondered which picture of himself Bill took.
20b. John wondered [which picture of himself] Bill took [which picture of himself]
20c. John wondered [[which x] [x picture of himself]] Bill took [x]

21a. John wondered which picture of himself Bill took.
21b. John wondered [which picture of himself] Bill took [which picture of himself]
21c. John wondered [which x] Bill took [x picture of himself]

(20c) is the presentation underlying the reading whereby the reflexive anaphor takes *John* as its antecedent. *John* c-commands the reflexive anaphor, but *Bill* does not. (21c) is the representation underlying the reading whereby the reflexive anaphor takes *Bill* as its antecedent. *Bill* is the nearest c-commanding subject to the reflexive anaphor. The correlation between the choice of the antecedent and the idiomatic versus literal meaning also follows from the representations in (20c) and (21c), on the assumption that the idiomatic meaning depends on the constituents of the idiomatic expression being adjacent. In (21c), where *Bill* is the antecedent of the reflexive anaphor, the constituents of the idiomatic expression are adjacent and therefore can give rise to the idiomatic meaning. In (20c), where *John* is the antecedent of the reflexive anaphor, the constituents of the idiomatic expression are not adjacent, thereby making the idiomatic meaning inaccessible.

The analysis extends to (22) which includes a reciprocal anaphor with a potentially ambiguous reference and an idiomatic expression *have attitude*:

22a. The students asked what attitudes about each other the teachers had.
22b. The students asked [what attitudes about each other] the teachers had
      [what attitudes about each other]

The reciprocal can in principle have as its antecedent either the embedded subject *the teachers* or the root subject *the students*. However, only the interpretation whereby the reciprocal anaphor takes the embedded subject as antecedent is available. According to Chomsky, this is tied to the fact that the idiomatic expression *have attitude* is not ambiguous, meaning it does not have an alternative literal meaning. (22) can either have the derivation outlined in (23) or the derivation outlined in (24):

23a. The students asked what attitudes about each other the teachers had.
23b. The students asked [what attitudes about each other] the teachers had
      [attitudes about each other]
23c. The students asked [what x] the teachers had [x attitudes about each other]

24a. The students asked what attitudes about each other the teachers had.
24b. The students asked [what attitudes about each other] the teachers had
      [attitudes about each other].
24c. The students asked [[what x] [x attitudes about each other]] the teachers
      had [x]

(23c) corresponds to the reading whereby the reciprocal anaphor takes *the teachers* as its antecedent. The embedded subject *the teachers* is the nearest c-commanding subject to the reciprocal anaphor. (24c) corresponds to the reading whereby the reciprocal anaphor takes *the students* as its antecedent. The root subject *the students* is the nearest c-commanding subject to the reciprocal anaphor. Only (23c), where the constituents of the idiomatic expression are adjacent, yields an (idiomatic) interpretation. Since the expression *have attitude* does not have an alternative literal meaning, (24c), where the constituents of the idiomatic expression are not adjacent, does not have an interpretation.

18.4   *A-chains*

The discussion so far has been restricted to A'-movement and A'-chains. The question arises as to whether the copy theory of movement extends to A-chains or is only restricted to A'-chains. If the theory does not extend to A-chains, (25a) will have the LF representation shown in (25b) where the object position is occupied by a trace. If, on the other hand, the theory extends to A-chains, (25a) will have the LF representation shown in (26b) where the object position is filled with a copy of the moved DP. At PF, the lower copy of the moved DP is deleted, as shown in (26c):

25a. John was killed.
25b. [John] was killed [t]

26a. John was killed.
26b. LF: [John] was killed [John]
26c. PF: [John] was killed

The situation with A-chains is arguably not as clear as it is with A'-chains. The argument from idioms suggests that the A-movement in sentences with an idiomatic expression such as (27) should leave a copy behind which enters into the idiomatic interpretation under adjacency with the verb:

27a. Several pictures were taken.
27b. [several pictures] were taken [several pictures]

On the other hand, the argument from reconstruction seems to suggest that A-movement does not leave a copy. Reconstruction is often claimed to be a property of A'-chains but not of A-chains. A-moved categories do not appear to reconstruct. Chomsky (1993) illustrates this claim with the example in (28):

28a. The claim that John was asleep seems to him to be correct.
28b. [the claim that John was asleep] seems to him [IP [t] to be correct]

If the raised DP in (28) is allowed to reconstruct, *John* will be c-commanded by the pronoun and a BC C violation is expected to arise. However, the pronoun can have *John* as its antecedent in (28). This suggests that the pronoun does not c-command *John* in the LF representation, which in turn suggests that the A-moved DP does not reconstruct in (28), which in turn suggests that A-movement does not leave a copy behind in (28). Note that there is independent evidence that the pronoun cannot have its antecedent inside the embedded clause in the context illustrated in (28), e.g. *I seem to him to like John* (with the pronoun and *John* having the same reference).

The same conflict is found in complex examples involving both an A'-chain and an A-chain such as (30) compared to (29). (30) includes a passive in the embedded clause which involves A-movement of the wh-phrase to the subject position, followed by A'-movement of the wh-phrase to the embedded Spec,CP:

29a. The students asked which pictures of each other Mary took.
29b. the students asked [which pictures of each other] Mary took
      [which pictures of each other]
29c. the students asked [[which x] [x pictures of each other]] Mary took [x]

30a. The students asked which pictures of each other were taken.
30b. the students asked [CP [which pictures of each other]
      [IP [which pictures of each other] were taken
      [which pictures of each other] . . .
30c. the students asked [CP [which x] [x pictures of each other]] [IP [x] were taken
      [pictures of each other] . . .

(29a) has the (only) representation shown in (29c), where the idiomatic interpretation is not available for the reasons explained in the previous section. In contrast, (30a) has an idiomatic interpretation. This suggests that the A-movement from the object position to the subject position of the embedded passive clause leaves a copy behind, as shown in (30c).

18.5 *Binding theory*

The reconstruction cases involving an anaphor discussed above show that BC A applies at LF, i.e. after reconstruction. Likewise, the reconstruction cases involving an r-expression and a pronoun show that BC C also applies at LF. This is a welcome result in a system which assumes LF to be the only level of syntactic representation, with the consequence that binding conditions are LF interface conditions.

However, it has been claimed that there are contexts where BC A must be concluded to apply at a pre-LF level, presumably SS. Chomsky (1993) illustrates this claim with the pair in (31) and (32), among others:

31a. John wondered which picture of himself Bill saw.
31b. John wondered [CP [which picture of himself] [IP John saw [t] . . .

32a. John wondered who saw which picture of himself.
32b. John wondered [CP who [IP [t] saw [which picture of himself] . . .

(31) is ambiguous in the by now familiar sense. The reflexive anaphor can have as its antecedent either *Bill* (the subject of the embedded clause) or *John* (the subject of the root clause). In contrast, (32) is not ambiguous. The reflexive anaphor cannot have *John* (the subject of the root clause) as its antecedent. Assuming that wh-in-situ undergoes covert movement to the embedded Spec,CP in (32), its derived position will be the same as the position of its overtly moved counterpart in (31). Yet the reflexive anaphor inside the wh-phrase cannot have *John* as its

antecedent in (32), contrary to its counterpart in (31). This difference is concluded to imply that BC A applies prior to covert movement of the wh-phrase in (32), that is, prior to LF.

The problem arguably does not arise in the context of the copy theory of movement. (31) is familiar from the discussion of idioms above. It can either have the representation shown in (33b) or the representation shown in (33c) which account for its ambiguity:

33a. John wondered which picture of himself Bill saw.
33b. John wondered [CP [[which x] [x picture of himself]] [IP John saw [x] . . .
33c. John wondered [CP [which x] [IP John saw [x picture of himself] . . .

On the assumption that wh-in-situ undergoes covert movement in (32), one could assume that deletion of the restriction *[x picture of himself]* applies to the operator position. This leads to the derivation of a representation similar to (33c) with *John* replaced by x. In this representation, the reflexive is not accessible to binding by the root subject, and hence the lack of ambiguity in (32b). However, this scenario only begs the question why deletion of the restriction has to apply to the operator position. An alternative scenario which delivers the desired result would be to rely on the idea that wh-in-situ does not undergo covert movement at LF. According to this scenario, (32) has the representation shown in (34c) which is consistent with the lack of binding by the root subject. The root subject is not the nearest c-commanding subject to the reflexive anaphor:

34a. John wondered who saw which picture of himself.
34b. John wondered [CP [who] [IP [who] saw [which picture of himself] . . .
34c. John wondered [CP [wh x, y] [IP [x person] saw [y picture of himself] . . .

The wh-operator binds both the subject variable and the object variable, an instance of what is sometimes called **unselective binding**. In both occurrences of the variable, the restriction is associated with the variable in the argument position.

It remains to be seen how the operator is linked to the variable in the object position despite the lack of (covert) movement. A possible solution, entertained in Chapter 19 in relation to wh-in-situ languages, is that only the wh-morpheme moves in instances of wh-in-situ. Assuming that the wh-morpheme corresponds to the operator, as suggested above, this movement links the operator to the variable in the direct object position in a derivational manner. Accordingly, (34a) has the more detailed derivation shown in (35):

35a. John wondered who saw which pictures of himself.
35b. John wondered [CP [who] [IP [who] saw [which pictures of himself] . . .
35c. John wondered [CP [which y] [who x] [IP [x person] saw
     [y pictures of himself] . . .
35d. John wondered [CP [wh x, y] [IP [x person] saw [y pictures of himself] . . .

The two separate wh-operators shown in (35c) then undergo what is sometimes called **absorption** which results in a single operator binding more than one variable shown in (35d). For reasons that will become clear later on in this chapter, let us call the process which moves the wh-morpheme/operator out of wh-in-situ **Cliticisation**$_{LF}$.

Bearing in mind the conclusions reached in relation to (33), consider now (36):

36a. John wondered which picture of Tom he liked.
36b. John wondered [which picture of Tom] he liked [which picture of Tom]
36c. John wondered [$_{CP}$ [[which x] [x picture of Tom]] [$_{IP}$ he liked
        [[which x] [x picture of Tom]] . . .
36d. John wondered [$_{CP}$ [which x] [$_{IP}$ he liked [x picture of Tom] . . .

In (36a) the pronoun in the subject position of the embedded clause cannot have *Tom* as its antecedent. This fact suggests that (36) requires reconstruction. The latter derives a representation where the pronoun c-commands *Tom* with the consequence that co-indexation between them will give rise to a BC C violation. As we saw above, obligatory reconstruction translates in the context of the copy theory of movement as non-deletion of the restriction from the argument position. This is shown in (36d). In view of this, it seems that while reconstruction is possible with anaphors, as concluded above in relation to (33), it is obligatory with r-expressions.

There is evidence that reconstruction is obligatory with pronouns as well. This is shown in (37):

37a. John wondered which picture of him Bill took.
37b. John wondered [which picture of him] Bill took [which picture of him]
37c. John wondered [$_{CP}$ [[which x] [x picture of him]] [$_{IP}$ Bill took
        [[which x] [x picture of him]] . . .
37d. John wondered [$_{CP}$ [which x] [$_{IP}$ Bill took [x picture of him] . . .

In (37a), the pronoun in the overtly moved wh-phrase cannot have *Bill* as its antecedent. This implies that (37) requires reconstruction. The latter places the pronoun in a position where co-indexation with *Bill* leads to the pronoun being bound in its local domain, in violation of BC B. In the context of the analysis which assumes the copy theory of movement, this means that the restriction in the argument position does not delete. This is shown in (37d). Thus, pronouns resemble r-expressions in that they require reconstruction.

Chomsky takes the noted difference between anaphors, on the one hand, and pronouns and r-expressions, on the other, to reflect a fundamental difference between BC A and BCs B & C. He then goes on to suggest an alternative analysis for cases of BC A which sets them apart from cases of BCs B & C. The alternative analysis relies on an LF-operation called **Cliticisation**$_{LF}$ which has the effect of moving the *self* morpheme of a reflexive anaphor to the I associated with the antecedent of the anaphor. To illustrate with simple examples, Cliticisation$_{LF}$ applies to (38a) to derive the representation shown in (38b), and to (39a) to derive the representation shown in (39b). The morpheme *self* is shown attached to the verb, but the original idea behind this analysis takes it to attach to the I associated with the antecedent:

38a. John likes himself.

38b. John **self**-likes [him t$_{self}$]

39a. Bill believes that John likes himself.

39b. Bill believes that John **self**-likes [him t$_{self}$]

Applying Cliticisation$_{LF}$ to an ambiguous example such as (40a), reproduced from above, yields either the representation shown in (40b) or the representation shown in (40c). Crucially, Cliticisation$_{LF}$ applies after wh-movement:

40a. John wondered which picture of himself Bill saw.

40b. John **self**-wondered [$_{CP}$ [which picture of [him t$_{self}$]]
     [$_{IP}$ Bill saw [which picture of himself] . . .

40c. John wondered [$_{CP}$ [which picture of himself]
     [$_{IP}$ Bill **self**-saw [which picture of [him t$_{self}$]] . . .

(40b), where *self* is cliticised to the I associated with the root subject, underlies the reading whereby the root subject *John* is the antecedent of the reflexive anaphor. (40c), where *self* is cliticised to the I associated with the embedded subject, underlies the reading whereby the embedded subject *Bill* is the antecedent of the reflexive anaphor.

Cliticisation$_{LF}$ distinguishes between cases of BC A and cases of BCs B & C by reducing the former to movement. However, Cliticisation$_{LF}$ still does not explain why reconstruction is obligatory with pronouns and r-expressions. To explain this fact, Chomsky assumes a **preference principle** which favours reconstruction, i.e. deletion of the restriction in the operator position. The preference principle is an exhortation to 'try to minimise the restriction in the operator position', understood as a kind of economy measure. The issue of preference does not arise for anaphors for reasons we do not need to get into here but which include the fact that their derivation involves movement.

According to the analysis outlined above, Binding theory applies at the interpretive level of LF, which is what is expected in the context of MP. In view of this, it is possible to have an interpretive version of Binding theory along the lines shown in (41), where D stands for 'domain' (Chapter 9):

41a. **BC A** If α is an anaphor, interpret it as coreferential with a c-commanding phrase in D.

41b. **BC B** If α is a pronominal, interpret it as disjoint from every c-commanding phrase in D.

41c. **BC C** If α is an r-expression, interpret it as disjoint from every c-commanding phrase.

BC A can be dispensed with under the Cliticisation$_{LF}$ analysis for anaphors. Chomsky explains that indexing can also be dispensed with in the context of an interpretive theory of binding of the type in (41).

18.6   *Quantifier scope interaction: Hornstein (1995)*

It was pointed out above that it is not clear whether A-movement leaves a copy or a trace behind. An optimal version of the copy theory of movement should be general in its scope, applying to all types of movement, including A-movement. In this section we will briefly present an analysis outlined by Hornstein (1995, 1998) which makes the claim that allowing A-movement to leave a copy behind makes it possible to account for quantifier scope ambiguities without having to resort to QR (Chapter 7). QR then becomes superfluous and therefore dispensable.

In the P & P framework, sentences which include a quantifier phrase, such as (42a) and (43a), have the LF representations shown in (42b) and (43b). The quantifier phrase is raised and left-adjoined to IP by QR, leaving a trace behind which translates as a variable bound by the raised quantifier phrase (Chapter 7):

42a. Mary attended every seminar.
42b. [$_{IP}$ every seminar [$_{IP}$ Mary attended t]]
42c. for every x, x a seminar, Mary attended x

43a. Someone attended Mary's seminar.
43b. [$_{IP}$ someone [$_{IP}$ t attended Mary's seminar]]
43c. for some x, x a person, x attended Mary's seminar

The scope ambiguities that arise from the presence of more than one quantifier phrase in a single sentence such as (44a) are resolved structurally in the manner shown in (44b) and (44c). (44b) is the representation underlying the reading whereby *every seminar* scopes over *someone*, and (44c) the (reverse scope) reading whereby *someone* scopes over *every seminar*:

44a. Someone attended every seminar.
44b. [$_{IP}$ every seminar [$_{IP}$ someone [$_{IP}$ t attended t]]]
44c. [$_{IP}$ someone [$_{IP}$ every seminar [$_{IP}$ t attended t]]]

In the context of the copy theory of movement, (44a) has the LF representation shown in (45b):

45a. **Someone** attended **every seminar**.
45b. [**someone**] I [$_{Agr_OP}$ [**every seminar**] Agr$_O$
     [$_{VP}$ [**someone**] [$_{V'}$ attended [**every seminar**] . . .

The subject moves to Spec,IP (where I is a collective term for merged Agr$_S$ and T), leaving a copy in Spec,VP (the thematic subject position). The direct object moves to Spec, Agr$_O$P, leaving a copy in the direct object position (the thematic object position). Verb-movement to Agr$_O$ is not shown as it is not relevant to the discussion.

Hornstein argues that given the representation in (45b), all that needs to be done to derive the two readings is to delete the appropriate copies of the quantifier phrase, as shown in (46b) and (46c&c'). The symbol [e] marks the position of the deleted copy:

46a. **Someone** attended **every seminar**.
46b. [e] I [$_{Agr_OP}$ [**every seminar**] Agr$_O$ [$_{VP}$ [**someone**] [$_{V'}$ attended [e] . . .
46c. [e] I [$_{Agr_OP}$ [e] Agr$_O$ [$_{VP}$ [**someone**] [$_{V'}$ attended [**every seminar**] . . .
46c′. [**someone**] I [$_{Agr_OP}$ [**every seminar**] Agr$_O$ [$_{VP}$ [e] [$_{V'}$ attended [e] . . . .

The reading whereby *every seminar* (c-commands and therefore) scopes over *someone* is derived by deletion of the copy of *someone* in Spec,IP and of the copy of *every seminar* in the direct object position. This is shown in (46b). The reading whereby *someone* (c-commands and therefore) scopes over *every seminar* can be derived in one of at least two ways shown in (46c) and (46c′). In (46c), the copies of the quantifiers in the functional structure above VP are both deleted, leaving the lower copies inside VP. In (46c′), the copies of the quantifiers inside VP are deleted.

Quantifier scope interaction is also found in contexts of (A-chains derived by) raising from the subject position of a non-finite clause as in (47a):

47a. **Someone** seems (to Bill) to be reviewing **every report**.
47b. [**someone**] I [$_{VP}$ seems (to Bill) [$_{IP}$ [**someone**] to be
       [$_{Agr_OP}$ [**every report**] Agr$_O$ [$_{VP}$ [**someone**] [$_{V'}$ reviewing [**every report**] . . .
47c. [e] I [$_{VP}$ seems (to Bill) [$_{IP}$ [**someone**] to be
       [$_{Agr_OP}$ [**every report**] Agr$_O$ [$_{VP}$ [e] [$_{V'}$ reviewing [e] . . .
47d. [e] I [$_{VP}$ seems (to Bill) [$_{IP}$ [e] to be
       [$_{Agr_OP}$ [**every report**] Agr$_O$ [$_{VP}$ [**someone**] [$_{V'}$ reviewing [e] . . .

(47a) has the representation shown in (47b) subsequent to movement, irrelevant details omitted. Deletion rules then apply to derive either (47c) where *someone* scopes over *every report* or (47d) where *every report* scopes over *someone*. Note that the reading in (47d) requires reconstruction (or **Quantifier Lowering**) under the QR analysis, but not under Hornstein's analysis.

In the examples discussed so far, deletion applies fairly freely. The only consideration has been to derive the right c-command and therefore the right scope relations between the quantifiers. There are contexts where additional considerations appear to determine which copies are deleted. For example, (48a) requires a representation where the copy of *someone* which c-commands the reflexive anaphor is not deleted:

48a. **Someone** seemed to himself to be reviewing **every report**.
48b. [**someone**] seemed to himself [$_{IP}$ [**someone**] to be [$_{Agr_OP}$ [**every report**]
       [$_{VP}$ [**someone**] [$_{V'}$ be reviewing [**every report**] . . .
48c. [**someone**] seemed to himself [$_{IP}$ [e] to be [$_{Agr_OP}$ [e]
       [$_{VP}$ [e] [$_{V'}$ reviewing [**every report**] . . .

(48a) has the representation shown in (48c), where the copy of *someone* in the embedded subject position is deleted. The copy in the root subject position must remain to bind the reflexive anaphor under c-command. Note, however, that (48a) is not ambiguous, unlike (47a), which is consistent with the conclusion that the copy in the root subject position does not delete. Thus, deletion is still determined by scope considerations holding between quantifiers in (48a).

Hornstein's approach succeeds in explaining quantifier scope interaction without having to resort to QR, clearly a welcome result in MP. However, the analysis suffers from what seems to be a major problem. In situations where the copy in the argument position is deleted, as is the case in numerous examples above, the chain link which enables the surviving copy to have a θ-role is broken. This results in a situation where the surviving copy does not have a θ-role. Hornstein (1998) solves this problem by reinterpreting θ-theory in a way which is consistent with his analysis as well as with MP. Here we will discuss an alternative analysis which solves the problem by combining Hornstein's basic ideas with Chomsky's ideas relating to the interpretation of wh-phrases outlined above.

In Chomsky's analysis of wh-phrases outlined above, the LF rules of interpretation apply to a wh-phrase such as *which book* to derive the representation *[[which x] [x book]]*. Suppose that the same rules apply to a quantifier phrase such as *every report* to derive the representation *[[every x] [x report]]* and to *someone* to derive the representation *[[some x] [x one/person]]*. These rules will derive representation (49c) from representation (49b) of example (49a) from above:

49a. Mary attended **every seminar**.
49b. Mary I $[_{Agr_OP}$ [**every seminar**] Agr$_O$
      $[_{VP}$ Mary $[_{V'}$ attended [**every seminar**] . . .
49c. Mary I $[_{Agr_OP}$ [[**every x**] [**x seminar**]] Agr$_O$
      $[_{VP}$ Mary $[_{V'}$ attended [[**every x**] [**x seminar**]] . . .
49d. [e] I $[_{Agr_OP}$ [**every x**] Agr$_O$ $[_{VP}$ Mary $[_{V'}$ attended [**x seminar**] . . .

Deletion rules apply to delete the restriction from the copy in the operator position, leaving *[every x]*, and to delete the operator from the copy in the argument position, leaving the variable with the restriction *[x seminar]*. These rules derive the representation shown in (49d) where the operator occupies the head position of the chain and the variable the θ-position. The higher copy of *Mary* is deleted purely for convenience of presentation.

The same analysis could be applied to (50a) from above, yielding representation (50d). The higher copy of *Mary's seminar* is deleted purely for convenience of presentation:

50a. **Someone** attended Mary's seminar.
50b. [**someone**] I $[_{Agr_OP}$ [Mary's seminar] Agr$_O$
      $[_{VP}$ [**someone**] $[_{V'}$ attended [Mary's seminar] . . .
50c. [[**some x**] [**x person**]] I $[_{Agr_OP}$ [Mary's seminar] Agr$_O$
      $[_{VP}$ [[**some x**] [**x person**]] $[_{V'}$ attended [Mary's seminar] . . .
50d. [**some x**] I $[_{Agr_OP}$ [e] Agr$_O$ $[_{VP}$ [**x person**] $[_{V'}$ attended [Mary's seminar] . . .

Deletion of the restriction in the copy in the operator position is consistent with Chomsky's guiding principle mentioned above: 'try to minimise the restriction in the operator position'. In (49) and (50) deletion of the restriction *[x person]/ [x seminar]* associated with the operator is actually not an option. It is forced by the fact that deletion of the restriction in the argument position will lead to the disappearance of the variable from the θ-position. The analysis outlined in (49) and

(50) derives a representation where the operator is located in the functional domain, while the variable it binds (together with the restriction) is located in the thematic domain (VP-internally). This is arguably an advantage.

Let us now move on to sentences with quantifier scope interaction. (51a) from above has the representation shown in (51c), subsequent to movement and the application of the LF rules of interpretation, but prior to deletion:

51a. **Someone** attended **every seminar**.

51b. [someone] I [$_{Agr_O}$P [every seminar] Agr$_O$
[$_{VP}$ [someone] [$_{V'}$ attended [every seminar] . . .

51c. [[some x] [x person]] I [$_{Agr_O}$P [[every y] [y seminar]] Agr$_O$
[$_{VP}$ [[some x] [x person]] [$_{V'}$ attended [[every y] [y seminar]] . . .

The reading whereby *someone* has scope over *every seminar* is derived by deletion of the restriction from the copy of *someone* in Spec,IP and from the copy of *every seminar* in Spec, Ag$_O$P. This is shown in (52) which is consistent with the observation that the operator is located in the functional domain and the variable in the thematic domain:

52.   [some x] I [$_{Agr_O}$P [every y] Agr$_O$ [$_{VP}$ [x person] [$_{V'}$ attended [y seminar] . . .

The derivation of the reading whereby *every seminar* has scope over *someone* is slightly problematic. The deletion rules affecting *every seminar* apply as for (52). To make sure *someone* is within the scope of *every seminar* we have to delete the higher copy of *someone* in the subject position and somehow transform the lower copy of it in Spec,VP into an operator-variable link. This could be done by moving the operator part of the expression to a VP-external position not higher than the position of the operator *[every y]*. Let us assume that the process which moves the operator part is an instance of Cliticisation$_{LF}$. Let us assume further that the operator part is cliticised to Agr$_O$. We then obtain the representation shown in (53) which is consistent with the observation that operators are located in the functional domain and the variables with their restriction in the thematic domain:

53.   [e] I [$_{Agr_O}$P [every y] [$_{Agr_O}$' [some x] Agr$_O$
[$_{VP}$ [x person] [$_{V'}$ attended [y seminar] . . .

The analysis applies to cases of subject raising such as (54a) from above in the same way. Movement and the LF rules of interpretation derive the representations in (54b&c):

54a. **Someone** seemed (to Bill) to review **every report**.

54b. [someone] seemed (to Bill) [$_{IP}$ [someone] [$_{I'}$ to [$_{Agr_O}$P [every report]
[$_{VP}$ [someone] [$_{V'}$ review [every report] . . .

54c. [[some x] [x person]] seemed (to Bill) [$_{IP}$ [[some x] [x person]] to [$_{Agr_O}$P
[[every y] [y report]] [$_{VP}$ [[some x] [x person]] [$_{V'}$ review
[[every y] [y report]] . . .

The derivation of the reading whereby *someone* scopes over *every report* is as outlined in (55a). The reading whereby *every report* scopes over *someone* requires Cliticisation$_{LF}$ of the operator *[some x]* to Agr$_O$, shown in (55b):

55a. [e] seemed (to Bill) [$_{IP}$ [**some x**] to [$_{Agr_O}$P [**every y**] Agr$_O$
     [$_{VP}$ [**x person**] review [**y report**] . . .

55b. [e] seemed (to Bill) [$_{IP}$ [e] to [$_{Agr_O}$P [**every y**] [$_{Agr_O}$′ [**some x**] Agr$_O$
     [$_{VP}$ [**x person**] review [**y report**] . . .

Finally, the unambiguous example (56a) from above has the representation shown in (56d). Only the restriction is deleted from the copy in the root subject position, thereby accounting for the binding of the reflexive anaphor. (56d) is also consistent with the idea that the operator is represented in the functional domain and the variable in the thematic domain:

56a. **Someone** seemed to himself to be reviewing **every report**.

56b. [**someone**] seemed to himself [$_{IP}$ [**someone**] to
     [$_{Agr_O}$P [**every report**] Agr$_O$ [$_{VP}$ [**someone**] [$_{V}$′ be reviewing [**every report**]..

56c. [[**some x**] [**x person**]] seemed to himself [$_{IP}$ [[**some x**] [**x person**]] to [$_{Agr_O}$P
     [[**every y**] [**y report**]] Agr$_O$ [$_{VP}$ [[**some x**] [**x person**]] [$_{V}$′ be reviewing
     [[**every y**] [**y report**]] . . .

56d. [**some x**] seemed to himself [$_{IP}$ [e] to
     [$_{Agr_O}$P [**every y**] Agr$_O$ [$_{VP}$ [**x person**] [$_{V}$′ be reviewing [**y report**] . . .

18.7 *Summary*

The copy theory of movement seems to have many advantages. It makes it possible to account for cases of reconstruction without having to appeal to lowering rules applying at LF. It also makes it possible to account for quantifier scope interaction without having to rely on QR. Finally, the copy theory of movement makes it possible to explain cases of binding previously thought to be determined at a pre-LF level. The latter is part of a general attempt to show that all syntactic principles apply at the interface level of LF, a necessary requirement in the MP which does not assume any syntactic level of representation other than LF.

19 Checking Theory and Language Variation

Contents

19.1 *Checking features and feature checking*

In the Principles and Parameters framework verbs were assumed to be inserted from the lexicon in their bare form, uninflected for tense and agreement. They pick up tense and agreement inflection as a result of syntactic movement which joins them with inflectional categories. The movement involved derives head-adjunction structures which form the input to morphological rules. The latter convert $[_{I^0}$ [V] I], for example, into an inflected verb. The inflectional heads are basically bundles of features which enter into the syntactic relation of spec-head agreement, among others, either separately or collectively. The complex which consists of the verb and the inflectional features is then spelled out at PF as a single phonological word.

Chomsky (1993) suggests, in the spirit of the Strong Lexicalist Hypothesis and 'lexicalist phonology', that verbs are inflected for features in the lexicon and inserted into derivations already inflected rather than in their bare form. The features carried by the verb are then checked against corresponding features encoded in inflectional categories. Taking I to be mnemonic for the inflectional categories, feature checking takes place in the configuration $[_{I^0}$ [V] I] derived by head-adjunction. If the features of [V] and [I] are compatible, [I] disappears and [V] proceeds to PF, eventually to be spelled out as a single phonological word. If the features of [I] and [V] are not compatible, [I] survives into PF and the derivation crashes at PF. PF rules are supposed to 'see' only inflected [V].

Once a feature is checked, it disappears, and is no longer available to the computation. At LF, all features must be checked. If a feature remains unchecked the derivation crashes at LF. This idea has the consequence that main verbs ultimately move to I if not overtly, then covertly. If the verb does not check its features overtly, it must do so covertly. Otherwise the derivation will crash at LF.

According to this scenario, the inflectional categories Agr_O, Agr_S and T have features which correspond to features encoded in the verb in the lexicon. Chomsky calls these features **V-features**. The latter have the function of checking the morphological properties of the verb, an important notion in the MP where movement is generally motivated by morphological considerations. The verb moves to Agr_O, T and Agr_S in order to have its morphological features checked. Movement of the verb and therefore checking of the V-features can take place at any stage in the derivation. It may take place prior to Spell-Out (overtly) or after Spell-Out (covertly).

Besides the function of checking the V-features of V, the inflectional categories Agr_O, T and Agr_S also have the function of checking the NP-features of the DP that moves to their Spec. This particular checking takes place under the Spec-head configuration and ensures that 'DP and V are properly paired'.

According to the theory of Checking outlined, the φ-features involved in subject agreement, for example, are represented in three separate categories prior to Spell-Out, V, Agr_S and the DP subject. Using a concrete example such as *John hits the ball*, the φ-features relating to subject agreement are encoded in *hits*, Agr_S and *John*. The verb checks its φ-features in the head-adjunction structure derived by V-raising to Agr_S. The DP subject checks its features in the Spec-head configuration derived by movement of the subject to Spec,Agr_SP. Recall from above that once an inflectional category such as Agr_S has performed its function of checking the features of a relevant category, it disappears. This means that only two sets of φ-features survive at PF and LF, one set associated with the verb and the other with the DP subject. Agr_S is said to 'play only a mediating role'. This is also true of T which checks the tense feature of the verb under head-adjunction and the nominative Case feature of DP under the Spec-head relation.

The domains of checking involve the head adjunction structure $[_X [Y] X]$ and the spec-head structure $[_{XP} Spec [_{X'} X]]$. The morphological features checked in these domains are called **L-features**. A position that is locally related to one of these features in the domains specified is said to be **L-related**. Thus, the position [Y] in the head adjunction structure $[_X [Y] X]$ is L-related by virtue of being in a local relation with the features in [X]. The Spec position in the spec-head structure $[_{XP} Spec [_{X'} X]]$ is L-related by virtue of being in a local relation with the features in [X]. Chomsky suggests that the adjoined position in the structure $[_{XP} [YP] XP]$ is also an L-related position, and therefore may enter into a checking relation with the head X of XP. Specifiers and adjuncts of XP are distinguished from each other in terms of the relations **narrowly L-related** (Specifiers) and **broadly L-related** (adjuncts).

19.2 *Economy principles*

An interesting consequence of the theory of Checking outlined in the previous section is that I-lowering previously thought to be involved in the derivation of English finite sentences is no longer needed. Prior to Spell-Out, (1a) has the representation shown in (1b):

1a. John often kisses Mary.
1b. [$_{Agr_S}$P [John] [$_{Agr_S'}$ [T] Agr$_S$ [$_{TP}$ T [$_{Agr_O}$P Agr$_O$ [$_{VP}$ often [$_{VP}$ kisses Mary . . .
1c. [$_{Agr_S}$P [John] [$_{Agr_S'}$ [kisses] [T] Agr$_S$ [$_{TP}$ T [[$_{Agr_O}$P [Mary] [$_{Agr_O'}$ [V] Agr$_O$ [$_{VP}$ often [[$_{VP}$ . . .

The subject raises overtly to Spec,Agr$_S$P to check its features. Presumably, T also raises overtly to Agr$_S$. The verb stays inside VP and so does the direct object. After Spell-Out, (1a) has the representation roughly shown in (1c), where the verb raises covertly to Agr$_S$ to check its own V-features and the direct object raises covertly to Spec,Agr$_O$P to check its own NP-features.

The discussion of example (1a) in Chapter 16 tried to answer a number of questions, among them why the main the verb does not raise overtly and (the different but related question) why the main verb is prevented from raising overtly. The first question is illustrated with example (1a). The second question is illustrated with example (2a), where the verb raises overtly, details omitted:

2a. *John kisses often Mary.
2b. [$_{Agr_S}$P [John] [$_{Agr_S'}$ [v kisses] [$_{TP}$ T [$_{Agr_O}$P Agr$_O$ [$_{VP}$ often [$_{VP}$ . . . Mary

Chomsky (1993) answers the question why the main verb does not (have to) raise overtly in English by relying on the idea that English Agr$_S$ is 'weak' (see Chapter 16). This idea is combined with the assumption that '. . . "weak" features are invisible at PF.', with the implication that if they are not checked overtly and eliminated they do not cause the derivation to crash at PF. Recall from above that when the V-features of [[T] Agr$_S$] have checked the corresponding features of a raised verb in a head-adjunction structure, they disappear. If they survive into PF, the derivation crashes at PF. Failure of the verb to move overtly to [[T] Agr$_S$] means that the V-features of [[T] Agr$_S$] survive into PF and may cause the derivation to crash. However, the derivation does not crash because the V-features of [[T] Agr$_S$] are weak in English. PF does not 'see' weak features. This explains why the verb does not (have to) raise overtly in English.

Although the verb does not raise overtly to [[T] Agr$_S$] in English it must do so covertly at LF. Recall that all features must be checked and eliminated at LF. Otherwise, the derivation crashes at LF. Notions such as 'weak feature', being phonetic in content, do not apply at LF. LF cannot distinguish weak features from strong features. All features, including weak ones, are visible at LF, and must be eliminated via checking.

The (second) question why the main verb is barred from raising overtly in English is accounted for in terms of an economy principle called **Procrastinate**.

The idea underlying Procrastinate is that (covert) LF operations are less costly than overt operations, arguably by virtue of being 'wired in'. The derivation 'tries to reach PF "as fast as possible", minimising overt syntax'. Because overt V-raising is not obligatory in English for the reasons explained above, it is barred by the economy principle of Procrastinate. The bottom line of this analysis is the old idea that categories move only if they have to, that is, movement as last resort. The difference is that the notion 'movement as last resort' is made relative to the level of representation in the MP. Overt V-raising is unnecessary (for the PF-related reasons explained above) and therefore barred. Covert V-raising is necessary (for the LF related reasons discussed above) and therefore obligatory.

Among the other questions that the analysis outlined in Chapter 16 tried to answer is why the English auxiliary verbs *be* and *have* raise overtly, contrary to main verbs. This is illustrated in (3):

3a. John is often in the garden.
3b. John has completely lost his mind.

Recall that according to Pollock (1989), auxiliary verbs differ from main verbs in that they do not assign θ-roles. Chomsky (1993) reinterprets this idea to mean that auxiliary verbs are semantically vacuous. They 'are placeholders for certain constructions, at most "very light" verbs.' As such, they are claimed to be invisible to LF rules, meaning they are not affected by movement processes which take place at LF. This combination of ideas has the consequence that if auxiliary verbs do not raise overtly, they will not be able to raise covertly, thereby causing the derivation to crash at LF.

Besides Procrastinate, Chomsky (1993) discusses another principle which drives derivations called **Greed**. This principle is motivated on the basis of a discussion of *there*-constructions of the type illustrated in (4):

4a. There is a strange man in the garden.
4b. [there] is [DP a strange man] in the garden
4c. [[a strange man] there] is [t] in the garden

The category *a strange man* in (4a), which we will take here to be a DP, is not in the checking domain of [[T] Agr$_S$] at Spell-Out. Therefore, it must raise to Spec,Agr$_S$P at LF to check its own features. Chomsky assumes that this is an adjunction movement which results in adjoining the raised DP to *there* regarded as an 'LF affix'. This movement derives the complex Spec [[*a strange man*] *there*], shown in (4c). The latter enters checking under the Spec-head relation with the complex head [[T] Agr$_S$].

Now, compare (4a) to (5a), where the same DP is included inside a PP:

5a. There seems to a strange man that it is raining outside.
5b. [there] seems [PP to [DP a strange man]] [that it is raining outside]

The Case feature of the DP *a strange man* is checked inside PP. Consequently, the DP does not need to raise to the position of *there*. By virtue of Procrastinate, the DP cannot raise to the position of *there*. The latter is not an obligatory 'LF affix'.

It can be a free standing 'LF word'. The derivation of (5) therefore converges at LF. However, it converges as 'semigibberish' according to Chomsky, due to *there* failing to receive an interpretation by being linked to a θ-marked position. This situation does not arise in the earlier example (4), where *there* is linked to the θ-marked position of the DP *a strange man* raised to it. Were the DP *a strange man* to move and adjoin to *there* in (5), the sentence would have an interpretation which Chomsky paraphrases as 'there is a strange man to whom it seems that it is raining outside'. However, the DP is banned from moving to the position of *there* as explained.

The point of the discussion is that even though movement of the DP to the position of *there* in (5) would have a beneficial effect, it does not apply. Chomsky takes this to reflect a crucial property of 'movement as last resort', namely that a category moves for the sole purpose of satisfying its own requirements (greed), not those of another category (altruism). Movement of the DP to the position of *there* in (5) would be altruistic, motivated by the need to assign *there* an interpretation. The DP has all its own requirements satisfied in its position inside PP.

The 'self-serving' nature of movement can also be seen in relation to example (6) which lacks *there* in the subject position:

6a. *Seems to a strange man that it is raining outside.
6b. [e] seems [pp to [DP a strange man]] [that it is raining outside]

The absence of *there* in (6) has the consequence that the Case feature of the complex head [[T] Agr$_S$] remains unchecked, causing the derivation to crash at LF. The derivation would be rescued if the DP moved to Spec,Agr$_S$P to check the Case feature. However, because this movement is not 'self-serving', it does not apply.

It seems that the 'self-serving' nature of movement prevails irrespective of whether overriding it would result in assigning an interpretation to a convergent derivation, as in (5), or in allowing a derivation to converge, as in (6).

The principle of Greed seems to face a problem in relation to the idea that T moves overtly to Agr$_S$ in English, if true. There seems to be no reason for T to move to Agr$_S$ other than to make it possible for the subject to check its Case-feature with [[T] Agr$_S$]. If this reasoning is correct, this movement is altruistic rather than self-serving (see Lasnik 1993 for discussion of such movements).

19.3   *Overt V-raising*

The discussion in Chapter 16 compared English to French where main verbs raise overtly, as shown in (7). (7a) shows that verbs move overtly, and (7b) shows that they have to move overtly:

7a. Jean embrasse souvent Marie.
    Jean kisses   often   Marie

7b. *Jean   souvent   embrasse   Marie.
    Jean   often   kisses   Marie

To explain overt V-raising in French, Chomsky (1993) borrows the idea that French Agr$_S$ is strong (Chapter 16), contrary to its English counterpart. Moreover, '"strong" features are visible at PF', unlike weak features. This means that the strong V-features of Agr$_S$ must be checked by Spell-Out in French. If they are not checked by Spell-Out, they will not have been eliminated when the derivation reaches PF causing it to crash at PF. This explains why French verbs move overtly, as shown in (7a), as well as why they have to move overtly, as shown in (7b). Note that Procrastinate does not apply in this case as movement is necessary for convergence. Procrastinate only applies when movement is not crucial for convergence, as is the case in English.

The discussion in Chapter 16 also included non-finite verbs in non-finite clauses, mostly in French. Chomsky (1993) does not discuss these contexts. Let us see what implications the facts of non-finite clauses have for the analysis outlined above. We will not address the question whether non-finite clauses include Agr$_S$ and T, and if they do what kind of features they encode. Our discussion will be limited to the lower domain of the structure, as in Chapter 16. Recall that French non-finite main verbs can undergo overt 'short movement' to a position immediately above VP, identified as Agr$_O$. This is shown in (8a). This movement appears to be optional as the pattern seen in (8b), where the VP adverbs precedes the non-finite main verb, is also possible:

8a. paraître   souvent   triste . . .
    to-appear   often   sad

8b. Souvent   paraître   triste . . .
    often   to-appear   sad

To account for (8a&b) it seems necessary to allow for the possibility that the V-features of an inflectional head, Agr$_O$ in (8a&b), can be either strong or weak. They are strong in (8a), thereby making overt V-raising necessary for convergence at PF. These features must be concluded to be weak in (8b). Otherwise, the derivation will crash at PF on the grounds that strong features have not been checked and eliminated. If this reasoning is correct, it follows that Agr$_S$ and Agr$_O$ may vary with respect to the strength/weakness of their V-features in the same language. The V-features of Agr$_S$ are invariably strong in French finite clauses, whereas the V-features of Agr$_O$ may be either strong or weak in French non-finite clauses. It is not immediately clear whether the V-features of Agr$_O$ have either property in French finite clauses due to overt V-movement to Agr$_S$.

The issue of optionality of strength and weakness of features, and the distinction between Agr$_S$ and Agr$_O$ in relation to it, arguably also arise with respect to the NP-features of Agr$_S$ and Agr$_O$. The NP-features of [$_{Agr_S}$ [T] Agr$_S$] are strong in both English and French finite clauses, given that in both languages the subject raises overtly to Spec,Agr$_S$P. Because the main verb does not raise overtly in English, thereby blocking raising of the direct object to Spec,Agr$_S$P (Chapter 17), it must be concluded that the NP-features of Agr_O are weak in English. The same is true of the French Agr_O. The order [ADV DP_{ACC}] in (7a) suggests that the direct object does not raise overtly to Spec,Agr_OP. The conclusion extends to Agr_O in French non-finite clauses with the same order.

In the next section, we will see that allowing the NP-features of an inflectional category to be optionally strong or weak is necessary to account for the properties of (VSO) languages which allow both the VSO and the SVO orders.

19.4   *VSO*

The VSO languages discussed in Chapter 13 were Welsh (Celtic) and Standard Arabic (Semitic). The former is a strict VSO language. It does not allow the SVO order in neutral finite sentences. Standard Arabic, however, allows both the VSO and SVO orders in neutral finite sentences.

The relevant Welsh example is reproduced in (9):

9.   Gwelodd Siôn   ddraig.
      saw   Siôn   dragon
      'Siôn saw a dragon.'

The analysis suggested by Sproat (1985) and discussed in Chapter 13 attributed the VSO nature of Welsh to raising of $[_I{}^0$ [V] I] to C. This movement is necessitated by the directionality restriction on the assignment of nominative Case by I which operates strictly rightward in Welsh. Obviously, the theoretical machinery of Sproat's analysis does not carry over to the MP.

Chomsky (1993) makes a suggestion on the basis of the related VSO language Irish (Celtic) which differs fundamentally from Sproat's analysis. It differs not only with respect to the theoretical machinery it uses, but also with respect to the more fundamental issue of what is responsible for VSO. According to Chomsky's suggestion, what is responsible for the strictly VSO nature of Irish is that the NP-features of Agr_S are weak. Consequently, the subject is barred from moving overtly to Spec,Agr_SP by Procrastinate. The verb raises overtly to Agr_S, implying that the V-features of Agr_S are strong. Extending the analysis to Welsh, (9) has the representation shown in (10) at Spell-Out. Purely for the purposes of presentation, the subject and the object are left inside VP:

10a. Gwelodd   Siôn   ddraig.
      saw   Siôn   dragon
      'Sion saw a dragon.'

10b. $[_{Agr_S}P$ [e] $[_{Agr_S'}$ [V gwelodd] [T] Agr_S] . . . $[_{VP}$ [Siôn] . . . [ddraig] . . .

The question whether Spec,Agr_SP is filled with some category at Spell-Out and whether the subject moves to Spec,Agr_SP at LF is discussed later on in relation to Standard Arabic. It remains to be seen whether an analysis developed on the basis of Chomsky's suggestion for Irish accounts for the properties of Welsh discussed in Chapter 13 and others.

Turning now to Standard Arabic, Chomsky's suggestion above is essentially similar in spirit to the suggestion made by Mohammad (1989) for Standard Arabic VSO sentences. Recall from Chapter 13 that Mohammad's analysis attributes the VSO order to failure on the part of the subject to move to Spec,IP. Movement of the subject to Spec,IP is optional and applies in the derivation of the SVO order. Recall also that there is a correlation between order and subject agreement in Standard Arabic. In the VSO order, the verb shows the default agreement features usually associated with expletive subjects, irrespective of the agreement features of the postverbal subject. In the SVO order, however, the verb agrees with the subject. The relevant examples are reproduced in (11a&b):

11a. raʔa-a   l-ʔawlaad-u   Zayd-an.
    saw-3S   the-boys-NOM   Zayd-ACC
    'The boys saw Zayd.'

11b. l-ʔawlaad-u   raʔa-w   Zayd-an.
    the-boys-NOM   saw-3PL   Zayd-ACC
    'The boys saw Zayd.'

To account for the availability of both the VSO and the SVO orders, Chomsky (1993) suggests that the NP-features of $[[T] Agr_S]$ can either be weak or strong in (Standard) Arabic. When they are weak, raising of the subject to Spec,Agr_SP is barred by Procrastinate, and when they are strong, raising of the subject is obligatory. The correlation between the position of the subject and the agreement inflection is simply a reflex of the weak and strong nature of Agr_S. The V-features of $[[T] Agr_S]$ are invariably strong in Standard Arabic with the consequence that the verb raises overtly to Agr_S. With V in Agr_S, failure of the subject to move to Spec,Agr_SP results in the derivation of the VSO order, and movement of the subject to Spec,Agr_SP results in the derivation of the SVO order. Accordingly, the Standard Arabic examples (11a) and (11b) have the representations shown in (12b) and (13b) at Spell-Out. Once again, the subject in (12) and the object are assumed to remain inside VP for purely presentational purposes:

12a. raʔa-a   l-ʔawlaad-u   Zayd-an.
    saw-3S   the-boys-NOM   Zayd-ACC
    'The boys saw Zayd.'

12b. $[Agr_S P$ [e] $[Agr_S'$ [V raʔaa] [T] Agr_S . . . [VP [l-ʔawlaadu] . . . [Zaydan] . . .

13a. l-ʔawlaad-u   raʔa-w   Zayd-an.
    the-boys-NOM   saw -3PL   Zayd-ACC
    'The boys saw Zayd.'

13b. $[_{Agr_S}P$ [l-ʔawlaadu] $[_{Agr_S'}$ [V raʔaw] [T] Agr_S . . . [VP . . . [Zaydan] . . .

Mohammad's analysis includes the idea that Spec,Agr$_S$P is filled with an expletive subject in the VSO order. The latter is null in (11a) and overt in the embedded context illustrated in (14):

14. za'amu-u   ?anna-hu ra?a-a   l-?awlaad-u   Zayd-an.
     claimed-3PL   that-it   saw-3S the-boys-NOM   Zayd-ACC
     'They claimed that the boys saw Zayd.'

The presence of an expletive subject in the VSO order is forced by the EPP. According to Chomsky, the EPP 'reduces to a morphological property of T: strong or weak NP features'.

It is interesting to work out what NP-feature, if any, the expletive subject in VSO checks. A clue is provided by the non-nominative Case form of the expletive subject in (14). This suggests that the expletive subject does not check the Case feature of the complex [[T] Agr$_S$] on the assumption that this feature is nominative. The expletive subject checks only the φ-features of [[T] Agr$_S$] which are the default third person singular features compatible with those of the expletive subject. The Case feature of [[T] Agr$_S$] is checked subsequent to LF raising of the subject and adjunction to the expletive pronoun, shown in the abstract structure (15b):

15a. Spell-Out: [$_{Agr_S}$P [EXP] [$_{Agr_S'}$ [V] [T] Agr$_S$ . . . [$_{VP}$ [SUBJ] . . . [OBJ] . . .
15b. LF: [$_{Agr_S}$P [[SUBJ] EXP] [$_{Agr_S'}$ [V] [T] Agr$_S$ . . . [$_{VP}$ . . . [OBJ] . . .

Movement of the subject and adjunction to the 'LF affix' derives a spec-head configuration where EXP checks the φ-features of [[V] [T] Agr$_S$] and SUBJ the Case feature. Note that SUBJ has different φ-features anyway, although it remains to be explained how and where these features are checked. This analysis is consistent with Chomsky's analysis of English sentences such as *There is a strange man in the garden*, where LF raising of the DP *a strange man* to the expletive *there* is also motivated by the need for the subject to check its Case feature.

19.5   *Wh-in-situ*

The discussion of the placement of wh-phrases in simple wh-questions in Chapter 11 was based on data from English, Japanese and Colloquial French. English requires overt movement of the wh-phrase in simple wh-questions. Japanese leaves the wh-phrase in-situ and appears to disallow overt movement of the wh-phrase. Colloquial French allows both the movement option and the in-situ option. The relevant examples from Japanese and Colloquial French are reproduced in (16) and (17) respectively:

16. John-wa   nani-o   kaimasita ka?
     John-top   what-ACC   bought   Q
     'What did John buy?'

17a. Tu   as   vu   qui?
    you   have   seen   who
    'Who have you seen?'

17b. Qui   as-tu   vu?
     who   have-you   seen

Wh-phrases are standardly assumed to move to Spec,CP. So far, we have not discussed this type of movement. If we take the view that all movement is motivated by the need to check morphological features, wh-movement to Spec,CP must also involve checking of some relevant feature. Chomsky (1993) takes the view that wh-movement to Spec,CP is also motivated by feature-checking considerations. The feature involved is [Q], encoded in both C and the wh-phrase. The domain of checking of the [Q]-feature is the spec-head configuration [CP Spec [C' [Q] . . . where Spec could include an adjoined wh-phrase. According to this scenario, Spec,CP must include at least one wh-phrase to check the [Q] feature of C, if not in overt syntax then in covert syntax. All wh-phrases in a given sentence must be in Spec,CP at LF to check their [Q]-feature.

Assuming the theoretical machinery just spelled out, it appears that all that needs to be said to explain the difference between English, Japanese and Colloquial French is to designate the [Q]-feature of C as either strong, weak or optionally one or the other. It is strong in English, thereby forcing overt movement of (at least one) wh-phrase to Spec,CP. It is weak in Japanese, thereby barring movement of a wh-phrase to Spec,CP by Procrastinate. It is either strong or weak in French. If it is strong, it forces overt movement (of at least one) wh-phrase to Spec,CP. If it is weak, overt movement of a wh-phrase to Spec,CP is barred by Procrastinate.

However, Chomsky (1993) takes a different view. Following Watanabe (1991), he suggests that the [Q]-feature of C is strong in all languages. This implies that all languages involve overt movement of a form of wh-phrase to Spec,CP. Japanese, where overt wh-movement appears to be barred, seems to be inconsistent with this view. Ironically, it was on the basis of data from Japanese that Watanabe (1991) concluded that Japanese has overt wh-movement. We will briefly discuss the background discussion to this conclusion here. Watanabe's discussion is couched in terminology associated with the Principles and Parameters framework, but the main point is fairly straightforward.

In Chapter 10, we discussed examples from English which show that Subjacency does not hold of covert LF movement, e.g. *Who likes books that criticise who?* Subjacency is basically a condition on overt wh-movement (applying at SS). This conclusion was originally reached by Huang (1982) on the basis of data from Chinese, a wh-in-situ language, as well as English. A wh-phrase included inside a complex noun phrase island or a wh-island does not give rise to a Subjacency violation in Chinese, according to Huang. The Chinese examples in (18a&b) are cited in Watanabe (1991):

18a. ni   xihuan [piping   shei de   shu]?
     you   like   criticise who REL   book
     'Who do you like books that criticise?'

18b. ni   xiang-zhidao [shei mai-le shenme]?
     you   wonder   who   bought what
     'What do you wonder who bought?'

Watanabe observes that while a wh-phrase inside a complex noun phrase island does not give rise to a Subjacency violation in Japanese, a wh-phrase inside a wh-island does. This is shown in (19a&b):

19a. John-wa   [nani-o   katta hito]-o   sagasite iru no?
     John-Top [what-ACC bought person-ACC looking-for Q
     'What is John looking for the person who bought?'

19b. ?John-wa [Mary-ga nani-o katta [ka dooka]]   siritagatte iru no?
     John-Top [Mary-NOM what-ACC bought [whether]]   want-to-know Q
     'What does John want to know whether Mary bought?'

Watanabe goes on to conclude that Japanese has overt wh-movement responsible for the Subjacency violation in (19b). The reason (19a) does not exhibit a Subjacency violation is due to the possibility that it involves pied piping of the whole complex noun phrase to Spec,CP (Nishigauchi 1986, 1990). The pied piping of the whole complex noun phrase in (19a) is a larger scale version of pied piping of noun phrases in English examples such as *[Which book of Mary's] did John buy?*

According to Watanabe, what moves overtly in Japanese wh-questions is a null wh-operator which originates inside the wh-phrase. Although the moved category is null, the movement applies in overt syntax and is an instance of wh-movement. If true, this leads to the conclusion that even wh-in-situ languages involve overt wh-movement. Citing Lisa Cheng, Watanabe points out that wh-islands such as in (18b) also give rise to a Subjacency violation in Chinese, at least for some speakers. Chomsky's suggestion that the [Q] feature of C is strong in all languages is consistent with the conclusion that even wh-in-situ languages involve some kind of overt wh-movement.

Finally, let us see how the type of expletive wh-questions found in Hungarian fit in with the idea that the [Q] feature of C is strong universally. Recall from Chapter 11 that this type of wh-question includes a wh-expletive in the root Spec,CP, with the wh-phrase remaining low inside the embedded clause. The relevant example is reproduced in (20a), together with an example which involves overt wh-movement of the wh-phrase itself (20b):

20a. Mit   gondolsz, hogy kit   látott   János?
     what-ACC think-2S   that   who-ACC saw-3S   John-NOM
     'Who do you think that John saw?'

20b. Mit   mondott   Mari?
     what-ACC   said-3SG-INDEF.DO Mary-NOM
     'What did Mary say?'

(20a&b) seem to be consistent with the idea that the [Q]-feature of C is strong. In (20b), the strong feature of C is checked by the overtly moved wh-phrase itself. In (20a), it is overtly checked by the wh-expletive element. The wh-phrase itself moves covertly and adjoins to Spec,CP to check its own [Q]-feature.

Presumably, the wh-phrase 'who' in (20a) does not move overtly to the root Spec,CP by Procrastinate. The ability of (20a) to converge at PF even though the [Q]-feature of C is strong seems to be dependent on the wh-expletive. The purpose of the wh-expletive appears to check the strong [Q]-feature of C, thereby enabling the derivation to converge at PF with the real wh-phrase lower in the structure. If correct, this scenario raises some interesting questions of economy which arguably also arise in relation to English sentences such as *There is a strange man in the garden*. The element *there* could be said to be inserted by Spell-Out for the purpose of checking the strong NP-feature of Agr$_S$, thereby enabling the derivation to converge at PF.

19.6 *Verb Second*

The discussion in the previous section focused on the feature of C checked in the Spec-head domain by a wh-phrase moved to, or inserted in, Spec,CP. It is interesting to see whether C also enters feature-checking in the head-adjunction domain created by head-raising to C. Head-raising would presumably involve an inflectional category, possibly including the verb. Using I as an abbreviation for inflectional categories, the checking domain created by I-raising to C would have the form $[_{C^0} [_{I^0} ([V]) I] C]$.

Chomsky (1993) suggests that feature checking in the head-adjunction domain created by raising of I to C is probably what underlies the Verb Second phenomenon (Chapter 13). The feature involved could be assumed to be a general operator-feature which covers topics/focus phrases in addition to wh-phrases. This suggestion implies that the operator feature in question must be encoded not only in C but also in I. The instance of the operator feature associated with C is strong, and, moreover, incompatible with the complementiser 'that'. This accounts for the Verb Second pattern found in languages such as German, where it is obligatory in root clauses and generally incompatible with the complementiser 'that' in embedded clauses. The relevant German examples are reproduced in (21) from Chapter 13:

21a. Den Ball hat Hans   gekauft.
     the ball   has Hans   bought
     'Hans has bought the ball.'

21b. Er   sagt   diesen Film   haben   die Kinder   gesehen.
    he   says   this film   have   the children   seen
    'He says that the children have seen this film.'

21c. *Er sagt,   dass   diesen Film   haben   die Kinder   gesehen.
    he says   that   this film   have   the children   seen

Languages which allow Verb Second (in embedded clauses) with the complementiser 'that' productively such as Yiddish and Icelandic do not appear to raise a problem, at least on the view that the Verb Second domain involves an additional projection with properties similar to those of CP (see Chapter 13 for discussion). The relevant examples from Yiddish and Icelandic are reproduced in (22):

22a. . . . az   dos yingl   vet   oyfn veg   zen   a kats.
    . . . that   the boy   will   on-the way   see   a cat

22b. . . . ad   Helgi   hevur   aldrei   hitt   Mariu.
    . . . that   Helga   has   never   met   Maria

In Chapter 13 it was pointed out that it is not clear whether I-raising to C triggers topicalisation of an operator to Spec,CP or the other way around. The two phenomena seem to correlate quite closely. This is also true in English wh-questions as well as declarative sentences with a negative topic, e.g. *Never have I seen anything like that.* Chomsky (1993) makes the suggestion that 'Raising of I to C may automatically make the relevant feature of C strong (the V-second phenomenon).' This suggestion appears to make movement of an operator to Spec,CP dependent on I-raising to C instead of the other around. I-raising to C makes the operator feature of C strong, thereby triggering overt movement of an operator to Spec,CP. This suggestion is consistent with the view that the operator feature of C is universally strong.

19.7   *Summary*

Lexical items are introduced into derivations already inflected for relevant morphological features. These features are also encoded in inflectional categories in the functional structure of the sentence. Inflectional categories play a mediating role and ensure that inflected verbs are properly paired with their agreeing arguments as far as their inflectional properties are concerned. Movement is driven by the need to check features. The verb raises to the inflectional categories to check its own features in the head-adjunction configuration, if not overtly then covertly. The subject and the object also raise to the Spec position of the relevant inflectional categories to check their own features in the Spec-head configuration, if not overtly then covertly. For a derivation to converge at LF, all features must be checked.

Whether features are checked overtly or covertly is determined by the parameter of strength/weakness. Strong features have to be checked overtly, and therefore trigger movement of the relevant categories in overt syntax. Weak features do not have to be checked overtly, and therefore do not trigger movement of the relevant categories in overt syntax. The parameter of strength/weakness of features can be exploited to account for the difference between overt V-raising versus non-overt V-raising languages, VSO versus SVO languages, overt wh-movement languages versus wh-in-situ languages, as well as for Verb Second versus non-Verb Second languages, among other distinctions.

20 Bare Phrase Structure and Antisymmetry

Contents

20.1 *Bare Phrase Structure*

X-bar theory was set up as an attempt to restrict the proliferation of Phrase Structure rules. X-bar schema are essentially abstractions of the core properties of PS rules, and generalise across categories (Chapter 6). X-bar schema have often been regarded as constraints on the projection of lexical items onto syntactic representations, particularly in the context of the strongly representational framework Principles and Parameters outlined in Parts II and III of this book. MP differs in being more derivational than representational in its drive. A theory of phrase structure befitting such a system is expected to be derivational in nature too. Chomsky (1995) outlines the broad aspects of one such theory called **Bare Phrase Structure (BPS)**.

In Chapter 17 lexical items were said to be selected and merged together into phrase markers by the operation GT. As pointed out there, GT is a complex operation which involves more than one step. Chomsky (1995) revises GT by dismantling it into two separate major operations called **Select** and **Merge**. Select and Merge introduce new items into the derivation. We will continue to assume that items are displaced in terms of the different operation Move α. The latter is a complex operation, too, particularly if movement is understood as copying (see

Chapter 18). Move α targets a category and merges the moved category into it, subject to the extension requirement (see Chapter 17).

The operation Select selects items from the lexicon in the form of feature complexes. The selected items are merged into phrase markers by the operation Merge. Merge takes two objects, α and β, and merges them to form a new object of the form {α {α, β}}. In the latter, α is said to **project** in the sense that the newly formed object has exactly the identity of α. Given that lexical items are essentially bundles of features, the new object has the features of the lexical item that projects. Put differently, when two items in the form of feature complexes are merged, it is the features of the item that projects (i.e. the head) which determine the newly formed category. Chomsky dismisses as unworkable the options whereby the newly formed category is an intersection or a union of the features of the merged items.

Taking α to be the determiner *the* and β the noun *man*, Merge derives the new object {the {the man}} with the bare structure roughly shown in (1a). (1b) is an alternative presentation of (1a) which includes categorial labels. (2) is the structure assigned to *the man* by X-bar theory:

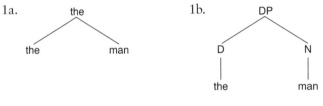

1a. (tree: the → the, man)   1b. (tree: DP → D (the), N (man))

2. DP
    |
    D'
    | \
    D   NP
    | |
    the N'
        |
        N
        |
        book

(1a&b) differ from (2) in many respects, among them the fact that it does not include the minimal, intermediate and maximal projections of the lexical item. X-bar theory determines the projections of lexical items in a somewhat absolute way. A lexical item X has the projections specified in the schema XP → (YP) X' and X' → X (ZP). X-bar schema yield the structure [$_{XP}$ (YP) [$_{X'}$ X (ZP)]] for X, irrespective of whether X has a complement or a specifier. Chomsky (1995) follows Muysken (1982) in taking projections of lexical items to be 'relational properties of categories' rather than inherent properties. Their presence is determined by the structure or context in which the lexical item is placed. In isolation, *the* and *man* are both minimal D/N and maximal DP/NP. When they are merged together a new context is created for both items. If *the* projects, it ceases to be maximal and becomes only minimal in relation to the newly created maximal object. The noun *man*, however, continues to be both minimal and maximal by virtue of being the member of the pair that does not project.

With this mind, let us try to trace the derivation of the sentence *The man saw it*. Recall that derivations are constructed bottom up, starting with the most embedded item. Select therefore selects the pronoun *it* first. Recall that *it* is both minimal (D) and maximal (DP) in isolation. The verb *saw* is also both minimal (V) and maximal (VP) in isolation. Merge merges *saw* with *it*, *saw* projects to form the new maximal object {*saw* {*saw, it*}}. Consequently, *saw* ceases to be maximal in relation to the newly created object. In contrast, *it* continues to be both minimal and maximal by virtue of not projecting. The structure derived so far is roughly as shown in (3):

3.

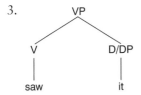

The next step is to merge the subject *the man* with (3), assuming the subject in VP hypothesis (see Chapter 8). The DP *the man* is formed in the manner explained above. The determiner *the* is merged with *man*, *the* projects to form the maximal object *[DP the [N/NP man]]*. The latter is then merged with the VP in (3), to form the new object shown in (4). Unlike (3), (4) includes the single-bar projection V' which arises as a result of introducing a specifier into VP:

4.

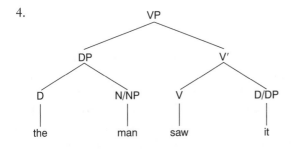

The next stage in the derivation involves merging the inflectional categories with (4). Let us take I to be a collective symbol for the inflectional categories Agr$_O$, T and Agr$_S$. I merges with (4), I projects to form the structure roughly shown in (5):

5.

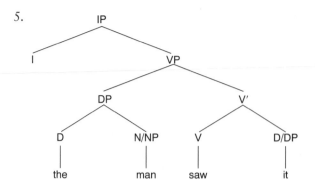

At this stage in the derivation, Move α applies to merge the subject with (5), leaving a trace or a copy behind. This derives the structure roughly shown in (6) which includes the single bar projection of I:

6.

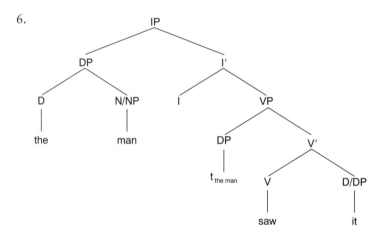

The discussion so far has been restricted to what were previously called the core X-bar structures, the head-complement structure and the spec-head structure. The operation which forms the head-complement structure creates a new object, as explained, and so does the operation which creates the spec-head structure. How about adjunction structures? In Chapter 17 we saw that adjunction is not subject to the extension requirement, with the consequence that adjuncts can be introduced non-cyclically (see also Chapter 18). This property of adjuncts already sets them apart from complements and specifiers. Chomsky (1995) suggests that adjunction structures are different in another (perhaps related) respect. The operation which introduces adjunction structures does not create a new object, unlike the operation which creates head-complement and spec-head structures. Rather, it only adds a new segment to an existing category, either a maximal category (adjunction to a maximal projection) or a head (adjunction to a head). Thus, BPS maintains a clear distinction between specifiers and adjuncts. They both exist, and with different properties. This aspect of BPS will be put in focus later on when we discuss another theory which obliterates the difference between them completely, basically by reducing specifiers to adjuncts.

20.2 *Some empirical issues*

20.2.1 Unergatives

The theory of BPS as outlined so far faces a problem with respect to a class of intransitive verbs. To see how, we need first recall the distinction between different types of intransitive verbs made in Chapter 7.

The traditional class of intransitive verbs, i.e. verbs with a single argument, has been shown to divide into two major sub-groups. One sub-group consists of verbs the single argument of which is an internal argument. These verbs are called unaccusative on the grounds that they do not assign accusative Case to their internal argument. The internal argument receives Case as a result of movement to the subject position in syntax. Accordingly, example (7a) is assigned the representations and derivation shown in (7b&c) in the context of the P&P framework. The internal argument *the vase* is base-generated inside V′ and moves to Spec,IP (see Chapters 7 and 8):

7a. The vase broke.
7b. DS: [$_{IP}$ [e] I [$_{VP}$ [e] [$_{V′}$ broke [the vase] . . .
7c. SS: [$_{IP}$ [the vase] I [$_{VP}$ [e] [$_{V′}$ broke [t$_{the\ vase}$] . . .

The other sub-group consists of verbs the single argument of which is an external argument. These verbs are said to be **unergative**. Their single argument is base-generated in Spec,VP and moves to Spec,IP in syntax. This is shown in (8), using the verb *laugh* as an example:

8a. Mary laughed.
8b. DS: [$_{IP}$ [e] I [$_{VP}$ [Mary] [$_{V′}$ laughed . . .
8c. SS: [$_{IP}$ [Mary] I [$_{VP}$ [t$_{Mary}$] [$_{V′}$ laughed . . .

In the context of BPS, VPs with an unaccusative verb are derived in exactly the same way as VPs with a transitive verb, except that they lack an external argument in Spec,VP. (7a) has the derivation shown in (9). The verb *broke* is merged with *the vase* to form the VP shown in (9b). I is then merged with VP to form the structure shown in (9c). Finally, *the vase* is merged into Spec,IP by Move α to form the structure shown in (9d):

9a. The vase broke.
9b. [$_{VP}$ [$_{V}$ broke] [$_{DP}$ the vase]]
9c. [$_{IP}$ I [$_{VP}$ [V broke] [$_{DP}$ the vase]]]
9d. [$_{IP}$ [$_{DP}$ the vase] I [$_{VP}$ [$_{V}$ broke] [t$_{the\ vase}$]]]

If we apply the same derivation to (8a), we obtain the representations shown in (10b–d). The order of the verb and the direct object inside VP is immaterial. It might as well be *[VP Mary laughed]* as we will see later on in this chapter:

10a. Mary laughed.
10b. [$_{VP}$ [$_V$ laughed] [$_{DP}$ Mary]]
10c. [$_{IP}$ I [$_{VP}$ [$_V$ laughed] [$_{DP}$ Mary]]]
10d. [$_{IP}$ [$_{DP}$ Mary] I [$_{VP}$ [$_V$ laughed] [t_{Mary}]]]

The representations in (10) are clearly inconsistent with the unergative nature of the verb. The argument of the verb is an external argument rather than an internal argument. It should be merged into Spec,VP rather than into the direct object position. However, there is no way the argument could be merged directly into Spec,VP in (10). BPS is simply technically unable to make a distinction between unaccusative and unergative verbs. If a DP is paired directly with a verb, it will always come up as an internal argument. It will only come up as external argument if it is merged with a set which consists of a verb and an object.

Chomsky (1995) solves the problem by adopting the conclusion independently reached in Hale and Keyser (1993) that all verbs, including unergatives, have an internal argument. According to Hale and Keyser, denominal verbs such as *laugh*, *sneeze*, *neigh*, *dance* are complex forms derived by incorporation of a complement N into an abstract V. The abstract verb is the equivalent of the 'light' verb in expressions such as *make trouble* and *have puppies*, so that *laugh* is roughly the spell-out of the complex 'make laughter'. The process of N-incorporation involved in the derivation of complex verbs is a syntactic one, as in Baker's (1988) derivation of overt N-incorporation structures (see Chapter 14). According to this analysis, the VP which includes the verb *laugh*, for example, has the form shown in (11) with N incorporated into V:

11.

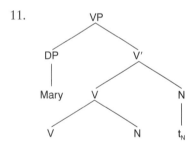

In view of (11), the DP *Mary* is not merged directly with the verb, but with a VP consisting of a verb and a direct object, the latter incorporated into V. Consequently, it correctly comes up as the specifier of VP instead of as direct object of V. Accordingly, (10a) has the derivation shown in (12):

12a. Mary laughed.
12b. [$_{VP}$ [$_V$ [V] [N]]] (= laugh)]
12c. [$_{VP}$ [$_{DP}$ Mary] [$_{V'}$ [$_V$ laughed] [N]]]
12d. [$_{IP}$ I [$_{VP}$ [$_{DP}$ Mary] [$_{V'}$ [$_V$ laughed] [N]]]]
12e. [$_{IP}$ [$_{DP}$ Mary] I [$_{VP}$ [t_{Mary}] [$_{V'}$ [$_V$ laughed] [N]]]]

20.2.2 Clitics

Another empirical issue that arises from BPS theory as outlined above relates to the idea that a given category can be both minimal and maximal. Chomsky (1995) points out that clitics are good examples of such categories.

In Chapter 15 we saw that VP-related clitics have the apparently conflicting properties of both heads and maximal projections. They are maximal projections in that they function as DP arguments and can move long-distance, particularly in clitic-climbing contexts. At the same time, they have properties of heads insofar as they appear to adjoin to a head and that their movement is blocked by head categories such as Neg and 'if'. The Italian clitic-climbing examples in (13a–c) are reproduced from Chapter 15:

13a. Gianni **li** vuole vedere.
    Gianni them wants to-see

13b. *Gianni **li** vuole non vedere.
    Gianni them wants not to-see

13c. *Non **li** so se fare.
    not them know-1S if to-do

In the context of BPS theory, clitics have the representation shown in (14) prior to their movement. They are both minimal and maximal by virtue of being the member of the set that does not project, as with direct object pronouns in English discussed above:

14.

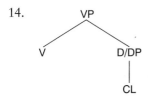

The ambiguous status of clitics means that they can adjoin to a head subsequent to their movement without giving rise to structural inconsistency. The question whether clitics move as heads, with the implication that cliticisation is an instance of head-movement, or as maximal projections, with the implication that cliticisation is an instance of XP-movements remains intriguing. The fact that they move long distance seems to suggest that they move as XPs. Note that the heads which block cliticisation, namely Neg and 'if', have independently been claimed to be associated with an abstract operator in their Spec position (Rizzi 1990, 1991). Perhaps, it is this operator that blocks cliticisation in the Relativised Minimality sense rather than the head. If this reasoning is correct, it may be possible to maintain the view that cliticisation is an instance of XP-movement. The fact that clitics adjoin to a head subsequent to their movement is not problematic in the context of BPS theory as explained.

20.2.3 Order

X-bar theory does not fix the order of heads in relation to their complement. In the P&P framework, the order is fixed in terms of an associated Head parameter, as we saw in Chapter 11. The head-first value yields the Head Complement (H-C) order and the head-last value yields the C-H order. The order of specifiers does not seem to be subject to variation, although there have been analyses in the literature which draw order distinctions relating to specifiers.

BPS resembles X-bar theory in that it too does not fix the order of heads in relation to the complement, nor for that matter the order of specifiers either. The notations {*saw* {*saw it*}} and {*saw* {*it saw*}} are essentially identical. In view of this, it seems possible to assume a Head parameter which fixes the order of heads in relation to their complement, as with X-bar theory in the P&P framework. However, Chomsky (1995) takes the view that 'There is no clear evidence that order plays a role at LF or in the computation . . . to LF'. He goes on to suggest that order is fixed at PF by certain mechanisms which apply to the output of Spell-Out. Among these mechanisms is the Linear Correspondence Axiom (LCA) suggested in Kayne (1994) in the context of theory of Antisymmetry discussed in the next section of this chapter.

For the moment, note that Chomsky's idea that order is fixed at PF represents a radical departure from previous theories all of which assumed order in the computational system, including Antisymmetry. In the P&P framework, assuming specific orders in the computational system is arguably the inevitable consequence of a view of PF which does not attribute to it mechanisms that can determine order. Attributing the role of fixing order to PF presupposes a comparatively richer level of PF with mechanisms that were not previously thought to be available to it. Whether this is the right move is an empirical question, although the burden of proof falls mainly on the theory which attributes the fixing of order to PF. The burden is a very heavy one indeed, as the typological literature upon which many studies of order in the P&P framework have relied, e.g. Greenberg (1966), includes many significant order universals, implicational and otherwise, which need to be explained.

20.3 *Antisymmetry*

20.3.1 Linear Correspondence Axiom (LCA)

Structures determined by X-bar theory do not establish a correlation between hierarchy and order. A set of hierarchical relations can be associated with more than one order. This aspect of X-bar theory is actually what makes order parameters such as the Head parameter possible and necessary. The verb and its object, for example, bear the same hierarchical relation to each other inside VP, but the two categories can have either the VO order or the OV order. Moreover, the hierarchical notions 'higher than X' and 'lower than X' do not necessarily always translate into linear relations of 'precede X' and 'follow X'. For example, a category that is right-adjoined to IP is higher than the subject in Spec,IP but does not precede the subject.

Kayne (1994) proposes an alternative theory of phrase structure which 'always completely determines linear order . . . ' such that different linear orders imply different hierarchical relations. At the heart of Kayne's theory, called Antisymmetry, is the axiom reproduced in (15). We will not try to discuss the formalism involved in the formulation of the axiom here. We will proceed directly to explore its consequences:

15. **Linear Correspondence Axiom (LCA)**

    d(A) is a linear ordering of T.

LCA presupposes a specific notion of c-command, namely 'asymmetric c-command', defined as in (16):

16. α asymmetrically c-commands β iff α c-commands β and β does not c-command α.

Note, crucially, that Kayne defines c-command in terms of the 'first node up', and not in terms of 'the first branching node up'.

Simplifying matters to a considerable degree, LCA can be interpreted to say that given two categories α and β, if α asymmetrically c-commands β then α precedes β. The asymmetric relation can either be between two terminal categories or between a terminal category and a maximal projection. If a terminal category α is in an asymmetric c-command relation with the maximal projection of β, then α is in an asymmetric c-command relation with respect to β. Moreover, asymmetric c-command, and therefore ordering, is transitive. If α asymmetrically c-commands β in the sequence $\{\alpha\ \beta\}$ and β asymmetrically c-commands γ in the sequence $\{\beta\ \chi\}$ then α asymmetrically c-commands γ in the sequence $\{\alpha\ \beta\ \gamma\}$. Ordering is also said to be 'total' in the sense that 'it must cover all members of the set'.

Kayne goes on to show how LCA derives some of the basic properties of X-bar theory. One such property is that the complement of a head cannot be a simple terminal category, but must be a maximal projection which dominates a terminal category. Using a concrete example, the VP *see John* has the representation in (17a), and cannot have the representation shown in (17b) where the terminal category N is not dominated by an NP:

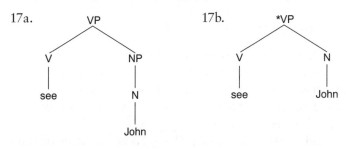

17a., 17b.

(17a) is consistent with the LCA as V asymmetrically c-commands N. (17b), however, is inconsistent with the LCA and therefore excluded. V does not asymmetrically c-command N in (17b). The two terminal nodes c-command each other, so that c-command in this structure is not asymmetric.

Another property of X-bar theory which follows from LCA is that an XP cannot have more than one head (see Chapter 6). An XP with two heads would have the structure shown in (17b) which is excluded for the reasons explained.

The property of X-bar theory that prevents an XP from dominating two maximal projections also follows from LCA. In Chapter 6, such a structure was considered for instances of topicalisation in English, and excluded on the grounds that it is incompatible with the requirements of X-bar theory. (18) is an abstract structure where a maximal projection dominates two other maximal projections. YP and ZP c-command each other, and neither Y nor Z c-command out of their projection:

18.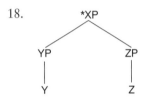

As a useful guide, LCA only allows structures that pair a head with a non-head. Structures which pair two heads such as (17b) or two maximal projections such as (18) are excluded.

20.3.2   Adjunction to a maximal projection

The observation that structures which pair non-heads are disallowed means that specifiers such as YP in (19a), and adjuncts such as YP in (19b), have no place in the theory. Neither of them meets the total asymmetric c-command requirement:

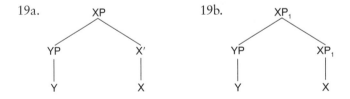

It turns out that structure (19b) can be accommodated in a way that will be explained shortly. Structure (19a), however, cannot be accommodated. Kayne goes on to conclude that subjects are structurally represented as adjuncts. In other words, the theory obliterates the X-bar distinction between subjects and adjuncts by reducing the former to the latter.

Kayne accommodates the adjunction structure (19b) by adopting the distinction between segments and categories suggested in May (1985), and defining c-command in a way that excludes segments. The definition in question is reproduced in (20). The motivation behind May's distinction between segments and categories is discussed in more detail later on:

20. α c-commands β iff α and β are categories and α excludes β and every category that dominates α dominates β.

Adjunction is said to create a category with more than one segment. In (19b), XP_1 and XP_2 are segments of the category XP. α is said to exclude β if none of the segments of α dominates β. In (19b), XP does not exclude YP, because YP is dominated by a segment of XP, while YP excludes XP. According to the definition of c-command in (20), XP_2 does not c-command Y in (19b), whereas YP c-commands X, deriving the asymmetric c-command relation needed for ordering.

(20) also has the effect of excluding multiple adjunction to a maximal projection of the type illustrated in (21):

21.

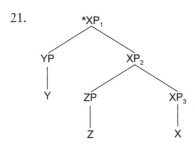

In (21) ZP c-commands Y and YP c-commands Z. Neither YP nor ZP is dominated by XP, resulting in mutual c-command between them. Kayne concludes that the exclusion of multiple adjunction derives the requirement incorporated in X-bar theory that a phrase can only have one specifier, assuming of course that specifiers reduce to adjuncts. Only one adjunct per maximal projection is allowed.

Kayne points out that the restriction of adjuncts of maximal projections to one leads to 'the pervasiveness of heads in syntactic structures . . .'. To see how, consider the topicalisation example in (22a):

22a. This (book), I don't like.

In Chapter 6, examples such as (22a) were assigned the structure shown in (22b). This structure is excluded by LCA as it includes a Specifier that is not an adjunct. Recall that specifiers reduce to adjuncts in the context of Antisymmetry. (22c) is also excluded, this time because it involves multiple adjunction to IP. (22c) is identical to (21), and therefore is excluded for the reasons explained. The only structure for (22a) consistent with the LCA is the one in (22d), where the topicalised category is adjoined to the maximal projection of a null head which exists over and above I/IP. The category in question is represented with the variable X.

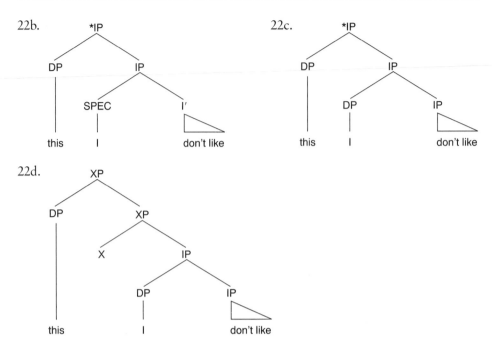

22b. *IP — DP (SPEC: this, I: I), IP (I', don't like)
22c. *IP — DP (this, I), IP (DP: I, IP: don't like)
22d. XP — DP (this), XP (X: I, IP: DP I, IP don't like)

Sentences that include an IP-adverb discussed in Chapter 6, e.g. *Presumably, John left*, must also be assigned a structure along the lines of (22d), where the adverb is adjoined to the maximal projection of a special null head. The view that adverbs are specifiers of special functional heads is outlined and defended in Cinque (1997).

We have discussed other contexts said to involve multiple adjunction to IP. Sentences with multiple quantifiers such as (23a) were said in Chapter 7 to involve multiple adjunction of the raised quantifiers to IP at LF:

23a. Every student admires some professor.
23b. $[_{IP_1}$ some professor $[_{IP_2}$ every student $[_{IP_3}$ t$_{every\ student}$ admires t$_{some\ professor}]]]$
23c. $[_{IP_1}$ every student $[_{IP_2}$ some professor $[_{IP_3}$ t$_{every\ student}$ admires t$_{some\ professor}]]]$

According to the discussion in Chapter 7, (23b) is the representation underlying the reading whereby *some professor* scopes over *every student*, and (23c) the representation underlying the reading whereby *every student* scopes over *some professor*. May (1985) points out that (23c) actually involves an ECP violation as the antecedent of the trace in the subject position is not close enough to the trace. Scope interaction between the two quantifiers must therefore be made possible on the basis of the single representation in (23b). May suggests that this could be done by allowing the quantifiers in (23b) to mutually c-command each other. This would be possible if the projection IP$_2$ that intervenes between the quantifiers does not block c-command. To achieve this, May makes a distinction between categories and segments such that only categories can block c-command. IP$_2$ in (23b) is only a segment and therefore does not block c-command.

Now, it is precisely because the two quantifiers in (23b) c-command each other that the adjunction structure that underlies them is excluded by LCA in the context of the theory of Antisymmetry. (23b) involves multiple adjunction to IP and is therefore identical to (21) above. The structure underlying examples such as (23a) must therefore have a different form in the context of Antisymmetry. A possible way of accounting for scope interaction in (23a) that is consistent with LCA is the theory outlined in Hornstein (1995) and discussed in Chapter 18. Another way would be to assume that raised quantifiers are adjoined to the maximal projection of a special (null) head. Such a theory is outlined in Beghelli and Stowell (1997).

20.3.3 Adjunction to a head

Head adjunction structures are involved in head raising contexts as well as cliticisation, as described in Chapter 15. Kayne uses clitics to illustrate the types of head-adjunction structures allowed in the theory of Antisymmetry.

(24b) is the head adjunction structure derived by cliticisation in a French example such as (24a):

24a. Jean **vous** donnera le livre.
Jean you$_{DAT}$ will-give the book

24b.

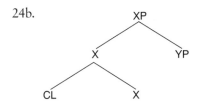

In (24b) X does not c-command CL because it does not exclude CL, the latter being an adjunct of X. However, CL c-commands X because CL excludes X, and every category that dominates CL also dominates X. Therefore, CL asymmetrically c-commands X in (24b). Single adjunction to a head is therefore allowed in the theory of Antisymmetry.

Let us now explore the structure involved in situations of multiple cliticisation found in French example such as (25a). (25b) is the structure derived by multiple adjunction of clitics to the same head:

25a. Jean **vous** **le** donnera.
Jean you$_{DAT}$ it$_{ACC}$ will-give

25b.   25c.

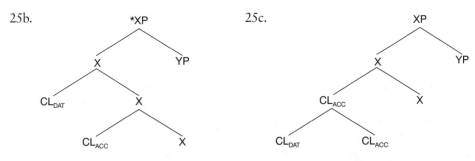

(25b) is similar to the structure which involves multiple adjunction to XP discussed above. In (25b), CL_{DAT} and CL_{ACC} c-command each other, in violation of the LCA. Multiple adjunction to a head is therefore excluded, on a par with multiple adjunction to an XP. Only one adjunct per head is allowed. A structure for (25a) consistent with the LCA is as outlined in (25c), where CL_{ACC} is adjoined to the head X and CL_{DAT} is adjoined to CL_{ACC} rather than to X. The head X has only one adjunct and the head CL_{ACC} also has only one adjunct. According to the analysis in (25c), multiple clitics form a constituent, which is arguably consistent with the traditional idea that adjacent multiple clitics form a 'cluster'.

20.3.4   Order

The theory of Antisymmetry incorporating LCA has radical implications for how language variation in linear order is derived. We will explore some of those implications here briefly.

Starting with the VO versus OV distinction and AuxVP versus VPAux distinction, let us remind ourselves how they are accounted for in the P&P framework (Chapter 11). Languages such as German are said to select the head-last value for V and I. This results in a structure where V is ordered to the right of O in VP and I is ordered to the right of VP. The German example (26a) therefore has the structure shown in (26b):

26a. . . . dass   Hans   den Ball   gekauft hat.
    . . . that   Hans   the ball   bought has
    '. . . that Hans has bought the ball.'

26b. [$_{CP}$ dass [$_{IP}$ Hans [$_{I'}$ [$_{VP}$ [$_{DP}$ den Ball] gekauft] hat]]]

(26b) is inconsistent with the LCA in more than one place, besides the fact that it involves a non-adjoined subject. The main verb asymmetrically c-commands the direct object inside VP, but follows the direct object. Likewise, the auxiliary in I asymmetrically c-commands the main verb in VP, but follows the main verb. Recall that in Antisymmetry, asymmetric c-command completely determines linear order. If constituent α asymmetrically c-commands constituent β, then α precedes β. In view of this, the German example (26a) must have a structure along the lines shown in (27), where every constituent asymmetrically c-commands the constituent that follows it, with the auxiliary being the most embedded by virtue of being the last constituent in the clause:

27.   [$_{CP}$ dass [$_{IP}$ Hans [$_{XP}$ den Ball [$_{YP}$ gekauft [$_{ZP}$ hat . . .

Presumably, (27) is derived by movement of the participle to a position above the position of the auxiliary, and movement of the direct object to a position above the derived position of the participle. An analysis along these lines is outlined in Zwart (1993).

Kayne makes the point that the German order shown in (27) is derived from an underlying representation where V is to the left of O and I is to the left of VP, as in

English. According to Kayne, all languages have the underlying order Specifier-Head-Complement (S-H-C), that is all languages are subject-initial and head-initial as far as underlying representations are concerned. Surface variation in order is the result of movement operations applying in the mapping onto surface representations.

Taking S-H to be the subject of the sentence and the verb, all languages are SVO underlyingly. The VSO order is derived by movement of the verb to a position above S. Recall from Chapter 13 that this is basically the scenario assumed by most analyses of VSO.

Taking H-C to be the verb and its object, all languages are VO underlyingly. The OV order is derived by movement of the direct object to a position above the verb, as explained above in relation to (27).

Taking H to be Comp and C to be IP, all languages have the order [C [IP]] underlyingly. English and German are consistent with this order. Japanese, however, is not. Judging from example (28), where the Q-element is clause-final, Japanese appears to be a Comp-final language with the superficial order [[IP] C]:

28a. John-wa   nani-o   kaimasita ka?
     John-top   what-ACC   bought   Q
     'What did John buy?'

28b. DS: [$_{CP}$ ka [$_{IP}$ John-wa nani-o kaimasita]].
28c. SS: [$_{CP}$ [$_{IP}$ John-wa nani-o kaimasita] ka [$_{IP}$ t$_{IP}$] . . .

Kayne suggests that the surface order [[IP] C] is derived from an underlying structure with the order [C [IP]], shown in (28b). The derivation involves movement of IP to the (adjoined) Spec position of CP, as shown in (28c). Kayne goes on to point out that this derivational property of Comp-final clauses may explain why languages which have them, such as Japanese, tend to lack overt wh-movement. Overt wh-movement displaces the wh-phrase to Spec,CP which in Comp-final clauses is occupied by the preposed IP. Recall that Japanese lacks overt wh-movement (Chapters 11 and 19).

Finally, taking H-C to be the preposition and its object, all languages have the order PO underlyingly. Postpositional phrases with the order OP found in some languages are derived by movement of the object of the preposition to a position above the preposition. Kayne suggests that the position occupied by the moved object could be the (adjoined) Spec position of an AgrP above PP, roughly as shown in (29). P may either remain in situ or adjoin to Agr:

29a. DS: [$_{AgrP}$ Agr [$_{PP}$ P [DP] . . .
29b. SS: [$_{AgrP}$ [DP] Agr [$_{PP}$ P t$_{DP}$ . . .

Kayne explains that (29b) may be the reason why overt agreement between P and its object is found in postpositional phrases more often than in prepositional phrases, on the assumption that agreement is triggered by movement of a category to Spec,AgrP.

20.3.5   Right-adjunction

It should be clear by now that right-adjunction is inconsistent with the LCA. Right-adjoined categories asymmetrically c-command the categories inside the projection adjoined to in much the same way that left-adjoined categories do. However, unlike left-adjoined categories, right-adjoined categories follow in linear order the categories inside the projection adjoined to. Thus, all constructions which have been assumed to involve right-adjunction, whether derived by movement or base-generated, must be reanalysed in a way consistent with the theory of Antisymmetry.

Among the right-adjunction structures derived by movement is the one associated with Heavy NP Shift (Chapter 4). (30a) is an example of Heavy NP Shift:

30a. John gave to Bill all his old linguistics books.
30b. John gave [[to Bill] [X^0 [[all . . . books] [Y^0 $t_{\text{to Bill}}$ . . .

In the traditional analysis of Heavy NP Shift briefly discussed in Chapters 4 and 6, (30a) is derived by rightward movement of the heavy direct object and, as we assumed there, right-adjunction to VP (or IP). In the context of the theory of Antisymmetry, the order in (30a) implies that PP is higher than the heavy DP rather than lower. DP must be the most embedded constituent. This means that (30a) is derived by leftward movement of PP to a position higher than DP. One such analysis is independently suggested in Larson (1988, 1990), and derives the order in (30a) by leftward movement of the string *[gave to Bill]* analysed as a constituent to a position above DP. The structure derived in Larson's analysis, however, is inconsistent with the LCA. In view of this, Kayne suggests to derive the order in (30a) by leftward movement of PP to a position above DP as shown in (30b). The underlying structure is one where PP is included in a small clause the subject position of which is occupied by DP. Kayne goes on to point out many advantages of the analysis in (30b) which we cannot discuss here for lack of space.

The other right-adjunction structure derived by movement is Extraposition. As far as extraposition of relative clauses is concerned, Kayne's reanalysis of it presupposes a specific structure of relative noun phrases we have not discussed yet (see below). However, the basic idea is pretty straightforward. Instead of deriving (31a) by rightward movement of the relative clause (Extraposition), they can be derived by leftward movement of the head of the relative noun phrase, roughly as shown in (31b). According to the analysis in (31b), (30a) is an instance of 'stranding' of the relative clause:

31a. Something just happened that you should know about.
31b. something just happened [$t_{\text{something}}$ that you should know about . . .

Turning now to base-generated adjunction, the typical context for it is relative noun phrases (Chapter 6). According to the analysis based on X-bar theory, relatives of the type found in English with the order [Det N CP] have the structure shown in (32b), where the relative clause is right-adjoined to NP:

32a. The picture of his mother that Bill saw

32b. [DP the [NP [N′ picture of his mother] [CP that Bill saw] . . .

(32b) is clearly inconsistent with LCA. Kayne points out that the only structure and analysis of relatives in the literature consistent with the LCA is the one suggested in the combined works of Smith (1969) and Vergnaud (1974). According to this analysis, relative noun phrases have the underlying structure roughly shown in (33b):

33a. The picture of his mother that Bill saw

33b. [DP the [CP [that [IP Bill saw [picture of his mother] . . .

33c. [DP the [CP [picture of his mother] [that [IP Bill saw t_picture of his mother · · ·

In (33b) the relative clause CP is the complement of D occupied by the definite article. The so-called head noun is an NP base-generated in the relativised position, which is the direct object in (33b). The order shown in (33a) is derived by movement of the NP *picture of his mother* to Spec,CP. This process is often called **promotion**, and the analysis outlined in (33b&c) is called the promotion analysis of relatives.

Relatives with a wh-word instead of the complementiser THAT, such as in (34a), are derived from the underlying representation roughly shown in (34b), where the wh-word and *picture of his mother* form a noun phrase arguably of the category DP:

34a. The picture of his mother which Bill saw

34b. [DP the [CP [e [IP Bill saw [DP which picture of his mother] . . .

34c. [DP the [CP [DP which picture of his mother] [e [IP Bill saw
[DP t_which picture of his mother] · · ·

34d. [DP the [CP [DP [NP picture of his mother] [which t_picture of his mother]]
[e [Bill saw t_which picture of his mother] · · ·

The constituent *which picture of his mother* is promoted to Spec,CP. This step is shown in (34c). Subsequently, the constituent *picture of his mother* is moved to a position to the left of the wh-word inside the noun phrase. This process derives the representation shown in (34d) with the order in (34a).

Relatives of the type found in English and illustrated above are called head-first relatives or **N-initial relatives**. These relatives have the order [N [CP]]. There are languages which have head-last or **N-final relatives** with the order [[CP] N]. N-final relatives are illustrated with (35a) from Amharic (Ethio-Semitic) (Fulass 1972). Amharic is generally a head-final language, where the direct object precedes the verb. English words are used in the derivation (35b–d) for purely presentational purposes:

35a. Kassa-n   yä-fällägä-w   lej
     Kassa-ACC   SM-wanted-the   child
     'The child who looked for Kassa'

35b. [$_{DP}$ the [$_{CP}$ [e [$_{IP}$ [child] [Kassa wanted]]] . . .
35c. [$_{DP}$ the [$_{CP}$ [child] [e [$_{IP}$ t$_{child}$ [Kassa wanted]]] . . .
35d. [$_{DP}$ [$_{IP}$ t$_{child}$ [Kassa wanted]] [the [$_{CP}$ [child] [e t$_{IP}$ . . .

Kayne suggests that N-final relatives are derived from an underlying structure identical to that of N-initial relatives. This is shown in (35b), ignoring the OV order inside the relative clause. Their derivation shares with that of N-initial relatives the promotion step to Spec,CP shown in (35c). It differs in that it involves additional movement of IP to the outer Spec,DP shown in (35d). This movement derives the order whereby IP is followed by the definite article and the latter by the head-N. Note that this is exactly the order in the Amharic relative noun phrase (35a).

20.4   *Bare Phrase Structure and Antisymmetry*

Kayne points out that LCA 'does underlie the entire set of syntactic representations and therefore that every syntactic representation is automatically associated with a fixed linear ordering of its terminal nodes'. The reasoning behind this statement is that LCA, together with asymmetric c-command, derives all the effects of X-bar theory so that phrase structure is determined by LCA and nothing else. It follows that LCA holds of all levels of syntactic representation insofar as they take the form of phrase markers, which they must do. Thus, even though there may be no direct evidence for linear ordering at LF, LF representations must be consistent with LCA. This is why discussion of the LF representation of sentences with multiple interacting quantifiers was included above.

Kayne's reasoning why LCA must hold of all syntactic representations does not extend to BPS. This is because phrase structure is not determined by LCA in BPS. It is determined by a separate mechanism which, moreover, does not impose linear ordering on terminal nodes. It is therefore possible to assume in the context of BPS that LCA holds only of PF, as Chomsky (1995) does.

There are however complications that arise from assuming LCA in the context of BPS. Here we will discuss one complication having to do with simple direct objects in sentence-final contexts such as (36a). (36a) has the bare phrase structure shown in (36b), where the pronominal direct object is a D:

36a. The man saw it.
36b.

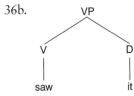

Note that (36b) is the kind of structure that was shown above to be disallowed by LCA, as V and D c-command each other. This fact has no implications for (36) in the computational system in BPS for the reasons explained. However, (36b) cannot survive as is at PF, where LCA is assumed to apply. V and D will not be assigned a linear ordering. To get around this problem, Chomsky (1995) suggests that D undergoes incorporation into V. This process is arguably more transparent with verbs that take particles such as *pick up*. With such verbs, a pronominal direct object appears between the verb and the particle, e.g. *The man picked it up* versus *The man picked up it*.

20.5 *Summary*

Two different theories of phrase structure were outlined in this chapter which were put forward as alternatives to X-bar theory. They are arguably both minimal in that they derive the effects of X-bar theory from independently needed requirements. Bare Phrase Structure relies at least in part on the operation Merge to derive phrase markers. The derived phrase markers have the property that their terminal nodes are not ordered. According to Chomsky, there is no evidence that the computational system relies on linear ordering. The theory of Antisymmetry differs radically in that its main aim is to set up a theory of phrase structure which completely determines linear order. According to this theory, the algorithm which determines phrase markers also determines linear ordering. It follows that the algorithm holds in all syntactic levels of representation insofar as they take the form of phrase markers.

Bibliography

Abney, S. (1987) *The English Noun Phrase in Its Sentential Aspect*. Doctoral dissertation, Massachusetts Institute of Technology.

Aissen, J. (1979) *The Syntax of Causative Constructions*. New York: Garland Press.

Akmajian, A. and F. W. Heny (1975) *An Introduction to the Principles of Transformational Grammar*. Cambridge, MA: Massachusetts Institute of Technology Press.

—— S. Steele and T. Wasow (1979) The Category AUX in Universal Grammar. *Linguistic Inquiry* 10, 1–64.

Allwood, J., L. G. Andersson and O. Dahl (1977) *Logic in Linguistics*. Cambridge: Cambridge University Press.

Anderson, S. (1982) Where Is Morphology? *Linguistic Inquiry* 13, 571–612.

Aoun, J. (1982) *The Formal Nature of Anaphoric Relations*. Doctoral dissertation, Massachusetts Institute of Technology.

—— (1985) *A Grammar of Anaphora*. Linguistic Inquiry Monograph 11. Cambridge, MA: Massachusetts Institute of Technology Press.

—— (1986) *Generalised Binding*. Dordrecht: Foris.

—— Benmamoun and D. Sportiche (1994) Agreement and Conjunction in Some Varieties of Arabic. *Linguistic Inquiry* 25, 195–220.

—— Hornstein and D. Sportiche (1981) Some Aspects of Wide Scope Quantification. *Journal of Linguistic Research* 1, 69–95.

—— and Y. A. Li (1991) The Interaction of Operators. In R. Freidin (ed.), *Principles and Parameters in Comparative Grammar*. Cambridge, MA: Massachusetts Institute of Technology Press, 163–181.

—— and D. Sportiche (1983) On the Formal Theory of Government. *Linguistic Review* 2, 211–36.

Aronoff, M. (1976) *Word Formation in Generative Grammar*. Linguistic Inquiry Monograph 1. Cambridge, MA: Massachusetts Institute of Technology Press.

Authier, J.-M. (1988) Null Object Constructions in Kinande. *Natural Language and Linguistic Theory* 6, 19–37.

—— (1989) Two Types of Empty Operator. *Linguistic Inquiry* 20, 117–25.

Awbery, G. (1976) *The Syntax of Welsh*. Cambridge: Cambridge University Press.

Bahloul, M. and W. Harbert (1993) Agreement Asymmetries in Arabic. *Proceedings of the West Coast Conference on Formal Linguistics 1992*.

Baker, C. L. (1970) Notes on the Description of English Questions: The Role of an Abstract Question Morpheme. *Foundations of Language* 6, 197–219.

—— (1978) *Introduction to Generative-Transformational Syntax*. Englewood Cliffs, NJ: Prentice-Hall.

Baker, M. C. (1988) *Incorporation: A Theory of Grammatical Function Changing*. Chicago: The University of Chicago Press.

—— K. Johnson and I. Roberts (1989) Passive Arguments Raised. *Linguistic Inquiry* 20, 219–51.

Baltin, M. (1983) Extraposition: Bounding versus Government-Binding. *Linguistic Inquiry* 14, 155–62.

—— (1984) Extraposition Rules and Discontinuous Constituents. *Linguistic Inquiry* 15, 157–63.

Bauer, L. (1983) *English Word Formation*. Cambridge: Cambridge University Press.

Beghelli, F. and T. Stowell (1997) Distributivity and Negation: The Syntax of *Each* and *Every*. In A. Szabolcsi (ed.), *Ways of Scope Taking*. Dordrecht: Kluwer Academic, 71–98.

Belletti, A. (1988) The Case of Unaccusatives. *Linguistic Inquiry* 19, 1–34.

—— (1990) *Generalised Verb Movement*. Turin: Rosenberg & Sellier

—— and L. Rizzi (1981) The Syntax of *Ne*. *Linguistic Review* 1, 117–54.

Benmamoun, E. (1992) *Functional and Inflectional Morphology: Problems of Projection, Representation and Derivation*. Doctoral dissertation, University of Southern California, Los Angeles.

Bennis, H. and T. Hoekstra (1984) Gaps and Parasitic Gaps. *Linguistic Review* 4, 29–87.

Besten, H. den (1983) On the Interaction of Root Transformations and Lexical Deletive Rules. In W. Abraham (ed.), *On the Formal Syntax of Westgermania*. Amsterdam: Benjamins, 47–131.

Bierwisch, M. (1963) *Grammatik des deutschen Verbs*. Berlin: Akademie.

Bobaljik, J. (1995) *Morphosyntax: The Syntax of Verbal Inflection*. Doctoral dissertation, Massachusetts Institute of Technology.

—— and A. Carnie (1996) A Minimalist Approach to Some Problems of Irish Word Order. In R. D. Borsely and I. Roberts (eds), *The Syntax of the Celtic Languages*. Cambridge: Cambridge University Press, 223–240.

Borer, H. (1984) *Parametric Syntax: Case Studies in Semitic and Romance Languages*. Dordrecht: Foris.

—— (1989) Anaphoric AGR. In O. Jaeggli and K. Safir (eds), *The Null Subject Parameter*. Dordrecht: Kluwer.

—— (1996) The Construct in Review. In J. Lecarme, J. Lowenstamm and U. Shlonsky (eds), *Studies in Afroasiatic Grammar*. The Hague: Holland Academic Graphics, 30–61.

Brame, M. (1981) The General Theory of Binding and Fusion. *Linguistic Analysis* 7, 277–325.

—— (1982) The Head Selector Theory of Lexical Specifications and the Non-existence of Coarse Categories. *Linguistic Analysis* 10, 321–5.

Bresnan, J. W. (1970) On Complementizers: Toward a Syntactic Theory of Complement Types. *Foundations of Language* 6, 297–321.

—— (1972) *Theory of Complementation in English*. Doctoral dissertation, Massachusetts Institute of Technology.

—— (1976) Non-arguments for Raising. *Linguistic Inquiry* 7, 485–501.

—— (1982a) Control and Complementation. *Linguistic Inquiry* 13, 343–434.

—— (1982b) *The Mental Representation of Grammatical Relations*. Cambridge, MA: Massachusetts Institute of Technology Press.

—— and S. Mchombo (1987) Topic, Pronoun and Agreement in Chichewa. *Language* 63, 741–82.

Brody, M. (1993) θ-Theory and Arguments. *Linguistic Inquiry* 24, 1–24.

Browning, M. (1987) *Null Operator Constructions*. Doctoral dissertation, Massachusetts Institute of Technology.

Burzio, L. (1986) *Italian Syntax: A Government-Binding Approach*. Dordrecht: Reidel.

Caplan, D. (1987) *Neurolinguistics and Linguistic Aphasiology: An Introduction*. Cambridge: Cambridge University Press.

Caramazza, A. and E. B. Zurif (1976) Dissociation of Algorithmic and Heuristic Processes in Sentence Comprehension: Evidence from Aphasia. *Brain and Language* 3, 572–82.

Cheng, L. (1991) *On the Typology of Wh-Questions*. Doctoral dissertation, Massachusetts Institute of Technology.

Chomsky, N. (1957) *Syntactic Structures*. The Hague: Mouton.

—— (1965) *Aspects of the Theory of Syntax*. Cambridge: Cambridge University Press.

—— (1966) *Cartesian Linguistics*. New York: Harper & Row.

—— (1968) *Language and Mind*. New York: Harcourt, Brace & World. (Extended edition 1972.)

—— (1970) Remarks on Nominalizations. In R. Jacobs and P. S. Rosenbaum (eds), *Readings in English Transformational Grammar*. Waltham, MA: Ginn.

—— (1972) *Studies on Semantics in Generative Grammar*. The Hague: Mouton.

—— (1973) Conditions on Transformations. In S. R. Anderson and P. Kiparsky (eds), *A Festschrift for Morris Halle*. New York: Holt, Rinehart & Winston.

—— (1975a) *Logical Structure of Linguistic Theory*. New York: Plenum.

—— (1975b) *Reflections on Language*. New York: Pantheon.

—— (1977a) *Essays on Form and Interpretation*. New York: North Holland.

—— (1977b) On Wh-Movement. In P. Culicover, T. Wasow and A. Akmajian (eds), *Formal Syntax*. New York: Academic Press.

—— (1980a) *Rules and Representations*. New York: Columbia University Press.

—— (1980b) On Binding. *Linguistic Inquiry* 11, 1–46.

—— (1981) *Lectures on Government and Binding*. Dordrecht: Foris.

—— (1982) *Some Concepts and Consequences of the Theory of Government and Binding*. Linguistic Inquiry Monograph 6. Cambridge, MA: Massachusetts Institute of Technology Press.

—— (1986a) *Knowledge of Language: Its Nature, Origin and Use*. New York: Praeger.

—— (1986b) *Barriers*. Linguistic Inquiry Monograph 11. Cambridge, MA: Massachusetts Institute of Technology Press.

—— (1987a) Transformational Grammar: Past, Present and Future. In *Generative Grammar: Its Basis, Development and Prospects*. Special Issue, *Studies in English Language and Literature*, Kyoto University of Foreign Studies.

—— (1987b) *Language in a Psycholinguistic Setting*. Special Issue of *Sophia Linguistica: Working Papers in Linguistics* 22. Tokyo: Sophia University.

—— (1988) *Language and Problems of Knowledge: The Managua Lectures*. Cambridge, MA: Massachusetts Institute of Technology Press.

—— (1991a) Linguistics and Adjacent Fields: A Personal View. In A. Kasher (ed.), *The Chomskyan Turn*. Oxford: Blackwell, 3–25.

—— (1991b) Linguistics and Cognitive Science: Problems and Mysteries. In A. Kasher (ed.), *The Chomskyan Turn*. Oxford: Blackwell, 26–55.

—— (1991c) Some Notes on Economy of Representation and Derivation. In R. Freidin (ed.), *Principles and Parameters in Comparative Grammar*. Cambridge, MA: Massachusetts Institute of Technology Press, 417–54.

—— (1993) A Minimalist Program for Linguistic Theory. In K. Hale and J. Keyser (eds), *The View from Building 20*. Cambridge, MA: Massachusetts Institute of Technology Press.

—— (1995) *The Minimalist Program*. Cambridge, MA: Massachusetts Institute of Technology Press.

—— R. Huybregts and H. van Riemsdijk (1982) *The Generative Enterprise*. Dordrecht: Foris.

—— and H. Lasnik (1977) Filters and Control. *Linguistic Inquiry* 8, 425–504.

Cinque, G. (1995a) On the Evidence for Partial N-Movement in the Romance DP. In *Italian Syntax and Universal Grammar*. Cambridge: Cambridge University Press, 287–309.

—— (1995b) On *Si* Constructions and the Theory of Arb. In *Italian Syntax and Universal Grammar*. Cambridge: Cambridge University Press, 121–98.

—— (1997) *Adverbs and Functional Heads: A Crosslinguistic Perspective*. Oxford: Oxford University Press.

Comrie, B. (1976) The Syntax of Causative Constructions: Cross-Language Similarities and Divergences. In M. Shibatani (ed.), *The Grammar of Causative Constructions*. Syntax and Semantics 6. New York: Academic Press, 261–312.

Culicover, P. (1992) Topicalisation, Inversion and Complementizers in English. In D. Delfitto, M. Everaert, A. Evers and F. Stuurman (eds), *OTS Working Papers. Going Romance and Beyond*. University of Utrecht, 1–45.

—— and Wilkins, W. (1984) *Locality in Linguistic Theory*. New York: Academic Press.

Curtiss, S. (1977) *Genie: A Psycholinguistic Study of a Modern-Day 'Wild Child'*. New York: Academic Press.

—— (1981) Dissociations between Language and Cognition: Cases and Implications. *Journal of Autism and Developmental Disorders* 2, 15–30.

—— (1982) Developmental Dissociations of Language and Cognition. In L. K. Obler and L. Menn (eds), *Exceptional Language and Linguistics*. New York: Academic Press, 285–312.

—— (1988) Abnormal Language Acquisition and Grammar: Evidence for the Modularity of Language. In L. Hyman and C. Li (eds), *Language, Speech and Mind: Studies in Honour of Victoria A. Fromkin*. London: Routledge & Kegan Paul, 81–102.

Czepulch, H. (1982) Case History and the Dative Alternation. *Linguistic Review* 2, 1–38.

Diesing, M. (1990) Verb Movement and the Subject Position in Yiddish. *Natural Language and Linguistic Theory* 8, 41–79.

Di Sciullo, A.-M. and E. Williams (1987) *On the Definition of Word*. Cambridge, MA: Massachusetts Institute of Technology Press.

Dobrovie-Sorin, C. (1990) Clitic Doubling, Wh-movement, and Quantification in Romanian. *Linguistic Inquiry* 21, 351–98.

Dougherty, R. (1969) An Interpretive Theory of Pronominal Reference. *Foundations of Language* 5, 488–508.

Durand, J. (1990) *Generative and Non-linear Phonology*. London: Longman.

Emonds, J. E. (1970) *Root and Structure Preserving Transformations*. Doctoral dissertation, Massachusetts Institute of Technology.

—— (1976) *A Transformational Approach to English Syntax: Root, Structure Preserving and Local Transformations*. New York: Academic Press.

—— (1978) The Verbal Complex V'-V in French. *Linguistic Inquiry* 21, 49–77.

—— (1980) Word Order in Generative Grammar. *Journal of Linguistic Research* 1, 33–54.

Engdahl, E. (1983) Parasitic Gaps. *Linguistics and Philosophy* 6, 5–34.

—— (1985) Parasitic Gaps, Resumptive Pronouns and Subject Extraction. *Linguistics* 23, 3–44.

Fabb, N. (1984) *Syntactic Affixation*. Doctoral dissertation, Massachusetts Institute of Technology.

Fassi Fehri, A. (1980) Some Complement Phenomena in Arabic, the Complementizer Phrase Hypothesis, and the Non-accessibility Condition. *Analyse/Theorie*, 54–114. Université de Paris VIII, Vincennes.

Fiengo, R. W. (1977) On Trace Theory. *Linguistic Inquiry* 8, 35–61.

—— C.-T. Huang, H. Lasnik and T. Reinhart (1988) The Syntax of Wh-in-situ. *Proceedings of the Seventh West Coast Conference on Formal Linguistics*, 81–98.

Fodor, J. A. (1983) *The Modularity of Mind*. Cambridge, MA: Massachusetts Institute of Technology Press.

Fodor, J. D. (1982) *Semantics: Theories of Meaning in Generative Grammar*. Brighton: Harvester Press.

Frampton, J. (1989) Parasitic Gaps and the Theory of Wh Chains. *Linguistic Inquiry* 21, 49–77.

Freidin, R. (1975) The Analysis of Passives. *Language* 51, 384–405.

Freidin, R. (1978) Cyclicity and the Theory of Grammar. *Linguistic Inquiry* 9, 519–49.
—— (1986) Fundamental Issues in the Theory of Binding. In B. Lust (ed.), *Studies in the Acquisition of Anaphora*. Dordrecht: Reidel.
Fromkin, V. and Rodman, R. (1988) *An Introduction to Language*, 4th edn. New York: Holt, Rinehart & Winston.
Fukui, N. (1992) The Principles & Parameters Approach. A Comparative Syntax of English and Japanese. MS, University of California at Irvine.
—— (1993) Parameters and Optionality. *Linguistic Inquiry* 24, 399–420.
Fulass, H. (1972) On Amharic Relative Clauses. *Bulletin of the School of Oriental and African Languages* 35, 417–513.
Gibson, J. (1980) *Clause Union in Chamorro and in Universal Grammar*. Doctoral dissertation, University of California, San Diego.
Giorgi, A. and G. Longobardi (1991) *The Syntax of Noun Phrases: Configuration, Parameters and Empty Categories*. Cambridge: Cambridge University Press.
Goldsmith, J. A. (1990) *Autosegmental and Metrical Phonology.* Oxford: Blackwell.
Green, M. G. (1974) *Semantics and Syntactic Regularity.* Bloomington: Indiana University Press.
Greenberg. J. (ed.) (1966) *Universals of Language*, 2nd edn. Cambridge, MA: Massachusetts Institute of Technology Press.
Grewendorf, G. (1988) *Aspekte der deutschen Syntax*. Tübingen: Narr.
Grodzinsky, Y. (1990) *Theoretical Perspectives on Language Deficits*. Cambridge, MA: Massachusetts Institute of Technology Press.
Gruber, J. S. (1965) *Studies in Lexical Relations*. Doctoral dissertation, Massachusetts Institute of Technology.
—— (1976) *Lexical Structures in Syntax and Semantics*. Amsterdam: North Holland.
Guéron, J. (1980) On the Syntax and Semantics of PP Extraposition. *Linguistic Inquiry* 11, 637–78.
—— and R. May (1984) Extraposition and Logical Form. *Linguistic Inquiry* 15, 1– 31.
Guerssel, M. (1986) On Berber Verbs of Change: A Study of Transitivity Alternations. Massachusetts Institute of Technology Lexicon Project Working Papers 9. Massachusetts Institute of Technology.
Haegeman, L. (1986) INFL, COMP and Nominative Case Assignment in Flemish Infinitivals. In P. Muysken and H. van Riemsdijk (eds), *Features and Projections*. Dordrecht: Foris, 123–37.
—— (1991) *Introduction to Government and Binding Theory*. Oxford: Blackwell.
Hale, K. and J. Keyser (1993) On Argument Structure and the Lexical Expression of Syntactic Relations. In K. Hale and J. Keyser (eds), *The View from Building 20*. Cambridge, MA: Massachusetts Institute of Technology Press.
Halpern, A. (1995) *On the Placement and Morphology of Clitics*. Dissertations in Linguistics. Stanford, CA: CSLI. Center for the Study of Language and Information.
Hazout, I. (1990) *Vebal Nouns: Theta-Theoretic Studies in Hebrew and Arabic*. Doctoral dissertation, University of Massachusetts at Amherst.
Heim, I. and A. Kratzer (1998) *Semantics in Generative Grammar*. Oxford and Malden, MA: Blackwell. .
Heny, F. and B. Richards (1983) *Linguistic Categories: Auxiliaries and Related Puzzles*. Dordrecht: Reidel.
Higginbotham, J. (1980) Pronouns and Bound Variables. *Linguistic Inquiry* 11, 679–708.
—— (1985) On Semantics. *Linguistic Inquiry* 16, 547–93.
—— and May, R. (1981) Questions, Quantifiers and Crossing. *Linguistic Review* 7, 129–67.
Holmberg, A. (1986) *Word Order and Syntactic Features in the Scandinavian Languages and English*. Doctoral dissertation, University of Stockholm.
Hornstein, N. (1995) *Logical Form: From GB to Minimalism*. Oxford and Cambridge, MA: Blackwell.

—— (1998) Movement and Chains. *Syntax* 1, 99–127.

—— and Weinberg, A. (1981) Case Theory and Preposition Stranding. *Linguistic Inquiry* 12, 55–99.

Horrocks, G. and M. Stavrou (1987) Bounding Theory and Greek Syntax: Evidence for Wh-movement in NP. *Journal of Linguistics* 23, 79–108.

Horvath, J. (1986) *Aspects of the Theory of Grammar and the Syntax of Hungarian.* Dordrecht: Foris.

—— (1996) The Status of Wh-expletives and the Partial Wh-movement Construction in Hungarian. MS, Tel Aviv University.

Huang, C.-T. J. (1982) *Logical Relations in Chinese and the Theory of Grammar.* Doctoral dissertation, Massachusetts Institute of Technology.

—— (1984) On the Distribution and Reference of Empty Pronouns. *Linguistic Inquiry* 15, 531–74.

—— (1989) Pro-drop in Chinese. In O. Jaeggli and K. Safir (eds), *The Null Subject Parameter.* Dordrecht: Kluwer, 185, 214.

Hudson, R. A. (1987) Zwicky on Heads. *Journal of Linguistics* 23, 109–32.

Hyman, L. M. (1975) *Phonology: Theory and Analysis.* New York: Holt, Rinehart & Winston.

Jackendoff, R. S. (1972) *Semantic Interpretation in Generative Grammar.* Cambridge, MA: Massachusetts Institute of Technology Press.

—— (1975) Morphological and Semantic Regularities in the Lexicon. *Language* 51, 639–71.

—— (1977) *X-bar Syntax: A Study of Phrase Structure.* Linguistic Inquiry Monograph 2. Cambridge, MA: Massachusetts Institute of Technology Press.

—— (1990) On Larson's Treatment of the Double Object Construction. *Linguistic Inquiry* 18, 369–411.

Jaeggli, O. (1980) *On Some Phonologically Null Elements in Syntax.* Doctoral dissertation, Massachusetts Institute of Technology.

—— (1982) *Topics in Romance Syntax.* Dordrecht: Foris.

—— (1986) Passive. *Linguistic Inquiry* 17, 587–633.

—— and K. Safir (1989) Parametric Theory. In O. Jaeggli and K. Safir (eds), *The Null Subject Parameter.* Dordrecht: Kluwer, 1–45.

—— —— (eds), (1989) *The Null Subject Parameter.* Dordrecht: Kluwer.

Jensen, J. (1990) *Morphology: Word Structure in Generative Grammar.* Amsterdam: John Benjamins.

Jones, M. and A. Thomas (1977) *The Welsh Language.* Cardiff: University of Wales.

Katamba, F. (1993) *Morphology.* London: Macmillan.

Kayne, R. S. (1975) *French Syntax.* Cambridge, MA: Massachusetts Institute of Technology Press.

—— (1984) *Connectedness and Binary Branching.* Dordrecht: Foris.

—— (1987) Facets of Romance Past Participle Agreement. MS, Massachusetts Institute of Technology.

—— (1989) Null Subjects and Clitic Climbing. In O. Jaeggli and K. Safir (eds), *The Null Subject Parameter.* Dordrecht: Kluwer, 239–62.

—— (1991) Romance Clitics, Verb-movement, and PRO. *Linguistic Inquiry* 22, 647–86.

—— (1994) *The Antisymmetry of Syntax.* Cambridge, MA: Massachusetts Institute of Technology Press.

Kempson, R. (1977) *Semantic Theory.* Cambridge: Cambridge University Press.

Kenesei, I. (ed.) (1985) *Approaches to Hungarian I.* Szeged: University Press.

—— (ed.) (1987) *Approaches to Hungarian II.* Szeged: University Press.

Kenstowicz, M. (1989) The Null Subject Parameter in Modern Arabic Dialects. In O. Jaeggli and K. Safir (eds), *The Null Subject Parameter.* Dordrecht: Kluwer, 263, 276.

—— M. and Kisseberth, C. (1979) *Generative Phonology: Description and Theory.* New York: Academic Press.

Keyser, S. J. and T. Roeper (1984) On the Middle and Ergative Constructions in English. *Linguistic Inquiry* 15, 381–416.

Kitagawa, Y. (1986) *Subjects in Japanese and English*. Doctoral dissertation, University of Massachusetts at Amherst.

Klavans, J. (1980) *Some Problems in a Theory of Clitics*. Doctoral dissertation, University College London.

—— (1985) The Independence of Syntax and Phonology in Cliticisation. *Language* 61, 95–120.

Koopman, H. (1984) *The Syntax of Verbs*. Dordrecht: Foris.

—— and D. Sportiche (1991) The Position of Subjects. *Lingua* 85, Special Issue on VSO Languages, ed. J. McCloskey.

Koster, J. (1975) Dutch as an SOV Language. *Linguistic Analysis* 1, 111–36.

—— (1984) On Binding and Control. *Linguistic Inquiry* 15, 417–59.

Kuno, S. and J. Robinson (1972) Multiple Wh-questions. *Linguistic Inquiry* 3, 463–87.

Kuroda, S.-Y. (1988) Whether We Agree or Not: A Comparative Syntax of English and Japanese. In W. Poser (ed.), *Papers on the Second International Workshop on Japanese Syntax*. Stanford, CA: Center for the Study of Language and Information.

Lakoff, G. (1968) Pronouns and Reference. Distributed by the Indiana University Linguistics Club, Bloomington.

Larson, R. K. (1988) On the Double Object Construction. *Linguistic Inquiry* 19, 335–91.

—— (1990) Double Objects Revisited: Reply to Jackendoff. *Linguistic Inquiry* 21, 589–632.

—— and G. Segal (1995) *Knowledge of Meaning: An Introduction to Semantic Theory*. Cambridge, MA: Massachusetts Institute of Technology Press.

Lasnik, H. (1976) Some Thoughts on Coreference. *Linguistic Analysis* 2, 1–22.

—— (1993) *Lectures on Minimalist Syntax*. University of Connecticut Working Papers in Linguistics 1. Distributed by Massachusetts Institute of Technology Working Papers in Linguistics, Cambridge, MA.

—— and M. Saito (1984) On the Nature of Proper Government. *Linguistic Inquiry* 14, 235–89.

—— —— (1992) *Move-alpha*. Cambridge, MA: Massachusetts Institute of Technology Press.

Lebeaux, D. (1988) *Language Acquisition and the Form of the Grammar*. Doctoral dissertation, University of Massachusetts at Amherst.

Lees, R. (1963) *The Grammar of English Nominalizations*. The Hague: Mouton.

Levin, B. and M. Rappaport (1986) The Formation of Adjectival Passives. *Linguistic Inquiry* 17, 623–62.

Lightfoot, D. (1976) The Theoretical Implications of Subject Raising. *Foundations of Language* 14, 257–86.

—— (1977) On Traces and Conditions on Rules. In O. Culicover, T. Wasow and A. Akmajian (eds), *Formal Syntax*. New York: Academic Press.

—— (1979) *Principles of Diachronic Syntax*. Cambridge: Cambridge University Press.

—— (1981) Explaining Syntactic Change. In N. Hornstein and D. Lightfoot, *Explanation in Linguistics*. London: Longman, 209–39.

—— (1991) *How to Set Parameters*. Cambridge, MA: Massachusetts Institute of Technology Press.

Longobardi, G. (1985) Connectedness, Scope and C-Command. *Linguistic Inquiry* 16, 163–92.

McCloskey, J. (1979) *Transformational Syntax and Model Theoretic Semantics*. Dordrecht: Reidel.

—— (1983) A VP in a VSO Language. In G. Gazdar, E. Klein and G. Pullum (eds), *Order, Concord and Constituency*. Dordrecht: Foris, 9–55.

Madeira, A.-M. (1993) Clitic-second in European Portuguese. *Probus* 5, 155–74.

Manzini, R. (1983) On Control and Control Theory. *Linguistic Inquiry* 14, 421–46.

Marantz, A. (1984) *On the Nature of Grammatical Relations.* Cambridge, MA: Massachusetts Institute of Technology Press.

Mathews, G. H. (1964) *Hidatsa Syntax.* The Hague: Mouton.

May, R. (1977) *The Grammar of Quantification.* Doctoral dissertation, Massachusetts Institute of Technology.

—— (1985) *Logical Form: Its Structure and Derivation.* Cambridge, MA: Massachusetts Institute of Technology Press.

Menn, L. and L. K. Obler (1990) *Agrammatic Aphasia: A Cross-language Narrative Sourcebook.* Amsterdam: Benjamins.

Mithun, M. (1984) The Evolution of Noun Incorporation. *Language* 60, 847–95.

—— (1986) On the Nature of Noun Incorporation. *Language* 62, 32–8.

Mohammad, M. A. (1989) *The Sentential Structure of Arabic.* Doctoral dissertation, University of Southern California, Los Angeles.

Mohanan, K. P. (1982) Grammatical Relations and Clause Structure in Malayalam. In J. Bresnan (ed.), *The Mental Representation of Grammatical Relations.* Cambridge, MA: Massachusetts Institute of Technology Press.

Muysken, P. (1982) Parametrising the Notion 'Head'. *Journal of Linguistic Research* 2, 57–75.

—— and H. C. van Riemsdijk (1985) Projecting Features and Feature Projections. In P. Musyken and H. van Riemsdijk (eds), *Features and Projections.* Dordrecht: Foris.

Napoli, J. D. (1989) *Predication Theory.* Cambridge: Cambridge University Press.

Newmeyer, F. (1980) *Linguistic Theory in America.* New York: Academic Press.

—— (1983) *Grammatical Theory: Its Limits and Its Possibilities.* Chicago: University of Chicago Press.

—— (1991) Rules and Principles in the Historical Development of Generative Syntax. In A. Kasher (ed.), *The Chomskyan Turn.* Oxford: Blackwell, 200–30.

Nishigaushi, T. (1986) *Quantification in Syntax.* Doctoral dissertation, University of Massachusetts at Amherst.

—— (1990) *Quantification in the Theory of Grammar.* Dordrecht: Kluwer.

Oehrle, R. (1976) *The Grammatical Status of the English Dative Shift Alternation.* Doctoral dissertation, Massachusetts Institute of Technology.

Ouhalla, J. (1988) *The Syntax of Head Movement: A Study of Berber.* Doctoral dissertation, University College London.

—— (1989) Clitic-movement and the ECP: Evidence for Berber and Romance. *Lingua* 79, 165–215.

—— (1990) Sentential Negation, Relativised Minimality and the Aspectual Status of Auxiliaries. *Linguistic Review* 7, 183–231.

Perlmutter, D. M. (1971) *Deep and Surface Structure Constraints in Syntax.* New York: Holt, Rinehart & Winston.

—— (1978) Impersonal Passives and the Unaccusative Hypothesis. *Proceedings of the Fourth Annual Meeting of the Berkeley Linguistics Society.* Berkeley: University of California, 157–189.

—— (ed.) (1983) *Studies in Relational Grammar* I. Chicago: University of Chicago Press.

—— and C. Rosen (eds) (1984) *Studies in Relational Grammar* II. Chicago: University of Chicago Press.

Pesetsky, D. (1987) Wh-in-situ: Movement and Unselective Binding. In E. Reuland and A. G. B. ter Meulen (eds), *The Representation of Indefiniteness.* Cambridge, MA: Massachusetts Institute of Technology Press.

Platzack, C. (1986a) The Position of the Finite Verb in Swedish. In H. Haider and M. Prinzhorn (eds), *Verb Second Phenomena in Germanic Languages.* Dordrecht: Foris, 27–47.

—— (1986b) COMP, INFL and Germanic Word Order. In L. Hellan and K. Christensen (eds), *Topics in Scandinavian Syntax.* Dordrecht: Reidel, 185–234.

Pollock, J.-Y. (1989) Verb Movement, UG and the Structure of IP. *Linguistic Inquiry* 20, 365–424.

Postal, P. M. (1966) On so-called 'Pronouns' in English. In F. P. Dineen (ed.), Report on the 17th Annual Round Table Meeting in Linguistics and Language Studies. Washington, DC: Georgetown University Press.

—— (1971) *Crossover Phenomena*. New York: Holt, Rinehart & Winston.

—— (1974) *On Raising*. Cambridge, MA: Massachusetts Institute of Technology Press.

—— (1979) *Some Syntactic Rules of Mohawk*. New York: Garland Press.

—— (1993) Remarks on Weak Crossover Effects. *Linguistic Inquiry* 24, 539–56.

—— (1994) Parasitic and Pseudoparasitic Gaps. *Linguistic Inquiry* 25, 63–117.

—— and G. K. Pullum (1982) The Contraction Debate. *Linguistic Inquiry* 13, 211–22.

Quirk, R., S. Greenbaum, G. Leech and J. Svartvik (1985) *A Comprehensive Grammar of the English Language*. London: Longman.

Radford, A. (1988) *Transformational Grammar: A First Course*. Cambridge: Cambridge University Press.

Raposo, E. (1986) On the Null Object in European Portuguese. In O. Jaeggli and C. Silva-Corvalan (eds), *Studies in Romance Linguistics*. Dordrecht: Foris, 373–90.

Reinhart, T. (1976) *The Syntactic Domain of Anaphora*. Doctoral dissertation, Massachusetts Institute of Technology.

—— (1983) *Anaphora and Semantic Interpretation*. London: Croom Helm.

van Riemsdijk, H. (1978) *A Case Study in Syntactic Markedness: The Binding Nature of Prepositional Phrases*. Dordrecht: Foris.

—— and E. Williams (1986) *Introduction to the Theory of Grammar*. Cambridge, MA: Massachusetts Institute of Technology Press.

Ritter, B. (1991) Two Functional Categories in Noun Phrases. *Syntax and Semantics* 25, 37–62.

Rivas, A. (1977) *A Theory of Clitics*. Doctoral dissertation, Massachusetts Institute of Technology.

Rizzi, L. (1982) *Issues in Italian Syntax*. Dordrecht: Foris.

—— (1986a) Null Objects in Italian and the Theory of *Pro*. *Linguistic Inquiry* 17, 501–58.

—— (1986b) On the Status of Subject Clitics in Romance. In O. Jaeggli and C. Silva-Corvalan (eds), *Studies in Romance Linguistics*. Dordrecht: Foris. 391–419.

—— (1990) *Relativized Minimality*. Cambridge, MA: Massachusetts Institute of Technology Press.

—— (1991) *The Wh Criterion*. Technical Report, University of Geneva.

Roberts, I. (1987) *The Representation of Implicit and Dethematised Subjects*. Dordrecht: Foris.

—— and U. Shlonsky (1995) Pronominal Enclisis in VSO Languages. In R. Borseley and I. Roberts (eds), *The Syntax of the Celtic Languages*. Cambridge: Cambridge University Press.

Roeper, T. and E. Williams (1987) *Parameter Setting*. Dordrecht: Reidel.

Rognvaldsson, E. and H. Thrainsson (1990) On Icelandic Word Order Once More. In J. Maling and A. Zaenen (eds), *Modern Icelandic Syntax*. Syntax and Semantics 24. San Diego, CA: Academic Press, 3–40.

Rosenbaum, P. S. (1967) *The Grammar of English Predicate Complement Constructions*. Cambridge, MA: Massachusetts Institute of Technology Press.

Ross, J. R. (1967) *Constraints on Variables in Syntax*. Doctoral dissertation, Massachusetts Institute of Technology.

—— (1986) *Infinite Syntax!* Norwood, NJ: Ablex.

Rothstein, S. (1983) *The Syntactic Forms of Predication*. Doctoral dissertation, Massachusetts Institute of Technology.

Rouveret, A. and J.-R. Vergnaud (1980) Specifying Reference to the Subject. *Linguistic Inquiry* 11, 97–202.

Safir, K. (1985) Missing Subjects in German. In J. Toman (ed.), *Linguistic Theory and the Grammar of German*. Dordrecht: Foris.

Saito, M. (1985) *Some Asymmetries In Japanese and Their Theoretical Implications*. Doctoral dissertation, Massachusetts Institute of Technology.

—— and H. Hoji (1983) Weak Crossover and Move α in Japanese. *Natural Language and Linguistic Theory* 1, 245–59.

Santorini, B. (1990) *The Generalization of the Verb-Second Constraint in the History of Yiddish*. Doctoral dissertation, University of Pennsylvania.

Scalise, S. (1984) *Generative Morphology*. Dordrecht: Foris.

Selkirk, E. (1982) *The Syntax of Words*. Linguistic Inquiry Monograph 7. Cambridge, MA: Massachusetts Institute of Technology Press.

Sells, P. (1984) *Syntax and Semantics of Resumptive Pronouns*. Doctoral dissertation, University of Massachusetts at Amherst.

Shlonsky, U. (1987) *Null and Displaced Subjects*. Doctoral dissertation, Massachusetts Institute of Technology.

—— (1997) *Clause Structure and Word Order in Hebrew and Arabic: An Essay in Comparative Semitic Syntax*. Oxford: Oxford University Press.

Siloni, T. (1994) *Noun Phrases and Nominalisations*. Doctoral dissertation, University of Geneva.

Smith, C. (1969) Determiners and Relative Clauses in a Generative Grammar of English. In D. A. Reibel and S. A. Schane (eds), *Modern Studies in English*. Englewood Cliffs, NJ: Prentice-Hall, 247–63.

Smith, N. V. (1989) *The Twitter Machine: Reflections on Language*. Oxford: Blackwell.

—— and D. Wilson (1979) *Modern Linguistics: The Results of Chomsky's Revolution*. Harmondsworth: Penguin.

—— and I. M. Tsimpli (1991) Linguistic Modularity? A Case Study of a 'Savant' Linguist. *Lingua* 84, 315–51.

Spencer, A. (1991) *Morphological Theory*. Oxford: Blackwell.

Sperber, D. and D. Wilson (1986) *Relevance: Communication and Cognition*. Oxford: Blackwell.

Sportiche, D. (1988) A Theory of Floating Quantifiers and Its Corollaries for Constituent Structure. *Linguistic Inquiry* 19, 425–49.

Sproat, R. (1985) Welsh Syntax and VSO Structure. *Natural Language and Linguistic Theory* 3, 173–216.

Steele, S. (1981) *An Encyclopedia of AUX*. Cambridge, MA: Massachusetts Institute of Technology Press.

Steriade, D. (1980) Clitic Doubling in the Romanian WH Constructions and the Analysis of Topicalisation. Paper presented at Chicago Linguistic Society meeting.

Stowell, T. (1981) *Origins of Phrase Structure*. Doctoral dissertation, Massachusetts Institute of Technology.

Szabolcsi, A. (1987) Functional Categories in the Noun Phrase. In Kenesei (ed.) *Approaches to Hungarian* I. Szeged: University Press.

Taraldsen, K. (1981) The Theoretical Interpretation of a Class of Marked Extractions. In A. Belletti, L. Brandi and L. Rizzi (eds), *Theory of Markedness in Generative Grammar*. Pisa: Scuola Normale Superiore.

Tellier, C. (1988) *Universal Licensing: Implications for Parasitic Gap Constructions*. Doctoral dissertation, McGill University.

Thiersch, G. (1978) *Topics in German Syntax*. Doctoral dissertation, Massachusetts Institute of Technology.

Travis, L. (1984), *Parameters and the Effects of Word Order Variation*. Doctoral dissertation, Massachusetts Institute of Technology.

Trithart, M. (1977) *Relational Grammar and Chichewa Subjectivization*. Doctoral dissertation, University of California at Los Angeles.

Vergnaud, J.-R. (1974) *French Relative Clauses*. Doctoral dissertation, Massachusetts Institute of Technology.

—— (1985) *Dépendances et niveaux de représentation en syntaxe*. Amsterdam: Benjamins.

—— and M.-L. Zubizarreta (1992) The Definite Determiner and the Inalienable Construction in French and English. *Linguistic Inquiry* 23, 595–652.

Vikner, S. (1990) *Verb Movement and Licensing of NP-Positions in the Germanic Languages*. Doctoral dissertation, University of Geneva.

Wahba, W. A. B. (1991) LF Movement in Iraqi Arabic. In C.-T. J. Huang and R. May (eds), *Logical Structure and Linguistic Structure*. Dordrecht: Kluwer, 253–76.

Wasow, T. (1972) *Anaphoric Relations in English*. Doctoral dissertation, Massachusetts Institute of Technology.

—— (1977) Transformations and the Lexicon. In P. Culicover, T. Wasow and A. Akmajian (eds), *Formal Syntax*. New York: Academic Press.

—— (1979) *Anaphora in Generative Grammar*. Ghent: E. Story-Scientia.

Watanabe, A. (1991) Wh-in-situ, Subjacency, and Chain Formation. MS, Massachusetts Institute of Technology.

Webelhuth, G. (1989) *Syntactic Saturation Phenomena and the Modern Germanic Languages*. Doctoral dissertation, University of Massachusetts at Amherst.

Williams, E. S. (1980) Predication. *Linguistic Inquiry* 11, 203–38.

—— (1981) Argument Structure and Morphology. *Linguistic Review* 1, 81–114.

—— (1982) Another Argument that Passive Is Transformational. *Linguistic Inquiry* 13, 160–63.

—— (1983) Against Small Clauses. *Linguistic Inquiry* 14, 287–308.

Yamada, L. (1990) *A Case for the Modularity of Language*. Cambridge, MA: Massachusetts Institute of Technology Press.

Zubizarreta, M.-L. (1987) *Levels of Representation in the Lexicon and in the Syntax*. Dordrecht: Foris.

Zwart, C. J. W. (1993) *Dutch Syntax: A Minimalist Approach*. Doctoral dissertation, University of Groningen.

Subject Index

Index of Languages and Phenomena